GEORGE WHITEFIELD CHADWICK

D1291570

GEORGE WHITEFIELD CHADWICK

THE LIFE AND MUSIC OF
THE PRIDE OF NEW ENGLAND

BILL F. FAUCETT

NORTHEASTERN UNIVERSITY PRESS | BOSTON

NORTHEASTERN UNIVERSITY PRESS

An imprint of University Press of New England

www.upne.com

© 2012 Northeastern University

All rights reserved

Manufactured in the United States of America

Designed by Eric M. Brooks

Typeset in Bulmer and Pastina by Passumpsic Publishing

University Press of New England is a member of the
Green Press Initiative. The paper used in this book meets
their minimum requirement for recycled paper.

For permission to reproduce any of the material in this book,
contact Permissions, University Press of New England, One Court
Street, Suite 250, Lebanon, NH 03766; or visit www.upne.com.

Library of Congress Cataloging-in-Publication Data

Faucett, Bill F.

George Whitefield Chadwick: the life and music of the pride
of New England / Bill F. Faucett. — 1st ed.

　　p. cm.

Includes bibliographical references and index.

ISBN 978-1-55553-772-2 (cloth: alk. paper)—

ISBN 978-1-55553-773-9 (pbk.: alk. paper)—

ISBN 978-1-55553-774-6 (ebook)

1. Chadwick, G. W. (George Whitefield), 1854–1931.

2. Composers—United States—Biography. I. Title.

ML410.C395F38　　2012

780.92—dc23

[B]　　　2012002173

5　4　3　2　1

For

COLLEEN, BILLY, *&* ADAM

with all my love

CONTENTS

ACKNOWLEDGMENTS

This book has relied on the goodwill and help of scores of people over a long period of time. I would like to start by offering my sincerest thanks to the family and heirs of George Whitefield Chadwick, especially Elsie Chadwick, Theodore Chadwick Jr. (now deceased), Nancy Knight, Fitts family genealogist Sylvia Fitts Getchell, and Virginia Chadwick Colby.

Several people have been closely involved with my work for more than twenty years. I am deeply grateful to Dr. Douglass Seaton, Warren D. Allen Professor of Music at The Florida State University, who is always willing to read about Chadwick and offer insightful advice even as doing so takes away from his own important research. Jean Morrow, director of libraries at New England Conservatory, and her right hand Maryalice Perrin-Mohr, also at New England Conservatory, have patiently answered questions, made photocopies, scanned photos, searched for elusive citations, and assisted in every way imaginable. This book is very much the product of their dedicated and cheerful effort.

Many others gave substantial help and advice. I especially wish to thank musicologist David Beveridge for his close reading of my chapter that includes Dvořák; Martin F. Grace, James S. Kemper Professor of Risk Management and Insurance at Georgia State University; Kathy Kienholz, archivist, American Academy of Arts and Letters; Jessica Steytler, archivist, Congregational Library, Boston; musicologist and dear friend Marian Wilson Kimber for her honest and gentle critiques; Julie Walker, librarian, Olivet College; Dorothy Sanborn, Boscawen town clerk; Pamela Olson and Martha Briggs, the Newberry Library; Diane O. Ota, curator of music, Boston Public Library; Richard Boursy, archivist, Yale University; Jennie Rathbun, Harvard College Library; David Peter Coppen, special collections librarian, Eastman School of Music; Wayne Shirley, division of music, Library of Congress (retired); MGySgt. Mike Ressler, chief librarian, US Marine Band ("The President's Own"); and Annie Bayly, reference services, Archives of American Art, Smithsonian Institution. To the countless others who have provided smaller bits of information over the years but are not mentioned here, please accept my warmest gratitude.

Richard Pult, my editor at the University Press of New England, was a patient and helpful sounding post; I sincerely appreciate his gentle manner of dealing with anxious authors. Enthusiastic thanks are also due to production editor Amanda Dupuis and copyeditor Lindsey Alexander. William K. Kearns, long recognized as *the* authority on Horatio Parker and his music, offered many insightful comments on my manuscript, and I am the happy beneficiary of his knowledge, which is both broad and deep. Naturally, this interpretation of Chadwick's life and music is my own, as are any errors of fact or omission.

Finally, I offer special thanks to my dedicatees, wife Colleen and sons Billy and Adam, for their love and encouragement throughout the long process of writing this book. They are my greatest satisfaction in life, and neither this work nor anything else would be possible without their patient support.

Professor Douglass Seaton's nineteenth-century music seminar at The Florida State University encouraged my discovery of many composers and scores. But of everything I listened to that semester, I was most taken by the compositions of a little known, to me at least, American composer named George Whitefield Chadwick. I "discovered," and then wrote a term paper on, his irresistible Second Symphony. It is melodic, inventive, and beautifully crafted. Since that time I have not only become familiar with much of his music, which a decade ago enjoyed a brief recording renaissance, but I also got to know aspects of his life and career that most musicologists have not been so fortunate to explore.

Much of what I learned was the result of several memorable summers spent in the company of Chadwick's grandson, Theodore (Ted) Chadwick Jr. and his wife, Elsie, in the small Massachusetts village of Duxbury. During those visits, in the 1990s, Ted Chadwick kindly gave me permission to root through a trunk of family belongings that had lain uninspected in an upstairs room for years. The contents were George Chadwick's personal documents. Ted and I talked late into the night about "Grandpa," his life, his music (of which Ted himself knew little) and his large reputation in family lore. We also pored over Chadwick's voluminous writings, now rescued from the trunk and stacked lovingly on the dining-room table. Ted read them eagerly and with a passion that led me to conclude that he had never before plumbed the trunk. Now and then he would even assume the elder Chadwick's voice and personality. After Ted's death these materials, along with others, were made a priceless gift to New England Conservatory by Chadwick's family and heirs. I cannot believe that George would have wished them to end up anywhere else.

The recent availability of this treasure trove enables the study of facets of Chadwick's life and work that were previously unknowable. These materials — memoirs, diaries, photographs, letters, and compositional sketchbooks — constitute one of the richest and most significant collections of primary sources that exists for an American composer of art music before the Great Depression. "They were begun as private soliloquies on the [Boston] Symphony concerts and other musical events at which I 'assisted' with no thought of any further continuation," Chadwick reflected on the origins of his efforts. "But writing is an industry which becomes a vice if encouraged, and the family was so much interested in these private observations that for their sake I started over at the beginning." Over time Chadwick's writings morphed from an insider's view of music as it was generally practiced in Boston, to a Chadwick family history, and finally to an intimate confessional. Chadwick's "vice" has made possible this examination and interpretation of his life, and I draw heavily on his own words to reach my conclusions.

What follows is not a strictly chronological account of Chadwick's life, although I have made it roughly so. Because Chadwick was prolific, and because at any given time he had many projects on his plate, I have sometimes elected to separate his oeuvre by genre. I have similarly provided separate consideration of aspects of his personal life and his professional career in order to give context and deeper meaning to the issues under discussion.

I have opted against the use of music examples in this book in an effort to make it more accessible for readers who are not musicians, music students, or musicologists. However, I have not hesitated to analyze important musical passages closely when discussion of the music itself seemed necessary. Generally speaking, I have offered more detailed harmonic and structural analysis for Chadwick's larger instrumental compositions, but I have approached this task with a minimum of music-theoretical jargon. When discussing form, I have used the language provided by Jan LaRue in his invaluable *Guidelines for Style Analysis*, 2nd edition (Harmonie Park Press, 1992), which may be summarized as follows: O refers to introduction/opening material; P refers to the theme associated with the principal key; S refers to the theme associated with the secondary key; N refers to a new theme; T (or t) refers to transitional material; and K (or k) refers to closing areas. (Lowercase letters refer to non-melodic material.) Traditional analytical language (exposition-development-recapitulation) is also used. Tables and appendices further illuminate aspects of Chadwick's life and music.

Not all of Chadwick's music is discussed here. The lion's share of my musical commentary has been devoted to Chadwick's body of instrumental music (with and without chorus) and to his stage works. Space limitations have forced me to give less attention to Chadwick's smaller works—his miscellaneous instrumental music and his choruses. I most regret that in this volume I have not fully examined his nearly two hundred songs. Chadwick wrote songs of every conceivable stripe: nonsensical ditties, sacred selections, occasional tunes, and art song, among them. In this volume, Chadwick's art songs have received the most attention. For detailed information about all his compositions, including a listing of premieres and other performances, critical reviews, and a discography, refer to my *George Whitefield Chadwick: A Bio-Bibliography* (Greenwood Press, 1998).

GEORGE WHITEFIELD CHADWICK

A Chadwick Sketch

No one who did not know would ever have taken George Chadwick
for a musical genius.
—William Dana Orcutt, *Celebrities Off Parade* (1935)

Less than a year and a half before Chadwick's death in 1931, the young conductor and musical savant Nicolas Slonimsky wrote an article titled "Composers of New England" for the then-influential periodical *Modern Music*. Assessing their contribution to a national art, Slonimsky asserted that Chadwick, along with his contemporary and friend Arthur Foote, "upheld New England's fame as a musical center without furthering the advance of a national idiom." He then scoffed, "There are few pages of purely American music in their voluminous works."[1] That conclusion, one shared by many others, effectively removed Chadwick and his confreres for the next fifty years from the collective consciousness of musicians, music critics, and musicologists, who were largely interested in the new, the original, and the modern.

It is fun to imagine the lively argument that might have ensued had Slonimsky, a character who was every bit as prone to verbal jousting as Chadwick, made these pronouncements to the older composer's face. Without a moment's hesitation Chadwick would have snapped that the entirety of his extensive contribution to music was American music. How could it be otherwise since he was an American? Naturally, Chadwick would have also pointed out that he made half a dozen contributions to a characteristic variety of "American music" in the wave of nationalism that washed over musical culture beginning in the last quarter of the nineteenth century. But it was well known among his contemporaries that Chadwick did not particularly care to join the American music fray that simmered from that time until the second decade of the twentieth century. Critic Olin Downes was quick to note, in Chadwick's *New York Times* obituary, that the Yankee composer was "not a propagandist for nationalism in art."[2] To Chadwick, as to many other American composers, nationalism was one way—not necessarily the best and certainly not the only way—to express oneself in tone. The vast majority of his several hundred compositions are skillfully crafted works firmly rooted in Western musical tradition, but they are of no particular nationalistic cast. It has been to Chadwick's extreme detriment—and to our own—that we have not given appropriate consideration to most of the vast body of his music outside of those compositions that are purportedly "American." In this biography I seek to illuminate heretofore unknown aspects of Chadwick's music, life, and times, and to provide a useful corrective to stubborn misconceptions about all three.

What emerges from an investigation of Chadwick's life is a portrait of a complex man and artist whose many layers of responsibilities and activities often created conflict. Tension was a fact of his life. Chadwick was the son of a mother who died only days after his birth, and it would be charity to say merely that he and his father did not get along; their relationship was at times positively rancorous, particularly as George entered adulthood. Chadwick also hustled innumerable jobs until he was in his forties, a situation that not only created financial uncertainty but did little to add to his renown as a composer. For most of his life he was a working musician and teacher; this contradicts the traditional view of Chadwick as the starched ruling authority at a flourishing conservatory. Chadwick resented that he was unable to procure some of the best musical positions in Boston because of the typically American propensity to revere foreign musicians more than native-born ones. In many artistic fields—and nowhere more than in music—Americans looked abroad for the finest talent, and they often failed to notice that artists of equal gifts were present right under their noses. Of course, the greatest source of tension for Chadwick, one that he managed remarkably well, was that between his employment as an administrator and his true calling as a composer.

As occurs to all of us during weaker moments, Chadwick sometimes disdained his day job as director of New England Conservatory (NEC), a position he assumed in 1897. Until then his connection to the institution had been slight. Although he taught a few classes, Chadwick made it a point to avoid conservatory politics, which were often thick. But he found much of the work rewarding, and he took pride in the success that came to him and the institution as NEC's reputation grew. His duties there included, in addition to administration, the teaching of theory and composition, and conducting a variety of choral and instrumental ensembles; these responsibilities occupied much of his time during the academic year. Once he got into a routine, he managed to complete some sketches in Boston, but he saved the "heavy lifting"—idea development, orchestrations, and such—for summers spent at his beach home at West Chop on the island of Martha's Vineyard. For Chadwick, composition was a pursuit saved for evenings, weekends, holidays, and moments stolen between classes and meetings. Nevertheless, his compositional work ethic was herculean. From the late 1870s until the mid-1910s, when he was into his sixties, Chadwick composed relentlessly, except for a one-year period when he was in Europe on sabbatical.

The very span of Chadwick's life and the diversity of his body of compositions make him an immensely attractive subject for historical inquiry. Born in 1854, just a few years before the first volley of the Civil War, he lived to see the devastation of the Great War and the turmoil wrought by the onset of the Great Depression. In his adopted hometown of Boston, he witnessed the establishment of significant New England cultural institutions, such as NEC, the Boston Symphony Orchestra, Symphony Hall, and Boston Opera. In New York he saw the rise and fall of Jeannette Thurber's National Conservatory of Music, the founding of the Institute of Musical Art (later known as the Juilliard School), and the glory of Carnegie Hall. Chadwick also watched as technology improved—and sometimes invaded—his life via electricity, the phonograph and the gramophone, the telephone, and the motion picture. He traveled widely —first by horse cart and train, then by steamship and automobile, and eventually by air—in the United States and abroad. Chadwick's travels enabled his presence at many of the age's most consequential musical events: Patrick Gilmore's second Boston Peace Jubilee (1872), the World's Columbian Exhibition in Chicago (1892), San Francisco's Panama-Pacific Exhibition (1915), and other smaller ones. His reports of these events, sometimes rendered in splendid detail, are often amusing and eloquent; they are always insightful.

If Chadwick's father had prevented him from experiencing an idyllic childhood, as an adult Chadwick enjoyed a wonderfully fulfilling family life. His wife Ida May is mentioned only obliquely in his writings, but her importance to his domestic steadiness and prolific compositional production cannot be overstated. We may take for granted that Chadwick dealt with issues common to everyday life: he paid his mortgages and other bills, invested his money (not always successfully), balanced the family checkbook, worried about his income and his ability to pay for his children's college tuition, and griped (often) about the performance and salaries of his household servants and other hired helpers. As a youth Chadwick desperately sought domestic tranquility, and, to his enormous gratification, the bitter, unrelenting feuds that he fought with his domineering parent during his teen years were virtually nonexistent in his adult household. His two sons grew up in a loving environment permeated with healthy communication and good cheer.

Chadwick had a captivating, in many ways uniquely American, personality and demeanor. He possessed a keen sense of humor, although his piercing eyes and sometimes torrential sarcasm could make even the not-so-timid wilt; Chadwick knew that, and he relished it—his brusqueness was often deployed as a matter of strategy. He always had amusing stories and anecdotes at the ready, but he could also display a thoroughly professional style and conduct himself in harmony with his status as a conservatory leader, a trait perhaps originating from the time he labored in his father's insurance business. Chadwick also possessed an inclination to intellectualism, but it was of a modest sort, uncluttered by pomp or arrogance. He was a reader, although not a voracious one, possessed of a robust curiosity. He always felt that his early family travails robbed him of the environment and the nurturing he needed in order to excel at his school work.

There are thorny issues to confront when exploring Chadwick's art and career. Besides the question of his "Americanism," one must also grapple with a huge corpus of music, most of which has never been published or even examined in any detail. Then there is the sometimes unpleasant metamorphosis in his personality as his status developed from an important and revered composer to an aging "old fogy," as he sometimes referred to himself. And there is little doubt that Chadwick's posthumous reputation has suffered as a result of his being what is derisively referred to as an "academic" composer. His music was nearly always "learned"—that is, molded by the norms of early-Romantic tradition, tuneful, and carefully planned in form and effect. This is not a situation that is unique to Chadwick; indeed, our perception of most American composers of classical music in the period from the beginning of the Civil War (and even before) to the end of the Great War is approximately the same. At that time, however, being "academic" was not a disparagement; being learned in one's field was a universal goal. Besides, work in an educational institution—in the college, the university, or the conservatory—is how most composers who wished to be engaged in music on a full-time basis made their livelihoods in a democracy, where patronage of individual composers and performers was not practiced. Most were no longer simply hanging a shingle and advertising their wares with the hope of establishing a prosperous private studio; they sought opportunities in the academy. Just as fretfully for Chadwick, avenues to professional conducting were almost completely closed to Americans; the nascent American orchestra industry intractably looked to Europe for its musical leaders. Absent the largess of monarchs, the government, and individual patrons—not to mention the impossibility of earning a living from publishing royalties—the academy was the sole refuge for a composer who wished to be in close daily contact with music.

Being in the "academy" can have a romantic overtone, and indeed in Chadwick's time, academia for the musician was a burgeoning and noble venture—serious musicians were involved in serious pursuits, not the least of which was the simple act of thinking deeply about one's artistic aims and composing profusely. For Chadwick, the conservatory was no ivory tower. NEC, bereft of funds and reputation, required a staggering amount of toil and fret. Under his dedicated and visionary guidance, the conservatory blossomed from its status as a musical finishing school mostly for young ladies to a significant conservatory based on European models he had researched diligently. And Chadwick's career as a conservatory leader set him entirely apart from his musical colleagues in Boston, although it was never what he considered a dream job. It was simply a job related to music, one that afforded him the ability to raise his family in some comfort and to travel now and then. Crucially, it freed him to compose from time to time during the academic year and constantly while on summer and holiday breaks. It also enabled him to regularly lead an orchestra, albeit it one comprising NEC students, and he could employ it as a laboratory for hearings of his own compositions.

Chadwick was at home in the company of intellectuals and artists of all stripes, and in fact his close friendships with visual artists especially are essential to an understanding of his art. His fleeting early experience as one of the famed Duveneck Boys not only had an effect on his music, but it created in him the desire to seek out painters, whose company he found stimulating. Chadwick aimed to learn about other fields, scientific and historical, as well as artistic. His association with visual artists, literary men, and scientists deepened throughout his career, as his later involvement in Boston's Thursday Evening Club and the American Academy of Arts and Sciences would demonstrate.

Nowhere, of course, was he more comfortable than among his fellow American composers, and it is impossible to accurately consider his life without taking stock of a group once known as the Boston Classicists but nowadays more popularly called the Second New England School of composers.[3] Chadwick's family musical background was not out of step with other composers of his era. It is generally thought that these composers have been collected into a "school" for their geographical proximity as much as their shared musical values, but that assumption overlooks the enormous influence they exerted on one another. Members of the group were familiar, if not always cordial, with one another's person and music. Its elder member was John Knowles Paine, the first to garner more than just regional fame. Paine's grandfather was an organ builder of some reputation, and his father, Jacob S. Paine, was the proprietor of a music store in Portland, Maine, where he also conducted the town's first band. Paine's extended family was musically active, and he was encouraged to take music lessons from an early age. Before he was twenty, Paine was producing his own concert series in an effort raise funds that would pay for the continuation of his education abroad. Paine's music is reserved and shows the heavy influence of Mendelssohn, Schumann, and other early Romantic composers. A humble man with a lackluster personality, he died in 1906 after having established a music degree–granting program—the first of its type at an American university—at Harvard.

Chadwick was closer to three other individuals nearer his own age, members of a group that, with him, came to be called the Big 4: Horatio Parker, Arthur Foote, and Arthur Whiting, whose company he relished. Parker, the most important composer of the group after Chadwick, was a church musician who, over the course of his brilliant career, was closely allied to the Anglican school of organ and choral composition. His mother introduced him to music; when he was fourteen years old, she noticed that his interest had surged, and she began to tutor him in piano and harmony.[4] Organ practice pedals were even installed in the Parker home so that little Horatio could begin his studies on that instrument. Within three years Parker was playing at a local church for the handsome sum of three hundred dollars per year. He was also known for several orchestral works, two prize-winning operas, and many choral works. Parker had been among Chadwick's first students and was heavily influenced by him. After further schooling in Munich and an early career start in Boston, Parker took a position in New York, where he lived and worked for several years. When he accepted a professorship at Yale University in 1894, he effectively removed himself from musical life in Boston.

Whiting and Foote did not compose prodigiously, and their careers, if perhaps not their talents, were modest. Whiting studied with Chadwick before leaving, as many of Chadwick's students would, to study in Munich. Although he left Boston in the 1890s, he maintained close ties to the group. Foote was a student of Paine and holds the distinction of having been the first person to receive a master's degree in music at an American university. Foote was also one of the few American musicians of his era to eschew the idea of studying in Germany; except for some minimal coaching in Paris, his schooling was acquired entirely in the US. More prolific than Whiting, who wrote only a handful of works, Foote's music has nevertheless been forgotten. Foote was by all accounts an exceptional teacher and, after four decades of goading, Chadwick finally convinced him to accept a position at NEC in 1920.

There were other members of the Second New England School. Amy Beach was well regarded as a pianist, but her career and renown as a composer was somewhat limited by her gender and her slim catalog of major compositions. The young wife of a prominent Boston physician, Beach was esteemed by the other composers in the group. Chadwick once wrote Beach a complimentary letter in which he stated that the merits of her music made it impossible not to consider her "one of the boys." His affection for her and his respect for her music were genuine.

Edward MacDowell was the only member of the group whose fame eclipsed Chadwick's. Born in New York in 1860, he had early on shown gifts as a musician.

By the time he was fifteen, he had already studied seriously with the Venezuelan pianist Teresa Carreño, who before long would herself be a legend. Soon Mac-Dowell left for Paris in the company of his mother. There he gained notoriety as a prodigy and was admitted to the city's famous Conservatoire before removing to Germany, where he began his career as a composer and teacher. Considered a master of "miniatures," smaller compositions often infused with poetic and pro-grammatic elements, MacDowell nevertheless produced a number of compelling orchestral works, including a piano concerto that maintains a small place in the modern repertoire. He was widely considered America's greatest composer of art song. MacDowell resided in Boston only briefly, and he was not particularly esteemed by Chadwick's circle—he possessed a serious and melancholy nature and was not attracted to the social aspects of life in which most of the Boston group, especially Chadwick, reveled. MacDowell died prematurely in 1908 at the height of his career. Effectively martyred, he left behind a reputation as the best composer in America's history; Chadwick often suffered by comparison to MacDowell, whose compositions, especially his songs and piano works, were widely known and performed by amateur musicians.

Although not a Boston man, or even a New Englander, Chadwick's exact contemporary and fast friend John Philip Sousa was considered something of an honorary member of the Big 4. In many ways Chadwick's career mirrored that of the bandmaster. Sousa was a prolific composer. His marches, of course, continue to be staples of modern band literature; during his own lifetime he was equally famous for his many operettas. Sousa was an able administrator, first managing the United States Marine Band and later his own phenomenally successful Sousa Band, which toured North America and the world. And, like Chadwick during his lengthy and very public reign over NEC, Sousa was a ce-lebrity who was constantly in front of an admiring public. Sousa had known Chadwick since at least the early 1890s, and he was fond of other members of the Boston group. He sought their company when in New England, and sometimes he even spoke to students at NEC, engrossing them with stories about his life and his career in music. Occasionally Sousa would sit in on one of Chadwick's NEC orchestra rehearsals and would generously offer performance tips.

During one of his visits, while conversing on a front porch with his colleagues and friends—members of the Big 4—Sousa, who knew Chadwick's talents well, called him the "Pride of New England."[5] Before Chadwick's implausible and estimable career was finished, he would be a music educator, a music adminis-trator, and especially a composer, in whom the entire nation could take pride.

"The Purest American Stock"
Chadwick's New England Roots

*The fact is that there were always amateur musicians, and
the amateurs — the real lovers — of an art are frequently those
who save it.*

—M. A. DeWolfe Howe, historian and Pulitzer Prize–winning
biographer, *The Boston Symphony Orchestra* (1931)

Music in the New World

George Whitefield Chadwick was born on November 13, 1854, the scion of
two venerable New England clans, the Chadwicks of the town of Boscawen and
the Fittses of the village of Candia, both situated in southeastern New Hampshire. By and large these families comprised farmers, craftsmen, and shopkeep-
ers. But there were also a few musicians, and plenty of music was made by them.
So much so that—with the benefit of hindsight—it is not impossible to imagine
that someone of George's modest station in the world could become an inter-
nationally renowned composer.

Music had long been an important part of New England life, and both sides
of Chadwick's family cultivated music in the ages-old fashion of their kinsmen
since their arrival in the New World sometime prior to 1650. They made music
at home and at church; they made music for their own edification and for entertainment. For some of the Chadwicks and the Fittses, music was a simple joy
cultivated casually in the idle moments spent away from their toils; for others it
was a passionate pursuit.

Music had been the passion of some individuals in America since the landing
of the Pilgrims at Plymouth, Massachusetts, in 1620. Because music's purpose at
the time was primarily to serve worship by illuminating the text of the Bible, the
Pilgrims and Puritans arrived with a variety of "Psalters," books that laid out the
texts of the Psalms along with melodies to which they could be sung. One of the
Pilgrims' most popular Psalters was Reverend Henry Ainsworth's *The Book of
Psalmes: Englished both in Prose and Metre* (Amsterdam, 1612), or the *Ainsworth
Psalter*. It comprised a total of thirty-nine monophonic tunes, some simple, others rather long and complex, especially in their rhythm. Another, older volume
that traveled to the shores of America with the Puritans was *The Whole Booke
of Psalmes* (London, 1562) by Thomas Sternhold and John Hopkins. Although
its music was simple, most thought its texts poorly set. A third Psalter that was

widely appreciated was Thomas Ravenscroft's *The Whole Booke of Psalmes* (London, 1621), which included a collection of 105 tunes. It presented a number of Psalms in a four-part setting, perhaps indicating the advanced musical ability of some of North America's earliest European settlers.

After a time, an American Psalter was certain to appear. It is entirely possible that a pioneering Chadwick or Fitts may have sung from his own copy of *The Whole Booke of Psalmes Faithfully Translated into English Metre* (Cambridge, Massachusetts, 1640), better known today as the *Bay Psalm Book*, the first book of any type published in the colonies. The *Bay Psalm Book* featured 150 psalms that could be sung to different well-known tunes—musical notation was not included in its earliest editions—after being matched to the appropriate metrical verse. As it turned out, most congregations utilized only a handful of familiar tunes to sing their Psalms. It is possible that the omission of printed music in the *Bay Psalm Book*, a steep simplification over earlier practice, caused a decline in music literacy in the colonies, although it may have been a response to an already enfeebled situation. There developed in the mid-seventeenth century a musical practice that came to be known as "the old style of singing" (or "the Old Way"). The Old Way, or congregational singing without accompaniment, featured the "lining out" of a song; that is, a principal singer, often but not always a church leader, would sound the tune, which would be repeated in rote fashion by the congregation. This method caused problems, including a continuing decline in musical literacy and huge variations in how the music was sung from congregation to congregation. Thomas Walter, in his *The Grounds and Rules of Musick Explained* (1721) remarked that the tunes featured in the Old Way are "now miserably tortured, and twisted, and quavered, in some churches, into an horrid Medley of confused and disorderly Noises."[1] To religions that sought uniformity in their church services, this problem was particularly vexing.

By 1720 there emerged a number of advocates of "Regular Singing," or singing from musical notation. One of these was Cotton Mather, whose portentous and impassioned 1721 tract, *The Accomplished Singer. Instructions first, How the Piety of Singing with a True Devotion, may be Obtained and Expressed; the Glorious God after an Uncommon Manner Glorified in it, and His People Edified. And then, How the Melody of Regular Singing, and the Skill of Doing it, according to the Rules of it, May be Easily Arrived unto*, pleaded for the universal adoption of Regular Singing. Mather and others argued that Regular Singing would naturally improve musical standards of the church service and, therefore, would reinforce the glorification of God. Learning the art of music would also provide an excellent and wholesome pursuit for singers during their leisure hours. Although adherents of the Old Way were quiet on the controversy (one historian has surmised that those supporting the Old Way felt little need to defend their choice[2]), they seem to have been unmoved by the Regular Singing advocates; the Old Way did not go away quickly.

Singing from notation naturally required individuals to learn to read music. Many did this in the numerous "singing schools" that began to sprout up all over New England. These schools, run by itinerant and fervid teachers of varying levels of musical ability, led to a number of important advances that would greatly benefit music in America. By the end of the eighteenth century, singing schools enabled music teachers to make their livelihoods by rendering music lessons. In turn, students required printed music, and that gave rise to music publishing and sales. The proliferation of publishing inevitably led to the composition of music by American composers. The impact of these developments was felt not only by church music, with its consequent increases in church choir participation, but secular music benefitted as well. The rise in musical literacy, as well as the increasing availability of imported instruments, also led to a growing participation in the performance of instrumental music.[3]

It was into this alluring and highly charged musical atmosphere that George Chadwick's family arrived and eventually flourished.

The Chadwicks of Boscawen

Much of the Chadwick family history is documented in three volumes: Charles Coffin's *History of Boscawen and Webster from 1733 to 1878*; Willis G. Buxton's continuation of Coffin's work from 1883 *to* 1933; and the Boscawen Historical Society's continuation, with corrections of both Coffin and Buxton, which covers 1933 to 1983.[4] Coffin's version of the Chadwick family tree had long been the accepted one, and it remains a valuable tool that attempts a thorough treatment of the Chadwicks.[5] His Chadwick chronicle contains several important errors beginning with his earliest entry; Coffin lists Charles Chadwick, born in England in 1596, as the first in the line to come to America. According to Coffin's account, Charles settled in Watertown, Massachusetts, in 1630. Perhaps in an effort to derail any potential disputes on the question of Charles Chadwick, Coffin boldly pronounced, "The Chadwicks of B.[oscawen] are without doubt his descendants."[6]

The more thorough genealogy is that by the Boscawen Historical Society, which makes no mention of a Charles Chadwick. Its 1983 revisions present a different origin to the family tree; its story is one that is more comprehensive, more thoroughly documented, and is based on research produced and submitted by the Chadwick family.[7] It is this family history that will be interpreted here.

The first listing for the clan is one John Chadwick, who was born in Lancashire, England, in 1601. He lived until 1681, when his will was probated on April 5 of that year. It is not known precisely when he arrived on American shores, but it is likely that he had emigrated by at least the 1640s. He resided in the villages of Watertown and Malden, Massachusetts.

John's son—also named John—was born in Malden in 1651 before moving to Boxford in 1686, and then to Bradford in 1701, where he died six years later.[8] (From this point Coffin and the Boscawen Historical Society continue in relative agreement.)

Edmund Chadwick, John's son, lived in Bradford, Massachusetts, and fathered nine children.[9] One of them was James Chadwick. We know virtually nothing about James's brief life and work, but his son Edmund Chadwick was one of the most celebrated members of the early Chadwick family. Edmund was active in Massachusetts political affairs; he signed controversial documents, such as the Boston Port Bill of 1772, and he reportedly soldiered "in [John] Stark's regiment, at the picket fence, at the battle of Bunker Hill."[10] Edmund participated in local governance; he became constable and tax collector in 1790, and later he served as deacon of the church in Boscawen. Edmund provided the first indication of the strong religious faith that ran through Chadwick's family. It is also possible that Edmund may have been among the earliest of the Chadwicks to live in the tiny New Hampshire town of Boscawen, for he is the first to be mentioned in close connection with it.[11] Edmund died on August 20, 1819, but his reputation among the Chadwick clan lingered; George Chadwick later declared that, on account of his exploits in the American Revolution, Edmund "had been a great 'ad' for the family."[12]

Edmund's children were an industrious lot. James Chadwick was the second of Edmund's six children, which included four boys and two girls. It is possible that James was a teacher, but details are sketchy. Joseph, James's brother, was a master clockmaker whose tall clocks are highly prized today.[13] He also donated the land on which the Boscawen Academy was built in 1827.[14] The eldest among Edmund's children, Samuel, was a farmer with extensive land holdings in Boscawen. He is remembered today by the hill and the road—"all but impassable now regardless of the fact that it is a full-fledged town road"—which bear his name: Sam Chadwick Hill Road. In recent years, and to the consternation of a few, it has been abbreviated to Chadwick Road.[15]

James's eldest son was George's father, Alonzo Calvin Chadwick. Little is known about Alonzo's early life. He began his career in Boscawen as a farmer, perhaps on one of his Uncle Sam's properties, but that endeavor did not last long, as we shall see.[16]

The Fittses of Candia

Chadwick's maternal family, the Fitts clan, was also of English stock according to the family genealogist, Sylvia Fitts Getchell. Siblings Robert, Richard, and Bridget were born abroad, but voyaged to America in approximately 1630. By 1638, Robert owned land in Cambridge, Massachusetts.[17] His son Abraham had been born in England several years before the family moved to America. As a young adult, Abraham participated in the Indian Wars that occupied settlers in the last quarter of the seventeenth century.[18] Abraham's descendants include his son Richard, a weaver by trade. Richard's son Daniel was a celebrated blacksmith who lived to his eighty-sixth year.

Among the most famous of the Fitts family was yet another Abraham, who was a highly regarded blacksmith with his father, but later speculated in land and became wealthy and powerful in local politics before picking up arms for the northern Continental Army in 1777.[19] It was Abraham who led the family to the New Hampshire town of Candia, where generations thrived; many Fittses inhabit the town to this day.

Abraham's son, also named Abraham, was active in municipal and church affairs in Candia; among the various offices he held was that of town assessor in 1808. He and his wife, Susannah, had eleven children, including Hannah Godfrey Fitts, George Chadwick's mother. As with many women of the day, we know disappointingly little about Hannah, but her four brothers were industrious in the typical New England manner. John Lane Fitts was a carpenter and eventually plied his trade in Lowell, Massachusetts; Abraham Fitts was a machinist; Jesse Remmington Fitts was a carpenter; and Isaac Newton Fitts was a machinist and a master mechanic in the Lowell textile mills. Hannah's many uncles, cousins, and nephews were involved in every small-town enterprise imaginable. Samuel Fitts was a cooper; Nathan Fitts a blacksmith-turned-shopkeeper; John E. Fitts ran a saw mill, one of many in and around Candia; and Moses Fitts was a shopkeeper who became known as "Master" Moses Fitts when, in 1818, he became Candia's first postmaster. Some of the more entrepreneurial members of the Fitts family experimented in silk production in the second quarter of the nineteenth century. It was soon recognized, however, that New England's climate was too cold for the delicate silkworms.[20]

The most remarkable musical Fitts was Hannah's cousin, Asa Fitz (1810–1878).[21] He established his own "academy" for the teaching of music. It eventually failed, but according to one account, "As a teacher he was quite popular, especially with the younger class of pupils."[22] He later taught music at the Teacher's Institute of Massachusetts and published a number of works, musical and philosophical. Fitz was prolific; he wrote or compiled over a dozen tunebooks between 1840 and 1870. They include such church-related titles as *The Congregational Singing Book* (ca. 1848), *The Sacred Minstrel* (ca. 1856), and *The Harmoniad and Sacred Melodist* (ca. 1857), as well as singing books for use in "common" or public schools. Among these are *The Primary School Song Book* (ca. 1843), *School Songs for the Million* (ca. 1850), and *The National School Songster* (ca. 1870). The philosophy behind Fitz's popular *The American School Hymn Book* (1855) was typical of the times in New England; that is, the songs reflected a broad, universal religious spirit—not a particular denomination—and all selections were morally uplifting. As Asa wrote in his preface:

> The Devotional hymns [included here] are believed to be entirely free from any sectarian peculiarities while they are highly elevated in their character, and adapted to all ages of pupils.
>
> The Songs contain pure moral sentiments, and are peculiarly adapted to render the exercises of the school room pleasant and refreshing.
>
> No teacher with this book can fail to have good music in his school. Even if he does not sing, there are always pupils enough who can sing many of the hymns in this book without the aid of a teacher.
>
> All schools, as far as possible, should commence and close the exercises of the day with a song of praise. This would tend greatly to refine and educate the moral elements of character, of which the pupil stands so much in need, and which, at the present day, is so much neglected.[23]

Besides the ages-old observation that children "at the present day" need character education, the preface may indicate the piety of at least one branch of the Fitts family, as well as the abiding faith in the power of music to improve one's life.

Asa was the most famous of Chadwick's musical relatives, but he was by no means the only one. Community and church music-making was a Fitts family habit. Many of them sang in the choir of the Congregational Society and participated as instrumentalists. George's uncle, Isaac Newton Fitts, has become famous in family lore for his varied musical activities; not only did he play the bass viol and direct the church choir, but, in a true measure of Yankee ingenuity, he once built an organ in his barn.[24] Uncle Jesse also played the bass viol, and Grandpa Abraham played the "clarionet."[25] At least four Fittses, cousins and uncles who would have been known to George, enjoyed membership in the Candia Cornet Band.[26]

One scandalous non-musical episode in Fitts family lore worth recounting is the strange case of George's cousin, Wilfred Fitts, the son of Uncle Isaac. On the evening of April 14, 1873, an ailing Wilfred, then living with his family in Lowell, broke into the home of his friend John Emerson brandishing an axe. After very nearly killing Emerson, Wilfred was captured and subsequently tried. As reported in a Candia town history, "A very large audience was present and a considerable number of the newspapers in the state were represented."[27] After a flurry of witnesses vouched for the boy's character, the judge in the case granted Wilfred release to the custody of his father under the promise that Isaac would seek help for his son. Considering the charge was attempted murder, the judge was unusually lenient. Although it was generally acknowledged that Wilfred suffered from some psychological malady, the special circumstances that surrounded this incident had no precedent in Massachusetts law, for the vicious attack on Emerson purportedly occurred while Wilfred was sleepwalking. Considering the mountain of publicity that was generated, there is little possibility that the eighteen-year-old George was unaware of his cousin's predicament.[28]

Chadwick's Parents

By the middle of the nineteenth century, the population of Boscawen hovered near 2,200. This included an area known as West Boscawen, which became the town of Webster in 1860.[29] The business of Boscawen was largely agriculture, along with related industries, but there also were lumber mills, tanneries, and the like, small businesses similar to those one might find in any rural community of the day. Naturally, at the end of long toilsome days, activities had to be found to combat the monotony and boredom of daily life. To that end, the Alonzo Chadwick family cultivated music.

Music historian Carl Engel, utilizing information he obtained from Chadwick, wrote that "the musical farmer," Alonzo, "for ten years taught a singing class. A member of that class he took for a wife."[30] Alonzo married Hannah Fitts on July 4 in what year we do not know, but probably in the mid- to late-1830s. Together they conceived two children, Fitz Henry Chadwick (called Henry), born in 1840, and George Whitefield Chadwick, born some fourteen and a half years later.[31] By the time George arrived, Alonzo had left Boscawen and moved his family to the industrial town of Lowell, Massachusetts. Within days of George's birth, at the family's home on Fifth Street in the section of town known as Centralville, Hannah died as a result of her difficult pregnancy and delivery. (As his own second son was about to be born, George Chadwick resented the stubborn unwillingness of the attending physician to give his wife ether to alleviate her pain, "merely because nature has so arranged it. I have no doubt that it was this merciless theory that cost my own poor mother her life."[32])

Alonzo was left to care for his children alone, in relatively new surroundings, far from family, and undoubtedly while living on a meager income. Not surprisingly for the times, Alonzo was not alone very long. Musicologist Victor Fell Yellin discovered that Alonzo married his Lowell neighbor, twenty-eight-year-old Susan Collins, on February 3, 1855, less than three months after the passing of his wife.[33] To modern ears the identification of a new spouse and a marriage within such a short span of time seems unusual, perhaps even unfathomable. At first glance, one might think that Alonzo was considering the needs of baby George; after all, Alonzo had a newborn infant to raise, and he needed a wife to help with that effort.

But in fact Alonzo and Susan did not raise infant George; he was left with his grandfather, James Chadwick, for about three years—presumably to enable Alonzo to forge a new career and establish his recent marriage. Once baby George was retrieved, Alonzo's new wife proved to be a fine mother to his children, although a rather rosy family-reunion scenario is vitiated by the fact that James died on December 29, 1857, just weeks after George's third birthday. It begs the question of whether Alonzo reclaimed George out of the desire to reunite with his son or whether he took George because, following the death of his father, he had no other choice. Other questions arise: Could Alonzo have blamed George for Hannah's death? And did this account for what would become a deep fissure between father and son forever? Could Alonzo's emotional detachment have animated the familial closeness that would develop between Susan and her toddler stepson?

Whatever the circumstances, the Chadwick family had finally been re-formed. Although Henry—whose whereabouts during the years when George resided with his grandfather are unknown—was by this time already a teenager, possessed of a fully developed personality and perhaps living on his own, Susan Collins raised little George like he was her own; in later years he would remember her with heartfelt gratitude, remarking that "her mission was to be the good angel of another woman's children and this she fulfilled with the utmost faithfulness. . . . No real mother could have lavished more tenderness and love on me than she did."[34] Of course, his love for the mother he had never known remained. On the occasion of her birthday in 1911, he confided, "One hundred years ago to this day Hannah Fitz was born. I have often wondered if my father's life would have been very different if she had lived. When she departed she left almost no trace behind, but I have always felt that in some unexplainable way, she has influenced my life, and if it is possible to love a parent whom one never saw, or heard from, I was sure I have felt that affection from her. She gave her life for mine, and greater love hath no man than this."[35] Chadwick maintained his ties to the Fitts family well into adulthood. His stepmother encouraged the relationship, and during his childhood summers with the Fittses in Candia, Chadwick was constantly kept at the family melodeon.

Chadwick later supplied details about the relationship shared by his biological parents. He recalled stories, told to him "by my favorite aunt," that his father had "a good tenor voice, he sang and played the bass viol in church and the bugle at musters." Hannah Fitts possessed "a fine contralto voice." Chadwick added,

> In the course of time [Alonzo] payed [sic] a visit to her in her home. There he was put through the third degree in religious matters by the young lady's father. He demonstrated familiarity with the tenets of Jonathan Edwards, his belief in the inspiration of the scriptures and the correctness of his views on foreordination and infant perdition, also the validity of his hopes for salvation for himself and for about two-percent of the neighbors, provided they were not Universalists, Unitarians, Episcopals, Catholics or other heathens. Then they made some music.[36]

Following the performance of several set pieces from "Deacon Gould's book" and a rousing performance of the *Marsellaise*, "This finished the young lady completely and they were married on the fourth of July. . . . Such was my father and such was my mother, whom I never saw, but who left to me the same love for music which had illuminated on her own short life. And for this blessed heritage I trust I may never cease to be grateful."[37]

In 1835 Alonzo was a teacher in New Hampshire's sixth and eighth school districts of Concord.[38] He is also reported to have organized a singing school there as well.[39] Alonzo had been a member of the Boscawen Musical Society and, when that group failed, he helped to reorganize and eventually preside over its reincarnation, the Martin Luther Musical Society.[40] Leadership of the Society was an important endeavor. Founded in 1821, at its zenith the society numbered approximately fifty of the finest musicians from the region. They swiftly set about purchasing music, which "required a much higher degree of culture than the music of by-gone days." Town historian Charles Coffin remarked that the society's library contained "music of a high order" by the likes of Handel, Haydn, Mozart, and Beethoven, but social and financial pressures were taking a toll. Coffin wrote that "emigration was telling upon the community, and other forces were at work to disintegrate the society, and the members, after a while, ceased to meet."[41]

While we know that Alonzo sang from "Deacon Gould's book,"[42] it is possible that he may have been personally coached by Nathaniel D. Gould, an expert on church music and one of the leading itinerant singing-school musicians of the day.[43] Gould propounded Regular Singing—that is, musical literacy—but as an adult he remembered with solemn adulation the pioneer spirit that could be found in the singing of those who practiced the Old Way. From all accounts, the Chadwicks concertized in a spirited manner. The family, Engel writes, was also known to produce musicales that included homegrown choruses and "orchestras" of varied, and sometimes curious, instrumentations.[44]

Alonzo Chadwick's home housed a piano that Henry took to immediately, and his talents were soon apparent. Later Henry would learn to play the organ, an avocation to which he clung for the rest of his life. It was Henry who gave young George his first lessons on piano and organ, and in the 1860s both Chadwick boys were playing for their mutual amusement and at church services. Critic and historian Louis C. Elson reported that as a boy Chadwick sang alto in the church choir and that "his first connection with organ-playing was at the handle of the bellows." In time he was "promoted from the blowing to the playing of the instrument."[45] George also played Beethoven and undoubtedly other composers as well, "'a quatre main' with brother Henry."[46] Engel further related that Chadwick's schooling interfered with his love for "following hand-organs all over town," and that music played a significant role at various Chadwick family events "when uncles, aunts, and cousins—some of whom were the possessors of excellent voices—sang praises to the Lord in rich and vibrant harmony."[47]

Chadwick's musical upbringing was not atypical. Early on he recognized that his family's cultivation of music was pivotal in his life, and he regarded it as a deeply important aspect of his cultural heritage, although he sometimes minimized its significance. As he matured, Chadwick reveled in many other aspects of his background and was proud of his humble New England roots, "that sturdy race [that] left us a heritage of good clean blood, useful brains, and steady nerves."[48] Chadwick was a Yankee to the bone, and he demonstrated a number of characteristics that we presently—if sometimes stereotypically—associate with that group: he carried himself with a pride and a confidence that sometimes bordered on arrogance; he was frugal and carefully watched every penny he ever earned, although as he prospered he rarely deprived himself of life's enjoyments. He was devoted to family, to work, to his own betterment, and to that of others. These traits Chadwick learned from his forbears, staid and solemn people who by and large looked to religion and music to ease their troubles. Elson was paying the composer a compliment when, in his famous *History of American Music*, he wrote that Chadwick "comes of the purest American stock."[49]

Musical Atmospheres
Early Life in Lowell, Lawrence, Boston, & Michigan
1854–1876

*Upwards of thirty thousand pages of music have been deposited at
the State Department, within thirty years, by American authors,
for copyright. Who says the Yankee can't whistle?*
—*Lawrence Daily Journal and Courier*, November 15, 1854

Lowell

By the time Chadwick was born, Lowell, Massachusetts, was already a thriving industrial town. It was popularly known as "The City of Spindles" because of its prominence in the American textile industry of the time, namely cotton cloth production.[1] The Chadwick family's removal to Lowell probably occurred because Alonzo Chadwick hoped to advance his position in the world by heading into industry and leaving small-town farming to those more apt to enjoy it. He may have been lured by the promise of factory life as it was described by the recruiters who were hired to keep the mill employment rolls filled.[2] Obviously professional prospects were limited in the hamlet of Boscawen, and, while we do not know too much about him, all indications are that Alonzo was an ambitious man.

Conditions at Lowell have been chronicled in detail primarily because of the town's early and extensive utilization of female employees, the so-called "Lowell Mill Girls." Author Charles Dickens became aware of the practice of hiring women as textile workers when he visited the United States in 1842. Dickens was one of hundreds of British writers who were curious about the new nation in the years between the War of 1812 and the outbreak of the American Civil War, and he sought to provide a sweeping chronicle of the New World for his readers back home. With a reporter's eye for particulars, he gave a colorful portrait of the times in his book *American Notes for General Circulation*. In a work focused on broad issues of American culture, Dickens provided a leisurely rumination on the small town. "I devoted one day to an excursion to Lowell," he explained. "I assign a separate chapter to this visit; not because I am about to describe it at any great length, but because I remember it as a thing by itself, and am desirous that my readers should do the same."[3] Dickens described the town in splendid detail: "Lowell is a large populous, thriving place. Those indications of its youth which first attract the eye, give it a quaintness and oddity of character which, to a visitor from the old country, is amusing enough."[4] He was intrigued by Lowell's newness: "One would swear that every 'Bakery,' 'Grocery,' and 'Bookbindery,' and other kind of store, took its shutters down for the first time, and started in business yesterday. . . . When I saw a baby of some week or ten days old in a woman's arms at a street corner, I found myself unconsciously wondering where it came from: never supposing for an instant that it could have been born in such a young town."[5]

Lowell has also attracted the attention of contemporary American scholars. Historian Brian C. Mitchell has written that, for the town's founders, "Lowell was a place where rational thinking and Yankee ingenuity combined to point the way to a bright future in a humane industrial environment. Lowell proved to the world that America promised and delivered on the promise, offering its residents an industrial setting which avoided the horrors of England's Lancashire."[6] If the residential conditions were attractive, employment conditions were far less so. Alonzo tended to the oiling of the cotton spindles in the mills,[7] and the work was arduous. The typical workdays for the mill girls were long, occasionally surpassing thirteen hours per day, and there is no reason to believe that Alonzo's hours were shorter.[8] After all, when the machines were operating, the oil had to be applied to keep them running smoothly.

Verena Rybicki's account of Lowell dispenses with the comparatively more romantic outlook expressed by Dickens. She notes that, in some of the mills, eight hundred to twelve hundred machines operated up to fourteen hours a day, producing a deafening noise and a thunderous rumble that could be felt throughout the shaking buildings.[9] Further, "Steam was constantly hissing into the room, providing the humidity essential to maintain the correct environment for the spinning and weaving of cotton. Windows were sealed shut to prevent the humidity from escaping, and temperatures would hover between 90 and 115 degrees. The window panes were grimed over by a brown deposit, reducing the light so that kerosene lamps would have to be lit—another smell to add to that of machine oil."[10]

Mill work was terribly dangerous. The use of oil in the mills was tightly controlled, not only because of its utility in maintaining the spinning machines and its expense, but also because of the ever-present threat of fire. "Throughout the mill," notes historian Laurence F. Gross, "cotton offered a ready source of fuel should a fire begin. Danger from oil-soaked floors, overheated bearings, accumulations of waste, and oil- or gas-lamps, offered a constant threat of fire capable of consuming a mill with great rapidity."[11]

Although the work at the Lowell mills was tough—Dickens observed that "they labor in these mills . . . [it] is unquestionably work and pretty [difficult] work too"[12]—there were many opportunities for the absorbing pursuit of the era: self-improvement. By the early 1840s "mutual Self Improvement Clubs" proliferated. Moreover, Massachusetts law required that the girls employed at the mills receive some education during the year and for that purpose local schools thrived, circulating libraries were numerous, boarding houses were often supplied with pianos, and churches of various denominations ensured the appropriate attention to moral education.[13] One of the most important outlets of knowledge and culture was *The Lowell Offering*, a magazine written by the girls in the mills, which endeavored to "inculcate habits of self-denial and content-ment, and teach good doctrines of enlarged benevolence. . . . It has very scant allusion to fine clothes, fine marriages, fine houses, or fine life."[14] As we have already seen, the Fitts family was no stranger to mill life; it is possible that Han-nah Fitts may have worked in them just as several of her brothers did.[15]

While still in Lowell, Alonzo had been looking for work outside the mill, perhaps in an effort to escape the grime, noise, and danger. It is equally likely that he hoped to make more money. Then, as now, climbing up the ladder to the professions, trading in mill work for a white-collar position, was commendable. Family lore has it that Alonzo began to sell inexpensive burial insurance poli-cies while still in Lowell, and in fact, his success at the endeavor enabled him to remove to Lawrence.[16] If that is the case, insurance was still a small part of Alonzo's activity; George's birth certificate lists Alonzo not as a machine tender or mill oilman or insurance agent, but as a carpenter.[17] But just as he left the Bos-cawen farm to forge a better life in the Lowell textile mills, he would soon put Lowell behind him in another effort to advance himself. Alonzo had determined that the end of the blue-collar drudgery of factory life lay upriver.

Lawrence
Alonzo had moved his family to Lawrence, Massachusetts, by at least 1859. Lawrence, an industrial community situated ten miles northeast of Lowell, had been planned and built by Boston businessmen in 1845. The town began with a population of 150.[18] Named for Abbott Lawrence, a prosperous Bostonian who owned substantial shares in various Lowell businesses, Lawrence differed from Lowell in at least one respect: its founders, Yankee utopians to the core, envisioned a "model city" that would not only make them a dollar, but would provide a firm foundation for the development of "proper" culture among the town's citizens. To wit, the aesthetic considerations of living conditions that were absent in Lowell were given substantial attention in the new burg. One town historian, chronicling the founders' attempts to enhance the lives of its residents, noted that "early pictures show that Lawrence was originally a pleas-

ant town with trees, grass, wandering animals, and children at play. Nor were these charms present by mere chance, since the founders had great interest in the physical appearance of their project. . . . They planted elms, laid out broad streets, and set aside many acres for a common and parks."[19] However, Lawrence's idyllic setting had a downside. Those who were employed by town companies were forced to abide by company rules that were strictly enforced by founders who were compelled to implement policies in a town that they, after all, had built from the ground up. The Pacific Mill, for example, would not hesitate to dismiss an employee "for lack of capacity and neatness, for unfaithfulness, for intemperance, for profanity, and for improper treatment of overseers."[20]

This authoritarian situation would not have been drastically different from that which Alonzo had already encountered in Lowell. But here it mattered little to him, for he was no longer a mill employee. In Lawrence he was his own man, the first independent insurance agent in town, and completely unbeholden to the town bosses. Lawrence's annual City Directories help ascertain the course of Alonzo's career. In the 1859 directory he is listed as secretary of the Fayette Insurance Company at 166 Essex Street. The next year he is listed as secretary and treasurer of the same company, and an advertisement in the back of the directory lists him as an agent for the Connecticut Mutual Life Insurance Company. In a common practice of the day, Alonzo's shop sold the wares of innumerable vendor companies, including Amazon Mutual, Quincy Mutual, Suffolk Mutual, and Dorchester Mutual, as well as a number of fire insurance companies. His title in the 1864 listing at 142 Essex Street is the somewhat more generic "insurance agent," and by 1871 Alonzo had moved the company to 283 Essex Street. George's name first appears in 1873, where he is listed simply as clerk. Appearing in the same directory is a small advertisement that lists only "A. C. Chadwick, General Insurance." Subsequent listings indicate that he remained at 283 Essex through at least 1877.[21]

Alonzo had found his calling. As a pioneer in Lawrence's insurance industry, he remained in business for many years, having founded his company when George was just five years old. By the 1860s and '70s, he was probably earning a very respectable living. For all of the many negative things that George would write about him later, there is no indication that Alonzo was a slouch. In fact, Alonzo's propensity to hustle various jobs throughout George's first two decades of life would not be lost on his impressionable younger son.

Lawrence's city fathers valued education and made its enhancement a community effort. Lawrence's Oliver High School had been founded in 1848–49 and named for General Henry Kemble Oliver to recognize his donation of "valuable philosophical and astronomical apparatus for its use."[22] In addition to being a popular politician, General Oliver was also an esteemed composer, music society organizer, and a friend of Lowell Mason. "Federal Street" (1832) is perhaps the most famous of Oliver's many hymn tunes.[23] By the time George attended Oliver High School, the general had already donated a number of art works, including "a fine engraving of the Landing of the Pilgrims, and also one of the Battle of Bunker Hill, together with busts of Cicero, Demosthenes, Socrates, Plato, George Washington and Benjamin Franklin, as well as statuettes of Galileo, Bowditch, Dante, Goethe, Schiller, Tasso, Ariosto, and Petrarch."[24] At Oliver High School, Chadwick's academic regimen was standard. In the fall of 1869, for example, he took courses in Latin ("which I hated and could never learn"), algebra, English, history, and physics ("then known as Natural Philosophy").[25] During this period, Chadwick's reading regimen was thorough. The family library was meager, with the highlights being Bunyan's *Pilgrim's Progress*, Josephus's *History of the Jews*, Richard Baxter's Puritan devotional, *The Saint's Everlasting Rest* (1650), and a dictionary. At school Chadwick read many classics, among them Shakespeare's *Julius Caesar*, *Macbeth*, and *A Midsummer Night's Dream*, Longfellow's *Hiawatha*, Scott's *Lady of the Lake*, Tennyson's *Idylls of the Kings*, as well as many ancient authors whose works were explored in his Latin class. Chadwick also pursued music at Oliver High School. His teacher was Reuben Merrill, "a funny little fat man who regarded himself as the only 'artist' in Lawrence," and a man for whom Chadwick had little respect.[26] Merrill was not a particularly patient man, and, in Merrill's defense, Chadwick was not a particularly attentive student. His stay in Merrill's class was brief.

Although it has been reported that Chadwick graduated from Oliver High School, the records indicate otherwise.[27] He actually attended for just over three years, from February 1868 until June 1871, and never received a diploma.[28] In preparation for his seminal article, "George W. Chadwick," which appeared in the *Musical Quarterly* in 1924, musicologist Carl Engel interviewed Chadwick at length. It seems that Chadwick may have been embarrassed enough about his high school situation to have given Engel bad information; throughout his life the composer lamented his lack of a strong secondary education. It is also possible that Chadwick was content to allow Engel to assume that he had matriculated from Oliver High School.

As noted previously, Chadwick's interest in music showed itself from an early age, but he was well into his teen years before he started to get serious. Although he clerked for his father in the insurance office, Chadwick had been involved with musical productions at Oliver High School. Rehearsal preparations for one particular school production were all-consuming and "the orchestra practiced so assiduously that they even gave 'al fresco' public rehearsals on their way home" from regular practices.[29] Chadwick worked doggedly on the music, an unidentified operetta composed by Sigmund Romberg: "The score I wrote out at great inconvenience from the parts in my father's office—when I should have been writing [insurance] policies. When we got through with it, it was a wreck and Romberg himself would not have known it."[30] The event included one of Chadwick's earliest conducting experiences; he remembered that his first baton was one of the pedals from the piano. As for his frustrations with the production, that baton "was eventually ruined on someone's head."[31] Despite the difficulties, "the performances were a great success, and we had to repeat it for the benefit of a church fair!"[32] For their dedication and verve, Chadwick and his group became known as the "irrepressible band."[33]

Chadwick's first important musical break came when he was asked to fill in for the ailing Sam Ellis, the regular organist and choirmaster at Lawrence Street Church. Up to that time, Chadwick had been a "blowboy," assigned to manually pump the organ bellows for the handsome sum of twenty dollars per year; but Ellis sensed that the youngster had talent. In addition to a salary, Ellis threw in the right to practice on the church's Cambridge, Massachusetts-built Stevens organ when it was available. Although not a remarkable talent himself, Ellis was very supportive of Chadwick, and he provided the young organist with his first glimpse into the varied life of a musician. Chadwick sounded an affectionate tone when he recalled that Ellis "kept a small music store, tuned pianos, sang a little, composed a la Lowell Mason and was a perfect type of the enthusiastic, incompetent, unsuccessful musician."[34] Within six months Chadwick secured the church's organ position full time and was paid the more substantial salary of a hundred dollars per year. Ellis, now a musical partner, remained the church's choir director.

Chadwick's tenure at Lawrence Street Church, however, was not without at least one sizable controversy, a widely discussed musical episode that even made the local newspaper. According to the writer (who did not disclose Chadwick's name or that of the church), the music being performed at the Sunday services was getting increasingly elaborate, a situation that was anathema to the church's conservative musical tradition. "The organist's efforts were highly artistic," he judged, "but they were apt to be somewhat livelier in movement than the bass-viol and trombone instrumentation, which in the days of the fathers carried the choir through the slow-motioned glories of the good old psalms and hymns."[35] Chadwick's improvisations had become long and far more complex than those to which the parishioners were accustomed. The chairman of the church music committee forwarded to Chadwick a message to "please make your response after the prayer short, distinct and impressive." With apparent glee the writer went on to explain that "nobody was quite prepared for the climax which followed":

> The minister said his "Amen," and then there came a response from the organ, which filled the musical committee's bill of instructions with a vengeance—just two chords sounded with the whole power of the instrument, every blessed stop arranged to do its loudest, and all of them, together, combining to give forth mighty and supremely startling strains like the trump of doom. The organist had loaded to the muzzle, and he fired down two ringing shots—"short, distinct and impressive"—and quit. There was stretching of eyes, in the congregation, of course, and of mouths in wonderment, and then of necks around and upward to the organ loft, and everybody smiled at everybody else whom he knew, and whispered to the people next to him. The committee, it is said, visited the organist after the service, demanding his reasons for what they considered an insult. The organist maintained, in defense, that his response filled the bill, and that, if they didn't like it, they must not assume to pass judgement on what they knew very little about, or convey their desires regarding the character of the church music, in a manner that was clearly offensive.[36]

"I only played this once," Chadwick later recalled, "for when I did I was fired out of that church like a shot out of a gun."[37] Without a hint of remorse, Chadwick left the Lawrence Street Church never to return.

Up to now Chadwick's formal musical education had been woefully inadequate. While working for his father, his burgeoning interest in serious music compelled him to do "the best I could to get ahead with my own work," but "much of the time it was groping in the dark."[38] Nevertheless, he continued to practice the keyboard and write his own music. "Before he received any instruction in composition," Engel reported, "he wrote anthems and songs."[39] Importantly, he was also being exposed to strands of music and culture that emanated from beyond New England.

The Irish potato famine coincided with the founding of Lawrence, and, as the Irish fled their desperate situation, they generally made for England where they then sought transport to Canada or the United States.[40] For those who arrived in New England, Lawrence was among the innumerable towns and cities where they began to rebuild their shattered lives. From its population of 150 in 1845, the year of the town's founding, Lawrence, now a small city, had grown to just under twenty-two thousand by 1865, a huge increase in just twenty years.[41]

Like many immigrant communities, Lawrence's Irish comprised something of a society unto itself. While it was not unheard of for a few of the immigrants to attain success on a par with some of the native Yankees, by and large they were common laborers, and remained among their own during work and play.[42] Nevertheless, Chadwick must have absorbed some aspects of their culture. We know, for example, that Chadwick encountered the Irish at Oliver High School, which "was full of Irish ruffians who traveled in a gang and woe to the Yankee boy whom they overtook when alone."[43] At least once, Chadwick scaled a fence to escape their wrath. But the Irish of Lawrence were also plainly visible. In 1865 alone the Lawrence Irish—more specifically the active political sect called the "Fenians"—staged three town parades, and later formed a Fenian Hall and a Fenian Sisterhood.[44] These events were accompanied by the expected cultural accoutrements—food, music, costume—that attend such ethnic activities. By the mid-1870s the Irish population, now 8,232 strong, was having a correspondingly large effect on Lawrence's local culture.[45] Surely young Chadwick, reared in a conservative Protestant Yankee household, found the Irish newcomers stimulating and colorful, perhaps even exotic.

Gilmore's Peace Jubilees

The seminal musical event of Chadwick's youth—and one of the most momentous in American music history—was Patrick Gilmore's 1869 Peace Jubilee, held in Boston to commemorate the fifth anniversary of the end of the Civil War. In his subsequent history of the event, Gilmore, referring to himself in the third person, recollected the Jubilee as it first sprang into his mind's eye:

A vast structure rose up before him, filled with the loyal of the land, through whose lofty arches a chorus of ten thousand voices and the harmony of a thousand instruments rolled their sea of sound, accompanied by the chiming of the bells and the booming of the cannon—all pouring forth their praise . . . in loud hosannas with all the majesty and grandeur of which music seemed capable. As his imagination reveled in the scenes his thought pictured, every nerve quivered with the intensity of his delight, and he was impressed with all the fervor of religious belief that it was his especial mission to carry out the sublime conception.[46]

Gilmore's mission took the form of a dazzling five-day festival that involved renowned guest artists and 103 community choruses recruited from Connecticut to Maine. Even Chicago's Mendelssohn Society, whose leaders included the famed music critics George P. Upton and W. S. B. Mathews, made the trip to Boston to be a part of the "immortal ten thousand," as Gilmore called them. Besides

Gilmore, the Jubilee included a constellation of leading New England conductors: Carl Zerrahn of the Harvard Musical Association; Eben Tourjée, the director of the newly-founded New England Conservatory; and Julius Eichberg, the admired longtime leader of the orchestra at the Boston Museum and a founder of the new Boston Conservatory of Music. Vocalists Euphrosyne Parepa-Rosa and Adelaide Phillipps were featured performers, as was the charismatic Norwegian violinist Ole Bull. Also among the choristers were George's brother Henry, who sang bass as a member of the "Boston Oratorio Class," and father Alonzo, also a bass singer and a member of the Lawrence Musical Association.[47]

Gilmore's Jubilee was quite unlike anything seen in New England before that time. Composer Arthur Foote reminisced that the Peace Jubilee was a "great awakening" in New England music, and he pointed to its enormity: "This was a monstrous affair, with its chorus of thousands, the orchestra of 1,000 (?), a 'Bouquet of 40 Artists,' with visiting German, French, and English bands, with Johann Strauss from Vienna to lead his waltzes. In certain compositions cannon [*sic*] were fired to emphasize rhythm, while one of the sights was to witness a group of red-shirted firemen in the street on their way to the 'Coliseum,' where they were later to strike their anvils, giving a final touch of sonority to the 'Anvil Chorus' of [Verdi's] *Il Trovatore*."[48]

Naturally, the event had many detractors. A particularly vocal one was John Sullivan Dwight. William Arms Fisher, in his valuable 1918 history *Notes on Music in Old Boston*, remembered that the influential critic and music journalist Dwight fled the city "to escape the cannons, anvils, bells, big organ, eighty-four trombones, eighty-three tubas, as many cornets, seventy-five drums, which with three hundred and thirty strings and one hundred and nineteen wood-wind, made 'an ensemble of fearful and wonderful sonority.'"[49] Had he remained to witness this occasion, Dwight would undoubtedly have found the entire affair "fearful."

Novelist William Dean Howells attended the Peace Jubilee and wrote a wonderfully evenhanded assessment. He commented on many of the same features that caught Foote's attention, although he admitted that he had "the natural modesty of people who know nothing about music," and therefore made few pronouncements about the quality of the performances. Howells nevertheless suggested that much of the spectacle had been musically successful, or at least impressive by virtue of immensity, and he penned—with a novelist's eye for detail—a most colorful account of the Jubilee:

Some thousands of heads nearest were recognizable as attached by the usual neck to the customary human body, but for the rest, we seemed to have entered a world of cherubim. Especially did the multitudinous singers seated far opposite [in the Coliseum] encourage this illusion; and their fluttering fans and handkerchiefs wonderfully mocked the movement of those cravat-like pinions which the fancy attributed to them. They rose and sank at the director's baton; and still looked like an innumerable flock of cherubs drifting over some slope of Paradise, or settling upon it. . . . Concerning the orchestra I had at first no distinct impression save of the three hundred and thirty violin-bows held erect like standing wheat at one motion of the director's wand, and falling as if with the next he swept them down. Afterwards files of men with drums and cymbals discovered themselves; while far above all, certain laborious figures pumped or ground with incessant obeisance at the apparatus supplying the organ with wind.[50]

Howells would not have agreed with Foote's generous assessment of the use of the anvils and the "final touch of sonority" their use added to Verdi's music. To Howells, in a critical alignment with Dwight that probably would have startled him, the spectacle was nugatory. He observed that "the choral and orchestral thousands sang and piped and played; and at a given point in the scena from Verdi, a hundred fairies in red shirts marched down through the sombre mass of puppets and beat upon as many invisible anvils. This was the stroke of anti-climax; and the droll sound of those anvils, so far above all the voices and instruments in its pitch, thoroughly disillusioned you and restored you finally to your proper entity and proportions. It was the great error of the Jubilee, and where almost everything else was noble and impressive,—where the direction was faultless, and the singing and instrumentation as perfectly controlled as if they were the result of one volition,—this anvil-beating was alone ignoble and discordant,—trivial and huge merely."[51]

Chadwick got involved in Gilmore's festivities when, in 1872, a second Boston event, the World's Peace Jubilee and International Musical Festival, was organized (see figure 2.1). This Jubilee, another "strange and mammoth enterprise" according to Dwight, was little more than an attempt to recapture the glory that accompanied the first Jubilee. Now Chadwick assisted Ellis in the preparation of choirs from Lawrence and, like his brother and father in 1869, he participated as a bass singer. New England choral singing was again a top feature. But Gilmore had gone to great lengths to make it a truly international affair by traveling to Europe himself to secure performances by famous military bands. Thomas Ryan, leader of the Mendelssohn Quintette Club remembered:

Gilmore's plans again showed his genius. They were bold, well conceived, but very costly. He went to Europe, and "talked the crown heads" (that was

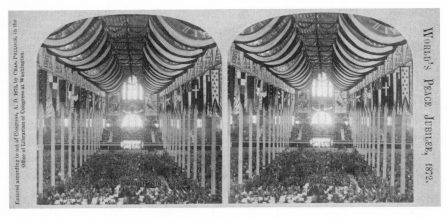

FIGURE 2.1. Inside the Boston Coliseum at Gilmore's 1872 Peace Jubilee. Courtesy of the Library of Congress Prints & Photographs Division, LC-DIG-ppmsca-17488 (stereograph).

the popular phrase) "into letting their crack" military bands come over to play in the Jubilee. He obtained the band of the Grenadier Guards from London, about forty-five strong . . . ; a German infantry band, about thirty-five men . . . ; and that of the Garde Republicaine, from Paris, of about forty-five men. It was said that this latter was reinforced by fine artists from the opera, and was not therefore a fair sample of French bands. There was also a little insignificant band, the Royal Constabulary, from Ireland. These bands had an English day, and German, French, and Irish days. The English band was good, the German, too brassy, the French, magnificent.[52]

When Chadwick reminisced about the Jubilee forty-nine years after it had occurred, his most vivid memories were of those very bands. Not only did they offer a sound unfamiliar to American ears by their emphasis of the reed section and a reduction in the power of the brass section, but they also exemplified perfection in technical and musical execution.[53] The European bands, which some considered the glory of the Jubilees—and Gilmore's true legacy—unquestionably contributed to the establishment of higher standards in American military band music.[54]

Boston

Chadwick clerked for his father's insurance company on a full-time basis following his stint at Oliver High School, but music continued to occupy his mind, even at the office. Alonzo was not supportive of his son's increasingly apparent absorption in music. Perhaps he feared that George would become a penurious musician; or perhaps he jealously sensed that the boy's talent in music eclipsed his own. Whatever the reason, Alonzo attempted to make remaining in Lawrence palatable to his son. According to Chadwick, his father "claimed that the [insurance] business would eventually be mine, that he was getting old, and that I must be learning it. That musicians were all godless bummers, and anyhow I had not enough talent to be anything more than second rate."[55] These words cut deeply, even as they inspired Chadwick to pursue an aggressive course of music study, which he was now hell-bent on procuring. This could be best accomplished in Boston where Henry now resided and worked as a clerk at the A. J. Wilkinson & Company hardware store. Soon Chadwick started receiving regular invitations to visit the city.

Henry enjoyed city life and its many diversions. He treated George to theatrical performances, as well as concerts, in some of which he himself performed. Henry sang bass in the Handel and Haydn Society, and Chadwick heard him perform Handel's *The Messiah* with the group at least once.[56] During another visit, on October 7, 1871, George and Henry attended a concert led by Theodore Thomas at Boston's Music Hall. Thomas had already performed a series of concerts earlier in the year, and those magisterial symphonic events had given local music fans something on which to ruminate. Thomas's programs were tailored to suit the tastes of Boston, and the Chadwick brothers were treated to an all-Beethoven performance. It included the Overture to *Coriolanus*, the G-major piano concerto, the Fantasie (op. 80), the Septet, and Symphony no. 3 (*Eroica*). In 1907, Chadwick remembered this experience—it was certainly more than just a concert to him—in a poignant article titled "A 'Touch' of Beethoven." In it Chadwick chronicled an imaginary encounter with the come-to-life statue of Beethoven, which formerly stood at the Music Hall and which oversees NEC to this day. Here Beethoven reminisces:

> I remember the first time I saw you. It was at a Thomas concert in the old Music Hall, where I used to be when I first came to Boston, you know. You were a little fellow, and were deposited in a seat in the middle of the hall by a gentleman who looked very much as you look now. He went away and came for you after the concert. . . . Pretty soon Thomas began with my *Eroica*, and how you did prick up your ears![57]

A month later, in November 1871, Henry visited Lawrence for Thanksgiving. He and George played duets at the piano, as they had done countless times before, and Henry was stunned by his brother's improvement. Perhaps less intimidated by Alonzo than his younger brother—and certainly more cognizant of George's immense talent—Henry urged the old man to send George to

Boston for serious music study. At first, Alonzo would have none of it, but, after a good deal of goading over many months, he relented. Naturally, his decision was not without self-interest; the firm of A. C. Chadwick required frequent trips to Boston, and George had been able to convince Alonzo that not only could he take care of company matters while in the city, but he could also travel there on a cheaper student-fare train ticket.

Chadwick pursued musical studies in Boston starting in 1872, when, during a ten-week summer term, he entered NEC, which then occupied the upper three floors of the Music Hall, as a "special student." Special students were heavily recruited during this period. They were mostly piano and voice pupils who were interested in little more than a few lessons here and there, but whose tuition kept the faculty paid and the fledgling conservatory afloat during lean financial periods—and there had been many lean periods at NEC since its founding in 1867. In the conservatory's early years, special students comprised the bulk of the enrollment.[58]

Nonetheless, it was entirely possible for a student of more serious aspirations to obtain an adequate grounding in the basics of music. Just a generation before, the possibility of training at an American conservatory was slim, and many had traveled to Europe to pursue their studies. Boston was just beginning to benefit from a wave of American professional musicians who had returned to practice their art in a field that most of their countrymen did not quite understand. Foreign artists had also discovered that the US was an attractive destination with enormous potential for career development. This was a boon to students who wished to take advantage of the new availability of qualified music instructors at NEC. Chadwick, for instance, studied piano with Carlyle Petersilea, a Leipzig Conservatory graduate who had studied with pianist-legend Ignaz Moscheles and conductor Carl Reinecke. George Whiting ("a nervous, irritable man whose patience I fear I sorely tried"[59]), who had only recently returned from his studies with the eminent Karl August Haupt in Berlin, tutored Chadwick in organ, as did Dudley Buck, who had studied with the famous organist Julius Rietz in Leipzig and Dresden. Also an accomplished composer and conductor, Buck ("a master of his instrument"[60]), was one of the most versatile American musicians of his generation, and he gained widespread notoriety for his NEC organ recitals. Chadwick also studied music theory with Stephen A. Emery and voice with H. L. Whitney. Each of these teachers was highly regarded in New England's musical circles, if their reputations outside the region were modest.

The priorities of the firm of A. C. Chadwick, and its youthful clerk George, would change drastically on the evening of November 9, 1872. At just after

7 p.m., a four-story granite building at the corner of Summer Street and Kingston Street in Boston caught fire. Charles Carleton Coffin, the regional historian and writer whom we have already met, heard the alarms and penned a compelling, if perhaps romanticized, account of the fire's opening moments: "I hear a booming of bells. Before the tones are flung out from the belfry and steeple there is a sudden lighting up of the sky, an illumination of spires, a red glare on roofs and windows. People in Summer Street,—the busy thoroughfare by day, the western boundary of this section of noble edifices,—are astonished by the bursting forth of flames in the upper stories of one of the tallest buildings."[61]

So began the Great Fire of Boston. The building, owned by Leman Klous, housed three businesses. Tebbitts, Baldwin & Davis, a dry-goods wholesaler, occupied the basement and first floor. Damon, Temple & Company, a dealer in hosiery, gloves, laces, and other finery, plied wares on the second and third floors. And the manufacturer of ladies' hoopskirts, Alexander K. Young & Company, was located on the fourth floor. There were no witnesses to the start of the fire, but there was plenty of speculation. As winter neared, Tebbitts, Baldwin & Davis and Damon, Temple & Company were well stocked with products. Some of these, it was believed, were located too near the basement furnace and a spark—"one little atom of fire," as Coffin put it—ignited the blaze that would destroy much of the city:

> There are bales and boxes of dry goods in the basement and on the ground floor, reaching back from Summer Street front one hundred feet or more. There are prints and muslins piled on counters ready for display,—a room full of tinder. In the stores above are cases, packages, and bundles of hosiery, gloves and laces,—and still higher, in the upper stories, piles of tape and muslin, thread and trimmings, shreds and ravelings, where sewing-girls have been at work manufacturing skirts and corsets. Tinder below and tinder above,—quick fuel for the flames from basement to attic.[62]

When the fire was finally quelled on Sunday morning, twelve hours after it had begun, the destruction was massive. Lost were a score of Boston's citizens, over 750 buildings in a sixty-five-acre area, and millions of dollars in product inventory. Because the scope of the fire was so vast and the damage so absolute, insurance companies, including A. C. Chadwick, were forced to work tirelessly on claims. George worked day and night for months, and there must have been a good deal of fear in the Chadwick household, for "Insurance companies, even the strongest, were failing by the score."[63] A. C. Chadwick was not bankrupted— owing largely to the fact that most of its holdings were in Lawrence—but those clients possessing Chadwick accounts were nervous. A good deal of George's time was spent convincing customers that the business was solvent and that their investments were safe, both of which were true.

Musically, the effect of the fire was more pernicious. Chadwick was forced to end his studies at NEC after the fall term of 1872. Given the increased workload brought on by the fire, there was little time for "trifles" such as music. It did not help matters that Alonzo had not been trained in business; he possessed few skills in management, organization, or accounting. Alonzo's talents lay in sales. It was his astute young clerk who managed the administration of the firm, and at this time his services were crucial.

Eugene Thayer

For George, difficulties in the insurance industry did not subside until well into 1873; by autumn he was able to resume his musical studies. Rather than returning to NEC, however, Chadwick elected to study privately with organist Eugene Thayer (1838–1889). Thayer was well known in Boston's musical circles. He began his own studies with John Knowles Paine, and later he attended the Berlin Conservatory, just as Paine had, studying organ with Karl August Haupt, the principal German disciple of Bach at that time. Composition was also pursued with Wilhelm Wieprecht. By 1863 Thayer was respected enough to have been one of only six organists in Boston selected to dedicate the new organ at the Music Hall.[64] One of Thayer's students was music journalist Sumner Salter, who wrote of his master's teaching priorities: "Clean and smooth pedalling was a special virtue to be cultivated, and to that end the use of a pedal piano was quite indispensable. The maxim so often repeated, that 'the keys should go down decidedly, should stay down *decidedly*, and come up DECIDEDLY,' was applied to overcome the tendency to sluggish pushing and poking as well as leaving of keys." Salter added that Thayer students became "missionaries to carry the gospel of Bach, Handel, Merkel, Rheinberger, Schumann, Thiele, Guilmant, and Widor to the benighted heathen."[65]

Chadwick did not consider Thayer a great teacher of organ technique, but was attracted by his enthusiasm and the personal relationships he routinely forged with his students. He was additionally enticed by Thayer's outstanding record of producing young organists who secured paying jobs in local churches. Thayer, "an interesting character with a decided personality," also appealed to Chadwick because he "played the big fugues of Bach and Handel concertos with tremendous conviction and earnestness."[66] Louis C. Elson, in his history of American music, gave Thayer special mention, assuring his readers that he became Chadwick's organ instructor "to such good purpose that at this time [the student] did such feats as playing several of Bach's greatest organ fugues from memory."[67]

Thayer was also a competent composer. His opus catalog, mostly comprising occasional works for the organ, numbers well into the forties. Chadwick wrote that Thayer's compositions "show a certain facility and melodic invention," but he did not include him among the first rank of Boston's composers.[68] Neither did his studies with Thayer put Chadwick in good stead with the city's other musical leaders, for Thayer was something of a musical black sheep. He was shunned not only because he was unaffiliated with NEC but also because he adhered to an opposing philosophy of organ playing. While most of Boston's organists were disciples of the more flamboyant school of performance founded by English organist W. T. Best (which Chadwick termed "the worst"[69]), Thayer's approach was decidedly more reserved.

Chadwick was still living in Lawrence when he began to participate seriously in musical activities in Boston. His debut performance in the city, under Thayer's auspices, occurred at the First Church of Boston at the corner of Berkeley and Marlborough streets in October 1873. Bach's music, always emphasized by Thayer, quickly became a Chadwick favorite. He performed Bach's Fugue in G Minor at his first recital; it was followed several months later with Bach's Fugue in A Minor.[70] Chadwick also played Bach at the 1874 Worcester Festival. If Thayer required the mastery of Bach, however, he also seems to have allowed room for other, more varied repertoires. In October 1874, for example, also as part of Thayer's concert series, Chadwick performed the C-minor *Concertsatz* by Ludwig Thiele.[71]

At approximately this time Chadwick composed the original overture *The New Prodigal* at the request of Sam Ellis, who intended to use it as the opening portion of his own cantata based on the story of the Prodigal Son. Although it was played regularly by Chadwick in a version for organ, he also orchestrated it. Chadwick's first serious attempt at writing for orchestra was aided in no small measure by Hector Berlioz's famous treatise on orchestration (1843).[72] To this point, Chadwick had studied orchestration only in books, and it showed. As he began to rehearse the overture he found that it contained a good many elementary mistakes: he wrote the viola parts in G clef; clarinets were scored in the wrong key; and, perhaps worst of all, he failed to sketch his work—he composed it directly onto orchestral score paper. "The noise was something awful," he remembered following its first rehearsal, "and I left in a state of discouragement." Its premiere "was a good deal of a mess."[73]

In 1875 Chadwick began producing his own series of organ recitals at Lawrence Street Church and Second Baptist Church of Lawrence. Six free concerts—the first of their kind in Lawrence—were presented between June and

October, and Chadwick demonstrated not only an acuity for programming, but also an entrepreneurial spirit. Thayer was featured prominently on the program, perhaps because Chadwick thought he might be an audience draw. Thayer performed Handel's Twelfth Organ Concerto, an improvisation "in the free style," and his own Variations on "Old Hundred." Movements from various organ sonatas and concerti by Handel, Merkel, and others peppered the program.

Often in these youthful recitals, an increasingly proficient Chadwick would simply improvise. Of course, he also continued to perform plenty of music by Bach—one concert was entirely Bach—but Chadwick's curiosity and eclecticism also forced the exploration of music such as Schumann's *Skizzen* and Hesse's Variations in A Major, and even arias by the likes of Mendelssohn, Gounod, and Faure. And he continued to perform his own works. His Postlude in C found a place in the October 1875 performance; it may have been composed specifically for that event. A month later, Chadwick again performed *The New Prodigal* in its setting for organ. The writer for the *Daily American* remarked that it had "effective registration" for the organ, and that it had been highly praised by Thayer.[74] Whether his master's music influenced this important early work is impossible to know, for *The New Prodigal* has been lost.

Chadwick's performances were beginning to garner attention. The *Daily American* critic observed that "the rendering of Thiele's *Chromatic fantasie* evinced the fact of Mr. Chadwick's ability to handle that king of instruments, the organ." The critic did not hesitate to scold those among the three hundred people in attendance who could not keep their attention fixed on the performance: "It is hoped that the persons who so outrageously inflicted their presence and noise upon the recital will hereafter bear in mind that the object of Mr. Chadwick's gratuitous efforts is the advancement of music, and that the auditors are not invited to indulge [in] an evening of annoying guffaws, to the evident discomfort of both performers and respectable auditors."[75]

Perhaps in an effort to eliminate further "annoying guffaws," Chadwick began to charge admission to his concerts in November 1875. Previously Chadwick's Lawrence performances had been free, but now patrons would be charged fifty cents. Attendance, hindered in part by New England's inclement winter weather, was dishearteningly slim. The size of the audience plummeted to 109 — "including dead-heads," reported the *Daily American*—and its failure to appear in numbers drew the ire of the critic, who had attended the earlier concerts and was steadfastly in Chadwick's corner. "It is rather deplorable as a commentary on our public taste as well as gratitude," he grumbled, "that Mr. Chadwick should have been allowed to lose money on the only venture he has undertaken in which he has asked patronage."[76] Chadwick was naturally disappointed, as was intimated by the critic, who speculated that everyone enjoyed the performance except "the energetic young gentleman who has been striving to do so much for us in a musical way, and who, after last night's experience, is, we fear, asking himself whether it is really of any use trying, and whether there is any such thing as gratitude."[77]

Chadwick's recitals continued at Lawrence's Second Baptist Church through the end of 1875. Although tickets remained at fifty cents apiece, the December attendance was remarkably good. One highlight of the concert (which was repeated a few days later at the Congregational Church in Salem, New Hampshire) was Chadwick's duet with Thayer on Hesse's *Fantasia* (op. 87). The *Daily American*, by now thoroughly familiar with the young musician and his efforts, reported that Chadwick's "skill and tireless application seem to destine him as an organist."[78]

If Thayer had been Chadwick's most influential mentor at this stage of his development, Stephen A. Emery was a close second. Emery was a well-known Boston harmony teacher and the best theory instructor at NEC. His résumé was singular. In Europe Emery had been profoundly influenced by the eminent theorists Moritz Hauptmann and Ernst Friedrich Richter. According to Arthur Foote, who took harmony lessons at NEC in the late 1860s, Emery taught from Richter's popular harmony text, *Lehrbuch der Harmonie*, which was first published in 1853 and translated into English in 1864.[79] The text, titled in its English translation as *Richter's Manual of Harmony*, quickly became the standard one in the United States. One thing that must have attracted Chadwick to the manual is Richter's insistence that the study of harmony was not to enable analysis but to aid in the creation of art; a good harmony book, Richter wrote, "must contain the essential fundamental principles of musical theory in the most concise and complete form possible; that these principles must be accompanied by practical directions for their application in order to qualify for future attempts in composition."[80] The manual is a practical guide that directs the student through harmony along a steady and methodical path; its musical examples are clear, although, with a few rare exceptions, they were straightforward theoretical formulations invented by Richter, not examples that had been extracted from actual musical compositions. But to Chadwick, a practical young man who was already beginning to map out his musical future, Richter's long view of the composer's musical journey must have resonated: "Our object is to reach a distant goal; it is to produce works of art."[81]

In the shorter term, Boston offered many other opportunities for eager young musicians who took the trouble to search for them. Engel reported that even as Chadwick was taking lessons, "The pupil in turn had begun to give lessons and concerts, attracting not a little attention in both."[82] Boston's appetite for music was voracious. "There was decided enthusiasm for chorus singing, and choral clubs and choruses were in a very flourishing condition," Engel claimed. "Moreover, there was a good deal of amateur instrumental music."[83] But, while there seemed to be a number of miscellaneous activities in the city, Chadwick dolefully concluded there was no way to immerse oneself in a musical atmosphere.[84] Obtaining lessons in organ or voice, or perhaps on a few wind instruments, was one thing, but learning the art of the composer in America at this time was quite another. Chadwick later remembered a telling episode: "Stephen Emery was once asked how one should go about the study of instrumentation. He said 'I suppose that Mr. [John Knowles] Paine [of Harvard University] will teach instrumentation, but I think no one else in this country can do so.' As a matter of fact, Mr. Paine was probably at that time [ca. 1870s] the only man in this country who really knew much about the subject. Contrast this with the fact that in Europe every capellmeister could teach it."[85]

Although a technical education was hard to obtain, the general musical culture was strong, and, as a young adult near the age of twenty, Chadwick had actually heard a good deal of distinguished music in New England. In addition to hearing many local performers in chamber and choral performances, as well as the tours of the Thomas Orchestra, Chadwick was impacted by a number of other musical events. Chadwick was present at the premiere in Boston of Verdi's *Aida* in 1874 at the Boston Theater; it made an unforgettable impression.[86] The same year Chadwick went to Boston's Globe Theatre for a performance — "the greatest event of my life up to that time" — of one of Wagner's operas. "The great crescendo at the entrance of *Lohengrin* in the first act nearly took me off my feet, and I was an unregenerate Wagner-ite from that time on."[87] Chadwick was not alone, for Wagner won legions of converts that day. "Many, with characteristic American (we may say, even Boston) haste," John S. Dwight thought, "rushed to the conclusion that they were suddenly newborn into the light of a new gospel, convicted Wagnerites in a breath, and ready to assert that verily this *is* the music of the Future."[88]

Chadwick's concerns about the creative atmosphere of America were shared by others. The Spanish-born American philosopher George Santayana, one of the most important voices on aesthetic matters in Chadwick's era, agreed that this phenomenon was endemic to all the arts in America. He observed that "beginners are still supposed to study their art, but they have no masters from whom to learn it."[89] For the duration of his stay at NEC, Chadwick did what student-musicians do: he practiced his instrument, but, having probably already determined that he lacked the skills to perform beyond the church setting, he did so with minimal effort; he studied music theory assiduously and dissected scores that were available to him; and he listened to as much music as was possible. His forays into Boston also brought him into close contact with experienced musicians who knew the esoteric ways of the European conservatories, and Chadwick had even begun studying the German language, although he had enjoyed "no systematic instruction," nor had he "learned the grammar properly."[90] Chadwick determined to be a composer in a musical city that, at the time, offered little to no preparation for that profession. "In this period," Chadwick wrote, "such a thing as American composition was unknown."[91] And all this he did while still in the service of his despotic father.

Chadwick dropped out of high school because his father's business required the kind of help that could only be gotten from his youngest son—that is, free labor, or nearly so. On George's twenty-first birthday, Alonzo had informed George that the firm would henceforth be known as "A. C. Chadwick and Son," but neither the storefront sign nor the stationery was altered to reflect the new partnership. And George's salary, which until now had merely been room and board irregularly supplemented by cash allowances, remained paltry. Chadwick, a grudgingly dutiful son, was growing furious. "It was the injustice of being compelled to give him the best years of my life without any compensation that rankled in my heart," he complained. "For a little steady and regular salary I would have taken a real interest in his business and even made some effort to increase it. But there was no object in doing so as long as I got absolutely no benefit from it."[92]

There were other alarming signs of a breakdown in the Chadwick family. Alonzo had taken to hiring young women to assist at the insurance office. We do not know how many were employed over the years, but they seem not to have stayed very long; and, as far as Chadwick could tell, they brought no discernible administrative skills to the position. The result was that, after a time, Susan Chadwick suspected that Alonzo was hiring the girls for reasons other than their business qualifications. Her jealousy, perhaps warranted, resulted in marital separation, and, given Alonzo's behavior toward him, it was easy for Chadwick to choose sides in the dispute. It was during this period of domestic strife that Chadwick determined to go abroad for advanced music study. Several years before, while Chadwick was toiling in the insurance office, his best friend Tom Scott had gone to Europe.[93] Scott was not a proficient musician—he played the piano "in a mechanical way," Chadwick observed[94]—but upon his return to Lawrence from Das Conservatorium für Musik in Dresden, he shared with Chadwick many compelling stories about his adventures there.

Chadwick needed money to venture to Europe, and he knew that it would not be forthcoming in Lawrence. In order to earn it, he was forced to travel deep into the heart of America, and into a region that was still quite remote. But his departure from Lawrence and his father's stern gaze was emphatic. While it seems clear that by now he had settled on music as his true calling, there is no question that he had settled against a career in the insurance business.

The Michigan Conservatory

In 1876 a young man of adventuresome spirit named Theodore Presser was offered the position of director at Olivet College's music department, newly formed in 1874.[95] That Olivet, an institution dedicated to "enlightened Christian education," was in faraway Michigan played little part in Presser's decision not to accept; he had already committed to another job. But he heartily recommended his close friend George Chadwick. Presser, six years Chadwick's senior, had been a fellow student at NEC, and, because he lived in Boston, Chadwick would sometimes stay with him when visiting from Lawrence. Chadwick subsequently met in Boston with the college's president, the improbably named Dr. Horatio Q. Butterfield.[96] Butterfield had been Olivet's president only since 1875, and he believed, as had his predecessor, that an active music department would provide the college with much-desired publicity and bolster its prominence. Olivet's official history describes Butterfield's character as one that would have resonated with Chadwick's Yankee traits. "He was the soul of honor, integrity, and sincerity. He loved honesty, truth, and righteousness. He hated duplicity, hypocrisy, and shams. He was not quick to discern character by intuition, but he brought others to the same touchstone he applied to himself, and pure gold only could stand his test."[97] Chadwick remembered that Butterfield was "rather aghast when he first saw me, as my face was innocent of any hirsute decorations. I probably looked younger than my real age which was twenty-one. But Presser's enthusiastic endorsement got me the position."[98]

Anyone who had been studying music seriously for a mere four years might have been elated to be named the director of a conservatory, even one in remote Michigan. Certainly Chadwick was pleased. He found Olivet a beautiful town, and in it he was surprisingly productive. Mostly he was happy to be on his own. "Altogether the place surpasses all my expectations," he wrote to a friend, "and I thank God every day for bringing me away from that damnable place — Lawrence."[99]

The Michigan Conservatory's music program was unexpectedly rigorous. Chadwick replaced Professor George H. Howard, who was on leave for family illness. (Chadwick later learned that Howard's wife had gone "insane.")

Howard "gave special prominence to classical music, and he thought it of great importance that those who aspired to eminence in music should have a good general education besides that in music."[100] At Howard's insistence, music students who passed the difficult entrance exams were required to take "some literary work," including three years of English. Also required were classes in "elocution" and "elementary singing," harmony, notation, and private lessons on either piano or organ.[101] Additionally, "A concert is given by the pupils of the conservatory at the close of each term, at which they are expected to perform when sufficiently advanced. These concerts are of a very high order, some of the best classical compositions being performed at them."[102]

We know only a few facts about "Professor" Chadwick's tenure at Olivet College, although surviving letters from this period indicate that he stayed busy.[103] Engel reported that Chadwick was "the head and rump" of the department, teaching piano, organ, and harmony. He also ran the glee club and the choir, performed weekly organ recitals, and gave lectures in music history, "each lecture requiring a hasty gathering of knowledge which he could pass on to his hearers."[104]

Chadwick's performing schedule while at Olivet was ambitious, as his desire to play the organ had not diminished since he produced his own recital series in Lawrence. Not long after assuming his new post, Chadwick played a "Grand Organ Concert" at the town's Congregational Church.[105] This and other concerts offered the chance to perform a wide variety of works—Hesse's Variations in A Major (op. 47), Handel's Second and Sixth Organ Concerti, Merkel's Canon in F-sharp (op. 39, no. 3), the English composer John Baptiste Calkin's *Andante con varia* (op. 520), Mendelssohn's Sonata (op. 65, no. 2), Smart's *Chorale and Variations*, and Thiele's *Chromatische fantasie*, among others. Bach again figured prominently; Chadwick played the Prelude and Fugue in C Major, the chorale prelude *An Wasserflüssen Babylons*, and the *Toccata Dorico*. An 1877 all-Bach performance concluded with the magisterial Toccata and Fugue in D minor.[106]

Besides tackling a full performance schedule, Chadwick's composing regimen accelerated at Olivet as well (see table 2.1). His own Canon in E-flat (op. 16, no. 1) for organ was performed in November 1876, along with the Canon in C minor (op. 16, no. 2) and an array of works that indicate Chadwick's increasing command of the organ. These were followed by the December premiere of Chadwick's song "King Death," performed at Olivet's Congregational Church. According to the program, Chadwick sang it himself. His March in B-flat (op. 24) was a highlight of the February 1877 organ recital, which, not insignificantly, featured only music by American composers. Chadwick played George Whiting's

TABLE 2.1. Chadwick's Music Composed before 1878

Asis—ca. 1869; hymn dedicated to S. A. Ellis; lost

"The Owl"—ca. 1872; song; lost

"The Sea King"—ca. 1872; song; published in 1885

"Is My Lover on the Sea?"—ca. 1873; song; later re-titled "Request"; published in 1883

Trio in D minor—ca. 1874; violin, cello, piano; lost

Cappricio [sic] in D minor—ca. 1875; solo flute; lost

Fantasie on a Chorale—ca. 1875; organ; lost

"Tho' Lost to Sight"—ca 1875; song; lost

Postlude in C—ca. 1875; organ

The New Prodigal Overture—ca. 1875; organ; lost

Canons in E-flat major and G minor, op. 16 nos. 1 and 2—ca. 1876; organ

"King Death"—ca. 1876; song; published in 1885

Soronian Concert Waltz—ca. 1876; piano; lost

Flute Sonata—ca. 1876; in three movements; lost

Piano Sonata—ca. 1876; lost

Overture—op. 19; ca. 1876; piano quintet; lost

Piano Quintette—op. 20?; 1876–1877?; Fantasie-Adagio-Scherzo-Andante; lost

Waltz in E-flat and Mazurka—op. 21, nos. 2 and 3; ca. 1876; piano?; lost

Carmen—op. 22; ca. 1877; Latin hymn; lost

Waltz in F—op. 23; ca. 1877; piano; lost

March in B-flat—op. 24; a.k.a. "Wedding March"; ca. 1877; organ

Concert Fantasy and Fugue—op. 25; a.k.a., Fantasie on "Last Rose of Summer"; 1877; organ; lost

Trio in C minor—op. 26?; ca. September, 1877; for violin, cello, piano; lost

"Löffelgesellschaft" Waltz—date undetermined; piano; lost

Postludium in G, Thayer's *Adagio religioso*, Dudley Buck's Variations on the "Star-Spangled Banner," and H. W. Fairbank's *Andante and Romanza*. The next month Chadwick performed his own *Carmen* at the "Annual Public Exercises of the Adelphic Society." *Carmen*, now lost, is an early example of Chadwick's use of Latin. It was also the first of several commencement ceremony compositions he would write over the course of his career.

Chadwick's composing schedule was robust, but over the next three years he would not consider most of his creations from this period good enough to preserve. Shortly after his departure from Olivet, he scrapped most of them and began the opus numbering anew. Chadwick does not explain this action, although we may be fairly certain he used some of his ideas in later compositions. The catalog of Chadwick's compositions that Engel appended to his biographical sketch began with the String Quartet no. 1 of 1878.

George Root and Chadwick's Earliest Songs

Chadwick's Olivet experience included a crucial episode that occurred as a result of his founding membership in the Musical Teachers National Association (MTNA), an organization created by Presser.[107] The association's first meeting, a landmark event in the history of music education in America, was held between Christmas Day and New Year's Day 1876, at the Ohio Wesleyan Female College in Delaware, Ohio. In Chadwick's first appearance on the national stage, he delivered what can only be described as an intemperate screed titled "The Popular Music of the day, wherein 'reform' is necessary."[108] The address, read to a distinguished assembly of musicians and music teachers, was hardly a measured and decorous rumination; it more closely resembled a tirade. In it the twenty-two-year-old composer of "serious" music could not understand how educated musicians would allow repugnant "popular" music to gain a foothold in civil society. Chadwick identified two problems with this low sort of music: first, popular music lacked "truth"; that is, it did not reflect the true and accurate sentiments of a thinking person. Second, and more disturbing to Chadwick, it lacked any measure of originality and creativity. A cursory inspection, he declared, demonstrated that in fact the entire body of American popular song was formulaic: "Let us see how much originality our popular music contains. For instance the songs; you have probably observed that the words of these songs are nearly all written in 8's and 7's metre. The music is distributed in rhythm after this fashion: Common time; a dotted quarter and five eighth notes in the 1st measure; a half note slurred to a quarter in the next, which finishes the phrase; the next phrase similar, leaving out the last quarter note, and so on throughout. . . . The harmony of course is the omnipresent and omni-prevalent Tonic, Dominant, and Subdominant."[109] Chadwick then asked rhetorically:

Why does all this weakness, this trash, this dishonest, miserable stuff—why does this flood our homes and choir galleries, and fill the whole land with its senselessness? Why will, and do, the people bow down to these brazen images instead of the true god? Because nothing better has been given to them. I believe the principal reason to be a want of a thorough musical education. Those who furnish the popular music have not paid, either in money or in mental discipline, the price of true and first-class musicians. Therefore they furnish to the people their wares, manufactured from the slender stock of knowledge they *have* acquired, at so cheap a rate that it floods the market to the exclusion of true music. . . . Our own business-like, avaricious, Yankee natures have caused us to forget, in this headlong race after money, that music as an art is a very different thing from music as a business. We want to get money. We want to get rich. Perfectly laudable desires, but have we any right to forget in our eagerness that we work for *art* first,—not money. Have we any right to debase our music simply to earn bread and butter? . . . Let the people's music be the popular music, but let us give the people music which will achieve a true popularity,—that is the popularity of *years*, not days. . . . I do not ask you to make popular music classical—I ask you to make classical music popular.[110]

The youthful Chadwick did not realize that he was valiantly fighting an ages-old battle—Dwight had made arguments in this vein for years—but he was certainly taken aback by an unexpected rebuttal.

Attending Chadwick's address was George F. Root, one of the main providers of "the popular music." More than thirty years Chadwick's senior, Root, a protégé of the pioneering music educator Lowell Mason, had been immensely successful in writing songs for the masses. During the Civil War several of his songs—among them "The Battle Cry of Freedom" (1862) and "Tramp! Tramp! Tramp!" (1864)—were known and beloved by untold thousands. In his own defense, Root refuted Chadwick's charges by describing the origins of his song-writing efforts:

Nathan Richardson started a large music store; [he] stacked the shelves with only the highest order of music. His relatives who were furnishing the money to keep up the store soon found out that they were in a money-losing enterprise. Something must be done, as the music published lay full of dust on the shelves. He came to me in this sorrowful time and wanted me to write him six songs. I did so, "Rosalie, the Prairie Flower" among the rest. My efforts were commended by some musicians of eminence. I was ashamed of having written songs in that measure at all. I was ashamed to put my name to them; I am ashamed of *that* now. I put the German of my name, "Wurtzel." I will only say that it shows what changes may come to any man. No matter if they are simple in character, I have no reason to be ashamed of them."[111]

Chadwick was embarrassed to be on the receiving end of Root's civil, even gentlemanly, reply. "I was perhaps rather too much in earnest," Chadwick recalled in 1926, "although there was nothing in the address which does not apply with even greater force at the present time." He admitted that Root "made a very courteous but effective reply, which I confess, modified my opinions to a certain extent. He was one of the finest gentlemen I have ever met, and a real folk-song composer."[112] Ordinarily, once Chadwick formed an opinion very little could be done to change it, and here the composer tries to have it both ways: he firmly maintained his negative stance on "popular" music, but he also issued absolution to Root. Chadwick even elevated him from a mere provider of popular music to a "real folk-song composer."

Chadwick's own small body of songs during this period includes "The Owl" and "Tho' Lost to Sight," both lost. "Is My Lover on the Sea?" was published by a New York printer in 1876; it had been retitled "Request" by the time Chadwick submitted it to the publishing house of Oliver Ditson, which rejected it on the grounds that it was "commercially no good," according to Engel. Finally, the firm of A. P. Schmidt published "Request" in 1883 as the first of Chadwick's *Three Little Songs* (op. 11).[113] "Request," with a text by Barry Cornwall (1787–1874), is in a simple ABA form. Although we cannot be sure how much Chadwick revised this song between the time he wrote it and the time it was eventually published, this effort shows ingenuity and promise. Like many art songs of the time, "Request" has elements of both nature—here evoking images of the sea—and romance. The vocal line is fetching and singable, and the piano accompaniments are unobtrusive and change little throughout the song. The intensity of the B section ("Let No Angry Wind Arise") is heightened by its modulation from the home key of F major into a darker F minor before quickly falling back to the tonic.

> Is my lover on the sea? / Sailing east or sailing west /
> Mighty ocean gentle be / Rock him into rest /
> Let no angry wind arise / Nor a wave with whitened crest /
> All be gentle as his eyes / When he is caressed /
> Bear him as the breeze above / Bears the bird unto his nest /
> There unto his home of love / And there bid him rest.

Another of Chadwick's characteristic early songs is "King Death," a two-part strophic song that begins in C-sharp minor:

> King Death was a rare old fellow / He sat where no sun could shine /
> And he lifted his hand so yellow / And poured out his coal black wine /
> Hurrah, Hurrah, Hurrah, Hurrah for the coal black wine.

> All came to that rare old fellow / He laughed till his eyes ran brine /
> He gave them his hand so yellow / And pledged them in Death's black wine /
> Hurrah, Hurrah, Hurrah, Hurrah for Death's black wine.

The subject matter is macabre for a composer barely into his twenties, but the text is buoyed by the piano part, which becomes increasingly more agitated. The harmonic language is advanced over "Request"; while Chadwick does not move past dominant-seventh chords, the music flirts with the related key of E major, and at its end slinks through the distant tonalities of F major and B-flat major, finally closing in A major. There is no attribution for the text of "King Death," and it seems likely that Chadwick wrote it himself. The song was published by Schmidt in 1885 as a companion to another watery creation, "The Sea King."

Chadwick took the teaching position in Michigan knowing that it was probably a temporary one, for Howard had been promised his job if and when personal circumstances permitted his return. There was a brief period when Chadwick was content at Olivet, and he seriously considered remaining there. "I am willing to make my life work here," he once confessed.[114] But toward the end of his first year, he determined that it would be impossible to forge a momentous career in Michigan. Of course, he had never intended to stay. He ventured to Olivet to get out from under his father's thumb and save money that would make it possible to pursue more rigorous studies in Europe, "the principal inducement in accepting it."[115] To the surprise of many, he quietly resigned in 1877.[116]

Naturally, Chadwick found some aspects of his life at Olivet distasteful. As his familiarity with the college leaders increased, he found them narrow-minded, intolerant of dissenting viewpoints, especially with regard to temperance, and appallingly strict with students who engaged in tomfoolery. Chadwick had already adopted a liberal view of Christianity, one to which he would adhere ever after. Further, Olivet was something of a social backwater. In Olivet there was simply no place to spend money, a fact that helped Chadwick to accumulate the funds he needed to pay for an extended stay abroad.[117] He was making twelve hundred dollars per year, a healthy sum for a novice college instructor, and he reported that "my expenses after I get my things in my room for 40 weeks will not probably exceed $300."[118] Additional concerts performed beyond Olivet earned Chadwick as much as a hundred extra dollars per year. He also sold sheet music to his students, an acceptable practice of the day, on which he made a commission.

Chadwick also pursued his own course of liberal education at Olivet; it is probable that he began his industrious regimen of reading during these years. He found time to audit a literature course and continued to study the German language seriously, on his own at first. Later, he enlisted the assistance of Johann Holzinger, a poor German student at Olivet, to tutor him.[119] Chadwick constantly conversed with him in an effort to learn the language he would soon need to know in earnest.

His plans to go to Europe "met with vigorous parental objections," but family disapproval and an ever-widening estrangement could not deter him, even as Engel tells us that "under the circumstances a father's love and wisdom felt constrained to point out that the insurance business was a good deal safer and more reputable."[120] Engel attempted here to put a positive spin on a turbulent relationship. In reality, demonstrations of paternal affection were absent from Chadwick's relationship with his father, and the son neither felt himself loved nor did he consider his father a sage advisor. On the contrary, Chadwick had long thought that he was being taken advantage of by his father at the family business, and he felt no particular need to ask Alonzo for either guidance or permission on any topic; once he left home he never sought from his father wise counsel or practical advice. Chadwick's experience was not unprecedented in the family, for Henry enlisted in the Union army against Alonzo's "violent opposition." Alonzo, in his anger, "made threats which he never carried out."[121] That Henry's relationship with Alonzo was also strained makes it is easier to infer that Alonzo was generally difficult to get along with as his children made their way into the world. Perhaps George had not been the first of Alonzo's sons to reject a role in the family business.

The young musician's growing bitterness and sense of betrayal resulted in his departure to a distant land. "The old man [Alonzo] never had any idea except that I would join him in the insurance business," Chadwick later told one journalist. "He strangled a bit when I accepted a position as a teacher of music in Olivet College, in Michigan, but when I announced a year later that I was going abroad to study music in Germany, there was real trouble. Music as a pastime appealed to him, but not music as a profession. But I had saved the money from my own earnings, and I went."[122]

Chadwick's unexpected departure—tantamount to an act of defiance aimed directly at his father—may have been the biggest indication to date of his pronounced rebelliousness. As we have seen, it was not the first such act.

Nor would it be the last.

Chadwick's European Education
1877–1880

I doubt if any of my generation, certainly of those whose experience did not extend to New York or the other side of the Atlantic, had ever heard a well-balanced orchestra.
—William Foster Apthorp, *By the Way* (1898)

Traveling Abroad

Chadwick arrived in New York City on September 4, 1877, a day and a half before his departure to Europe. This was his first visit to the city. While there he attended a performance by Teresa Carreño, the legendary singer-turned-pianist, at Madison Square Garden, where she enraptured her audience with a blazing performance of Mendelssohn's *Rondo Capriccioso*. Carreño performed "with a fleetness and grace that was inimitable," Chadwick later remembered. "Of all the artists male & female I have ever known I think she was the most magnetic, the most interesting, and the most inspiring."[1] Chadwick could have chosen to attend the "Triumphant Inauguration of the Series of Grand Concerts" to aid the Gilmore Band's "European Fund." Tickets were fifty cents for the performance, which was presented at "Gilmore's Concert Garden." There were many other options for entertainment and edification.

The chief musical story of the week was not a happy one. On the morning of September 3, a fire started at Hale & Company, a reputable piano manufactory at Thirty-Fifth and Tenth Streets. Chadwick could not have failed to notice the news about the fire, which left in its wake "a scene of utter destruction."[2] Starting on the fourth floor—in the "drying department" where just-glued piano sounding boards were placed to cure—the fire quickly spread and eventually ravaged eighty surrounding homes and businesses.[3] Initially it was thought that hundreds died in the fire, but within days officials determined that, miraculously, only six lives were lost. Nevertheless, the devastation was severe. As a neighborhood smoldered and crowds gathered to view the damage from a safe distance, one reporter described the sickening scene: "Dead horses, cows, chickens and cats, partially roasted, a pile of singed pickles, heaps of iron-work, and the remains of trucks and ice wagons were strewn all about."[4]

Chadwick left New York Harbor on the Hamburg-America Line steamship *Gellert* on September 6, 1877, bound for Hamburg, Germany.[5] It was a gloomy, drizzly day, but his hopes and goals for the excursion were not dampened.

"My great object, which I had never lost sight of in the previous five years," he wrote, "was to get thorough training in composition, absorb as much music as possible, learn the [German] language and eventually produce some orchestral work of some value and spend as little money as possible while carrying out this program."[6]

Chadwick befriended a number of passengers aboard the *Gellert*, several of whom were musicians. There was a German tenor named Fritsche, who had sung with the Theodore Thomas Orchestra. From Chicago there was C. E. Richard Müller and his sister, both of whom were music students. The collection also included Gustav Heubach, a young businessman from Brooklyn who was "very fond of music cultivated in a small way." Harry Eaton was not a musician but a medical student who was "a very gay and cheerful boy who kept us in roars of laughter with his funny yarns and anecdotes." But the most important friendship Chadwick forged on the *Gellert* was with Samuel L. Herrmann of Philadelphia. Herrmann, another budding musician, was voyaging to Germany to pursue his dream of becoming a conductor. He was "already a very fair pianist and organist and had been exhibiting the big organ at the Philadelphia Centennial" of 1876. Herrmann was a Jew, probably the first that Chadwick had ever known.[7]

If Chadwick's aims upon his departure had been clear, his initial steps upon arrival seem surprisingly improvisatory. When the ship arrived in Hamburg, Chadwick proceeded to Berlin, where he contacted organist Karl August Haupt (1810–1891), with whom he hoped to study. There is no evidence to suggest that Chadwick had contacted Haupt prior to his arrival in Berlin. In the days before easy international communication, we may reasonably assume that Thayer, who had been a Haupt student, provided a letter of introduction for Chadwick, as was customary. Haupt was an impressive talent. A master improviser and a leading advocate for the music of J. S. Bach, Haupt had studied with August Wilhelm Bach (1796–1869) before embarking on his career at various churches in Berlin.[8] Later he taught at the Königliches Kirchenmusik-Institut, a prestigious post in Berlin. For all his renown as an organist, Haupt composed very little. Even so, Chadwick was surprised when he learned that Haupt had no interest in examining his compositions. Haupt plainly told Chadwick that he could not—or would not—instruct him in composition, and he suggested that Chadwick make an effort to study with Immanuel Faißt (1823–1894) in Stuttgart. Faißt, a talented and largely self-taught organist who garnered considerable fame as the founder of the Stuttgart Conservatory, was also not recognized as an abundantly talented composer. Nor did the Stuttgart institution have a strong composition faculty aside from Faißt. The Stuttgart school gave minimal structure to its American students, who were often more interested in sightseeing and cultural exchange;

FIGURE 3.1.
Salomon Jadassohn, composer and teacher at the Leipzig Conservatory [undated photo]. Courtesy of New England Conservatory, Boston.

and unlike some other conservatories in Germany, there were few Americans there who actually excelled in music.[9] In any event, Chadwick dispensed with the idea of pursuing studies in Stuttgart. Simply noting that Stuttgart "did not suit my ideas at all,"[10] Chadwick made for Leipzig and Das Königliche Conservatorium der Musik zu Leipzig, or the Royal Conservatory of Leipzig. He had been urged to go there by his new friend Herrmann, who had already enrolled for the conservatory's fall term.

Leipzig

Arriving in Leipzig in October, Chadwick went to the Hôtel du Pologne, where he intended to reside until he could find an acceptable apartment. At approximately this time he made the acquaintance of William Henry Thaule of New York, a young musician who had recently studied at the Royal Conservatory, and who had serious reservations about the institution. Thaule, a pianist, advised Chadwick not to enter the conservatory, but urged him instead to study privately with composer-theorist Salomon Jadassohn (1831–1902). Thaule also helped him secure a job as an accompanist at concerts sponsored by the singing club Gesang Verein Merkur, where Chadwick became acquainted with composer Franz Abt, who was renowned for his huge body of music and especially for his works for male chorus.

FIGURE 3.2.

Carl Reinecke, teacher, composer, and conductor of the Leipzig Gewandhaus Orchestra, 1902. Courtesy of New England Conservatory, Boston.

Chadwick heeded Thaule's advice. Jadassohn, a member of the conservatory faculty who also maintained a teaching studio at his home, already enjoyed a reputation in Germany as a skilled composer and a fine teacher (see figure 3.1). In the 1870s, however, he was still relatively young, and much of his best work lay ahead of him. Jadassohn had himself been a student at the Leipzig Conservatory and even studied piano with Liszt in Weimar for a time. Chadwick's brief experience in Jadassohn's studio proved richly rewarding, musically and personally. However, he soon found that he could save a great deal of money by registering at the conservatory. Enrollment had another upside, as it would also enable him to study with another major personality in Leipzig's musical life, composer and conductor Carl Reinecke (1824–1910).[11] (See figure 3.2.)

Chadwick entered the conservatory as a regular student on January 3, 1878. His first impressions of the conservatory were disappointing. His schedule of courses was dictated to him, and, when he learned that he was expected to attend ten hours of classroom instruction per week in six subject areas, Chadwick was appalled. "I only wanted Jadassohn and Reinicke [*sic*] and appealed to Jadassohn about it. He laughed at me and said 'Don't you know you don't have to go to all those lessons unless you want to?' And so I never went."[12] Since the conservatory did not require strict attendance, absenteeism was prevalent. Nevertheless, Chadwick attended at least a few of his courses, which included—besides counterpoint with Jadassohn and composition with

Reinecke—piano with Johannes Weidenbach (1847–1902); harmony with Ernst Friedrich Richter (1808–1879); and music history with Oscar Paul (1836–1898). (One anecdote illustrates the laxity of the conservatory's administration and its policies. Chadwick had been scheduled to study organ with Benjamin Robert Papperitz [1826–1903], and just before he left Leipzig, Papperitz spoke to him with unusual warmth and kindness about one of his compositions. Chadwick was unsure from whence the organist's affection came; apparently Papperitz "had *entirely forgotten that I had never been in his class.*"[13])

Naturally, it never occurred to Chadwick to miss his lessons with Jadassohn. They occurred on Saturday evenings at six o'clock, and, although it was a long walk from his residence, "I needed the exercise and was so full of enthusiasm from my lesson that I felt like running all the way home. Jadassohn often kept me long after my hour was up and often played his new compositions to me. He corrected everything I brought with great care but he never gave me any reasons except for 'sounds better.' He never mentioned strict or tonal counterpoint and did not require C clefs except for string quartet."[14] Jadassohn's pedagogy resonated with Chadwick; both were more interested in compositional results than they were in the methods of arriving at those results. And Chadwick enjoyed learning from Jadassohn precisely because he was not pedantic—the "sounds better" approach would later inform his own teaching and become a hallmark of his compositional aesthetic.

Not that Jadassohn was inept or looking for easy solutions. If Jadassohn failed to instruct his students in counterpoint, as suggested by Chadwick, it certainly was not because he lacked a thorough knowledge of its procedures. In addition to teaching harmony, counterpoint, composition, and instrumentation, Jadassohn was also a prolific composer whose oeuvre approaches 150 compositions and includes four symphonies, two overtures, a piano concerto, and many vocal and chamber works. With the publication in 1883 of his estimable *Harmonielehre*, Jadassohn also ensured his reputation as a pedagogue. By the time he died, he had published over a dozen theoretical and instructional treatises.

Chadwick not only respected Jadassohn's teaching and compositional skills, but the two were also developing a close personal relationship. In Chadwick's Lehrerzeugniß (official transcripts), Jadassohn, writing on behalf of himself and Reinecke, wrote, "Herr Chadwick possesses a completely exceptional talent for composition, as is sufficiently demonstrated by his work, two string quartets, overtures [*sic*] for orchestra, etc., which are far beyond schoolwork. The lessons were always a pleasure for me."[15] Jadassohn's kindness undoubtedly helped Chadwick to forget his own father's harshness; indeed, he considered Jadassohn as something of a father figure.

By contrast, Reinecke's name is conspicuously absent from most of Chadwick's later conservatory ruminations. Reinecke, an acquaintance of Schumann and Mendelssohn, and the conductor of the Leipzig Gewandhaus Orchestra since 1860, cut a broader swath in Leipzig musical circles than Jadassohn; he almost certainly had less time than Jadassohn to devote to his pupils. And although better known as a conductor, Reinecke was in fact a virtuoso pianist who toured widely and vigorously advocated for Mozart's music at a time when much of Germany was reveling in the just-rediscovered works of J. S. Bach. He was also a gifted and prolific composer whose works encompass a wide range of genres. Given Chadwick's idolization of Theodore Thomas, it is possible that he had already discovered his own desire to conduct. His contact with Reinecke, however, was limited to composition lessons.[16]

String Quartet No. 1 (op. 1)

Chadwick brought with him to Leipzig two instrumental trios that he had produced at Olivet College, his first in D minor (ca. 1874) and a second in C minor (ca. 1877), both now lost. "It had some rather good things in it," Chadwick remembered about the latter work, "and I thought it was a great work because I had put so much time into it. But neither Jadassohn or Reinicke [*sic*] told me its real defects which were glaring in the technical handling of the instruments as well as in the material [and neither of them] made me burn it or write it over. As an effort it really showed promise. As a result it was inadequate."[17]

More successful were the two movements of his String Quartet (no. 1, op. 1) in G minor which were composed wholly in Leipzig and selected for performance at the conservatory's Hauptprüfungskonzert (conservatory final exams) of May 29, 1878. The exam concerts were greatly anticipated events during which conservatory student-musicians performed the best works produced by conservatory composition students. Chadwick's quartet movements were played by two German students, Arthur Beyer, violin, and Max Eisenberg, cello; and two Americans, Georg Schäfer, violin, and Edgar Coursen, viola, from Baltimore and San Francisco, respectively. Dedicated to Sam Herrmann, it was the first selection of a concert that included piano music by Richard Rickard of Birmingham, England; songs by Edward Schütt of St. Petersburg, Russia; a selection for three violins and viola by Henry Schoenefeld of Milwaukee; and a piano sonata by Hans Schmidt from the city of Fellin in what is now Estonia. Chadwick thought Rickard the best pianist at the conservatory, but he admired Schütt for his versatility and his wide-ranging talents. "Another musician who plays, paints, composes poetry and music, speaks five languages and not yet 22 years old," Chadwick wrote enviously. Schütt was studying with the legendary violinist

Joseph Joachim, but, in a moment of sarcasm, Chadwick conjectured that the young Russian "doesn't know anything about the insurance business."[18]

Chadwick was unable to complete the final two movements of his First Quartet in time for the Hauptprüfungskonzert, but his reviewers seemed not to mind, and Chadwick's first brush with the German music critics was a positive one.[19] The reviewer for *Die Neue Zeitschrift für Musik* wrote: "The work exhibited a good working knowledge of harmonic principles as they apply to compositions of this nature. . . . When the composer is not original in his invention it is not obvious, and certainly what he has said in this piece demonstrates clear thinking."[20] Considering it his first professional-quality composition, Chadwick numbered it opus 1.[21] He also admitted with pride to his friend Charles Saunders that the quartet was favorably received by his fellow students; it "made me quite a lion among the Americans at least."[22] Chadwick had predicted this success; he told Saunders that Jadassohn and Reinecke were both pleased with the quartet, as was Friedrich Hermann (1828–1907), a Gewandhaus Orchestra violist and a teacher at the conservatory. A composer of modest achievement, Hermann had studied composition with Mendelssohn, and Chadwick shared his quartet with Hermann as it progressed. Chadwick again exhorted to Saunders, to whom he had sent sketches of the quartet's themes, "I am sure of a success on it and I hope a great one as it is really a great advance in originality and definiteness."[23]

The first movement of the quartet is a straightforward sonata form in G minor marked Allegro con brio. The taut, anxious main theme sounded by the cello outlines the tonic triad. At first the music is a simple melody with accompaniment, but Chadwick develops the material quickly, giving special attention to rhythm. Note values gradually decrease, hemiola confuses the pulse, and bits of stretto create conversations between the instruments. The secondary theme, sounded in the relative major key of B-flat, is a rhythmically sophisticated one that increases in complexity with the addition of triplet and dotted-eighth/sixteenth figures.

The music's quickened vibrancy is enhanced by its rather exotic pentatonic sound. The passage is not strictly pentatonic, as it uses six tones—F-G-B-flat-C-D-E—in its four-measure statement. Musicologist David Beveridge, referring to music by Dvořák, has observed that pentatonicism is not a "closed system" that composers followed strictly. Rather, he writes, "What we think of as the pentatonic feeling may be more dependent on certain peculiarities of melodic motion than on strict adherence to the scale."[24] As we shall see, Chadwick's music sometimes leans on these pentatonic peculiarities to provide a folksy style, but in this work its rusticity is understated. Fugato is another distinguishing feature of the development section, and its heavy chromaticism includes a particularly pungent non-functional diminished seventh chord that is used solely for its jarring effect.

The second movement, Andante non troppo lento, was also rendered at the Hauptprüfung concert. A gentle, songful invention in E-flat, it evinces Chadwick's skill at creating long, flowing lines that modulate almost imperceptibly. Its simple form (ABA'B' with a coda) enabled the composer to concentrate on the variation of themes and motives, while also taking pains to develop rhythm. The first section presents the lyrical theme without introduction. After a brief episode in C minor, Chadwick introduces not a new theme but a simple descending motive in B-flat. That motive dominates and rapidly seeps into the instrumental fabric. A compact movement at just 120 measures, it is surprisingly powerful and undoubtedly bedazzled Chadwick's conservatory adjudicators. Steven Ledbetter asserted that this movement "grows in a lyrical surge from a straightforward melodic gambit to a dramatic climactic phrase."[25]

"Shoot the Pipe," a folk song that was familiar to Chadwick (its source remains undiscovered), is a most important element in his third movement, Menuetto: Poco vivace. Actually a scherzo—it has "little connection with eighteenth-century courtly dance," says Ledbetter—the fiery ABA movement is in C minor.[26] Its opening theme (A) bears a striking resemblance to the main theme of the first movement. One sees here Chadwick's penchant for hemiola and a rhythmic imagination that is second to none. The Trio section (B) introduces "Shoot the Pipe" in the key of F major, but fewer than twenty-five measures later the A theme returns as the result of another seamless modulation. Following a dramatic pause, the first movement's principal idea returns (thereby making the relationship between the two movements explicit) before several fragments of "Shoot the Pipe" bring it to a close.

The melody of the quartet's final movement, a G-minor sonata form, is imbued with a distinctive Scottish spirit. From the outset a characteristic fiddle tune, Finale: Allegro ma non troppo, blazes in the fashion of an elaborate jig, one richly decorated with trills and shakes. Here Chadwick stretches the virtuosity of the ensemble by presenting difficult arpeggiations throughout. The movement's contrasting theme, branded Marcato, arrives in B-flat major; it is a homophonic passage reminiscent, as Ledbetter observed, of a march. The development section explores the rhythmic possibilities of the jig tune before moving smoothly and without a caesura into the recapitulation in the expected home key, G minor. Here Chadwick modulates from the minor to G major and introduces a new theme—the hymn tune—before gradually ramping up his rhythmic activity. The furious coda, Allegro quasi presto, brings the movement to a brilliant close.

What conclusions may be drawn from a close analysis of Chadwick's first large-scale composition? To begin with, as his first serious composition to be forged directly under the eyes of Reinecke and especially Jadassohn, Chadwick could hardly have broken free from the tethers of form. His sonata forms closely adhere to accepted tenets, and so do his simpler forms, those which comprise the inner movements. Nevertheless, it is impossible to ignore the hymn tune theme that appears in the recapitulation in the finale movement. Chadwick clearly views the recapitulation as an area the can withstand further development, and soon he will discover that coda sections can withstand the same. Second, Chadwick's music demonstrates a strong sense of forward propulsion. His meters and rhythms are daring; his predilection for $\frac{3}{4}$ (only the finale is in duple meter) enables the use of hemiola and lends to his music an additional layer of complexity; and Chadwick takes great pains to develop rhythmic ideas. Finally, Chadwick's use of ethnically shaded melodic materials — pentatonicism — in the 1870s puts him at the forefront of a developing school of American nationalism and well in advance of his American colleagues. The first movement presents a nearly pentatonic melody based on folk song, and the principal melody of the fourth movement, with its jig-like construction, is modeled on Celtic or Gaelic dance. Similar musical strokes will be heard soon in his Second Symphony, and much later in his orchestral tour de force, *Tam O'Shanter*.

Chadwick in the Old World

For the most part, Chadwick adapted easily to his new European environs. He was able to combine his ever-widening musical interests with his need for social interaction in relatively short order. In Leipzig he joined the Gesang-Verein Concordia, a men's chorus in which he sang "2nd bass."[27] The fellows of the chorus would sometimes invite Chadwick to their homes. At the club's regular rehearsals, which were social as well as musical, the group would fill up on "the vilest form of beer ever concocted," dance with the ladies present, play Kegel ("outdoor ten pins"), and, of course, sing. From these events sprang Chadwick's friendship with the society's conductor, Moritz Creidel, who offered Chadwick lodging at his home. Creidel's father was a cantor, and Chadwick often had occasion to play the organ for the older man at synagogue.

Chadwick's membership in the Concordia improved his German-language skills in a hurry, but he admitted that "my blunders were a never-ending source of amusement" to his fellow choristers.[28] His increasing fluency in German was enhanced by his attendance at performances of light operatic works by Johann Strauss, Franz von Suppé, and Carl Millocker, often under the direction of a young Arthur Nikisch, who would later conduct the Boston Symphony Orchestra. In addition to companionship, the Concordia also provided a platform for at least one of his own works to be performed. Chadwick's now completed Trio in C minor was heard at the Concordia's concert of March 11, 1878.[29] Chadwick, playing the piano, was joined by violinist Edwin Reim and cellist Carl Bayrhoffer in the salon of the Hôtel du Pologne. Concordia events were the epitome of "miscellaneous" concerts; that is, while most of the performance was structured around the men's choir, there were a number of other musical offerings by a variety of singers and instrumentalists. This recital featured, in addition to the chorus, music for cello and piano, songs for piano and vocalist, and, of course, Chadwick's now lost four-movement trio.

A curious Chadwick began touring greater Germany almost immediately. His first Christmas, in 1877, was spent with Herrmann at Cöthen, where they stayed with the family Herzberg. Chadwick befriended Fannie Herzberg, whom he described as "very pretty, very sweet, and inclined to be sentimental."[30] Their friendship, perhaps even a mild romance, resulted in the recitation of a great deal of German poetry. Fannie adored Schiller, Chamisso, and Heine, and read their works to Chadwick often. At this time the music student also was inspired by a number of German painters, including Karl von Piloty, Wilhelm von Kaulbach, and Hans Markart, among others.

The summer of 1878 was spent in continental exploration, mostly in Switzerland, with Herrmann and two other companions. Chadwick did little composing during this journey, but he enjoyed the sights at Lucerne, Zurich, Interlaken, Bern, and Lausanne, among other cities. The young travelers were awed by the magnificent scenery — the Alps, the Grindelwald glacier, the Wetterhorn, and others — so much so, in fact, that Chadwick would make several return journeys to Switzerland.

When he returned to Leipzig to ready for the fall term at the conservatory, he was forced again to confront what became a seemingly never-ending quest for an acceptable home. Accommodations had been a huge source of tension for Chadwick since his arrival in Leipzig, and his stay at the boarding house of Frau Wehsener, whom he had met shortly after his arrival, had not been a pleasant experience. The payment of fifty marks per month provided a roof over his head but not much else. The rent included meals, but the menu was routinely mediocre. "For breakfast I had a very poor 'Blümchen-caffee' and one 'semmal' fresh and good. . . . For lunch, always cold, a little cold ham, veal, or cheese with 'schwarz brod' and sometimes a little potato salad. For dinner . . . one cotelette or schnitzel with carrots and peas or potato and a little 'compot' of green salad, and of course beer which was extra."[31] Frau Wehsener's portions were small, and at day's end he often was hungry.

Chadwick had additional appetites. He was a smoker, even something of a tobacco connoisseur. "Fair but tasteless cigars cost 6 pf. apiece," he reported, "but I usually smoked a pipe at home. I smoked Durham when I could get it which was not always the case. The only pipe tobacco in Germany is an awful brew called 'Canaster' which the Germans smoke in long porcelain pipes."[32] Many evenings he would venture out to eat and grab a quick smoke before bed. Eventually the hunger issue and his general discontent would cause him to leave Frau Wehsener's for good.

A succession of residences followed: he briefly resided with the Klausnitz family, but, besides being a long walk to the conservatory, there were few restaurants in the vicinity. Chadwick then moved in with fellow conservatory student Charles Carter on Poniatowski Strasse; as roommates they proved incompatible. Then to the Berger family residence, where his room depressed him; there was little direct sunlight, and meals with the family grew tiresome—he suspected that they were interviewing him as a prospective husband for their daughter, "a pale, silly creature without an idea in her head except to catch a husband." That housing arrangement lasted only a few weeks.[33]

Chadwick finally made arrangements to live with Boston friend Theodore Presser, who had recommended him for the position at Olivet College. Presser unexpectedly arrived in Leipzig about a year after Chadwick. Of course, the two had already cultivated a close relationship as classmates at NEC, and in Europe Presser quickly became one of Chadwick's most ardent supporters. Chadwick would later recall that, while at the conservatory, Presser "did not learn a d—— thing," but "his constant good cheer endeared him to the other American students."[34]

Presser provided much moral support as Chadwick's composing career started to advance, and his good humor was a crucial balm as Chadwick's family and financial crises started to erupt. During the summer of 1878 Chadwick appealed to his father for money, the only time that he did so as far as we know, but to no avail. Alonzo Chadwick was not forthcoming with financial assistance, and he was even mean-spirited in his response. In one correspondence Alonzo proved "so impaternal, so bitter, and so vindictive that I fully made up my mind never to appeal to him again under any circumstances. He claimed that I had always acted against his advice and wishes, that I have sided with my mother against him, that I was making the failure he had always predicted and have only myself to blame. Therefore he did not propose to assist me either then or at any future time. The whole tone of the letter showed no affection for me, but it almost exulted over my difficulties."

Chadwick answered his father's letter with a savage diatribe of his own: "And

I did not spare him in the slightest. I was burning with indignation and with a sense of the monstrous injustice of it. After all, he was responsible for my existence, if not for much else since it began."[35] He sent the letter to his brother, who, as Chadwick learned only later, did not forward it to Alonzo. Henry was up-front about the matter: "George, it was all true and I don't blame you in the least, but you will be glad I did not give it to him."[36] After a time—when a cooler head could prevail—George agreed. But Alonzo must have known that he had heard the last from young George.

String Quartet No. 2 (op. 2)

By the time rehearsals of his First String Quartet began in preparation for the conservatory's May 1878 Prüfungskonzert, the composition of Chadwick's Second String Quartet was already under way. Considered "the first flush of Chadwick's maturity," it indeed shows a remarkable advance over his first effort in terms of thematic invention, rhythmic and harmonic imagination, development of ideas, and proportion.[37]

Chadwick commenced the Second Quartet, which he dedicated to Jadassohn, at least by May and finished the second movement in July; the third and fourth movements were completed in November. The time lag perhaps reflected Chadwick's inability, or lack of desire, to compose during what was an adventure-filled summer. It is also possible that the complexity of the new score may have required extra time to complete.

The first movement, a sonata form in C major, opens in $\frac{12}{8}$ meter and provides hints of the principal theme to come. When finally reached, the spirited main melody, another pentatonic one, emphasizes the relationship between the tonic (C), the dominant (G), and the submediant (A). Unlike themes heard in the First Quartet, the themes here indicate that Chadwick was anxious to make the pentatonicism more obvious. The tune is folksy and sprightly, and it allows ample inspiration for manipulation. A noble, sweeping secondary theme, marked *cantabile*, provides a welcome relief to the principal melody, but it lasts only briefly. In an unusual move—but one that becomes increasingly typical of his music—Chadwick interrupts the development section with a brief new idea, here marked Lento, immediately preceded by an ad libitum string passage and a grand pause. This surprising gesture garners the listener's attention not only because the music's flow is stemmed by the pause, but because here Chadwick presents his boldest harmonic passage yet, one that emphasizes with a fermata a startling diminished-seventh chord built on the second scale degree (D-F-A-flat-C) to provide a transition to the tonic key (C) and the start of the recapitulation. As in his First Quartet, Chadwick manipulated his material in the recapitulation and coda sections. Rhythmic figures first heard in the development section are recalled, the music modulates briefly to D major, and another bold harmony, a dominant-ninth chord, rings loud and clear.

The second movement of the quartet may be Chadwick's finest achievement to this point in his career. This section, Andante espressivo, ma non troppo lento, demonstrates the composer's sure handling of the instruments and a new insistence on the independence of their musical line. It is an approach that differs somewhat from Chadwick's earlier writing, much of which featured melody with accompaniment. Within its ABA form, one observes a noticeable increase in Chadwick's mastery of counterpoint and a willingness to give each instrument a bite at the melody. He also gives play to the expressive elements of his music with indications like dolce and espressivo, as well as carefully placed crescendi and diminuendi. Several harmonic twists—including an emphasis on B-flat (the minor third degree of the tonic G major)—add to the movement's pungency.

The third movement, Scherzo, is a passionate yet playful five-part creation (ABACA) in E minor. The main theme, in flourishes presented by the viola and the cello, is rich in its rhythmic variety, as is the elegant B theme, which lilts slightly off-balance metrically, owing to its use of hemiola. A passage of pizzicato in the accompaniment presents a welcome change of texture and is expanded upon in the C section.

Syncopation is the most compelling aspect of the finale, a brisk sonata form stamped Allegro molto vivace. Cast in the tonic C major, the exposition presents a jaunty quickstep theme in small-note values. The music moves briefly through E-flat major before the appearance of the wistful secondary theme in a brief episode of G major. The development section sounds motives derived from the main theme, and soon includes decorative elements, like pizzicato and sul ponticello, as well as a variety of harmonic shifts, and even a new theme, which is accompanied by the rhythms of the habañera.

On the eve of the premiere performance of the Second Quartet at the conservatory's Hauptprüfungskonzert of May 30, 1879, Chadwick wrote to Charles Saunders, "The rehearsals of my quartette go on swimmingly—The fellows like it and especially praised its 'Geigenmässigkeit' (I don't know how that word is in English)."[38] The "Geigenmässigkeit," literally "violin moderation," that garnered praise from classmates may refer to the expanded role the Yankee composer gave to the second violin, viola, and cello parts—in other words, Chadwick "moderated" the typical dominance of the first violin part. He had made strides in his scoring since his First Quartet; the Second demonstrates a confidence and surety that the earlier composition lacks. Chadwick had taken pains to master the instruments he was writing for, and he admitted to Saunders several months after the quartet's completion that he had been studying the violin conscientiously: "I hired a fiddle for 25¢ a month, box [case] and all, and in these last two terms [at the conservatory] learned the fingerings so that I know exactly what not to write although I can't play anything."[39] He also benefitted from advice given by the musicians who premiered it, Hans Winderstein, Imanuel Muck, Bruno Oelsner, and Edmund Röthlisberger, all fellow students at the conservatory.

Critical assessments of the quartet echoed those of his classmates. *Musikalisches Wochenblatt* related, "In this manuscript work nothing of interest was wanting, and there was a suitable character and sentiment, for example in the first and third movements. The musical materials of this composition are not unskillfully handled, nor overly burdened with polyphony, and the form of the individual parts [movements] is restrained and not disproportionate to its contents. The workmanship of the composition displays careful planning."[40] Other reviews were similarly favorable. The critic for the *Neue Zeitschrift für Musik* noted the "fine impression" that resulted from the first movement's "considerable inventive power, sentiment, and good planning."[41] The critic for the *Signale für die Musikalische Welt* gave some credit to the performers; he detected, "besides natural and resourceful invention, a nicely prepared and graceful execution."[42]

When Chadwick finally returned home to Boston, the Second Quartet—notably unlike the First—received something of a revival. In 1881 the local and rather prominent Beethoven Quintette Club, led by the ambitious violinist Gustave Dannreuther (1853–1923), performed Chadwick's quartet at least three times in the first half of the year. Shortly after its performance at a Euterpe Society concert on January 5, 1881, Dwight wrote that the Second Quartet was "fresh and pregnant in its themes and yet free from extravagance, and full of spirit and legitimate effect." Dwight also reported that Chadwick was in the audience and "being persistently called out, he stepped upon the platform and modestly bowed his thanks."[43] The quartet had become familiar enough by midyear that a columnist for the *Boston Evening Transcript* included it in an article that surveyed "Some Recent American Music." "In a concise and admirably rounded form," the writer exhorted, Chadwick's invention "brings material of really great value, and is one of the most promising works that we have known to come from the pen of a young composer."[44] In 1882 Chadwick arranged the lovely and delicate second movement of his quartet for string orchestra, titling it simply *Andante.*

Rip Van Winkle Overture (op. 3)

That Chadwick had been able to concentrate on composition at all following the long-distance wrangles with his imperious father is remarkable. It had not been easy; at one point his melancholy was so pronounced that Presser urged him to seek professional help. He reluctantly agreed and sought therapy with a local psychologist. Chadwick initially was determined to finish his course of studies at the conservatory, but by December 1878, fifteen months after his arrival and just a few weeks after he completed his Second Quartet, Chadwick matter-of-factly wrote to a friend, "On the whole I have concluded that I have stayed in Leipzig about long enough."[45]

Another source of anxiety for Chadwick was an ailing Jadassohn, who had never enjoyed robust health. Not only was it stressful for Chadwick to see his beloved master ill, but the situation also kept him from his composition lessons. Other musical problems piled on. "My piano playing doesn't improve any," he wrote, and "I have no opportunity to practice organ music. I can't compose— everything I write I put in the fire." The state of musical programs in the city also exacted his resentment. "The orchestra and the opera has [sic] become miserable, and the prices put up [i.e., raised] at that. They keep giving the same things [i.e., repertoire] over and over."[46] Chadwick's distaste for conditions in Leipzig was growing: "I'd like to know why the devil I was born with an ambition to stand on the highest mound and have to spend my life reaching for it from a second class place."[47] His depression was perhaps attributable to homesickness, but certainly his living conditions were a contributing factor. (Wryly commenting in his memoirs on the contents of his correspondence, Chadwick wrote that "this letter shows that living in a dark room without sunlight, eating fried German food, [and] drinking bad coffee and dark beer was having its effect."[48])

Additionally, Chadwick feared for his own financial well-being. "I sometimes think that I shall come home without having accomplished much except getting dead broke," he bemoaned, although it seems doubtful that money was the root of his problems. At no time during this sojourn did Chadwick starve, and, on the contrary, even though he was always watchful of his spending, he often treated himself to delights: cigars, beer, concerts of every hue, and late-night suppers. Nor was he completely without a safety net. After all, brother Henry, who was watching Chadwick's money for him while Chadwick was in Europe, was employed and almost certainly would have sent funds in an emergency. Chadwick probably believed that even Alonzo would have sent his desperate son money, although not without adding an "I told you so" or two.

Chadwick's depression was rather short-lived and would never become chronic. It was substantially mitigated as he began, probably in autumn 1878, what would be the most important composition of his Leipzig period, *Rip Van Winkle* Overture. Little is known about the overture's genesis, although the orchestral score was prepared from a four-hand piano version that was played by and for a number of his fellow conservatory students.

He completed its scoring on March 18, 1879. Chadwick, anxious to hear his first serious orchestral work, immediately secured for the overture a short rehearsal with a local beer-hall orchestra of about thirty musicians. He had befriended the orchestra's leader, "who was a good routined man. After one or two 'kneips' [i.e., drinks] with him he readily consented to let me have a part of the rehearsal to try over the overture and find possible mistakes in the parts. I had corrected them with great care, but was still afraid I might have overlooked some."[49] Presser accompanied Chadwick to the beer-hall rehearsal and was "wildly enthusiastic." Within a month after placing the finishing touches on *Rip Van Winkle*, at approximately Easter, Chadwick, apparently believing that he had learned as much as he could in Leipzig, withdrew from the conservatory.[50]

Despite his withdrawal, *Rip Van Winkle* Overture was a featured selection at the conservatory's June 20, 1879, Hauptprüfungskonzert, his third work in two years to be featured at that event. Chadwick, whose reputation as the best student composer at the conservatory was swelling, reported that a celebration ensued following the premiere. Chadwick and classmates Karl Muck, Herrmann, Carter, and others, "adjourned to Barman's [Tavern] where we had a 'Taufung' [baptism] and nearly drowned the poor old Rip in beer."[51] Much to his surprise, his German classmates admired the work. But Chadwick was dismayed that his best friend, Theodore Presser, failed to attend. Chadwick suspected that Presser might have been jealous of his success.

In Chadwick's day, Washington Irving's *Rip Van Winkle*, a tale of German origin, still resonated with the American public. It gained particular momentum in the 1860s and 1870s when the legendary American actor Joseph Jefferson (1829–1905) portrayed Rip in a theatrical version that toured the United States, to remarkable critical and popular acclaim. It is not clear whether Chadwick saw Jefferson in the role of Rip, but given that he dedicated his overture to Jefferson, it seems likely. Naturally, *Rip Van Winkle* Overture is programmatic, but at the time, Chadwick preferred to let his music speak for itself rather that provide details beyond what would already have been known to the average American reader.

Rip Van Winkle Overture is scored for paired woodwinds; a brass nonet of four horns, two trumpets, and three trombones; timpani; and strings. Chadwick's instrumentation is rather lean by the progressive standards of the late

1870s, but an aggressive system of doubling made his orchestra sound larger and fuller than it actually was. *Rip Van Winkle* is founded on the traditional principles of sonata-allegro form. While its sonata structure, with the inclusion of an introduction and a coda, is obvious, Chadwick cleverly modified the form to fit his programmatic purpose. Fundamental to his presentation of the form is his use of melody. Although the overture is constructed within the bounds of tradition, within its carefully crafted though somewhat unbalanced architecture five related themes pepper the overture, each occurring within the exposition section. Throughout the overture his melodic ideas undergo subtle changes and adaptations, and, while upon close inspection they prove to have shared origins, they nevertheless maintain distinct profiles. Included within the organically generated tunes are subtle motivic references that make regular appearances throughout the music. Although the organic generation of musical material was not a new technique by this time, in his first works Chadwick demonstrates that he is one of America's earliest masters of it.

Rip Van Winkle Overture benefitted from Chadwick's exposure to the abundant artistic culture of Leipzig. He reported regular attendance at myriad events, including the opera and the choir performances at the Thomaskirche. At the latter he heard motets and sometimes even entire cantatas by J. S. Bach. Chadwick recalled: "The first time I heard it I could not believe it was boys' voices. Neither did I appreciate the fine old contrapuntal stuff. It was never called to my attention or explained to me."[52] He also made a point of attending the Gewandhaus Orchestra's open rehearsals and concerts often led by his teacher, Reinecke. Programs emphasized the early Romantic canon; Chadwick heard copious amounts of late Beethoven, Weber, Schumann, Raff, and especially Mendelssohn, with whom so many of his German teachers had enjoyed a direct relationship. He usually prepared himself for these events by thoroughly examining the scores to be played, most often symphonies and programmatic concert overtures. Jadassohn and Reinecke, of course, helped to develop that aesthetic with Chadwick in his lessons. Chadwick also enjoyed exposure to contemporary trends in the music of the day, for Brahms, then Europe's leading composer, was active in Leipzig during Chadwick's time there. Chadwick attended the premiere of Brahms's Violin Concerto; he also heard a private Gewandhaus rehearsal, on January 8, 1878, of Brahms's newly minted Symphony no. 2, for which he "sneaked in with the orchestra by carrying a fiddle box for one of the boys." He listened intently from behind a curtain in the gallery.[53] Brahms's bold polyphony was something of an epiphany to the young Yankee, although he could not quite decipher it yet. Chadwick may have been most invigorated by the free public garden concerts performed by military bands and orchestras,

TABLE 3.1. The Form of *Rip Van Winkle* Overture

	Introduction		Exposition			Development	Recapitulation		Coda
Part:			I			II			
Section:			1		2	3	4		
Theme:	O1	O2	P	T	S		O1	P	k
Key:	F		F		C		F	F	F
Measure:	1	8	38	60	108	154	302	315	531–62

and he rarely failed to attend local operetta productions. "I did not miss many of these shows and from them learned much, especially about how to make a small orchestra *sound*."[54] That lesson would serve him well in his new overture.

The most distinguishing feature of *Rip Van Winkle* is its wealth of gentle and often lighthearted melody. Chadwick was an inventive tunesmith and his first overture bursts with two introductory themes (O1 and O2), the principal key theme (P) followed by a transitional melody (T), and a secondary key theme (S) (see table 3.1). The opening melody, an innocent, wistful tune stated by the solo cello, is Chadwick's sonic depiction of Irving's "pleasant valley" in upstate New York. Like Mendelssohn, Chadwick's artistic outlook was strongly affected by both painting and landscapes. Europe's majestic scenery, which he was currently experiencing, and Irving's masterly descriptions, which he could readily imagine, incited him. In the opening cello melody the vast expanse of Rip's mountainous terrain is illustrated by the music's wide range, and its lengthy ascent is an important characteristic of its later manifestations. A jaunty theme depicts the careless Rip, while a sweeter theme, marked *cantabile*, introduces the character of Rip's daughter.

Rip Van Winkle Overture was enthusiastically received by the German press. The critic for *Musikalisches Wochenblatt* appreciated Chadwick's self-assuredness in the handling of a large form and declared that he clearly possessed his "own poetic intentions." Further, his creation teemed with "color and physiognomy."[55] The writer for the *Signale für die Musikalische Welt* frankly considered the overture "by far the best" composition on the program. "The contents," he judged, "are fresh, it is architecturally well knit and adroitly orchestrated."[56] Likewise, the writer for the *Neue Zeitschrift für Musik* compared Chadwick's work to Mendelssohn's *Midsummer Night's Dream*; he declared that his study of the older master had obviously given the youngster "constant and fruitful pleasure."[57] When, in 1939, composer Sidney Homer called *Rip Van Winkle* Overture a "landmark" work, he was undoubtedly considering not only its adept construction, but also its subject matter and its geniality.[58]

Perhaps realizing that *Rip Van Winkle*'s success would be the apex of his Leipzig experience, and feeling that he had little to gain by remaining in the city, Chadwick departed almost immediately following its Hauptprüfung performance. Jadassohn failed to understand why Chadwick was compelled to leave, and even made the promise to secure for him a position as a capellmeister in a town near Leipzig if he would agree to stay. But Chadwick had already made up his mind: "I felt that I needed a change and that another man's ideas would be valuable and that a different environment would be interesting."[59]

There were additional reasons to leave: "I had been in Leipzig for two years and got to know the dingy old place pretty well, but I never did get to thoroughly like the Saxons or get reconciled to their meanness or dirt." Chadwick was also disgusted by north German anti-Semitism. He often heard discussions about the "smützige Juden" ["dirty Jews"] and, by virtue of his having acquired many Jewish friends and acquaintances, including Herrmann and Jadassohn, thought them unjustified. Finally, his challenge to find acceptable living quarters had reached a breaking point. A brief stay with Presser resulted in an intense scrape with their landlady, a "dirty old widder with a miserable mangy dog that was always underfoot."[60] His complaints about the quality of the coffee and the infrequent changing of the towels and bedding resulted in almost immediate confrontation. Chadwick, ever the crusty Yankee, was not shy about matters he judged unjust. "Presser was too meek to kick, but I was not and in about two days there was a row that could have been heard for miles. Presser came in in the midst of it and remarked with much enthusiasm 'I knew it! I knew it would come!'" The argument resulted in some positive change at the apartment, "and I was not sorry I could command a few cuss words in the Saxon dialect."[61]

Chadwick's plans upon leaving Leipzig were nearly as ambiguous as those he had upon his arrival in Europe. He left for Dresden with the idea of taking organ lessons from Gustav Merkel (1827–1885) of the Dresden Conservatory. Merkel had taught there since 1861 and also conducted the Dreyssig Singakademie. His compositional output was modest, although he composed many works for organ, including noteworthy pedagogical studies. Chadwick was familiar with Merkel because of Thayer's advocacy of his music in Boston.

Chadwick had been dissatisfied with his keyboard studies in Leipzig—the teaching had not been remarkable and finding an instrument on which to practice proved nearly impossible. With Merkel he may have simply hoped to improve his skills without the burden of conservatory enrollment. Merkel agreed to give Chadwick lessons, but had no place for him to practice and, like Haupt before him, was unwilling to look over Chadwick's orchestral compositions. Although

Merkel was "altogether the best organist I had heard in Europe," he saw little point in studying with him given the limitations.

He liked Dresden, though. Following another brief sojourn to Switzerland, this time with Presser and several others, Chadwick happily returned to Dresden, where he rented a pleasant, inexpensive apartment on Racknitz Strasse. He remained for the duration of the summer. Unlike Leipzig, Dresden was charming and entirely compatible with his temperament. The city's cultural offerings were unparalleled—his daily visits to the local gallery and museum were interrupted only by day trips to the countryside—and Chadwick attended Merkel's regular recitals at the Hofkirche. At this time he also became acquainted with another former member of the Theodore Thomas Orchestra, conductor Bernhard Gottlober, who led the Concert-Kapelle des Königliche Belvedere. To Chadwick's surprise, Gottlober was captivated by his new overture and offered to perform it at one of his concerts. "When one reflects that such an opportunity as this was an [absolute] impossibility at that time anywhere in America," Chadwick remarked, "it shows why ambitious music students went to Europe to get their education."[62] Gottlober conducted *Rip Van Winkle* Overture on September 17, 1879.

Munich and the Duveneck Boys

For all its many charms, Dresden was not to last for Chadwick. Charles Carter had already matriculated to Munich to study at that city's Königliche Musikschule (Royal Conservatory, later renamed the Academie der Tonkunst). He persuaded Chadwick to follow. Leading the conservatory in the composition department was the imposing Josef Rheinberger. Chadwick knew little about Munich, but he was familiar with Rheinberger's brilliant reputation as a master artist and an authoritative instructor. After reading Carter's enthusiastic reports about the place, Chadwick arrived in late September 1879.

A decade before, American writer Charles Dudley Warner (1829–1900) had visited Europe—as he did many times during his lifetime—and wrote about the adventure in his absorbing travelogue, *Saunterings* (1872). Writing in 1869, Warner painted vivid descriptions of his travels in London and Paris, before he pressed through the Low Countries, Switzerland, and finally into Germany. Warner described in close detail the Munich that would have greeted Chadwick a few years later; he had an especially strong sense of the mood and the history that enveloped the Bavarian capital:

> Munich needs the sunlight. Not that it can better spare it than grimy London; for its prevailing color is light gray, and its many-tinted and frescoed fronts go

far to relieve the most cheerless day. Yet Munich attempts to be an architectural reproduction of classic times. . . . The old portion of the city has some remains of the Gothic, and abounds in archways and rambling alleys, that suddenly become broad streets and then again contract to the width of an alderman, and portions of the old wall and city gates; old feudal towers stand in the market-place, and faded frescoes on old clock-faces and over archways speak of other days of splendor. . . . You see, it is easy to grumble, and especially in a cheerful, open, light, and smiling city, crammed with works of art, ancient and modern, its architecture a study of all styles, and its foaming beer . . . only seven and a half kreuzers to the quart. Munich has so much, that it, of course, contains much that can be criticized.[63]

Late-nineteenth century Munich teemed with music. Warner, an inveterate music lover, made it a point to attend concerts and other musical events, as "we felicitated ourselves that we should have no lack of music when we came to Munich," and, he said,

I think we have not; though the opera has only just begun, and it is the vacation of the Conservatoire. There are first the military bands: there is continually a parade somewhere, and the streets are full of military music, and finely executed too. Then of beer-gardens there is literally no end, and there are nightly concerts in them. There are two brothers Hunn, each with his [own] band, who, like the ancient Huns, have taken the city; and its gardens are given over to their unending waltzes, polkas, and opera medleys. Then there is the church music on Sundays and holidays, which is largely of a military character; at least, has the aid of drums and trumpets, and the whole band of brass. . . . I think there was some sort of yearly fair in progress, for the great [town square] was filled with temporary booths: a circus had set itself up there, and there were innumerable side-shows and lottery-stands; and I believe that each shanty and puppet-show had its band or fraction of a band, for there was never heard such tooting and blowing and scraping, and pounding and dinning and slang-whanging, since the day of stopping work on the Tower of Babel. The circus band confined itself mostly to one tune; and as it went all day long, and late into the night, we got to know it quite well; at least, the bass notes of it, for the lighter tones came to us indistinctly. You know that blurt, blurt, thump, thump, dissolute sort of caravan tune.[64]

Warner was cannily aware of the city's musical politics when he observed that "the present director of the conservatoire and opera, a Prussian, Herr [Hans] von Bülow, is a friend of Wagner. There are formed here in town two parties:

The Wagner and the conservative, the new and the old, the modern and the classical; only the Wagnerites do not admit that their admiration of Beethoven and the older composers is less than that of the others, and so for this reason Bülow has given us more music of Beethoven than of any other composer. One thing is certain, that the royal orchestra is trained to a high state of perfection: its rendition of the grand operas and its weekly concerts at the Odeon cannot easily be surpassed."[65] Chadwick would probably have felt at home in a concert hall run by Bülow, for the conductor's musical personality and predilections were strikingly similar to those of Theodore Thomas.

Chadwick's first order of business was the taking of exams for entry into the conservatory. It was not a pleasant experience. Chadwick could not understand why, having proven himself in Leipzig, he was forced to take the exams to begin with. Once they started, Chadwick sensed he was in for a dose of humiliation:

> The entire faculty of the music school, many of whom wore very pessimistic countenances, sat about in a ring and watched the victim write Harmony and Counterpoint exercises on the blackboard. These were all in C clef, with which I was none too familiar. . . . Besides I was a good deal rattled by the presence of the ogres who surrounded the altar on which the victim was immolated. The consequence was that I made a pretty poor showing, which elicited some ironical remarks about graduates of the Leipzig Conservatory.[66]

In what can only be described as a colossal failure, Chadwick was not accepted to the conservatory. Believing that he botched the test not on account of a lack of talent, but because of his anxiety, he appealed to a key member of the faculty: "I tried to protest to [Josef] Rheinberger and he finally said that if I would bring him a new fugue and canon in two days, that perhaps he would let me in the class. I did so to his satisfaction, but it was impossible for him to understand why I could not do the same thing on the blackboard under the eyes of the faculty."[67]

Rheinberger (1839–1901) was the principal reason for a young composer to go to Munich. In Leipzig Chadwick familiarized himself with several of Rheinberger's organ works and his popular symphonic poem, *Wallenstein* (op. 10), all of which had made a favorable impression. Rheinberger's fame in Germany was expansive; in 1869 Hans von Bülow, who was not an easy man to impress, sang the composer's praises: "Rheinberger is a truly ideal composition teacher, whose skill, refinement and love of detail are unrivalled in all of Germany and the surrounding area, in short, one of the most respectable musicians and men in the world." Bülow stopped short of a complete endorsement, though, continuing

"I am not yet willing to guarantee the immortality of his compositions."[68] A posthumous entry in *Baker's Biographical Dictionary of Music and Musicians* (1919) accurately sums up Rheinberger's life and work: "As a composer [Rheinberger] falls just short of greatness; he never rises to the height of passion and only occasionally does he touch the strings of real emotion. Nevertheless, his dignity, formal finish, and consummate technical mastery, compel respect and admiration."[69]

Chadwick was assigned to courses in canon, fugue, and instrumentation, and Rheinberger permitted him to attend advanced classes in single and double counterpoint, as well. The studies were rigorous, quite unlike Chadwick's experiences at Leipzig. At Munich's conservatory attendance was expected, testing was frequent, and nonsense was not tolerated. Besides his official classes, Chadwick took class organ lessons with Rheinberger. Because the organ class numbered only four pupils, Chadwick became more familiar with the older composer than would have been possible in the regular classroom. Rheinberger's pedagogy was severe: "He always made us improvise a Prelude before we began to play our lesson. He wanted it strictly conventional and at any hint of abrupt modulation or modern dissonances, he would make a wry face. Sometimes he would improvise for us himself, although he had a bad sore on one of his fingers." The "bad sore" was a lesion that had caused Rheinberger grief for years; in 1871 it burst and did not heal for well over a decade.[70] Despite that handicap, Chadwick admired Rheinberger's sure skill at improvisation: "It was always clear and characteristic in both form and part writing as though it were written out and was certainly a splendid model for the rest of us."[71] If Rheinberger was an inspiring performer, however, his stolid nature did not allow him to lavish praise upon his students. Chadwick was sometimes praised faintly with "Verhaltnismässig, sehr gut" ["Comparatively, very good"]; his classmates seemed not to merit as much as that.[72] It has been generally concluded that Chadwick's skill at the keyboard was negligible, but Rheinberger's remark, like others we have heard since Chadwick's early days in Boston, suggests otherwise.

Whether or not he was a favored student, Chadwick had but slight appreciation for Rheinberger's imperious classroom manner: "He had absolutely no idea of the students' point of view and he was pedantic, not to say pig-headed to a degree. This was even more noticeable in the instruction on orchestration than in his counterpoint lessons. He never quoted anybody after the time of Weber; most of his examples being from Gluck, Mozart, or Beethoven. These we were obliged to write out on the blackboard and copy, even though we owned the score ourselves. He never mentioned Berlioz, Wagner, or Liszt and if he had, it probably would have been with contempt."[73]

Rheinberger was a teacher of the old school. His attention to detail was leg-endary and he drilled his students thoroughly in the basics of compositional technique. Musicologist E. Douglas Bomberger has pointed out that "Rhein-berger did not use a textbook; instead he had the students copy his lectures verbatim, thereby making their own textbook for future reference."[74] Sidney Homer (1864–1953), a Chadwick student who, in the mid-1880s, was urged by Chadwick to study in Munich, remembered not only the mental and physical difficulties of Rheinberger's methods, but also the sheer excitement of them:

All the classwork was done on a blackboard, and the piano was rarely touched. In that silence the most exquisite counterpoint was written on the board either by Rheinberger or by one of the students. The tension was tre-mendous, and after two hours . . . we were exhausted. What a strange sight for an outsider who should occasionally look in! A long bare room badly lit by gas. A small gray-bearded man with burning eyes and expressive hands; twenty completely absorbed students watching a blackboard on which notes were being written, waiting breathlessly in absolute silence for the next progression: a beautiful passage in the alto, a thrilling touch in the tenor, a delicate, satisfying melodious step in this or that voice—the whole *sounding* wonderful. Sounding! When you could hear a pin drop? Yes, every student was listening, and the little white notes were sounding out clearly as they were written.[75]

Chadwick also developed a close association with painters while in Munich, and it would prove to have a lasting effect on him and his music. It began when he attended an informal gathering at a local tavern. Among those present were the aspiring young American painters Joseph Rodefer DeCamp, John Twachtman, William Merritt Chase, Ross Turner, Charles Mills, Julius Rolshoven, Charles Forbes, and others, each feasting on snacks of black bread and turnips, which they washed down with copious amounts of good beer. This collection, called the "Duveneck Boys," sought, much like their musical brethren, the inspiration and atmosphere that would lend their work individuality. Their leader and men-tor was "the Old Man" (never mind that he was scarcely a decade older than his followers), Kentuckian Frank Duveneck (1848–1919), an American who had found his artistic voice in Europe. He started out in Munich's Royal Academy, where he excelled under the influence of Wilhelm Leibl and the more conserva-tive Karl von Piloty. Duveneck enjoyed success, and, as his own renown grew, so did his entourage. Young American artists eschewed studies in the academy in order to lead a bohemian life and to learn from a budding American master—notably, one whose talents had been sanctioned by Europeans. Students flocked to him. Part of their experience included exploration of the continent, living on a shoestring, and, of course, painting, all the while in the company of sympathetic and like-minded artistic companions. On at least one of these journeys, Chadwick tagged along. The magnificent natural scenes of Europe—among which Chadwick composed while his fellows were sketching or painting—moved him immensely.

Most intriguing to Chadwick were the Duveneck Boys' discussions of art in its largest sense. He remembered that first meeting in the tavern: "They were all wrangling about ART and it interested me very much. . . . Under the influence of these fellows my views about art began to change quite rapidly. I found that I had been looking for the wrong thing and not seeing the qualities that make art permanent and valuable. . . . I began to see *color* and *relation* as I never had seen it before."[76] Chadwick was with the Boys only briefly; he returned to Munich while Duveneck led them to Italy, where they emigrated seasonally, to winter in Florence and summer in Venice.

Following the habit he had formed in Dresden, Chadwick began to frequent Munich's museums, now in the company of his newly acquired artist friends, those who, like him, elected not to continue their travels with Duveneck. They were men Chadwick thought would be able to enlighten him further on matters pertaining to the visual arts. Under their considerable influence Chadwick learned to approach his world as a creative artist: "My association with painters gave me an interest in Art, all the arts in fact, which has altered my life very materially. . . . And from these associations I have learned more of music itself as an art than I ever learned from any music teacher except in a purely technical way."[77] Chadwick would continue to meet and befriend countless visual artists; several of the best known among them were Childe Hassam, Daniel Chester French and John Singer Sargent. More than a few of the Boys became his life-long friends.

How did these experiences manifest themselves in Chadwick's compositions? What exactly did he mean by "color" and "relation" as it pertains to music? Generally speaking, we will hear in Chadwick's post-Munich works more adventuresome orchestrations; that is, a more adept utilization of the tonal "colors," or timbres, of musical instruments. We will also observe an imaginative use of instruments in solo passages or in combination, and we will note that his orchestral palette is greatly broadened. His increasing mastery of this facet of composition will, as we shall see, enable him more effectively to convey programmatic, extra-musical ideas. Chadwick's compositions will also demonstrate a heightened awareness of textural possibilities, perhaps instigated by his greater understanding of perspective or "relations." Competing interests of melody and countermelody become surer, more confident in his later works. In the end, however, the degree to which we can link his newfound appreciation of the visual arts to his musical advances is a matter of speculation; after all, Jadassohn and Rheinberger were towering influences, as well.

Going Home

Chadwick officially withdrew from the Munich Conservatory on December 13, 1879, two years and three months after his arrival on the continent.[78] His Munich experience had proven to be an artistically invigorating, and perhaps even a watershed, event in his career, although when he arrived there he had already been thinking about home and his future. In the previous September, Chadwick wrote hopefully to a friend, "I have got my eye on a good position *for me* in America and if you hear about me coming home about New Year's Eve you will know that I have got it—however keep mum till the time comes."[79] That unidentified possibility did not materialize.

Additionally, matters of finance were becoming worrisome. His brother had been the custodian of his money, and Henry wrote to Chadwick in February 1879 to inform him that his account at Lawrence Savings Bank was nearly depleted. To make matters worse, what little money remained in the account was unavailable because of "stay laws," which purported to avert widespread financial crisis by severely limiting the amount of money an account holder could withdraw. Banks were eager to make loans against one's own deposits, but Henry had already borrowed as much as he could on his brother's behalf. Chadwick was used to living close to the edge, financially speaking, although, as we have seen, he seems not to have lived in the poverty that has been described elsewhere.[80] Nevertheless, his present financial straits were serious. As Henry put it, "The bottom of the pail was in sight."[81]

At approximately this time, Chadwick was presented a rare musical opportunity: he unexpectedly received an invitation to conduct his *Rip Van Winkle* Overture at the Triennial Festival of Boston's venerable Handel and Haydn Society. Chadwick had sent the laudatory German reviews of his overture to Boston months earlier, and his successes were touted in *Dwight's Journal of Music*. Dwight was an advisor to the Handel and Haydn Society and certainly had a hand in encouraging the organization to perform Chadwick's overture. This was an enormous opportunity for a young American composer, and after considering his financial plight, Chadwick decided to return to New England. "I was sorry to leave Munich without finishing my year with Rheinberger," he recalled, "but I saw that the opportunity to conduct the Overture was too valuable to be lost."[82] With characteristic impatience and minimal fanfare, Chadwick—

who was also homesick and tired of his austere lifestyle—simply packed up and left. He took with him many memories and maintained relations with many of his new German and American friends. He also sent a steady stream of his own students to both Leipzig and Munich, although more to the latter, which perhaps reflects his respect for the teacher and/or his love of Munich's cultural life. Louis C. Elson, then an American music student, first met Chadwick in Cologne as the latter was preparing to return to Boston. He sensed Chadwick's confidence and artistic ability and recalled that in Chadwick he had found "an American who had just finished his music studies abroad and was going home to begin a great career."[83] Both Rheinberger and Jadassohn told Elson that Chadwick had been a brilliant student.

Chadwick's journey home was more leisurely than his arrival had been. On his way to London he stopped over in Paris, where he ended up in a seedy hotel. His lack of proficiency in the French language compounded his problems, but he managed to visit the Louvre, the Opera, and a concert that featured Berlioz's *Symphonie fantastique*. Chadwick also heard the great Belgian violinist Martin Pierre Marsick play a concerto by Saint-Saëns at which he took particular note of French concert etiquette. "I was astounded to hear the audience break into applause in all the tuttis of the concerto."[84] A visit to Chopin's grave stirred Chadwick deeply and resulted in his mazurka for piano titled *Reminiscence* (published in 1882). Once in London, he heard the legendary English organist W. T. Best in recital at Albert Hall, and he saw Minnie Hawk sing the title role in Bizet's *Carmen*. Sir Charles Hallé performed chamber music with an out-of-tune Joseph Joachim; it was a terrible disappointment.[85]

The eighteen-day journey to New York was arduous. "No sooner had we gotten out of the English Channel," he wrote, "than we ran into a gale which lasted most of the way to New York. . . . Most of the time we were not allowed on deck."[86] When the ship arrived in port Chadwick found himself on the verge of pneumonia and disastrously short of money. He disembarked with several friends, and between them they pulled together the price of a few cheap hotel rooms and train tickets from New York to Boston.

Chadwick was ill when he arrived at his mother's home in the Boston suburb of Malden. Although his health remained a concern for six weeks—in one undated letter from this period he wrote, "I have not been up at all today and my lungs are fearfully sore"[87]—he slowly recovered. During recent months his musical productivity had declined precipitously, but he was now rested and renewed. And with his newly earned German musical pedigree and several good compositions under his arm, Chadwick set out to make his mark on the landscape of musical Boston.

Getting Started in Boston
1880–1882

*Success in composition it seems to me is so uncertain; the way
is so long; there are so many and such insurmountable difficulties
in the way, that it is not strange many are frightened from even
attempting the first steps, to say nothing of persevering until a
reasonable amount of success is obtained.*

—George E. Whiting, "An American School of Composition" (1884)

First Jobs

Chadwick re-entered Boston's musical world with a perspective that was vastly different from the one he possessed a few short years ago. Now a professional with an enviable German conservatory imprimatur—although not a diploma—he would spend the next several years busying himself with numerous conducting and performing jobs. Importantly, he would also establish his own teaching studio. An advertisement placed in *Dwight's Journal of Music* lists Chadwick's profession as "conductor and solo organist," and offers his services for piano and composition lessons, as well.[1] Chadwick devoted much of his youthful career to organ playing, but he disdained serious practicing from his earliest days and practically stopped playing altogether once his career as a teacher and composer advanced, with one or two notable exceptions. He never harbored the desire to be a performing musician. Nevertheless, on those occasions when Chadwick performed he was typically regarded as technically competent. Jadassohn thought that he had little natural ability for the keyboard, but emphasized that when he did play it was with fine musicianship, even if "proper piano technique" was absent.[2] Chadwick never held any of the most coveted church directorships in Boston, such as the Episcopal Trinity Church or the Anglican/Unitarian King's Chapel, two plum posts. But his early career as a church musician was not unimportant (see table 4.1).

In Malden Chadwick often practiced on the new organ at the town's Methodist church, and even gave a few lessons. He also briefly substituted at Boston's Grace Episcopal Church, where he wrote his diminutive *Te Deum*, before securing the full-time organ post at St. John's Church in Roxbury. St. John's had "a miserable little organ, a poor church, a mixed, very mixed choir," and paid him five hundred dollars a year for two services per week. "But it was a *start* and that was all I asked for."[3]

TABLE 4.1. Chadwick's Church Positions

Years	Church
ca. 1875	First Church of Boston; Eliot Church, Newton; Lawrence Street Church, Lawrence (substituting variously for S. A. Ellis and E. Thayer)
1880	Grace Episcopal Church, Boston (as a substitute)
1880?–81	St. John's Church, Roxbury
1881–82	Clarendon St. Baptist Church
1882–84	Park Street Church
1884	Hollis Street Church
1887	Hollis St. Church merges with South Congregational Church
1893	"Resigns" from South Congregational Church
1893–1904	Second Universalist Church, Columbus Avenue
1894–1900	Trinity Church, Boston (substituting for Parker)

By May 1881, Chadwick had taken the presumably more lucrative, or at least less time-consuming, position as "Musical Director" of Boston's Clarendon Street Baptist Church, having left St. John's just after Easter. One journalist who reported on Chadwick's new position and discussed several of his compositions predicted for him "a brilliant career, if his present successes do not overcome him. From what we know of him, we have no fears in that direction, and shall watch his progress with much interest."[4] Chadwick was enticed to Clarendon Street Baptist Church by its organ, the finest he had played since leaving Europe. It helped, too, that the choir included six seasoned performers, four men and two women, who gave more polished performances than were possible at Grace Episcopal Church.

When Chadwick left Clarendon Street Baptist Church ("the minister desired to make the music more evangelistic in character"[5]) in April 1882, he took the position of organist at Boston's now-historic Park Street Church, perhaps the most important, or at least the most visible, church post Chadwick would ever occupy. (It is worth mentioning that earlier in the church's history its music director was none other than Nathaniel D. Gould.[6]) Chadwick was hired as organist for a small salary plus the use of a residential room.[7] It seems possible that he had not intended to stay at Park Street Church for very long, or was hired only for a temporary engagement, for the church records of May 25, 1883, state that "The organist is not yet engaged. Mr. Chadwick is occupying the position at present at the rate of $300 per annum."[8] It is also possible that Chadwick did not wish to sign a contract that would leave him unable to take another position, although the room that came with the job provided a strong incentive to keep it. His current quarters at 149a Tremont Street exposed him to "a bedlam of thumps and shrieks all day," due in large measure to the throngs of music teachers who resided in the neighborhood. In his new room at Park Street Church, which overlooked the serene Boston Common, he would be able to enjoy "the most public place in Boston and yet the most secluded." And while the organ was no match for the one he left at Clarendon Street, it nevertheless was "old, but very sweet in tone."[9] Chadwick began his tenure at Park Street Church on the first Sunday in May 1882 and left after more than two years, in July 1884. Church records do not mention a successor by name until 1886.[10]

Within two months Chadwick was appointed to another post, this time as organist at Hollis Street Church, led by the charismatic and poetic Reverend Henry B. Carpenter.[11] Chadwick may have secured that position after working closely with Carpenter on music for the dedication of the church; Carpenter provided the text and is the dedicatee of Chadwick's 1883 *Dedication Ode* (op. 15). Chadwick, a Christian but not an especially devout one, appreciated Carpenter's approach to religion and characterized Hollis Street as a church intended largely for people who did not attend church; that is, there was relatively little fire and brimstone in the sermons, and interactions among congregants of the church—the strengthening of its social fabric—was a high priority.

In 1887, Hollis Street Church merged with another Unitarian congregation, South Congregational Church.[12] Records are not intact for much of this period, for a later fire destroyed many of them,[13] but the merger created at least one headache for Chadwick. South Congregational Church's organist was B. J. Lang, who had held the position for some twenty-five years. Lang had studied in Berlin in the late 1850s and was highly regarded in Boston as a teacher, an organist and, later, as a composer, although his works were seldom performed. One of his best students was composer Arthur Foote, who wrote that Lang was "remarkably gifted as an organist, excelling in improvising." Another student, Henry Dunham, was more critical: "Mr. Lang was neither a great pianist nor organist. . . . For many years we dubbed him 'The Musical Dictator of Boston,' which in a large degree was true."[14]

Lang was a man known for high standards and precious little patience, and the church merger seemingly provided a convenient excuse for Lang's firing, which had long been sought. When Chadwick inquired about the elder musician's future prospects at South Congregational Church in the wake of the merger, the hiring committee stated curtly, "Mr. Lang will not be considered."[15] On Lang's general direction of the musical activities at South Congregational, Foote reported, "I have never heard any church service with a quartet choir to equal the sort of thing they gave you at Sunday afternoon Vespers."[16] If his quest for excellence was appreciated, his temperamental shortcomings were equally irritating. Lang was not pliable on matters of repertoire, and he exuded the sort of gravitas that likely would not be welcome in a family church. Naturally, Lang, a valued commodity in musical Boston, would not be out of work for long. Following his ouster, he took the position of organist at Boston's historic and prominent King's Chapel, where he remained until his death in 1909. As we shall see, the careers of Lang and Chadwick intersect at many points.

That Chadwick stayed at South Congregational Church for six years in the wake of someone of Lang's caliber speaks well of his musical and administrative acumen. But if he had been attracted to Reverend Carpenter's easygoing style, one wonders how he reacted to South Congregational Church's fiery Edward Everett Hale, who now led the church. Hale was a social activist in the city. The author of numerous tracts and books, including the enormously popular Civil War story, *The Man Without a Country* (1863), Hale was energetic and strong-willed, and Chadwick assuredly got from Hale's pulpit an earful of sermons relating to current events. Reverend A. Z. Conrad probably had Hale in mind when he reflected that "the Congregational Church in Boston has been a powerful factor in shaping the religious and social activities which have done so much to further the interests of the kingdom of God in America." Conrad proudly pointed out that "the Congregationalists also originated, abetted and supported every great moral reform movement that has ever been carried on in the city."[17]

South Congregational Church was not to last for Chadwick. Amid circumstances that remain unclear, Chadwick was forced to resign on March 22, 1893, at which time, he reported with evident satisfaction, "The entire choir did the same." Chadwick was shocked at his dismissal, for he fully believed that administrators and parishioners alike were satisfied with his artistic results. It is true, however, that several of the church's soloists—each politically connected to the church's leadership—did not always see eye-to-eye with Chadwick's methods and standards. Whether this contributed to his departure is not known, but, unfathomably, he lingered for more than a month. On April 30, "I shook the dust off Hale's church for good."[18]

No matter. Chadwick's next stop, the Second Universalist Church on Columbus Avenue led by Dr. Stephen Roblin, offered "a better organ, a better quartet, the same salary ($1,000) and no extra services."[19] The new congregation delighted in Chadwick's talent, and he often played for them well beyond the time required by the service. The church elders so appreciated Chadwick's work that they gave him a budget that enabled the formation of an eighteen-member paid choir: "They only got $1 or $2 apiece but I made them earn it and after some rigorous training [they] got to do unaccompanied things in good tune and with artistic shading."[20] In time he hired twenty singers, who were anchored by a strong vocal quartet. The increased range of repertoire possibilities, the outstanding choir, and the admiration of the congregants combined to make Second Universalist Church the most satisfying church position Chadwick ever held.

Chadwick left Second Universalist Church in 1904, but he did not give up church music completely. When Horatio Parker took a professorship at Yale in 1894, he retained his position as organist at Trinity Church and often relied on Chadwick to cover weddings (including that of Dr. H. H. A. Beach to his betrothed, the composer-pianist Amy Cheney), funerals, and other special services during the week.[21] Chadwick assisted for the next six years. And although he would have agreed with Edward Dickinson's slightly later observation that church music in America did not keep up with developments in art and concert music, Chadwick nevertheless prized the social aspects of church work.[22] One should not fail to mention that, as his family began to grow, his extra income was becoming increasingly necessary.

Chadwick experienced considerable success as a conductor. His decision to abandon his studies at Munich's conservatory in mid-session for the festival performance of *Rip Van Winkle* was not simply a matter of wanting to hear his own music played—Chadwick relished the chance to conduct. In Boston he had the opportunity to direct a respectable organization before enthusiastic audiences and influential critics, many of whom, he knew, were aware of his European triumphs. Following his debut with the Handel and Haydn Society, critical comments about his conducting were uniformly positive. The *Musical Herald* observed that Chadwick kept the players "well together" and gave "shading and expression in a thorough manner," while the *Boston Evening Transcript* concluded that he led his group with "verve and splendid effect."[23]

His *Rip Van Winkle* successes in Boston led to other conducting engagements. He led John Knowles Paine's incidental music to Harvard College's signal production of Sophocles's *Oedipus Tyrannus* (op. 35) in Boston and New York in 1882. Chadwick had attended the premiere of *Oedipus Tyrannus*, which was conducted by Paine, who had never been accused of being an adept conductor. From his seat in the front row, Chadwick helped Paine keep the orchestra together, thereby saving the performance and Paine's reputation.[24] Later in the year, Miss E. H. Ober, manager of Boston Ideal Opera Company and something of a musical speculator, engaged Chadwick, with Paine's blessing, to conduct *Oedipus* on tour. The *Transcript* review, probably penned by critic William Foster Apthorp, noted that Chadwick "held his forces with a firm hand"; the *Musical Record*'s journalist was greatly impressed by the Yankee's efforts, and even went so far as to state that Chadwick "has few equals as an orchestral conductor."[25]

Chadwick maintained a lifelong fascination with the conductor's art, and from early in his career he yearned to wield the baton professionally. However, it was excruciatingly plain to him—as it was to all American musicians—that American conductors could expect little support. There was Theodore Thomas, a naturalized German-American, but after him there were very few Americans who could inspire a young musician with ambition. Dudley Buck had enjoyed success as an assistant to Thomas, and B. J. Lang had conducted the Apollo Club, the Cecilia Society, and eventually the Handel and Haydn Society. But both Buck and Lang suffered by standing in the long shadow of Boston's leading conductor, Carl Zerrahn (1826–1909), a German. After that there was the Ohioan Arthur Mees (1850–1923), who, just four years Chadwick's senior, had launched his successful career in 1880 as conductor of Cincinnati's May Festival; as yet, however, Mees was not widely known.

Chadwick's mature thoughts about conducting may be deduced from comments made in a speech in 1912, by which time he had distinguished himself by leading many major orchestras and choral festivals in New England and throughout the states. In "Orchestral Conductors and Conducting," Chadwick described to his largely dilettante audience many of the technical requirements of conducting, among them a keen sensitivity to pitch, a heightened sense of musical time and rhythm, and a thorough understanding of the "capacities and limitations" of all orchestral instruments. Chadwick was also savvy enough to know that other factors contributed to a conductor's success. "It is a fact that personality has as much, and probably more, to do with a conductor's success," he admitted, "than his musical knowledge, or even his musical talent; for the conducting gift is primarily an executive one and much more akin to that of a military or naval officer than to the genius of the composer or virtuoso, or other artist." Even more than personality, Chadwick believed that a conductor should be "imbued with a broad and catholic spirit toward the musical art."[26]

The conductor, in Chadwick's estimation, "must not allow his personal prejudices to influence his work as an interpreter of the composer's intentions, whether he is in sympathy with them or not. A conductor who believes that music expired with Beethoven is not likely to be very enthusiastic over the atmospheric combinations of Debussy or the hair-raising harmonies of Richard Strauss. On the other hand, if his appetite craves these musical chutneys and hot stuff, he is likely to find the classics rather mild breakfast food. I think, however, that although there are some who are temperamentally unable to understand compositions with which they are not in sympathy, very few conductors are lacking in conscientiousness."[27]

Chadwick's Early Boston Compositions

Chadwick's major compositional efforts during his early years in Boston included the orchestral waltz, *Schon München*; the dramatic composition, *The Viking's Last Voyage*; the *Te Deum*; and several songs. *Schon München*, completed in October 1880, is a Viennese-style waltz that was considered stylish and even suave at its initial performance, and it demonstrates Chadwick's remarkable talent in the lighter vein of composition.[28] *The Viking's Last Voyage*, an engaging work for baritone soloist, male chorus, and orchestra, was completed in March 1881 and premiered the next month by Boston's Apollo Club. Chadwick conducted. This was no minor event in Boston, for it celebrated the ten-year anniversary of the club and marked the sixty-eighth concert led by B. J. Lang.[29] The program also included music by Raff, Mendelssohn, Saint-Saëns, and New England composer George E. Whiting. Chadwick's music, composed for men and on a manly topic, reflects the influence of the Concordia Singing Society that he had loved so well in Leipzig. Dwight thought Chadwick's *Viking* music similar to efforts by Max Bruch in his *Frithjof* cantata (op. 23), and described it as "heroic, gloomy, wild, tempestuous, now mournful, now exulting." He further thought it compared well to Bruch's score in its "vivid graphic power, felicitous invention, [and] mastery of the art of thematic development and instrumental coloring."[30]

The Viking's Last Voyage was the first indication of Chadwick's brief infatuation with the northern hordes. He composed *The Song of the Viking* for men's chorus and piano in 1882, but we know very little about its first performances. Ostensibly premiered by Boston's short-lived Mozart Society in the 1882–1883 season, we have no further information about this performance following the concert announcement.[31] The Apollo Club rendered it in 1886 at the Music Hall, but the writer for the *Transcript* was only slightly moved. "Though the music has not much that is strikingly original," the critic complained, "it has a certain strength, which was well expressed by the club."[32] In 1904 Chadwick prepared *The Song of the Viking* in German, and in 1914 he orchestrated it. Both versions are dedicated to his beloved Concordia Singing Society.

Chadwick's songs and choruses of the early 1880s were his first published works. They include the song "The Miller's Daughter," which he later orchestrated, and "Reiterlied" and "Margarita," both for men's chorus. One of his most popular songs, "Before the Dawn," was also composed at this time, as was "The Danza." His piano miniature "Scherzino" was popular in Boston at the time.[33] These compositions, suitable for performances by capable amateurs, helped Chadwick to win his first professional positions. Indeed, at this point his career was not unlike that of Nathaniel D. Gould, or even his second cousin, Asa Fitz, men who taught, conducted, and published music to increase their fame around New England.

Chadwick's varied activities paid off in short order. In the fall of 1882 it was announced in the *Musical Herald* that he would direct the local Arlington Club in three performances.[34] Reviewing the May 1883 concert, a critic for the *Musical Record* congratulated Chadwick "upon the proficiency of the club, whose singing is marked by precision and fullness of tone, and by a delightful clearness of enunciation."[35] This was a brilliant result considering the club comprised "young business men, with rather poor voices but lots of enthusiasm."[36] Chadwick would soon add to his résumé the title Musical Director of the Schubert Club in Salem, Massachusetts. He led the club through the whole of its sixth and part of its seventh seasons, in 1883 and 1884.[37] Club concerts were anticipated occurrences in the town, and the eclectic repertoire included selections from Schubert and Schumann to Gade, Rheinberger, and George E. Whiting. One writer noted that the club, founded in 1878, "has given the people of Salem an opportunity of hearing the better class of cantatas, part songs and glees, performed by a well-drilled chorus with the best of solo assistance."[38] The Schubert Club was also a social institution. Besides the more serious fare, "novel and original entertainments," which utilized actors in addition to the singers and musicians, were also counted among the club's activities. We do not know the circumstances of Chadwick's withdrawal from the club, but in all likelihood it was amicable. His friend and colleague Arthur Foote (1853–1937), a Salem native, took over the reins through the 1886 season.[39]

Chadwick as Teacher

Chadwick's generation, having returned from music study abroad, was the last to simply hang a shingle, post an advertisement or two, and begin a music teaching business. By the end of the nineteenth century, musicians—especially composers—would increasingly look to colleges and conservatories for employment; those institutions promised financial security and avoided the requirement of cobbling together a livelihood from students who may or may not show up for lessons or pay their lesson fees on time. Affiliation with higher education also gave composers increased respectability at a time in America when employment in the arts was highly suspect. In the early 1880s, Chadwick had already begun to build a noteworthy career as a music instructor from his home studio, where he taught theory and composition; as he began his employment in the local churches, he could give organ lessons, as well. It was common at this time for music teachers to travel to the homes of their students, but Chadwick drew the line at that, and as a result his pupil roster grew slowly. There were other reasons for his slow start. Chadwick's studio began to fill with students from outside Boston, largely because students from the "best" Boston homes were already studying with B. J. Lang. Lang not only enjoyed local renown as a church organist, but he was also a teacher of piano, theory, and composition. He had managed to secure the trust of Boston's leading patricians and was engaged by many of them to teach their children, especially their daughters.

Lang and Chadwick waged something of a turf war over music students in Boston. Chadwick reported at one point that he was "very seriously advised to make my peace with Mr. Lang as nothing could be done without his powerful protection."[40] Chadwick was probably considered a youthful and energetic threat to Lang's teaching empire, which had been forged over many years. Following an eventual truce, Chadwick began to see a stream, albeit a small one, of students who came to him from within the city. He was aided by his increasing renown in both musical circles and high society, including his membership, in 1880, in Boston's tony St. Botolph Club.

If the premiere of *The Viking's Last Voyage* on April 22, 1881, marked an important evening for Chadwick, certainly the earlier part of the same day was even more memorable, for it marked the beginning of Chadwick's long association with NEC. On that day, Eben Tourjée, director of the conservatory, hired Chadwick to teach "free composition." While this was a huge boost for Chadwick's professionalism—and his pocketbook—his tenure did not begin easily, for he did not immediately accept the offer. Chadwick had been contemptuous of NEC since he had left it a few years before, mostly because Tourjée had shown no interest in his talents at all. For his part, Tourjée seemed unable to completely forgive Chadwick for leaving NEC, which he considered a personal slight. Nevertheless, a compromise was reached and Chadwick began teaching for $1.50 per hour, a substantially lower salary than his new colleagues commanded. Almost instantly Chadwick proved himself a popular teacher, and by mid-November, his studio at NEC had swelled to twenty students, and he was teaching at least four capacity classes.[41]

But all was not well at NEC. Tourjée, always something of an entrepreneur, was attempting to get the conservatory out of its cramped quarters at the Music Hall and into a larger property. He had his eye on the massive, six-story St. James Hotel in Franklin Square. Not only would the new site supply more classroom space, but it would provide NEC with another much-needed revenue stream—Tourjée had determined to get into the dormitory business. By furnishing dorm space at the St. James, in the very same building that housed classrooms, a recital parlor, and a library, Tourjée could stress to parents that their children would be safe under his watchful care. He also reckoned that a comfortable housing complex could entice those living outside Boston to send their children to the conservatory, thus furnishing an entirely new market for his ambitious musical empire. Living quarters, he estimated, would also bring in a steady flow of cash.

As was often the case, though, Tourjée had neither money nor prospective backers to buy the hotel outright. So he then initiated an unwelcome campaign to raise financial guarantees from his faculty, which would provide collateral for the necessary bank loans he would borrow. Chadwick, like many of his colleagues, was coerced into signing a promissory note for $500. While the young teacher never had to make good on a payment, the questionable tactic was not without a detrimental effect; Tourjée, never particularly well trusted by his underlings, was now closely watched by many and completely avoided by some. However, Tourjée was adored by a host of others. "But so far as I know," Chadwick wrote, "Dr. Tourjée was the acme of integrity. Certainly he had many friends who believed in him and were devoted to him."[42]

Perhaps fearing the financial volatility of Tourjée's NEC, Chadwick continued to teach privately at his apartment. Horatio Parker, who would become Chadwick's most famous student and his best friend, began his lessons at Chadwick's home during this period. The date—November 13, 1881—is memorable because Parker appeared on Chadwick's twenty-seventh birthday. The teacher noted with an uneasy blend of pride and envy that Parker "did not come many times before I realized that he was a character who would have to be seriously reckoned with."[43] Within months Parker's talent was such that Chadwick knew he needed "an older and firmer hand than mine to guide him"; by Chadwick's recommendation, Parker went to Munich to learn from Rheinberger in the summer of 1882.[44]

Other remarkable talents visited Chadwick's apartment. Arthur Whiting began his lessons on September 20, 1882. He, along with Parker, would later become a leading voice in musical New England. Sidney Homer (1864–1953) studied with Chadwick in approximately 1883. He reported that Chadwick tutored him in harmony, counterpoint, double counterpoint, and "all forms of canon and simple fugue." On his experiences at Chadwick's studio, Homer reflected that "music is an easy study under a great master."[45] About three years later, Henry Hadley, who would later enjoy a tremendous career as a composer and a conductor and become one of Chadwick's most famous students, would also seek him out. Hadley, among all of Chadwick's many composition students, left perhaps the most compelling account of his teaching:

My experience and friendship with him began when, as a lad of fifteen [ca. 1887], my father took me to Mr. Chadwick's home in Boston and arranged for me to have lessons in counterpoint with him. These hours which I spent every week at the South Congregational Church, where Mr. Chadwick played the organ and had a little studio, were and still are lovely memories, very precious to me. George Chadwick did much to instill in my young mind the love of all things beautiful in Art. As a teacher he was painstaking and thorough, and never failed to interpolate his instruction with witty remarks and anecdotes drawn from his inexhaustible knowledge of the masters. He could always illustrate his points most aptly with examples from the great writers, and in many subtle ways he enlarged the vision and stimulated the imagination of his students.[46]

Chadwick stressed technical proficiency in composition. He gave his students thorough instruction in counterpoint, fugue and canon, and instrumentation, even as his own knowledge of the latter subject was still ascendant. We can also imagine that he gave his students tips on the establishment of a hardy work ethic.

Chadwick cherished the memories of his students, especially of those from his earliest years. In a nostalgic essay he penned and submitted to the *Boston Herald*, he remembered the eager students who visited his Park Street Church studio for lessons: "To that room came, among others, Horatio Parker and Arthur Whiting, with their fugues and canons. Perhaps they brought with them more than they carried away from their teacher."[47]

John Knowles Paine and the American Symphony

Chadwick was prolific for the simple reason that he was easily bored. During those first few years in Boston following his German sojourn, he could easily have spent more time milking the success of his *Rip Van Winkle* Overture; however he chose not to rest on that triumph. Having gotten his foot solidly in Boston's musical door with his first overture and a few smaller works, he was eager to turn his attention to another major project. High on his list of goals was the completion of his already begun second composition for orchestra, the First Symphony.

In the minds of many young American musicians, the true test of a composer's mettle was the symphony. Chadwick had already successfully tackled many of the technical requirements necessary for the crafting of music for the orchestra in his superlative first effort, *Rip Van Winkle*. Although composing a weighty four-movement work is a far different matter than composing a concert overture, the overture had been fine preparation for the task. At the time, symphonies by American composers were decidedly rare. The best known in the mid-nineteenth century were those by Anthony Phillip Heinrich (1781–1861), William Henry Fry (1813–1864), George Frederick Bristow (1825–1898), and Louis Moreau Gottschalk (1829–1869). Heinrich was actually a self-taught Bohemian, but he became a beloved and respected personage in American music. Having taken music to the distant west in the first half of the nineteenth century, he was called variously "The Beethoven of Kentucky" and even "The Beethoven of America." Heinrich was a prolific composer in many genres, but he had a special affinity for orchestral works; he composed a number of them on grand descriptive subjects with subtitles such as "sinfonia eratico fantachia" (for his *The Indian Carnival* [ca. 1845]) and "sinfonia patriotic-dramatica" (for his *The Empress Queen and the Magyars* [ca. 1845]). Others — none simply titled "Symphony" and followed by a number — include *The Hunters of Kentucky* (1837), *Schiller* (ca. 1830), and *The Tomb of Genius: To the Memory of Mendelssohn-Bartholdy* (ca. 1847). Heinrich's music matched his rather idiosyncratic personality. It is short on technique — mastery of form, counterpoint, and the like — and much of it was never heard. But it is certainly imaginative.

William Henry Fry hailed from Philadelphia, where his musical predilection became apparent early on. Like Heinrich, Fry also composed symphonies, most of which bear descriptive titles such as *Santa Claus: Christmas Symphony* (1853), *Childe Harold* (1854), and others. A more knowledgeable and gifted composer than Heinrich (although arguably less inventive), Fry nevertheless lacked either the craftsmanship or the inclination to compose symphonies couched in traditional forms. Critics chastised these works not only because Fry tended to compose his "symphonies" in single movements but also because he almost completely ignored the idea of the development of abstract ideas; if most arbiters of the day considered Beethoven's works the finest efforts in the symphonic genre, Fry's symphonies could only suffer by the comparison.

Bristow and Gottschalk were professional musicians whose symphonies demonstrate a more thorough handling of form and instrumentation, although they too utilized programmatic elements. Bristow's five symphonies include his Sinfonia in E-flat (op. 10, 1848), the Jullien Sinfonia (op. 24, 1853), Symphonie in F-sharp (op. 26, 1858), Arcadian Symphonie (op. 50, 1872), and perhaps his best known work today, the Niagara Symphony (op. 62, 1893). Bristow did not rely on programmaticism to the degree that Heinrich and Fry did; he was more willing to compose according to tradition and utilize four-movement structures with expected key relationships. His music is often compared to Mendelssohn, whose influence on American composers in the mid-nineteenth century was palpable. Gottschalk's two symphonies, Symphony no. 1 (*La Nuit des tropiques*, 1859) and Symphony no. 2 (*Á Montevideo*, 1868), are melodic and captivating, but without the formal rigor that might have made them more palatable to knowledgeable critics and audiences. The former symphony is in two movements and the latter, a single-movement romp in three parts, can more accurately be called an overture. Gottschalk's gift lay not in his symphonism, but in his ability to interweave fetching tunes and rhythms — many of them redolent of an American spirit, and sometimes including direct quotes of beloved American folk tunes — into simple symphonic molds. Gottschalk's symphonies, premiered and performed in Latin America, were unknown to American audiences until well into the twentieth century.[48]

The greatest and most recent precedent for a symphony composed along traditional lines by an American composer had just been set down with dazzling results. At about the time of Chadwick's return to the United States, Paine's Symphony no. 2 in A major (*Im Frühling*) was premiered, on March 10, 1880, at Harvard's Sanders Theater. Paine's First Symphony had appeared in 1876, and, although less well-known today, at the time it too exerted a signal influence over composers. Chadwick himself reflected that, even though Paine's Mass and his oratorio *St. Peter* garnered praise, the First Symphony brought Paine enormous renown. The work "at once attracted attention by its interesting melodic material, its masterly use of the symphonic form and its sonorous orchestration." He continued, "The simple and benighted music lovers of those days had not been taught by . . . critics that the sonata form was a worn out fetish, that noble and simple melody was a relic of the dark ages, and that unresolved dissonance was the chief merit of a composition."[49]

Paine's symphony is none too innovative, but it is beautiful. To Chadwick, who heard the First Symphony performed on January 26, 1876, by the Theodore Thomas Orchestra and considered it a masterwork, it was little wonder that it "should have been a stimulus and an inspiration to more than one ambitious young musician of that time."[50] It affected Chadwick so strongly that, following that performance, he sought composition lessons with Paine. The arrangement did not work out, mostly because of the difficulty of travel to Paine's residence in Cambridge, but Chadwick nevertheless spoke highly of Paine and considered him the quintessential American composer of his time.[51] Paine was unusually supportive and respectful of his younger colleague.

Paine, fifteen years Chadwick's senior, was a native New Englander. Born in Portland, Maine, he had the good fortune to grow up in a musical household. Paine later traveled to Europe, where he resided for three years and studied organ with Haupt, with whom he developed a close musical and personal relationship, at the Berlin Conservatory. Shortly after his return to Boston, he became associated with Harvard University, where he quickly established the archetype for music and its role in the university setting. Not only was he highly regarded for his work as a composer, but his approach to the "scientific" aspects of music — through lectures on theory, analysis, and especially music history — gave him a great deal of clout in Boston's intellectual circles. Paine's posthumous *A History of Music to the Death of Schubert* (1907), lovingly edited and introduced by Albert A. Howard, demonstrates a solid command of its subject.

The positive reception of Paine's First Symphony was handily eclipsed by that of the Symphony no. 2. Dwight believed that the performance of the Second Symphony "formed an event of unusual significance in our musical world," and that it was one of the finest productions yet manufactured by a native American. He further wrote, "We cannot but regard this 'Spring' Symphony as a remarkable, a noble work, by far the happiest and ripest product, thus far, of Prof. Paine's great learning and inventive faculty, and marking the highest point yet reached in these early stages of American creative art in music. It is worthy to hold a place among the works of masters, and will reward many hearings wherever the symphonic art can find [an] appreciative audience."[52] The Second Symphony is seldom heard today, but it lives on in American music history by virtue of its publication by the A. P. Schmidt Company in 1880, the first American symphony ever to achieve that distinction.[53]

"Genuine Symphonic Respect":
Chadwick's First Symphony (op. 5)

To explore the symphonic aspect of Chadwick's art, it is necessary to revisit his European experience. Chadwick had been eager, curious, and industrious in Leipzig, but there is no indication that his studies with his primary mentor, Salomon Jadassohn, in any way prepared him specifically for the task of writing a symphony, although Jadassohn himself was an accomplished symphonist with four to his credit. Chadwick always revered Jadassohn, although he did not think that Jadassohn's pedagogy was terribly systematic. Jadassohn's "sounds better" approach would later inform Chadwick's own teaching style and enable him effectively to unleash his own musical imagination without too many pedantic constraints, but at the time Chadwick did not appreciate the unusual freedom it allowed him. In fact, Chadwick himself thought that his close relationship to the Duveneck Boys, with their bohemian lifestyle, their concentration on expression as well as technique, and their often freewheeling ways, had affected his musicianship more than his German teachers.[54]

Rheinberger probably had a more consequential impact on Chadwick's symphonic aspirations than Jadassohn. By the time he arrived in Munich, Chadwick was gripped primarily by orchestral composition, and Rheinberger's reputation loomed much larger than that of his Leipzig mentor. Chadwick, who had been impressed by Rheinberger's popular symphonic poem, *Wallenstein* (op. 10), observed in Rheinberger a pedagogue whose strict values were the polar opposite of Jadassohn's. And, even though later on Chadwick would advise many of his own students to seek study with Rheinberger (it is not clear that he ever sent a student to Jadassohn), he was not completely pleased with Rheinberger's more rigorous methods. Nevertheless, Chadwick admits: "I learned much from him, especially about canonic writing, of which I had done very little, and about the regular development of a contrapuntal education."[55] Indeed, the skills that Chadwick acquired from his composite education were a foundation of his genius. His freedom of musical expression—enabled by Jadassohn and encouraged by the Duveneck band—was complemented by strict attention to fundamental compositional procedures demanded by Rheinberger.

As mentioned previously, prior to his move to Munich to study with Rheinberger, Chadwick had spent a part of the summer of 1879 in Dresden. There his days were filled with regular visits to various museums, and he delighted in countryside excursions; he even took a brief walking trip through Switzerland. Although he was captivated by Dresden, his time there was not a musically fruitful period: "I did not accomplish much of any work in Dresden; I seemed to have had no ideas and the summer there was practically wasted as far as composition was concerned. Whether it was a reaction from the excitement of my success in Leipzig [with *Rip Van Winkle*] or an attack of [a] paucity of ideas, I do not know. At any rate, I accomplished very little."[56]

But a feature article in the *Boston Sunday Herald* contradicts Chadwick's recollection. It reported that he had been working on his own First Symphony in C major (op. 5) for several years, including while he was in Dresden. According to the writer, who undoubtedly gleaned his information from Chadwick, the symphony was begun in Leipzig in winter 1877, and "many of the sketches were made for it during the next two years, especially in Dresden and Switzerland."[57] Chadwick's first mention of his symphony occurs in a letter to his friend Charles Saunders dated October 1879, wherein he reported from Munich that, after having been there since just September, the first movement of his new symphony was nearly complete. He confided to Saunders, "I have got (or shall have by the time you get this) the first movement of my symphony ... finished. If I can get it played as soon as I get home (May Festival, for instance) I would have the parts made here and bring them home. Music copying is cheap here compared to America and I think quite a savings could be effected by having it done here."[58]

Considering that Chadwick was newly arrived in Munich when he wrote to Saunders, it is unlikely that Rheinberger advised him regarding the first movement of his symphony. Not only was it already completed, or nearly so, but Chadwick complained that most of his classes with Rheinberger involved only musical exercises and that, after the completion of a large number of class assignments, he had little enthusiasm for "real composition." Later Chadwick regretted that he "never got any chance at the school orchestra," either as a conductor or a composer; in that respect he undoubtedly missed Leipzig, where he had cut a wide swath.[59] Nevertheless, Chadwick gained much from his Munich studies, although there is little to indicate that he did much in the way of music composition beyond Rheinberger's disappointingly academic assignments. One might speculate that Jadassohn may have had some input on the first movement since it was begun while Chadwick was under his tutelage, and, at the very least, it is reasonable to suggest that Jadassohn would have had occasion to discuss general principles of symphony composition—form, organicism, key relationships, and the like—with the young composer. According to the *Herald* report, the best source of information on the First Symphony's genesis, the final three movements were finished in Boston. The exact dates and order of their completion are not known.[60]

Chadwick conducted the premiere of his First Symphony, which was the centerpiece of a varied program that included an overture by Cherubini, vocal duets by Mozart and Berlioz, and Rossini's Overture to *William Tell*. All but Chadwick's composition were led by the regular conductor of the Harvard Musical Association Orchestra, Carl Zerrahn, at the Boston Museum—which in fact was a curiously named twelve-hundred-seat playhouse—on Thursday afternoon, February 23, 1882. The premiere of Chadwick's symphony was heralded as a major event in artistic circles. One writer wrote that "the symphony commanded the closest attention and interest of one of the most exacting audiences that ever filled a music house in Boston."[61] In a town whose love of all things orchestral was rapidly growing, a new work by a young and credentialed American composer was not to be missed.

What that audience heard would have sounded familiar to them. Chadwick's First Symphony is a traditional four-movement creation: an Allegro movement in C major; a scherzo in C minor; an Adagio in A-flat major; and a finale marked Allegro moderato in the tonic key. The instrumental forces resemble those favored by Brahms: pairs of flutes, oboes, clarinets, and bassoons; four horns, two trumpets, and three trombones; timpani and strings.

Chadwick's main melody begins in $\frac{3}{4}$ meter with C-major triadic contours that relate it closely to the first theme in Beethoven's *Eroica* Symphony, a fine, not too surprising model for a young composer's first effort at a symphony—the gambit may be considered a tribute both to Beethoven and Theodore Thomas. As the music progresses to the theme associated with the secondary key, we find a static melody within a rather narrow range. Here Chadwick sets his theme in E minor, rather than in the more typical dominant, in this case, G major. This decision is not a rarity in nineteenth-century music, but it is a rather bold and unexpected step for the youthful Chadwick to undertake. Structurally, it has the effect of giving the second area less tonal tension, and Chadwick's later emphasis on C major and C minor confuses the matter even more. The movement's development section, with elaborate and far-ranging harmonic treatment, swirls through the major keys of B, E, C, E-flat, and G minor, and even presents a brief statement in the distant F-sharp major. Chadwick includes a brief area of fugato, perhaps as a proof that, like his teachers Jadassohn and Rheinberger, he has command of learned techniques. Certainly his studies in Europe would have led him to regard this as a common and expected practice. The recapitulation begins with the main theme in the tonic key and offers relief from the tension that had continued to build since the end of the exposition. The theme itself, however, is quickly overshadowed by frequent appearances of the secondary theme; it is couched in an elaborate harmonic canvass that emphasizes the submediant and, briefly, even the supertonic.

Possibly using Schumann's symphonies as a model, Chadwick closes the movement with a very long coda in four distinct sections. Because the development and the recapitulation venture far afield harmonically, it was necessary to close with a coda that could hammer home the tonic. Chadwick utilized this section to explore further the rhythmic and metrical possibilities of his theme, starting out in $\frac{3}{4}$ and then moving through $\frac{6}{8}$ before closing in $\frac{4}{4}$. Like Beethoven, Chadwick viewed the coda as a perfectly appropriate place to take care of unfinished business.[62]

The symphony's second movement is a devilish scherzo in five parts (ABABA) marked Allegro molto vivace. Chadwick may have used as models scherzi by Schumann, in his First Symphony, or Brahms, in his Second Symphony. He invented a main theme that has great potential for development, as well as a subsidiary theme that, like those in his earlier string quartets, is pastoral in character. In the noteworthy fourth section, the music not only moves from the tonic C minor to the key of F major, but within that area it emphasizes mediant and submediant harmonies. As in the first movement, Chadwick's proclivity to spice up his music harmonically is in full view.

The slow third movement, Adagio molto espressivo, begins with a sweeping melody played by the first violins. Chadwick does little in its ABA form to develop the music harmonically, although the move from the opening key of A-flat major to the distant G major in the second part is striking. Most unusual, though, is the lightness of texture; the movement has the delicacy of chamber music, unlike some of the more plodding Adagios he might have known. While Chadwick had created a number of solo passages in *Rip Van Winkle* Overture, that music does not give the impression that it is for other than a full orchestra. But here Chadwick uses to his advantage the solo capabilities of several instruments (especially oboe and English horn) in intimate scoring, a technique that he will continue to favor and one that will surface again in his music.

The finale, an Allegro moderato sonata-style movement, owns characteristics that distinguish it from the first movement and demonstrate that Chadwick was thoroughly exploring the possibilities of the form. Here he emphasizes the difference between his principal and secondary themes, the former punchy and march-like, and the latter conjunct and lyrical. But the proportions of the finale have been altered significantly: following the long introduction that dwells nearly entirely on the dominant, the brief exposition and slightly longer development segments are followed by an enormous recapitulation. While the development, at only 116 measures, progresses through myriad keys—it even introduces fugato and a new theme—the 217-measure recapitulation remains largely in the home key, although it spends a good deal of time on subdominant harmonies. Chadwick does not relent at the end, for in the three-part coda the music continues to visit a number of tonalities, several of them quite remote from the tonic. What begins as a hopeful and well-proportioned musical essay ends as a lumbering, somewhat tedious affair.

Chadwick's conception of his First Symphony and its ultimate form are inextricably bound to his German education and to his youthful professional experiences in Boston. Chadwick himself considered it a crowning achievement of his early career, and its use of musical materials, forged over what for Chadwick was a lengthy germination period, shows remarkable ingenuity and thoroughly competent handling. One noteworthy omission is any hint of pentatonicism, which Chadwick had used to good effect in his string quartets. Nevertheless, contemporary reviewers consistently thought it a compelling artwork indicative of burgeoning young talent. The writer for the *Transcript* hesitated to offer an opinion about "a work of the pretensions and importance of a symphony . . . on a single hearing," but that did not stop his review. "The composer had endeavored to produce a work," he concluded, "which should be truly symphonic; one, that is, in which a theme should be regularly developed or treated, as one may say, with genuine symphonic respect."[63] Louis C. Elson, writing as "Proteus" in *Church's Musical Visitor*, thought that parts of the symphony showed "striking originality." He even compared the young Yankee to Paine: "When we think that Chadwick is a very young man, and that Professor Paine, the leading American composer, in my eyes, had not achieved as much at his age, we find that there is great hope and promise in the already prominent composer."[64]

For his part, Chadwick had been disappointed in the performance, which he attributed to the poor rehearsals held at the Chickering piano store, "where everything made a horrible noise and it was impossible to hear whether the parts were right or not." He was, however, pleased by the response. "The work was very much praised by the critics," Chadwick noted dryly, "especially the parts which deserved it the least."[65] Portions of the First Symphony were performed at the 1886 meeting of the Music Teachers National Association convention, but for various reasons, not the least of which was its failure to attract a publisher, the symphony's performance history ground to a halt after that.

Alonzo Chadwick did not live to see his son at the start of a promising musical career in Boston, for he had died on December 5, 1878, during Chadwick's travels abroad. Upon George's return to the states, the onerous business matters that he had literally escaped caught up with him. "My father left no debts but many debtors," Chadwick despaired. "He had carried insurance for a lot of old bucks about Lawrence who paid as little as they could on [their] account and [Alonzo] lent his ready money to some of them on very poor security. The consequence was that they had to be sued to get anything out of them and I had to spend several days in the witness chair in Lawrence as I was the only one who knew anything about his books."[66] Legal wrangles of this sort were not much different than they are today, for, as Chadwick reported, "We won the suits but the lawyers got all the money and some more."[67]

The family was left with little or no money, but Alonzo owned property that he did not wish for Susan Chadwick to possess. "In order that my mother should not profit by it my father put all of his property into my brother's hands before he died. . . . But brother Henry, who had some old fashioned ideas of justice and honesty," proposed to George that the assets be divided equally among the three. Chadwick's share came to more than five thousand dollars, a staggering sum. "If I had only had this money while I was still in Europe," he later lamented, although his funds evaporated in short order. Chadwick invested much of his inheritance in stocks that "declined so that I got very little good in the end from my father's money—which was his intention."[68]

The end of the lawsuits marked the end of any possibility—tenuous as it may have been—that the firm of A. C. Chadwick would endure. A disenchanting, often tumultuous relationship was finally over, although its memories would engender an uneasy combination of regret and resentment for the remainder of Chadwick's life. But he was finally free. No more guilt; no more discomfiting estrangement; no more family drama.

And with freedom won, Chadwick was elated. Not by the death of his father, but by the promise of a career in music that neither he—nor certainly Alonzo—could have imagined just a few years before.

"That Fatal Facility"
Chadwick's Boston
1880s

Verily, music is getting so low-priced in Boston that the
poorest man can have his little symphonic enjoyments.
—Louis C. Elson (writing as "Proteus") in
Church's Musical Visitor, 1882

Musical Life in "The Hub"

The decade of the 1880s saw a number of impressive gains in Boston's musical life. Of course, musical life in "the Hub"—as Boston was nicknamed by Oliver Wendell Holmes to reflect the position it claimed as the educational and cultural center of the universe—had already been vibrant, even though it was not quite the "musical atmosphere," as Chadwick put it, that one could find in Europe so readily. Nevertheless, the city's musical progress was strong and steady, and its recent strides, particularly in instrumental music, seemed unstoppable.

Many of the advancements in music mirrored the social progress of the city in the last third of the nineteenth century. After the horrors of the Civil War, Boston, which had a rich history of charity, gave to various institutions with near abandon. Children and health were at the forefront of Boston's social causes: the Massachusetts Society for the Prevention of Cruelty to Children was founded in 1878; the New England Home for Little Wanderers in 1889; Vincent Memorial Hospital in 1890; and the Boston Floating Hospital in 1894. Among the cultural, non-musical institutions supported by Boston's citizens, the Museum of Fine Arts, established in 1870, stands out as one of the city's noblest endeavors. The Boston Public Library was begun in 1887. A grand edifice of pink granite (which has since been bleached by the sun) with a marvelous collection of books and a courtyard that provided a haven for readers, the library was built expressly for the masses, as the motto chiseled above the entryway, "Free for All," proclaims. To these charitable efforts one could add countless others.

The famous Handel and Haydn Society had been founded in 1815, and its reputation as a company of excellence gave Boston plenty of distinction. It emphasized choral music, oratorios, and the like; instrumental music served primarily to undergird the word.[1] Serious orchestral music got its start much later. Louis C. Elson believed that the inception of orchestral activities dated from the 1840s, when the leadership of Boston's Academy of Music decided that it was fruitless to continue in vocal competition with other organizations — such as the Handel and Haydn Society, which invariably offered better results — and it founded an orchestra. By the end of the decade the academy orchestra comprised mostly professionals and was regarded as the best ensemble in the city.[2]

The Harvard Musical Association (HMA), organized in 1837, initiated much in the way of music lectures and chamber music, and it was a crucial organization because of its endorsement of music as a fine art — as distinct from music as simply an activity for amusement or leisure — thereby setting the stage for the cultivated landscape that would dominate late-nineteenth-century musical Boston.[3] The association offered a series of orchestra concerts from 1865 until 1882. Its musical improvements were modest for some time, although the concerts continued to flourish because they were attractive social as well as educational events. But the association was not the brilliant ensemble that was longed for. The respected critic William Foster Apthorp remembered that in 1869 Theodore Thomas and his New York orchestra, "unquestionably one of the finest in the world," began giving concerts in Boston.[4] The concerts put local organizations, especially the HMA orchestra, to shame. According to Apthorp, Thomas's concerts "gave us Bostonians some rather humiliating lessons in the matter of orchestral technique."[5] Apthorp lamented that the association leaders did not take the lessons of the Thomas experience to heart, and soon the association's demise was a foregone conclusion. Apthorp's remedy for a bad orchestra was a simple one that he thought had originated with Thomas: engage better musicians and give them more time to rehearse. Naturally, both solutions required increased funding.

The matter of musicians, rehearsals, and finances could be grappled with; more stubborn was the HMA's inability to come to grips with "musical progress." The association had been spearheaded by the music journalist John Sullivan Dwight, whose allegiance to the "old masters" was unshakeable. According to Apthorp, "Dwight was inexorable and would not yield an inch" in matters of programming. His stubbornness resulted in a widespread and not always deserved perception that the concert programs were lackluster. Even Chadwick had to admit, however, that association leaders "made few concessions to those who yearned after the flesh-pots of Egypt. The names Berlioz, Liszt, and Wagner were sometimes represented, but they were regarded with considerable suspicion."[6] The program of March 3, 1870, is typical. It included, in order, Schumann's *Genoveva* Overture; vocal selections from Gluck's *Orfeo*; a Chopin Piano Concerto (op. 21); vocal selections from various Handel works; and Beethoven's Symphony no. 3 (*Eroica*). The piano soloist was twenty-six-year-old Anna Mehlig, a well known young artist and former student of Liszt. But

Mehlig was not exactly a star. Although the concerts were not entirely without star power, most of the solo talent was local, and the repertoire rarely ventured beyond a rather narrow chronological scope. These facts led to a decline in subscriptions from which the association could not recover. Apthorp laid part of the blame on Boston's musical public: "If the Harvard Musical Association's concerts stuck pretty fast to the classics, they had at least an excuse in the coldness with which almost all new things were received—no matter how loudly press and public might have clamored for them. The public persistently cried for the new things, and turned up its nose when it got them."[7] Nevertheless, Apthorp could not help but notice that the expression "'dull as a symphony concert' almost passed into a proverb."[8]

The Harvard Musical Association held a central place in Chadwick's early career. Its orchestra, in its final year and under the direction of the respected Carl Zerrahn, offered Chadwick the chance to conduct the premiere his First Symphony in 1882. Zerrahn, a gifted conductor and organizer, as well as a cherished personality, had been a fixture in musical Boston for years. He was first with the Germania Musical Society, a traveling orchestra of immigrant German musicians that had been founded in 1849, and then with any number of lesser musical ventures, including an Orchestral Union in the 1860s, which initially prospered before failing in the wake of the Civil War.[9] Zerrahn figures into the life of Chadwick in numerous ways, not the least of which is that in later years the families would intermarry.

For its part, the HMA faced many competitors. Traveling orchestras and ensembles, such as Theodore Thomas's and others, were noteworthy features of the cultural landscape of the time, and were pilloried by Dwight in his insightful 1876 article "Musica Peripatetica."[10] Dwight concluded that the nation unquestionably owed the Thomas Orchestra, which performed widely, a debt of gratitude "for much good music which it otherwise would not have heard, and even for awakening the musical perception, doubtless, in thousands." Dwight also credited Thomas with increasing the nation's exposure to an eclectic repertoire and for raising the general standards of orchestral performance, putting musicians everywhere upon their mettle. The downside of the traveling groups, according to Dwight, was the flight of musicians from Boston, whose employment opportunities were sapped by "imported" ensembles. "If [local musicians] are not encouraged by all the orchestral employment that can be given them," he wrote, "if these nobler tasks are withdrawn from them; if, instead of twenty symphony concerts, or even one every week throughout the season of the year, they cease to find support for ten only in a year, what motive have they any longer, either artistic or material, for continuing to reside with us?" Dwight saw the tremendous value of having a community of musicians in Boston. He lamented that traveling chamber ensembles were creating the same effect that he observed from the visiting orchestras, complaining, "Never before has it been so hard to keep among us first-class violinists, cellists, etc." Dwight maintained an abiding fear—one perhaps issuing from his experience with Gilmore and his jubilees—that Boston "may have to depend on speculating impresarios" for good music. Indeed, that had long been the case with opera in the city.

It mattered little in the wake of what would soon occur. Neither the attempts by Dwight to maintain musical purity at the HMA, nor the legion of smaller associations, such as the Boston Philharmonic Society—another of the city's countless shoestring orchestral operations, and one in which Chadwick had participated as a board member—could keep up with the newest symphonic threat in town. Henry Lee Higginson's full-time, fully professional, and fully funded Boston Symphony Orchestra (BSO) was founded in 1881. Elson bluntly claimed that the HMA orchestra and the Boston Philharmonic "gave up the ghost" because of the BSO.[11]

The Rise of the Orchestra

The founding of the BSO reflected the city's general fondness for orchestral music, and by the 1880s that attraction was strong and undeniable. Elson, an enthusiastic lover of music for orchestra, thought that symphony concerts "more than the number of concerts [of any variety offered by a city], indicates the true musical atmosphere," and many of the city's philanthropists agreed.[12] Bolstering his conclusions were the facts that "the leading composers of America have their residence here" and that "conductors are plentiful, orchestras are numerous."[13] A mere two years later Elson could exclaim: "Symphony! Symphony! Symphony! That is about all that one can write from Boston at present. The Bostonian gets symphony with his breakfast, he whistles the 9th with his dinner, he takes the Raff symphonies as a nightcap after his suppers."[14]

What had precipitated the city's love of music performed by an orchestra? Stephen A. Emery cited three advantages of orchestra performance "which may not be elsewhere attainable. First, a refinement of taste resulting from a constant intensifying of musical feeling as expressed in intensified and extreme musical effects." This, Emery argued, was not possible through the piano recital or a chamber music concert. Emery also pointed out the "indescribable beauty of tone-colors, with their infinite degrees of light and shade" that emanated from an orchestra, and finally "the enthusiasm of numbers," by which he meant the excitement incited by the substantial body of players involved in music-making.[15]

As mentioned earlier, there was more to the symphony experience than just the music. Symphony concerts had by this time also become a required social convention for the middle and upper classes. The popular New England novelist Arlo Bates described a scene in his Boston-set 1889 novel, *The Philistines*, wherein one of his characters, Miss Merrivale, is engaged in the current cultural craze. Miss Merrivale, Bates wrote, "had assisted at that sacred rite of musical devotees, the Saturday night symphony concert, where a handful of people gathered to hear the music, and all the rest of the world crowded for the sake of having been there."[16]

Getting to the point where the symphony was a "sacred rite" had not been easy in Boston. Higginson, the scion of a well-known New England business family, was himself a devoted musician and even briefly considered pursuing it as a career. Once he realized that he lacked the requisite talent, he set about on several soul-searching adventures. Eventually he made his way into the family business, the prosperous banking firm of Lee, Higginson & Company. In time, of course, Higginson prospered as well. His stated aim in founding an orchestra was uncomplicated: he shared the typical New Englander's belief that every person was responsible for the uplift—financial, moral, cultural—of his fellow citizens. This notion was heightened following the turmoil of the Civil War, and Higginson thought that he could best uplift his countrymen by providing music. Higginson, who had served in the war, argued that "war taught a great many men that if we were to have a country worthy of the name, we must work for it, educate it, as well as fight for it, and this duty lay upon every individual citizen, be it man or woman. Such had been the creed of the men with whom I had lived from boyhood, and as most of them were killed in the war, my duty was greater in order to fill up the gap which their death had left."[17] As a student in Europe, Higginson found good music readily available, affordable, and enjoyed by all, rich and poor. Moreover, music there was considered an integral part of a normal upbringing. Higginson had long hoped that his contribution to America's betterment could be in some way musical, and he spent a fortune to ensure that the BSO's concert admission prices were kept within reach of those of even the most modest of means.

Higginson chose as the first conductor of his new organization Georg (later George) Henschel (1850–1934). A singer of achievement, Henschel had very little knowledge about leading an orchestra, although he had done some composing for it. In the early days of the BSO its members were largely made up of the same players—generally mediocre ones—who had already been performing in the HMA and other ensembles. Chadwick's assessment was that no conductor could have made them much better, but especially one "who, though very enthusiastic, had no idea of orchestral discipline further than to get the notes right."[18]

Henschel was not an uneducated musician; in fact, ten years before Chadwick, he was at the Leipzig Conservatory, where he studied piano with Moscheles and theory and composition with Reinecke. His BSO programs were eclectic and featured contemporary works by Wagner and Brahms, as well as Berlioz, Liszt, and others. And if Henschel was not a vociferous advocate of America's nascent composers, he at least demonstrated a genuine interest in Chadwick's work.

Also contributing to the surge of musical activities in Boston was the parallel growth of NEC. Eben Tourjée founded the institution in 1867. By the 1880s, concerts at the conservatory were well-attended events, "the hall being crowded to overflowing" at one November 1881 performance. This was the rule rather than the exception.[19] Concerts of that year included recitals by vocalists, pianists and organists, and violinists. In addition, the Conservatory Symphony Concerts formed "an important element in our winter's music," even though the orchestra was "to be made up of picked up musicians," rather than students.[20] By summer 1882 the conservatory was openly boasting that it would soon be "the largest musical college in the world," with course offerings broadened and European musicians filling out its roster of teachers.[21] In that year, the conservatory celebrated the occasion of its thousandth concert by making it a faculty event; Chadwick contributed a performance of Bach's "St. Anne's Fugue" (BWV 552) on the organ. In 1883 Elson reported that NEC concerts were occurring at the rate of about twenty per week.[22] As the conservatory's reputation increased, so did the number of visits to its facilities by the legions of guest artists who were lured to the city by the BSO, the reputation of which was also increasing.

In the shadow of Boston's thriving orchestral movement, musical clubs and organizations of every imaginable type cropped up throughout the decade. In 1888 the Dilettante Club, the Bach Club, and the Manuscript Club were among the most popular, each offering "music of a high order, but in a semi-private manner."[23] Art clubs were also very popular in Boston, and Chadwick, who often asseverated his close affinity to painters, compared the composer's lot to that of artists:

> The painter is a gregarious animal and likes the companionship of his kind even when he does not entirely approve of their performances. He is usually glad of a frank criticism from a professional brother whom he respects and is not suspected of malice if he is equally frank in his own expressions. The composer is perhaps a little more reticent. It may be that he does not ordinarily live in so rugged an artistic atmosphere—if indeed he lives in an artistic atmosphere at all. And yet it is only in such an environment that he can really

thrive and grow strong. And it is not only musical surrounding that he needs. To be sure, he needs the companionship of his great predecessors as much as the painter does, and their works ought always to be accessible to him for study "for doctrine, for reproof and for instructive insightfulness." But besides this, he must have artistic stimulus of all possible kinds if he would pursue the ideal with joy and happiness and with artistic success. Then let him go, as the painter does, to *Nature* herself.[24]

Chadwick shared criticism and camaraderie with a number of his musical fellows, as Arthur Foote recounted in his article "A Bostonian Remembers," written for the *Musical Quarterly* long after most members of the New England school had perished. "One of my cherished remembrances," Foote wrote, "is of the meetings several times a year of Chadwick, Parker, Whiting, and myself, at which we each offered manuscript compositions for criticism, sometimes caustic, always helpful. The talk was honest and frank to a degree, and one was certainly up against the unadorned truth. I learned a lot from it."[25]

One possible reason for musicians and artists to spend more time among themselves and less time in more well-rounded company may have been the changing character of some of the social clubs, such as the St. Botolph Club and the Tavern Club. It was a phenomenon that was noticed by Arlo Bates, once again in his novel *The Philistines*. The changes in this instance occurred at his fictional St. Filipe Club: "The temper of the clubs, like that of individuals, changes from time to time, however constant remains its temperament. Those who reflected upon such matters noticed that at the St. Filipe Club, where a few years back there had been much talk of art and literature, and abstract principles, there had come to be a worldlier—perhaps a Philistine would say a more mature—flavor to the conversation. There were a good many stories told about its wide fireplaces, and there was much running comment on current topics, political and otherwise. There was, perhaps, a more cosmopolitan air to the talk."[26]

Chamber music also abounded in Boston. Violinist Franz Kneisel's celebrated quartet concertized regularly, as did the Adamowski Quartet; both groups were known for exceptional playing, and the Kneisels felt an obligation to perform the works by American composers—especially local ones—or at least give them a play-through in rehearsal. The Boston Chamber Music Society was founded in 1886, and 1890 saw the formation of the NEC Chamber Music Club, which had been established to spotlight faculty members and give unusually scored compositions their due on the concert stage.[27] And even though opera was but a side dish on the city's musical menu, throughout the 1880s miscellaneous performances flourished mostly because of the many traveling companies that visited Boston. As is still the case today, there seems not to have been a great deal of crossover audience; Elson observed that "our symphony audiences and our operatic ones are entirely different in their composition."[28] Naturally, in the puritanical musical environment of Boston, opera was viewed as mere spectacle, while music of the orchestra—abstract and sober—was preferred by the cognoscenti. Aside from modest local efforts such as the short-lived American Opera Company of Boston, touring troupes—including the Mapleson Opera Company, the Damrosch German Opera Company (known in Boston for its performances of "sauerkraut operas"), the Ideal Opera Company, the Emma Juch Opera Company, and the New York German Opera Company—visited frequently.

By decade's end, "popular entertainments" were more popular than ever. The famous band leader Patrick S. Gilmore returned to Boston in 1889 for a "revivified Jubilee," an attempt to recapture the success that he had scored at the great National and World Peace Jubilee concerts of 1869 and 1872, respectively. Gilmore gave nine concerts, all very well attended, proving to the cultured classes "beyond doubt that there is a very large public in Boston, as elsewhere, who do not rise to the symphonic level, and whose wants can be catered to in a noisy manner."[29]

Chadwick's composing regimen heated up in 1881. Prior to then he had completed just a couple of works per year, but 1881 saw him bring out a half dozen, and for the remainder of the decade he averaged that number annually. By 1882 the ambitious composer was writing to Theodore Thomas to request assistance that he hoped would lead to performances of his music. Chadwick had already sent Thomas the *Rip Van Winkle* Overture, and he now offered Thomas his *Andante* for strings and the First Symphony.[30]

Thalia (op. 10)

In 1819 William Tudor, a co-founder and editor of the important literary magazine *North American Review*, dubbed Boston the "Athens of America," an appellation that clings to the city to this day. Boston, Tudor astutely observed, was not only a center of political thought and commerce, but also of learning, philosophy, and science—the city boasted a marvelous collection of minds and institutions that harkened back to the golden age of Greek thought. Boston adopted the "Athens" mantle in many ways, but nowhere was its affection for ancient times better reflected than in the city's architecture. Throughout the nineteenth century, Greek-style buildings began to appear in Boston, among them the Merchants Exchange (1842); the Custom House (1847); Horticultural

Hall (1865); the massive South Station (1898); and, of course, Symphony Hall (1900), the Greek façade of which is articulated inside by plaster statuary on classical subjects. The venerable Boston Athenaeum—its very name reflective of ancient Greece—had been founded in 1807, but its none-too-Greek building did not appear until 1849.

It was in this environment of veneration for Greece that Chadwick composed his concert overture *Thalia*, which may be viewed as his first contribution to Boston's continuing Greek revival movement. Thalia is one of the nine muses, all daughters of Zeus in Greek mythology, and each representing disciplines in the arts and sciences. They are Thalia (comedy); Melpomene (tragedy); Terpsichore (dance); Euterpe (music and epic poetry); Calliope (epic poetry); Erato (lyric and love poetry); Klio (history); Urania (astrology and astronomy); and Polyhymnia (sacred poetry and geometry). In Chadwick's day, references to Greece were ubiquitous; as far as his own art goes, he may have been drawn to the subject by Harvard's recent performance of Sophocles's *Oedipus Tyrannus* accompanied by Paine's incidental music to a play that was, as already noted, quite influential on him. Chadwick's homage to the Greek atmosphere that permeated Boston culture at the time was not intended to be "authentic." Like Paine, who had briefly considered making his music to *Oedipus Tyrannus* authentically Greek (as ancient Greek music was understood at the time), Chadwick simply hoped to capture in his music the spirit of the muse. He also later remarked that "I frankly intended [*Thalia*] for the theatre," even though the work is in sonata form and is scored for greater forces than would have been typical, or practical, for a theater orchestra.[31] On his manuscript Chadwick used Greek letters for the title for his work. Just below he tells us that "the principal subjects are intended to suggest the sentiment, humor and dramatic action of an imaginary emotional comedy."[32]

Chadwick completed *Thalia* in November 1882, and on January 12, 1883, he led the BSO in its premiere. There was no paucity of enthusiasm for *Thalia*. Apthorp, writing for the *Boston Evening Transcript*, observed that "Mr. Chadwick's new overture took all hearts by storm. Judging merely from the first impressions, we have nothing but admiration to express. The tuneful, melodious character of the themes, the ingenuity with which one brilliant effect is made to follow close upon the heels of another, the sharply drawn, but never exaggerated, contrasts of coloring, and, above all, the genial Hellenic cheerfulness of the whole fill[s] the listener with delight."[33] Chadwick himself was more captious of it in his later years and even criticized Apthorp's jubilation, which, he thought, "only showed how an ass [i.e., Apthorp] can write himself down."[34]

If Chadwick proved himself to have a firm grasp of formal and developmental procedure in both of his previous orchestral statements, in *Thalia* he produced a work that is obviously for and of the theater. Perhaps owing to its dedication to fellow Duveneck Boy Ross Turner, Victor Fell Yellin thought that the overture "may be considered a musical memoir of his student days in Germany."[35]

Although *Thalia* adheres to sonata principles, several traits establish its distinctiveness. The lengthy opening clarinet cadenza, a large battery of percussion, including castanets, triangle and tambourine, and the free use of the brass in sectional and solo passages, each lend colorful aspects that portend the rise of the proscenium curtain. Its themes have immediacy; they are lighthearted and gossamer, and Chadwick ingeniously employed an attractive conversational style between the instruments while steadfastly avoiding the thick, protracted development that he had used in *Rip Van Winkle* and the First Symphony. Again, his self-taught lessons on "how to make an orchestra sound," gained as a result of his having attended many operettas and garden concerts in Germany, affected this overture.

The premiere of *Thalia* marked another important occasion. It was the first of what would be many performances of Chadwick's music by the BSO. Chadwick's association with the organization—its founder, conductors, and musicians—would exert an enormous influence on his career. It is not too much to say that, without the BSO's formation, the course of Chadwick's career and influence as a composer would have been very different, perhaps even negligible.

The Boston Orchestral Club

The shadow cast by the BSO was indeed long, but it did not forestall the formation of many other symphonic organizations, some of which made a significant mark on the city's musical life. The Boston Orchestral Club was formed in 1884 and presented its first concert in January 1885 at Boston's hallowed if not entirely adequate Horticultural Hall at its location then on Tremont Street. The revered and ubiquitous Bernhard Listemann, the club's founder, conducted; among its officers were president J. C. D. Parker and vice president John S. Dwight. Elson reported that the orchestra was "composed chiefly of amateurs, both ladies and gentlemen, but it does not play in an amateurish manner."[36]

Chadwick surmised that Listemann and the members of the orchestra had simply tired of each other. Listemann departed, and in 1887 the aspiring young conductor was offered the job.[37] The first reports of Chadwick and the Orchestral Club appeared in 1888, when he led the group of fifty-eight musicians (to which he quickly added a chorus) at Bumstead Hall, a small venue utilized principally for rehearsals and located directly beneath the Music Hall. Although the first performance of that season "was not without blemish to be sure," the varied program, featuring selections by Beethoven, Haydn, Rameau, and Suppé, satisfied the crowd.[38] Critical praise was tempered somewhat following the second concert of that season. Although the program was a captivating one—Arthur Foote played piano in Saint-Saëns's septet—the *Musical Record* wondered if "some criticism might be made concerning [the] desirability of such a concert."[39]

Chadwick's tenure with the Boston Orchestral Club gave him much-desired regular practice rehearsing an ensemble, one that was larger than his usual forces at church. He acknowledged that the orchestra, while full of enthusiasm, "did not really like to study or submit to too much discipline."[40] Its Monday evening weekly rehearsals and handful of performances per season, which lasted from November through April, did not allow time for perfection. Nevertheless, the club gave him an opportunity to explore the music of diverse composers, aided by Wilhelm Gericke, who provided tips on matters of both repertoire and conducting. Chadwick programmed works by Bruch, Gounod, Delibes, Gade, Mendelssohn, and many others. Two Wagner selections—"The Prayer" from *Lohengrin* and the Overture to *Tannhäuser*—were played in 1889, and from among his own circle of acquaintances he performed Jadassohn's Serenade in D and Reinecke's *Fest-Overture*. At one point he had also considered performing Raff's famous symphony, but ultimately decided against it, perhaps because of its difficulty.[41] This placed him apart from Listemann, who selected music that was often technically beyond the reach of the amateur group. Chadwick approached the ensemble with two relatively modest goals: to give the members music they could play successfully, and to train them to play in tune. For Chadwick, the entire experience was "a liberal education in practical conducting."[42]

In matters of repertoire, Chadwick was never one to forget his friends and colleagues. He vehemently supported the cause of American composers, but he seldom did it with speeches and fanfare. When it was within his power, he programmed their music, sometimes even when he found the music distasteful. As for his work with the Orchestral Club, he wrote to Parker: "I am busy as the devil—have a first rate, regular nickel plated chorus with the orchestral club and I think that our season will be a great success. I would like very much to do [Parker's] *King Trojan* but I am afraid of the [manuscript] parts which our girls and boys are not used to. However if you can send me the orchestra parts to try I should like to make the experiment."[43] Chadwick's young student Henry Hadley was given the rare opportunity to conduct several of his own early waltzes with the club, and naturally, Chadwick also used the orchestra to try out his own music.[44] During the 1886 season several of his songs were performed, including "He Loves Me," "I Know Two Eyes," and "The Danza"; "Allah" was sung during the fourth season (1888); and both *Lovely Rosabelle* and *Rip Van Winkle* Overture were featured during the sixth season (1889).

Chadwick's tenure with the BOC ended in 1891.[45] "I resigned having too much to do," he remembered, "and being tired of bad intonation & attack. The Club busted up with *money in the treasury*."[46] But other problems followed: "After 1893 the subscriptions fell off, interest languished, and the club was discontinued." Additionally, members of the BSO, especially wind players who bolstered the club's forces, were forbidden by the BSO management to continue to participate.[47] Another competitor had also reared its head: by November 1890, the latest version of Boston Philharmonic, a group that for years had moved in and out of existence under various conductors, appeared on the scene with none other than the ever undeterred Listemann conducting. The concerts were reportedly "of a popular class, but not at all of a cheap order."[48]

There was one small bit of good news in the BOC's demise. When the ensemble disbanded, most of the club's music library went to NEC.

Life at Home

If the 1880s were heady days for Chadwick professionally, his personal life was also flourishing. It changed dramatically of course when he married Ida May Brooks (see figure 5.1) on June 16, 1885, at Hollis Street Church in a service led by Reverend Henry B. Carpenter. Chadwick had taken notice of her at least by 1881, when he reported seeing Ida May at a Euterpe Concert in which his own String Quartet no. 2 was the featured work.[49] The newlyweds honeymooned in Europe; during that trip Chadwick visited Horatio Parker, who was pursuing his education in Munich, as well as Rheinberger and Jadassohn and a number of the Duveneck Boys, who "adopted the bride with great alacrity."[50]

For all the affection that Chadwick directed to Ida May, he rarely discusses her in his writings with much directness; in fact, his references are unusually oblique—most often he mentions her in relation to others. As a result, and despite the existence of her own diaries (mere log-books really), she remains something of a mystery. She was born Ida May Brooks in 1851; Chadwick was her second husband.[51] But despite the haze that often obscures our knowledge of women of the period, now and then we are able to glimpse Ida May's character. She was devoted to many lady friends, but she also enjoyed close relationships with a number of Chadwick's male friends, especially Parker, with whom she had a very cordial and proper friendship, and Samuel Sanford, Parker's colleague in the music department at Yale, who was himself an extraordinary pianist and former student of Anton Rubenstein. We get an indication of Ida May's loyalty when, following the tragic death in Boston of their longtime friend, painter John

FIGURE 5.1.
Ida May Chadwick, 1881.
Courtesy of New England
Conservatory, Boston.

Leslie Breck, she went to Auburndale to inform Breck's mother of her son's demise, thought by some to be suicide. "It seems to be her fate," Chadwick wrote of his wife, "to lend her own character and strength to other women in time of trouble and this is not the first time she has been called on for her sympathy."[52]

Ida May also proved an asset to Chadwick's professional stature. Ever the good wife, she accompanied him to many performances and festivals around the country and became acquainted with many of his colleagues. She often kept company with the wives of other artists while the men went about their musical business. Although there is no indication that Ida May was musical, there is every reason to believe that she enjoyed music; later on she would collaborate with her husband on the text of *Noël: A Christmas Pastoral*, one of his large-scale works. Curiously, Chadwick dedicated none of his compositions to her.

"To a professional musician living in a great city," a long-time Chadwick associate observed, "a certain amount of club life of the right sort is little short of necessity."[53] Chadwick quickly comprehended this and was developing a richly textured social life in Boston. He joined both the St. Botolph Club and the Paint and Clay Club in the 1880s. Intended for men with an appreciation of the arts and letters, the former was modeled on New York's famed Century Club, and naturally its members included an elite group: the president was historian Francis Parkman (1823–1893); the secretary was novelist and essayist T. R. Sullivan

(1849–1916); and other members came from a variety of artistic and professional fields. There were painters, architects, writers, and a few musicians. Among the latter were Julius Eichberg, B. J. Lang, Foote, and Henschel. Chadwick was a bit surprised at how "clubbable" he was, that is, how immediately and easily he took to not only the social aspects of club life but also with how much he enjoyed its intellectual aspect. At the time there was a serious effort to combine the artistic and the intellectual, as Chadwick remembered about the St. Botolph Club:

> Every Saturday night there was a supper after which congenial souls gathered about the tables and discussed the artistic and other affairs of the town and the nation. And as many members came directly from the Symphony concert we often had the male soloist of the evening with us. In this way the club soon got a reputation as a place where artists were made welcome and in that way added materially to the musical prestige of Boston.[54]

Chadwick penned the St. Botolph Club song, "Greet the Old Man with a Smile," which he would later incorporate into his burlesque *Tabasco*, and he met Robert Grant, a club member whose libretto *The Peer and the Pauper* Chadwick set to music. "There was no action in it and the dialogue was rather stilted," he admitted, "but certain numbers are quite 'catching.'"[55] In 1883 Chadwick also joined the Papyrus Club, a more strictly literary guild that was a splinter group of the St. Botolph Club. And in 1888 he was elected to the Tavern Club—a mostly social fraternity—to replace the departing Gericke. Bicycling had long been a hobby for Chadwick, but his membership in the Boston Bicycle Club was interrupted by his new marital relationship.[56]

Naturally, Chadwick was also carving a living. By the time he arrived at the Hollis Street Church, he was making a thousand dollars a year, a nice sum that was supplemented by substantial income from organ, composition, and theory lessons. Most of this additional income was derived from his private studio (for which he charged three dollars per forty-five minute lesson), and from NEC (where he was earning $3.50 per hour). Add to these his miscellaneous music lectures, for which he received ten dollars an hour. Chadwick's orations typically elucidated the music that was being performed around the city, especially by the BSO. In addition, he received publication royalties, principally from the firm of Novello, which printed and distributed many of his songs and choruses.

By the late 1880s Chadwick's work schedule had become routinized. He spent two afternoons a week teaching at NEC; private students received lessons at his home (see table 5.1) from one o'clock until the early evening; late evenings were spent at rehearsals and performances, as necessary. Most importantly, his mornings were left available for his consuming passion: composition.

TABLE 5.1. Chadwick's Residences from 1880

1880	149a Tremont Street, Boston (in the Lawrence Building)
1882	Park Street Church, Boston (loft apartment)
1885	99 Boylston, Boston (apartment)
1887	133 Boylston, Boston (Mrs. March's boarding house)
1888	Williams Street, Brookline (house)
1892	903 Boylston, Boston (apartment)
1893	Moved into West Chop, Martha's Vineyard (summer home; built in 1892)
1902–1931	360 Marlboro, Boston (house)

Symphony No. 2 in B-flat Major (op. 21) (1883–1885)

Chadwick's Second Symphony was not originally conceived as a symphony at all, but it turned out to be an exceptional example of the genre. It is widely considered one of the freshest and most original pieces of American music up to that time, and represents a huge leap in quality over his First Symphony. That was recognized immediately by a perceptive press: "No more satisfactory effort in this line of writing has yet been put before the public by a native born citizen."[57] Chadwick wrote the F-major Scherzo movement first, in the winter of 1883 ("in score and in ink without sketching it at all except the main themes"[58]), and then, in a fit of excitement about the Scherzo, he composed on its heels an Allegro movement in B-flat. To these he added two more movements, which are thematically related to the Allegro, a happenstance that accounts for the stark individuality of the Scherzo.

Chadwick encouraged the performance of the first two movements upon their completion. Henschel led the BSO in the premiere of the Scherzo on March 7, 1884, at the Music Hall, and Chadwick himself conducted the first movement a year later, on April 29, 1885, in an Apollo Club concert, also at the Music Hall. He made it known that the two movements were related and now part of a single work, for the reviewer from the *Boston Daily Advertiser* thought the movement in B-flat "was highly interesting, full of freshness, originality, and charm, and in fact it seemed more than worthy to belong to the same composition with the scherzo, which has already excited so much admiration."[59] Following his marriage in 1885, Chadwick busied himself with the completion of what would become the third and fourth movements. We do not know the exact dates or the order of their completion, although the finale was inspired by a mountain excursion taken during his honeymoon in Europe. The premiere of the completed four-movement symphony featured Chadwick conducting the BSO on December 10, 1886, at the Music Hall. He was reported to have earned thirteen dollars that evening.[60]

The reviews of the performance were generally favorable, but some disparaging remarks were sounded here and there. One critic who was evidently knowledgeable about the young composer's music wrote, "Mr. Chadwick, who is capable of better things, has sacrificed artistic truth to a desire to please and to produce brilliant effects; and he will come to grief if he persists in writing symphonies, at any rate, in this vein." The writer could not help but notice that the other listeners seemed quite satisfied: "the applause and enthusiasm were, for a Boston audience, almost unbounded."[61] Chadwick's cultivation of "brilliant effects" was a pejorative charge that would haunt him for the next several decades.

As in his First Symphony, Chadwick's Second shows him to be an able craftsman: his forms are clear, his melodies are attractive, and his developments are thorough. The Second Symphony goes beyond these qualities to demonstrate the composer's sharp rhythmic imagination, as well as his ear for tantalizing instrumentation, especially demonstrated by his writing for the woodwinds and brass. These traits were obvious in *Rip Van Winkle*, although less so in the First Symphony.

The Second Symphony's first movement begins with a permeating pentatonic horn call, which is also heard in the third and fourth movements, demonstrating Chadwick's awareness of cyclic relationships. Although this movement is in the key of B-flat major, its long and turbulent introduction begins in D major and perhaps suggests Beethoven's Ninth Symphony. The main theme, energetic and heroic in a Straussian manner, is sounded by the first flute and the horns in a passage closely related to the opening bars. Chadwick's secondary melody occurs in the conventional dominant key and again features a horn solo and dialogue among several instrumental groups. Like *Rip Van Winkle*'s contrasting theme, this one is a tender melody that contrasts starkly with what has come before. Chadwick's development section is brief, at fewer than a hundred measures, and in it the composer revels in a kaleidoscopic variety of keys. In another Beethoven-inspired gesture, a false recapitulation lures us back to the home key and a restatement of the main theme; and, in one of the movement's most compelling moments, we hear a full-blown trumpet solo on the secondary tune. Chadwick's predilection for both new themes and furious conclusions is demonstrated in the coda.

The second movement, Allegretto scherzando, is one of the most heralded creations in all of American orchestral music. Although it is built as a two-part form with a coda, and is harmonically unremarkable, its arresting melody, rhythm, and instrumentation gained it immediate accolades. The pentatonic principal melody is first sounded by the solo oboe, although it includes several stray passing tones. In this movement Chadwick also utilized sixteenth-eighth-sixteenth note rhythms to energize the accompaniments, and the oboe solo, unusual enough in itself, includes several trills. These characteristics convinced Apthorp to muse in the *Boston Evening Transcript* that the melody exuded a "quasi-Irish humorousness."[62] In this same vein, the *Boston Post* reviewer enjoyed its "pleasing Scotch flavor."[63] These perceptions may be the result of the oboe's melodic decorations and reedy, bagpipe-like timbre, as well as that of a bassoon solo that occurs later in the movement. Chadwick would use similar instrumental gestures to affect a Celtic/Gaelic sound much later in portions of his *Tam O'Shanter*. Already, however, the *Transcript* critic thought the orchestration "that of a master, and full of delicious bits of color, without ever becoming outrageous."[64]

Again echoing Beethoven, Chadwick's D-minor third movement, Largo e Maestoso, offers a stirring pathos. It is more "learned" than some of Chadwick's earlier music and includes a section of intense fugue alternated with passages of utter jubilation. One critic wrote, "There is much beauty in the largo, and if one finds restlessness and motion where quiet would have been preferred, the result is an evidence of the composer's affection for the brasses, without which he could scarcely be called an American."[65]

The finale, Allegro molto animato, is in a wonderfully executed sonata form in the home key, B-flat major. It begins with motives derived from the first movement's opening horn call, but it is quick-paced and jolly. The movement introduces a number of new ideas, all of which are closely related to those heard in movements 1 and 3. The contrasting secondary theme, engulfed in brass flourishes, makes its way around the orchestra, and it quickly arrives at the brief but harmonically daring development area. As the movement draws to a close, listeners would not have failed to notice the brass fanfares and its bold martial character. The *Post* reviewer thought some of Chadwick's strategy a failure: "In the last movement some clever use is made of themes taken from the previous movements, but the constant changes of tonality and tempo give this movement a certain patchwork character which is much to be regretted."[66]

So what was "brilliant" about the Second Symphony? Clearly Chadwick created a work that is engaging, well crafted, even bracing, but that could be said of many other symphony scores. Apthorp, unable to put his finger on the precise character of this composition, wrote: "And yet there is that in the general character and animus of the symphony which baffles all attempts at comparing it with known models of any school. We, for one, cannot remember any music of this character being written in the symphonic form. One feels like saying, with Friar Lawrence, 'Art thou a symphony? Thy form cries out, thou art.'"[67]

Indeed, Chadwick's forms adhere to accepted practice, but other aspects jolted the audiences and the critics alike.

The Second Symphony's supposed Irish and Scotch roots, especially in the second movement, have garnered for it a permanent place in histories and textbooks as an early example of "characteristically American" music. But other contemporary reviewers noted similarities to music by Beethoven, Mendelssohn, and Niels Gade, although none pointed to specific examples. On the other hand, the respected critic Philip Hale thought it a very American creation, "a jolly, jocose movement which approaches the edge of vulgarity," with the "smell of American soil" and rhythms that reminded him of "Roustabouts dancing on the levy [sic]."[68] Obviously there was disagreement about the cultural lineage of Chadwick's music, a situation that foreshadowed the controversy over matters of origin in Dvořák's music less than a decade later.

Chadwick's adept instrumentation certainly contributes to the work's luminescence. Numerous solos, especially in the wind instruments, pepper the work and most of them soar over very light accompaniments, making them easily heard. Also, the composer's frequent use of motoric rhythms, often syncopated and in quick tempi, breathes energy into well-worn forms. Unlike Paine's First and Second Symphonies, both of which are staid and predictable, Chadwick's music, with its "patchwork" forms, Celtic/Scotch themes, daring instrumentation, and scintillating rhythms, offered the promise of a more exotic future for American symphonism.

In 1888 Chadwick sent Higginson a copy of his newly available Second Symphony, which A. P. Schmidt had just published. Chadwick was understandably proud of it—no American symphony had been published since Paine's Symphony no. 2, and, given the rapid demise of Chadwick's own First Symphony, having a published one in hand would provide at least some possibility that it would be performed and perhaps even achieve a position in the repertoire. Higginson responded with a letter of thanks and encouragement ("I wish we had more good native work—but patience! It will come"), but it was apparent that just a few years into his leadership of the bso he was tired. Running the orchestra, Higginson confessed, "is a duty which I will perform if the load is not too heavy."[69]

Chadwick was frequently his own harshest critic. He later observed that "this symphony has serious defects. The movements were assembled separately with the result that the inspiration, such as it is, is not sustained, and there are other evidences of youth and inexperience. I shall not mourn if it is never played again as a whole, although the scherzo might perhaps be rescued."[70] Some critics were also sour. One of them was Apthorp, who by and large relished it; but, as critics are wont to do, he added several jabs. The Second Symphony, the critic averred, "falls short of what may be called symphonic dignity." Although "brilliant, often very fascinating," it is also "fitful, capricious, and, if we may be pardoned for saying so, even frivolous." Apthorp considered its orchestration inferior to that of *Thalia*. He concluded that "it seems as if the composer had not yet sufficiently drilled his powers to cope with so severe a task as a symphony."[71]

Chadwick was enraged at these remarks. "What the critics said was mostly wrong, especially Apthorp," he recollected in 1926, following its short-lived revival by the People's Symphony Orchestra. "My reply was *Melpomene*."[72]

Quartet (no. 3) in D Major (1886)

With characteristic candor, Chadwick wrote of his Third Quartet, "For some reason or other I never cared much about this piece, although it was well made and had some good themes in it."[73] He began the quartet in the early part of the decade, between 1882 and 1884, just at the time when his enthusiasm for composing orchestra music was on the ascent. That zest kept him busy, and, unlike his previous string quartets, which were composed to be played immediately at the Leipzig Conservatory, this one seems to have been commenced with no particular opportunity for performance in mind. For this reason, the Third Quartet remained at the bottom of the piles on his work desk until it was finally completed on May 25, 1886. It then had to wait nearly a year for its premiere performance.

That Chadwick was able to finish it at all was the result of an incredible work ethic that simply did not allow him to stop composing. We catch a glimpse of this aspect of Chadwick in a letter he wrote to Parker in 1886, just a few weeks before he completed the Third Quartet: "I have made some new songs for one and four male voices[,] scored my Dedication Ode[,] and am at present at work on a string quartet in D maj[or] which I hope to show you completed when you come [to Boston]." Chadwick went on to excoriate another member of the Big 4 whose accomplishments had been negligible: "[Arthur] Whiting has done *Nothing*. Niente! Gar Nichts!! He says he hasn't any ideas. Perhaps I haven't either but I don't mean to forget how to make [notes] while I am waiting for some."[74] Essential to an understanding of Chadwick is his unrelenting lifelong desire to work, which, as illustrated here, did not allow him to take a break from putting notes on paper, even though he may not have had "any ideas." This single-mindedness, coupled with the fact that he spent very little time revising works once they were completed, makes him one of the most prolific American composers ever.

Chadwick's work methods were indeed challenged as he attempted completion of the quartet. From 1885 through early 1886, besides being in the throes of completing a number of songs and the orchestration of the *Dedication Ode*, he had also been creating choruses and organ music, and he was probably engaged in preparations for the premiere of the entire four movements of his recently completed Second Symphony. By early 1886 he was almost certainly working on the song and overture *The Miller's Daughter*, which he would complete in June 1886; and of course he was planning his next major orchestral work, *Melpomene*, at this time as well. Between the large-scale compositions that kept his ego satisfied, and the smaller works that he intended for instruction and publication, a piece such as the Third Quartet was something of an afterthought.

The quartet includes a number of remarkable traits, beginning with its lack of an introduction, a unique feature in Chadwick's sonata form movements in this genre. Chadwick begins the music straightaway with the plucky principal theme in D major. In another manifestation of his predilection for triple meter, Chadwick imbues the initial measures with rhythmic variety, especially by use of a dotted-eighth-sixteenth note figure, which dominates the music's texture. Hemiola is also prominent.

The second movement of the quartet is a theme and variations in D minor. Chadwick rarely used this form, although he possessed the requisite ingenuity to pull it off successfully. Following an expansive presentation of the theme in an Adagio tempo, the music scurries through five variations, each of which is quick-paced and inventive. Critic Henry Krehbiel remarked that Chadwick owed a debt to the theme and variations movement of Schubert's *Death and the Maiden* quartet, although Chadwick himself typically remained silent about such influences.[75]

The brief third movement is an affable, beautiful essay in ABA form. Chadwick's G major melody is breezy, and the harmonies are uncomplicated until something altogether unexpected occurs. Near its end the music progresses through the flat second degree and its dominant (that is, the Neapolitan-sixth chord, or A-flat, and then E-flat) to give the music a novel harmonic twist. These fresh sounds are wrapped in ambiguous rhythmic clothing that accelerates (più animato) at the close in full pizzicato. Its combined effect makes this one of the best moments in all of the composer's chamber music.

The finale is a fiery tarantella in a straightforward D-major sonata form. It exhibits the verve that one expects in a finale, and includes the welcome appearance of fugue in the middle section. Chadwick rarely hesitated to use fugue as a developmental device, even though by this time it was considered a bit old-fashioned. But in his view, its employment was perfectly legitimate, the test of a composer's ability to combine tones logically.

The performance history of the Third Quartet is not a distinguished one. It was premiered by Boston's Euterpe Society, at that time led by Arthur Foote, its dedicatee, in 1887. The quartet was performed again later that year at the American music concerts produced by Frank van der Stucken in New York. The reviewer for the *Times* gave a generally good write up to the first three movements, although he found the last "somewhat trifling in character."[76] Critic Henry Krehbiel's assessment was more positive. He enjoyed the Third Quartet and was relieved that in it Chadwick "stops talking when he has nothing more to say."[77] A third performance, the last heard during Chadwick's lifetime as far as can be discerned, was undertaken by the Kneisel Quartet in January 1888.

Boston's Music Journals and Wagner

One key to understanding the musical culture of Boston in the latter half of the nineteenth century is recognizing the important role of music critics and their journals. The foremost, the journal among journals in Boston, was *Dwight's Journal of Music: A Paper of Art and Literature*. It was founded in 1852 by John Sullivan Dwight, who was also its editor. *Dwight's Journal*, distributed weekly and then fortnightly, never had a huge base of subscribers; critic W. S. B. Mathews suggested that its circulation never exceeded five- to six-hundred. "The number circulated, however . . . conveys no just idea of the influence wielded by the journal."[78] A strange, somewhat iconoclastic figure without formal training in music, Dwight was nevertheless respected as a tireless worker on behalf of the art. He was also a leader in the city's musical circles; he founded and presided over the Harvard Musical Association and advised other musical organizations in Boston. Dwight was a Unitarian minister and a Transcendentalist, and both pursuits informed his musical perspective. In Dwight's thinking, music, especially abstract instrumental music, was wholly expressive and required no further explanation. On the other hand, those musical forms that had to rely on words, scenery, or programmatic idea to provide effect were considered inferior.

In his lengthy, appreciative obituary of Dwight, colleague William Foster Apthorp thought the revered older critic was "essentially a Hellene and an idealist" for whom music was sacred. But Apthorp made no attempt to disguise Dwight's well-known shortcomings:

> He never developed anything that could fairly be called a musical facility; he never handled musical notation with the ease of a craftsman, and always found some difficulty in following performances from the score, especially when things went at a rapid tempo. His naturally musical ear never developed to more than an average pitch of delicacy; technical slips seldom disturbed

him, and "rough performances" fully satisfied him, if only the right spirit was there.

Apthorp concluded that, despite these deficiencies, "his musical instincts and perceptions were, in a certain high respect, of the finest."[79]

Naturally not everyone thought so. Stephen A. Emery may well have had Dwight in mind when he wrote in an 1880 issue of the *Musical Herald*, "Of genuine musical criticism, we have too little; of poor attempts at this, too much."[80] It has been in vogue in recent decades to condemn Boston's perceived infatuation with an early Romantic canon we now regard as classic and especially to pillory Dwight for having maintained his devotion to these compositions. Music histories, dictionaries, encyclopedias, and textbooks abound with references to his "conservative" perspective. In a particularly invidious recent attack, cultural historian Joseph Horowitz excoriated him, writing, "Ultimately, Dwight is a puritan for whom art is purest religion; a purist intent on sanitizing music; a prude on guard against 'promiscuous' alliances with popular, sensuous, or sentimental genres. He is a dogmatist prone to a priori judgments." Horowitz then plays the race card, pitting Dwight against the Irish founder of the Peace Jubilees, Patrick Gilmore: "[Dwight] feels secure in his Boston bastion, but incipiently embattled by a roisterous immigrant mob, chiefly Irish."[81]

Apthorp's view of Dwight's "conservatism," based on his firsthand knowledge of the man, is more generous. "His utter distaste," the critic remembered, "for music of the more modern schools, for Berlioz, Liszt, Wagner, and even Raff and Brahms, has too often been ascribed to sheer prejudice. No doubt prejudice did play some part in the matter; these modern men came upon Dwight somewhat late in life, when, although he retained all his naiveté and enthusiasm, his musical receptivity had become to a certain extent anchylosed into immobility, and he found it difficult to throw off old habits and adopt new points of view." But more than simply the inability of an old dog to learn new tricks, as the saying goes, Foster had observed that the music of the moderns was anathema to Dwight's personality: "the whole essentially modern spirit which pervades their work, with all of its high strung nervous energy, restless striving, and lack of serenity and repose, the way their music reflects the characteristic strenuousness and turmoil of modern life, were totally antipathetic to his nature."[82]

The extent of the influence of *Dwight's Journal of Music* has been the subject of debate; we cannot calculate with any certainty the number of subscribers or the number of copies of each issue printed monthly. Nevertheless, it seems reasonable, given Dwight's longstanding leadership role in musical Boston—as well as his *Journal's* miraculous nearly thirty-year run—that it was read by musically inclined locals; but any true estimate of the scope of its readership or its influence is just that. When the last edition of *Dwight's Journal* appeared in September 1881, after the publication of a staggering 1,051 issues, a competing music magazine with a similar physical format but a decidedly different editorial perspective had already been in publication for nearly two years. It was perfectly poised to replace Dwight's venerable *Journal* and help to remold the musical atmosphere of Boston.

The *Musical Herald* was founded under the managing directorship of NEC leader Eben Tourjée, and it featured a number of significant features that distinguished it from *Dwight's Journal*. First, Tourjée's magazine embraced the latest music and encouraged its writers—among them such prominent local music leaders as Louis C. Elson, William Apthorp, and Stephen A. Emery—to cover it. Although editorially *Dwight's Journal* had been nearly a one-man show since its founding, Dwight had employed contributors; but he rarely seems to have given them the aesthetic leeway that Tourjée gave his stable of critics.

Second, the *Herald* gleefully accepted advertising, which Dwight mostly resisted until it finally caused the demise of his *Journal*. Many *Herald* advertisements were for locally produced goods, such as pianos and sheet music, and services, mostly for private vocal and instrumental instruction. Music instructors associated with NEC often advertised, among them organist Henry Dunham, piano tuning instructor Frank Hale, and Stephen Emery, who taught private students in theory and counterpoint. Needless to say, Tourjée also gave prominent advertising space to his own NEC.

Thirdly Tourjée assigned more space to local and regional issues than did Dwight, and therefore one could read, for instance, about the latest developments in public-school music education in New England. One final feature distinguished the *Herald*: Tourjée included sheet music for practice and performance in the home in the pages of his journal. Dances, studies, and songs for the piano occupy several pages of every issue. Perhaps because Dwight was himself not a pianist, nor a practicing musician on any instrument, music rarely made it into the *Journal*. Later, he was forced by economic conditions to include music in the form of separately bound supplements printed by the publishing firm of Oliver Ditson, which took control of the printing of the *Journal* in 1858. Unlike Tourjée, however, Dwight was not particularly interested in reaching the home musician, which he would have regarded as entirely too practical; Dwight loved music for its religious, philosophical, and moral value. He had no interest in promoting music as a pastime; he was intent on elevating it to the position of high art. It is easy to imagine that the founding of the *Musical Herald* was at least in part a response to Dwight's aims and his nearly unswerving devotion to a more severe aesthetic, one that judged Beethoven and the early Romantics as the ne plus ultra of composers.

The *Herald*, on the other hand, was intent on exploring new music topics, and in fact may well have been successful because of it. By the mid-1880s there was a decidedly pro–new music tenor to the journal, as evidenced by its increasing discussion of Wagner. One of the more momentous events of the day, Boston's first Wagner Festival, held from April 14–17, 1884, received ample coverage in the *Herald*. Conducting six concerts over four days, Theodore Thomas led a 150-member orchestra, solo vocalists, and a six-hundred-member chorus that included local singers at the Massachusetts Charitable Mechanics' Association Building. The programs included selections from *Tannhäuser*, *Die Walküre*, and *Siegfried*. Although over the four days of the festival there were no complete performances of any single opera, and all works were presented in concert settings, the *Herald* reviewer observed that "the festival has been throughout a great success, and without doubt educated Boston in a school of music of which it previously knew very little. It has paved the way for a full representation of Wagner's operas with scenic and all other effects."[83] Some of Thomas's Wagner concerts attracted as many as eight thousand listeners.[84] By May 1888 a writer for the *Herald* could remark that there remained a widespread interest in good French and Italian music, "[in] spite of the pronounced Wagnerian tendencies in Boston."[85]

Chadwick found himself becoming something of a Wagnerite. He and Ida May made another trip to Europe in 1888, "our special errand being to attend the Bayreuth festival" and to see performances of Wagner's operas.[86] In less than a week the couple heard two performances of *Parsifal* conducted by Hermann Levi and *Die Meistersinger von Nürnberg* under Hans Richter. Of the former opera, Chadwick remarked, "It is of the stage, stagey"; it was not a work he appreciated as he thought the music "often commonplace," and the plot and staging needlessly elaborate yet somehow still forgettable. On the other hand, the *Meistersinger*, Chadwick exclaimed, "was a great joy" with a "buoyancy and exuberance." Before their homebound voyage, the Chadwicks even took the time to visit Wagner's grave.[87]

Melpomene (1887)

Chadwick had for some time sensed the city's "Wagnerian tendencies." Even before his Bayreuth trip, Chadwick began his Wagner-inspired "dramatic overture," *Melpomene*. He completed his sketches on July 15, 1887, started the orchestration the very same day, and completed it on September 30. Chadwick

TABLE 5.2. Boston Symphony Orchestra Conductors through 1949

George Henschel	1881–1884
Wilhelm Gericke	1884–1889
Arthur Nikisch	1889–1893
Emil Paur	1893–1898
Wilhelm Gericke	1898–1906
Karl Muck	1906–1908
Max Fiedler	1908–1912
Karl Muck	1912–1918
Henri Rabaud	1918–1919
Pierre Monteux	1919–1924
Serge Koussevitzky	1924–1949

titled the work after the Greek muse of tragedy, intending to craft a work that would be a companion piece to *Thalia*, as well as an overture along more serious lines than he had heretofore composed. *Melpomene* would be his fourth overture; to his great disappointment, the previous three did not catch on with either conductors or the public. *Rip Van Winkle* Overture had been an imposing musical essay on a beloved figure from American literature; *Thalia* was a light-hearted, comical thrill ride; and *The Miller's Daughter*, completed in 1886 but not performed in Boston until 1892, is a clumsy "song and overture," and, while tuneful, was widely considered ineffectual. That these works were performed only a few times and had not attracted a publisher was disheartening. Chadwick realized that he was in need of more than a passing success — his next overture had to engage the public. But first it had to captivate a conductor.

Wilhelm Gericke (1845–1925) had been persuaded to come to America by Higginson, who needed to replace Henschel at the BSO. Gericke came to his new post with an authority that Henschel had not even closely approached. With wide conducting experience learned under the tutelage of Hans Richter, Brahms, and others, he was regarded as not only a gifted conductor and interpreter, but also as a builder of orchestras. Gericke's term was to start with the 1884 season, and Higginson was happy to have him (see table 5.2). If his new man did not have Henschel's dash and charisma, Gericke possessed a surpassing ability to drastically improve an orchestra, a quality Henschel lacked.

Gericke was not impressed by the orchestra in his first season, and he made his dissatisfaction known to Higginson. Few players were virtuosi; the concept of ensemble playing was a foreign one; and even something as basic as good intonation was challenging. But Gericke's personality would not allow his own defeat. Following his first year, Higginson remembered, Gericke "went back to

Vienna, engaged an excellent concertmaster (Franz Kneisel) and a large number of good musicians, and brought them here. With a certain number [of good musicians] already in Boston and New York, he began his second year, and worked hard to form an orchestra. The concertmaster and, indeed, the first desks of the first violins were excellent, but still there was much room for further improvement." Higginson further reflected, "Before the end of the winter we had a fair orchestra. Again, people would ask [Gericke] if it was not splendid, and got the same reply, 'Not yet.'" [88]Chadwick recalled one episode during which Gericke intended to lead the BSO in the Boston premiere of Brahms's Third Symphony. The rehearsal "did not go to suit him," and he substituted a Haydn symphony at the concert. "This was a good example of Gericke's artistic conscientiousness and an exemplification of his standard."[89]

Although accomplished in a variety of repertoires, both in the concert hall and on the operatic stage, Gericke had an affinity for music by contemporary Austro-German composers, including Wagner, Bruckner, Brahms, and Strauss, works that, then as now, are considered serious and titanic. Gericke, not insensitive to his audience's preferences, also packed in copious amounts of Beethoven and other favorites. Chadwick knew that in order to get a hearing for his works from the BSO, they had to meet certain standards not only in terms of their craftsmanship but also of their gravity. If the Second Symphony was frivolous, as Apthorp thought, Chadwick's next major composition would be among his most serious.

The Teutonic pedigree of *Melpomene* sealed its success with the Austro-German conductors who dotted America's musical landscape, including Gericke. It was appreciated for its seriousness—or its "earnestness," to use a word that was popular in the contemporary reviews—a trait that some had felt to be lacking thus far in much of Chadwick's work. The overture also benefitted from the loftiness of its subject matter. Chadwick's earlier muse overture, the comic *Thalia*, was not to be taken as a solemn work of art, but *Melpomene* offers the essence of gravity. As if to demonstrate visually its serious, classical orientation, Chadwick wrote its title on the manuscript cover page in Greek letters. It was plain that Chadwick had reached a new level of austerity in his music with this new overture.

This time Apthorp was pleased. He observed in the *Transcript* that the overture proved that Chadwick could compose music of consequence: "Not that [in it] he tries to curb his innate fondness for the romantic and the brilliantly effective . . . but that in spite of an occasional tendency toward the sensational, the music shows that he has looked deeper into human emotion and passion than ever before. More than this, he has plainly trusted less to that fatal facility of his, and has put more thought and real energy into his work."[90]

Much of *Melpomene*'s popularity has issued from the doleful opening measures, which instantly remind the listener of the first strokes of Wagner's Prelude to *Tristan und Isolde*. Chadwick begins his work with pensive solo statements in the English horn which then progress through a series of chords that resolve conventionally. Chadwick also created a gauzy, mysterious mood, heightened by pianissimo timpani rolls, subtle crescendi and diminuendi in the winds, and hushed pizzicato passages in the strings. Taken together, Chadwick has obviously constructed a composition that owes a debt to Wagner, although perhaps not a huge one. One of the more interesting assessments of *Melpomene* comes from musicologist E. Douglas Bomberger, who analyzed it in light of Harold Bloom's theory of poetic influence. Bomberger writes that Bloom's theory "involves the notion that poets in the modern era . . . are oppressed by a sense of belatedness, brought on by 'the embarrassments of a tradition grown too wealthy to need anything more.' The tradition is more than a rich source of inspiration; it is a burden that leads weaker poets to imitate their predecessors or despair of writing anything original."[91] Applied to Chadwick, the theory suggests that Wagner's greatness inspired Chadwick while at the same time paralyzing him to some extent.

Chadwick's opening measures recall Wagner's in instrumentation, harmony, melodic contour, and mood. Additionally, *Melpomene*'s relationship to Wagner is confirmed when Chadwick writes at the end of his manuscript "Vorhang fällt!!!" [curtain falls], a humorous counterpoint to Wagner's instructions at the end of his *Tristan* prelude, "Der Vorhang geht auf" [curtain rises]. Beyond these similarities, there are few Wagnerian elements. Nevertheless, portions of the overture offer important insights into Chadwick's own development as a composer. For example, the leitmotifs that Chadwick used to generate this overture demonstrate an understanding of the organic process. He had already experimented with motivic generation and its possibilities for building a complete work in three movements in his Second Symphony, where the motivic cells predominantly are used to give the themes their similar shapes. In *Melpomene* the technique was applied assiduously, not with motives but with longer melodic strains, and more conscientiously—nearly every measure of the work bears a relationship to its two opening ideas. Our preoccupation with Wagner's influence on *Melpomene* has hampered the full appreciation of Chadwick's novel and effective approach to its construction.

Although the overture is plainly based on sonata form, Chadwick has taken

TABLE 5.3. The Form of *Melpomene*

	Introduction		Exposition							Development	Recapitulation		Coda
Part:			I							II			
Section:			1						2	3	4		
Theme:	O1	O2	P	T1	T2	T3	T4	S			P/T2	S	T3/O1
Key:	d		d					F		f		D	
Measure:	1	18	31	62	80	92	114	131		148	245	294	312

several liberties that contribute to its sometimes unsettling, but ultimately satisfactory, countenance (see table 5.3).

Two short opening themes (O1 and O2)—the first a torturous, ascending theme that moves from piano to fortissimo in short order; the second a pastoral *tranquillo* melody—establish its D-minor tonality and provide fodder for the rest of the composition. The principal theme (P) is a heart-pounding and tumultuous revel marked Allegro agitato. Four distinct transitional areas (T1, T2, T3, and T4) take the music to the gentle contrasting theme (S), also marked *tranquillo*, and now in the key of F major. The development section, one rich in counterpoint, is based on the main theme. It is perhaps surprising that Chadwick would elect to include in a composition ostensibly inspired by Wagner a segment of academic fugue that Wagner, by the 1880s, would have abhorred. What could be farther away from music drama and *Zukunftsmusik* ("music of the future") than Chadwick's dense counterpoint? Clearly Chadwick was not too concerned or "anxious" about Wagner's influence over him. On the contrary, Chadwick took Wagner's unresolved effort and finished it off. The fugue leads to another brief portion that presents the principal and the second transitional melody in combination. This will be the last time we hear the principal theme, and its appearance is rather weak, especially as it shares space with the brassy transitional theme. Nevertheless, it is the closest Chadwick comes to offering a recapitulation. Following the reappearance of the secondary theme firmly in the new key, D major, a long coda comes to a turgid close. The overture ends in a dark, pensive mood, but one that is slightly less ominous than previously on account of its major tonality.

Gericke loved *Melpomene*, although Chadwick later reported that the conductor requested changes. Chadwick reflected that "Gericke was really worse than Rheinberger as a hide bound pedant," when it came to requiring conformance to certain models of composition.[92] Chadwick seems to have complied, and—in a move perhaps more political than affectionate—he dedicated the overture to the conductor. Gericke led the work several times, including its premiere performances in December 1887, and again the next concert season, in March 1889. *Melpomene* was also heard during several BSO tours of the northeast US.

American conductor Frank van der Stucken got hold of the score and performed *Melpomene* at least twice, once with New York's Arion Society in 1888, and again at the Exposition Universelle in Paris in 1889. Following Gericke's 1889 performance one critic reported that at its premiere "it at once made the impression of being the strongest work the composer had yet given to the public." The latest rendering, the writer related, "made a doubly fine impression."[93] When A. P. Schmidt published the score in 1891, performances of the overture began to proliferate.

Melpomene was by far the most frequently performed of Chadwick's works during his lifetime. Its success stood in stark contrast to Chadwick's dismal experience with his Second Symphony. Following the Symphony's publication in 1888, also under the aegis of Schmidt, it had a grand total of two performances, in 1891 and in 1893; it would remain virtually forgotten until it was revived in the 1920s. *Melpomene*, on the other hand, benefitted from Boston's current appetite for Wagner, as well as Chadwick's deft blending of Wagner-influenced melody and instrumentation with a musical form that was digestible to American audiences. Chadwick found an artistic way to reconcile two competing aesthetic paradigms. In doing so, he created one of the great monuments of American music literature.

Other Works from the Late 1880s

Just over a year before the completion of *Melpomene*, in June 1886, Chadwick composed his odd little "song and overture," *The Miller's Daughter*. Featuring words by Alfred Lord Tennyson, from his well-known *The Lady of Shalott and Other Poems* (1832), the composition is for baritone accompanied by pairs of woodwinds, four horns, two trumpets, and strings. *The Miller's Daughter* was appreciated for its treatment of a then-familiar poem, and some critics were enthusiastic. At its New York premiere one writer thought it "most ingenious and musical," primarily because in it Chadwick quoted from Mendelssohn's "Wedding March."[94] Others, including the writer for the *Boston Evening Transcript*, thought that "one may pass over his *Miller's Daughter* in silence."[95] Philip Hale was even more forthright. After establishing that Chadwick's themes "are not happily invented," and that the work suffered in both development and instrumentation, he succinctly stated, "In a word, the work is dull."[96] Never published, it has been heard only three times, in 1887, 1890, and 1892.

Following *Melpomene*, Chadwick returned to a more intimate form. Although there seemed to be little reason to compose a chamber work—by this point he had accumulated but a handful of performances of his three string quartets—he nevertheless completed the Quintet for Piano and Strings on October 28, 1887, in the cozy confines of the St. Botolph Club. This was less than one month after he had put the finishing touches on the score of *Melpomene*. The decision to produce a work that included piano may have simply begun with the wish to finally write something substantial for that instrument. Although he was a respected organist, Chadwick had never been an accomplished pianist; it was a source of mild embarrassment for him throughout his life. A number of prominent Boston composers were also respected pianists, and many local organists were more technically adept than him, if not more musical. Although Chadwick recalled that "once in Leipzig I managed to wiggle through Mendelssohn's B minor capriccio with the [conservatory] orchestra," beyond that experience and a few youthful piano compositions, he showed little interest in the instrument.[97] Another time he remarked with evident jealousy that Edward MacDowell had enjoyed the considerable advantage of having started his keyboard training at an early age. MacDowell's gifts on the piano had given him a substantial leg up on other American composers, partly because he could play his own compositions, including especially his two Piano Concertos (1884 and 1890), which still garner the occasional performance. To improve his own situation, Chadwick began to take lessons with B. J. Lang, for which he practiced diligently. He was determined to perform his Quintet at its premiere with the Kneisel Quartet, and he did so with considerable pride on January 23, 1888, at Chickering Hall.

The quintet is, in fact, Chadwick's major composition for the piano, but it failed to find a position in the repertoire of Chadwick's day, undoubtedly on account of its inclusion of the piano. The three string quartets were at least portable—that is, they could easily be performed by a traveling string ensemble. The addition of a piano to the mix almost ensured that the Quintet would receive few performances, and indeed that was the case. Following its premiere there is evidence of only five more performances between 1890 and 1930; only one of those occurred outside Boston.

The quintet's dedicatees, violinist Gustave Dannreuther and his wife, seem to have been ambivalent about the quintet. Dannreuther had been a student of the great Joseph Joachim in Europe, and had even played in the BSO briefly. In 1884, while in New York, he formed the Beethoven String Quartette, which he later renamed the Dannreuther String Quartette. Shortly after the publication of Chadwick's Quintet, Dannreuther got into a heated argument with the publisher, A. P. Schmidt. At issue was Dannreuther's inability—or more likely his refusal—to pay for the published version of the music. Chadwick implored Schmidt to send Dannreuther a complimentary copy, but Schmidt refused—

Dannreuther, he argued, should buy the music like everyone else. Although we cannot be sure, it seems that Dannreuther decided against the purchase, and therefore against a performance of a composition that is dedicated to him. At this writing, there is no evidence that the Dannreuther group ever performed Chadwick's Quintet.

One of Chadwick's last hurrahs with the Boston Orchestral Club was a performance of his ballad for chorus and orchestra, *Lovely Rosabelle* (1889), based on Scott's *Lay of the Last Minstrel* (1805). He dedicated the work to the chorus and orchestra of the club and premiered it with them on December 10, 1889, in Association Hall. Chadwick was apparently fond of the piece, for he was eager to share it with Parker, to whom he wrote, "I have been too devilish[ly] busy to write letters, but have managed to knock out a short ballad for chorus and orch. which I shall be glad to turn loose on you."[98] *Lovely Rosabelle* garnered only a few more performances, but the critics were mostly generous toward its gentle melody and lithe orchestration. Henry Hadley was an admirer of the ballad. He reminisced, "[Chadwick] had fine taste and sure judgement and always chose the richest, the most expressive colors from his musical palette. I well remember the beauty of a certain passage in his 'Lovely Rosabelle' . . . which he had just then published. He had adroitly combined the low quality of the altos of the chorus with the high register of the tenors, and by thus blending them to the text in unison, he produced a passage with a peculiarly ghost-like, unearthly effect—a very impressive and indescribably beautiful one."[99] Chadwick sold the publishing rights to Schmidt, but he later admitted that was probably a mistake, figuring that the Novello firm might have exerted more effort to sell it. Nevertheless, Chadwick always found this ballad endearing—"it is not only easy and practical, but it has character."[100]

The Pilgrims, a work for chorus and orchestra based on Felicia Hemans's patriotic text, occupied part of 1889. Chadwick had begun the piece as an exercise for his fugue class at NEC. He also busily worked on two orchestral miniatures during the summer of 1890, possibly for use by the Orchestral Club, although he had resigned following that year's spring series pleading that he was too busy to continue his conducting duties. The *Serenade in F* for string orchestra was inspired by a similar work by Victor Herbert and bears a dedication to the St. Louis Musical Club, where it was premiered. Chadwick originally conceived the *Serenade* for strings, but he briefly considered adding winds. "Nobody wants to let all the wind and brass twirl their thumbs by themselves for half an hour while the strings play alone," he wrote, before deciding to leave well enough alone.[101] *Pastoral Prelude* was also completed in 1890. Intended to "suggest a June morning with all the birds singing at once," it is dedicated to

Horatio Parker and scored for a small orchestra of piccolo, pairs of woodwinds, an English horn, four horns, two trumpets, timpani, and strings.[102] Arthur Nikisch, who had taken over the mantle of the orchestra from Gericke in 1889, conducted it with the BSO in the winter of 1892. It was generally thought that Nikisch did much to widen the scope of the BSO's repertoire, but that he did not improve the orchestra. And while amiable, he did little to bolster the cause of American music. For his *Prelude*, Chadwick borrowed from William Wordsworth its preambular line, "Feel the gladness of the May," although the piece is surprisingly unpastoral. This was pointed out by the *Transcript* writer who observed "here we have a bright, lively, chattering movement, full enough of a certain rusticity . . . but in no wise suggestive of that peaceful repose."[103]

Songs & Choruses, Fairs & Festivals
Chadwick & America's Vocal Traditions
1890s

And now we dare claim for America that today she stands
foremost as a land of vocal music, her choral organizations
and resources standing pre-eminent.
— F. N. S., "American Choral Societies" (1872)

The Springfield Festival (1890–1899)

The 1890s have long held a special place in the popular imagination of Americans. The decade has been variously termed the "Gay Nineties," the "Mauve Decade," and the "Reckless Decade." Mark Twain cynically called the last quarter of the nineteenth century "the Gilded Age," while literary critic and historian Van Wyck Brooks optimistically designated the entire period from 1885 to 1915 the "Confident Years."[1] Chadwick might well have called it the "Choral Decade," for he reached the pinnacle of his choral experience when, in August 1889, he was elected to head up the Hampden County Musical Association's Springfield Festival. He would spend much of the rest of the decade engaged in the hot pursuit of choral excellence at one of New England's best festivals.

Chadwick had been associated with organized choral groups since his youth. Whether at family gatherings, or at Oliver High School; whether leading small groups at Olivet College, or performing in Leipzig's Concordia Singing Society; running Boston's Arlington Club or Salem's Schubert Club; or conducting various church ensembles, choral work was a central and ongoing aspect of Chadwick's musical life. But Springfield held a promise that many of his earlier endeavors did not. Nestled in the Connecticut Valley in central western Massachusetts, Springfield was a city that appreciated the arts and did not to have the bias to foreign conductors that was irritatingly prevalent in Boston. In fact, Springfield embraced the notion of an American leader. Additionally, it was a musically sophisticated city. Incorporated in 1852 and with fewer than forty-five thousand inhabitants when Chadwick arrived, Springfield boasted musical clubs that could rival Boston's in enthusiasm if not in quality.

Springfield's instrumental organizations included the Orchestral Club, an ensemble that commingled amateurs and professionals to give regular concert series. The beloved Little Brass Band, often no more than a sextet, achieved local acclaim because it "furnished the music for the roller-skating rink." And the Coenen Orchestra, named for its visionary leader Louis Coenen, enjoyed a popularity that few groups could match. Coenen had arrived in Springfield in 1865 and began his career as a composer, violinist, organist, and choirmaster, but he found his stride as an organizer of events. One writer noted that "Springfield probably owes more to him than to any other person for untiring efforts to raise the standard of musical taste in the city."[2]

The popularity of choral music surpassed even that of instrumental music. Zuchtmann's Conservatory of Music, run by Frederick Zuchtmann (1829?– 1909), "one of the leading local instructors in vocal music and the culture of the voice," aimed to impart to the masses the pleasures of singing, while the Spring- field Tonic Sol Fa Association endeavored to educate residents by "conduct- ing institutes, singing-classes, and musical instruction" throughout the town's school system. The Orpheus Club was "devoted to the study and singing of male part-songs," while a more inclusive Handel Chorus—with as many as 125 participants of both sexes—included "carefully selected and cultured singers for performances of oratorios and other important choral works."[3] The Handel Chorus, with its popular Connecticut Valley Musical Association annual festi- vals, formed the basis of the Springfield Festivals.

Chadwick initially was engaged only for the upcoming season to include the traditional December performance of *The Messiah* and the next three-day festival in May 1890, "the managers preferring to retain the right to select the concert director when the time comes."[4] For his efforts, rehearsals as well as performances, he was to be paid five hundred dollars. The board members of the association had good reason to keep Chadwick on a short leash during his first season; the May Festivals, as they were often called, had only been initi- ated in 1888, under the direction of the veteran conductor Carl Zerrahn and Zuchtmann, who was "retiring" after a single year. Zuchtmann had impressive local credentials, having served as a local public-school music supervisor and as an instructor at Amherst College, but he lacked both the musical ability and the celebrity needed to bring wide attention to the festival. If the board had been unhappy with the efforts of Zuchtmann, it certainly would not have wished immediately to retain another director for the long term.

In any event, the association's chiefs were ebullient about Chadwick and his prospects for success, for he was regarded as "the coming man" in American music at the time, and "the action of the [festival] officers is likely to place the association in the front rank of musical organizations in New England."[5] Chadwick accepted the opportunity not only to hone his skills as an organizer, programmer, and conductor, but also as a composer. We should remember that, at this time, Chadwick was still a humble church organist and harmony teacher, who lectured part-time to students at NEC and led his own studio of private students—only some of whom were pursuing composition. The Springfield Festival would be by far the most important post he had held up to now. Besides conducting, Chadwick would be expected to bring in high-caliber guest artists and elevate the quality of the festival orchestra, which included the likes of concertmaster Emil Mollenhauer and Victor Herbert, who, in addition to being the principal cellist, was Chadwick's associate conductor. An additional inducement, if one was needed, was the excellent prospect he would have to produce his own works for chorus and orchestra.

During the early 1890s, Chadwick spent a large portion of his time composing smaller works: sacred and secular songs and choruses, as well as studies and occasional pieces for piano and organ. These were compositions that had the benefit of practicality—not only could Chadwick make use of them when teaching, but they were also attractive to amateur singers. Choral works such as "Art Thou Weary," "Autumn Winds are Chill," "God Be Merciful," "Love is Fleeting as the Wind," and "My Sweetheart Gave a Crimson Blossom" are not overly long and proved suitable to schools, singing societies and clubs, and churches. That made them attractive to publishers and, therefore, capable of generating for Chadwick an added stream of income. Chadwick had learned from his recent experience that expansive compositions, while wonderful for one's reputation and ego, did little for the wallet. Big works also occupied an enormous amount of time. Although his Second Symphony had been published, his other major works—*Rip Van Winkle* Overture and the First Symphony, to name two—remained in manuscript. Chadwick realized this, but was not prepared to bypass the chance to compose for his new Springfield group. Any hesitation was undoubtedly tempered in part by his knowledge that compositions for chorus and orchestra could easily be reduced to piano-vocal versions, which made them much more attractive to publishers.

Phoenix expirans (1891)

One of the earliest fruits borne from Chadwick's Springfield position was the cantata *Phoenix expirans* (The Dying Phoenix) for soloists, chorus, and orchestra with organ. The cantata borrows a text attributed to William Alard (1572–1645), which was included in Richard Chevenix Trench's 1849 volume, *Sacred Latin Poetry*.[6] *Phoenix expirans* proved to be among Chadwick's most popular sacred choral works, mostly owing to Schmidt's piano/organ-vocal score, brought out swiftly on the heels of its completion. It contains many features that lend themselves to widespread popularity among singing groups: at thirty minutes the piece is not unbearably long; the choral writing is approachable by associations of modest ability, there being surprisingly little contrapuntal activity; the solo parts are not too numerous and are similarly singable; and the problems of retaining orchestral accompaniment are ameliorated by Chadwick's judicious keyboard reduction. Chadwick recognized that one of the biggest problems that performers of the cantata might face would be its Latin text. Not only was the Latin language losing influence in American society, but among New England Protestant congregations, who were Chadwick's audiences and his performers, its use might have smacked of "popery" at a time when the Catholic faith raised suspicions chiefly due to its close relationship with the Irish population.

Phoenix expirans was begun and completed within the month of August 1891. It was premiered at the Springfield Festival on May 5, 1892, with the composer leading the festival orchestra. Among the singers was tenor Max Heinrich, who would become a leading proponent of Chadwick's vocal music. Chadwick dedicated *Phoenix expirans* to the Springfield Festival and scored it for a substantial orchestra: pairs of woodwinds, brass including four horns, two trumpets, and three trombones, timpani, organ, and strings. The choral forces are also substantial, as it requires soprano, alto, tenor and bass (SATB) soloists and an SATB chorus. Lucien Hosmer, one of Chadwick's most devoted students and a competent composer in his own right, copied the orchestra score, while the parts were completed by Frank Fiala, who would remain Chadwick's go-to copyist for the next twenty-five years.

Phoenix expirans is presented in five carefully designed movements (see table 6.1), although the poem itself is in six stanzas.

Looking at the score, one senses Chadwick's increased assuredness, especially in his writing for the orchestra. Harmonic progressions are confident, instrumental combinations are intelligent, and the overall effect is thrilling. His setting of Latin was less successful, for he was not fluent in the language, and he had only experimented with it once before. Nevertheless, several portions are striking: the feathery textures of the second movement deserve a hearing; the utilization of only clarinets, bassoons, strings, and vocalists in the canonic first section of the third number is masterful; and the thunderous final chorus, with its extended fugato, would undoubtedly be appreciated by modern audiences.

Phoenix expirans generated considerable local excitement; the *Springfield Daily Republican* critic even made a point of attending at least one rehearsal. Following its performance he sensed that Chadwick had "absorbed the devotional feeling of the Christian poet" and that the composition demonstrated "a comprehensive knowledge of both voices and instruments."[7] After noting the sparse counterpoint, critic Philip Hale, who had made the journey from Boston

TABLE 6.1. The Structure of *Phoenix expirans*

Section number	type	key	title
No. 1	Chorus	g	"Amore vulneror" ("Wounded with love I lie")
No. 2	Solo—Chorus	E-flat	"Fulcite floribus" ("Let flowers their strength impart")
No. 3	Quartet	A-flat	"An amor dolor sit" ("If love pain may be")
No. 4	Chorus	c/C	"Quid amor crucias?" ("Why love dost thou torment?")
No. 5	Chorus	G	"Jam vitae flumina" ("Burst through thy bonds, O soul!")

to Springfield, concluded that, in addition to "melodic expression," the harmonies are "often exceedingly happy, and here and there a return to Gregorian tonality lends churchly dignity."[8] Hale bluntly stated that the cantata "deserves the attention of any choral society of pretension."[9] Louis C. Elson agreed. He found *Phoenix expirans* "fresh and lovely in melody, dignified and consistent in conception, delicate and rich in orchestral scoring, and warm and churchly in its harmonies." Indeed, Elson thought this composition "the finest fruit of [Chadwick's] genius."[10]

Chadwick was duly impressed by his own creation. When the Handel and Haydn Society performed it in 1913, he immodestly observed, "this piece must have been ahead of its time when it was made."[11]

The World's Columbian Exposition and Chadwick's *Columbian Ode* (1892)

Two months before the premiere of *Phoenix expirans*, in February 1892, Chadwick was called on in Boston by his boyhood friend, George H. Wilson. A native of Lawrence and one of Chadwick's classmates at Oliver High School, Wilson had since made a name for himself in music journalism, writing reviews for the *Boston Traveller* while also laboring at Boston's Custom House, where copious numbers of cargo ships destined for the city's ports were inspected and registered. Following a stint with the *Boston Post*, he was also responsible for the "musical yearbooks" that had been produced in that city since 1884. Wilson had written program notes in the early years of the Boston Symphony Orchestra, but more recently, in 1891, he had purchased Tourjée's *Boston Musical Herald*.[12] Now living in Chicago, Wilson was in the employ of the World's Columbian Exposition Company as secretary of the Music Bureau. The company was the producing organization of what would be one of the most successful World's Fairs in history.

Wilson was something akin to the private secretary of Theodore Thomas, who had been elected the fair's music director. He was responsible for assisting in what promised to be one of the greatest music spectacles in America in decades, perhaps the greatest since Gilmore's jubilees. Wilson visited Chadwick to offer him a commission for a work that would be performed at the "dedication of the buildings" ceremonies in Chicago in October, 1892, just eight short months away. This was a huge opportunity for Chadwick, for it would place him in a musical constellation that included, besides Thomas, composers John Knowles Paine, Dudley Buck, and John Philip Sousa, each of whom would also compose music for the fair. Chadwick accepted Wilson's offer. The result, his *Ode for the Opening of the World's Fair held at Chicago, 1892*, or *Columbian Ode*, is a work for massive forces, but is brief at only twenty minutes. The *Ode* would become the most important commission of Chadwick's early career, even if the enterprise proved one of the more trying episodes of his musical life.

At the end of the 1880s, the cities of Washington, St. Louis, New York, and Chicago each vied for the opportunity to host the World's Columbian Exposition, under the sanction of the United States Congress. Scheduled to open in 1892, the Exposition would celebrate the four hundredth anniversary of Christopher Columbus's discovery of the New World. Chicago was eager to win the bid; city fathers quickly formed a 250-man committee and raised five million dollars—and later an additional five million dollars—by the issuance of company "stock" to lay the groundwork for what promised to be a spectacular event. The organizers sought to celebrate the anniversary "by holding an international exposition of arts, industries, manufactures, and products of the soil, mine and sea."[13] Chicago had a number of things going for it. Being nearly in the geographical dead center of the US, and with dozens of railroad lines leading directly into the city, it promised to lure throngs of people. And, still considered a "western" town, Chicago had the additional advantage of being somewhat exotic to those in the east whose travel experience had never extended beyond the Allegheny Mountains. More practically, Chicago—unlike New York—had plenty of vacant land needed to produce such a grandiose event; and it also had—unlike St. Louis—ample hotel accommodations for the expected thousands of fairgoers.

Congress conferred upon Chicago the right to hold the exposition, and President Benjamin Harrison signed the measure into law on April 25, 1890. The Exposition Company quickly set about forming committees to oversee everything from finance and transportation to fine arts and "machinery and electrical appliances." When all was said and done, two and a half years of frantic preparation led to dignified dedication ceremonies in October 1892, followed by the actual opening of the Exposition to the general public in May 1893, amid bad weather and an approaching financial panic.

Expositions of the day attempted to put on display the world's progress in all fields, and Chicago's was no less ambitious. States, nations, races, creeds, professions, and pursuits of every imaginable cast were celebrated with their own special days. Among them were "Stenographers' Day" (July 22); "Colored Peoples' Day" (August 25); and "Carriagemakers' Day" (October 5). Five consecutive days, September 4–8, were dedicated to the International Eisteddfod, a celebration of music and poetry derived from Welsh bardic tradition. Although attendance lagged below the initial forecasts, the Exposition was generally deemed a success.

Congress had by law set the closing day to be Monday, October 30, 1893 — Columbus Day — and Chicago intended to produce a jubilee that would not soon be forgotten. But two days before the closing, on October 28, the city was shaken when Carter H. Harrison Sr., mayor of Chicago, was assassinated at his home. Naturally, the spirit of the day's activities was dampened. Harrison was an admired politician who had served as mayor for most of the 1880s and had just been re-elected earlier that year; most agreed that the exposition could not have been secured for Chicago without his untiring leadership. Columbus Day 1893 turned out to be one of mourning. As the Exposition drew to a close that day, stragglers stayed until the array of flags, at half-mast since the shooting, were taken down and carefully folded. "Many of those who witnessed this simple act could not restrain tears of sorrow for the sad ending of the glorious Exposition."[14]

A weary H. N. Higinbotham, president of the Exposition Company board of directors, acknowledged the trauma that attended Harrison's assassination. Later he could more accurately assess the import of the event in its full measure, despite the tragedy. In his final report, Higinbotham saluted the wonder of the Exposition, its inclusiveness, and its representation of human advancement. "An exposition," he wrote, "is the apotheosis of civilization, in which all that is beautiful, useful, wonderful, or for any reason attractive, must play its part."[15]

Chadwick's *Columbian Ode* was to set to a poem by Harriet Monroe, a poet of renown in the Midwest and formerly a *Chicago Tribune* music and arts critic. Monroe was regarded in some circles as a malcontent and an opportunist. When she learned that the fair's artistic offerings did not include poetry, she lobbied one of the governing councils and secured for herself a commission to write an ode to be read at the dedication ceremonies.[16] But Monroe struggled to deliver her poem on time. This gave some members of the selection committee—those who had been less susceptible to her arm-twisting—second thoughts about Monroe's qualifications. Her health problems gave them an opening to ask questions about whether she could deliver the *Ode* in time for its recitation on October 21, 1892, at the "dedication of buildings ceremony." That date was intended primarily to summon publicity, for the fair did not officially open until well into the next year, and in fact many of the structures being "dedicated" in 1892 were little more than scaffold.

Adding to Monroe's irritation was the always controversial issue of copyright. Without Monroe's permission, the *New York World* obtained a nearly complete version—albeit a draft—of her *Ode* and printed it in the September 25, 1892, issue. How the newspaper obtained the poem is a mystery, but Monroe was livid, and the *World*'s piracy created a minor scandal. Since the dedication and the performance of the *Ode* were closing in quickly, Monroe had little choice but to put the episode behind her—for the time being.[17] When at last the committee decided that Monroe's *Ode* would be featured at the exposition, she was asked to recite it herself, but deferred to the suggestions that the respected New York actress Sarah Cowell LeMoyne—"six feet tall, handsome and vocally magnificent"—deliver the lines with some of its stanzas set to music.[18] There is no indication that Monroe had a say in the matter of who would set her *Ode* to music.

For his part, Chadwick was enthusiastic about the project, and he determined to make music that would befit this historic event. He began the eventual 103-page score on May 17, 1892, and completed it less than two months later, on July 10, while summering in Hingham, Massachusetts. Chadwick requested a mid-July meeting with Thomas at his home in Fairhaven. There they discussed the *Ode* in detail, and Chadwick made a number of alterations to his score based on Thomas's suggestions, although we do not know the specifics of the changes. Chadwick wrote for a standard full orchestra supplemented by piccolo, English horn, contrabassoon, four percussion, and harp. Monroe's words would emanate from soprano and tenor soloists and a double SATB chorus. Most intriguing is Chadwick's addition to the orchestra of three military bands ("to the north," "to the south," and "to the east") for which he employed all manner of brass, saxophones, and percussion. To at least one critic, Chadwick's compositional plan conjured up shades of Berlioz.[19]

Chadwick had his own problems with copyright. The contract he signed with the fair commission explicitly stated that the fair had a right to the first performance, but not to the music itself. Unknown to Chadwick, however, fair officials printed copies of the piano-vocal score to sell to the participating choristers. This left Cincinnati's J. Church Publishing Company, the firm with which Chadwick had already arranged to publish the *Ode*, in the lurch. Chadwick deemed it "a matter of flagrant injustice" that the fair pirated his music; not only did it rob Chadwick of potential royalties, but it also exposed him to a lawsuit from Church.[20] For Chadwick, the inducement for joining the fair was twofold: he wished to be in the lofty musical company headed up by Thomas, but he also fully intended to reap a financial benefit through publishing royalties. This event alone promised the sale of hundreds, if not thousands, of copies of his music.

Monroe's lengthy poem charts a voyage from the Old World to the New in three stages: departure, journey, and arrival. Chadwick's *Ode* is similarly constructed in three movements. The first, to the words "Over the wide unknown," begins with a rhythmically vibrant instrumental introduction in C major (Allegro moderato). Chadwick utilized fanfare flourishes and agitated passages in the instrumental parts, but the chorus parts are obstinately homorhythmic. Not only does the music evoke the ocean's vastness by cleverly using musical space, but Chadwick astutely understood that his music would be performed in a mammoth venue which would make homorhythm essential. Perhaps his experiences at Gilmore's jubilee served him well here. "Columbia, Men Behold Thee," Chadwick's second movement, reflects the passage across the Atlantic to the New World. Solos by the tenor and soprano, as well as a soprano/alto duet, provide the narrative, and Chadwick created another spatial leap when, at "Now let the sun ride high o'er head," the music transitions from the tonic A-flat major to the distant E major. The final portion, "Clasp hands as brothers 'neath Columbia's shield," is also powerfully homorhythmic. Small note values, the composer knew, simply would not be heard by the audience in the enormous performance space, and perhaps not even by the musicians sitting on opposite sides of the stage. Besides, there would be precious little time for the chorus to learn intricate passages. Instead Chadwick created contrast by tempo, harmony, meter, and vocal variety (i.e., solos vs. full chorus). The *Ode* comes to a robust conclusion, Maestoso assai, on the words, "Along her blessed, blessed shore, one heart, one song, one dream."

Most critics panned the venue. The writer for the *Springfield Graphic*, who attended the fair, remarked that Chadwick must be proud of his music "even if no one could hear a note or distinguish a word of it in the great building."[21] W. S. B. Mathews, the illustrious Chicago critic, was dispirited by the treatment of American composers generally, but especially Chadwick, at the fair. "It [the

Ode] was rendered and paid for," Mathews remarked, but he doubted whether Chadwick "got much information as to the success or non-success of his work from witnessing the performance."[22]

Despite the problems composers faced at the fair, Monroe's memory of the dedication ceremony fifty years later was generally favorable:

> I remember the warm sunshine streaking through the newly glazed roof on the vast audience and kindling to splendor the reds, blues, greens, of the gay costumes of women. Every little while there was applause in the audience, music in the band at one end of the hall, and a flutter of white in the chorus at the other end, as some distinguished person or group entered and was recognized—governors of states, foreign ambassadors in grand array. There was no chance to be bored before, at last, at eleven o'clock, the audience hushed as the program began with Professor Paine's "Columbian March" and a prayer, followed by the Director General's introductory address, and a welcome from [former] Mayor Washburne, granting freedom of the city to the distinguished visitors from Washington and across the sea.
>
> The "Columbian Ode" came next on the program, and Mrs. LeMoyne, statuesque and beautiful, looked like a queen as she advanced to the front of the platform and recited her lines. Her voice traveled farther than any other on that day unblest with microphones, and the signals worked perfectly, so that the chorus rose promptly to the two songs, "Over the wide unknown" and "Lo, clan on clan," and thrilled us with the beauty of Mr. Chadwick's music as it rolled from end to end of the great hall."[23]

The poem itself was not the success Monroe had hoped for. She commissioned a "pamphlet edition" which she sold at a quarter apiece, but Monroe found her vendors unenthusiastic—in her words, "unresponsive"—and unwilling to exert effort to promote the poem. Monroe later lamented, "So all winter I used the ode for fuel in the little stove which heated my bedroom-study in the large old-fashioned house where our double family lived. . . . I well remember the emotions between laughter and tears . . . which came over me every time I stuffed that stove."[24] A later, handsomer "souvenir edition" of her ode was also commercially unsuccessful. Monroe naturally, and perhaps correctly, blamed poor sales on the fact that it had been illegally pirated and given away for free by the *World*. But she would have her revenge. Monroe sued the Press Publishing Company, the *World*'s parent company, in 1896 for twenty-five thousand dollars. She stipulated in court that she not only suffered monetary damages, but also "shame, mortification and great personal annoyance." Monroe was awarded $5,000.[25]

Chadwick's memories of the fair's dedication were mixed. The venue was too big to get a valid assessment of his music, and the sales of the published music and the number of subsequent performances was a disappointment. He could not afford to attend the actual exposition the next year, although several of his compositions—*Melpomene*, the Second Symphony, and the Finale of the *Ode*—were performed. Nevertheless, he was happy to receive a specially struck gold medal to commemorate the event. "Mine was used for several years for the boys"—his two sons—"to roll on the floor," Chadwick recalled.[26] The medal remains in the possession of his family and heirs.

For Thomas, the exposition ended disastrously. The orchestra operations were disbanded in early August 1893—nearly twelve weeks early—after months of ill-will between Thomas and the organizers. Never one to put up with having a boss, a combative Thomas had been a thorn in the side of management nearly from the start. If Chadwick's copyright calamity were not enough, Thomas had earlier skirted the rules of exposition sponsorship by allowing performances on a piano that was not an "official" instrument brand of the exposition. Shortly after this unpleasant discovery, exposition leaders began to find many faults with Thomas's classical music enterprise: audiences at the concerts—who in most cases had paid an additional admission fee—were small; programs were "too severely classical"; and they failed to reflect "the spirit and the animation" that was conspicuous elsewhere on the fairgrounds.[27] Perhaps not wishing to bad-mouth classical music, the board's executive committee used the pretense of cutting costs to ouster Thomas; it was, they flatly stated, simply too expensive to maintain an orchestra. But clearly the money was there. The exposition's run, from May to October, had netted nearly eleven million dollars.[28]

Tabasco (1894)

Chadwick spent the latter part of 1893 working on *Tabasco*, a "burlesque opera" with a libretto by Robert Ayres Barnet. Their collaboration was part of an effort to raise funds to help Boston's fashionable First Corp of Cadets build a new armory. The cadets formed a unique institution in Boston's military and cultural history. Chartered in 1741, they were part of Massachusetts's pre-Revolutionary War volunteer militia and often attracted the city's most prominent young men, many of whom were Harvard graduates. John Hancock, a celebrated signer of the Declaration of Independence, was once a commander of the First Corps. But as their utility as a military brigade faded, the cadets became a sort of hybrid military and social organization, not unlike the many other clubs that dotted Boston's landscape, although as the group became more social it stubbornly clung to the pretense of being a military organization. In the 1870s, leaders of the cadets determined to build a new armory, not only to replace the inadequate space that currently held their meetings, but also to symbolically guard the city against the recent wave of invaders whom they thought represented a dire threat to their society: the Irish. According to Barnet's biographer and great-granddaughter, Anne Alison Barnet, "There were reasons to build an armory other than the comfort of the prestigious First Corps. With the upsurge in immigration of the mid-1800s and the perceived threat of labor unrest and anarchism, Boston's Yankees had begun building fortresses."[29] The cadets' new armory was indeed a fortress. Begun in 1891, the huge granite edifice sits like a castle at the intersection of Arlington and Columbus Avenues. The prominent Boston architect William Gibbon Preston designed it to include such unnecessary features as watchtowers and even a drawbridge. By the time it was completed, in 1897, the cost was just short of a staggering seven hundred thousand dollars.[30]

To raise the money needed to build the armory, the cadets began to stage shows in 1890 (although they had flirted with the presentation of minstrel shows as early as 1884). Barnet wrote and produced *Injured Innocents*, an "operatic farce-tragedy," performed in 1890 and 1891, and *1492*, an "operatic extravaganza," which premiered in 1892. *Tabasco* was the third show Barnet had written for the group; he even performed in its premiere alongside the cadets, although he himself was not a member of the Corps. True to the style of such theatricals, the cadets performed both the male and the female roles; this of course accounts in part for the popularity of the shows.

Renowned for his ability to forge collaborations, Barnet, posthumously called the "Extravaganza King," probably asked Chadwick to contribute the music for *Tabasco* for the sport of it. It is possible that Barnet might also have hinted at the show's chances for future financial success. Chadwick, of course, had already enjoyed limited success for his theatrical efforts. In early 1883, he composed *The Peer and the Pauper* to a libretto by the prominent Boston attorney (soon to be a judge) and novelist Robert Grant. Although never performed, Chadwick used portions of *The Peer and the Pauper* in various later compositions—including *Tabasco*—for years. Chadwick's now-lost *A Quiet Lodging*, his second attempt for the comic stage, had been premiered in 1892 at Boston's private Tavern Club. An operetta—a farce really—in two acts, *A Quiet Lodging* featured characters with unlikely names like "Ariminta Blowbellow," "Maria Smutchbread," "Professor Erasmus Blowbellow," and the like. That work gave Chadwick a small taste of the bustling world of the stage; he had composed much of *A Quiet Lodging* on the train to Springfield, "and the whole thing was composed, rehearsed and performed in a month. A regular Rossini pace in fact."[31] Chadwick's student and NEC colleague Wallace Goodrich conducted two more performances of *A Quiet Lodging* in 1914, again for the Tavern Club, twenty two years after its premiere. While the location of the score was known as late as April 20, 1927, when it was performed for the final time, again under the auspices of the Tavern Club, it subsequently disappeared. *A Quiet Lodging* has yet to be recovered.

Barnet was a forward-thinking man. He generally attempted to craft his writings in such a manner that, following their performance with the amateur cadets, they could then appeal to a professional producer. The cadets began their five-day run of *Tabasco* on January 29, 1894, and filled the seats at Boston's Tremont Theatre, where the show earned a profit of $18,500 for the cadets to put toward their armory.[32] Shortly thereafter, Barnet's scheme to sell the show paid off. Producer E. E. Rice purchased the rights from Barnet and Chadwick, and quickly sold them to actor-comedian Thomas Quigley Seabrooke (1860–1913). An impresario himself, Seabrooke, who had legally changed his name from Thomas James Quigley in 1893, intended to take *Tabasco* on tour.

Seabrooke had made a reputation for himself in *The Cadi* (1891), and especially in *The Isle of Champagne* (1892), an enormously popular show that gave him a measure of clout in the business. His deal with *Tabasco*'s creators included script changes, for, as Chadwick annoyedly reported, "Seabrooke's part had to be fattened at any cost."[33] Chadwick seems to have surrendered to the changes without argument. Once Seabrooke's professional company had assembled, the whole group, which now included females, and Chadwick, moved to New London, Connecticut, for rehearsals that went on nearly around the clock for three days prior to the first performance on April 6, 1894, in Norwich, Connecticut. Following a second performance on April 7 in New London, the troupe returned to Boston, where performances commenced at the Boston Museum on April 9.

By and large, the casting delighted Chadwick; in addition to Seabrooke himself, it included Joseph F. Sheehan ("a stupid Irishman with a beautiful tenor voice"); Elvia Crox, who was Seabrooke's wife; Otis Harlan ("a much better actor than Seabrooke") and Walter Allen.[34] Chadwick was particularly impressed by the show's exemplary conductor, Paul Steindorff, a veteran of the stage who had previously led acclaimed performances of *The Charlatan* (1889) to music by John Philip Sousa. Chadwick's opinion of Seabrooke was another matter; he thought him "a stupid ass without any natural talent," although he had mastered the arts of the vaudeville stage. Seabrooke "had learned a lot of horseplay and silly tricks which he could put over on the average audience."[35] Chadwick was intensely curious about modern theatrics and the rising popularity of Broadway, but, as we have seen, his opinion of popular culture was low. If Chadwick's music is captivating and often memorable, *Tabasco*'s plot is little more than a rather thin vehicle on which to mount generally imbecilic jokes, visual gags, and double-entendre witticisms. There was no denying that Seabrooke's onstage antics garnered acclaim for *Tabasco*, a typical example of the vaudeville genre.

The inspiration for Barnet and Chadwick's *Tabasco* was the famous hot sauce, developed by Edmund McIlhenny, who started producing it in 1868 in Louisiana. Tabasco sauce was widely used throughout the United States by the mid-1870s, and it has maintained its popularity. The burlesque's story revolves around a ruler in Tangier, the Pasha, who is introduced to the condiment by Dennis, an Irish vagrant. The Pasha immediately becomes enamored with the sauce and rewards Dennis by promoting him to the position of household chef. Side plots develop, and a number of theatrical conventions are carried off by stock characters, including Fatima, a member of the Pasha's harem; Marco, the Spanish trader; and Lola, Marco's sister. The main thread of the story line involves the growing shortage of Tabasco sauce and the threats made to Dennis's safety by the Pasha if he does not procure more.

Although *Tabasco* is more a trifle than a masterpiece, one feature that lends it significance is its polyglot musical profile. For this work, Chadwick drew on a number of musical styles to create characters and promote the exotic. Hence, among its songs there is the plantation ballad, "O Darkies Don't Yer Member"; a Spanish "Bolero"; and the Irish-inspired "The Shamrock Blooms White." Although the music is not complex, it is quite sophisticated and generally well suited to its book. After spending valuable time in the creation of the music, Chadwick was happy to let his student Lucien Hosmer write the orchestrations.

The critical acclaim for Seabrooke's Boston performances ran high, as it had just nine weeks earlier when audiences flocked to the cadets' show. Chadwick reported that *Tabasco* "opened to a very swell and enthusiastic audience."[36] A writer for the *Transcript* noted that, although the dialogue had been considerably altered from its earlier version, "so far as the music is concerned there is very little change." He also remarked that "the vocal portions gain in effectiveness by the addition of female voices."[37] A *Boston Journal* critic noted that *Tabasco*'s "tuneful music, catchy songs, its costumes, its mirth, is nightly enjoyed by large audiences." According to this reviewer, "there is no intimation of its withdrawal" from the stage.[38]

Despite the *Journal*'s hopeful reporting, "the houses fell off after just a week" and Seabrooke looked to New York, where *Tabasco* opened at the Broadway Theatre just a month later, on May 14, 1894. The New York press was not as generous to Chadwick and Barnet as had been their hometown arbiters. The day after its premiere a *New York Times* writer flatly declared that "Mr. Chadwick's music does him no credit whatever."[39] *Tabasco* was nevertheless successful with audiences, and it played "well into the summer."[40] After forty-eight performances the final curtain fell on June 23. Seabrooke's version of *Tabasco* was not a smash hit, but it went off well enough to give him the idea of taking the show on the road. And if the burlesque did not add to Chadwick's fame as a serious composer—one loud voice of disappointment was Philip Hale, who, writing about the cadets' performance, declared that he would "reserve in a measure judgement until his work receives a more adequate performance"—at least he and Barnet could benefit from the modest extra income.[41]

Barnet and Chadwick did not venture on the road with Seabrooke and his troupe, and before long there was a noticeable slowdown in royalty payments. Barnet began to investigate the matter, and Chadwick was happy to let him do so. Eventually, collecting royalties became a near impossibility. The duo considered dispatching a representative to oversee Seabrooke and his shenanigans with their box office receipts, but in the end they estimated that that solution would cost them more than they stood to gain. Nonetheless, when Seabrooke boldly altered the plot and re-titled the show *The Grand Vizier* in an effort to escape the royalty payments altogether, Chadwick and Barnet were compelled to act.

Seabrooke's thievery was brazen. When *The Grand Vizier*—a purported "successor" to *Tabasco*—opened in New York at the Harlem Opera House in March 1895, very few missed its similarity to the original. Writing about the show's lead character, one critic observed, "Dennis O'Grady appears . . . as a wandering Irishman whose talisman is whisky instead of pepper sauce. Through whisky he secures the favor of a potentate, rank and fortune. He still sings 'Swim Out, O'Grady' [one of the biggest hits in *Tabasco*]. He is still irrepressibly dull [i.e., stupid]." The critic also reported that new words had been supplied by Edgar Smith, and that the music "is ascribed to" Frederick Gagel.[42]

Chadwick confided to a friend that "I anticipate a legal battle with Seabrooke which might require my presence."[43] Seabrooke in fact returned to Boston and was promptly jailed. "He finally escaped all responsibility by going into bankruptcy and taking the poor debtors oath," Chadwick recalled. "Not very long after this he died."[44] (Chadwick's facts here are not entirely correct. In 1898, Seabrooke filed in New York a "voluntary petition" for bankruptcy—he owed a hundred creditors a total of nearly forty thousand dollars. One reporter claimed that his assets at the time included only "a scarfpin."[45] Following years spent on the national vaudeville circuit, he died in Chicago on April 3, 1913.)

If the Seabrooke episode embittered Chadwick at the time, in later years he would reflect upon the whole adventure more philosophically; he would even consider it one of his great lessons in life. Besides, Chadwick enjoyed his brief brush with the theater, and of course there was some modest financial reward. Nevertheless, "It seemed a pity to waste practically a whole year's time on such unworthy stuff," he wrote. "But I have never regretted it."[46]

Chadwick seems to have been interested in another comic project at approximately the same time he took up *Tabasco*. He corresponded with the American author and poet Edgar Fawcett (1847–1904) about setting one of his works to music. Fawcett, a prolific and enormously popular writer in the 1880s and 1890s whose works included many bizarre and forward-looking themes, had written in 1885 the now obscure *The New King Arthur: An Opera without Music*. Contrary to its title, Chadwick hoped to turn it into an opera with music, for which Fawcett prepared a libretto. Fawcett remarked that *King Arthur*, "altho' surely not *opera comique*, it is not raw farce, and has been written with extreme care, believe me." Finally, Chadwick had discovered an appealing, competently crafted libretto by a celebrated author. He even saw something comparable to Wagner in the text, to which Fawcett responded, "I fear you over-rate my libretto. It seems to me that it is all burlesque. . . . I tried to make it respectable; but, ah, I fear the work itself is far more flippant in conception, far less serious and less *truly comedy*—than the libretto of the *Meistersinger*."[47] If Chadwick had designs on finally starting a "real opera," his hopes would soon be dashed. For reasons that are unclear, Fawcett lost interest and the project screeched to a halt.

Whether or not *Tabasco* was actually a waste is questionable. Certainly whatever Broadway fame Chadwick gained on its account was short-lived, but there is little doubt that his music should be considered, if not some of his best, at least his farthest reaching. Publisher B. F. Wood printed the piano-vocal score in 1894 (the year it premiered), as well as an arrangement for band titled *Tabasco March*, which also had been scored by Lucien Hosmer under Chadwick's close guidance. Chadwick sold the rights to the tune to B. F. Wood for a mere four hundred dollars; Wood went on to sell more than a hundred thousand copies, an astonishing number that did not benefit the composer financially in the slightest.[48] Several other band, orchestral, and even vocal versions of the *March* were retitled *The New Hail Columbia March*; they sold briskly throughout the 1890s. J. B. Claus arranged the tune for use by Sousa's band in 1894, and subsequent versions were prepared and published, in Berlin in 1899, and again by B. F. Wood in 1917. To these may be added a half dozen songs from *Tabasco* that were published individually.

The Lily Nymph (1895)

Although Chadwick's brush with vaudeville had not completely soured him, he was anxious to return to his comfort zone and a more dignified style of music. He had worked diligently in 1894 on his "dramatic cantata," *The Lily Nymph*, another in his series of collaborations with Boston novelist Arlo Bates. His preparation of the orchestra score, which was begun on November 5, was interrupted by the arrival of Noël Chadwick, his second son, on December 21.[49] In fact, Chadwick did little compositional work of any kind in the first six months of 1895 (besides making a few sketches) until the family made its annual pilgrimage to West Chop, on the island of Martha's Vineyard; once settled, he resumed his scoring. On the Fourth of July he worked from 9 a.m. to 6 p.m. on *The Lily Nymph*, "about the longest day's work I ever put in at one time. I never had the endurance of Parker or Hadley at writing notes."[50] He finished orchestrating *The Lily Nymph* on July 21.

The first performance of *The Lily Nymph* occurred on December 7 at New York's Carnegie Hall. It was led by Frank G. Dossert, leader of the New York Musical Society. *Tribune* critic Henry Krehbiel summarized Bates's story in program notes prepared for the event:

> The subject is a familiar one in fairy lore—the fatal result of love between mortal man and a supernatural creature—but Mr. Bates has localized the story in harmony with a tradition which attaches to a lake in the Black Forest of Germany. The lilies of that lake, according to the old tale, are enchanted maidens, who once a year, on Midsummer night, are permitted to resume their original forms. Should mortal man meet one of them and both yield to their charms, death is the result. This is what happened to Sir Albrecht, in the story, who fell prey to one of the sirens, while on his way to meet his bride. In choosing such a subject Mr. Chadwick was plainly seeking to combine the lyric or romantic, the dramatic or tragic and the picturesque. To help to this end, Mr. Bates created groups of Elves and Dryads to contrast with the Knights of Sir Albrecht's retinue and serve the romantic, and also a demon, who, besides representing the evil principle and aiding the rational[e] of the story, supplies a picturesque element.

> The composition is divided into seven scenes and an epilogue. In the first we are introduced to Sir Albrecht and his Knights, and the Elves and Dryads, who serve later as commentators on the woeful tragedy, assuming for that purpose a character like that of the classic chorus. In scene II Albrecht is made acquainted with the danger that threatens, but which he continues resisting, in fancied security in the love of his bride. The next scene [3] brings

us the picture of the lilies and their magic awakening; the next [4] the love scene between the Knight and the Nymph in which the domain of opera is frankly entered on. In Scene V we find the chorus of Dryads and Elves telling us of what the absence of dramatic spectacle will not permit us to see. The sixth scene pictures the reweaving of the spell, and the seventh, the punishment and farewell of the lovers.[51]

Even by the standards of the day, *The Lily Nymph* was a bit precious. While fairy tales, with their combination of prancing elves and unlikely plots, were by no means unusual to contemporary audiences, they were increasingly regarded as archaic. Nevertheless, this was a piece of music that Chadwick expected would be admired by those who sang it, for it was both attractive and easily performable by amateurs. One critic thought Chadwick had missed the mark on the latter point, remarking, "It is a pretty, sad story, suitable for the good young ladies and gentlemen of the typical provincial singing school. But Mr. Chadwick has made the music a little too difficult for such organizations." Nevertheless, "It is very sweet and fluent music without a single harsh or discordant phrase."[52] Dossert's concert also featured the great pianist Ignaz Paderewski performing his own *Polish Fantasy*. Chadwick admitted that the eager, capacity audience attended mainly to hear Paderewski, a situation that "side tracked the poor little 'Nymph' pretty effectually."[53] In other words, *The Lily Nymph* did not attract the spotlight that night. But when Chadwick finally heard his score he was well satisfied, "although the orchestra took no pains to give it a finished performance."[54] Chadwick and Paderewski agreed that Dossert was inept.

Although *The Lily Nymph* had originally been intended for the Springfield Festival of 1896, Chadwick sanctioned the New York performance, as well as a second one in New Bedford, which occurred in January 1896. Chadwick himself conducted a third performance, by the Philharmonic Society of Montreal, on April 2. The Philharmonic Society had agreed to perform it on the condition that Chadwick dedicate it to the group, and he complied. We know few details about *The Lily Nymph*'s early performances in New York, New Bedford, and Montreal, although the chorus master of the Montreal Society, G. Couture, was "a French gentleman and musician, educated in Paris, and an authority on Gregorian music."[55] Couture carried with him a score of Saint-Saëns's *Samson et Delilah*—"*his own*," an impressed Chadwick exclaimed—and he thought that Couture's ideas for conducting it were insightful.[56] Chadwick would soon immerse himself in Saint-Saëns's score and learn a great deal from it.

Chadwick was generally pleased with his Montreal principal singers, all of whom followed him to Springfield for the May festival performances. Among the cast leaders, Chadwick admired Emma Juch and Giuseppe Campanari, but Barron Berthald was "a second rate German opera singer."[57] By the time the group reached Springfield, they were familiar with the nuances of Chadwick's score; the orchestra also caught on quickly. Considering it a landmark, one reporter thought that the festival had reached a turning point in its history with *The Lily Nymph*, for it was "one of the smoothest and most finished performances that the association has ever given. If the [remaining] concerts are held up to the same level the festival will take a higher rank than any of its predecessors."[58] The same writer admitted that "the chorus has indeed made immense progress during the year. . . . Three years ago such singing would have been out of the question."[59] The *Springfield Daily Republican* critic thought, as many others subsequently admitted, that Bates's libretto was weak. Nevertheless, the score was one of the finest creations yet in American music, "a real midsummer night's dream and the elfish spirit strongly predominates. No American composer, not even Mr. MacDowell, has a surer sense of orchestral color, and the light and tricky touches . . . would have been admired by Berlioz."[60]

Rupert Hughes disagreed. Hughes, known today for an early history of American music, was a writer for *Godey's Magazine*, a prominent monthly. Since May 1895 he had been documenting various composers in America at the rate of one per month; it was Chadwick's great misfortune to be chronicled in the February 1896 issue.[61] Most of Hughes's review revolved around the just-premiered *The Lily Nymph*, "the only orchestral work of Mr. Chadwick's that I have ever heard," he confessed without a trace of embarrassment. It is clear from the outset that Hughes is no admirer of Chadwick.[62] Hughes had little patience for the dainty, the genteel, in American music, and he clearly thought that *The Lily Nymph* represented just that: "Is it possible that music is so gentle an art that all its writers are going to evolve into lady-like persons?" Hughes was sickened by what he referred to as "the namby-pamby," which was "the deadliest poison known to art," and he had no patience for those who might "flutter and simper 'How nice, how lovely,'" over a piece of music.

In fairness to Hughes much of his vitriol concerning *The Lily Nymph* is aimed at Arlo Bates, "who ought to know better." But Chadwick was not spared. "I cannot coax myself into accord even with the general enthusiasm," Hughes grumbled, about Chadwick and his music. "I should hate to deny that in certain instances he has reached a high plane indeed. But to me he must remain a man of much talent and industry, and little of the sacred fire of genius. It is ghastly to think of a composer of experience and ability squandering and perverting his talent to such uses. Better a thousand pot-boiling Bowery tunes and topical songs than a cantata such as this 'Lily Nymph'"[63] One can only imagine that Chadwick was relieved that Hughes had never heard *Tabasco*.

The Lily Nymph was performed twice more, on September 28, 1898 and September 27, 1899 at the Worcester Festival in Worcester, Massachusetts. The former occurred with miserable results. Chadwick recalled that the 1898 performance "was nearly wrecked by the stupid old sopranos of the semi-chorus who were staring at the new gowns in the audience and missed their cue for the 'elves.' Having started a measure late nothing could stop them and the orchestra who were frantically reading at sight did not know enough to repeat a measure. It was the worst mess I ever got into before or since."[64] Critic Philip Hale attended both performances, and, in his review of the later concert, he thought that *The Lily Nymph*, "which was poorly performed last year, had evidently been rehearsed with special loving care."[65] Hale could have added that Chadwick was not one to make the same mistake twice.

Lochinvar (1896)

The day after *The Lily Nymph* premiered at Springfield, Chadwick's setting of *Lochinvar*, from Walter Scott's epic poem *Marmion* (1808), was given its first performance, also at Springfield. Interjected into the "canto fifth" of Scott's grandiloquent work is the story of the young Scottish knight Lochinvar, who, returning from war, interrupts a wedding-in-progress to claim his true love—the English, fair, and about-to-be-wed Ellen. Ellen also has feelings for Lochinvar, but her parents would not permit them to court ("I long wooed your daughter, my suit you denied"). Lochinvar and Ellen conspire to run away together. Fortunately her near-husband proved not to be an obstacle to their union ("For the poor craven bridegroom said never a word"), but Lochinvar and Ellen are forced to flee from her family, the Netherby clan, whom they eventually elude ("There was racing and chasing on Cannobie Lee; but the lost bride of Netherby ne'er did they see").[66]

The story of the chivalrous romance of Lochinvar and Ellen had been popular since Scott published *Marmion*, and by the 1890s it had lost none of its appeal. A dramatic narrative poem, it perfectly suited the talents of baritone Max Heinrich, who premiered it and to whom Chadwick dedicated it. Heinrich was a marvelously talented fellow. A German by birth, he had toured with Theodore Thomas's orchestra before taking a position at London's Royal Academy of Music, where he taught for five years. Following his tenure there, he returned to the US and embarked on a concert career that took him around the country with many of the leading conductors of the era. Chadwick recalled that at the premiere of *Lochinvar* Heinrich "got a great ovation. He certainly put it over in great shape. Nobody has since been able to match his performance of this ditty."[67]

At forty-three pages of score, *Lochinvar* is a diminutive work, composed for baritone soloist and a standard orchestra plus harp, an instrument that Chadwick began to rely on for its coloristic potential. The music moves through myriad tonalities and meters in eleven distinctly articulated sections, and Chadwick utilized a variety of moods and textures to convey the couple's reunion, their mutual tenderness, and subsequent perilous escape. *Lochinvar*'s Scottish pedigree also gave Chadwick an opportunity to exploit once again a musical nationalism associated with his own British heritage. Musically, the most noteworthy section is number eight, the "Introduction and Strathspey." A Strathspey is a slightly slower version of another Scottish dance called a reel; in it we find the rhythm known as the "Scotch snap." In this section the composer introduces, through the pervasive use of the oboe, a variety of sounds and rhythms that will remind the listener of bagpipes. As the music intensifies, Chadwick adds a military drum to splendid effect, but he unexpectedly gives the harp some of the score's most compelling passages, including—in the penultimate segment—a full cadenza.

Critics and audiences adored *Lochinvar*. Thankful that Chadwick had not "pressed realism to extremes," the writer for the *Springfield Daily Republican* asserted that "the skirl of the bagpipes, the tread of the dancers, and the racing and chasing of Cannobie Lee are effectively delineated."[68] *Lochinvar* enjoyed a brief revival after the turn of the century. The renowned baritone David Bispham sang *Lochinvar* in 1909 at Carnegie Hall as part of the program at a concert presented by the American Music Society. The next day Henry Krehbiel called it "a fluent piece of writing, frankly melodious," with a captivating "Scotch color."[69] Chadwick's friends found unintended humor in it. "[Horatio] Parker liked it but refused to take it seriously," he remembered, and "the first time Max read it through with me he roared out 'Love smells like the subway' instead of 'Love swells like the Solway.' Great fun!"[70]

Subsequent accounts of his music often rank *Lochinvar* among his finest compositions. It was heard on the all-Chadwick concerts that cropped up in his later years, and received at least thirteen performances with orchestras around the nation, the last occurring in 1943. Despite Parker's ribbing, *Lochinvar*, published in its piano-vocal version by A. P. Schmidt in 1896, proved to be Chadwick's most celebrated work for voice and orchestra. It was also a crucial springboard to his later works in the Scottish style, including his symphonic tour-de-force, *Tam O'Shanter*.

By 1898 Chadwick believed that the Springfield chorus was "in splendid condition, full of fresh voices, well balanced, and full of enthusiasm."[71] By and large, the group had achieved the goals he set for it when he started. Not only had Chadwick managed to improve his chorus, but he was mentored by BSO conductor Arthur Nikisch, who offered valuable tips in matters of orchestral technique and discipline. Chadwick learned from Nikisch that the surest way to success required a blend of patience and a healthy dose of high expectations. When Paderewski toured the US in 1891, Chadwick noted with interest the orchestra's response to Nikisch's manner at one of the rehearsals with the BSO: "If any of the orchestra had up to that time labored under the delusion that Nikisch was 'easy' their minds must have been disabused by that rehearsal. Not the smallest detail escaped him. They found themselves going to school as much as they ever did to Gericke. It was this quality that retained their respect for Nikisch no matter how easy going and apparently careless he might be at times."[72]

Theodore Thomas also proved helpful when, in 1898, the Springfield group performed Beethoven's Ninth Symphony. The previous April, Thomas had visited with Chadwick, Wallace Goodrich, Franz Kneisel, and Parker. Thomas generously shared his ideas on Beethoven's masterpiece: "We had a jolly dinner at the [St. Botolph] club and after the table was cleared he laid out the score on it, set up a metronome, and talked oh so *lovingly* about it until after one o'clock." Together they explored the score in close detail, and Thomas demonstrated wide familiarity with performances of the Ninth Symphony by other conductors and orchestras: "His discussion of Wagner's suggested alterations and of some made by other conductors of the traditional tempi, of the treatment of the voices especially in the solo quartet and in the composition as a whole, was the most valuable and profitable lesson I have ever had from anybody at any time." The experience was unforgettable, and "no money could have paid for the information I got."[73] The next month Chadwick wrote ebulliently to Thomas, who had been lending him scores for the festival concerts for several years, about his group's performance.[74] "The hints that you gave me I found of the very greatest service and they were received by the orchestra with many expressions of approval. I have never heard the place for the wind[s] in E flat in the slow movement sound so beautiful. Mr. [Emil] Paur's running time for the first three movements was fifty three minutes. Ours was forty five. I only regretted that we had so few basses and cellos, but as they were all excellent players the effect was quite impressive. The chorus did magnificently, altogether the best work they have ever done."[75]

Omaha

"It was a rough and smelly place," Chadwick sourly recalled about his 1898 visit to Omaha, Nebraska. He had been invited there to attend the Trans-Mississippi and International Exposition, where he would provide music lectures, play the organ, and lead "conducting exhibitions"; organizers intended to highlight American music. These activities held far less interest to Chadwick than the opportunity to take a two-week journey to the wild and wooly West. Two years earlier, he had accepted an invitation to conduct his own Second Symphony in the far more cosmopolitan city of St. Louis. ("There was not much money in the job but a lot of glory and advertizing besides."[76]) Now, with Wallace Goodrich in tow, Chadwick traveled through Chicago and arrived in Omaha on the morning of July 1. Lost in transit was their luggage; as their irritating search for it began, Chadwick warily ambled near the train station. "While I was loitering about I was accosted by a rough looking man who asked me what I was doing there. I explained that I was waiting for my luggage. 'What's yer name?' said he. His manner was so impudent that I resented it and plainly told him that it was none of his business. Whereupon he threw back the lapel of his coat and showed a policeman's badge. I told him that I was registered at the Paxton house and what I had come for at which he expressed much incredulity & hinted that he contemplated 'pulling me in.'"[77] Chadwick reckoned that this incident was the closest that he had ever come to being arrested.

Visited by nearly three million people, the exhibition itself was a miniature version of Chicago's Columbian Exposition, "handsome and interesting," Chadwick thought, but far less memorable than the gleaming White City. But where Chicago featured world cultures and American industry, Omaha gave pride of place to American Indian culture and American agriculture. The Indian exhibits included a huge array of tribal representation—Omaha, Wichita, Winnebago, Blackfoot, Sioux, among many others—punctuated by "sham battles," violent reenactments of inter-tribal wars. Strangely juxtaposed with these attractions was an emphasis on farming and food production, which found its artistic representation in the large statue of Ceres, the Roman goddess of agriculture. Ceres, the foremost of many statues on the grounds, oversaw the exhibition's Greek- and Roman-style buildings, which, in Chicago Fair style, surrounded a lagoon dominated by the "Fountain of Neptune." Among the most elaborate edifices were the enormous Manufacturer's and Electricity Building, the Fine Arts Building, and the Music Pavilion, a magnificently well-lit outdoor concert stage that looked remarkably like a Roman triumphal arch. Oddly, most of the performances of serious music took place in the comparatively modest auditorium.

Music did not hold at Omaha the exalted place it occupied in Chicago, although it did not fail to attract musicians of note. Louis C. Elson had joined Chadwick and Goodrich, and the new "Theodore Thomas Chicago Orchestra" was also there. Among its members was violist Frederick Stock, a future conductor of the orchestra. The orchestra was led by Arthur Mees, as an aging and somewhat grumpy Thomas had had enough of the fair experience. Chadwick conducted the Chicagoans in two of his own works, including the first three completed movements of his *Symphonic Sketches*; these were considered the highlight of the event.[78] Chadwick later wrote Thomas that the "boys" in the orchestra treated him "handsomely."[79] He raved about the quality of the group, and off-handedly compared the Chicago band to Boston's orchestra: "It is not in good taste for me (especially) to make any comparisons at least not on paper. But I will say that before they had played four measures I recognized the effect of *discipline*. They played both my pieces beautifully and I promised them that I should so state to the 'old man.'"[80] Little else of musical importance occurred at the Omaha exhibition; in fact, not too different from Chadwick's Chicago Fair experience, he thought its organization "a very mixed up mess." The chief administrator was muddled, and "he had no real authority & it was with much difficulty that we found out what was expected of us or from whom we should get our money."[81] As he complained to Thomas, "*Omaha* is a one horse town."[82]

Having taken stock of his future during the long journey home, Chadwick decided to resign his post at the Springfield Festival. Publicly he cited his obligations at NEC, but in truth he had already started rehearsing another chorus the year before in Worcester—which everyone in Springfield knew—and he had grown increasingly frustrated by his situation in Springfield. Chadwick had winnowed out many of the weaker singers, and by 1898 he was pleased, although not unreservedly so. But in the 1899 series of performances, there was a distinct "'decrescendo' from our previous high standard."[83]

In a letter to composer and critic Frederick Grant Gleason, Chadwick laid out several of his problems in Springfield.[84] Gleason had sent several scores to Chadwick, longing for their performance, and Chadwick promised to try to include them in the season's lineup. But he was not hopeful. "I have been looking them over," Chadwick wrote, "and if I can possibly find a place on our Springfield program I shall try to put on one of the entr'actes. If I do not however you will understand that these are the reasons. 1st: We only have two miscellaneous concerts. 2d: We have to play things to a large extent which have been previously rehearsed and performed by the orchestra. 3d: We have so little time for rehearsal that it is difficult to do a new [manuscript] work full justice. I know that you think as I do that it is better not to have any performance than a bad one."[85]

Chadwick could have cited several other dilemmas that were ruining his Springfield experience. As early as 1892, he suffered poor relations with the singers, which, to everyone's embarrassment, became a matter of public record. The *Springfield Graphic* recorded that "the Musical Association chorus is sadly in need of male voices, but it is safe to say that there are men who enjoy singing with the chorus who do not enjoy Mr. Chadwick's sarcasm, which at times verges on impoliteness. Mr. Chadwick is immensely funny, and his wit is keen; but there is a kind and courteous treatment that even bass and tenor singers appreciate. Perhaps this is only a symptom of Bostonese manners."[86]

Additionally, the Springfield Festival was not financially successful, and Chadwick did not have the time — nor is it likely that he had the interest — to assist the fundraising effort. Financial constraints caused a noticeable slip in the quality of the guest artists toward the end of Chadwick's tenure, but that problem did not keep him from programming a final extravaganza. In his last season he would invite pianist Teresa Carreño to appear in a performance of Tchaikovsky's B-flat Piano Concerto. It was, he remembered, "one of the greatest moments of my life."[87]

Chadwick had intended to resign in 1898, but, at the urging of the board of directors, he agreed to stay on through the 1899 season. The Springfield Festival molded him in a very positive way — although he was quick to admit that "it probably did little to enhance my reputation as a conductor" — and taught him several important lessons that would soon prove useful.[88] He learned how to administer a complex organization that comprised many parts; how to navigate the politics of a board of directors; and how to build, drill, and perfect an orchestra; and all this while he was becoming intimately familiar with a wide repertoire of music and programming many of his own works. Chadwick reveled in performances of Paine's Prelude to *Oedipus Tyrannus* (which he had conducted to general acclaim years before), Parker's *Northern Ballad*, and Mendelssohn's *Ruy Blas* Overture, among many others (see Appendix 1).

In the end, however, Chadwick was bittersweet. "So ended my ten years of service as conductor of the Springfield Festival," he wistfully reflected. "They could not afford to pay me to continue, and in fact only paid me half my salary for the last year. I never pressed them for the rest."[89] Although the job had never been without serious challenges — financial, musical, political — Chadwick had turned a community chorus into an accomplished musical ensemble that was better than it had a right to be. Sadly, it could not withstand his departure; shortly after Chadwick resigned, the festival disbanded.

The Worcester Festival (1897–1901)

Chadwick was named the director of the Worcester Festival in October 1897 while still leading the Springfield Festival. He succeeded the revered Boston conductor Carl Zerrahn (already mentioned in connection with the Springfield Festival and the HMA) and edged out fellow conductors and sometime musical adversaries Emil Mollenhauer and Jules Jordan for the post. Chadwick was actually the committee's second choice, for the job had initially been offered to Horatio Parker, but his "inclination was not in this direction."[90]

The Worcester Festival's history was distinguished. Zerrahn, now seventy-one years old, had run the organization for an astonishing three decades, but in recent seasons his health had been in question; not the least among his problems was his increasing deafness.[91] But Zerrahn's physical condition was not the only issue at play, and it may not have even been the most decisive one. For several years attendance at the festival had been in decline and admission collections had fallen off sharply, in part because of complaints about the programming and the lack of "stars" to carry the concerts.[92] In the season before Chadwick took over, the festival had seen its smallest attendance in years and showed a financial loss of over four thousand dollars. The official notices of Zerrahn's retirement do not mention these dilemmas.

One episode neatly encapsulates the problems the festival faced. In 1896, the legendary pianist Leopold Godowsky arrived in Worcester to perform Carl Tausig's arrangement of Chopin's E minor Concerto. Zerrahn did not conduct. That was left to his able assistant Franz Kneisel, who was the only one on stage using Tausig's arrangement—the orchestra had parts for Chopin's unedited original version, while Godowsky played his own exquisitely elaborate composite of the two. Regardless of whom the selection committee invited to head the next festival, it was clear that Zerrahn's successor would have to be an effective administrator so as to eliminate such embarrassing predicaments. Further, it would be incumbent upon the new leader to lure exceptional soloists and musicians—"stars"—to Worcester, and to energize the increasingly impatient audience base. It was well known among festival leaders that Chadwick had done exactly this in Springfield.

Chadwick was to commence rehearsals in January 1898, well before the beginning of the festival, which occurred annually in September. His chorus was lackluster. It included acceptable upper voices, but "the tenors are very poor and very scarce and the basses [are] mostly relics of the glacial period with a few pinfeather baritones who could not read [music]."[93] However, the quality of the singing was the least of his problems: "And overall was the blight of 'we always did it that way' which included no end of wrong notes and absolutely no idea of phrasing or expression."[94] As he had done at Springfield, Chadwick quickly assessed his forces and aggressively recruited new talent.

Chadwick's first festival included seven concerts, but the critical response did not reflect its huge musical advancement over previous years. The chorus seemed no more brilliant than in years past, and the soloists, although notable artists, were not as stellar as many had expected. They included the dramatic soprano Johanna Gadski, local musical celebrity Gertrude May Stein, and tenor Dudley Buck Jr. Chadwick's musical selections fared better. As he had done in Springfield, he gave an important place to the American composer—himself included—on his programs. Besides Mendelssohn's *Elijah* and Grieg's *Olaf Trygvasson*, his own *The Lily Nymph*, Parker's *Hora Novissima*, and Amy Beach's cantata *The Rose of Avontown* were featured. The orchestral menu included Brahms's Second Symphony, Raff's Third Symphony (*Im Walde*), and an eclectic assortment of music by Massenet, Haydn, Mozart, Leoncavallo, Wagner, and Rheinberger. As was the style of the day, Chadwick liked to mix things up: soloists, orchestral works, and choral numbers were often featured on the same program.

Despite some flat reviews, Chadwick's imaginative programs (see Appendix 2) drew the crowds the managers had hoped for, and set the stage for Chadwick's next three seasons. Raymond Morin, the festival's historian, wrote that audiences from throughout New England purchased tickets far in advance of the festival, and, as a consequence, local hotels were filled to capacity.[95]

By his second season, Chadwick had instituted several important changes. The chorus had improved dramatically, partly because the members "submitted to reorganization, a small chorus for special work having been selected from its ranks."[96] Chadwick had also insisted on "the continual practice of singing whole tones," which forced them to sing in tune.[97] And the Boston Symphony was engaged to accompany the chorus, "a sure guaranty of noble and beautiful performances."[98] Chadwick contracted better soloists, including the Metropolitan Opera's great coloratura soprano Marcella Sembrich (1858–1935) and the Ukrainian pianist Vladimir de Pachmann (1848–1933), an eccentric performer, a former student of composer Anton Bruckner, and the era's foremost interpreter of Chopin. American music figured prominently with a reprise of Chadwick's *The Lily Nymph*, Parker's *King Trojan*, MacDowell's Suite no. 1 (op. 42), and the first movement of Frederick S. Converse's new symphony. The highlight of the season was Berlioz's *Damnation of Faust*, which had been requested by the festival board. Chadwick consented "on condition that the chorus be weeded out and fresh blood added. To their surprise the chorus committee found that it was *this dead wood* that had been keeping the good singers of Worcester—of whom there were quite a few—out of the festival chorus."[99]

The American premiere in English of César Franck's *Les béatitudes* was the major achievement of the 1900 Worcester Festival. Chadwick believed that marked improvements in the chorus and orchestra would allow him to program this difficult piece, and, while he still feared that it was beyond their reach, he wrote excitedly to Theodore Thomas: "Our performance of 'Beatitudes' at Worcester comes on the 27th and it would be a matter of great pride and pleasure to all the Worcester people, not to mention myself, if you could hear it. The work is certainly very impressive and there are many large effects for both the chorus and the orchestra. The instrumentation is clear and simple, but very sonorous." Chadwick was not without reservations. "I fear that the work as a whole may give a slight impression of monotony, as each of the eight numbers ends with the same kind of effect, to wit: celestial chorus pianissimo, molto moderato, etc. There is a very large proportion of slow tempo in the work and the parts which are fast are not particularly interesting musically."[100] Chadwick's hesitation did not relent; only two weeks later he backtracked on his invitation to Thomas: "Our Beatitude performance comes on the 27th and from present indications it will be bad. Chiefly from want of rehearsals and very poor material in the chorus. We shall be glad to see you if you come—but honestly I would much rather you would come next year when I have particular reasons for wanting you."[101]

The concert went better than Chadwick expected, and in another letter to Thomas, who did not attend, Chadwick thought that "the effect of the work on the audience was immense. They were enthusiastic from beginning to end. The solo and ensemble parts are so effective that they relieve the heaviness of the chorus to some extent. I was really surprised that the work did not seem to flag, as I wrote you it might do."[102] Chadwick included on the same program the Brahms Requiem with which "the Worcester chorus really had no business, but I submitted it on account of the immense training the chorus got from it; and much of it went very well indeed."[103] Later Chadwick performed the *béatitudes* in Boston, and, as he wrote to Thomas, "Our performance here was much better than at Worcester and created a good deal of enthusiasm among musicians. I think unmusical people liked most of it but were bored in spots. We shall undoubtedly repeat it at Worcester next year."[104] Chadwick's enthusiasm may have influenced Thomas, who programmed the *béatitudes* at Cincinnati's May Festival at least as early as 1902.[105]

Critical appraisals of festival performances were increasingly favorable, and Chadwick "justified his appointment" after the 1899 season, his second. (Chadwick's continued employment at the festival had by no means been assured following his first.[106]) Ernestine Schumann-Heink was contracted for the 1900 season, and she proved to be the only big draw. Singer David Bispham and pianist Richard Burmeister starred in the 1901 concerts. The programming during this period included Brahms's Third Symphony, MacKenzie's *Coriolanus* Suite, and Bizet's *Jeux d'Enfants*. American highlights were MacDowell's orchestral work *Lancelot and Elaine* and Edgar Stillman Kelley's *Aladdin* Suite. Chadwick invited Kelley to conduct his work. At one point during a rehearsal, a nervous Kelley demanded more time for rehearsal. Chadwick reluctantly consented, although he resented it because not only had it been sufficiently rehearsed in his opinion, but it took rehearsal time away from his own "lyric drama," *Judith*, which was being readied for its premiere (see Chapter 9). "He took an hour!" Chadwick complained. "This is only another specimen of musicians' gratitude. But for my pertinacity with the Worcester committee these Chinese jingles of Kelley's would have remained forever unplayed and unheard as far as Worcester was concerned but I liked the piece in spite of Kelley's angular conducting and thought it ought to be heard. But it was an experience that rather soured me on 'boosting' my rival composers!"[107]

As at Springfield, Chadwick had never been completely satisfied with the quality of musicianship of the Worcester chorus, although in his time it had many fine moments. In the end, he believed that his experiences in Worcester "led to *nothing*—except trouble and anxiety."[108] One annoying, rampant problem was nepotism, and oftentimes Chadwick was compelled to admit an unqualified singer simply to appease a board member who happened to be a relative. Further, he found working with the program committee, which questioned his every decision, to be irksome. By his final season, Chadwick found the situation improved, "but at what expense of nerve force, physical fatigue, and will power against the stupid, narrow and conceited ideas of some of the powers that had the running of the Association?"[109] Chadwick's resignation in 1901 surprised the board members. Once tendered, however, he worked tirelessly to ensure the festival's future success.

Chadwick's intense political maneuvering resulted in the appointment of Wallace Goodrich to the director's post. Goodrich was quickly becoming known as Chadwick's protégé. An able organist, and later administrator, he had performed at a number of Springfield Festival concerts. One of the programs featured a brief estimate of Goodrich, probably penned by Chadwick: "J. Wallace Goodrich, although quite a young man, is already one of the leading organists in Boston. He has been a close student in theory and composition; gives evidence of unusual versatility and ability, and from the talent already displayed, it is fair to expect results of no mean order in later years."[110] Violinist and conductor Franz Kneisel hoped to resign from the festival simultaneously with

Chadwick, but Chadwick knew that Goodrich's success would require guidance and leadership from the veteran concertmaster. The politics of the festival required no small amount of savvy, and Kneisel could act as a liaison between Goodrich and the board, chorus, and orchestra. Following a contentious argument with Chadwick, Kneisel agreed to stay through 1902, in the sole effort to ensure Goodrich's success.

When all was said and done, an exhausted Chadwick was relieved that his career at Worcester was over. He left the festival in better shape than he found it, and—unlike the Springfield organization—the Worcester group would continue to flourish after him.

7

"A Hell of a Job for a Composer"
Taking Charge at New England Conservatory
1897

And this is the motive, the mission, of the conservatory
system in this country, inasmuch as organized is more potent
than individual effort to elevate our national taste, to prepare
the way for the future artist, that he may be born under the
right conditions, his divine gift fostered and directed to become
worthy of its exalted destiny.

—Frank Damrosch, "Conservatory Life in Boston" (1880)

Tourjée and Faelten

By the 1890s, the situation at New England Conservatory was a mess. But, then again, the situation at NEC had long been a mess. The conservatory was founded in 1867 by Eben Tourjée (1834–1891), a genuine zealot for the cause of music, although he himself was not a particularly remarkable musical talent. Born in Warwick, Rhode Island, Tourjée was mostly self-taught, but by age seventeen he had already opened his own music store in Fall River, Massachusetts, where he had determined to teach others in the art he loved. Soon he would travel to Europe to begin lessons at the Berlin Conservatory with organist Karl August Haupt and carefully observe the administration of a successful music school. The lessons with Haupt would ensure some musical legitimacy back in the states, but Tourjée's main intent upon his return to the US was to establish his own conservatory.

What Tourjée had in quantity was ideas, bolstered by charisma and a bottomless pail of fortitude. He arrived in Boston from the Providence Conservatory of Music, which he had founded, with the intention of developing a musical institution that could be made economically feasible. Tourjée advocated what he termed the "class system." That is, rather than one instructor tutoring a single student, private lessons and other music courses could be taught in groups or classes, much like university courses were taught. Although today, from preschool through graduate school, class instruction in music is the rule, in the nineteenth century one-to-one tutelage was typical. One writer, commenting on Tourjée's activities as a music journalist earlier in his career, judged that "even at that time he gave hints in his paper of the radical change in the system of musical instruction, which he later inaugurated and which he has since carried out so grandly."[1] Tourjée wondered "why our system of education in classes, which has proved so successful in every other study, should not be applied to music; why the advanced instruction in music should be put beyond the reaches of the great masses by the old method of personal lessons; and why the favored few, who are able to pay for private instruction, should be shut up to the solitude and disheartening atmosphere of private study, and be denied the stimulus and help which come from contact with congenial minds."[2]

Naturally, there were also practical reasons for this shift from individual to collective instruction. If more students could pay for fewer teachers, Tourjée correctly believed, there were many benefits to be reaped: tuition costs would be reduced; a smaller pool of teachers could handle the throngs of students who desired music instruction; the culture would be improved by the enlightening qualities of good music on larger numbers of its citizens; and, of course, more money would be made by teachers and the conservatory.

It is perhaps too much to say that Tourjée was a musical version of the great impresario P. T. Barnum, but he certainly attempted to have both artistic and financial success. On the one hand, he firmly believed—not unlike Dwight—that great music could have a hugely positive moral, educational, and aesthetic effect on his fellow citizens, and he hoped that he could be the one to provide those meaningful experiences. Educator and journalist Thomas Bickner, who was sympathetic to Tourjée's aims in this regard, wrote that Tourjée "is America's great Commoner in music."[3] On the other hand, after only a brief moment of hesitation, Tourjée agreed to assist Patrick Gilmore by organizing the choral department of the 1869 Jubilee. Not only was he attracted to Gilmore's legend and the prospect of being a principal in the greatest musical event in the history of the nation, but he was partially motivated by the possibility of snaring more than a few talented singers and instrumentalists from throughout the region to help fill out his NEC classrooms. Naturally, Tourjée's brand of entrepreneurialism would never have occurred to Dwight—it was precisely this aspect of Gilmore's personality that so disgusted the critic.

Founding a conservatory required the identification of a venue that could house classes, rehearsals, and performances. Tourjée began his modest NEC at Boston's Music Hall, where he let a few rooms and began to peddle private lessons with the assistance of several faculty members. Built in 1852, the Music Hall had a stately audience chamber, which sat 2,500, but its exterior was dismal; mere steps away from the picturesque Park Street Church and Boston Common, it was situated at the end of a short, dark alley and was devoid of any decoration.[4] Nevertheless, Tourjée's relentless advertising of NEC led to a rapid and unexpected expansion in enrollment; soon he required three times the space. As the Music Hall facilities started to burst with students, he began to plot the conservatory's move to a larger, more suitable facility. Tourjée settled on an abandoned building situated at Franklin Square, the enormous, three-hundred-room St. James Hotel. The hotel would require a one-million-dollar renovation, but it promised to easily accomodate the conservatory's rapidly growing student body. As a former hotel, it could also provide students with dormitory rooms, and thereby supply NEC with a new, much-needed stream of revenue. (The hotel also benefitted Tourjée personally, for he and his wife lived in a comfortably appointed suite.[5]) The hotel lacked an auditorium, of course, but in 1885, Tourjée would add Sleeper Hall to the Franklin Square complex. Named for its principal benefactor, Jacob Sleeper, the intimate 550-seat concert venue housed the hundreds of recitals and concerts in which NEC faculty and students performed each year. It also contained the great Walcker organ, formerly housed in the Music Hall and purchased for NEC in 1884 by conservatory trustee W. O. Grover.[6]

When Tourjée died on April 12, 1891, pianist Carl Faelten took over as director of NEC. Faelten had been on the conservatory faculty since 1885 and had a reputation as an efficacious teacher as well as a fine artist. His résumé was impeccable: he began piano and violin as a child and excelled on both; he was friend and confidante to Joachim Raff, the revered German composer; and prior to his arrival at NEC he had taught at Frankfurt's Hoch Conservatory and the Peabody Institute in Baltimore. Faelten performed widely in New England, and critics were mostly awed by a sure virtuosity. Elson called him "one of the most brilliant artists I have ever heard."[7] But Faelten's administrative acumen, and perhaps his enthusiasm, was less than the struggling institution needed at this critical time. To make matters worse, his elevation to the top post of the conservatory occurred without the consent of the faculty. Faelten was unpopular with the teachers for one chief reason cited by Chadwick: his "incorrigible German methods of which nepotism was a prominent feature."[8] Faelten had recruited his own brother, who was widely considered incompetent, to teach at NEC. Equally vexing to faculty members was Faelten's routine appropriation of the best students for his own studio and classes. Unlike Tourjée, whose interest lay primarily in the number of paying students admitted—and not so much the quality of their musicianship—Faelten often attended student auditions, but mostly for selfish reasons. When he heard a student of promise, he had little compunction about assigning that student to his own roster of pupils. This enraged many faculty members; not only was Faelten stealing talent and filling their studios with the musical leftovers, but he was also horning into an area in which they thought he, as an administrator, should not be involved. Under Tourjée's leadership, student auditions and studio assignments had been left entirely to the faculty.

Faelten was not without a few successes at NEC. He lured the Italian piano virtuoso and composer Ferruccio Busoni (1866–1924) to Boston in 1891, a noteworthy achievement that occurred in his first year.[9] This hiring did not get the publicity that Jeannette Thurber would enjoy a few years later upon securing the services of Dvořák at her National Conservatory of Music, but the purpose of Busoni's invitation had not been dissimilar. Faelten hoped that Busoni would give NEC some much-needed positive press, and within local circles there was much talk about the Italian composer and pianist. But Busoni was not interested in the prospect of involving himself deeply in Boston's musical culture, and, despite his pronounced respect for tradition, he was a modernist composer in a city that worshipped classicism. Moreover, Busoni's morale suffered when Faelten assigned to his studio a number of poor-quality piano students simply to keep him busy—"To make him earn his salary," as Chadwick put it.[10] Busoni's compositional aesthetic, with its chromaticism, dissonance, and angularity, was in line with neither Boston's historical preference for the Masters nor the latest currents of nationalism. In any event, he had yet to produce his finest compositions—Busoni's chief concern at this time was his performing career. He hoped that his appointment to NEC would provide a cozy home base, as he fully intended to tour widely. "Boston," Chadwick later recalled, "was too small for a man of his caliber at that time."[11]

In the end, not even importing a major artist could help Faelten to save his job. One NEC associate believed "if Faelten were to resign, the faculty would throw their hats in the air."[12] As the ire of the faculty continued to rise, one eventful meeting began with "venomous" attacks on Faelten and ended with music theory instructor Percy Goetchius, a beloved teacher and competent historian and theorist, demanding Faelten's resignation, to no avail. Chadwick attended the meeting but wisely kept quiet; unbelievably, this was the first faculty meeting he had ever attended even though he had been associated with NEC for more than a decade. He was shocked by what he heard. Several instructors spoke intemperately, and soon, as the grumbling continued among the faculty after the meeting, the alumni became aware of Faelten's shortcomings. Once that happened, the conflagration quickly became public. Trustee Richard Dana defended Faelten and promised changes, but when, at the end of the year, a number of the "revolutionist" faculty members were fired by Faelten, the alumni stepped in. Chadwick recorded that "they wrote letters and talked to the trustees and in every way made it as hot for poor old Faelten as they could."[13]

As bad as the internal turmoil was, the public airing of the issues at NEC did not help anyone's cause. "The registrations dropped off and the annual deficit, already large, began to increase," Chadwick reported. "The moral reputation of the school which had been little short of scandalous under Dr. Tourjée was dragged in to fuel the fire."[14] By his own admission, Chadwick was not fully informed about the circumstances of either side, as he had astutely maintained a low profile at NEC even as his reputation as a composer of national importance was surging. Not being one of "Tourjée's boys"—there were many of them still in place at NEC—Chadwick hesitated to be too candid, and at times he even considered himself a bit out of place (not unlike how his mentor Eugene Thayer had felt). Chadwick's schedule at this time was also frenzied; up to now he simply showed up at NEC, taught his classes, and went home to his other, more engrossing activities, which included composing, running the Springfield group, and tending to his young family.

But Chadwick's professional life was about to change forever. On New Year's Day 1897, NEC business manager Frank W. Hale arrived at his home to discuss conservatory matters in harsh detail. Hale advised Chadwick of the faculty's wish to oust Faelten and elect him as the new director. Chadwick's acceptance, argued Hale, was the only solution that would unite the faculty and save the conservatory. Chadwick had gained the trust and support of the faculty not simply on account of the quality of his work as teacher, composer, and organist, but because they knew that he was straightforward and reliable, unlike Tourjée (whom Henry Higginson once called "a damned old liar"[15]) and Faelten. Chadwick had also garnered the faculty's admiration with a simple act of kindness, when, in the fall of 1885, his former teacher and now-colleague Stephen A. Emery had a breakdown. As a result, Emery was unable to teach his classes, but as the head of a family and its principal breadwinner, he was in desperate need of a paycheck. Chadwick assumed Emery's class load, and did so without pay. Emery remained on the NEC payroll during his recovery.[16]

Chadwick was surprised at the directorship proposition; he wondered why he was being offered the sizable sum of five thousand dollars per year to run a conservatory and lead a faculty, neither of which he had ever done before. "I had never dreamed of the possibility of such a thing and it was the last position in the world that I desired," he later wrote. In fact, it is surprising how little he knew about the machinations of NEC. "I knew nothing of their graded system, their requirements for graduation, or their business methods and had little respect for the results of their teaching. I was on good terms with all the teachers although some of them I knew but slightly."[17] Chadwick's references to "them" and "their" underscore how foreign the place was to him. Soon his hesitance became a matter of public record. In a page-one report, the *Boston Morning Journal* exclaimed "there is a possibility that the newly-elected Director will not accept [the job]. He was first informed of his election by a *Journal* man, and he stated to the reporter that unless everything was made right he should refuse to accept. This he made emphatic by repetition." The reporter quoted Chadwick: "The position of Director is filled with details calling for a vast amount of work and worry."[18]

Chadwick was warned by friends not to take the job, and he dreaded the notion of its requirements, which inevitably would include public speaking, fundraising, and presiding over meetings; he especially dreaded the latter, given his recent harrowing experience at the NEC faculty assemblage. These were not Chadwick's only concerns: he knew that his acceptance of the position would take a large slice of time away from his composing regimen and from his growing family. However, besides earning twice the largest salary he had ever had and enjoying a steady income he could not count on as a freelance music teacher, the position offered a few musical payouts that were hard for him to ignore. As the master of his own universe, Chadwick could implement his ideas for a serious orchestra program, and he could take a more active role in the recruitment of gifted young musicians. He could also teach the subjects of his choice and — perhaps ironically, especially after Faelten's misdeeds — Chadwick could also appropriate the best students for his own studio; as it was now, he tended to get the dullards. And if he could not make a go of NEC, what was there to lose? He was an established composer whose star was still on the rise; he would remain a professional conductor and organist at least for a while longer; and he had enough private students outside NEC to pay the rent.

The precise details of his negotiations are not known, but apparently "everything was made right," for Chadwick accepted the position. He promptly wrote to Theodore Thomas that he did not "expect to have to give up my composing or conducting on account of it, otherwise I would not have accepted the place."[19] Clearly he was not prepared to give up the Springfield Festival, and free time for composing was crucial. But Chadwick had in mind more than a comfortable administrative job and its handsome salary. Not unlike Tourjée, he had large designs for NEC; but he had no intention of becoming music's "great Commoner." On the contrary, Chadwick's NEC would be a place for professional development in music, and high expectations for students and teachers would be the norm. True to himself and his own unrelenting drive to excel, he confidently asserted to Thomas, "I do expect to be able in time to develop a school on broad artistic lines which shall be a power in the land. I shall have very little teaching but much scheming and planning."[20]

Chadwick in Charge

Chadwick's tenure as director of NEC officially began in February 1897, but Faelten's ouster was slow. Time remained on his employment contract, and Faelten, who we may imagine was hugely discomposed by the situation, generously consented to assist Chadwick in the transition. To Chadwick's surprise, Faelten was genuinely helpful, even congratulatory. Faelten got along with Chadwick and proved to be surprisingly gracious in defeat—at that year's spring graduation ceremony, he insisted that Chadwick sit on the podium alongside him and the board members.

During Chadwick's first months, he learned the inner workings of the conservatory and became acquainted with the many personalities who populated it. He had not ventured far from his teaching studio since he started there, but now Chadwick attended board meetings—most often saying nothing—and he got to know the alumni, who proved to be a potent, sometimes meddlesome, force in conservatory politics.

Chadwick was officially in charge, and without the assistance of Faelten, when fall registration opened on September 2, 1897. The student turnout was strong, numbering approximately thirteen hundred, and perhaps represented confidence in the conservatory's new administration. The following week Chadwick called the faculty together to offer his support and to ask for theirs. He outlined his philosophy of teaching and pledged not to interfere with their methods, but made it plain that he expected results. Chadwick attended all NEC recitals in the effort to evaluate the students, but he was especially keen to hear the performances by the faculty, as he fully intended to execute a short-term plan that would weed out those who were not pulling their weight artistically. Chadwick also established regular office hours, which enabled anyone with a problem or a question to consult with him directly, something that had been all but impossible under Tourjée and Faelten.

Chadwick remained an active classroom instructor, and his teaching load comprised two composition classes, a second-year harmony class, and "sight playing." Elsewhere in the curriculum, steps were taken to forge a more structured and logical approach to teaching young artists. Chadwick scrapped an ineffective "fundamental training" class and replaced it with ear training and dictation courses. As he began to assert his authority, some of the changes instituted at the conservatory naturally met with resistance. The German teachers especially had difficulty working for the greater good of the conservatory because "they had for so long run little private conservatories of their own."[21] From the intractable German contingent advice was given freely, and Chadwick was annoyed that he was being lectured about how conservatories were run in

Germany. Against such complaints, Chadwick pointedly reminded faculty members that he had attended *two* German conservatories and that he had done so more recently than some of the self-proclaimed conservatory experts. Chadwick further explained that Boston was not Germany, and, as he would from that time onward, he made it clear that he was the boss. He was not afraid to bark orders to older musicians or insist—sometimes harshly—that his rules be followed. "After this I did not hear quite so much about 'Chermanie.'"[22]

Harmony: A Course of Study (1897)

Once Chadwick was elected director of the conservatory, the completion of his textbook, *Harmony: A Course of Study* took on a greater urgency. He had been planning the book since 1893, when he began making notes and drafting exercises for possible use at a summer school at West Chop. Now that he was leading NEC, Chadwick supposed that having his own published textbook in hand would increase his authority as an educator in the eyes of his faculty. *Harmony* included studies he had composed during his years as a private harmony instructor, as well as many new music examples that had been created while on the train to the Springfield Festivals. Once the music examples were in hand, Chadwick turned to the writing of the text: "However I found that *definitions* that would hold water were not the easiest things in the world to make. To cover the ground *without saying too much* requires both skill and knowledge. . . . I was ambitious to make the book a model of expression, most of the books on harmony being more or less poor translations from the German."[23]

Indeed, Chadwick's *Harmony* was something of an oddity in a musical world that relied mostly on translated textbooks. Chadwick himself had been schooled by *Richter's Manual of Harmony*, which, at that time under the able editorial hand of John P. Morgan, retained its popularity well into the twentieth century. Nevertheless, when Chadwick mentioned his own book to B. F. Wood, the respected publisher with whom Chadwick had already established a professional relationship, Wood asked Chadwick to give him a chance to review it for possible publication. Conservatory business administrator Frank Hale urged Chadwick to let NEC publish it privately—and thereby reap the profits—but Chadwick dismissed the idea, "not being at all confident that I would *always* be the [NEC] director, and having a very strong feeling that it would be more successful if published in the regular trade."[24] A settlement was reached when Chadwick negotiated from Wood a favorable purchase price for NEC students, and the institution was credited on the inside cover.[25]

The first edition of *Harmony* was utilized by Chadwick in various NEC classrooms with the assistance of his newly appointed theory department head, Benjamin Cutter (1857–1910). Cutter had been on the conservatory staff for some time, but his considerable talent had been completely overlooked by Faelten. Chadwick recognized that Cutter was in fact one of the brighter lights among the faculty, a splendid theorist and teacher who was both popular and amicable. The classroom use of *Harmony* enabled the location of a few errors, but in general "the book worked admirably and Cutter was very enthusiastic about it." Other teachers also responded positively. "The book met with little unfavorable criticism," Chadwick later remembered, "and a good deal [of] warm commendation. The old fogies thought it was too 'advanced' and too difficult for the average student—which was perhaps true." That, he concluded, "depends on how much they want to learn!"[26]

Chadwick's purpose is succinctly stated in his preface:

The object of this book is to give the student a working vocabulary of chords for the harmonizing of melodies in the order of their practical value and harmonic importance. The author has endeavored to encourage the student to use his ever-increasing chord material,—not so much by warnings against what is bad, as by examples of what is good, as musicians understand it, and by maxims deduced from such examples.

This book is not intended to deprive the teacher of his occupation, but rather to furnish him with useful text and material, systematically arranged, which he is to illustrate and elucidate as much as is necessary. To this end copious references and elaborate explanations of details have been avoided as much as is consistent with lucid statement.

The student is supposed to have already a rudimentary knowledge of the intervals, scales and chords given in the introduction.[27]

There is no evidence that Chadwick wrote his text with the hope that it would usurp Richter's manual, although he knew its strengths and weaknesses. Richter's book, comprising a total of twenty-six chapters, is divided into three main parts: (1) "The fundamental harmonies and the chords derived from them," in which Richter examines a wide range of chords including ninth, eleventh, and thirteenth chords, and modulation; (2) "Accidental chord formation. Tones foreign to the harmony," in which he discusses suspensions, pedal point, passing tones, and the like; and (3) "Practical application of the harmonies. The exercises in their use in the pure harmonic structure," or the utilization of harmony to undergird melody.[28] Richter's book is intended for self-study. The verbal explanations are sometimes lengthy, there are few exercises to complete, and scant musical examples are drawn from actual compositions. The text also relies heavily on the comprehension of figured bass, and the final sections lead the student into the first stages of church polyphony; that is, sixteenth-century counterpoint.

Chadwick's text, by contrast, is far better suited to its American audience. The mastery of harmony had long been Chadwick's driving preoccupation, and he later said that "as the training of the literary man consists largely of learning the weight of words, so the harmony student must learn the subtle significance of chords as well as the laws of their progression."[29] With that in mind, *Harmony* comprises seventy-two brief, sequential chapters that outline the qualities and uses of chords. These are supplemented by numerous practice exercises, which students are expected to complete. As Chadwick wrote in his preface, he intended his text to be used by a teacher in either a private or a classroom setting. The simple explanations prepared by Chadwick were to be explored in detail by the music instructor. Music examples, while mostly created by Chadwick, also include excerpts of compositions by Bach, Haydn, Mozart, Beethoven, Mendelssohn, and Wagner. Perhaps most unexpectedly, *Harmony* includes virtually no figured bass, and preparation for the study of counterpoint is completely absent. Chadwick's main purpose was to help the student write harmonies that would support melodies. He plainly addresses the novice composer in his text and is refreshingly undogmatic in his beliefs: "In the matter of counterpoint, I would not insist on any one method. We know that composers are not made by the study of an arbitrary system like strict counterpoint in the church modes, but if the object of study in composition is to acquire a command of the polyphonic style, such studies are of a great advantage."[30] A unique feature of the book is Chadwick's inclusion of a variety of graphs and visual aids that assist the student in the understanding of complex harmonic relationships.

Notably missing from the first edition of *Harmony* is the oft-quoted passage by Chadwick that "if the effect justifies the means, *any* rule may be disregarded. This usually involves considerations other than purely harmonic ones; orchestral color, rhythm, and the dramatic effect often give striking significance to harmonic combinations and progressions which would otherwise be offensive, or at least unsatisfactory."[31] These words have been cited as early evidence of Chadwick's progressive tendencies, but did not appear until later, when Chadwick added a substantial appendix to address the staggering changes that were occurring in modern harmonic and compositional aesthetics. He admitted with melancholy that, since the book was first published, "much water has flowed under the bridge."[32]

Within two years of its initial release, Chadwick had softened his stance on the text's difficulty as he came to realize that perhaps the book was too challenging for some of his students at NEC. This change of heart gave him an opportunity to demonstrate his confidence in Cutter, whom he encouraged to prepare and publish—this time under the auspices of the conservatory—*Exercises in Harmony: Simple and Advanced Supplementary to the Treatise on Harmony by G. W. Chadwick*.[33] Its publication was a winning situation; it ensured that it would be used by everyone at NEC, it enabled Cutter to put his own stamp on Chadwick's work, and Chadwick earned more in royalties.

Harmony enjoyed widespread popularity for well over a quarter of a century; by 1925 Wood was printing its eighty-eighth edition. If Chadwick had already exerted pressure on his staff to excel, *Harmony* is one of the first manifestations of his own desire to impress high standards on students at NEC. It also reveals much about Chadwick's own compositional aesthetic—he appreciated tradition but he could also muster a good deal of innovation within conventional bounds. More immediately, however, *Harmony* demonstrated to his faculty that he knew a thing or two about teaching music and could express ideas with authority and eloquence.

The Conservatory Orchestra

Tourjée and Faelten had been generally content to recruit pianists and singers to NEC. Although there had been early, and even mildly successful, efforts to build an orchestra program, neither leader was particularly knowledgeable about running one. Tourjée, after all, favored vocal music and was himself an organist, and Faelten was a pianist who had no experience with the ensemble except for occasionally performing in front of one. In any event, success may have seemed so remote as to make the effort hardly worth it. However, Chadwick postulated that the best way to give NEC legitimacy and a sense of community importance would be to form an ongoing, permanent orchestra; it had also been obvious to him for some time that if the conservatory remained a school for singers and pianists, it simply would not thrive. It might not even survive.

Orchestra-loving Boston, Chadwick knew, would support an orchestral enterprise. Not only that, but Chadwick's own first love was the orchestra and its music; had there not been the prospect of developing one, he probably would not have accepted the post. In a letter to Theodore Thomas in 1902, Chadwick explained the strategy he had adopted: "I have tried to organize this school on a university basis,—that is to say, making it a complete school in each department, Voice, Pianoforte, Organ, Composition, Orchestra, etc., while combining them all for theoretical work, and I am beginning to be quite happy over the result."[34] Indeed, Chadwick gave due attention to all of these areas, but the orchestra was his first priority. When he addressed the Music Teachers' National Association in 1909, he stated plainly, "An orchestra is an indispensible adjunct to a fully equipped school of music. For not only does it teach its own members the necessary routine of orchestral playing, but it is a sort of laboratory in which every singer, player, conductor and composer may work, besides giving the most convincing examples of the rendering of music to those students who are debarred from active participation."[35] Chadwick sought to devise an orchestra that would be NEC's common ground.

A crucial element in the development of NEC's orchestra concerned the reorganization of the string department. It was apparent to Chadwick that he would have to deal immediately with the two warring factions in the violin department led by teachers Emil Mahr (1851–1914) and Eugene Gruenberg (1854–1928). Both men were imposing musicians. Mahr had been a student of the legendary Joseph Joachim and was a veteran of several Bayreuth Festivals, at which he hobnobbed with many of the greatest musicians in Europe. Gruenberg, a composer of ambition, had performed for ten years in the Leipzig Gewandhaus Orchestra and had remarkable teaching credentials that included several published volumes of pedagogical works for violin. Each man operated his own string studio, and each ran his own ensemble class; this was a variety of isolationism that had been tolerated at NEC since its founding. "Neither of them had anything to do with the other," Chadwick complained. "Between them there were perhaps twelve or fourteen violins and violas and one or two violoncellos. So I informed both these gentlemen that the two classes were to be united under *my* direction and 'advised' them to send their students to the class."[36]

With fewer than fifteen string players accompanied by an organ performing the wind parts and music borrowed from the Harvard Musical Association, Chadwick began the conservatory orchestra in earnest in 1897. By 1898, winds and percussion—including two flutes, one oboe, two clarinets, two horns, two cornets, plus timpani players—had been added. The remaining wind parts were realized on the organ by George S. Dunham, whom Chadwick coached in the art of score reading; the rehearsals were moved into the cramped quarters of Sleeper Hall. As concerts neared, the orchestra's roster was bolstered by paid players.

The orchestra performed its first complete program without reinforcement from Dunham on March 7, 1902. Selections included the more manageable portions of Beethoven's *Egmont* Overture, which had been performed by the group (with Dunham's assistance) the previous autumn, and at which the orchestra had worked tirelessly since the beginning of the academic year.[37] "This was the first audible result of more than four years of scheming, planning and working," Chadwick wrote. And he knew he would have to continue to do all of these to maintain his standards. Nevertheless, he was proud of the results.[38]

A reviewer for the *Boston Evening Transcript* noted only that it was "a very interesting event."[39]

The orchestra performed again in June at the considerably larger Tremont Temple. The occasion was NEC's annual commencement exercises, which were highlighted by the ensemble's rendering of the first movement of Rheinberger's Organ Concerto in F (op. 137). The audience comprised students, parents, faculty, and conservatory supporters. While many may not have known the music, few could have failed to recognize how far the orchestra had progressed.

Prior to Chadwick, the conservatory had regularly operated with annual losses made up by generous contributions from a few individuals. Although he had not originally planned to do so, Chadwick immediately involved himself—not without some resistance—in conservatory finances. NEC's accounting reports had long been consolidated, combining the business side (dorms, capital expenditures, and the like) and the artistic side (teachers' salaries, performance-related costs, etc.). Where Tourjée and Faelten had been content to leave the business side in the hands of others, Chadwick intruded and quickly discovered that the conservatory's perennial fiscal shortfall was due to the residence hall and other physical plant amenities, including Sleeper Hall.

Although the dormitory complex had been advantageous for NEC's marketing efforts—contemporary advertisements cited its "collateral advantages," such as a gymnasium, a library, and even a resident physician—housing hundreds of students at the St. James Hotel and maintaining the buildings had proven to be a money-losing proposition. On the other hand, the musical component of the conservatory operation—student tuition, salaries, and administrative costs—had done surprisingly well from a fiscal standpoint, as Chadwick found when he separated the financial ledgers.

In short order, Chadwick concluded that the future solvency of NEC depended on abandoning its present Franklin Square location to move to another part of town and into a less expensive facility, and perhaps even a new building of its own. This notion Chadwick intended to proffer at the annual meeting of the conservatory's trustees, but he feared a cool reception. Who could blame him? Given the institution's shaky financial history, its bad luck—or poor judgement—with property investments, and its mildly scandalous reputation, he had little reason to think that the trustees would even consider moving forward with such an ambitious project. Nevertheless, Chadwick believed that a new site was crucial. His current classroom space was inadequate, and the performance venue was entirely too small, especially given his orchestral aspirations. That situation required Chadwick and his staff to schedule orchestra rehearsals and performances across the city at halls that the conservatory was forced to rent, often at excessive rates. Chadwick was also anxious to get out of the dorm business. Running a dorm, with all its attendant concerns of caretaking and security, was an aspect of NEC management that Chadwick neither wanted nor needed. The trustees, Chadwick assumed, would argue that even if the dormitory created annual losses, it provided much-needed short-term cash flow. The end of dormitory rental income, combined with the responsibility of a large mortgage on a new building, would be a burden the conservatory could ill-afford.

But Chadwick misjudged his trustees. When he eventually discussed his findings and ideas with them directly, not only were they in agreement with his conclusion, but one trustee suggested the immediate initiation of a subscription to pay for a brand-new facility. He even kicked it off with his own contribution of fifty thousand dollars.[40] That was Eben D. Jordan Jr., perhaps the most important trustee in the institution's history. According to one NEC chronicler, Jordan, a millionaire, was "a fine type of the modern business man, having the distinction of managing the affairs of a giant mercantile establishment and yet finding leisure and inclination to devote his money and time to other projects than the acquisition of wealth."[41] Jordan was precisely the sort of generous rich man that socially conscious Bostonians could admire. After a deal was brokered for the sale of the St. James Hotel, ardent fundraising began, and before long the conservatory fund had built up to an impressive $150,000. Even Henry Higginson gave a five-thousand-dollar contribution. It was not a huge gift from a man known to be philanthropic toward the arts, but Higginson's personal efforts on behalf of NEC raised many more dollars. Chadwick had longed to be released from the tribulations of dormitory management, and, now that he would soon be untethered from that millstone, he could focus on transforming the conservatory into the musical institution he had dreamed of creating.

In later years Chadwick was very sentimental about the NEC orchestra's 1902 premiere performance. "It was the first of a long series of similar performances," he remembered, and "as long as we could keep it going the standards of the conservatory would be safe. I felt too that as soon as we could rehearse and give the concerts in a suitable place it would be recognized by the public and give the conservatory a prestige which it had never before achieved."[42]

By 1914 the orchestra had progressed to a point where it started "with 16 new candidates for the 2nd violin section and 16 veterans for the 1st violins. . . . On the whole, a very promising lot."[43] That "promising lot" paid off; in 1915, the orchestra, led by Wallace Goodrich, performed an evening of music by Wagner.[44] Chadwick thought it one of the best concerts in conservatory history.

Included were the Prelude to *Die Meistersinger*, the Introduction to Act 3 of *Lohengrin*, and selections from *Tristan und Isolde*, *Parsifal*, *Das Rheingold*, and *Die Walküre*. Chadwick wrote, "This went with remarkable smoothness and effectiveness. I was really proud of the orchestra." Karl Muck, conductor of the Boston Symphony Orchestra, was in attendance; he was overwhelmed, for he had no idea that NEC was able to produce such outcomes.[45]

Louis C. Elson had been involved, either as an observer or a teacher, at NEC for years and was regarded as a knowledgeable music critic and an astute historian. When he reflected on his time at NEC, he gave Chadwick appropriate accolades. "Only a few of the older teachers can fully appreciate the difficulties of his task here and how he overcame them," Elson wrote. "There had been dissension, acrimony, plot and counterplot, and the Conservatory was decidedly a 'hothouse.' Under the new [Chadwick] regime, there came not only peace but prosperity. There was full recognition of the work of each teacher, [and] there was a unity of purpose that was exhilarating. There was also a constant advance in the curriculum. Mr. Chadwick did not aim to make 'the biggest school in America' (although that came also in the train of events), but the best and most thorough."[46]

By the century's end, with Tourjée's Franklin Square dormitory enterprise on the wane, the NEC orchestra on the rise, and his trustees enthusiastically on board, Chadwick could set about planning for the conservatory's new home. It would be the centerpiece of his blueprint to make it the best music school in the nation and one on par with the greatest European institutions. Chadwick's ideas—grandiose yet still practical in the old New England way—would require further consultation with Mr. Jordan.

Sketches in Americanism
Chadwick's Instrumental Music
1890s

The new American school of music must strike
its roots deeply into its own soil.
—Antonín Dvořák, *New York Herald*, 1893

The Bohemian Dvořák

Czech composer Antonín Dvořák was already over fifty years old when he came to the United States in September of 1892. Hired by music lover and philanthropist Jeannette Thurber (1850–1946) to provide leadership and to serve as a figurehead for her National Conservatory of Music in New York City, Dvořák was well established, with a long list of compositions to his credit, including eight operas, several large works for chorus and orchestra, eight symphonies, numerous other orchestral pieces, and an impressive catalog of chamber music. Many of his works were widely admired. Dvořák's fame in the US was such that one anonymous journalist believed that "it was unnecessary to introduce him to the American public with a hymn and a sermon."[1]

Thurber was passionately devoted to the cause of American music. She had, along with her husband, the prosperous New York food wholesaler Francis B. Thurber, developed a taste for music philanthropy by starting the English language–only American Opera Company in 1885. Although that endeavor was short-lived, Thurber was undeterred. She founded her conservatory in the same year, 1885, and it received its national charter in 1891 at no small cost to her time and personal fortune. "A more thoroughly unselfish project cannot be found," wrote a *Washington Post* reporter.[2] Thurber had a remarkable and visionary dream. Music historian Joseph Horowitz concluded that "Thurber's agenda stressed the self-sufficiency of an American musical education. She espoused an American idiom based on native sources. She offered scholarships for women, minorities, and the handicapped. African-Americans were prominent students at every level of study."[3]

By the time Dvořák arrived, the National Conservatory had already developed a reputation for excellence. Modeled on the Paris Conservatoire, the conservatory aimed to provide free tuition for its students, and thus attracted some very talented ones.[4] Its faculty boasted many of the city's best musicians, including pianists Rafael Joseffy and James Gibbons Huneker (who was also well known as a music journalist); music history teacher and *New York Tribune* critic Henry T. Krehbiel; and Horatio Parker, whose tenure at the conservatory had begun just prior to Dvořák's arrival and lasted for a single year, until 1893. Like many Americans, Thurber believed that freedom from European musical fetters had yet to be won and that an outstanding American school of composition must be established in order to win that independence. To that end, she acquired excellent teachers and hired Dvořák with the expectation that he would spearhead the effort to create an American school of composers that would spring from her conservatory. Thurber's intentions were admirable, but the irony of enlisting a European composer to reveal the possibilities for creativity in American musical art was not lost on American musicians.

Dvořák, far from being a peasant naïf, as he was commonly portrayed, understood that Thurber expected him to be a visible institutional leader, and he wasted little time in making his first public statements. In an interview with a writer from the *New York Herald* (widely suspected to have been James Creelman), titled "Real Value of Negro Melodies" and appearing on May 21, 1893—less than a year after his arrival—Dvořák made his stance on the future of American music known. "I am now satisfied," he told Creelman, "that the future of music in this country must be founded upon what are called the Negro melodies. This must be the real foundation of any serious and original school of composition to be developed in the United States."[5]

He clarified his initial thoughts a week later in a letter to the editor of the same newspaper, writing that his conclusions were arrived at after months of research and observation. "This is not a sudden discovery on my part," Dvořák wrote. "The light has gradually dawned on me."[6] His thoughtful essay considered the nature of music as currently practiced in America and addressed two principal themes: first, he acknowledged that there was a paucity of educational opportunities available to musicians in America; professional instruction was nearly impossible to find except in the largest cities and towns. Indeed, the nation was woefully short of both teachers and educational institutions, as formal music education and performance had only just begun to expand their reach into colleges and universities. Increasing the possibilities for music education was a cause that could unite many musicians, music lovers, and philanthropists; it was, of course, central to Thurber's mission. Dvořák didn't stop there; his second point, regarding potential sources of inspiration of the American composer, brought with it something of a firestorm. "It is my opinion," he declared, "that I find a sure foundation in the Negro melodies for a new national school of music, and my observations have already convinced me that the young musicians of this country need only intelligent directions, serious application and a reasonable amount of public support and applause to create a new musical school in America."[7]

That single sentence stoked to a blaze the embers that had already been lit by "Real Value of Negro Melodies." It also generated mounds of censure. Musician and music educator William T. Mollenhauer's response was typical. He wrote to *American Art Journal*, "The idea of using Negro melodies as a basis for a new school of American music appears ridiculous. These melodies are so incipient [*sic*] and trivial that an American would be ashamed to derive his inspiration from such trash; besides the Negro is a Negro and belongs to Africa, not to America. These so-called Negro songs are not original; if they were, we would find them in their native land (which is not the case)."[8]

Chadwick was not unaware of the controversy, although in his usual reticent Yankee way he was rather indifferent to, perhaps even slightly dismissive of, the whole thing. In light of the controversy, the *Boston Herald* asked for additional commentary from local composers and musicians. Among those who offered up their thoughts on the matter were John Knowles Paine, Amy Beach, B. J. Lang, George Whiting, and Chadwick. While most provided lengthy missals about music in America and its possibilities for advancement by the use of ethnic musics, Chadwick wrote laconically, "I am not sufficiently familiar with the real Negro melodies to be able to offer any opinion on the subject. Such Negro melodies as I have heard, however, I should be sorry to see become the basis of an American school of composition."[9]

If Chadwick dismissed the notion of utilizing Negro melodies, he would have been hard-pressed to disagree with some of Dvořák's other observations. "The new American school of music must strike its roots deeply into its own soil," the Bohemian insisted. "There is no longer any reason why young Americans who have talent should go to Europe for their education. It is a waste of money and puts off the coming day when the Western world [i.e., the US] will be in music, as in many others, independent of other lands. . . . I find good talent here, and I am convinced that when the youth of the country realizes that it is better now to stay at home than go abroad we shall discover genius, for many who have talent but cannot undertake foreign residence will be encouraged to pursue their studies here."[10]

Surely Chadwick must have had some sympathy for Dvořák's personal travails, many of which he had also endured. Dvořák undoubtedly hoped to inspire and endear himself to the American public by advancing his own story of hardship and self-sacrifice in the service of his art; after all, it was a compelling tale that reflected very closely several quintessentially American ideals. "If in my own career," Dvořák stated,

I have achieved a measure of success and reward it is to some extent due to the fact that I was the son of poor parents and was reared in an atmosphere of struggle and endeavor. Broadly speaking the Bohemians are a nation of peasants. My first musical education I got from my schoolmaster, a man of good ability and much earnestness. He taught me to play the violin. . . . Then I spent two years in the organ school in Prague. From that time on I had to study for myself. It is impossible for me to speak without emotion of the strains and sorrows that came upon me in the long and bitter years that followed. Looking back at that time, I can hardly understand how I endured the privations and labor of my youth.[11]

Dvořák wrote his Symphony no. 9 (*From the New World*) between January and May 1893. It was his first work composed in the US and the first of several to demonstrate traits he thought "American." Although Dvořák's identification of his symphony as American in style was usually oblique, he may have intended it to serve as a model for American composers. He certainly claimed to have imbued the work with American traits, and he said as much in his correspondence. To his friend Antonín Rus, he wrote: "Just now I am finishing a new *Symphony in E minor* and I'm very pleased that it will again be different from my earlier ones. Maybe it will be a little *American!!!*"[12]

The Bohemian had been inspired by Henry Wadsworth Longfellow's epic poem *The Song of Hiawatha*, which first appeared in 1855.[13] Houghton, Mifflin & Company brought out a new edition in 1891, one which featured hundreds of simple ink sketches and several elaborate portraits of Native American scenes and artifacts. The book's illustrators included artistic luminaries Frederic Remington, Maxfield Parrish, and N. C. Wyeth. As a result of the grandeur of the volume, *The Song of Hiawatha* saw its popularity renewed; it seems likely that Dvořák was familiar with this edition.

The *New World* Symphony was premiered at an open rehearsal on December 15, 1893, with Anton Seidl leading the New York Philharmonic at Carnegie Hall. A hugely anticipated event, it naturally generated torrents of critical assessment. Among the most important voices in favor of Dvořák's ideas was the sedulous Henry Krehbiel. Krehbiel enthusiastically endorsed Dvořák and considered him, if not the savior of American music, then certainly a divinely inspired prophet of American music's potential. He could not understand why some rejected Dvořák's advocacy of indigenous materials. "Music is seeking new vehicles of expression," he affirmed, "and is seeking them where they are most sure to be found—in the field of the folk-song. We have such a field and it is rich. Why not cultivate it? Why these sneers at the only material which lies to our hand?"[14]

But others would have none of it. James Huneker was one critic among many who saw no single nationalistic influence on the symphony. He predicted that "when the smoke of criticism has cleared away it will be noticed, first, that Dr. Dvořák has written an exceedingly beautiful symphony; secondly, that it is not necessarily American, unless to be American you must be composite. The work, thematically considered, is composite, sounding Irish, Slavic, Scandinavian, Scotch, Negro and German. The latter nationality enters into its construction, for the form is purely symphonic in the conventional style, as exemplified by Beethoven, while the coloring and treatment is modern and altogether Dvořák's—meaning Czech."[15] Huneker seems subtly to be saying that a composition *from* the New World need not necessarily be *of* it.

Dvořák concurred. He was annoyed at the perception that he had simply quoted from American musical sources, and, although the symphony clearly reflects his impressions of America, the composer could not—and would not—escape his own strong Czechness. In a letter to Oskar Nedbal, who had been Dvořák's pupil in composition in Prague and was about to conduct a concert of Dvořák's works in Berlin (including the *New World* Symphony), the composer wrote: "I'm also sending you Kretschmar's analysis of the symphony, but leave out that nonsense that I used Indian and American motives, because it's a lie: I only tried to write in the spirit of those American folk [*národní*] melodies!"[16]

Chadwick sided with Huneker on the matter. After hearing the BSO play the *New World* Symphony on December 30, 1893, he had a bit more to say on the subject. "The style was certainly new and some of the themes . . . resembled Negro spirituals and Indian dance tunes. But some of the best tunes were like other composers especially Schubert and Dvořák himself."[17] Chadwick did not dwell, as many did, on Dvořák and his impact on music in America, although it is worth mentioning that (for reasons that are unclear) he copied a brief excerpt from the Bohemian's *American* Quartet (no. 12 in F major) into his compositional sketchbook in 1894.[18]

Chadwick expressed his hopes many times that America would produce a great composer, but never did he indicate that the "Great American Composer" would or should compose in a nationalistic style. By the mid-1890s, the drive to identify the Great American Composer was acute; equally intense was the desire in some quarters for American composers to write "American" music, whether according to the Dvořák prescription or otherwise.

Symphony No. 3 (1894)

Of course, one way to identify the Great American Composer was to sponsor a competition, and shortly after the new director's arrival in New York, the

National Conservatory did exactly that. "Desiring to celebrate the engagement of Dr. Dvořák," a *New York Times* reporter explained in 1893, a competition had been founded that would "award large prizes" to composers in the categories of "best opera, libretto, symphony, oratorio, suite or cantata, and piano or violin concerto."[19] Competing composers were to have been born in the US and under thirty-five years old. Chadwick, along with many of his peers, did not meet the latter requirement, which was intended to induce younger musicians to apply. Instead, Chadwick served as a judge in the "Grand Opera" category; at that time he probably first met Dvořák and other National Conservatory leaders.

The results of the first competition, put before an audience on March 30, 1893, were, in the eyes of one writer, underwhelming. "On the whole," he lamented, "the concert was exceedingly dull." It included music by four winners, three of whom were virtually unknown and one who was recognized as a rising star: Henry Schoenefeld of Chicago won for his symphony; Joshua Phippen of Boston for his piano concerto; Frederick Bullard of Boston for his string orchestra suite; and Horatio Parker, now living in New York, for his cantata *The Dream-King and His Love.* Although he saw in them slight indications of talent, the reviewer found that "the symphony, the concerto, and suite all proved to be extremely crude works." But Parker's youthful cantata, the hands-down sensation of the evening, was "a melodious, fluent work, excellently written." Schoenefeld, who later in his career would be known for his "Indianist" predilections, was on the receiving end of the writer's harshest criticism. "The symphony competition must have been of a poor sort," he concluded, "to permit the award of the prize to such an immature composition."[20] Clearly Dvořák and his conservatory's plan to hold an annual contest for American composers was not off to an auspicious start.

Chadwick's Third Symphony was begun at least by the summer of 1893, and possibly even as early as 1892, well before the announcement of the National Conservatory's second annual competition, which was tucked into Creelman's famous article in the *New York Herald.*[21] Chadwick dedicated his symphony to Theodore Thomas, possibly as a gesture of thanks for Thomas's having featured the *Columbian Ode* so prominently at the World's Fair. His devotion to Thomas, whom he had deeply admired since his youth, had intensified in the years since the fair preparations began. Of course, Chadwick's possible ulterior motives must also be acknowledged. No stranger to musical politics, Chadwick may simply have thought that by dedicating his symphony to Thomas he would have a better chance of getting it performed (see figure 8.1). Whatever his reason—ultimately unknowable and likely a combination of the two—this symphony

FIGURE 8.1. George Whitefield Chadwick, 1893.
Courtesy of New England Conservatory, Boston.

may have been intended as a signal to the world that America already possessed a composer of no small talent, and that there was little need in the United States for a pontificating Bohemian.

Chadwick carefully sized up his potential competitors—easy enough to do at the time, as American symphony composers of standing were few—and concluded that the only composers of merit who could submit a work were Paine, whose compositional pace had slowed considerably and who in any case would not be able to compete (the maximum age had been pushed to forty), and Parker, who he knew had neither a completed symphony in hand nor time to produce one.[22] In any event, Parker had just won a prize in the previous contest and might not have cared to enter the second one. And Chadwick may have believed that recent professional connections established with the National Conservatory might help his efforts to win the prize. These conclusions made him more cocksure than he had ever been about the prospects for his music—as he placed his Third Symphony in the post, he was already certain he would win.

Indeed Chadwick did win the competition, and he was notified in April 1894 via telegram from Dvořák himself. Dvořák also waived the National Conservatory's right to premiere the symphony in view of Chadwick's desire to "produce it without delay."[23] We may surmise that by this time Chadwick had already been assured of its performance by the BSO. At any rate, when Chadwick informed Horatio Parker that he had won, Parker, who had an intimate knowledge of the conservatory and its finances, only half-jokingly urged him to cash the three-hundred-dollar prize check posthaste. In a moment of classic understatement, Chadwick suggested that Parker "was dubious about the financial stability of the Thurber Conservatory."[24]

Before the National Conservatory contest winner was announced, Chadwick eagerly peddled the Third Symphony not to the BSO but to Theodore Thomas. Chadwick wrote to Thomas twice in October 1893, the first time to ask if Thomas would review the symphony during his vacation at his home in Fairhaven, Massachusetts, near Boston. Chadwick even offered Thomas the use of an apartment during a planned visit to Boston, during which he hoped to share the score with the conductor.[25] In the interim, Thomas had apparently agreed to perform the symphony: "The score I can show you at your leisure while here, and I thank you for your offer to play it. If it holds good after you see it I will be delighted to accept."[26] But the performance did not materialize, and Chadwick received an explanation, although it has been lost to history. He again wrote to Thomas: "I was very glad to receive your kind letter although it was not necessary to reassure me of your continued interest in my work for I know that you will do all you can for me and for all of us."[27] Thomas had not yet seen the symphony that was dedicated to him. "You may have heard that I received the prize for my Symphony as you predicted I would do," Chadwick wrote. "I have not received the money yet but when I do I propose to spend a portion of it on a ticket . . . to Fairhaven that you may look over the score at your leisure."[28]

The BSO premiered the Third Symphony on October 19, 1894. Shortly thereafter, Chadwick was still enticing Thomas with it. In yet another letter, he wrote: "I can also send you the parts of my new Symphony at any time if you can find a place on your program for it. It was very well received here & condemned by some of the newspaper men as a 'dry and uninspired work' by which you may guess that it has some features which were not altogether trivial. Besides the orchestra are quite enthusiastic over it which is enough to condemn it for a newspaperman."[29] After innumerable delays, Thomas finally conducted the symphony on January 8 and 9, 1897, with his Chicago Symphony Orchestra. Thomas was ecstatic about the final result and soon began recommending it to European conductors.[30]

The symphony was deeply meaningful to Chadwick. "I could not help feeling that the slow movement reflected the sacred joy of our young motherhood and fatherhood," he later recalled; "the first movement, the aspiration and ambition of newly won power and maturity; and the last movement the exaltation of victorious achievement. For in this work I tried my utmost for perfection of architectural form, for beauty and nobility of melodic expression, rithmic [*sic*] variety and for sonorous and rich orchestral color rather than tricky decorative effects." Chadwick went on to note that the symphony, dignified and pure in expression, included "no muted strings, 'sul ponticello' or 'col legno' effects and muted horns only once."[31]

Thomas's apparent enthusiasm was well founded, for the Third Symphony is an ambitious and compelling work. The first of its four movements is an F-major sonata structure marked Allegro sostenuto. Melodic, richly orchestrated, and restless in its rhythms, some of its originality is vitiated by the striking initial measures that will immediately remind the listener of Brahms's Symphony no. 3, also in F major. Although the opening chord in Chadwick's movement is resolved differently than in Brahms's symphony, the closeness between the two was recognized by the most astute listeners. His melodic gifts are obvious in this movement, as well, especially in the opening of the secondary section, which features a beautiful folk-like tune in the oboe and horns. Chadwick's effective orchestration is sometimes clouded by less attractive imitative passages, which, when combined with several ponderous transitions, bog down the forward momentum.

The second movement, Andante cantabile, easily ranks among Chadwick's most alluring orchestral creations. It is redolent of themes that resemble folk song, but Chadwick's German training led him to introduce several relentless stretto and fugal passages that his more progressive listeners considered pedantic. Importantly, these sections never obscure the many gorgeous string passages, punctuated by rich, powerful yet unobtrusive brass chords. The movement, an ABA form in D minor, stresses unusual harmonic choices, including several Neapolitan-sixth and diminished-sevenths chords and a number of colorful minor sonorities. The rhapsodic, doleful ending is one of the best moments in all of Chadwick's music.

Marked Vivace non troppo, the third movement is also constructed in ABA form. Its main theme closely resembles a saltarello and rapidly leads to the middle section, which highlights the horns and strings in pentatonic passages. Here the oboes also perform strains that have a slightly oriental tint. There is in this movement a Mendelssohnian lightness and grace that most contemporary writers found deliciously appealing.

Chadwick's fourth movement, Finale: Allegro molto energico in sonata form, opens with a muscular flourish, again in the horns. The main melody that follows in the cellos is reminiscent of contemporary British music, broad and pastoral, and is perhaps even suggestive of Edward Elgar. Much of what follows, however, is difficult to follow. Chadwick parses his themes in any number of ways, and the result is a form that, while discernible after careful study, is difficult to follow at first hearing. This aside, there are several striking soli passages for the trumpets, horns, and oboes, each of which reflects Chadwick's desire to write music for winds that is more than mere accompaniment.

Although in retrospect we are able to recognize the Third Symphony as one of Chadwick's finest achievements—perhaps the watershed of his early maturity—it was not considered so at the time, despite, or possibly because of, winning the National Conservatory prize. The writer for Boston's *Saturday Evening Gazette* considered it rather "intellectual," and he went on to damn it with faint praise: "uninspired as it is, Mr. Chadwick's Symphony is the finest product that American musical art has produced."[32] But that was a minority opinion. Others found the symphony a total artistic failure, including Philip Hale, a generally well-regarded critic, who thought the composition a "disappointment."[33] Hale believed that Chadwick had been "sitting at the feet of Johannes Brahms," especially in the first movement—no surprise there—and he sarcastically guessed that the composer "has also listened—no doubt unconsciously—to the pleasing performance of Mr. Antonín Dvořák on the celebrated instrument known as the Negro-Indian American pipe, which I believe is the invention of Messrs. Krehbiel & Company." This was a blatantly disparaging comment directed toward Krehbiel, whom Hale blamed for encouraging the use of ethnic musical sources, a practice Hale thought misguided. While the remark is a bit snide, it nevertheless makes the point that Chadwick's contemporaries recognized that his music was mildly tinged with African American or Native American traits, as suggested by Dvořák.

Reviewer Louis C. Elson was similarly disenchanted. He observed that "when Mr. Chadwick came upon the stage to direct his symphony there was a most spontaneous outburst of applause; but the applause was not quite so un-hesitating after the first movement had come to an end." Admitting his aversion to "pampering the American muse," Elson thought that in the first movement of the symphony Chadwick fell "into the style of Brahms in giving many small thoughts rather than one continuous one." Elson was pleased by the second and third movements, but concluded that "all in all, one finds much to praise in the work, but at the end must confess that the great American symphony is not yet written."[34]

Warren Davenport, of the *Boston Herald*, echoed a number of Hale's com-ments when he judged that "as a whole, the music is labored and dry; the themes lack nobility; the thematic development is disappointing; the ideas advanced are without purpose, or over-elaborated and weighted down with a loud and noisy orchestration; the progressions in the wind passages are often discordant and ear-splitting in their violence and are not mollified in the least by the efforts of the strings, which are employed also with an overabundance of vigor, at times, while the whole work moves on in patches, incoherent and obscure, as regards true musical form." Davenport's summation was unambiguous: "Mr. Chadwick has failed to achieve a success."[35] Comments in this vein are found in review after review.

When Thomas was considering the symphony for another Chicago perfor-mance, in the 1900–1901 season, Chadwick confessed to him, "I have always felt that it was as good as I could do at that time, but it was roundly abused by the newspaper reptiles in this town, largely, I think, because they knew I received a prize for it. They are a precious lot, as I don't have to tell you."[36] Chadwick was particularly distressed that his symphony's merits escaped the notice of his Bos-ton audiences. And as he aged, his disgust with the "newspaper reptiles" would only intensify. His disdain for a nefarious press undoubtedly contributed to his abandonment of the "classical" symphony as it was conventionally conceived.

Symphonic Sketches (1895–1904)

Chadwick's greatest "American" musical statement is his *Symphonic Sketches*, which was begun in the winter of 1895. It was music that Chadwick knew would be performed—a rare thing for an American composer—for the request for a composition from his pen had originated with George W. Stewart, whose Boston Festival Orchestra had provided musicians for the Springfield Festival during Chadwick's time there. In addition, Stewart, a business agent and impre-sario, planned to send a small orchestra on tour throughout the United States, and he asked Chadwick to conduct.[37] Chadwick declined Stewart's conduct-ing offer, but he happily provided a composition; he was certain his *Sketches* "would be heard by very miscellaneous [i.e., diverse] audiences all over the country."[38]

As we have seen, some of Chadwick's music to this point had been considered characteristically American, but in his *Sketches* he was determined to confront head-on the recent controversies over what is or is not stylistically American. Although he did not explain his compositional methods with any specificity—and we know that he was not particularly moved by Dvořák's recipe—he nevertheless determined to make them "*American* in style—as I understand the term."[39]

The most striking manifestation of Chadwick's Americanism is his emphasis on rhythm and the syncopations that reflect an energy commonly associated with the "typical" American persona. Contemporary critics also remarked on the ebb and flow of mood that resulted from constant shifts in rhythm and tempo. *Transcript* critic H. T. Parker thought the *Sketches* reflected the obvious tendency "in the American temperament to turn suddenly serious, and deeply and unaffectedly so, in the midst of its 'fooling,' to run away into sober fancies and moods, and then as quickly turn 'jolly' again."[40] Philip Hale explained to his readers that in the *Sketches* "there is an originality, a swing, an audacity, a recklessness, and irreverence" in the music that is utterly captivating and largely based on rhythm and tempo.[41]

Chadwick's melodies strike the pentatonic chord we have seen in his music since *Rip Van Winkle* Overture, including several of the string quartets, and even in his recent Third Symphony, although rarely had the composer placed pentatonicism so obviously before his audience. His instrumentation also left a distinctly American impression: a huge number of exposed brass and percussion passages as well as wind solos give the *Sketches* a distinctive sound, one that is at times boisterous, even rather unorchestral, and more redolent of a band. There is little wonder that over the years this work attracted the attention of bandmasters, including John Philip Sousa and others, who performed the *Sketches* in arrangements for band.

The first movement, "Jubilee," completed in 1895, a barn-burner if there ever was one, is heard frequently on concert programs and radio today, especially on festive occasions, such as Independence Day. Chadwick's slow movement, "Noël," so titled for the dual reason of its having been conceived in winter and also reflecting the name of his second son, Noël, had its origins in an organ improvisation, which "I made in church after 'the long prayer.'" It, too, was completed in 1895. The last movement, the picturesque "A Vagrom Ballad," was composed from an idea that came to Chadwick during one of his many rail journeys to Springfield to lead the town's annual festivals. Chadwick watched "the hobos and tramps who infest the woods" near the tracks and developed "the idea of a narrative, related by any one of them."[42] "A Vagrom Ballad," completed in early 1896, includes a variety of humorous sonic gestures, including hiccups. Chadwick thought that in this movement, which delighted him, he had accurately depicted the American hobo, whose life—strange and little-understood—was still romanticized during Chadwick's time.[43]

The three *Sketches* were first performed in New Bedford, Connecticut, before being featured on the tour that also included *The Lily Nymph*.[44] Chadwick conducted the Boston premiere of these movements on November 21, 1904. A performance of the completed four-movement work had to wait until 1908, when the scherzo-like third movement, "Hobgoblin," (composed in 1904) was added. This turned the suite into what amounts to a four-movement symphony, his unofficial "Fourth."[45] Karl Muck led the premiere of the whole with BSO at Symphony Hall.

The word "sketches" requires a bit of explanation here, as in Chadwick's day it was a term in wide circulation with many applications. "Sketches" denoted not only works of visual art—portraits, landscapes, and the like, most often drawn by pencil or pen—but also descriptive writings, such as biographies, travelogues, and histories. Perhaps the most famous example of literary sketches in America is Washington Irving's 1820 masterpiece, *The Sketch Book of Geoffrey Crayon*, which included *Rip Van Winkle*, *The Legend of Sleepy Hollow*, and other tales, essays, and observations. Another popular volume was William Dean Howells's 1871 *Suburban Sketches*, a compilation of essays and ruminations, many of which concern activities in Boston. The book was reissued in 1898 with drawings by Augustus Hoppin, a respected illustrator of books. Howells, in his chapter titled "Jubilee Days," wrote about Gilmore's 1869 Peace Jubilee in Boston. As discussed previously, Howells penned a mostly positive account of the Peace Jubilee; he was charmed by the music but was much more awed by the sights and sounds of the crowd and its response to the spectacle. Howells remarked that, as time passed, the Jubilee crowds dwindled, but not on account of worsening weather. He observed that the Jubilee's "general expression had changed: it had no longer that entire gayety of the opening day, but had taken on something of the sarcastic pathos with which we Americans bear most oppressive and fatiguing things as a good joke. The dust was blown about in clouds; and here and there, sitting upon the vacant steps that led up and down among the booths, were dejected and motionless men and women, passively gathering dust, and apparently awaiting burial under the accumulating sand,—the mute, melancholy sphinxes of the Jubilee, with their unsolved riddle, 'Why did we come?'"[46]

Chadwick had a different recollection of the Peace Jubilee. While Howells, an Ohioan, looked at the event with the eyes of an outsider, Chadwick beamed with hometown pride; the Jubilee not only cemented Boston's position on the musical map, but two members of his own family had even participated in the chorus. Might Chadwick's first *Symphonic Sketch*, "Jubilee," be the composer's response to Howells's impressions of the Peace Jubilee? It is not possible to know with certainty, of course, but all signs indicate that these *Sketches* are extraordinarily personal documents.

Chadwick prefaced each movement of the *Sketches* with a mood-establishing text that he penned himself. ("Very few people," he later wrote gleefully, "know it to this day."[47]) The text prefacing "Jubilee" features a number of references to color, but most telling is Chadwick's emphasis on the word "MY," which suggests his own experience of Gilmore's great event:

No cool gray tones for me!
Give me the warmest red and green,
A cornet and a tambourine,
To paint MY Jubilee!
For when pale flutes and oboes play,
To sadness I become a prey;
Give me the violets and the May,
But no gray skies for me.

Chadwick's loud and brassy main theme, styled in the manner of a fanfare, begins without introduction in A major (Allegro molto vivace). The contrasting theme, in C major, is marked *cantabile*, a favorite indication for the second theme in Chadwick's sonata forms. Here a graceful folk-song melody in the unison violins and horns soars over an attractive, if slightly out of place, habañera rhythm. Why did Chadwick move to C major, the mediant key, rather than the more expected dominant, E major? Several reasons are possible: Chadwick had explored the possibilities of mediant relationships since his earliest works, and the reduction in large-scale harmonic tension more easily enabled the emphasis of other musical elements such as melody and rhythm. More practically, however, the move to C major placed the music, and especially the horn part, within a comfortable tessitura.

The development section is harmonically adventuresome. It swirls through a number of keys, and the principal tune even makes a brief appearance in the remote key of C-sharp minor. Once the recapitulation arrives—with a thunderous chord and a halting two-measure misplacement of the principal theme—the music again travels down an unexpected road for a final restatement of the secondary theme, now in F major rather than the principal key. The five-section coda of "Jubilee" not only restates the two main themes but introduces an altogether new one.

A glance at the proportions of "Jubilee" will demonstrate that the extended manipulation of materials is key to Chadwick's style in this instance: the exposition is a mere eighty measures in length; the development, recapitulation, and the codas, wherein the materials undergo tremendous transformation, constitute the remaining 253 measures. As he had done so many times in the past, Chadwick treated the recapitulation and the coda as localities in which to develop his material. The constantly changing dispositions of "Jubilee" were paramount to H. T. Parker; he paid scant attention to its melodies or architecture. Parker also dismissed the hints of Negro melody, as he believed that "the American quality of the music lies little in that. Rather it is in the high and volatile spirits of the music, the sheer rough-and-tumble of it at its fullest moment" that made this work "American."[48]

The music of "Noël," lyrical and tranquil, unfolds fluidly throughout its ABA structure in D-flat major, an unexpectedly distant key from the first movement's A major tonality. Chadwick matched the music with the following lines:

Through the soft, calm moonlight comes a sound;
A mother lulls her babe, and all around
The gentle snow lies glistening;
On such a night the virgin mother mild
In dreamless slumber wrapped the Holy Child,
While angel-hosts were listening.

It is impossible to avoid the conclusion that Chadwick's opening melody, a plaintive, pentatonic tune rendered by a lone English horn, was influenced by the first measures of Dvořák's famous Largo from his *New World* Symphony. But the similarities end there; Chadwick's music is not only more intimate, but it features several unusual harmonic twists and passages of hemiola.

"Hobgoblin" is Chadwick's answer to the scherzo, although it is constructed as an F-major sonata form. Chadwick summons images of Puck by prefacing the movement with a line borrowed from Shakespeare's *A Midsummer Night's Dream*:

That shrewd and knavish sprite called Robin-goodfellow

After an introduction stated by the horns, the jolly main tune appears. Vividly depicting the devil-may-care attitude of its subject, it is followed closely by the C-major secondary theme, a brisk Celtic jig. The movement spins through a ka-

TABLE 8.1. The Form of "A Vagrom Ballad"

Section:	Introduction	1	2	3	4	5	Coda 1	Coda 2
Theme:	O		P	P	P	t	N	k	k
Key:	a		a	d	g	a	A	A	A
Measure:	1		16	55	87	146	202	245	281

leidoscopic sequence of keys, and, according to his customary habit, Chadwick developed materials in the recapitulation and in the two-part coda.

The most important of the four *Sketches* from the standpoint of "American-ism" is "A Vagrom Ballad." In a burst of self-congratulatory exuberance, Chadwick later singled out this movement: "I was highly elated by the effect of the Vagrom Ballad. I knew I had said something in that piece!"[49] His prefatory lines set the tone:

> A tale of tramps and railway ties,
> Of old clay pipes and rum,
> Of broken heads and blackened eyes
> And the "thirty days" to come!

In this piece Chadwick has abandoned the structural principles of sonata form to place the music in an eclectic five-part structure (see table 8.1), which is perhaps an admission that he did not have faith in sonata form's ability to convey his programmatic idea. Chadwick had already proven the flexibility of sonata form in "Jubilee" (and several other compositions), but, by using a less rigid formal scheme in his fourth movement, he eliminated the requirement to develop the music in the traditional symphonic manner. Chadwick emphasized minor tonalities starting with A minor before proceeding through D minor, G minor, and A minor again. A dream-like section of new material (N) couched in the language of impressionism and marked Lento misterioso, is followed by a two-part coda, which brings the composition to an exhilarating close.

Several features serve to identify this movement as "American." First, there is a pronounced display of an American sense of humor; not only is "A Vagrom Ballad" marked "alla Burla" (i.e., "in Burlesque style"), suggesting a vaudeville-inspired whimsy, but several solos by unlikely instruments, most notably the bass clarinet and the bassoon, are offered with tongue in cheek. Chadwick's writing for the brass sometimes suggests the military band, and a passage of strumming strings is an attempt to imitate the banjo. One can hear the "ragged" rhythms borrowed from a music that was presently growing in popularity, as well as melodies with a pentatonic hue. H. T. Parker understood Chadwick's musical jokes. He asked rhetorically, "Is Mr. Chadwick's final 'sketch' . . . anything else than musical 'fooling' and musical 'jollying,' American in spirit and expression, and often at its loudest and most careless?"[50]

Symphonic Sketches represents Chadwick's clear departure from the "classic" symphony model. But why would Chadwick abandon a genre that was the ne plus ultra of his epoch and place, and especially at a time when the pursuit of a "real American symphony"—not unlike the dream of a "Great American Novel"— was in full swing? Of course, he didn't. Chadwick, by deploying popular styles, altered the genre slightly to provide music that may have sounded vaguely familiar. By doing so, he created greater accessibility for his listeners. His rejection of strict forms, especially in "A Vagrom Ballad," also freed him to explore novel narratives and more innovative musical relationships. It is worth noting that, like Beethoven's trek from his first three relatively contrapuntal symphonies to his less-so Fourth Symphony, the dense counterpoint—any trace of the "learned" that had been an expected and distinguishing feature of Chadwick's first three symphonies—is completely absent in his *Sketches*.

The nature of the *Symphonic Sketches*—what they are "about"—has been a topic of some debate. Musicologist Victor Fell Yellin emphasized the programmatic elements of the movements rather than their technical and structural features. Couching his argument in terms of another variety of modernism, he called the *Sketches* "realistic" portraits of American life, ones that are void of "the concern for exotica, the bizarre, or the romantic."[51] I later offered an alternate view that, far from being works of realism, they are exemplary essays in American Romanticism and strongly reflect the burgeoning interest among American composers in musical exotica, which included forays into plantation songs, ragtime, and habañera.[52] Although not an extended multi-movement narrative, these pieces may easily be related to the programmaticism of the type exemplified in Berlioz's *Symphonie fantastique*, Strauss's *Also Sprach Zarathustra*, and others. In the *Symphonic Sketches* Chadwick begins to tread ever so lightly into the realm of hyper-Romanticism and even approaches modernism.

Any analysis of *Symphonic Sketches* requires a consideration of Chadwick's growing awareness of recent trends. Several critics detected resemblances in form and orchestration to music by Wagner and Strauss, as well as to Debussy in the brief area of "A Vagrom Ballad" (Lento misterioso) that uses the techniques of impressionism and provides a striking relocation of Chadwick's narrative. One reviewer remarked on the score's "modern orchestral coloring, freedom of form and treatment [and] bold and fiery mood-painting."[53] Another thought it could reasonably be considered an "American *Till Eulenspiegel*"[54] But not all writers gloried in its modernism. Philip Hale was simply gratified to experience pleasant music. Upon hearing the *Sketches* again in 1918, he reflected that "in these days when young composers are gloomy, pessimistic in music, when they strive to translate tragedy into tones, to express the Infinite in a symphonic poem, it is a good thing to be reminded that music may be gay, exhilarating, and thus beneficent."[55] Indeed, the critical acclaim was nearly as great for *Symphonic Sketches* as had been the disappointment in the Third Symphony.

There is no question but that *Symphonic Sketches* evinces some of the musical elements related to modernism and nationalism as had been suggested by Dvořák; these traits were detected by many critics, particularly those who had heard the first performances of Chadwick's work and were still swept up in the Dvořák controversies. More than one critic, however, reminded his readers that Chadwick had written music that recalled the plantation long before the Bohemian composer had arrived in America. But if *Symphonic Sketches* gave a voice to modernism and American musical nationalism, its expression was still fully recognizable to his audiences in Boston, for it was impossible for Chadwick to tear away from his primary compositional imperatives: melody, form, and directness.

The Fourth Quartet (1896)

In his diary entry of December 2, 1895, Chadwick recorded that he had "made all the tunes" for a new string quartet, his fourth in the genre. The Fourth String Quartet is one of Chadwick's most American works, and indeed at times it sounds at least as characteristically American as the better-known *Symphonic Sketches*, although it contains no element of programmaticism. Chadwick's quartet was composed close on the heels of Dvořák's F major *American* Quartet (op. 96), which had been premiered in Boston on New Year's Day 1894, by the Kneisel Quartet. The ensemble, founded by Franz Kneisel, the eminent concertmaster of the BSO, was a remarkable performing group. It was widely known in New England and around the nation, but it was especially beloved in Boston. Chadwick did not attend the premiere of the Dvořák piece; at that time he was preoccupied with his own *Tabasco* project. But he completed his own quartet within a year of that performance, on November 1, 1896, and dedicated it to Kneisel, with whom he was developing a close personal relationship. Following an unimaginable fifteen rehearsals, the Kneisel Quartet premiered the Quartet no. 4 in E minor on December 21, 1896, at Boston's Association Hall. Although Chadwick missed the performance—that night he had been called on to replace the ailing B. J. Lang as conductor of a Handel and Haydn Society rehearsal—

the Kneisel band and the audience adored the quartet. The ensemble would perform it many more times in Boston and elsewhere. The parts (notably not the score) were published by G. Schirmer in 1902, making this the first of Chadwick's quartets to be made commercially available.

If Chadwick had been inspired to write his own American quartet by Dvořák's example, he was no novice at creating characteristically American works, as we have seen. The first movement, firmly couched in sonata form, utilizes familiar features: syncopation, themes that recall hymn tunes, and pentatonic or nearly pentatonic melodies. It opens with a dolorous, syncopated melody presented by the viola, but by the fourth measure a dotted-note motive in the first violin appears that resembles the opening of his own Second Symphony. By the time the main theme is reached, a vast amount of development is already at play. Stretto passages, rhythmic displacement, and hemiola, none of which are new to Chadwick's style, are sounded boldly. Hymn-like music is reached at the section marked *tranquillo*, but it is quickly overshadowed by a pentatonic theme that closely resembles, in both sound and shape, the main theme of *Rip Van Winkle* Overture, although it is not likely that any of those who heard the quartet would have caught the reference to his older work. Often overlooked in this movement is Chadwick's imaginative use of harmony. In one clever stroke, he used an unresolved augmented-sixth chord and dominant-seventh chords that resolve not to the tonic, but to mediant harmonies. These progressions offer a scintillating freshness that adds substantially to the movement's American sound.

Chadwick's second movement "revels in unabashed lyric song,"[56] and in fact it is a diminutive gem among Chadwick's quartet movements, a musical tour in which the composer strolls rather than runs. Crafted in an ABA form and marked Andantino, it begins with an affable main theme that is punctuated by passages of *quasi recitativo* solo cello. A slightly more anxious contrasting B section lasts only briefly before the main melody, in a varied form and played by the second violin and the cello, is restated. In the coda, pizzicato and harmonics in all parts effect a nostalgic remembrance of what has come before.

Critic William Foster Apthorp was probably remembering the third movement when he remarked that the quartet was imbued with a "characteristic Irish brogue."[57] Although it has been compared to musical types as disparate as New England fiddle tunes and comic opera, the principal theme of this movement is clearly a hornpipe, a rustic, traditional dance-type native to the British Isles.[58] A perfectly acceptable replacement for the traditional scherzo, Chadwick's C-major hornpipe keeps up a sturdy virility throughout, and gives every sense of having been adapted from the bagpipes, complete with flourishes and trills. The "quasi-Irish humorousness" that so captured the imaginations of audiences who heard Chadwick's Second Symphony years before can also be heard here, for Chadwick subtly quotes from that earlier composition. A trio section is plaintive in character—darker in its mood, but not pessimistic. It may be argued that among all of Chadwick's inventions this area most closely follows the recipe for the utilization of Negro tunes in American music as prescribed by Dvořák.

Ledbetter has called the finale "in some ways the most unusual movement of the quartet," and indeed from a formal standpoint it is somewhat perplexing.[59] It has the qualities of a passacaglia, but, unlike the textbook passacaglia, Chadwick does not utilize the bass theme throughout. He has also avoided a clearly articulated sonata form, preferring instead to build the movement in thematically related sections, but in a diverse array of tonalities. In other words, Chadwick has made a fairly free composition that wanders in and out of his main thematic idea.

The music begins with a chant-like modal chorale cast in Brahmsian garb. Yellin heard in it a tinge of New England psalmody,[60] but it is worth mentioning that Brahms utilized the passacaglia in the finale movement of his Fourth Symphony. There follows an imitative section; it sounds pedantic, rather like an exercise. This is especially noticeable in light of a number of novel passages that have come before. A beautifully melodic area (Lento espressivo) reaches a sudden pause that brings the whole to an unexpected halt. A fugal section gives Chadwick a chance to tackle the dense polyphony he had thus far avoided. At this point in his manuscript Chadwick etched the words, "And I shall shake," a biblical reference that gives Yellin's notion of psalmodic influence increased credibility. Chadwick may have borrowed from Hebrews 12:26, "Yet once more I will shake not only the earth, but also heavens." His fugue subject, related to the movement's opening theme, is a powerful one that escalates tension through its brisk Allegro con brio tempo and increasing volume. As the music reaches its final key, E major, the main theme is sounded in an augmented form. The movement closes with a sweeping, heroic coda.

Like Kneisel, Apthorp admired the Fourth Quartet. He thought it more characteristic of true quartet writing than was typical of the times, wherein orchestral sonorities were the norm. "And how genial, charming, fresh, and truly musical it all is!" Apthorp cheered. "A single hearing affords no sound basis for detailed criticism; but the first impression is inexpressibly delightful."[61]

The Fifth Quartet (1898)

Chadwick had been buoyed by the success of his Fourth Quartet, and immediately began thinking about another. Although his acceptance of the NEC directorship had interrupted his composing schedule, by the summer of 1898, while returning from Omaha, he had progressed far enough to show Wallace Goodrich a collection of themes worked out in his sketchbook.[62] These were his first ideas for what would eventually become his String Quartet no. 5 in D minor. Chadwick toiled on it through the autumn, and the Fifth Quartet, which he dedicated to the brothers Adamowski, was completed on Thanksgiving Day 1898. The Adamowski Quartet, with violinist Timothée and cellist Josef, was a leading string ensemble in Boston; although not as well known outside Boston as the Kneisel Quartet—largely because of Franz's towering musicianship, charisma, and renown as the BSO's concertmaster, not to mention the group's greater willingness to tour—the Adamowski band was nevertheless esteemed. In an early attempt to hear the Fifth Quartet, Chadwick asked the Kneisel group to give it a play-through, which they did. But the honor of the premiere went to the dedicatees who gave its first public performance on February 9, 1900, at a Harvard Musical Association concert.

The first movement, a sonata form marked Allegro moderato, includes pentatonicism (in the secondary theme) and a hulking, complex development. Chadwick demonstrates his mastery of melodic invention, for the first theme—by no means identifiably American—is fetching and rhythmically charged. Naturally, Chadwick had the Adamowski group in mind when writing this quartet, for there are numerous solos and brief instrumental "conversations" for the brothers and the other players. The viola part, premiered by ensemble member Max Zach, is also very soloistic, a fact that prompted him to remark to Chadwick, "you should call this a quartet for viola and three other instruments."[63]

Eschewing a slow movement, Chadwick's pace in the second movement is a brisk Andantino. Its ABAB plus coda structure is noteworthy not only for its tonal scheme, but also its inventive interplay of the instruments. It begins in B-flat major with a lyrical melody punctuated by solos in the cello marked "quasi recitative." A gentle song-like secondary theme moves through D-flat major, before arriving at a restatement of the main theme, again in B-flat major, this time underscored with the recitative solos in the violin part. Chadwick cleverly cloaked the final appearance of the B theme in the rather dark-hued key of G-flat major, and the instrumental parts in the final section are muted, which enhances the ethereal quality of the music. The movement closes with rhythmic lines in the viola part that will again remind the listener of passages in the Second Symphony.

Chadwick's third movement is unique to his music (see table 8.2). A scherzo, it lacks the ferocity of many of his similar creations, although its tunes brim with rhythmic vigor. It is crafted in two large sections—both of which may be further subdivided as ABAC and A'AB'C, respectively—plus a coda. The main

TABLE 8.2. The Form of String Quartet no. 5 (movement 3)

Section:	1				2				Coda
Theme:	A	B	A	C	A'	A	B'	C	k
Key:	F	C	F	B-flat	F/f	F		D-flat	F
Measure:	1	58	90	129	177	260	291	315	331–59

melody is an animated one that is fully plumbed; it contrasts with the smoother, more elegant secondary theme, which is encountered only briefly and without elaboration. Much of Chadwick's energy was focused on the slow portion, theme C, the first appearance of which is marked by a languorous viola solo, soon repeated in the cello part. The pattern is roughly repeated in the highly developmental second section. Beginning with the main melodic material, the music passes in imitation through the ensemble, and, after sounding hints of the B theme, the final appearance of the A theme serves as a sort of recapitulation. Another slow section utilizes music from the C theme, before a brilliant but relatively brief coda ends the composition.

The final movement is a sonata-form march in D major. Just a few measures into the movement Chadwick utilized stretto to transition to an attractive, lyrical second theme, marked "mit Humor," a perfect foil to the angular principal tune. One may reasonably conclude that Brahms's sophisticated deployment of rhythmic displacement procedures had an effect on Chadwick. Two fiery codas bring the quartet to a riveting close.

By many measures, the Fifth Quartet is a successful composition; it is entertaining, inventive, and artfully crafted. But to my ears it is less impressive than the Fourth Quartet. Several sections are plodding—more labored, less fluid than one encounters in Chadwick's best writing. Harmonically it is far less adventuresome, and the rhythms lack the verve of the earlier quartet. It is simply less fun, and less "American," than the Fourth Quartet. Chadwick may have had similar thoughts on the matter. He admitted in 1903 that "I have never been quite satisfied with my d minor quartet although it had been played several times with success."[64] He revised it, but even those changes did not fully compensate for what I perceive is an overall stodginess that is not present in the Fourth Quartet.

William Foster Apthorp's experience was ambiguous. Writing a full year after its premiere, he observed, "Of Mr. Chadwick's new quartette my first impressions are considerably vague. Although evidently written with a certain fluent mastery, it is not a work which lays its full meaning bare at the first dash. . . . I heard graceful, ear-wooing themes, could perceive a good deal of natural, unforced development; but I felt still more strongly that there was much in the composition that would become clearer on repeated hearing. The real gist of the work escaped me."[65]

The Fifth Quartet would be Chadwick's last. It naturally begs the question: Why did he abandon a genre he enjoyed, one with which he had experienced a modicum of success? As ingenious as the final quartet is in selected portions, the lukewarm reviews from critics and even his own comments may ultimately tell the tale. And there are other possible answers. Chadwick, like his fellow Bostonians, was naturally enamored with the orchestra; writing music for it was his passion. Although in the next decade he would become more involved with works for the stage, at no time did he relinquish his desire to compose music for the orchestra. Perhaps he simply sacrificed chamber music on the altar of time management. Besides, chamber music, while an engaging enterprise artistically, did not add to his renown. His music for orchestra was widely played before large audiences, but the five quartets, only two of which were published during his lifetime, were infrequently heard. When they did garner the odd performance here or there, they usually occurred at small concert venues or in private homes. Nor did Chadwick's chamber music add to his pocketbook. Some of his larger works, especially those composed for choral societies, often were commissions that produced an income, much needed for the support of his growing family. Likewise, his increasing body of songs and works for community and school choruses generated a steady stream of income from royalties. Such was not the case with the string quartets.

Chadwick may have intended to abandon writing chamber music following the completion of his Third Quartet and the piano quintet (1886 and 1887, respectively). He only renewed his acquaintance with the genre a decade later when Dvořák arrived in the United States and produced "American" works, thereby providing solutions to problems that many American composers did not know existed. Although Chadwick publicly professed not to have interest in Dvořák's ideas about potential sources of music for American music, in several works, including his last two quartets, he was anxious to put his own authorial stamp on an American sound.

The Fifth Quartet was played on November 4, 1913 — a full decade after the composer made his revisions — by the Kneisel Quartet at Boston's underground Steinert Hall. ("I should like the place," the composer wrote a few years earlier, "if it were not so much like a mausoleum."[66]) Chadwick, perhaps chuckling under his mustache, remarked that all the critics responded to the composition as if its ink had just dried. To them, it sounded new and fresh.

But their response mattered little. More important to him on this night was his company. Son Theodore accompanied him to the recital, and Chadwick remembered with evident pride that the young man, now in his early twenties, gained for his father a substantially enlarged respect. Theodore had witnessed few scenes of his father in the composer's limelight; mostly he was familiar with the informal music-making among friends at their summer home. But at Steinert Hall, Theodore saw his father's genius acknowledged in the rain of applause that followed the performance of the Fifth Quartet. His impression of his father had been instantly heightened by his companions on the program, for that night Chadwick was a god in a veritable musical pantheon. Kneisel sandwiched Chadwick's music between venerable quartets by Beethoven and Brahms.[67] Elson, who also attended the concert, assessed that Chadwick's composition "was by no means crushed between the upper and nether millstone."[68]

"This Particular Game": Chadwick and Americanism

In 1911 Chadwick had the opportunity to hear the *Comedy Overture on Negro Themes* by Henry Gilbert performed by the BSO. Gilbert, just into his forties, was becoming known as a staunch advocate of American music, a vocal proponent, à la Dvořák, of using native material as a basis for an American school of composition. And he didn't just espouse it; over the course of his career he made "aboriginal" elements central to his musical style, producing the incidental music to *The Redskin, or the Last of his Race* (1906) and many other works with equally evocative titles, such as *Indian Sketches* (1911) and *Negro Rhapsody* (1912) for orchestra, and *Negro Dances* (1914) for piano. Much of Gilbert's fame as a composer today rests on his symphonic poem *The Dance in Place Congo* (1908), intended to represent a revel of slaves on the Louisiana bayou. It was revised a few years later to make it more suitable for ballet, and in that guise it was presented to impassioned critical acclaim by the Metropolitan Opera in 1918 on a double bill with Charles Wakefield Cadman's "Indian opera," *Shanewis*.

Gilbert's fame also grew as he became a public spokesman for the cause of American music. In 1918 he wrote a lengthy article for the *New York Times*, headlined "Composer Gilbert on American Music."[69] In it he exclaimed that "Musical America is in the grip of Europe" and that "Europe dictates to us what music we shall hear, tells us the kind we should prefer, and, worst of all, insists upon dictating to our composers what kind they should write." Gilbert's remarks are especially ironic considering he was writing precisely the kind of music that Dvořák had suggested throughout the mid-1890s. Nevertheless, his point about European musical domination was clear and widely believed; Chadwick would have agreed with it. But, Gilbert being Gilbert, he then went too far: "Let me say at once that music written by American composers in conformity to European models is not American music. . . . I am not one of those who insist that there is a large quantity of meritorious American music as yet unheard. There is almost no real American music at present in existence. But there are tendencies, somewhat blind and groping as yet, but still earnest and sincere."[70]

The passion Gilbert demonstrated in this newspaper article had been obvious to Chadwick several years earlier. Following the 1911 BSO concert, Chadwick wrote of Gilbert, "He is an odd stick—full of talent and a firm believer in 'American music'—whatever that may be—but somewhat lacking in technique and still more in good taste."[71] These comments are telling. Chadwick simply did not subscribe to an American style—he did not think a single type of such music was possible; he did not believe that his definition of American was the same as anyone else's; and, despite now being considered an American composer, that is, a composer whose compositional style is consistently in some sense "American," he certainly did not think of himself in the same vein as Gilbert, a composer whose fame was and is built on the treatment of "aboriginal" musical ideas. On the contrary, Chadwick was certain that Gilbert's career was in jeopardy: "Gilbert is a deserving fellow, a sort of rough diamond (in a dirty shirt) but I fear that he will soon come to the end of his rope if he tries to work this particular game."[72]

"This particular game," of course, was the writing of purportedly American music. What compelled composers to attempt Americanist works? Some undoubtedly wished to express the feelings of national identity that would enable the composer of serious music to affect the masses in the same way a Stephen Foster melody did. Others might have thought that their music would have a better chance of being accepted and performed by European conductors if it struck some national chord; after all, more traditional compositions were merely imitative of European models, or so it was generally thought. Certainly after a time critics expected American music to veer toward nationalism; and throughout the 1880s and '90s—since the World's Fair phenomenon had begun—"ethnology" and the study of North America's indigenous people were fashionable areas of inquiry. It is true that several of Chadwick's compositions are flavored with the same seasonings that Gilbert utilized: syncopated rhythms; melodies based on folk-song styles or pentatonicism; simple harmonies that included little or no chromaticism; and the diminished importance of formal considerations. But to this point in his career there are only a handful of works by Chadwick that may reasonably be considered stylistically or characteristically, Americanist: the First Quartet, with its inclusion of an undiscovered folk song titled "Shoot the Pipe," and the Fourth Quartet; *Rip Van Winkle* Overture; the second movement of the Second Symphony (which most critics of the day considered "Scotch");

portions of the Third Symphony (although at the time it was widely compared to Brahms); and the outer movements of *Symphonic Sketches*, which he admitted he intentionally made American according to his own definition.

Of course, the difficulty in defining American music and in forging an American musical style is that an American style can only be created by the use of two musical parameters: melody and rhythm. There were, in the 1890s, no particular Americanisms associated with harmony, form, instrumentation, and texture.[73] The melodies suggested for use by Dvořák—the Negro and Indian varieties—besides being virtually unknown to American composers were not considered particularly American by those whose ethnic heritages were predominantly British and whose compositional predilections were entirely German. As for rhythm, those which Dvořák recognized as American were, to many American composers including Chadwick, simply without a particular national tint; or if there seemed to be some relationship to a particular nation or culture, most often they were recognized as Scotch or Irish or Gaelic or Celtic. And very often it seems to me that at issue are not the rhythms of an individual beat or a single measure, but rather the large-scale rhythmic, metric, and temporal plan of a given work and its somewhat indefinable characterization as jaunty or buoyant or spirited or some other like adjectives.

There is one more feature of a work, a non-musical one, that bears on a composition's nationalism; that is, its suggestive or "programmatic" title. In Chadwick's case the most suggestive title used in his American works was for his *Rip Van Winkle*. There is, however, little in that overture to suggest that it is American other than its title. *Rip* was a famous and beloved tale of the unusual life of a "Dutchman" who resided in the mountains of upstate New York. The widely held perception of Chadwick's overture as a piece of Americana rests— for now—almost solely on its programmatic appeal.

Let us briefly relate this to American literature. When that art was developing in America, its nationalism was not a product of its form; that is, the novel's form did not make the American novel American—its American subject matter did. The American novel achieved an even deeper level of Americanism when authors began using speech rhythms that were particular to some regional American subculture. Music did likewise by utilizing melodic inflections and rhythms that were somehow identified with the American experience. That their forms did not change drastically from their European models is a central fact of both American literature and American music. Many American composers, including Chadwick, eschewed nationalism precisely because of its melodic and rhythmic limitations. Just as the lilting voice of a Boston Brahmin or the plaintive drawl of a Southern Belle could not have a lasting appeal for authors, neither could the incessant utilization of pentatonic melodies and syncopated rhythms maintain a composer's fascination. For Chadwick's part, formal expression was paramount. The metamorphosis of melodic germs into full-blown symphonic structures cast in traditional, recognizable forms is the very essence of Chadwick's symphonic art.

In an untitled 1922 essay, Chadwick made a veiled reference to his own Second Symphony; he wrote that "Dr. Dvořák was not the first to adopt this distinctive style in American composition." He continued, "In the early days of the B. S. O., certain works were played which were irreverent enough to be classed as 'American' in style, but they were not flavored with Negro or Indian rithms [*sic*]; neither is the most characteristic music of the present generation of American composers, although sometimes the influence is quite evident. Finally: These Indian and Negro tunes, although picturesque and strong in local color, do not contain the germs from which serious art forms may be developed. As soon as we begin to apply to them the modern processes of thematic development which are necessary to an organic structure, they lose the naïve simplicity which is their principal characteristic."[74]

Americanism was a game that Chadwick himself had played successfully if only sporadically. In light of the spread of nationalism and the enormous pressure that Dvořák brought, perhaps unwittingly, to bear on American composers to compose in an "authentic" American musical style, Chadwick may have felt compelled to try his hand at it a few times. Or he may simply have been inspired by a widely admired visiting composer. Chadwick had composed characteristically American music ten years before the Bohemian had arrived, in the early 1880s. When he sought to compose American works again, in the 1890s, he simply drew from and improved upon techniques he had mastered previously. However, Chadwick never strayed far from his own artistic impulses and priorities. Although he likely would not have admitted it, it is clear that Dvořák had a brief and not unimportant impact on him. But by the turn of the new century, Chadwick's Americanist flirtation, his playing of "this particular game," was largely over.

Chadwick, Modernism, & the End of an Era
Adonais to *Cleopatra*
1899–1905

And so by degrees, and little by little, the chains of tradition were
loosened, the fetters of convention and arbitrary theory broken;
this limitation disappeared, that restriction ceased to bind.
— Reginald De Koven, "The Modern Revolt in Music" (1907)

Adonais (1899)

Critic William Foster Apthorp thought that Chadwick's *Adonais* Overture was "the most modern in spirit of anything I know from his pen."[1] But it defied easy and immediate comprehension. Beautiful and imaginative though it is, Apthorp could not fully grasp it at first encounter. Upon savoring its early 1900 premiere at Boston's Music Hall, Apthorp admitted, "After but a single hearing, I understand Adonais no more completely than I did Tchaikovsky's 'Pathetique,' the Prelude to Tristan, or Beethoven's eighth symphony. But I have an inkling that it is splendid music, all the same."

Indeed, we can see in *Adonais* a departure from some aspects of Chadwick's earlier style, especially from the Americanism that he had recently cultivated. Dvořák's impact on composition in the United States, though not without actual consequences, probably looms larger in history than it did in reality. In 1904 critic Richard Aldrich, a Dvořák admirer, had to admit that "the strange controversy" that surrounded the Bohemian's proposed utilization of Negro and Native American sources "is now well-nigh forgotten."[2] Having left Americanism behind, Chadwick proceeded to explore other techniques, especially those related to impressionism. *Adonais* is couched in a recognizable form, but it includes the unexpected presentation of new themes, feathery chamber music–like textures, metrical ambiguities, and brief hints of exotica. These elements, far removed from the dense passages of counterpoint in the Third Symphony and the rambunctious spirit of "Jubilee," were enough to confound Apthorp at his first encounter.

Chadwick began his *Adonais* Overture shortly after the death, on July 26, 1897, of his longtime friend Frank Fay Marshall, a prominent music teacher in Boston. Their friendship reached back to their days together as classmates at the Leipzig Conservatory. Marshall was at Chadwick's side as *Rip Van Winkle* emerged and "had been my constant, sympathetic friend and confidant." Chadwick continued, "He loved me like a brother. . . . He knew of my struggles and troubles and did his best to cheer me in all my darkest hours." Marshall had long suffered from a number of physical ailments and was forced to contend with his wife's insanity, the symptoms of which began to appear immediately after their marriage. Much of Marshall's life had been tragic, and, while saddened at his death, Chadwick could not "wish him back to a life of sure unhappiness."[3]

Chadwick's composition was inspired by the poem *Adonais: An Elegy on the Death of John Keats* by Percy Bysshe Shelley. Shelley began his fifty-five-stanza poem shortly after Keats's death on February 23, 1821. In the preface to his detailed analysis of Shelley's poem, W. M. Rossetti stated that *Adonais* was the one poem by Shelley that was reasonably popular. Further, he judged, Shelley's poem "is elevated in sentiment, classical in form,—in substance, biographical in relation to Keats, and in some minor degree autobiographical for Shelley himself."[4] Shelley's elegy lamented the premature death of a genius, the twenty-four-year-old Keats, whose loss to poetry and literature was immeasurable. Chadwick regarded Marshall's death in much the same way; that Shelley's *Adonais* brims with musical references greatly added to its attraction. While not named for a muse, Chadwick's overture nevertheless demonstrates the composer's continuing fascination with all things Greek. Adonais—a French variation of Adonis—was a complex figure in mythology. He occupies a place among the so-called "vegetation gods," that is, those who die but are then reborn, in a similar fashion to the seasonality of plants. Adonis as a metaphor for death and rebirth has been a common theme in art and literature for centuries.

Chadwick was unable to complete *Adonais* until January 27, 1899, nearly a year and a half after it was begun. The long period of its creation was largely the result of the constraints that Chadwick's new position as director of NEC placed on him. But there were other distractions; besides continuing to serve as the director of the Springfield Festival, Chadwick was still an active organist. His family also required his attention.

Chadwick molded *Adonais* in sonata form, but he took a number of liberties within that scheme. Emphasizing a sentimental rhetoric, the overture opens in E minor with a slow, funereal introduction. It is followed by a brisk main theme, Allegro patetico, the initial character of which—smooth, calm, conjunct—is reflective of the beauty of its protagonist, Adonis. Soon more ominous and percussive strains assert themselves. Chadwick's secondary theme marks a departure from his usual pattern, for it is not an especially sweet one—there is no *cantabile* marking, as we have seen so often in his music—although it occurs in the expected dominant key, B major. Chadwick here pits his $\frac{6}{4}$ melody against an accompaniment in $\frac{4}{4}$ and uses a variety of rhythmic shifts that reminds one of Brahms. More startlingly, Chadwick invents two new melodies in his development section, the second of which features a mournful chorale in the low brass punctuated by pizzicato strings and solemn passages in the harp. The principal theme is sounded prominently at the arrival of the recapitulation, but moments later the listener is barraged by the other melodies in a lush wall of orchestral sound. Chadwick brings *Adonais* to a striking close when, within the final measures, the music moves from a full-orchestra fortissimo to pianissimo, still in E minor, as if to signal his reluctant farewell to Marshall, who was among the first of his friends and colleagues who would depart in the coming years.[5]

Apthorp did not think that the modernism of the overture was to be found in its architecture. He observed that "if the scheme is practically the same [as several of Chadwick's earlier works], the spirit and treatment are different: both are modern and romantic. The very character of the thematic material in 'Adonais' is modern, in sharp contrast to the classic reserve found in the 'Melpomene'; his expression is more outspoken, more purely emotional and dramatic. . . . Here we have essentially modern and romantic musical development, not the old classic structure."[6] By now it came as no surprise to Chadwick that Apthorp would use his best-known work, *Melpomene*, as the point of comparison.

Chadwick approached Wilhelm Gericke to conduct his new overture. Gericke had returned to lead the BSO in 1898, nine years after his successful first term with the orchestra came to an end, ostensibly from "overwork."[7] It was generally recognized that Gericke, having inherited a lackluster, undisciplined band from Henschel, had molded the BSO into an orchestra of astonishing brilliance. While his two successors through the 1890s, Arthur Nikisch and Emil Paur, brought something of their own personality to the orchestra's performances and to the institution, the BSO had essentially been Gericke's creation. American composers could celebrate his return; neither Paur nor Nikisch were considered resolute advocates of American composers and their music, although neither could be accused of ignoring native artists altogether.

Gericke was no huge fan of *Adonais*. He conducted its premiere on February 2, 1900, but the rehearsals had not gone well, and this time errors in the orchestral parts were not to blame. The problem, Chadwick thought, was Gericke's icy attitude.[8] After the second rehearsal, Gericke "had worked himself into a bad humor, he turned to me and said angrily 'This is too long. You must make cut.'" Chadwick was livid, and he refused to recoil. Neither would he compromise. "I came down the aisle and said, 'Mr. Gericke if this piece annoys you so much I prefer you should not play it at all.' At which he said 'I must play. It is on the program.' To which I replied 'Very well. Play it as it is. I shall not cut it.' He slammed the score down on the rack and took up the next piece. This conversation took place while the whole orchestra listened with their mouths open."[9]

Chadwick had the support of the musicians on stage, especially the Alsatian musician Charles Martin Loeffler, a composer and violist in the orchestra, who later confided to Chadwick that he was well within his rights to limit Gericke's savagery.[10] It was widely known in Boston that Gericke, implacable by most accounts, had little respect for the composer's art, at least when it conflicted with his program design. Chadwick regarded Gericke as an abhorrent and unsentimental butcher of other artists' music, and, as one who frequently borrowed music from the BSO music library for use at NEC, he was in a position to know the extent of what he termed Gericke's "vandalism" of musical scores.[11]

Chadwick tried unsuccessfully—and perhaps only half-heartedly—to enlist Theodore Thomas's support for *Adonais*. Five months following its premiere he wrote to Thomas, "I will send you the score if you would like to see it. I doubt, however, if you would find it quite effective for your concerts. It is a memorial to a friend of mine and a little too 'ernst' [i.e., serious] in sentiment to be appreciated by the casual listener. At least, that was my impression of it at the concert."[12] (In 1998 this author tried to interest Neeme Järvi, then conductor of the Detroit Symphony Orchestra and an ardent Chadwick fan, in *Adonais*. Järvi also found it "ernst," and determined that it would be a hard sell on his programs, especially when, after studying the score for mere moments and then turning to the final pages, he saw that the composition closed pianissimo.[13])

Adonais's performance history is a regrettably brief one, and it is unclear whether Chadwick tried very hard to have it published; he made no mention of any effort to contact publishers. Perhaps he calculated that given Gericke's tepid response, the overture's quiet, introspective ending, and a newspaper review that touts its modernisms, there would be little hope of ever seeing *Adonais* in print. As with so many of Chadwick's compositions, *Adonais* was destined to be heard again only rarely during the composer's lifetime. Its only performances, in 1916 and 1917 respectively, were both by the NEC orchestra. But Chadwick vigorously defended *Adonais*, claiming it a personal favorite among his music. "Lest some fool scribe should jump at the conclusion after I am dead when it will be played that I did not think it was near enough my own standard to be worth publishing," Chadwick declared, "I will put on record my opinion, formed after hearing several performances and many rehearsals, that it is as good as I have ever been able to do and is in some respects the best of my works."[14]

Judith (1900)

Chadwick had flirted with the stage a number of times since conducting Paine's *Oedipus Tyrannus* in 1881. His greatest personal triumph in that arena had been in 1894 when the First Cadets performed *Tabasco* to popular and critical acclaim. But that was a comic vehicle. Chadwick was no snob, but he recognized that such works—burlesques in reality—tended to have a short shelf life. He thought that the boost *Tabasco* gave to his reputation was not commensurate with the time spent and hardships endured to write and produce it. In his search for a suitable serious work he found *Judith*, which, although it owns a respected spot in his oeuvre, failed to gain a foothold in the American operatic repertoire.

It is unclear precisely when Chadwick determined to set the Apocryphal story of Judith to music, but both Ledbetter and Yellin have suspected that Saint-Saëns's *Samson et Delilah*, a work that had enjoyed a good deal of notoriety in the US in the 1890s and one that Chadwick himself had conducted at Springfield, might have provided him with a model.[15] *Samson et Delilah*, an opera, was perfectly suited to a concert presentation, and indeed that was the performance format that was most familiar to America audiences. Its flexibility would have appealed to Chadwick—while he longed for *Judith* to be staged in full glory, he knew it would be more widely performed in oratorio style; that is, with singers and an orchestra, but without the scenery, costumes, and other paraphernalia typical of operatic productions. Chadwick called *Judith* a "lyric drama," perhaps hoping that the unique nomenclature would endow it with an appealing pliability that would in turn expand its possibilities for performance. In fact the label thrust upon his work a stubborn and problematic ambiguity. Chadwick's "lyric drama" occupies an uncomfortable space between the worlds of opera and oratorio, and, despite beautiful passages of music and several compelling dramatic scenes, neither audiences nor critics knew quite how to grapple with it.

If the nature of *Judith* was a problem, another was Chadwick's choice of librettist. William Chauncy Langdon (1871–1947), seventeen years Chadwick's junior, had written the book for *The Vision of the Throne* (1898), a sacred cantata dedicated to the memory of his father, who died in 1895. Chadwick heard it sung by the choir of Grace Church in Providence, Rhode Island. He was delighted; Chadwick considered *The Vision of the Throne* and Langdon's verse well crafted and poetic, and he even shared it as a model of cantata structure with his composition pupils. He commissioned Langdon, an unseasoned librettist by any measure, to set the text from a scenario Chadwick had already sketched. In rather short order, Langdon's hiring proved to be a mistake—*Judith*'s text was its weakest element. Although in the next twenty years Langdon would become an important librettist for America's pageant craze—contributing works such as *The Pageant of Cape Cod* (1914) and *The Pageant of Corydon* (1916)—his present effort left Chadwick disheartened. He later thought that Langdon "was given to extravagant expression, sometimes not in good taste, had little facility and was probably too inexperienced dramatically for such a big job."[16]

Not that Chadwick was faultless in the matter. Langdon was excited about the prospect of writing for the famous New England composer, and Chadwick observed and appreciated that enthusiasm. But Langdon was "rather up against it when it came to extending lines of music." Chadwick admitted that he ended up crafting a good deal of the text himself, "which is not my job."[17] Following the excruciating birth of the libretto, Chadwick's progress on the music was rapid, and he never again mentioned the problems with the text, although it is unlikely that he forgot about them.

Chadwick has left us a fairly complete account of *Judith*'s creation. He began to work with Langdon on the text in 1898, at which time he was also jotting down musical ideas for the work.[18] Detailed sketching of its music commenced in May 1899, and he had completed the first act by July. Chadwick worked on act II through the rest of the summer and into autumn, when he began its orchestration. The final act was drafted in an astonishing eleven days, also in the summer of 1900, and scoring continued through the fall. He put the finishing touches on *Judith* on December 12.

Chadwick's approach to *Judith*'s orchestration diverged tremendously from *Tabasco*, for here he clearly had a modern opera in mind, not merely a small theater piece. Besides the mezzo soprano, tenor, baritone and bass vocal soloists, and the SATB chorus, he scored *Judith* for a large orchestra that includes pairs of flutes, clarinets, oboes, and bassoons (with some doubling on English horn and bass clarinet); four horns, three each of trumpets and trombones, and one tuba; harp; strings; and a large battery of percussion.

Judith, spanning three acts and fifteen scenes, tells the story of Holofernes, who is ordered by Nebuchadnezzar to travel to Judea to punish the Israelites for failing to assist his armies in battle. Holofernes constructs a blockade around the town of Bethulia in an attempt to starve out the rebels there. Town leader Ozias agrees to surrender Bethulia to Holofernes in five days, by which time he hopes God will have intervened on the Israelites' behalf. God does so in the form of Judith, a widow, who uses her beauty to enter Holofernes's camp. After several lusty days together, Judith gains Holofernes's trust. Following a banquet, Judith finds him passed out on a couch and proceeds to cut off his head with three blows of his own sword. Judith then makes for Bethulia, with Holofernes's head in hand, and the townspeople thank God before vanquishing what remains of the enemy troops.

Because Chadwick was the director of the Worcester Festival at the time, securing its premiere there was not difficult, although it had to wait nearly a year, until it was performed on September 26, 1901. The matter of a second performance was more problematic, but he had high hopes that Theodore Thomas would produce it. A month before *Judith* was finished he proudly exhorted to Thomas: "I have just finished a new work for chorus and orchestra . . . the libretto of which was written especially for me from my own scenario. It is shortly to be published by Schirmer and is already accepted for performance at the next Worcester Festival. It will sing about two hours, has four principal solo parts and one small one. The principal part, that of Judith, I have written especially for Gertrude May Stein."[19] Chadwick offered it for performance at the Cincinnati May Festival, and Thomas considered squeezing sections of it—not the complete work—onto an already crafted program. That did not suit Chadwick; he wrote to Thomas, "if the works for the whole evening are already selected, I am inclined to think it would be better not to consider mine at all. It is a dramatic work in the form of continuous scenes and I don't see how any of it could be left out without leaving part of the story unexplained. At any rate, I fear it would be difficult to combine it with a miscellaneous concert, and my feeling now is, that I would rather wait for some future festival than try to cut it down."[20] Chadwick undoubtedly wrestled with this decision, for even a partial performance by Thomas would have been widely reported. A "miscellaneous concert," one that featured a variety of musical selections, including songs, single movements of symphonies, and the like—would not have been appropriate for the unveiling of a serious new dramatic work. Given concerns Chadwick probably already had about *Judith*, he may have thought that a fully staged performance was imperative to its long-term survival.

Critics were generally baffled by *Judith*. Langdon's ineffectual libretto, coupled with Chadwick's musical setting, which defied easy categorization, contributed to what can at best be considered a modest success, if not an outright failure. Frederick R. Burton of the *New York Times* was among the more supportive critics; he noted that its premiere "aroused no end of discussion among visiting musicians." Observing that the choruses are the finest feature of *Judith*, Burton continued, "Some of them are massive and simple, with long passages *a cappella*; others are frankly in oratorio form, though nonetheless dramatic. There is a highly developed fugue in the first act that lends its structural peculiarities capitally to the requirements of the situation, theatrically speaking. It might be remarked in passing that when the word 'theatrical' slips into this commentary it is not used in any disparaging sense. The music of *Judith* is not cheap."[21]

Opinions such as those represented in the *Boston Evening Transcript* were oftener sounded. Upon the publication of the piano-vocal score in late 1901, a reviewer wrote: "Both book and music suffer from a lack of distinct purpose. . . . It [the music] suffers, to be sure, from the want of unity that mars the whole work, for one-half is pure oratorio and in the other dramatic half there are perhaps half a dozen different styles of opera represented."[22]

Chadwick, whose disgust with his situation in Worcester was growing, naturally blamed his musical forces. He invited Thomas to attend the premiere, but his faith in the organization was weak. "I must give you warning," he wrote acerbically, "not to hold me too much responsible for the result musically, for I have had to contend with the most absurd and benighted ideas among the Festival officials. Such mountains of prejudice, ignorance and conceit . . . would be incredible in any town in the world but Worcester."[23]

Judith received several performances during Chadwick's lifetime, and selections from it found their way onto recital programs, especially in Boston, for the next twenty years. When the Worcester Festival revived *Judith* on October 8, 1919, critic Olin Downes was in the audience. In a report that clearly relies on information obtained from Chadwick, Downes remarked that "the composer did not feel that he had written a cantata or [an] oratorio. Nor yet had he made a music drama." Many years later the precise taxonomy of *Judith* had remained elusive and controversial. Downes, a genuine music lover if ever there was one, closed his review sympathetically and generously: "It was an unusually interesting performance, of a singularly uneven work, by one of the greatest of American composers."[24]

Building Jordan Hall

Chadwick, like many musicians, composers, and music lovers of his day, considered the orchestra the acme of musical expression and communication. For Chadwick this had been true for decades. From his childhood days when his brother dropped him off at concerts of the Thomas Orchestra, through his student years in Leipzig, where he regularly heard the unrivalled Gewandhaus Orchestra, to the Harvard Musical Association and then to the Boston Symphony Orchestra, where he eventually heard his own music performed, the orchestra had imprinted itself on him as a medium of musical expression more deeply, and more ineluctably, than any other. Chadwick craved not only the sensual thrill that the large ensemble provided, with its ever-changing variety of sounds and its remarkable potential for harmony, rhythm, timbre, and texture; he also coveted the accolades that orchestral success could bring him. And as he advanced into the music education realm in a serious way—as director of NEC—he judged that the conservatory would not survive if it retained Tourjée's model of operation, that is, as a piano school. Chadwick dreamed not only of a new building with classrooms and private teaching studios, but also of a concert hall which could hold assemblies, graduation ceremonies, and, of course, performances. His fledgling NEC orchestra was presently performing all over Boston, often in inconvenient locations and under undesirable conditions that included cramped quarters and poor lighting. One important objective of Chadwick's orchestral enterprise was to facilitate a new building that would in turn clear the way for a new conservatory, a new performance hall, and a more promising future.

In remarkably short order, Chadwick's scheme was underway; by April 1901 NEC's cash contributions for the classroom and administrative portions of the new building approached $150,000. In a fantastic act of philanthropy, Eben Jordan Jr. agreed to pay for the concert hall, which would subsequently be named Jordan Hall in his honor, and to contribute an additional fifty thousand dollars for the Hutchings electric organ intended to be the crown jewel of the entire edifice. Chadwick was present when Jordan signed the contract to purchase the organ, an elaborate one inspired by an instrument in Siena, Italy.[25] Chadwick gleefully recalled that Jordan "was not a man who ever regretted his own good impulses."[26]

Jordan had many good impulses. Bespectacled, routinely calm, and always concerned about the needs of others, he was the son of Eben D. Jordan Sr. (1822–1895), the founder of the Jordan, Marsh & Company Department Store empire and coiner of the phrase "the customer is always right." Jordan Sr. had long sought to assist in the uplift of his fellow man. One of his most public philanthropic gestures had been to fund Gilmore's 1869 Peace Jubilee, and he had even served as treasurer on its board of directors. By the time Jordan Jr. died in 1916, he had overseen a number of business concerns and had given generously to scores of causes. As it had with his father, music figured prominently in his philanthropy: NEC benefitted first, and in several years the Boston Opera Company would also profit from his largess.

Chadwick envisioned a conservatory along the lines of the most famous ones in Europe. He was advised to travel there by NEC's recently retained architect, Edmund Wheelwright (1854–1912), who had begun working on the blueprints for a new facility. Wheelwright's involvement in this effort was crucial, for it signaled to city leaders, local philanthropists, and music lovers that NEC was now to be taken seriously. Wheelwright, a pensive and industrious man, had been involved in the construction of Higginson's Symphony Hall (completed in 1900) when he worked for the firm of McKim, Mead & White, and he was currently a principal in his own prominent Boston architectural firm, Wheelwright and Haven. His company was responsible for a number of structures that are now considered landmarks in the city, including Horticultural Hall, the Longfellow Bridge, and the now-demolished Boston Opera House. Insofar as the design of Jordan Hall was concerned, Wheelwright and Haven "were practically given carte blanche."[27]

Chadwick's European mission was well defined. It would include touring and evaluating the best music schools in Britain and on the continent to ensure that Boston's facility would have the features necessary to put it on the same high level. Chadwick also planned to learn about conservatory administration, an area in which he was a novice, and especially about the establishment and operation of a good school for the training of orchestral musicians.[28] Naturally, he had every intention of seizing opportunities that might advance his own composing career, especially given that Chadwick had not been to Europe since the 1880s. Now a fully credentialed and accomplished artist, Chadwick intended to meet as many composers as he could, and he hoped to share some of his scores with musical leaders who might perform them.

Chadwick disembarked from Boston on May 4, 1901, bound for Liverpool, England, on the steamship *Devonian*. He took the score of *Judith* and several of its manuscript string parts, which he planned to have copied cheaply in Europe. The trip would occupy several months, during which Chadwick would visit London, Berlin, Paris, and several smaller cities as time permitted. But on May 5, just his second day aboard the ship, Chadwick fell on the deck and fractured his ankle. The pain was excruciating; it was compounded by the fact that the *Devonian* would not arrive in harbor until May 13, leaving Chadwick to suffer on board for nine days. And suffer he did. Chadwick was in severe pain, and, never reticent, he complained loudly that his daily doses of morphine were insufficient. He had little confidence in the ship's physician ("a drunken brute," Chadwick thought[29]), and another physician on board set his leg. Chadwick surmised that that act saved him from "permanent lameness" or worse. When the *Devonian* pulled into harbor Chadwick was sent directly to Liverpool's Northern Hospital, where he remained for nearly two long and emotionally draining weeks.[30]

By May's end, Chadwick had recovered enough to maneuver about, although uncomfortably, and he was ready to begin his work. He arrived in London on May 28, set up residence, and began to accept a parade of well-wishers. Scottish composer Sir Alexander MacKenzie was among the first to call on him. Mac-

Kenzie, just a few years Chadwick's senior, was not only a celebrated composer but was deeply involved in the administration of the Royal Academy of Music (RAM), where he also taught composition. MacKenzie and Chadwick got along splendidly. Chadwick watched as Mackenzie conducted his own incidental music to Shakespeare's *Coriolanus*, which had just been premiered a month before. While Chadwick remained silent about MacKenzie's score, we may imagine that he appreciated MacKenzie's unabashed love of melody and the utilization of harmonic and rhythmic resources that reflected Chadwick's own style.

As his physical discomfort abated, Chadwick rededicated himself to his task and to concert attendance. He saw Henry Wood conduct Eugene Ysäye and Ferruccio Busoni in a concert of music by Beethoven. Another performance featured Hans Richter leading music by Wagner. Chadwick was also most impressed by MacKenzie's student orchestra at the RAM. Chadwick declared, "Student orchestra of 120 quite remarkable (We can do it too, in time.)"[31] Chadwick also met Frederic Cowen, Charles Villiers Stanford, Hubert Parry, Alberto Randegger, and others. He lamented that the most brilliant of the new school of British composers was not available: "Elgar I missed which I very much regretted. He is the most serious composer the English have produced for many years."[32] Chadwick's affection for the latest currents in English music was growing, and he noted that Elgar's newly minted overture, *Cockaigne*, "is very effective."[33]

Chadwick was unable to journey to the continent. The pain in his ankle subsided little, and the medication he continued to require kept him from venturing far from London. He headed for home on June 22, 1901, less than two months after his distressing sojourn began. Chadwick's injury was an impediment not only to his investigations of the conservatories, the primary purpose of the tour, but also to his personal musical aspirations. Parker traveled to Europe later that year and may have been attempting to temper Chadwick's sour feelings about his own trip when he wrote to Ida May from Paris that "Chad seems to have left a luminous trail of good-will behind him."[34] Parker even requested that Chadwick's scores *Lovely Rosabelle* and *Phoenix expirans* be forwarded to his British address, for he had already pledged to share them with a number of musicians in Europe.

Their year of contact with the most eminent British artists had a profound impact on both Chadwick and Parker, although it was certainly a more profitable endeavor for the latter. By 1902 Parker could write to Chadwick, "There is so much to be said about the state of music in this country [England], that I dare not begin writing about it. It must wait till we can talk until some very late hour. Generalities are so untrue, and I should hate to mislead you."[35] Parker's "generalities" are unknown to us; but Chadwick's brief seven-week stay could not have given him much of a chance to experience them firsthand.

Parker's relationship with English culture and its school of composers was a close one. Partly by virtue of his affiliation with the Episcopal Church in America, Parker's music, especially his choral music, was performed frequently in England and lauded by the locals, who appreciated its refinement and nobility. Parker was proud of his Anglo-Saxon roots, and he made no secret of the fact to Chadwick, whose own delight in his heritage was blossoming. "In spite of your pain and distress," Parker wrote to his friend, "you must have enjoyed British hospitality. It is a fine and a unique thing."[36]

Construction of the new conservatory began in the autumn of 1901 (see figure 9.1). Wheelwright retained the services of Professor Wallace C. Sabine of Harvard University to lend advice on the acoustics and soundproofing of Jordan Hall. Sabine had been a significant principal in the design of Symphony Hall, although his input had not been welcomed by the project's lead architect, Charles Follen McKim. McKim had already designed a space purported to embody the best qualities of the Leipzig Gewandhaus when Higginson asked Sabine—without McKim's knowledge—for his assessment. After much hesitation, McKim finally relented to Sabine's suggestions, but made it a point to distance himself and his firm from the acoustical results, which he erroneously thought would be poor. (While the design of Symphony Hall more closely reflects that of the old and familiar Boston Music Hall than the Leipzig Gewandhaus, it acquired for Sabine considerable fame. He was much sought after once the building was complete.[37]) The acoustics of Symphony Hall were recognized as excellent in very short order.

Naturally, Jordan Hall could not replicate Symphony Hall, for their needs and uses were entirely different. Whereas Symphony Hall would host up to a hundred professional musicians and guest artists playing for capacity crowds, Jordan Hall would feature student recitals, a novice orchestra that rarely numbered as many as sixty, and many chamber music performances, often for small audiences. A forgiving hall, one suited to the purposes of teaching, was imperative, and its shape mattered. Writer Frank Waldo observed that there were two types of music halls, "and each has its admirers; the long, rectangular shape, and that of a horseshoe curve or truncated ellipse. Curiously enough Boston possesses the best specimens [of] these two forms to be found in America; and they lie within a stone's throw of each other."[38] Jordan Hall was the latter, of course, with its horseshoe-shaped audience chamber and a stage designed to push as much sound forward as possible. Waldo himself conducted a study in which he

FIGURE 9.1. New England Conservatory, ca. 1904. Courtesy of the Library of Congress, Prints & Photographs Division, Detroit Publishing Company Photograph Collection, LC-D4-17046.

thoroughly inspected Jordan Hall and then tested its acoustical properties by listening "at eight localities on the floor."[39] From Waldo's perspective,

> The dimensions of Jordan Hall are such that even for solo performances no part of the hall is outside the sphere of sympathy. The continual slant of the floor which makes every seat a raised seat prevents the absorption of sound at the front to such an extent as to impair the tones reaching the audience towards the rear and provides for a uniform diffusion of tone. The steep slope of the outer sides of the floor beneath the balcony is so arranged as to give almost equally distributed advantages to the space there; and these are all the advantages of a low ceiling which are so much appreciated acoustically. This arrangement has been so finely adjusted that at no point in the hall has the tonal balance been more exquisitely preserved than in the rear beneath the balcony. The same steep pitch to the balcony secures to every seat there almost uniform exposure toward the direct vibrations coming from the stage meeting but little interference and suffering no absorption from intervening bodies. Here the slight continual decrease in the intensity of the direct tones with increased distance from the stage is made good by the reflected sounds that come from the ceiling and the walls.[40]

Waldo concluded, "As a whole, the musical tones come to all parts of the house with a strength, fullness and clearness of remarkable uniformity and in such a condition as to satisfy the most exacting of musical natures."[41]

Chadwick shared the opinion that Jordan Hall was indeed excellent, but the conservatory design was not without flaws. "The architects took the most elaborate steps to make the teaching rooms sound proof," he later recalled, "calling in Prof. Sabine of Harvard to assist them and testing different kinds of sound proofing material (cabot quilt, etc.) all of which in the end did very little good because the steel girders and wood floors conducted the sound all over the building. Singularly enough, the organ rooms which were not sound proofed were more nearly silent than any in the building."[42] Construction progressed smoothly through the spring of 1902 until a workers' strike halted progress. Although the classrooms were finished according to schedule, the completion of Jordan Hall had to wait an additional year.[43]

Pontius Pilate (1903)

Between running the conservatory and overseeing the construction of the new building, Chadwick had little time to compose. "I have not written a d—— thing since Xmas," Chadwick complained to Parker in 1902, "but I mean to begin very soon now. I have got a book which I think is a perfect corker, although it will be no such snap to work it out. However I mean to take a couple of years to do it in."[44] That book was *Pontius Pilate*, another biblically inspired composition in the mold of *Judith* that Chadwick worked on steadily for nearly a year. From the beginning the work was to be rather modernistic, for Chadwick intended to "dodge $^6_4$ chords, four bar phrases, fugato choruses & a few other vices."[45]

Pontius Pilate's librettist was writer Henry Copley Greene, whom Chadwick had met at the St. Botolph Club. Greene may have been recommended to Chadwick by his student Edward Burlingame Hill, who had already utilized verses by Greene for a handful of songs (Greene dedicated his play *Saint Ronan of Brittany* to Hill). Chadwick and Greene shared ideas about a dramatic work based on the life of Pontius Pilate, and together they plotted the story of Pilate's life and legend following the crucifixion of Jesus Christ utilizing stories from the Book of the Apocrypha and elsewhere. The pair also made use of "the legend of Mt. Pilatus in Switzerland to which Pilate retreated after the Crucifixion and which his unforgiven spirit still haunts." Greene published his libretto, "a play in verse," in 1902 and dedicated it to Chadwick.[46] It is steeped in nineteenth-century Victorianism, full of stilted, rather archaic language and plenty of "lo" this and "ye" that. Nevertheless, the drama itself is compelling, and it gives the vilified Pilate an unexpected humanity. Chadwick summarized *Pontius Pilate*'s plot as follows:

> It was in three parts the first ending with Pilate's surrender [of Jesus], against his will to the Jewish priests. The second, a description of the resurrection, and the last a wonderful scene in the snow on Mt. Pilatus, where Pilate bearing the inanimate form of Procla, is [threatened] with death by a herdsman who discovers his identity. A hermit, a symbolical figure of The Saviour, appears and assures him of Divine forgiveness as he dies.[47]

Musically, Chadwick had much to work with. The first act, the only one that Chadwick completed, comprises seventy-eight pages of piano-vocal score. It presents characters, including Pilate, Procla, Longinus, Annas, Caiphus, Mary Magdalene, and Jesus Christ, as well as Servants, Women, and The Jews, who populate the various choruses. The dark subject matter of the crucifixion naturally lends itself to the minor mode, and the D minor beginning ("Lo many things") introduces Pilate conversing with himself in his "inanimate form," Procla. The second section, "Living though he hath lain three days," ends up in B major, but not before passing through a transition of dense chromaticism. One of the most moving portions of the piece is Pilate's F minor recitative, "And so perchance let rope and murder miss their due reward," wherein the Roman general responds to Procla's urge to grant Jesus's release. There follows a dramatic, powerful conversation between Pilate and "the Nazarene," highlighted by a stark alternation of unaccompanied vocal parts and some of Chadwick's thickest harmonic writing.

Ultimately Greene and Chadwick's creation is one of redemption for Pilate, for in his final moments among the living, Pilate accepts Jesus as his Lord and Saviour and rests assured that he will be saved as he exhorts to Procla:

Procla, since He hath kissed my brow—oh wake
And hear!—angels are singing for thy sake.[48]

However, that scene occurs at the end of Greene's act III, and Chadwick gave up on *Pontius Pilate* after he completed the first act. Why he stopped his work we cannot know for sure, although he had reservations about its immediate possibilities for performance. Perhaps Chadwick simply lost interest in *Pontius Pilate*. Or perhaps he thought the work too unorthodox: "This would have been a wonderful piece for the stage—except that it would not be permitted," he later wrote, "except in Oberammergau."[49] That he left it uncompleted certainly was not characteristic of his work ethic.

In many ways the composition is eerily similar to *Judith* in that there is again a curious blend of opera and oratorio—*Pontius Pilate* could well pass for another "lyric drama." There are no opportunities for soaring melody, á la Verdi, and, while the overly large cast offered lots of possibilities for dialogue, giving any of them featured melodies would make for a very lengthy work. In my opinion, Chadwick's music—as with several of his other theatrical scores—is better than its libretto, but by now we can no longer avoid the conclusion that he was simply not cut out for the operatic arena. Chadwick was an extraordinary melodist and craftsman, but his gift for thematic development—which worked so splendidly in his instrumental works—did not translate to the stage.

What we do know is that Chadwick would not be deterred. He desperately yearned for triumph on the serious stage, and he continued to search for libretti that would confront challenging topics and provide fertile ideas for musical development. But a compelling one was still several years away.

As NEC construction progressed through the summer of 1902, Chadwick prepared for the start of the new academic year. There was much trepidation because no one knew exactly what to expect on registration day; while the new edifice had generated discussion throughout Boston—and in fact throughout the whole of New England—as yet there had been little to indicate that a magnificent facility would do much to increase student registration. Add to that the unfinished state of the building. On September 18, 1902, the first registration day, "There was a great deal of confusion, many rooms not finished, plumbing not at all working (the men had to make journeys across the street to Symphony Hall). There was some kicking [by the faculty] about the assignment of rooms. The little teachers wanted the big rooms of course. Jordan Hall was one big staging [area], but that we could spare in view of our other blessings. Everybody was so full of enthusiasm."[50]

The new conservatory attracted many visiting musicians, among them Theodore Thomas, who gave his approval of Jordan Hall in 1903. Thomas had arrived in Boston to pursue research in the music library, after which he and Chadwick went to inspect the hall. It was still set with scenery from a recent opera performance, but Thomas was able to get around the stage, clap his hands, and stomp his feet. He succinctly declared, "This is a good hall!"[51] Similarly, Gericke, in his imperfect English, thought the hall beautifully displayed orchestral resonance. "It makes a goot, lonk sound," he said.[52]

Chadwick, never missing an opportunity for publicity, was able to keep NEC front and center in the public mind because of the number of "firsts" it sponsored. On the occasion of the first commencement ceremony held in Jordan Hall, on June 24, 1903, the *Boston Globe* reported: "The occasion marks the formal opening of the hall, which is considered to be one of the best of its kind in New England."[53] Chadwick may not have been encouraged by this remark after having aspired to build one of the great halls in the world. No matter. He could see for himself that "everybody admired it [and] the sound was all we could desire and has been ever since."[54]

A second "first," and a genuinely important occasion in Boston's musical life, was the official dedication of Jordan Hall on October 20, 1903. Chadwick intended the event not simply to mark the opening of another performance venue in Boston, but to signal the conservatory's reinvention. To that end he produced a lavish gala concert unlike anything that had ever occurred at NEC. Henry Higginson immediately aided the cause by offering a BSO performance at Jordan Hall at no cost to NEC. Chadwick accepted, and, although Gericke would conduct most of the program, Chadwick led the group in his own *Melpomene*. As rehearsals commenced, Chadwick, who was none too certain about how the hall would respond acoustically to an imposing professional orchestra, made sure he was in attendance at Gericke's first rehearsal. He was not disappointed. "I heard all the rehearsals in the hall," Chadwick remembered, "and was overjoyed at the sweetness and power of the orchestral tone."[55] In addition to *Melpomene*, the program included Bach's Prelude and Fugue in C major performed on the new organ by Wallace Goodrich; Schumann's A major concerto with pianist Antoinette Szumowska (Mrs. Joseph Adamowski) as soloist; and, perhaps predictably, Beethoven's *Eroica* Symphony. The audience that night numbered a thousand people, "the cream of society."[56]

In what can only be judged a smart political decision, the keynote address was delivered not by Chadwick, but by Henry Higginson, who had been invited to speak for ten minutes. Once onstage, Higginson—in equal parts irrepressible and irresponsible—went on for more than a half hour, during which time he said "some very tasteless things about Tourjée, whose family were present and about some of the musicians of his own generation."[57] Higginson's indecorous remarks did not reach the level of scandal—they were ignored in the local press coverage—but the delays created headaches for Chadwick, who reported that "Gericke was wild" about the unexpected wait. "He pranced up and down the tuning room and scolded me as if it was my fault. 'What shall I do with *Eroica* at ten o'clock in the night?' he roared. I did not blame him, but I could not give Uncle Henry the hook after once he got started [*sic*]."[58] Nevertheless, Chadwick's main objective was met. The grand performance was well received by audiences and critics, and with near-boundless satisfaction he recalled that "The audience included all the musical people that counted [and] I think they went away with the idea that 'the old Conservatory' was on the map from that time on."[59]

Euterpe (1903)

Named for the goddess of music (and, in later Greece, of lyric poetry), *Euterpe* is Chadwick's third muse-inspired overture, following *Thalia* (1882) and *Melpomene* (1887). As with those two compositions, he has not intended in *Euterpe* to relay a descriptive program; in fact, Chadwick originally planned for the composition to serve as the fourth movement of his lighthearted symphony-like abstract composition, *Sinfonietta. Euterpe*'s relationship to anything "Greek," therefore, must be taken with a grain of salt. The piece is simply intended to convey the joy that attends the art of music. The composer began *Euterpe* at West Chop on July 26, 1903; he completed it on November 4, and dedicated it to his longtime friend, Sam Sanford.

Euterpe is crafted on the principles of sonata form, but, having become a master of it, Chadwick now thoroughly explores its possibilities. A broad and somber introduction in D minor, set against a wash of strings and woodwinds in descending motion, creates instability by displacing the main beats and winding through a variety of harmonies. The music's character reminds one of the introduction to the first movement of Brahms's Symphony no. 1, also begun in a minor mode, and, as if to further embrace the older masters, Chadwick echoes Beethoven's famous use of a false entrance in his Symphony no. 3 (*Eroica*) by presenting the first moments of an introductory theme (performed by the principal trumpet), before its full statement is sounded.

Much has been made of *Euterpe*'s brilliant principal theme, with its unique rhythmic profile and cheerful disposition. Yellin—giving credit to Gottschalk's influence on Chadwick—believed that the theme "modulates into a kind of Antillean *tresillo*, or syncopated three-beat rhythm within a duple meter bar," which brings it into conformity with modern ragtime.[60] Chadwick manipulates the theme almost immediately, pushing through C major on the way to a giant downbeat on a Neapolitan-sixth chord (an inverted major chord on the flatted second scale degree, or D-flat/F/A-flat). The instrumental color is heightened by the prominent use of the harp, as well as upper woodwinds in their high register.

A soaring secondary theme, marked Cantabile espressivo, is introduced in F major. Like others of Chadwick's contrasting themes, this one is sentimental and lies within a fairly narrow range. It is performed by one of Chadwick's favored instrumental combinations, horns doubled with violins. Soon the main theme reappears in the upper woodwinds set against the opening theme, now in E major, and again counterpoint pervades. As the recapitulation arrives, the main theme, now returned to the tonic D major, is extensively transformed, and its harmonic vestment is surprisingly unstable. The overture closes with three volcanic codas.

Following its completion, *Euterpe* was swiftly premiered by the BSO on April 22, 1904, under Chadwick's direction. Gericke had recently been stung by the success of "novelty" concerts performed under the auspices of the Chickering piano company, many of which featured works by local composers. In effect, Gericke had been "scooped." Chadwick knew this and offered *Euterpe* to Gericke, who looked it over before deciding to give it a hearing on the condition that Chadwick conduct. "This was a great surprise to me," Chadwick reflected, "as it was entirely contrary to his precedents, but I subsequently discovered that it was to save himself trouble and that he had not studied the piece much himself."[61]

Critics immediately concluded that *Euterpe*, despite its attractiveness, was not an artistic milestone for Chadwick. The *Boston Evening Transcript* reporter wrote that "it did not seem interesting although it was agreeable."[62] The *Herald* critic predicted that it would not "enlarge his reputation, for it is not conspicuously imaginative or brilliant."[63] Nevertheless, *Euterpe* generated occasional performances until 1924, after which it disappeared from the concert hall. Mason Redfern, the respected but now obscure music critic of the *San Francisco Examiner*, appreciated *Euterpe* more than most. He heard it in 1915 when Chadwick conducted it at the "American Composers' Day" celebration and concert at the Panama-Pacific International Exposition in California. Redfern relished the overture's classical reserve, but was surprised that there was not so much as a hint of "Americanism."[64] Plainly Redfern would have disagreed with Yellin's later assertion that *Euterpe* bore a relationship to ragtime.

Several compelling features in *Euterpe* serve to give it a modern tint. It displays an exhilarating exoticism not so much in its melodies, but by its utilization of colorful chords at pivotal structural points. Chadwick's use of the harp, as well as several wind instrument solos (especially in the oboe and trumpet parts), contributes to its novel countenance, as does the large-scale harmonic interplay between D minor and D major, which is unique in Chadwick's output.

Sinfonietta in D (1904)

Chadwick sketched his *Sinfonietta in D* during the summer of 1903, but did not begin its orchestration until February 11, 1904. The passage of six or seven months between the sketches and the orchestration can be attributed to the fact that he was occupied with other projects, and indeed, if we consider only his orchestral works that were in progress at the time—the final movement of *Symphonic Sketches*, *Euterpe*, and a new work, *Cleopatra*—he had much on his plate. One can add to this prodigious compositional workload numerous songs and choruses that were being written and published during this period. Nevertheless, *Sinfonietta* was finally completed on May 3, 1904.

Sinfonietta is in effect Chadwick's Fifth Symphony, although it is far less ambitious than his earlier ones in terms of its dramatic intensity, the size of its instrumental forces, and its length. Chadwick's use of a diminutive suffix in the title perhaps demonstrates that he intended to downplay it as a work of artistic significance. But that should not suggest that *Sinfonietta* is uninteresting, or that he considered it an unimportant work. In fact, by virtue of its use of any number of modernist techniques, the *Sinfonietta* is one of Chadwick's most innovative little gems, and in it one senses a great deal of experimentation. This may be because Chadwick expected it to be a teaching piece for his NEC orchestra, an attractive, innovative, and playable demonstration work that would have been enlightening to his composition students.[65] *Sinfonietta* is scored for three flutes, pairs of oboes, clarinets and bassoons, four horns, two trumpets, and three trombones. Also included is a large battery of percussion: timpani, snare drum, bass drum, triangle, cymbals, and harp, as well as a full complement of strings. The four movements that comprise *Sinfonietta* are standard to the symphony genre: a medium tempo, sonata form first movement, Risolutamente, is followed by a Canzonetta: Allegretto, in $\frac{2}{4}$ time. A brisk, third-position scherzo bursts with some of Chadwick's most inventive rhythmic writing, while the Finale: assai animato is typical of Chadwick's rousing closers. *Sinfonietta* was premiered at an "all-Chadwick" concert on November 21, 1904, in celebration of his fiftieth birthday. Chadwick conducted members of the BSO, many of whom had become friends.

Like *Euterpe*, *Sinfonietta* makes noteworthy use of exotic elements, including bits of impressionism, a modal melodic language—in this instance Phrygian mode—that offers up a Middle Eastern flavor, and the use of instruments that effect Middle Eastern sonorities. Chadwick has here followed French composers of the turn of the century, especially Debussy, who had utilized these techniques in an effort to invigorate his music, relying less on form and more on mood and atmosphere. Chadwick's use in the first movement of the Phrygian mode creates something of an imbalance, one that momentarily transports the listener off terra firma. That feeling is enhanced by the "Chinoise" effect produced by the combination of swirling woodwinds, harp, and cymbals.

The second movement Canzonetta is a three-part creation in the style of a march. Its military character reminds one of the farandole movement of Bizet's first *L'Arlesienne Suite*, although the quiet close in the first section, at the appearance of the viola solo, echoes Berlioz's *Harold in Italy*. *Transcript* critic H. T. Parker wrote in 1930 that "Ravel himself might envy the fancy and felicity of the distant horns against the sustaining viola," at the movement's end.[66] This is a remarkable, uncomplicated, and fetching movement, one that would be appreciated by young performers and audiences today.

Chadwick's third movement, an F major Scherzino: Vivacissimo e leggiero, is also a wonderful example of his writing in a light style, and hearkens back to the clever second movement of his Second Symphony. It shows a considerable advance in Chadwick's rhythmic thought, as shifting meters and syncopation keep the listener on his toes. The B-flat major Trio section presents a lovely pastoral melody, one of the most memorable in the piece.

The Finale, like most of Chadwick's final movements, is spine-tingling. A *Boston Evening Transcript* critic thought that "Mr. Chadwick seems preeminently a composer of scherzos and brilliant finales," and that in them he was nearly without peer. "In this line he has something personal to say, and a distinctly personal way of saying it, very far removed from the commonplace which he is like to approach in his slow music, and also far away from an imitation of German orthodox composers."[67]

Sinfonietta appeared quickly on the heels of the now fully completed *Symphonic Sketches*, and it was thought by some to be a quintessentially American work. Indeed, given its jovial character and tunefulness, it may be considered so, although, unlike other characteristically American works by Chadwick, there is little here that conjures folksiness, except perhaps the main tune in the third movement. Nevertheless, we find threads in the fabric of the work that indicate that Chadwick was familiar with trends in the musical world around him, and clearly he was curious enough to give some new techniques a try.

To twenty-first century ears, the music seems rather unchallenging: pleasant melodies are set in comfortable harmonies, routine rhythms, and clear phrases. A *New York Sun* reviewer, writing as *Sinfonietta* was being revived in 1910 in New York and Boston, "sat up and rejoiced" because he was able simply to enjoy beautiful music without having to plumb the depths of modernism. The writer was ecstatic that the piece did not require from him the close intellectual and analytical brand of listening that was demanded by many other compositions of the day. "There was no pitfall for the unwary," he wrote gleefully. "No concealed meanings, no pathological or other –ological subtleties, but just a bit of lovely musical landscape, filled with the sunshine of a happy disposition and vocal with the songs of spontaneous fancy."[68]

The full score of *Sinfonietta* was published by G. Schirmer in 1906. A sympathetic, if technically imperfect, recording was produced in 1959 by Karl Krueger and the American Arts Orchestra. Despite its attractive qualities, *Sinfonietta* never caught on in the American canon. In its more than one-hundred-year history, it has received just over a dozen live hearings.

Cleopatra (1904)

In 1904, Chadwick spent a good deal of time studying scores by his contemporaries, but, like many others, he was especially drawn to music by Richard Strauss. Chadwick may have been inspired in part by Strauss's widely heralded first tour of the United States. Strauss arrived in New York in February 1904 as the most famous—and infamous—composer of the day. A Strauss Festival at Carnegie Hall signaled his arrival, and the three-day event was attended by "everybody who counts in the culture of our metropolis. There were princes of finance, dictators of society, queens of opera, autocrats of the baton, lords and ladies of the piano and violin, and all the rest."[69] Following several more days of recitals in New York (during which he conducted the world premiere of his *Sinfonia domestica* on March 21) and Philadelphia, Strauss proceeded to Boston, where he led both the touring Philadelphia Orchestra and the BSO in performances of his *Till Eulenspiegel* (1895), *Tod und Verklärung* (1889), *Don Quixote* (1897), and *Don Juan* (1889).

Strauss's music had been a subject of impassioned discussion in America for years; he was, at the turn of the century, considered the most modern of the moderns, and what he was attempting to do in music—or what some thought he was attempting to do—created enormous controversy. In 1899 critic James Gibbons Huneker wrote that Strauss "has attempted the delineation of thought, not musical thought, but philosophical ideas in tone." According to Huneker, Strauss sought "to seize not only certain elusive psychical states, but also to paint pure idea." Huneker elaborated, "Strauss's German brain with its grasp of the essentials of philosophy, allied to a vigorous emotional nature and a will and imagination that stop at nothing, enabled him to throw into high relief his excited mental states. That these states took unusual melodic shapes, that there is the suggestion of abnormality, was to be expected; for Strauss made a flight into a country in which it is almost madness to venture."[70]

If Huneker thought that Strauss's "psychical" flights approached insanity, his assessment of Strauss's music was more sober. "Formalism is abandoned," Huneker declared. "Strauss moves by episodes; now furiously swift, now ponderously lethargic and one is lost in amazement at the loftiness, the solidity and general massiveness of his structure. The man's scholarship is so profound, almost as profound as Brahms's; his genius for the orchestra is so marked, his color and rhythmic sense is so magnificently developed that the general effect of his rhetoric is perhaps too blazingly brilliant."[71] As for *Also sprach Zarathustra*, Huneker predicted that "the tremendous sincerity of the work will be its saving salt."[72]

In *Cleopatra*, Chadwick sought to confront modernism more directly than he had before. It occurred to him that "I had never written for a big modern orchestra. . . . [I] made up my mind to try my first on a big decorative piece on which I could let myself go."[73] Chadwick got the idea to write *Cleopatra* from his reading of Plutarch's *Life of Antony*, which "struck me as a very picturesque subject and I made a plan in free symphonic form with a very elaborate and decorative introduction, suggested by a description of Cleopatra's barge on the Cydnus, a martial war-like theme for Antony, a lush and amorous one for Cleo[patra], a big clashing battle scene ending with the defeat of Antony, Cleopatra's love music again with death music at the close, and an imposing Finale with the three themes worked together."[74] The plan for this composition, Chadwick's first to carry the label "symphonic poem," was ambitious. He worked on the piece steadily during the summer, having begun sketches on June 20; the compositional plan was completed by the end of August, and after laboring industriously through the autumn, he completed it on New Year's Eve.

Cleopatra was first performed at the Worcester Festival on September 29, 1905, with Franz Kneisel, who succeeded Wallace Goodrich as director, conducting. Earlier that year, in April, Chadwick had shared the score with Wilhelm Gericke in hopes that he would play it with the BSO. Gericke thought it too long ("As I knew he would," wrote an irritated Chadwick), but he reluctantly agreed to present it that season between a scheduled performance of Schumann's A-major piano concerto and Strauss's *Ein Heldenleben*. To Chadwick, "This looked a good deal like 'skying' the piece"; that is, tossing it in the air and letting it land on a program randomly. In disgust, the composer rejected Gericke's offer. Kneisel, a loyal friend, might have been pleased to premiere *Cleopatra*, but Chadwick knew that it would attract little critical notice in Worcester.[75]

Chadwick shared his programmatic vision of *Cleopatra* with Philip Hale, who prepared program notes that were "sanctioned by the composer."[76]

> The Life of Antony by Plutarch contains many vivid situations which are susceptible of musical illustration in the modern sense, and those having the most direct reference to Cleopatra have been chosen for musical suggestion in this piece, although the action of the tragedy is not literally followed.
>
> The symphonic poem opens (F major, Andante sostenuto) with an undulating motive for flutes and harps, suggesting the voyage on the Cydnus [O1], which, after a climax for the whole orchestra, is succeeded by an Allegro agitato [O2] depicting the approach of Antony and his army. A bold military theme [P] (Allegro marziale, D major), in which the brass and percussion instruments play an important role, is worked up to a powerful climax,

TABLE 9.1. The Form of *Cleopatra*

	Introduction		Exposition		Development	Recapitulation	Coda
Part:	I.				II.		
Section:			1	2	3	4	
Theme:	O1	O2	P	S		O1, P, S	S, P
Key:	D	d	D	F	D-flat	D	D
Measure:	1	33	84	123	205	329	452

but soon dies away in soft harmonies for the wind instruments and horns. The Cleopatra theme [S] then begins, first with a sensuous melody for the violoncello (F major), repeated by the violins and afterwards by the whole orchestra.

The key now changes to D-flat (Molto tranquillo) [development section]. Strange harmonies are heard in the muted strings. The English horn and clarinet sing short, passionate phrases, to which the soft trombones later on add a sound of foreboding. But suddenly the Cleopatra theme appears again, now transformed to vigorous allegro, and Antony departs to meet defeat and death. (F minor, Allegro moderato).

The Antony theme is now fully worked out, mostly in minor keys and sometimes in conjunction with the Cleopatra motive. It ends with a terrific climax on the chord of C-flat, and after a pause the introductory phrases are again heard [recapitulation]. A long diminuendo, ending with a melancholy phrase for the viola, suggests his final passing, and Cleopatra's lamentation (D minor) follows at once.

In this part much of the previous love music is repeated, and some of it is entirely changed in expression as well as in rhythm and instrumentation. At last it dies away in mysterious harmonies with muted horns and strings.

The work closes with an imposing Maestoso [coda] in which the burial of Antony and Cleopatra in the same grave is suggested by the two themes now heard for the first time simultaneously. For this, Shakespeare's line is, perhaps, not inappropriate: "She shall be buried by her Antony. No grave on earth shall hold a pair so famous."[77]

While Strauss exerted an increasing influence on Chadwick, and undoubtedly provided inspiration in this case, *Cleopatra* may be the best proof we have that Chadwick thought about musical construction predominantly in terms of sonata form (see table 9.1). According to Hale, there was a clear intention to paint a musical illustration "in the modern sense" and render "musical suggestion," although he admitted that there was no attempt to follow the tragedy to the letter. Of course, Chadwick was familiar with Strauss's attempt to capture sonically and in close detail events and occurrences common to everyday life, many of them trivial, but he chose not to emulate that scheme. And despite his declared use of modern technique and "free symphonic form," Chadwick's music is cast in a fairly traditional mold. *Cleopatra*'s form—and its programmatic narrative of masculine versus feminine—is not vastly different from that of *Rip Van Winkle* Overture, a work composed fully twenty-five years before. In fact, the two compositions share an eerily similar design: a two-part introduction is followed by a brief principal theme; upon the arrival of the contrasting secondary theme the music undergoes complex development even before reaching the development proper. A fermata (or in the case of *Cleopatra*, two fermati) mark a break from the development and the arrival of the recapitulation using themes from the introduction. The initial introductory, principal, and secondary themes soon follow, and the works close with a dazzling multi-sectional coda. Although *Cleopatra* could well have ended quietly based on the narrative, which leaves both characters dead at its end, Chadwick learned in *Adonais* that quiet endings can meet with even quieter responses from conductors. *Cleopatra*'s form was a pattern Chadwick knew well, and despite his desire to stay up with new trends, he was unable to change his stripes, at least for now.

But Strauss resonates among *Cleopatra*'s musical parameters, and, because of them, the work strikes an unmistakably modern chord. Chadwick believed that, with his increased instrumental forces, "I was acquiring quite a new kind of technique. To this I have ever since adhered. With the big halls of this country a big orchestral sound is necessary for any imposing effect."[78] Chadwick's "new kind of technique" was achieved by a huge orchestra of three flutes (the third doubles on piccolo); pairs of oboes, clarinets, and bassoons, plus English horn and bass clarinet; four horns, three each of trumpets and trombones, and a tuba; five percussion and three timpani; harp and celesta; and a full string section. Not only does his orchestration include plenty of doubling within and between instrumental families to ensure that musical lines are heard, but *Cleopatra* is, quite simply, a very loud piece of music. The volume of the music (which, to be sure, is not at a constant forte) is aided by an unusual amount of homorhythm, wherein instrumental parts move along in block-chord fashion. The absence of counterpoint, a hallmark of Chadwick's earlier style, is also noteworthy. In addition, *Cleopatra* is imbued with a colossal variety of shifting meters and tempi, and, while Chadwick does not go far beyond his usual harmonic language, striking large-scale relationships—including the D major/D minor duality in the long introduction, the shift to D-flat (a remote tonal center from the tonic D) at the start of the development, and his ongoing preference for the mediant relationship (in this case F) in the secondary key area—makes for an intelligently crafted and persuasive composition.

Chadwick was in Europe when he entrusted to Kneisel the premiere of *Cleopatra* at the Worcester Festival. He first heard it in 1906 when the recently appointed conductor Karl Muck took it up with the BSO. In Chadwick's view the rehearsals did not go well. Chadwick had never been entirely appreciative of Muck's preparation of the orchestra, and he flatly detested some of his practices. "Dr. Muck was much criticized for his programs," Chadwick railed. "His theory was; first that *everything* by a great composer is better than *anything* by a minor practitioner. That would make the overtures Ruins of Athens & the Jubal overture by Weber better than the Verkäufte Braut or Melpomene which is not the case (If I do say it as shouldn't)." Chadwick furthered complained that, according to Muck's theory, music from the Classical and Romantic eras should not be mixed on a program and "the audience had no rights as to the length of a program." Muck's programs fluctuated between less than an hour to several hours in length, and audiences were free to take it or leave it. The conductor was also panned by more than a few observers, including Chadwick, for offering concerts that "appeared to have been assembled like a washing day luncheon."[79] Nevertheless, Muck deserves some credit for the small place he gave to American music on his programs, although it was often done with Chadwick's prodding. Despite the conductor's shortcomings, even Chadwick had to admit that Muck's preparation of *Cleopatra* "finally ended by a brilliant performance."[80]

Cleopatra garnered a mere dozen performances before it vanished among the stacks of Chadwick's manuscripts, unpublished and rarely touched; it did not even rate a mention in John Tasker Howard's comprehensive history, *Our American Music* (1930). The reviews were mostly lukewarm, although some writers found it mildly alluring. Hale, now reviewing the BSO in his role as critic for Boston's *Sunday Herald*, considered *Cleopatra* "more modern in its sentiment" than some of the composer's more recent works.[81] *Cleopatra*'s final hearing occurred in 1908, when Frederick Stock led the Chicago-based Theodore Thomas Orchestra in its home city. Critic and historian William Lines Hubbard reviewed the performance, and in his estimation its themes "are wanting somewhat in distinctiveness." But Hubbard could not deny that "the manner in which the themes are handled and the instrumental color employed make the score brilliant and attractive."[82] *Cleopatra* awaits a modern hearing.

Chadwick continued to write a number of songs in the first years of the new century. Some of them were sacred, like "The Good Samaritan" (1900) and "Hark!

Hark! My Soul" (1903), and were prepared for publication, principally during this period for the firms of Church, Scribner, and especially Schmidt. Chadwick's secular songs also had a following; one of his key song collaborators was another of his St. Botolph Club companions, Nantucket-born businessman and poet Arthur Macy. Chadwick set no fewer than seven of Macy's texts, including "Faith" (1899); the drinking song "Saint Botolph" (1902), composed to celebrate the twenty-fifth anniversary of the club; Six Songs for Mezzo-Soprano and Baritone (1902) of which five are Macy's; and Three Songs for Mezzo-Soprano or Baritone (1902), of which one, "Thou Art to Me," numbers among Chadwick's most popular songs. Chadwick also set Sidney Lanier's evocative "A Ballad of Trees and the Master" in 1899; the song won first place and a seventy-five-dollar prize in *The Musical Record & Review* competition.

Chadwick's success as a composer of sacred works for chorus continued unabated with "While Shepherds Watched" (1899), "Morn's Roseate Hues" (1903), "Teach Me O Lord" (1903), "Saviour, Again to Thy Dear Name" (1904), "Sun of My Soul" (1904), and a number of collections for women's voices. Among his miscellaneous instrumental works of this period are *Ten Little Tunes for Ten Little Friends* (1903), a pedagogical piano album for children, and an arrangement for orchestra of Handel's Concerto in B-flat (no. 12), scored in 1903 for use by the NEC orchestra.

The Death of Theodore Thomas

If Chadwick was elated at the completion of *Cleopatra* on New Year's Eve after six months of toil, within a week he was devastated by the news that Theodore Thomas had died on January 4, 1905. Thomas succumbed to a brief bout with pneumonia that Chadwick suspected had been contracted at a rehearsal in Chicago's new orchestra hall, which was "unfinished and damp."[83] Tucked into the pages of his 1905 memoirs, Chadwick inserted three typed pages of Thomas-related anecdotes that demonstrate his immense admiration and affection for the elder statesman of American classical music, the very man who had most inspired his own career.

Chadwick also knew that Thomas could be intemperate. Critic Philip Hale, commenting on a Boston concert led by Thomas in his maturity, wrote: "The years have frosted his hair, but his figure is as erect, his bearing as graceful, his quiet authority as supreme as when he first visited us. I know of no conductor who has such despotic control over his men and at the same time commands [them] so imperceptibly."[84] For his part, Chadwick recalled, "He had a strong will and resolute purpose indispensable to a great leader and on that account was sometimes accused of being arbitrary and intolerant. It was one of his principles not to allow himself to be made responsible for things he could not control, and this sometimes led him into conflicts with authorities whose standards were lower than his own."[85] We may reasonably surmise that here Chadwick was referencing the unfortunate events of the Columbian Exposition.

Thomas's musical legacy was widely considered transformative. John Tasker Howard, writing in 1930, viewed Thomas as "an epic figure in American history—one of our great heroes. Compare the state of musical culture at the time of the Civil War with conditions today, and then thank Theodore Thomas for the difference."[86] Thomas's soaring musical standards launched America's advances in symphonic music in the last quarter of the nineteenth century, and his touring orchestra brought great music to scores of thousands of listeners who heard everything from Mozart and Beethoven to the latest works of Wagner. Indeed, Thomas played no small role in establishing in America the repertoire we now consider classic. As we have seen, Thomas was also a great friend to the American composer, whose music he insisted be heard. "He did not give entire programs of American music, as one would exhibit a collection of curiosities," Chadwick related. "He believed, and rightly, that such booming [i.e., advocacy] does the composer more harm than good. But he placed their works on his programs where they could be fairly compared with the compositions of their contemporaries—French, German and Russian. He could do them no greater service."[87]

The famous Thomas concerts in Lawrence and Boston in the 1870s were seminal musical events of Chadwick's early life, and it is not too much to say that Chadwick soon became something of a "groupie." Chadwick sought to meet Thomas as early as 1882, when he was in New York to conduct Paine's Prelude to *Oedipus Tyrannus*.[88] Thomas was then the conductor of the New York Philharmonic Orchestra, a post he had held since 1877. Chadwick, never shy, used his acquaintance with Thomas to pitch his own music, but soon, at least by 1892, what had begun as a business relationship developed into a personal one. From that point their bond strengthened. To Chadwick's great delight, Thomas owned a summer home in Fairhaven on Massachusetts's coastline, and the two men managed to reunite often in New England, although probably not as often as Chadwick would have wished.

Chadwick's correspondence with Thomas began at least by 1882 (again, the year of *Oedipus Tyrannus*), and continued steadily for the next twenty-two years. Their final dispatches ended just prior to Thomas's death. In his letters Chadwick often offered up his music for Thomas's inspection, and, by the mid-1890s, he was regularly sending scores to Thomas; sometimes they met at

Fairhaven or in Boston to peruse them together. At one time or another, Chadwick tempted Thomas with the first three Symphonies, *Symphonic Sketches*, *Pastoral Prelude*, the *Andante for String Orchestra*, *The Lily Nymph*, *Adonais*, and *Judith*, among others. Chadwick also kept Thomas apprised of the news of Boston's Big Four—Parker, Foote, and Whiting, in addition to himself— and regularly sent him updates on happenings at NEC and the Springfield and Worcester festivals. Chadwick knew that Thomas's experiences in Cincinnati, where he founded and administered that city's May Festival and its College of Music, could be instructive. As the years passed, their relationship grew less formal, more personal. Chadwick sounded positively giddy when he requested a photograph of Thomas such as the one the conductor had recently presented to Kneisel. "Should you be inclined to confer a like honor upon me," he wrote, "it shall occupy a place of honor on the walls of this Emporium [i.e., NEC] of beauty and virtues, incense shall be burned before it, and no Conservatory girl shall pass it without genuflecting."[89]

Several years after Thomas's death, Chadwick read the memoirs penned by his wife, Rose Fay Thomas.[90] The book rekindled many memories for him and provided new insights about the man he had admired for decades. Chadwick harbored sympathy for the musician and the many trials through which he suffered, not the least of which was his inability to find a home city that appreciated him. "And in spite of his wonderful, stupendous success he never had smooth sailing until he finally settled in Chicago [and] for good and all made his mind to stay there."[91] As for Thomas's reputation as a tyrant, "Undoubtedly some of his fights were caused by his own obstinacy and pig-headedness," Chadwick thought, "but even these qualities were a part of his unflinching devotion to the cause of art."[92]

Thomas's death marked the end of an important chapter in American musical life. With the possible exception of John Philip Sousa, there was no other American leader who had impacted the musical culture—or who could commandeer an audience—with the same epic force. Certainly no American composer of art music could now claim the mantle of leadership. Not MacDowell; not Parker; not even Chadwick himself.

At Thomas's death Chadwick was eight years into his tenure as director of NEC and exactly fifty years old. Although a nationally respected composer and administrator, he was not a famous, revered musical leader—he was not Theodore Thomas—and it was a situation that by now he knew was not likely to change. As NEC surged—with a new building and concert hall, increasing enrollment, and heightened reputation—his compositional productivity was starting to wane. Despite his sturdy New England constitution, Chadwick had reached a point where he needed a respite, a bit of time to take stock and re-assess his life and career at its mid-point.

As he often had, Chadwick turned to Europe.

"Our Great Pilgrimage"
Chadwick's Grand Tour
1905–1906

Horatio Parker

Chadwick yearned to return to Europe to accomplish some of the goals that he failed to achieve during his ill-fated 1901 trip, perhaps because he felt as though he was running out of time. His recent fiftieth birthday occasioned a special tribute performance of several of his compositions and a reception at which he received gifts and affectionate accolades from students, faculty, and board members. Chadwick was mildly despondent even as he thought those gestures "certainly did a good deal to reconcile me to the loss of my youth."[1] If his youth was slipping, however, his ambition remained intact. Chadwick may well have been inspired to undertake a trip by Horatio Parker, whose year-long journey to Europe, also in 1901, had produced for him marvelous musical results. Their voyages of that year nearly overlapped, for Parker wrote to Chadwick, "We expect to welcome you on your return, to condole and congratulate [you], though we shall probably leave the next day ourselves."[2]

Parker had been to England several times, most recently in 1896 (see figure 10.1). At the time he "was very thick with the Novellos," owners of a British publishing firm, "& made real progress toward the future performances of his works in England."[3] A coveted 1899 invitation to Parker to conduct his own compositions at England's renowned Worcester Festival resulted in additional requests from other festivals over the next several years. By 1901 Parker could venture to Britain with a résumé that was singular. Although he had come to music as a teenager, he got a good grounding in piano from his mother and other local teachers in his hometown of Auburndale, Massachusetts. Soon he learned organ, which he played in church, and composition. His earliest works were hymns, anthems, and songs for school children.[4] Parker began serious study in harmony and composition with Chadwick in November 1881; his progress was rapid and within just a year he had his eyes set on Europe and its renowned conservatories. At Chadwick's urging, Parker went to Munich to study with Rheinberger. In July 1882, Chadwick sent advance notice of Parker's arrival to his beloved German mentor:

> During the summer a young student and friend of mine will probably appear in Munich. His name is "Parker" and he is not yet 19 years old, and I would

like to ask sincerely for your valued interest in him. I believe he has a very special talent for composition and needs only to study for a few years with you in order to accomplish something extraordinary.

This year he studied harmony and counterpoint very diligently with me and also something of form as well, but he should review it all and start the whole thing over again. He can also play some of the large fugues of Bach on the organ, and hopefully it will be possible to have lessons with you. He is somewhat stubborn and conceited, but one can't expect otherwise from a 19-year-old. May I perhaps hope that you will have the same friendly interest for him that you showed for me?[5]

Parker, a more patient, staid, and predictable student than Chadwick, remained at the conservatory for three years. The major accomplishment of his European adventure was an orchestral work; in Parker's case his First Symphony, which he dedicated to Chadwick. The symphony was premiered in 1885 in Munich, but it is an undistinguished composition. Parker's biographer, William K. Kearns, observed that the composer's "single attempt at composing a symphony also lacks originality. In organization and style, it reveals a model no later than early Beethoven."[6] He had also gained modest notoriety as an organist and as a composer of chamber music. When Parker returned to the US in 1886, he breezed through a number of church positions in New York City and taught briefly at Thurber's National Conservatory. In 1893 he accepted the organist and choirmaster position at Trinity Church in Boston, an important post at the time. The same year Parker composed *Hora novissima*, the oratorio that brought him his greatest renown. Chadwick's role in what is generally considered Parker's finest work was not insubstantial. Parker, who was most apt to compose music when stimulated by words, was inspired to look to Latin texts by his familiarity with Chadwick's *Phoenix expirans*. In 1894 Parker accepted the position of professor of music at Yale University, where he stayed for the rest of his life; he retained his position at Trinity Church until 1902. Both posts gave him a good deal of visibility, but, as the musical leader of one of America's largest Episcopal churches, known as the Church of England in earlier times, Parker naturally came to the notice of English composers.

Chadwick was always supportive of his musical friend. When Parker made a brief trip to England in 1900, as he had done before, Chadwick reminded him, "You are now a missionary whether you will or not, of the American Board of Musicians, and I know that you will continue the conversion of the British [to the appreciation of American music], which you began with such great results last year. None of us could do it as well, and we are all proud of your success 'im voraus' [in advance]. You deserve all and more."[7]

Cambridge University elected in 1902 to confer upon Parker the degree of Doctor of Music. He wrote the news to Chadwick almost apologetically: "You have perhaps heard that Cambridge has offered me the degree of Mus. Doc. I have always respected and shared your prejudice against musical as well as other doctors, but there are Doctors and Universities and Cambridge has been conferring the degree for so many hundreds of years that they can probably do it by now so that it will stick. At any rate I shall be in very good company and lucky if I don't turn out to be the worst of the lot."[8] Chadwick had received an honorary master's degree from Yale University in 1897, in no small part due to Parker's influence, and he would finally get an honorary doctorate, the highest honor Boston's Tufts University could bestow, in 1905 in recognition of his service to the Universalist denomination. Chadwick gratefully accepted both degrees, although his views on honorary "doctors" were in keeping with the contemporary majority opinion; he "never encouraged its use," and was only rarely referred to as "Doctor Chadwick," as "this matter of indiscriminate honorary degrees was much criticized at the time." Chadwick also admitted that "Such an honorable institution as Yale has not been altogether blameless in this matter, and I have sometimes felt that my degree from that Institution of which I was once so proud, had depreciated in value since 1897."[9]

Parker's travels and his musical successes in Europe probably inspired

TABLE 10.1. Chadwick's European Travels

September 1877–1879	New York to Hamburg	Education
June 2–September 20, 1883	New York to Antwerp	Vacation
June 20–September 12, 1885	New York to Antwerp	Honeymoon
June 4–September 2, 1888	New York to Antwerp	Vacation
May 4–July 4, 1901	Boston to Liverpool	NEC business
September 1905–August 13, 1906	Boston to Naples, Italy	Sabbatical

Chadwick to pursue his own grand tour. While Chadwick had made several return visits since his own conservatory days, they had all been accomplished as an independent musician/composer with the exception of his 1901 trip, which turned out to be a brief and painful debacle (see table 10.1). Now, however, he possessed an imposing arsenal of compositions, a reputation as an accomplished institutional leader, and a salary which would be paid *in toto* while he was away. He also had some personal savings upon which to draw, which had not been the case during his prior visits. It was finally possible for Chadwick to present himself to his European peers as a successful artist and conservatory administrator, and he fully expected this would be a trip to remember.

Sabbatical

Chadwick had many reasons to plan this sabbatical, which is traditionally an opportunity for college professors to refresh themselves artistically and intellectually by taking time from everyday drudgeries to rediscover aspects of their chosen field and to reclaim their passion for it. After eight years of challenging, stressful work to get NEC's finances and administration in order — not to mention the monumental task of building the conservatory and Jordan Hall — Chadwick needed both a respite and a chance to refresh his musical imagination. While he had managed to complete a few works in the past five years, and he even began several major projects, his output now compared to just a few years ago had dwindled significantly.

He started planning his European sabbatical during the summer of 1905, "with eager anticipation."[10] It would be a year-long trek during which Ida May, along with sons Theodore and Noël (see figure 10.2), both of whom were now old enough to enjoy the adventure, would be in tow. Chadwick may have been jealous of his younger colleague's recent European successes; Parker, nearly ten years his junior, had broken into elite British musical circles like no American composer before him. Chadwick longed to forge similar artistic bonds abroad, but he realized that his time for making an international reputation for him-

FIGURE 10.2.
Sons Noël (left) and Theodore
Chadwick, ca. 1901. Courtesy of
New England Conservatory, Boston.

self was running out, as was his energy for making the arduous transatlantic passage.

The family's immediate destination was Lausanne, Switzerland; that location would provide a home base during much of their stay on the continent. To get there they journeyed via the steamship *Romanie* through the Azores and Gibraltar, before they landed at Naples, Italy, where "we were welcomed by a marine orchestra of four."[11] Much of the family's time in Italy was spent not on music business, but simply as tourists. Chadwick was enthusiastic about Mt. Vesuvius, which was "pouring forth black clouds of smoke and at night there were two gashes of livid red from the molten lava."[12] After a quick trip to Pompeii and a disappointing tour of Genoa, Chadwick heard "some very good organ playing of the German style" in Milan. To get to Lausanne from Italy, the Chadwicks traveled over the Simplon Mountain via the famous Simplon Pass (Passo del Sempione) in a carriage "by 'extra' post," or stagecoach, rather than go around the mountain the long way. The now-famous Simplon Tunnel, begun in 1898, was not yet completed. The Alpine journey was not without discomfort; it was even a bit risky: the weather is unpredictable, and the pass itself, at an altitude of 6,589 feet, is cold and desolate, and at that time it was poorly maintained.

But the adventure made for memorable moments. One of them occurred when the family had dinner at a town located two hours below the summit of the pass. One day, as the snow cleared, "the sun came out, and a landscape of such stupendous grandeur and beauty was revealed as is beyond the power of words to describe. Beethoven must have had such visions when he wrote the Ninth symphony, and as for Bach, he must have lived them." Chadwick's music only rarely references nature or "sounds of place," but the splendor of this view captivated him.[13] It also inspired a profession of faith—a facet of Chadwick's personality that he seldom demonstrated—when he admitted, as he gazed at the scene, that "there is only *one* artist."[14]

Following their descent to the foot of the Simplon Pass's northern slope to the town of Brig, the Chadwicks proceeded to Lausanne through the Rhône Valley ("which I tramped in 1878").[15] The family was soon settled and the boys were enrolled in a local private school. Although homesickness set in almost immediately, Chadwick quickly got to work.[16] He planned to travel to Geneva with the hope of paying a visit to violinist Henri Marteau, who was then teaching at the Geneva Conservatory. Chadwick also intended to devote some of his time there "to Mr. Higginson's affairs," which included helping to lure a new conductor to the BSO.[17] Naturally, he intended to leverage his visits into performances of his own music.

As Chadwick was making plans for his sabbatical, he visited publisher Gustav Schirmer in New York. Schirmer was eager to publish American music "apart from commercial considerations," and Chadwick hoped he would consent to publish *Euterpe*, *Sinfonietta*, and the now-completed four-movement *Symphonic Sketches*, which Chadwick would then be able to share with conductors throughout Europe. Despite his promises, Schirmer did not come through with his part of the bargain until long after Chadwick's return to the United States. Although all three compositions were eventually available through Schirmer, the delay resulted in Chadwick's anger and disappointment; the only orchestral scores he had to show in Europe were the Third Symphony, *Melpomene*, and *Cleopatra*, which was not likely to be performed on account of the extra instruments required. There is ample reason to suspect that Chadwick might have postponed his sabbatical trip had he known that Schirmer would fail to live up to his pledge.

Nonetheless, in November, Leipzig's Concordia Singing Society devoted an evening entirely to Chadwick's music. The program included *Melpomene*, *Ecce jam noctis* (for men's chorus and orchestra), and Symphony no. 3. Chadwick relayed few details of the Concordia concert, but press reports made their way—probably through Chadwick himself—to Boston. In one article, "Leipsic Discovers a Boston Composer," the critic noted that, "As he [Chadwick] had only an orchestra from one of the regimental bands of the garrison, the performance must have proceeded under some difficulties."[18] The writer went on to quote (in translation) a German reviewer who had attended the concert and gave a glowing report about Chadwick's Third Symphony: "I declare that I consider this symphony the best of all that have been written since Brahms. It is extraordinarily rich in tone color and masterly in construction and instrumentation. It is hard to say what most strongly seizes the listener—the joyous energy of the first movement, the original humor of the third, or the sturdy manliness of the last, which closes in such splendid romp."

1906

If the 1901 visit had been disheartening, Chadwick made up for it five years later. Through the early months of 1906 he traveled nearly constantly, visiting musicians and conservatories in an effort to learn the art of music administration. In the spring he penned "A Greeting to '06 from Over the Water," an open letter that was read to NEC's graduating class. "I have visited the Conservatories of Frankfurt, Leipzig, Berlin, Bale, Zurich, Florence, Venice, Rome, Milan and Paris, and have three or four more yet to add to my collection," he wrote in his four-page missal,

> but it has not made me ashamed of ours—no, not a little bit! There are many virtues that only come with age, and these old schools, like old wine, old violins, and old shoes, have acquired their peculiar halo in many cases by the history they have made, and of which they have been a part. But here are some of the things I saw in these schools. In Leipzig a young student of Prof. Nikisch, conducting *Romeo and Juliet* by Tchaikovsky with the greatest authority, sureness and enthusiasm, and with hardly a glance at the score. In Paris, an organ student of Guilmant improvises a fugue on a subject which I gave him myself, and it was not only correct but musical and interesting. And most wonderful of all, in the Paris Conservatory I heard a little girl in a short dress sing an exercise in five clefs at sight, which not one of you could have played in the same tempo on the piano! And the whole class, many of whom were much younger, wrote a passage from a violin concerto from dictation. Think of *that*, ye solfeggio grumblers![19]

Because Chadwick planned to spend the last five weeks of his sabbatical in England, much of the spring of 1906 was spent in an attempt to procure summer performances of his music or schedule meetings in London. But those efforts came to nothing. When Theodore and Noël completed the academic term at their private school at the end of June, the family made for England, where they arrived on July 4.

Chadwick secured many appointments in England, although performances of his music were not forthcoming. He returned to the Royal Academy of Music to see Parry and Stanford, "who were very cordial,"[20] and he finally met with Edward Elgar, of whom he seemed strangely suspicious. "Had a very jolly and interesting visit," Chadwick reported. "Elgar is probably the best one of the English composers at present, but I am not quite prepared to recognize him as the great original genius that his cult would make him out."[21] Elgar had made a name for himself in recent years with *Variations on an Original Theme*, better known as the *Enigma Variations* (1899), the overtures *Cockaigne* (1901) and *In the South* (1904), as well as two oratorios, *The Dream of Gerontius* (1900) and *The Apostles* (1903). In 1909 Chadwick would hear the Boston premiere of Elgar's new Symphony in A-flat (op. 55), and, despite his high hopes, he was disappointed by it. "It is all *invented* with tremendous skill to be sure," Chadwick wrote, "for his craftsmanship is not to be denied, but still one does not feel it to be the result of a genuine and overmastering impulse of a desire to express something that will not stay in."[22] Chadwick's cool attitude toward Elgar's scores would thaw in later years.

In London Chadwick renewed his acquaintance with Sir Alexander MacKenzie, a man who by and large shared his own musical viewpoint. MacKenzie introduced Chadwick at a meeting of the RAM, where he met Edward German, Myles B. Foster, John E. West, "and other well known S. A. T. B. composers."[23] MacKenzie was sympathetic to a number of Chadwick's preoccupations. Like Chadwick, MacKenzie was a prolific composer who created clever and effective works in nearly every genre. He had already composed a dozen stage works, almost as many choral compositions, and a great deal of chamber and vocal music. A native of Edinburgh, he had also produced orchestral music that was highly characteristic of Scottish culture. Among these are two *Scottish Rhapsodies*, *Britannia* Overture, a *Highland Ballad*, and his *Scottish Concerto*. In 1911 MacKenzie would produce his third *Scottish Rhapsody*, based on Robert Burns's *Tam O'Shanter*, a poem that would capture the imagination of his Yankee colleague just a few years later.

Chadwick also renewed his friendship with Alberto Randegger, whom he had met briefly in 1901. He observed as Randegger, a renowned conductor and voice coach, worked with several students, none of whom were remarkable talents. Nevertheless, the older master was able to draw much from them; Chadwick thought it little wonder that Randegger was so highly regarded and thought him "the smartest old chap I know."[24] Other activities included a performance of Rossini's opera, *Armida* ("Never again!"), at Covent Garden; lunch at the RAM Club, where he was eloquently introduced by MacKenzie; and a brief visit to the town of Chester, where Chadwick met church organist Joseph Bridge. With mild irritation, Chadwick related that Bridge mentioned Parker, "with whom I always seem to be connected in the English mind."[25] A more positive experience was an encounter with Percy Pitt, "one of the ablest of the younger English conductors and composers."[26] Pitt's training mirrored Chadwick's; he studied with both Reinecke and Jadassohn in the late 1880s, and then traveled to Munich for instruction with Rheinberger. When Chadwick met him he was a repetiteur at the Royal Opera at Covent Garden; the next year he would assume the mantle of principal conductor. Chadwick enjoyed Pitt, and generally speaking he loved the British people, although he wondered: "How is it that the English, who are usually so brutal and selfish when traveling on the continent, are absolutely considerate, good natured and courteous (in their way) when they flock together in their own country?"[27]

What are we to make of Chadwick's sabbatical journey? Clearly he accomplished most of his stated goals: he met with many composers and musicians and he toured more than a dozen conservatories. While disappointed that he was unable to secure performances of his music outside of Leipzig, that problem was perhaps vitiated by his revelatory rediscovery of England, which he came to regard as his "mother country" more profoundly than ever before. Not only did his own personality and compositional aesthetic resonate with those of the English school, but the very place gave him comfort and solace.

Chadwick was deeply affected by the Tower of London and Westminster Abbey. Although a spiritual man, if not a particularly religious one, Chadwick had inspected many holy sites. He observed that some English churches matched those in Rome and Paris in architectural majesty, "But not one [of those] expresses in its exterior and interior that 'The Church's one Foundation is Jesus Christ our Lord' in the way that we of Anglo Saxon blood feel and believe it, as does Westminster." Chadwick believed that "this place stands for the very foundations of Anglo Saxon civilization." Perhaps sensing the impending chaos in global politics, he was prescient when he wrote, "And if we are to end in anything but anarchy and confusion this civilization must eventually dominate the world."[28] Chadwick was now making the first mature connection with his own ancestral Britishness, which, as we shall see, will assert itself musically in the coming years.

The Chadwick family boarded the *Winifredian* from Liverpool on August 4 and arrived in Boston on August 13, following a thankfully uneventful passage. "Thus ended our great pilgrimage," Chadwick recorded forlornly. "In many ways it was a disappointment but no amount of foresight could have prevented it under the circumstances. Personally I accomplished very little that I hoped to do but as time goes on I have come to feel that it is not very important. And we certainly did gather a fund of experiences which have been a joy to us ever since."[29]

Chadwick and His Milieu

There was little to distinguish Chadwick's sabbatical. As an artist whose compositional work ethic had been herculean for the past thirty years, he did little creative labor in Europe, but for minimal work on his Christmas oratorio. Thomas's death compelled Chadwick to recognize that one phase of his life had ended; as he returned home—eager and chock full of fresh ideas—another, he knew, would begin. The focus now was not squarely on what he had done well as a composer but on what else he could do, and do better, in the time that remained. While he may not have intensely practiced his art for a year, Chadwick certainly returned refreshed by his encounters with artists in Europe, and especially England. Chadwick was also gradually settling in to the notion that his role in music education and conservatory administration in America would perhaps loom as large—larger?—over his posthumous reputation as his career as a composer. But as much as he wished to direct his waning energy on writing music, he also desired to be an attentive husband, as well as a faithful father and friend.

Chadwick's youthfulness was disappearing. Early portraits show a young man of steely confidence with a high forehead, thick eyebrows, a compact chin, and full lips. His complexion was fair and his face smooth, a welcoming counterpoint to his penetrating eyes. The mustache that he sported for much of his life was a product of his desire to look older and to be taken seriously. Chadwick sought a sober demeanor because, at a scant five-feet-six or -seven inches tall, he lacked what the great Roman historian Tacitus called "the accidental advantage of impressive stature."[30] If he was unable to tower over students, faculty members, board members, and professional musicians, Chadwick would have to rely on charisma, charm, and his famously quick wit. These endeared him to many, but not all.

Later photos show a distinct softening of many of Chadwick's features and the expected weight gain, some of which may be ascribed to his 1901 shipboard injury and the onset of gout, both of which prevented extended physical activity. In 1895 Chadwick fell off his bicycle ("Most of my weight seemed to have fallen on the big toe of my right foot"). The doctor pronounced it "traumatic gout."[31] Gout, a condition caused by elevated levels in the body of uric acid, has historically had a close connection to the ingestion of certain foods and alcohol, and can also be activated by physical trauma. Its symptoms include extreme pain and swelling generally located in the big toe, but other joints can also become affected by arthritis-like features. Naturally, movement becomes highly restricted. Gout is often chronic, and when it arrives it typically stays for a while. For the remainder of his life Chadwick's gout would put him out of commission in stretches from anywhere between a few days to several months. In February 1910, he endured "a very trying time, in fact the most serious of any so far experienced."[32] He did not wear a shoe for ten days.

Besides gout, Chadwick also suffered serious dental problems. In the late 1890s he started wearing a dental plate after the loss of a tooth to pyorrhea; over the next several decades he would lose many more.[33]

Chadwick reveled in the companionship of his large circle of friends, whom he often met at social and professional clubs. Although a member of the Tavern Club, his true love had been the St. Botolph Club, which was named for the patron saint of travelers and is the purported source of the city's name, "Botolph's Town," corrupted as "Boston." His membership in these clubs—as well as his frequent attendance at the meetings of the other clubs in which he was not a member—enabled him to meet some of the city's most prominent citizens, not just in artistic circles but throughout an expansive intellectual universe. By 1908 Chadwick was tiring of his beloved St. Botolph. It was expensive, and "many of the old members are bores."[34] The new members were more interested in its social aspects, including alcohol consumption, rather than its intellectual and artistic aspects. The St. Botolph Club had acquired the traits of the Tavern Club, and "the conversation," he observed, "is sometimes diverting but not often stimulating or suggestive and the time might be much more profitably spent."[35] Not that Chadwick disdained drink; he "kneiped," as he called it, habitually, although for the most part he drank in moderation. (One instance of Chadwick's drinking has remained alive in historical memory. Following a lunch with Horatio Parker, the two returned to Parker's classroom at Yale. A student in the class was Charles Ives, who, sitting directly in front of the older composer later wrote of Chadwick, "Lord! [What a] beer breath!"[36]) Despite Chadwick's general enjoyment of the Tavern and St. Botolph clubs, Chadwick would soon begin to look elsewhere for intellectual nourishment.

Chadwick was a family man first and foremost, and success at that enterprise was as important to him as composing or running NEC. Ida May was a loving mother and a faithful partner who tended to the daily management of the Chadwick household, and that often meant overseeing nannies and supervising domestic servants. That was not an easy task: the household staff was relied upon to cook and clean in Boston, as well as in West Chop, where they were sent ahead of the Chadwicks to prepare the house for the arrival of the family. Competence among the servants was critical because, in order to compose, Chadwick required calm. In the domestic turmoil that boiled over in 1912, Chadwick made it plain that Ida May oversaw this aspect of their lives: "I am told that I do not need to worry about these matters, but I simply can't do any work when the equilibrium of the home is destroyed for any reason, and the time might as well be crossed off the calendar as far as my work is concerned."[37]

Chadwick's fatherhood was to some extent ahead of its time. While he did not dote on Theodore and Noël (he left that to his wife and their hired help), he was always engrossed in their activities and was very affectionate toward them. As fathers do, he beamed with pride at their accomplishments, and he recognized that he was probably too lenient when they deserved to learn a harsh lesson. Chadwick embraced his role in his sons' lives, and he admitted their importance in his: "But if there is anything that a father absolutely needs it is the love and respect of his sons," he later wrote. "Nothing can comfort and sustain him in his old age like that. And for a son, his father's loyalty and affection should be a bulwark all his life."[38] It should be remembered that he came to fatherhood rather late in life (and Ida May was three years older than her husband), especially given the norms of his era. Theodore arrived in early 1891 and Noël at the end of 1894, when Chadwick was thirty-six and forty years old, respectively. Naturally, it is impossible to consider Chadwick's close relationship to his sons without recalling the chasm that separated him from his own father, a man who by all accounts was emotionally remote from his children.

Like many of the men in his circle—and in his time—Chadwick was contemptuous of those who were different from himself. Today it is often difficult to imagine, but, in an age that was less afflicted with utopian notions of equality, Chadwick was not afraid to project an air of superiority. Most of his ire was directed toward European Jews, whom he viewed as encroaching on American soil to steal jobs from American artists. His writings are peppered with insults, some more direct than others. For example, when, at the end of the BSO's 1902–1903 season, Kneisel, Loeffler, and others resigned—much to the astonishment of both Gericke and Higginson—Chadwick wrote to Theodore Thomas with buoyant optimism. Although the orchestra might suffer temporarily by such a change in musical personnel, he thought, it might well bring a number of new and able musicians to Boston. "The more the better," Chadwick averred, "but I'll make an even bet there will be more Jews than Christians if Gericke engages them."[39] Following the annual student assessments at NEC, Chadwick casually remarked that he had just sat through "Junior (and Jewnior) exams."[40] At this time, of course, immigration into the US was at historic heights, and newcomers of many stripes were in his crosshairs. Chadwick was tremendously irritated

with what he perceived as the unrelenting onslaught of "Jews, Italians, Arme-
nians and other scum," who were, in his opinion, changing the ways of old New
England drastically.[41]

Foreigners aside, there were still plenty of others to denigrate. Chadwick
was not impressed by blacks; he often referred to them as "niggers," and he
resented the recent emphasis on their music ("plantation melodies" and such)
as a wellspring for the creation of American art. The African melodies that he
had heard were not only inauthentic, he believed, but they also failed to resonate
with his own tastes and ideas. Chadwick appreciated Irish-Scots music types,
if he dismissed the Irish themselves as troublesome drunkards. In his youth in
Lawrence, Chadwick had had skirmishes with the Irish; he sometimes directed
insults toward them, although he seems not to have been blatantly anti-Irish.
As for the rapidly growing Italian population in Boston, Chadwick made few
condescending remarks, and in fact he frequented several Italian restaurants in
the ethnic enclave of North Boston.

Having mentioned Chadwick's prejudices, it is only fair to note that his
animosities were of a general sort and that examples of his thoughtfulness and
generosity toward these "different others" are abundant. He had many Jewish
friends, and once, as a student in Leipzig, he was in love with a Jewish girl. And,
as we have seen, Chadwick revered Jadassohn.

As concerns money, Chadwick was rarely driven by it, but he was not unaware
of its utility, especially as his family grew. In his youth he seemed always to be
living on the financial edge, although he never lived in abject poverty. Chadwick
was a "jobber," an itinerant musician who hustled from gig to gig to earn his
bread. And he was good at it; from the time he arrived in Boston fresh from his
European student experience, he consistently enjoyed a steady, if often small,
salary cobbled together from teaching, organ playing, lecturing, and conducting.
As for his compositional work, he negotiated with publishers and kept a careful
accounting of his royalties. These efforts were not all-consuming, however, as a
negligible amount of Chadwick's income was earned from the publication of his
music. Moreover, his relationships with publishers were routinely a source of
disappointment and irritation.

Of course, once he became its director, Chadwick's NEC salary comprised
the largest portion of his income. He started with compensation in 1897 of five
thousand dollars per year, and at first his raises were modest. But by 1912 he was
making twice that amount, and in 1922 he was paid a handsome fifteen thousand
dollars annually.

Thursday Evenings & the Sea
1906–1912

Karl Muck & the Thursday Evening Club

Karl Muck's term as the fifth conductor of the Boston Symphony Orchestra was announced in June 1906, during the final leg of Chadwick's European sojourn. This followed Higginson's lamentable inability to come to terms with Wilhelm Gericke earlier that year prior to his sudden and unexpected resignation. Chadwick's efforts to retain Muck had proven invaluable, for he had been asked by Higginson to help to persuade Muck to come to Boston from his prestigious post at Berlin's Royal Opera House. "Tell him the advantages and the disadvantages (if any)," Higginson instructed Chadwick, "of his position here."[1]

Muck, whose contract Higginson had negotiated with German authorities, was eminently qualified for the post (see figure 11.1). BSO historian M. A. De-Wolfe Howe has written that he, "of all the men who have directed the Orchestra . . . came to his work with the most firmly established reputation."[2] Chadwick knew Muck's credentials well—and in fact had even known him when both were students in Leipzig—because he had sought to hire the great conductor to teach at NEC. Chadwick admitted that, in this instance, Higginson had bested him by offering Muck a better paycheck; with mild bitterness Chadwick wrote that the old man obtained Muck's services, "But I doubt if it was the same terms which I offered him."[3]

Muck had studied music as a child, although he never intended to pursue it as a career. However, after earning a doctoral degree in classical philology in Heidelberg, he devoted himself to music full-time at the Leipzig Conservatory. Muck was an excellent pianist, and although he never studied conducting formally, it did not take long for him to distinguish himself. He demonstrated an unusual genius in the interpretation of opera and held several posts with small opera companies before finally taking over Berlin's Royal Opera in 1892. Muck possessed traits that bedazzled musicians and audiences alike. In an age that appreciated conductors with flair, Muck was economical, erudite, and supremely well prepared. He was known to run rehearsals efficiently, and he heavily marked his own scores—Muck did not believe in score memorization—with colored symbols ("red, blue and green triangles," Chadwick noted) to indicate

special problems of expression or technique. Muck insisted that the markings be transcribed onto each musician's part; after that "a technically imperfect performance was impossible."[4]

Muck's mastery of a diverse repertoire was also appreciated. He was more at ease in a broader range of music than his predecessors, especially Gericke, and he prepared it more expertly. His performances were widely considered stunning. The programs were of a quality such that Chadwick kept many of the playbills and made numerous annotations on them; he included references to the music's general effect, strengths and defects in their interpretation, and the audience's reaction.

It was Muck himself who commanded the Yankee composer's attention and admiration. Chadwick, never one to heap praise, wrote of Muck's "signal and unusual virtues, not the least of which was his remarkable versatility. He would give a most noble & dignified performance of a Beethoven Symphony, the next week an elastic interpretation of Tchaikovsky or Liszt, and then a hair raising & simply devilish 'rendition' ... of *España* or the Spanish Caprice."[5] Muck also possessed the advantageous gift of being able to elicit more from a score than perhaps was actually there. On Beethoven's Symphony no. 6—considered in the nineteenth century one of the composer's weaker creations—Chadwick concluded that "on the whole Muck made more of the symphony than I ever heard before."[6]

During Muck's first season those pining to hear more American music had to be pleased with the number of selections programmed. That year the BSO performed, among other compositions, Paine's Prelude to *Oedipus Tyrannus* (1881), MacDowell's *Indian Suite* (1895), Converse's *Mystic Trumpeter* (1904), and Hadley's tone poem *Salome* (1907), an intriguing and eclectic group of works by anyone's standard, and one that gives a quick survey of serious music in America since Paine. Chadwick became more closely acquainted with the conductor when Muck took up his *Cleopatra*, although, as discussed previously, their collaboration was not without fireworks. Most unusual was the fact that Muck himself, not Chadwick, conducted it. While previous BSO conductors tended to hand the orchestra over to composers for the performances of their own music, Muck deigned few fit to lead his band. Chadwick surmised that, prior to Muck, opportunities were extended to composers to conduct their own works so the regular conductors did not have to trouble themselves learn the scores. But Muck "seldom expressed any opinion about the merits of compositions; of American music, never. To him, it was all in the day's work and he always did his best to get things to sound, even when badly written for the orchestra."[7] Muck's interest in his music, whether real or feigned, undoubtedly pleased Chadwick.

Muck became a towering figure in musical Boston. Chadwick thought him a master of tempo, but he was especially awed by his ability to teach the members of the BSO. "It would have been impossible," Chadwick recorded, "for any conductor to be more conscientious in the training of his orchestra than Dr. Muck especially in music that he disliked."[8] Not that Muck was perfect. He had a "certain insensibility to impure intonation," that sometimes combined with "over-accentuation" and a preference for "earsplitting trumpets and drums," which often detracted from otherwise impeccable performances. At times Chadwick also considered Muck's programming ineffectual, as Muck rarely mixed Classical period music and music of the Romantic era on the same bill. That variety of musical pigeonholing made it easier for audiences to pick and choose which concerts they would attend. For his part, Chadwick—no great fan of Mozart or any composer before Beethoven—would simply skip concerts that did not appeal to him; he could do so knowing that he would not miss much.

The Chadwicks and the Mucks were neighbors in Boston, and Ida May was friendly to the couple, as she was to most of her husband's colleagues. Mrs. Muck proved well educated, fluent in English, and friendly, but her husband was not particularly social; in order to avoid conversation Karl faked the inability to speak English—which annoyed Chadwick—and he was fond of vulgarity, which he used indiscreetly and in quantity. Muck was a serious musician who was known to spend most of his time engaged in the study of music. Chadwick observed that while Muck was generous almost to a fault when it came to sharing his time and knowledge with young musicians, "Society functions he abhorred, and was not easily dragged away from his studies to take part in them."[9]

In time the warmth of his growing Boston circle of friends softened Muck. Chadwick observed an easing in his temperament and noted in early 1908 that Muck "is getting to be very gemütlich."[10] As he neared the end of his tenure with the BSO, Muck attended a succession of farewell receptions given to honor his genius and acknowledge the debt musical Boston owed him. His reputation as a sensitive but demanding conductor had grown into legend, and he stepped easily within the circles of high society and among musicians. When Max Fiedler took over the BSO in Muck's substantial wake, Chadwick could not help but compare the two. He liked Fiedler personally and had known him in Leipzig—their compositions had even shared the bill of a conservatory Prüfungskonzert—but he did not think much of the newcomer's conducting. At the end of Fiedler's first year with the BSO, Chadwick chided that the ensemble "has degenerated in a marked degree under his leadership—or followship."[11] It was clear to all that Fiedler was no "Mückerl."[12]

If Muck and the BSO occupied much of Chadwick's attention during the latter half of 1906, a new activity would become equally engrossing. That year Chadwick was elected to "that most Bostonese of Boston institutions," the venerable Thursday Evening Club.[13] Club life in Boston had a rich tradition, and organizations flourished in many forms: athletic clubs, business clubs, political clubs, social awareness clubs, and clubs of other sorts coexisted in the city. Artists flocked to the St. Botolph Club and the Tavern Club, founded in 1879 and 1884, respectively. It is not clear why two clubs with similar artistic and literary aims were established within the space of five years, but each endeavored to keep its dues low, and neither was a dining club. Although cocktails and cigars were de rigueur, fancy meals and a paid kitchen staff would have been out of the financial reach of most members. Chadwick was an active member of the more social St. Botolph Club; he thought it "diverting, but not often stimulating or suggestive."[14]

The Thursday Evening Club, however, was a recognized scholarly institution in the city, and it proved a wonderful outlet for his own substantial intellectual curiosity. It had been founded in 1846 to facilitate discussions of science, commerce, and social policy, but by Chadwick's time it had broadened its vista to include many other areas of inquiry. That it was comparatively old and revered in the city—not to mention that it was a dining club—only added to its luster as far as Chadwick was concerned.[15] Managed by an assemblage of Harvard University faculty, the club met on alternate Thursdays from December to April.

The meetings were fairly routinized: "Three papers of exactly thirty minutes each are read, on scientific, artistic, literary and social subjects and eminent scientific men from abroad are often present."[16] This was precisely the type of camaraderie that Chadwick had long sought and enjoyed among men who were eager to better themselves.

Topics explored at the Thursday Evening Club meetings were wide-ranging and reflected the members' interests in history, travel, and many of the newest developments in all branches of science and sociological studies. Muckraking journalist and political reformer Lincoln Steffens delivered a paper on socialism in 1909, just a few years after his important book *The Shame of the Cities* (1904) appeared. One 1914 meeting featured Morefield Story describing the impeachment of President Andrew Johnson ("at which he was present," Chadwick wrote in amazement). Professor Wallace Sabine described the acoustics of several theaters with emphasis on the Century Theater in New York. And Harvey Cushing kept his audience rapt "in an interesting and entirely comprehensible" presentation about the human body's glandular system.[17] Chadwick judged the success of the speakers not only by their mastery of their respective topics, but also by their delivery. He was electrified by Reverend George A. Gordon's lecture on "the practice of medicine for the unfit," a commentary on recent developments in the burgeoning science of "psycho-therapeutics." "His paper," Chadwick wrote, "was full of keen, searching criticism and humor, impeccable English and delivered with a simplicity, dignity and power which even [Harvard] Pres. [Charles W.] Eliot could hardly surpass."[18]

Guests were sometimes invited to read on musical topics. One much-admired paper was shared by John A. Lomax, who, in 1912, delivered his research on cowboy songs. Lomax was an authority on the subject, for his important *Cowboy Songs and Other Frontier Ballads* had just appeared in 1910. (Lomax is also known for being the father of Alan Lomax, a pioneering folk singer and musicologist.)

Chadwick's contributions to the club meetings included at least six papers on varied musical topics (see table 11.1). As most members of the club were not musicians, on the occasion of his first presentation Chadwick was advised to make it "specially adapted to the rudimentary [musical] intelligence"[19] of his audience. When Chadwick joined, well-known Boston organist B. J. Lang was the sole musical member; later, composer Frederick Converse and critic Philip Hale were enlisted.

Naturally, Chadwick also delighted in the club's social aspects. Good cigars and free-flowing champagne were rituals following the readings, and the membership roster, mostly made up of college professors and a few artists, was carefully crafted to include selected wealthy patrons whose responsibility it was to

TABLE 11.1. Chadwick Papers Read before the Thursday Evening Club

March 19, 1908	The Evolution of the Musical Idea
January 6, 1910	Some Early Program Music
January 18, 1912	Orchestral Conducting and Conductors
January 19, 1922	Untitled essay on Americanism in music [Folk Songs]
[Date undetermined]	A Plea for Choral Singing
[Date undetermined]	English Folk Songs

provide the venue—usually a private home or an upscale meeting room—and pay for the receptions. Chadwick often procured the evening's entertainment, as he did at a 1915 meeting at which Charles Bennett "sang a string of old ballads much to the pleasure of the dusty old pedagogues present."[20] Like any such pursuit, the evenings were not uniformly engaging. Following one particularly uninspiring meeting, he reported that the event was "stupid as ever."[21]

Die Bude

In his first years as director of NEC, it was difficult for Chadwick to escape his often onerous administrative duties. Fortunately he had come across a talented musician, his former student and protégé Wallace Goodrich, who had proven himself capable of managing the conservatory (according to carefully drafted plans) when Chadwick was away. Goodrich, sixteen years Chadwick's junior, was a native New Englander and an early NEC success story. He studied composition with Chadwick and organ with Henry Dunham before going to Leipzig for advanced instruction. Goodrich was among the first generation of American musicians to opt for France, where he became a student of the great organist Charles Marie Widor in Paris. His fortunes upon his return to Boston were spectacular; while in the employ of NEC, Goodrich was also the organist at Trinity Church and the BSO, and additionally ran the Worcester Festival and his own Boston Choral Arts Society, one of the city's most successful choral ventures.

Goodrich was an excellent NEC steward; when Chadwick returned from Europe he found that everything was pretty much as he had left it. Chadwick had strived over the years to rid the conservatory of some of its historical institutional drama, and after a while his job became routine. He gradually managed to devote more time to composition, although less energetically than in his youth. It is a sad fact that Chadwick finally started to have free time just as he was losing his stamina, which in any case had never been as great as several of his colleagues', especially Parker's. Composing during the academic year meant mostly jotting down melodies and making sketches; the real work of developing ideas, scoring, and the like, often had to wait until the summer break, and much of this Chadwick accomplished at his summer home, affectionately called Die Bude ("the shack"). Located at West Chop on Martha's Vineyard, the famous vacation island off the coast of Massachusetts, it offered much-needed relaxation, seascapes, and an escape from the city.

Chadwick was persuaded to purchase the large parcel of land at Main Street and Quinsigamond Avenue—known popularly as the Lighthouse Lot because it abutted the US lighthouse on West Chop—in 1892.[22] The home he eventually built there became a haven not only for his family, which held onto the property until after World War II, but before long it became a gathering place for many of his friends and colleagues.[23] In fact, the town had virtually become a seasonal mecca for musicians and their families. Horatio Parker rented a home nearby, as did singer Max Heinrich, and composer/conductor Henry Hadley.

By the end of the first decade of the new century, the Chadwicks' respites at West Chop had become routine. Before breakfast there was a bracing swim; work and/or study was then pursued until about noon, "with an occasional vacation for sailing, racing or tennis." Until dinner there was a "bathing festival," that is, another romp in the water, followed by a nap; a late game of tennis was followed by an even later supper.[24] Evenings were often spent making music with friends, especially the Heinrichs, who delighted in entertaining the others with song as they sat on the piazza of the Chadwick home. For Theodore, at least, these evenings were excruciating. Chadwick made scant effort to engage his children in music—he did not force them to learn to play an instrument or sing beyond a rudimentary level. As a consequence, the children, especially Theodore, were not particularly enamored by music.[25] Chadwick was insistent that his sons receive a "proper Boston boy's education" of the type he never got; to him, at least on the surface, it mattered little that music had a small role in their upbringing.

The whole point of West Chop was a new atmosphere and seaside frolicking, and to that end Chadwick and family fished and boated with fervor; both boys had participated on school crew teams—Noël had even been a champion crew captain—and were competent sailors. But as his sons were able to entertain themselves, Chadwick mustered more time and inspiration to compose. As we are told by one anonymous NEC insider, at Die Bude "he is able to develop the compositions that have been planned during the busy winter and spring. Among the pines near the house is a little open space, to which the ocean breezes penetrate and in which many of the works familiar to concert goers as Chadwick pieces have been peacefully elaborated."[26]

In fact, West Chop proved critical to his work, for there he most often completed the musical thoughts that were begun in Boston; at West Chop he could do the "heavy lifting" of composition—sketches could be given full treatment and once finished the scoring could begin. Because the distractions were few, Chadwick could work rapidly. Not that his time there was completely trouble-free: one memorable story he told was of the time when, while sketching his Fifth Quartet, the wind blustered and sent leaves of his manuscript into the surf. As he rewrote the lost portions, Chadwick was not at all sure that his work was faithful to the original.[27]

Suite Symphonique (1909)

Chadwick's final orchestral work in the form of a symphony is his four-movement *Suite Symphonique*, another piece which, like the Symphony no. 2 and *Symphonic Sketches*, was not originally conceived as a unified composition. He worked at the *Suite*—Chadwick did not worry too much about the nomenclature used for this composition; he referred to it many times as a "symphony"[28] —off and on in piecemeal fashion beginning in 1904, but it languished and was mostly forgotten during his European jeremiad. The first movement, sketched and scored in 1907 and 1908, was submitted as an independent concert overture, titled *La Vie Joyeuse*, to a competition sponsored by the National Federation of Music Clubs in 1910. Chadwick created the second movement, "Romanza," by borrowing material from his Fifth String Quartet, although he also utilized themes that he had invented while in West Chop in 1907.[29] The *Suite*'s third movement, "Intermezzo e Humoreske," was constructed of material he had invented earlier but never used. To these three Chadwick added a finale, the main theme of which was sketched in 1906 while sitting in a steamboat café near Ouchy, Switzerland. The whole was brought together as a single composition in 1909.

While the stand-alone *La Vie Joyeuse* did not win the music club's prize, the completed *Suite Symphonique* won "Best Orchestral Work by an American Composer," awarded by the same organization, the very next year, 1911. Chadwick suggested, in something of a slap to the 1910 judges, that the high quality of the later panel, which included Frederick Stock, Henry Hadley, and Victor Herbert, contributed to his victory.

Schmidt's 1911 published edition of *Suite Symphonique* is dedicated to Frederick Stock and the Theodore Thomas Orchestra of Chicago. Stock, a German, shared the aesthetic ideals of the Boston composers, and he was respected because it was felt that he carried on Thomas's traditions of strict discipline and sense of purpose. He arrived in Chicago with a thorough knowledge of the conductor's art, but Stock learned a great deal from Thomas. After playing viola with the orchestra for just four years, he became assistant conductor and then principal conductor when Thomas died in 1905. Stock was also an accomplished composer; he studied at Cologne's conservatory with Engelbert Humperdinck, and had to his credit a number of chamber and orchestral works, including one symphony; he would add another symphony within a decade. His was an enormous talent; when Stock led the Theodore Thomas Orchestra in Boston in 1912, Chadwick conceded that the event was "the most wonderful thing we have had in Boston in years."[30]

True to its original title, the suite, especially its first movement, is indeed a joyful work, and its elaborate scoring reflects lessons learned since *Cleopatra*. Included are three flutes, pairs of oboes, clarinets and bassoons, four horns, two trumpets, two trombones and a tuba, timpani, six percussionists, harp, and strings. Here Chadwick's gift for orchestration and his imaginative, often rollicking rhythms are displayed in full glory. Less noticeable, however, is the adventuresome large-scale harmonic palette that rings throughout the *Suite*.

The first movement, Allegro molto animato, is rooted firmly in sonata form, although Chadwick dispensed with the traditional harmonic patterns. For instance, while the work begins in the tonic E-flat major, Chadwick ends the exposition not in the expected B-flat major, but at a distant harmonic point, D minor. This is not completely new in his oeuvre, but here he takes it a step farther from the mediant preferences to which he turned so often in earlier compositions. As his harmonic procedures went modern, Chadwick was willing to rely on his themes to create unity in the work; he also stretched his own boundaries to take us into a sound world that reminds one of Debussy, where lovely, slightly foreign themes are couched in mildly unstable harmonies.

The second movement, a saccharine, somewhat nostalgic "Romanza," with the main melody in the solo saxophone part (or alternatively the celli), offers light, transparent textures and ambiguous harmonies, as well as a section of orientalism. This is Chadwick's most overt use of Debussian harmonic practice in the composition thus far. The third movement is set in two parts, an "Intermezzo" and a "Humoreske." In the latter, Chadwick cleverly set "Yankee Doodle" in full impressionist garb, prompting one reviewer to observe that it added "a blithesome touch, being true to its classification in the marked air of whimsicality."[31] The Finale is an attenuated sonata form and includes morsels of the oriental effects that were encountered previously; here the allusion to a Janissary band is obvious. One senses that Chadwick is trying to emulate the finale of his earlier Third Symphony, but the music doesn't quite measure up to that standard: the main tune is laborious, the orchestrations are strained, and very often the momentum slows.

Given its impressionist twists and evident weaknesses, the critics were split in their opinion of the *Suite*. Following its premiere on March 29, 1911, at Philadelphia's Academy of Music the reviewer for the *Inquirer* assessed that "the texture of the opening allegro is so loose that it communicates an impression of fragmentariness and incoherence, which would probably be removed by a better acquaintance with the music." He admitted, however, that "it contains much that is ingratiating and sympathetic and easily holds the attention."[32] But when *Suite Symphonique* was performed in Boston on April 13, 1911—two weeks after its premiere—the *Transcript*'s H. T. Parker mocked the *Suite* for not escaping "the easy obviousness of prize music."[33] Its geniality and glorious bombast, he concluded, had been invented solely for the purpose of swaying the contest's judges, and he continued to negatively compare it to the wonder of *Symphonic Sketches*, which had garnered high praise from him just a few years before. Parker warmly remembered the *Sketches* for its "American sentiment, American humor, American jubilation, of the quick shiftings of mood, which are very American, of the frankness of one feeling crowded upon another."[34] He had no such plaudits for the *Suite*, in which, he curtly proclaimed, "Mr. Chadwick's invention of melody flags." The "Romanza," Parker chided, "barely escapes a rather thin and commonplace sweetness in matter and in manner"; and in the third movement, "Neither the rattle of the xylophone nor the tinkling of the triangle, nor yet again the mockery of Debussian and Pucciniesque dissonances and progressions is in itself amusing." As for the finale, Parker simply thought it tedious: "Mr. Chadwick's music needs freshness, needs spirit, and, above all, brevity." Parker was not alone in his assessment. Even critic Olin Downes, a Chadwick admirer, dryly commented that, although the piece was not without some delectable passages, "it is not the opinion of this writer that the composition increases Mr. Chadwick's reputation as a composer."[35]

The *Suite* fared better when it was performed in 1912 by Chadwick and the New York Symphony. The *Times* reviewer (probably Richard Aldrich) applauded Chadwick's third movement, and described it as: "A 'Cake Walk' in five-four time, and a bit of parody in the modern French style, the 'whole tone' scale of Debussy, the consumptive frogs in dismal pools of the decadent poets." He admired Chadwick's restraint in imitating the all-too-easy-to-imitate Debussian style.[36] Another critic applauded the *Suite*'s tunefulness and gaiety, "being destitute of atmosphere, psychology, metaphysics, pathology, idealism, realism, or even snobbism": this, the critic wrote, "is just old-fashioned music."[37] Chadwick was generally pleased with the *Suite*'s New York reception ("The papers are all kind to me"), although, as with Parker's review of the Boston performance, the element of having composed a "prize winner" could not be escaped. "They can't quite forgive my getting $700 for that piece," Chadwick complained.[38]

At least one Philadelphia critic expected that *Suite Symphonique* would become a welcome part of the American repertoire; and even H. T. Parker, who pummeled it at the earlier Boston performance, reconsidered the *Suite* in 1912, when he wrote that it deserved "many a repetition."[39] Despite these views, following its 1913 performances in Chicago and San Francisco led by Stock and Henry Hadley, respectively, *Suite Symphonique* began its trek into obscurity. In 1924, Chadwick led the People's Symphony Orchestra in a number of his own compositions at Boston's St. James Theatre. Only one movement of his *Suite*, the lyrical "Romanza," made it into the evening's program. Maybe the other movements were deemed too difficult, or perhaps there was simply too little rehearsal time available. In any event, fifteen years after its completion, few would have been sufficiently familiar with the *Suite* to have fond memories of it rekindled.

The Norfolk Music Festival

The founding of the Norfolk Music Festival was one of the more fascinating musical developments in the United States at the turn of the new century. The first festival performance occurred in 1899 with concerts by the Litchfield County Choral Union, the fruit of a cooperative effort of five Connecticut choirs that included the Norfolk Glee Club, the Winsted Choral Union, the Salisbury Choir, the Canaan Choral Society, and the Torrington Musical Association. Their combined performing forces usually numbered between 350 and 400 voices, although the actual total membership was nearer to 700.[40] The festival had been founded by millionaire philanthropist Dr. Carl Stoeckel and his wife, Ellen Battell Stoeckel, to honor the memory of her father, Robbins Battell, a successful attorney who had also been a music lover and a dilettante composer. Carl Stoeckel was also from musical stock; his father, Gustave, had been a fixture in musical New England for nearly fifty years, first as an instructor and then as the first dean of Yale University's music department from 1849–1896.[41]

Founded as a modest festival that would present the standard choral-orchestral repertoire, within a decade it grew to reflect the ambition of Dr. Stoeckel. By 1905, the public was no longer charged admission to hear the concerts, and the Stoeckels bore the costs in their entirety, an amount that by decade's end approached $10,000 per year (approximately $250,000 in 2009 currency).[42] In 1908 Stoeckel enlisted Yale's University Club, which comprised "men of means and culture who are interested in individual research in other branches of learning, as well as in music," to assist with the commissioning of works by American composers, an initiative that would be "the first regular organization for the encouragement of American composition."[43] In other words, this was not an association that would sporadically offer prizes; the Norfolk Festival would exist in large measure to foster new American music. Composers were requested "to write at their pleasure a musical work, choral or orchestral, of any length, in any style, upon any theme, and demanding any number of interpreters, to be produced for the first time at these concerts."[44] Not only would the selected composer receive a fee upon the delivery of his composition, but his music would be performed by top-notch musicians, as the Choral Union was routinely undergirded by professional musicians from the Boston Symphony Orchestra and the New York Philharmonic, among others.

Another draw was Litchfield's sumptuous natural setting. The festival was located in the scenic hills of northern Connecticut, where the Stoeckels built on their immense estate an auditorium still known as the "Music Shed," a fine hall that, at the time, accommodated almost fifteen hundred people. The choral festival was a premiere event. Townsmen recognized that not only was it a boon to musical art in New England, but it also had decided economic benefits. Special trains were chartered to transport singers and their guests, musicians, and dignitaries into town, and hotel rooms were booked well in advance.

Composer and editor William Arms Fisher wrote about the festivals with admiration, remarking that "they gave the first performances anywhere of more new choral works than can be credited to any other American festival series."[45] Chadwick was swept away by its more general but nevertheless enormous contribution to American culture. He observed with astonishment that the festival was free to music lovers, generous to artists, and existed for no other reason than "the uplift of the people." And yet "we are called a nation of sordid materialists, with no God but money, and no ideals but commercialism. But where in the wide world can such another enterprise be found?"[46]

A highlight in the distinguished history of the Norfolk Festival occurred in the summer of 1914, when Finnish composer Jean Sibelius was invited to compose and conduct his new tone poem, *Nymphs of the Sea* (better known today as *The Oceanides*), which had been commissioned by Stoeckel. Chadwick had the opportunity to spend a good deal of time with Sibelius; their conversations occurred in German, of which neither was a master. Nevertheless they managed to communicate, and Sibelius even spoke to a group of American musicians at a dinner hosted by Stoeckel. "Sibelius quite let himself out and talked freely and interestingly about his national music," to company that included Charles Martin Loeffler, Henry Hadley, Frederick S. Converse, Louis C. Elson, Philip Hale, and others.[47] Chadwick's affection for Sibelius is evident in the appreciation he wrote shortly after the festival. "Learned reviewers usually consider it safe to sneer at music which is composed for special occasions," Chadwick wrote from experience, but Sibelius's *Nymphs of the Sea* "is a piece which shows the power and individuality of the composer in its strongest light. It is very dignified and sustained in character but relieved by interesting decorative phrases, mostly for the wind instruments." Sibelius's unfeigned modesty was also admirable. "He was quite evidently embarrassed," Chadwick observed, "by the storm of applause which greeted his appearance and he acknowledged it with the awkwardness which is the privilege of genius."[48]

Insofar as the festival's artistic standards are concerned, composer and correspondent Henry Gilbert would declare that "the orchestra is the best that can be obtained, bar none. The chorus, which is composed of the best singers in Litchfield County, has had constant ensemble training and practice for years and has attained to a degree [*sic*] of artistic finish well-nigh unsurpassed anywhere."[49] If Gilbert's observations about the ensemble's technical achievements were sober and reflective, Stoeckel viewed his artistic and philanthropic endeavor with a religious zeal that reminds one of John Sullivan Dwight. As the Music Shed was being built, he summed up New England's devotion to music:

> The nearest gateway to divinity is by the road of truth in art. We shall not find truth if we look about the pasteboard scenery, the tinsel and the trapdoors of the operatic stage, so feebly exploited by commercial managers as educational and even consecrational. We must look for it rather in the great choral and orchestra works which are standing the test of the ages and which appeal to the poetry and imagination of every pure nature. To such end our organization is committed. It is blazing a narrow path which succeeding generations will widen, until all can enter the Olympian temple by the broad highway of truth in art.[50]

The first work commissioned for the festival was Horatio Parker's cantata *King Gorm the Grim*, premiered in Norfolk on June 4, 1908. *King Gorm* is the tragic tale of a Danish sovereign whose only son is lost in battle. Although not well known today, Parker's score includes a number of beautiful choruses and orchestral interludes. In all likelihood Parker secured this commission from the festival leaders, whose membership included Stoeckel, by virtue of his close association with Yale University. It is also likely that, having procured the festival's first commission, Parker helped his best friend land the second one. The result was Chadwick's second commission (see table 11.2) and the first in more than a decade.

TABLE 11.2. Chadwick's Major Prizes and Commissions

1892	*Columbian Ode*	Commissioned by the World's Columbian Exhibition — $500
1894	Symphony No. 3 in F	1st Prize in annual composition competition; National Conservatory of Music (New York) — $300
1899	"A Ballad of Trees and the Master"	1st Prize in the "song category" of competition sponsored by *The Musical Record & Review* — $75
1908	*Noël: A Christmas Pastoral*	Commissioned by Norfolk Music Festival — $1,000
1909	*Everywoman*	Commissioned by Henry W. Savage, producer — $1,500
1911	*Suite Symphonique*	"Best Orchestral Work by an American Composer"; National Federation of Music Clubs — $700

Noël: A Christmas Pastoral (1908)

Although he had begun a portion of the work while he was in Lausanne, Switzerland, in the winter of 1905–1906, Chadwick began to compose his cantata *Noël* in earnest on January 7, 1908. The score was completed on February 29, 1908. *Noël* was already underway when Chadwick received an invitation from Stoeckel to submit a composition to the Norfolk Festival commissioning committee for its consideration. The committee reviewed the incomplete manuscript, and, finding the work "to be one of great merit," offered to feature it at the 1909 festival.[51] Upon learning that *Noël* had been selected, Chadwick wrote a lengthy acceptance letter in which he stated that it was not only an honor to follow Parker's *King Gorm the Grim*, but that the board members' profoundly heartfelt beliefs in the aims of the festival closely mirrored his own. "It is my conviction," Chadwick declared, "that if musical art and taste is to be kept alive in this country, it will be not alone by performances of grand opera, symphony concerts and great schools of music, but by the cooperation of the people themselves as singers and players in the performance of good music."[52] These were tenets to which Chadwick had long subscribed, and he related them to his family's long tradition of participation in community music-making: "it is, therefore, a matter of peculiar pleasure and pride as a New Englander and descendant of New Englanders that I should be invited to compose this work for you."[53]

One element of the festival that was perceived as an innovation was actually recognized by Chadwick as something of a throwback to his father's era. The

Choral Union's five independent choirs each contributed funds to maintain a full-time choirmaster, Richmond P. Paine, who traveled from town to town to rehearse his forces.[54] By now, the itinerant music-master was the exception, not the rule; it harked back to the days when Nathaniel Gould roamed throughout New England to instruct children and adults with the hope of both civilizing the populace and carving out a decent living for himself. In what was no small accomplishment, Chadwick actually respected Paine, as, by all accounts, the chorus for *Noël* had been consummately prepared. Chadwick even gave public accolades to Paine, "who through all the season past has so faithfully, ably and enthusiastically drilled the chorus and interpreted the whole work."[55] Following the first rehearsals of *Noël* in the Shed, Chadwick, in a direct insult to Boston's vocal clubs, remarked that Paine's group "put the city singing Societies to shame."[56]

Noël was compiled from various sources by Chadwick and Ida May. It constitutes one of the few instances in which we have proof of Ida May's active involvement in her husband's compositional endeavors. The cantata is in two parts, each comprising six movements, and is prefaced by a prelude, *The Star*, which Arthur B. Wilson described as "a little symphonic poem, which may be played independently if desired."[57] The texts are largely adapted from ancient and medieval sources, including English poet John Milton (1608–1674), Roman Christian poet Aurelius Prudentius Clemens (348–413?), German Protestant poet and hymnist Gerhard Tersteegen (1697–1769), and others, and each is presented in English with the exception of "Parvum quando cerno deum," by an anonymous Latin source. Chadwick scored *Noël* for SATB soloists; a double-chorus; and a large orchestra that includes triple woodwinds, full brass and string sections, as well as harp, timpani, and organ. Wilson wrote effusively about the work. "The theme of *Noël* partakes of the quaint, idealized beauty of the olden-time Christmas, which is portrayed by the soft tints, the quiet devotion and reverence of an 'Adoration' rather than the ruddy hues of festive jollity and merry good cheer, which our modern Christmas has borrowed from the English customs of the day."[58]

There was tremendous excitement on the part of the chorus to take part in these annual world premieres, as the music was fresh and the guest artists were routinely eminent. In this instance, it seemed not to matter that the "Christmas Pastoral," as Chadwick called *Noël*, was being premiered in June. The soloists were soprano Marie Rappold, alto Louise Homer, tenor George Hamlin, and bass Herbert Witherspoon. Chadwick conducted.

Critic George W. Judson proclaimed *Noël* a success. He reported that the ovation Chadwick received exceeded any that had ever occurred at the festival, and that "this work, like all of Mr. Chadwick's compositions, shows the influence of the Wagnerian motif and method, and for this reason in part received the enthusiastic praise of the members of the orchestra who assisted so ably in its rendition last night. Indeed, the orchestral score is the pronounced feature of the whole work."[59] Judson continued, "The solo parts are not prominent, but as it is needless to say of such accomplished artists . . . they were all well executed and gave much delight."[60]

Noël was rendered in Boston by the Cecilia Society under the direction of Arthur Mees in 1913. The performance was a weak one (Chadwick once derisively referred to the conductor as "Arthur Mess"); in fact, it was so bad that Chadwick threatened to produce it again at his own expense simply so Bostonians would have the opportunity to hear it adequately performed.[61] But the poor Cecilia performance seems not to have had an effect on its general acceptance. It was published in an organ-vocal score by the New York firm of H. W. Gray in 1909; "Parvum quando cerno deum" became its most popular excerpt. *Noël* continued to be performed, and by the 1920s had become a staple of the Christmas season repertoire. Not only was *Noël* a moving seasonal work, but it was also within the reach of a training ensemble; that is, it is playable and singable by student performers at NEC and elsewhere, and is a satisfying artistic creation besides. Perhaps in an attempt to demonstrate that any hard feelings he had with Edward Everett Hale and the leadership at South Congregational Church over his summary dismissal had long since faded, Chadwick conducted a performance of *Noël* there—using the version in which the organ replaces the orchestra—in 1923.

Everywoman: Her Pilgrimage in Quest of Love (1910)

Chadwick's greatest success on the stage by far was realized with his incidental music to the play *Everywoman: Her Pilgrimage in Quest of Love*. Ironically, it was an endeavor in which he had but a minor role; unlike several of his earlier stage collaborations, here Chadwick was not enlisted to conduct, nor did he have much say in the production. *Everywoman* was written by Walter Browne, a novice librettist and playwright, who partnered with producer Henry W. Savage to stage what they branded a "modern morality play." Browne, a veteran performer with the D'Oyly Carte Company, had created noteworthy characters in American performances of Gilbert and Sullivan's *Iolanthe* and *Patience*. Browne's own lyrics, "of which there are only five or six," Chadwick assessed, "are very rhythmical and singable and he knows how to make them to music."[62]

But if Browne was a relative newcomer to Broadway, Savage was an old hand. Along Broadway, Savage was a prominent commodity whose fame had been guaranteed by a 1907 *New York Times* feature story that heralded him as "the Yankee Impresario."[63] A Harvard man, he had only begun his theatrical career in 1895. Savage additionally was a successful real-estate investor in Boston, an endeavor he did not give up when he began to pursue his theatrical muse. Before taking on *Everywoman*, Savage had produced some thirty-six shows in New York City. One of those was a hugely successful American production of Lehár's *The Merry Widow* (1905), which Savage produced with at least three touring troupes. "The two companies now playing—in New York and Chicago—," a *Times* essayist pointed out, "are located in immense theatres and are enjoying patronage that is positively abnormal. Desirable seats at the New Amsterdam Theatre are practically sold out for six weeks in advance, and the capacity of the house seems to be the only real limitation to the income at the box office."[64] Savage's success was not only artistic but also commercial—he had become a millionaire.

Chadwick's involvement in the project may be gleaned from a *New York Daily Tribune* interview with Savage, who, when asked if Chadwick composed all of the music for the production, said, "Yes. Mr. Browne read his play to Mr. Chadwick and Mr. Chadwick became very interested. He wanted to write the music as a labor of love, but I could not accept such a sacrifice."[65] The notion that Chadwick wished to take on the project as a "labor of love," that is, without receiving a fee, appears to be an invention, for he actually requested a fee of fifteen hundred dollars.[66] But, if pressed, Chadwick may indeed have done the work for free. Although he was not without other important projects at this time, his last stage effort, *Judith*, had a disappointing run. And since many of his friends and colleagues were beginning to take advantage of the increased popularity of American stage works—opera and Broadway alike—he may simply have wished to give it another try, paycheck or not. That Savage was a seasoned theatrical professional may have made the offer too difficult to pass up. It is also possible that Chadwick became interested in *Everywoman* precisely because the onus of the show did not rest on him alone; he had only to focus on the music. And Savage's genuine enthusiasm may have added to its allure. *Everywoman* would be, the producer assured Chadwick, "another Ben Hur."[67]

Chadwick's *Everywoman* has remained a bit of a mystery in the annals of American music history for several reasons, not the least of which is that a Broadway show scored by him does not line up well with our image of a Boston composer. Additionally, the score and instrumental parts are lost and with them any possibility of a close examination of Chadwick's work. The music was completed near Christmas in 1910, and a piano-vocal score was published in 1911; several of the songs were published as separate leaves, but they offer no opportunity to judge his instrumental coloring. There is no doubt that the music was intended to be a primary component of the play as Browne emphasized in the introduction to his bound edition of the play, *Acting Version of Henry W. Savage's Production of Everywoman: Her Pilgrimage in Quest of Love*, (1911):

An important feature of "Everywoman" will be its musical equipment of twenty-six numbers, especially composed by George Whitefield Chadwick, one of the few Americans to achieve high standing as a symphonic writer. The numbers include three solos, a trio, four choruses, a male quartette, several dances, and incidental and entr'acte numbers. For the rendering of the score an orchestra of forty pieces will be employed.[68]

Browne structured *Everywoman* in five "canticles," or acts, and provided the following synopsis:

Canticle I. Everywoman is shown her quest for love. With Youth, Beauty and Modesty she sets out.

Canticle II. Her travels take her first to the stage of a metropolitan theatre where she mistakes Passion for Love and where Modesty deserts her. She learns in time that Passion is not Love and, pursuing her quest, leaves the playhouse.

Canticle III. At a gay dinner party, lasting until dawn, Beauty dies and Everywoman, looking at her mirror sees not Flattery as she did at first but Truth. Wealth comes to her side, whispers in her ear and, desperate, she enters into a mad, drunken dance with him. Conscience seeks to dissuade Everywoman, but Wealth temporarily triumphs.

Canticle IV. Disappointed finally, Everywoman finds herself alone with Youth, her body clad in a cheap and shabby dress on Broadway on New Year's Eve. Time, the callboy, comes to rob Everywoman of Youth and Everywoman, in her plight, tries to regain the affections of Wealth. Wealth passes her by and takes up with Vice instead.

Canticle V. The Truth comes and reveals her Beauty to Everywoman. "Love," says Truth, "is my son." Everywoman returns to her home and there finds Love waiting for her. At first she does not recognize Love, but Truth makes her see Love aright and, as Everywoman and Love clasp hands, Modesty returns and clings to Everywoman's garments.

Despite its precious subject matter—in this respect it is rather like *The Lily Nymph* of fifteen years earlier—*Everywoman* enjoyed an impressive run. After premiering off-Broadway on February 9, 1911, at Parsons Theatre in Hartford, Connecticut, it then opened at the Herald Square Theatre on Broadway on

February 27, 1911, where it remained until mid-May. During the rehearsals Chadwick thought that Hugo Frey (1873–1952), the conductor, probably could have done a fine job, although he was "harassed to death" by nearly everyone involved in the production and was not able to focus on musical preparation.[69] "Everyone" was no small matter in this case; there were thirty-five members in the opening night cast. Frey had a slight Boston connection; early in his career he was the violist with the Listemann String Quartet (the figure of Bernhard Listemann crops up regularly in Boston's music history), and later on he would arrange music for the Victor Phonograph Company. He even wrote stock music for a number of film scores. Chadwick's generous assessment of Frey took into consideration his singers, who, as Chadwick discovered when he rehearsed them, were appallingly weak.

Following the Herald Square Theatre performances, the production moved to the Lyric Theatre (then owned by musical polymath Reginald de Koven), where it opened on May 29 and ran the entire month of June, closing on July 1. There followed an eight-month span during which Savage took the production on tour to Chicago, Boston, and elsewhere, and it re-opened in New York on February 19, 1912, again at the Herald Square Theatre. *Everywoman*'s final performance occurred on March 23. By the end of its Broadway run, it had played 189 times.

Naturally, the production did not always run smoothly. In November 1911 Chadwick attended a rehearsal prior to *Everywoman*'s Boston premiere. When he discovered that changes had been made to his orchestrations, he stormed Savage's office and demanded that the score be restored to its original form. This episode made the local newspapers, and, because it was deemed by some as a slap to the face of a Boston son—and by a New Yorker, no less—Savage was forced to explain that the changes were the result of rising costs incurred by an inflexible Musicians' Union. With eyes ever on the bottom line, Savage's changes stood.[70]

Chadwick was generally pleased with his score to *Everywoman*. "The music certainly does enhance the effect of the situation," he later wrote, "which is more than can be said of a good many grand opera."[71] However, its description as a morality play did not resonate with everyone. Philip Hale believed that "it is in fact a spectacle with music, with a pleasing dash of musical comedy."[72] Another commentator, writing more sarcastically, thought it "a musical comedy without the comedy." "What Everywoman lacks most as a play," the critic continued, "is real movement and action."[73]

Chadwick had been here before; like *Judith*, *Everywoman* suffered from a lack of distinct identity, a situation that hampered its long-term success. Chadwick thought it an amusing project, however, and, despite the problems with Savage, *Everywoman* must be put down as his most noteworthy stage success. But—like *Tabasco*—it was not a serious work, which prompted the composer to remark, "I shall be mighty careful what kind of stage piece I shall tackle next time."[74]

Aphrodite (1911)

The Norfolk Festival's primary mission was to bring together singers and musicians for the performance of major choral-symphonic works. But, as was the case for Chadwick's next major composition, music for orchestra alone was also welcomed. Chadwick began sketching his "symphonic fantasie," *Aphrodite*, on July 5, 1910. He completed it within a month on August 3, an astonishing feat especially considering that at 748 measures it was his longest and most complex single-movement composition to date. Almost a year passed until he began its orchestration—Chadwick planned the work "in my mind" for months "before I put down a single note of music"—and the entire work was finished on August 26, 1911, at West Chop.[75] He prepared a piano reduction of the score, and two months later, on October 29, he played it for friends Edward Burlingame Hill and Charles Martin Loeffler, who remarked on it favorably.[76]

Aphrodite is scored for three flutes and pairs of oboes, clarinets, and bassoons supplemented by an English horn, a bass clarinet, and a contrabassoon; a large brass section comprising four each of horns and trumpets, three trombones, and a tuba, all of which are joined by an off-stage trumpet section; a sizable percussion battery, including timpani, two additional percussionists, harp, celesta, and field drums; and a full string section. As Elson tells us, it is "only to be attempted by a grand orchestra."[77] Following his usual practice, Chadwick sent the score to Europe to have the parts copied; those for strings were back in hand in March 1912. He dedicated the piece to the Stoeckels.

Aphrodite had already been published by A. P. Schmidt by the time it premiered at the Norfolk Festival on June 4, 1912. The timing of the performance was wrenching for Chadwick and the Norfolk audience, for there was still much distress about the disastrous sinking, just six weeks earlier, of the steamship RMS *Titanic*. Chadwick was listless. The catastrophe, he wrote, "has so overshadowed all other affairs that I could not get into any mood to write."[78]

Aphrodite, named for the Greek goddess of love and beauty who is perhaps better known today by her Roman name, Venus, was inspired by a number of sources. Art collector and philanthropist Francis Bartlett donated a marble bust of Aphrodite to the Museum of Fine Arts in Boston in 1900. A magnificent piece, now referred to simply as "the Bartlett Head," it dates from the late Classical/early Hellenistic era (330–300 B.C.E.) and is thought to originate from

Attica, a peninsular province of southern Greece that juts out into the Aegean Sea. Within Attica's borders lies the capitol city of Athens, a city Bostonians had long compared to their own. The Bartlett Head is yet another symbol of New England's—and especially Boston's and Chadwick's—ongoing infatuation with classical Greece. Indeed, Chadwick later wrote of his introduction to the bust with uncommon reverence: "I well remember the very first idea I had for 'Aphrodite.' When she was first installed in the basement of the old Art Museum I used to worship at her shrine and I never came away without a feeling of elation—of inspiration not only from her marvelous [beauty] but from her wonderful history."[79]

Aphrodite was also inspired by the sea, as is reflected in the verse that prefaces the published score:

> In a dim vision of the long ago
> Wandering by a far-off Grecian shore
> Where streaming moonlight shone on golden sands
> And melting stars dissolved in silver seas,
> I humbly knelt at Aphrodite's shrine
> Imploring her with many a fervid prayer
> To tell the secret of her beauty's power
> And the depths of the ocean whence she sprang.
> At last the wave-born goddess raised her hand
> And smiling said: "O mortal youth, behold!"
> Then all these mysteries passed before mine eyes.[80]

These lines created some consternation for Chadwick. He had recently read "On a Statue of Aphrodite by the Seashore" from Lilla Cabot Perry's well-known compilation, *From the Garden of Hellas: translations into verse from the Greek Anthology*.[81] In an age and a place that worshipped an idealized Greece, this book, one of the era's many translations of ancient Greek poetry, sought to remove some of the romantic excesses that often accompanied other volumes. Chadwick attempted his own ode to Aphrodite, one that he hoped would retain the dignity of Perry's translations and lend his own voice to the goddess's story, but it met with little success. After several frustrating attempts, Chadwick asked Henry Copley Greene to prepare it. Greene, who had collaborated with Chadwick on *Pontius Pilate* in 1902, produced an eloquent rendition.

Using elements of Greene's verse plan, Chadwick developed *Aphrodite* with a clear formal scheme in mind. "The scenes," Chadwick noted in the program guide that accompanied the music's premiere, "are preceded by a short introduction in the nature of an apostrophe, [and] might be characterized as follows:"

Moonlight on the Sea	Andante con moto
Storm	Allegro con fuoco
Requiem	Andante lamentabile
The Lovers	Andante amoroso
Children Playing	Allegretto semplice
Approach of a Great Army and	
Hymn to Aphrodite	Maestoso
Moonlight scene partly repeated	Andante con moto
Finale	Molto maestoso

"Although each of these scenes, several directly inspired by Perry's verse, is complete in itself," Chadwick explained, "they are connected together by an *Aphrodite* motive which is developed throughout the whole piece in various forms and is given originally to the English horn in the first scene."[82] Here, in an unusual departure, Chadwick built an episodic work rather than the sonata form that he so often applied to his music. In this respect, *Aphrodite* is not unlike Richard Strauss's *Also sprach Zarathustra*, which he heard the BSO perform in 1909 and admired enormously.

Aphrodite begins with a serene, rather lugubrious solo by the viola. Its first moments have been compared to the opening of Wagner's *Tristan und Isolde*, mostly because of its melodic shape and its air of harmonic unsurety. The comparison is apt to a point; Wagner's theme has long been heralded for its avoidance of a resolution, its utterly unfinished nature. Chadwick viewed the sea in much the same manner, as an ever-changing body, without beginning or end. He also summoned harmonic and thematic techniques that he had used in *Melpomene* (in which the memory of Wagner was also conjured) to lend the composition added aesthetic heft.

Chadwick's main *Aphrodite* theme, which sounds throughout the work in various guises, is first issued by the English horn. The setting at this point owes a debt to Debussy. Chadwick had heard Debussy's *La Mer* when the BSO performed it in the 1906–1907 season but he was not particularly enthusiastic about it, and in fact thought it a distinct falling off from the composer's *Prelude to the Afternoon of a Faun*. "I found very little *salt* in it," he wrote caustically.[83] Nevertheless, Chadwick succeeded in capturing the elusive nature of the sea by using Debussian techniques.

The remainder of the score is equally captivating. The "Storm" scene, with pounding percussion and bold brass writing, offers up the turbulence of an angry sea, while "Requiem" utilizes high, static winds countered by low, trembling bass lines and spacious harmonies to create a haunting austerity. Weaker inventions follow: "The Lovers" and "The Approach of a Great Army" are less arresting than the opening segments, although the animated finale, cloaked in resplendent Lisztian harmony, is Chadwick at his best. *Aphrodite* is rife with displaced rhythms that create impressions of a sea breeze and shimmering waters. Solos are exchanged throughout the orchestra, especially in the winds, and accompanimental figures are often lightly textured, swirling passages. *Aphrodite*'s harmonies—now sober, now passionate—also find themselves farther afield; while not as adventuresome as Debussy, Chadwick demonstrates a mastery of chromatic writing. He also utilizes the instruments with a skill that was appreciated by critics. Taken as a whole, *Aphrodite* paints an evocative and potent picture of the sea.

The critical reception was largely favorable. *New York Times* reviewer Richard Aldrich made the trip to Connecticut to review the premiere. Chadwick had met Aldrich in New York several months before, and even visited the critic's home, where he was impressed by Aldrich's large library and his collection of music-related items. Chadwick took an instant liking to him. "Why can't all music critics be modest and able like him?" Chadwick wondered.[84] Aldrich found power and beauty in Chadwick's vision of the sea. "There are many passages," he thought, "of a tonal richness and color that signally illustrates Mr. Chadwick's skill in orchestration."[85] Louis C. Elson also believed *Aphrodite* a brilliant work "in the modern vein," and reported that the audience was ecstatic: "Five times was Mr. Chadwick obliged to rise from his seat in the audience and bow his acknowledgements."[86] Philip Hale, commenting on the music's picturesque qualities, thought it worthy of the cinema: "The most fastidious composer may yet welcome the opportunity of writing program music for motion pictures."[87]

H. T. Parker was the lonely censorious voice. His opinion, written after Karl Muck's 1913 BSO performance, identified the work as a "tone-poem." Parker recognized in Chadwick's score "the mysterious creeping of amorous longing into human hearts," and "the ardor of tremulous desire." He even remarked that its "musical fabric is beautifully luminous." Parker nevertheless complained that, "in spite of a measure of imagination with harmonies and timbres, progressions and dissonances, the outcome is no more than well-made and appropriate music."[88]

"A Beautiful but Costly Exotic"
Opera in Boston, the Met, & *The Padrone*
1913

*There is no branch of music so subject to the caprices
of fashion as the opera.*
—John Knowles Paine, "The New
German School of Music" (1873)

Opera in Boston

Chadwick's forays into the world of stagecraft had very much been a hit-and-miss proposition up to this time. Several of his previous works had been disappointing; *Pontius Pilate* was left in the lurch, and *Judith*, a work that he had reason to expect would be a sensation, was wholly uneven in its theatrical approach. He had tasted Broadway success with *Tabasco* and *Everywoman*, but Chadwick was not comfortable staking his reputation on those two. Indeed, he considered them diversions that were well removed from his artistic ambitions. Despite a number of personal creative missteps, opera still captivated Chadwick; he believed that opera represented an enormous opportunity not only for his own career, but also for the continued advancement of NEC.

Since he began his tenure at NEC in 1897, Chadwick had developed the institution in a carefully paced, astute, and logical manner. He first took steps to bolster the morale of the faculty by championing the good teachers and scaring off the bad ones. Then he addressed the challenges of advancing the curriculum, increasing the quality of the students, and replacing its wholly unsatisfactory facility. Chadwick used the orchestra program to recruit young instrumentalists of promise in order to give NEC good standing among Boston's musical elite, many of whom were enamored with the conservatory's symphonic aspirations. However, opera at NEC was never far from Chadwick's mind, and within a few years of taking the reins he would begin to hatch a plan to establish an opera program, a tricky endeavor that had defeated his predecessors Tourjée and Faelten.

Chadwick began by hiring in 1901 Oreste Bimboni, a Corsican opera director who arrived in Boston with professional credentials from Moscow and Vienna. Bimboni first came to Chadwick's attention when he was touring with the Mapleson Opera Company, and shortly after accepting the job the new NEC opera chief was producing astounding results. Bimboni offered excellent organizational skills and was scrupulous in his attention to detail. By 1902 Chadwick could boast that "the Opera school was quite flourishing under Bimboni, and we stimulated it by offering some scholarship[s] outside the school"; that is, the standard conservatory course for singers was supplemented by performing experiences with local and traveling opera organizations. A principal benefactor to this effort had been Eben Jordan Jr., who had long wished to see opera thrive in the city.[1]

Bimboni's first production opened at the Boston Theatre on May 23, 1902. The program included scenes from Verdi's *Aida*, Wagner's *Lohengrin*, Donizetti's *La favorita*, and others, and featured NEC vocal and orchestra students. Bimboni's leadership was exemplary. "He knew every detail of his work," Chadwick marveled, "costumes, scenery, action & all and was absolutely tireless."[2] The performance was a triumph, as "all Boston was there and we probably got our expenses back (It was a free show) in advertising."[3] Plans were quickly laid to repeat the format, and the following year, 1903, Bimboni and his students performed scenes from Rossini's *The Barber of Seville*, Meyerbeer's *Les Huguenots*, Flowtow's *Martha*, and Verdi's *La Traviata* and *Il Trovatore*, as well as Gluck's *Orfeo*. Chadwick again wrote admiringly that "all this show Bimboni put through without any row or any more fuss than was inevitable with such [an] amount of detail. He ran the whole bloomin' show himself, costumes, scenery, action, chorus, orchestra . . . a wonderful job."[4] During his time at the helm of the NEC opera department, however, Bimboni had not produced anything more than miscellaneous scenes, although from a wide variety of operas.

Ironically, the first complete opera production at NEC occurred on May 18, 1906, shortly after Bimboni's death in late 1905. The opera department, under the temporary leadership of Wallace Goodrich, performed Ignaz Brüll's *Das goldene Kreuz* (*The Golden Cross*) in Jordan Hall.[5] It is not insignificant that, at a time when Italian opera was the rage, Goodrich selected for performance an English version of Brüll's 1875 work, a melodic and easily performed work that is thoroughly German. Although the cast needed "thorough drill in the elemental principals of dramatic action," an excellent fifty-member NEC orchestra, led by Goodrich, buoyed the event. It was, wrote a critic, "a good omen for the future."[6] As he was in Europe at the time, Chadwick missed this signal event in NEC history.

Opera at NEC continued with uneven results, but had progressed sufficiently by 1908 for the production of Ambroise Thomas's *Mignon* (1866). Mounted for the benefit of the Chelsea Relief Fund, the opera was a local smash, and Chadwick was thrilled by the students' performance. The opera department had "a completeness—and wholly from its own resources—that only a few European schools of music could match," concluded one reviewer.[7] The conservatory's talent pool was strong, although it had fewer truly exemplary musicians than it had enjoyed in the past, and the spirit of teamwork and camaraderie was remarkable.

The conservatory's venture into opera stretched the resources of a staff that was already toiling assiduously. *Mignon* would be NEC's final experiment in opera, and Chadwick could not have been happier. "But no more Conservatory operas for me!" he cheered. "We have accomplished everything that we could be expected to accomplish. The singing, playing and acting all studied under our own roof and with our own material, and now that it is all over, what is the result? A certain amount of experience to be sure, but at what expense of time, trouble, friction, bother, hurry and nervous energy without any artistic result in proportion."[8]

Opera did not end at NEC, of course, but thereafter it would be produced only sporadically. The results were never entirely satisfactory and were often severely limited by leadership and money (which are not unrelated). As late as 1926, when opera at the conservatory was enjoying a renaissance, hopes ran high that renewed efforts would have more success than past ones. Chadwick never ceased to believe that NEC needed a great opera school in order to be a great conservatory. "I believe that we can build such a school," he asserted, "but it will take time, money and room. With these things supplied, I would gladly put my remaining energy into it."[9]

In the first years of the new century, Chadwick's efforts to build opera at NEC had been enhanced by its growing popularity, as evidenced by a steep increase in performance activity, in Boston. Visiting companies attracted sizable crowds, and this was especially true of New York's Metropolitan Opera. But the Met was also the bane of Boston opera lovers, who were embarrassed that their city did not possess a company of its own; more humiliating was the possibility that it could not support one financially even if it had one. This was all part of an ongoing war for cultural superiority between New York and Boston, one which extended to nearly every imaginable field. If Boston had the upper hand in higher education, New York held sway in commerce; the two cities, then as now, also vied for dominance in baseball. Opera was simply another battlefield on which the war would be waged. Up to now, New York had scored the most victories.

Gustav Mahler brought the Metropolitan Opera Company to Boston in April 1908 for six days of performances of Verdi's *Il Trovatore* and Wagner's *Tristan und Isolde*. Chadwick confided that it was "about the best I ever heard."[10] Mahler's work in opera may have reminded some Boston audiences of the harsh lessons learned about orchestral technique thirty years before, courtesy of the Theodore Thomas Orchestra. It is worth noting that Thomas also sought operatic success in Boston. In 1887 he led the National Opera Company, formerly known as the American Opera Company, in English-language operas, and while the performances were well attended, the receipts could not keep pace with the expenses. The company, based in New York and spearheaded by philanthropist Jeannette Thurber, folded in short order. A variety of other traveling opera companies, most of them long since forgotten, also performed in Boston. They included the Savage Opera Company, the Manhattan Opera Company, the Mapleson Company, and the San Carlo Opera, all of which performed regularly in the city. Their repertoires were mostly of the Italian bel canto variety—simple, tuneful operas with thin plots and uncomplicated staging. Among the several venues that were available to opera producers were the Howard Athenaeum near Scollay Square, Boston Theatre, Park Theater, the Majestic, and Jordan Hall. Chadwick was eager to let Jordan Hall to reputable companies not only because it brought professional practitioners of the art form into closer contact with his students, but also because of the additional operating revenue that the rents poured into NEC's coffers.

Opera impresario Henry Russell managed the San Carlo Company and utilized Jordan Hall for rehearsals during its December 1907 tour. The San Carlo Company gave admired performances of Puccini's operas, which were then the newest rage, but more importantly the company's local success initiated a new round of discussions in Boston about the formation of a resident organization.[11] The notion of forming a "permanent opera company" had been considered off and on for years, but now audience appreciation—fostered in part by the successes of Chadwick and NEC—and philanthropy converged. The time seemed right, the initiative seemed possible, and Russell seemed to be the man best able to take on the task. Possessed of a gift for making ordinary productions spectacular, Russell had lured many noteworthy Boston citizens into the idea of building a local opera company. Chief among them was Jordan, who, as the opportunity unfolded, would become increasingly consequential to the cause of opera in Boston.[12]

Chadwick had high hopes about the possibilities for professional opera in Boston. Not only would it be a positive development for musical culture in the city, but, in keeping with Chadwick's current plan, it would enable opera at NEC to die with little notice. Chadwick also saw in Russell's scheming another opportunity for NEC—and for himself—to get into the opera business without bearing the burden of total responsibility. At the end of 1907, fewer than six months before *Mignon* was produced at NEC, Jordan had already hinted to Chadwick that he was considering the construction of an opera house that Boston could call its own. "If he does," Chadwick wrote excitedly, "it will probably be [located] next to the NEC. And we shall have a large hand in the management."[13]

The Boston Opera Company

The aspirations of the Boston Opera Company, visibly represented by its opulent, if smallish, new opera house, were lofty. Frank H. Jackson outlined them in the 1909 souvenir book that accompanied its inauguration and related that the leaders of the company sought

[a]n Opera House of beautiful proportions and unlimited resources; a company of gifted and eminent singers; a chorus a proportion of which are American singers; a ballet of American dancers; an opportunity to enjoy grand opera at lower rates than was ever known before; and best of all, the definite launching of a movement which will make grand opera in America what it is in Europe, — an institution adapted to the native spirit and temperament and calculated to develop the dormant American musical instinct, — all of these things are realized with the inauguration of the Boston Opera House.[14]

One year earlier writer and music editor Joe Mitchell Chapple offered another perspective; he defined the project based on what it was not: "The purpose is not to make grand opera a mere social or show event, but to satisfy the musical demands and to provide an ensemble of talent rather than depend upon the glory of a single star as an attraction. The unnecessary expense of stellar exploitation exclusively entails disastrous economy in other ways to the usefulness of music as music."[15]

Built nearly entirely through the generosity of Jordan—whose philanthropy, we have seen, had led directly to Jordan Hall—construction of the opera house began in August, 1908. Jordan's scheme was a straightforward one and was almost certainly advocated and advised by Russell. Jordan would pay for the construction of the building and guarantee expenses for three years on the condition that other philanthropists and opera lovers would band together to form and incorporate an opera company.[16] The Boston Opera Company would then agree to raise an additional $150,000 in cash to help both the company and the Boston Opera House with start-up capital needs, such as stage machinery, costumes, and scenery. This funding would also enable the hiring of singers, musicians, and a production and administrative staff.

Jordan was savvy; he knew very well that Higginson had spent years strapped to difficult BSO finances, and he had no wish to take on the same role at the opera. He therefore required the Boston Opera Company leaders to sign a three-year lease agreement, as well as secure three-year subscriptions for the opera house boxes at the rate of two thousand dollars per box, per year. The conditions having been met, fifty-four boxes were sold immediately, bringing in a total of $108,000.[17] To raise the remaining forty-two-thousand-dollar shortfall, "shares" in the opera house were sold to the public at the cost of a hundred dollars per share. According to Jackson, "The rapidity with which these were taken up is in itself an assurance of the success of the new institution."[18] Performance tickets were then sold; Chadwick wrote that they were "liberally subscribed for," with the best seats going for three dollars. Gallery seats could be had for a mere seventy-five cents. The plan from the outset was to produce at least fifteen operas a year, each receiving four performances.

By the time the cornerstone was laid on November 30, 1908, Jordan's threshold for "stockholders"—one of whom was Chadwick—had been met, and excitement for the enterprise had reached a fever pitch. The laying of the cornerstone was itself an extraordinary event in Boston's musical history; it featured appearances by politicians all the way up to the governor, a crowd of musicians and music lovers, and all manner of philanthropists and socialites. Although Chadwick was mildly offended that his presence was not mentioned in the newspaper coverage, in fact he shared the stage with the other dignitaries. A band played; speeches were made by Governor Curtis Guild Jr. (1860–1915) and Jordan; and the cornerstone, a half-ton hunk of solid granite, was laid over a bronze box that held items that were relevant to the occasion, priceless relics of Boston's now-mature musical culture.

The box contained programs and yearbooks from an array of local music organizations; copies of compositions, mostly by New England composers, including Beach's Mass in E-flat, Chadwick's *Judith*, Converse's *The Pipe of Desire*, Damrosch's *The Scarlett Letter*, Foote's *The Wreck of the Hesperus*, Hadley's *Merlin and Vivian*, Loeffler's Psalm 137, MacDowell's *Hamlet and Ophelia*, and Parker's *The Legend of St. Christopher*. The relatively new technology of phonograph recording also made its way into the bronze box. Recorded sound excerpts from a wide variety of operas sung by the likes of Lillian Nordica, Louise Homer, Geraldine Farrar, Christina Nilsson, David Bispham, and the most popular leading man of the day, Enrico Caruso, were also entombed in the cornerstone. Newspapers ran congratulatory messages from Farrar, Emma Eames, Caruso, and the chairman and directors of the Met, among many others.[19]

One major task that the organizers of Boston Opera faced was making the enterprise morally savory. Heretofore one reason Boston had not cultivated opera was because it was deemed inappropriate in polite society. While singers, especially "stars," were lauded for their virtuosity, opera itself was seen by many, especially those of Puritan stock, as slightly racy. While abstract orchestral music permitted flights of the imagination and was universally loved by the city's musically informed, opera often comprised a public display of private matters: love, ambition, treachery, and death. Many thought that these should remain private and undiscussed. Even worse, opera, particularly in its turn-of-the-century guise, often depicted seedy, distasteful aspects of human activity: crime, poverty, sex, and murder.

Despite the efforts of many writers and artists, the concept of "realism" was slow to penetrate Boston's artistic, especially musical, circles. Its requirements, after all, did not resonate with the grace and dignity that Boston's composers sought in their music. It seems almost unfathomable that, given the bloody and horrific experience of the Civil War, realism in music by American composers did not occur routinely until after the Great War. But Boston's composers clung to tradition. Their reaction to the horrors of the Civil War was to restore civility; that is, the balance, logic, and gentility of their works was a reposeful response to the strife of the 1860s. "Realism," and its associated depravities, was simply not wanted.

Further, Bostonians abhorred the pretentious displays of wealth that often accompanied events like opera at which glamour sometimes overshadowed art. Add to this the fact that opera was often prohibitively expensive; Chadwick referred to it as "a beautiful but costly exotic."[20]

At least one speaker at the cornerstone-laying ceremony could relate the potentially controversial matter of opera in terms that the locals could understand and appreciate. Here in Boston, America's Athens, opera was, according to Governor Guild, of a wholly Greek pedigree. In a lengthy, sometimes rambling speech that was carefully transcribed by an ambitious reporter, Governor Guild declared to a crowd of two hundred, "Grand Opera, I need scarcely remind you, was originally a religious performance and in its origins essentially Greek, for the tragedies of Sophocles and his rivals were but little other than grand opera."[21] By relating opera to classical Greece, the governor was placing the art form in the same artistic sphere that was already occupied by Boston's architecture (as well as several of Chadwick's compositions). The crisp, clean lines of Boston's many Greek revival buildings lay within the comfort zone of the governor's audience. As an able politician, he knew that, once his audience was reminded of opera's relationship to Greek theater, arts patrons in Boston could support the enterprise. It was incumbent upon music lovers, Governor Guild explained, to receive opera warmly; it mattered little that his discourse on ancient music history was rather far-fetched.

Contrary to his earlier hopes, Chadwick was out of the loop in the opera house's administration well before its construction began. As NEC's *Mignon* came to a close, he decried all the work involved in producing opera and bitterly remarked that opera in Boston can now be run "at Russell's new operatic Hippodrome," at the corner of Huntington Avenue and Opera Place. That, he assessed, would "leave us to our quiet study of music as an art."[22] Chadwick was a member of the opera's board of directors, and two of his closest NEC captains were employed in significant positions of responsibility. Wallace Goodrich was one of two music directors, and Ralph L. Flanders, a longtime NEC administrator, was managing director. Goodrich was an excellent local choice in the musical area, and Flanders had distinguished himself as an astute business manager at the conservatory. With his friends and associates employed at Boston Opera it is clear that by early 1908 Chadwick knew he was on the outside looking in. He met with Russell several times to propose the incorporation of NEC's opera program into that of the Boston Opera for the benefit of the conservatory students, but that effort seems to have met with silence.

Chadwick had no role in the vision or the direction of the opera house; in fact, there is an obvious animus on the composer's part toward Russell. Chadwick described a meeting at which he "took the opportunity to tell him [Russell] exactly where I stand on the opera question. It is not very likely that he will ever hypnotize *me*, and therefore he may distrust me."[23] The issue at hand was not disclosed, but their association was further complicated by Chadwick's growing resentment of Russell, who was occupying both the time and attention—not to mention the funds—of several of his most important donors, Jordan and Higginson among them. Chadwick's suspicions about Russell would not subside; in 1912, after listening to "one of his usual asinine speeches," Chadwick wrote, "What a success that man would have made as a head Barker for a circus!"[24]

Chadwick's already strained relationship with the Boston Opera administration declined precipitously when Flanders "resigned" from his position under Russell on October 26, 1909, less than two weeks before the grand opening of the opera house. Much of our information about this event comes from H. T. Parker's article that ran the next day in the *Transcript*. As the story reads, it is obvious that Parker obtained most of his information from Russell himself. His opening sentence is personal and diabolical: "The withdrawal of Ralph M. Flanders from the general management of the Boston Opera House removes a material obstacle to the accomplishment of the plans and the maintenance of the standards that it has announced and reiterated." Throughout Parker not only speculated that Flanders's resignation was forced, but accused him of inciting "recurring friction, misunderstandings, delays and blunders."[25]

Parker held Flanders responsible for the considerable discord between administrators and the architects and builders of the opera house, but he resisted the temptation to blame Flanders for the bomb that was exploded on March 27, 1909. Although investigators were certain that the bombing was the work of disgruntled construction employees, no arrests were made. Chadwick acidly complained that "even if the culprits are discovered, our easy going American public sentiment would not punish them."[26] No one was injured in the blast and the damage resulted in only a small financial setback for the organization. Nevertheless, the workers' dissatisfaction was blamed on Flanders's inability to deal effectively with contracting issues.

As if that was not enough, Parker maliciously wrote that Flanders was "wholly unversed in operatic affairs." Naturally, given Flanders's long association with NEC, Parker could not help but throw a punch in that direction. In Parker's view, Flanders "seemingly, but mistakenly, saw in the Boston Opera a local and provincial undertaking, closely allied with his music-school." In what can only be judged a jab at Chadwick himself, Parker—who had apparently learned of NEC's hopes for a Boston Opera partnership—concluded that "the opera must exist, first of all, for itself and its public and not for the advantage of any music school or any balance sheet." A reporter for the *Boston Herald* offered a more sober assessment of the scandal. He wrote simply that Flanders resigned citing the neglect of his duties at NEC and the huge toll the workload was taking on his health. Perhaps in an effort to quash further controversy, Jordan, then president of the opera, invited Flanders to remain on the executive committee.[27]

With the passing of the Flanders scandal, the Boston Opera Company inaugurated its new stage on November 8, 1909, with a gala performance of Ponchielli's *La Gioconda*. This was a watershed moment for the city's music lovers. One effusive critic wrote, "For the present it seems no exaggeration to say that it is a matter of epochal significance and will prove the one thing needed to make secure Boston's high standing among the musical centres of the world."[28] The featured singers were Lillian Nordica and Louise Homer, both of whom had studied in Boston. Summarizing the activities, Chadwick wrote: "The great event . . . has come and gone, and Boston has now moved up from the position of a deserted village, abandoned farm, or at least one horse town."[29] The performance was a great one, "thoroughly metropolitan," as he sarcastically put it, a "brilliant social event." On this plane at least, Boston indisputably was competing with the Met.

Despite his many moments of disappointment, Chadwick was actually quite proud of the opera house. His affection for the operatic art had recently grown along with that of Boston, although he did not predict a long future for it. In this he proved prescient. When, several years later, the opera house fell on hard times, he began to suspect that all the troubles were landing squarely on Jordan's shoulders.[30] Before long, Chadwick maintained, the opera house would be a "vaudeville theater," one that would inevitably be "leased to a Jewish syndicate."[31] But now, at the end of October 1909, just before the opera house's grand introduction to an enthusiastic public, Chadwick took Ida May for a tour of the new building. He confessed, "It is very beautiful and I am glad we have got it." He asserted more laconically, "I am not so sure I am glad we have got Russell."[32]

Fred Converse

Opera was at the forefront of Chadwick's artistic life during this period, and it was not a coincidence that several of his most devoted former students, among them Horatio Parker and Frederick Shepherd Converse (1871–1940), were also steeped in Boston's operatic efforts. If Parker had been Chadwick's best student, the younger Converse came in a close second. Converse had studied with Paine at Harvard and with pianist Carl Baermann and Chadwick at NEC before travel-ing to Munich to take his place among the legions of American students who learned composition from the German master, Rheinberger. Upon Converse's return to Boston, Chadwick quickly hired him to teach harmony at NEC, and he took little time to establish himself as a talented composer and an excellent instructor. Like Chadwick, Converse also proved to be a thoroughly able and level-headed administrator. He left NEC after two productive years to take a posi-tion at Harvard University, but his family fortune enabled him to resign in 1907 in order to devote himself entirely to composition. Before long, however, he was deeply involved in the opera house project as the first vice chairman of the board of directors; he was also one of its key fundraisers. In all likelihood Converse's close association with Boston's opera led to one of his greatest achievements as a composer. He distinguished himself in the annals of American music when, on March 18, 1910, his opera, *The Pipe of Desire*, was the first American opera to be performed at the Met in New York City.

The Pipe of Desire, Converse's first opera, was not new. It had already been presented in a concert version at Jordan Hall in 1906, where it was conducted by Wallace Goodrich and directed by Robert Barnet, Chadwick's collaborator on *Tabasco*. Chadwick was in Europe at the time, but he undoubtedly heard good reports about the music; he may have even inspected the score as Converse was composing it. When the opera was mounted at the Boston Opera House in 1911, a year after the Met premiere, Chadwick gave it his full estimate: "This piece is hardly an opera at all. It is an idyll—highly poetic in places and always beautiful in color especially in the orchestra but totally lacking in action and therefore [lacking] in real dramatic effect."[33] Despite its failure as a theatrical work, *The Pipe of Desire* nevertheless demonstrated that a convincing opera could be written in the English language, for its text setting struck a very positive note. Chadwick was further impressed that Converse managed to traverse "that hotbed of Italian graft, the Boston Opera House," a feat which he considered "little short of a triumph." "If such a piece can get that far," Chadwick hoped, "it would seem as though *Judith* which at least contains characters of real flesh and blood ought to be heard some time or other."[34]

Converse's second opera, *The Sacrifice*, was also performed by the Boston Opera Company in 1911 in a production reported to be elaborate "both musically and mechanically."[35] The opera's libretto, based on the actual mid-nineteenth century memoirs of an American soldier who was based in Mexico, was crafted by Converse himself. *The Sacrifice* gave Converse immediate and unexpected standing as one of America's greatest opera composers. Chadwick also missed the premiere of this opera, but he had had plenty of chances to hear it in rehearsal at Jordan Hall. He was not persuaded. Chadwick "found some things to admire but many things to disappoint." The opera, he thought, lacked real action, gave way to too much chatter by the principals, and was completely void of melodic interest in the vocal parts. Chadwick predicted "this opera will not last beyond the end of the Boston season."[36]

Chadwick was not surprised by Converse's rapid rise to success. Converse had been a remarkable student, and years ago Chadwick had given him a hearty recommendation to Rheinberger—and later even a job—without hesitation. Chadwick thought that Converse had "fine imagination, indomitable energy and masterly technique, for he is as good a workman as can be found in any country." The two were more than teacher and student—their families often dined together, and Converse was "almost my most sympathetic colleague [and] in spite of the differences in our ages he seems to belong in our own class more than any others of the younger American composers."[37]

But Chadwick was a competitive man. He had been toiling as a composer for twenty years longer than Converse, and there can be little doubt that although publicly supportive, he was privately jealous. His student's triumphs only fueled his determination to write a meaningful—and hopefully successful—opera of his own.

Parker and the Met

Chadwick's first significant association with the Metropolitan Opera Company occurred in 1910 when he was invited to judge submissions for the Met's

"American opera competition." The competition was the brainchild of Italian opera impresario Giulio Gatti-Casazza (1869–1940), whose tenure at the Met had just begun in 1908. Now a legendary historical figure in the opera world, Gatti-Casazza had spent the previous ten years at Milan's La Scala, where he turned a good local opera house into the best in Italy and the most famous in the world. His idea for a competition had been proposed to the board of directors and was formally announced on December 15, 1908. At stake was the enormous amount of ten thousand dollars to the winner, along with the promise of a coveted performance at the Met. The deadline for submissions was set twenty-one months hence—all operas would be due on September 15, 1910.

Composition competitions were not unique in America, but the prestige and the sizable purse of the Met competition enticed qualified composers from near and far. But not all of them. Chadwick was already committed to *Noël*, on which he had been working for a year and would finally complete in early 1909. Converse, likewise, had already received the promise of a Met performance from Gatti-Casazza himself for *The Pipe of Desire*; he may have thought that, even if he had the time to write a new opera, entering the contest would be futile given that a performance of his work was in the offing. For Horatio Parker, however, the timing could hardly have been better. His cantata, *King Gorm the Grim*, had been premiered in Norfolk on June 4, 1908, and his *Legend of Saint Christopher*, composed a decade before, had been successfully performed in Boston just days before the Met contest was announced. Energized by these two triumphs, Parker found himself in a compositional slow period and eager to get to work on a new project.

Within two months of his decision to compete, Parker received *Mona*, a libretto by Brian Hooker, and he immediately set to work. Hooker's creation, set in ancient Britain, is the story of Mona, a warrior princess, who falls in love with Gwynn, the son of the ruling Roman governor. Mona eventually kills her lover, and in turn she is murdered by the vengeful Romans. Parker delighted in the work; he composed steadily, interrupted only by family matters and his own poor health, until he finished the scoring on August 24, 1910. As he was putting the final touches on his manuscript, a scandal erupted at the scandal-ridden Met.

In July 1910 it was reported that the Met planned to extend the competition deadline exactly one year from its original date, to September 15, 1911. Critic Henry Krehbiel was quick to note that this was "in direct violation of the conditions of the contest," and, while there were undoubtedly a number of contestants for whom the later deadline would be beneficial, Parker was outraged.[38] Not only had he been toiling on *Mona* to the exclusion of many other responsibilities, but he was irate that composers who were not able to finish their own works in a timely manner would be given an extra year to catch up to him. Parker fully expected that the extended deadline would create a larger pool of competitors and place him at a distinct disadvantage.

On the face of it, the Met administration may have been worried that there would be a paucity of entries. Other than hearsay, there was no way for them to know how many operas would come in at the original due date. Krehbiel, ever curious and intrepid, had other suspicions about this matter. In correspondence with Chadwick, Krehbiel surmised that Otto H. Kahn, the powerful Met board chairman, may have floated the idea of extending the deadline in order to help Arthur Nevin, a contestant whom he covertly favored.[39] It mattered little. Just two days before the deadline, the Met board released a statement that explained that the competition date had not been extended, and in fact that by rule it could not be extended except by the judges, who had not yet been impaneled. The statement maintained that, if the jury agreed that none of the entries merited the award, more time could be granted. Given the controversy, one can imagine the general relief among Met leaders when more than thirty operas were received.[40]

The following December, Krehbiel was asked by the Met board to identify two judges to join Walter Damrosch and Alfred Hertz, both of whom had already been impaneled. Krehbiel proposed Chadwick and Charles Martin Loeffler. The board acted quickly; by January 2, 1911, Chadwick's services had been secured, and he had already received four opera scores to review. The work was not easy. "It is a horrible job," Chadwick complained just two weeks into his task. "Lucky for me I like to read score."[41] It did not escape Chadwick's notice that, among four judges reviewing American operas, he was the only native-born American.

By early March, Chadwick had finished evaluating another group of operas. Under the terms of the competition rules, the identity of all composers was concealed from the jury and the Met administrators; each opera was labeled with a fictitious name and was accompanied by a sealed envelope, the contents of which identified its creator. On his score, Parker replaced his own name with "Mona." Naturally, Chadwick instantly recognized Parker's music, which "is decidedly the best of the lot but suffers as do most of them from too many *words*, and too little *action*." Otherwise Chadwick admired "the beautiful music, masterly scoring and poetic lines."[42]

Despite the fact that the deadline did not change—and therefore the whole episode ended up a non-event—Parker continued to stew over the matter. As his irritation festered, he became belligerent. "Parker has worked himself up to such a frame of mind," Chadwick wrote, "that he really believes the prize belongs to him—whether anybody else thinks the play will go over the footlights or not."

> He assured me that he know[s] a great deal more about dramatic music than I do, or any of the people in the Met Opera House. Whereat I hinted that it was a great loss to the country and to Art that he was not one of the judges. He had a great deal to say about Kahn's dishonesty as he called it in proposing to extend the time of the competition, declared that he had no respect whatever for the judgment of Martin Loeffler (which was funny considering that Martin has expressed his admiration of Parker's opera). He hinted that Walter Damrosch was not above trying to get square with him for some little personal misunderstandings they had had, & that Hertz *of course* would have to vote as Kahn dictated. He did not say this but hinted it unmistakably. His attitude was in the highest degree supercilious and arrogant, and although I think I kept my temper I was pretty much disgusted.[43]

Chadwick determined to get to the bottom of the matter. He wrote to Krehbiel to learn "the true history of Mr. Kahn's action."[44] But Chadwick was careful here, for he also distrusted Krehbiel and suspected that the critic, "a meddlesome old Tabby," had done "a lot of gossiping and meddling in this matter." Krehbiel responded that, although the idea for extending the deadline had emanated from Kahn, at least one other judge also wished to extend it (although he refused to name names). In the meantime, Krehbiel had read the competition rules and wondered to Chadwick, "tell me if you can how it came that a jury of four men was appointed when the rules required a majority of two-thirds?"[45] In an era of muckraking journalism, Krehbiel smelled a story.

Krehbiel admitted to Chadwick that he believed that the jury still might extend the deadline, since, per the rules, it was within its power to do so. There was also some thought that none of the entries met the expected standard. Krehbiel laid the situation out to Chadwick: "If the jury decides on 'no award' [and] an extension I scarcely believe its membership will be continued unless you are unanimous." He then asked Chadwick: "If you are not willing to remain on the jury will you give me your reasons for publication?"[46] We do not know how Chadwick reacted to this letter, but Krehbiel's intrusive inquiries were getting uncomfortable. In any case, it is likely that by now the jury had already made its decision, for within three days of Krehbiel's correspondence Parker's *Mona* was publicly declared the contest winner.[47]

Performances of *Mona* were delayed nearly a year. When finally staged in March 1912 the reviews were mixed; three subsequent performances did little to alter opinion. Daniel Gregory Mason dismissed it out of hand, writing, "One has the feeling that, except for occasional passages of individuality, almost any-body of Professor Parker's attainments might have written *Mona*."[48] Richard Aldrich was more generous. He claimed in his *New York Times* review that the opera was "warmly welcomed" by the audience, and although Hooker's libretto missed the mark, Parker's musical style contained "remarkable originality."[49] *Mona* had already been forgotten when, a year after its premiere, a *New York Times* editorial urged the Met to produce the opera again.[50]

For his part, Chadwick was pleased when the episode concluded. "So this is the end of the fearful and wonderful Metropolitan Opera $10,000 competi-tion," he confided to his diary, "and we are all relieved."[51] Fellow adjudicator Walter Damrosch was simply glad "we came out alive and kicking."[52] Chadwick recognized that Parker's opera was the only one of the lot that worthy of perfor-mance consideration, and he speculated that the field of contestants was weak because neither Converse, Frank van der Stucken, nor Hadley had submitted an opera; neither had Chadwick. Once those names were out of contention, who else was there? Nonetheless, Chadwick was not completely sold on *Mona*. "It still remains to be demonstrated," he declared, "whether Parker's opera is really dramatic in the theatrical sense."[53]

Chadwick was pained that his friend ever after harbored resentment about *Mona* and the shifting deadline episode. Parker's attitude toward Loeffler had always been cool—Chadwick would later remark that a 1916 speech made by Parker in honor of Loeffler was very flattering "if it was sincere"[54]—but he did not expect that the matter would affect his own relationship with Parker. It did, however, and Parker became increasingly aloof. He rarely bothered to share news of his own compositional work, and he seemed disinterested in that of his Boston colleagues. "Verily grand opera," Chadwick wrote, "is the root of all evil."[55]

Why is the intrigue that surrounds l'affaire Parker and the Met pertinent to Chadwick's biography? Although other American works followed the produc-tion of *Mona*, that opera clearly set the tone for Gatti-Casazza's reception of American works in the future. In his 1933 ruminations on opera in America, Gatti-Casazza withheld no punches with regard to Parker. He flatly declared that *Mona* "is a cold and arid thing," and that its creator "did not possess cre-ative power." Gatti-Casazza ranted against Parker, who by the time of his writing had been dead for more than a decade: "He was not an artist, deep down in his soul. He was simply a cerebral, a pedagogue. And from conversations I had with him I could not help but be convinced that he believed himself on the right road and that he considered the public mistaken."[56] And this was the Met competition winner! Because Chadwick was one of the judges—and perhaps even an outspoken one—the odds of a Met performance of an opera of his own now seemed very long.

Although rife with challenges, opera inexplicably remained a rage among American composers, and performances of one's own opera became a sort of musical Holy Grail that was to be pursued at any cost. Part of the allure of opera was that success in it was so unattainable. While operas by Converse and Parker were not wholly appreciated (Gatti-Casazza noted that *The Pipe of Desire* was "coldly received" at its Met premiere[57]), the apparent willingness of the Met and the Boston Opera to support and perform American works, albeit on a modest level, made the endeavor exciting and worth tackling.

For Chadwick, however, there was more than mere ego at stake. He sought redemption. His earlier stage works had not achieved the acclaim he expected, and he was simply appalled at the lowly state of dramatic writing for the American stage, even by his own friends and associates. For all of Gatti-Casazza's complaints, Chadwick would have been hard pressed to disagree.

Chadwick knew that the Great American Opera had yet to be written. And, despite its many perils and pitfalls, the opera bug had not left him.

The Padrone (1913)

Chadwick had not fully gotten over the inefficacies—if not, in some ways, the total failure—that had befallen *Judith*. At issue was not the quality of the music in his "lyric drama," which some thought uneven, but its failure to fit the profile of either an opera or an oratorio. He had the opportunity to rethink his approach to the operatic form on April 26, 1911, when *Judith* was performed in Philadelphia, its first complete presentation since 1902.

Two Pennsylvania Quakers, Justus Strawbridge and Isaac Clothier, had founded their department store just after the Civil War, in 1868, and, not unlike the employees of the Lowell mills of Chadwick's parents' youth, the company's workers banded together for mutual education and enjoyment. The Strawbridge and Clothier Chorus—a surprisingly talented collection of "dry good clerks" led by the store manager Herbert J. Tily—performed *Judith* to orchestral accompaniment provided by members of the Philadelphia Orchestra.[58] The performance was excellent, but it forced its creator to conclude "that no amount of excision would make the first act seem anything but like an oratorio."[59] Chadwick had considered producing a staged performance of *Judith*, but after this revelation he realized the futility of the effort. He had neither the energy nor the ambition to revise the work, and he continued to lay most of the blame for *Judith* squarely on the libretto. As he gradually abandoned hope for its future possibilities, he started to explore fresh avenues for making an opera. Naturally, a good libretto was his first priority. Within a few days after the Philadelphia performance of *Judith*—and, not coincidentally, on the same day the Met contest panel awarded Parker its prize for *Mona*—Chadwick lamented, "But oh for a good opera book. A book that will *act*—and act without any words, and sing—sing without any necessary action. A book without Indians, negroes, cowboys, Mexicans or other aborigines, but with a real atmosphere and with real emotions."[60]

The atmosphere and emotions Chadwick sought were close at hand in the burgeoning Italian community of Boston's North End. This area—once inhabited by the English, then Germans, and then Irish—was by 1906 home to twenty-two thousand Italians out of the total population in that neighborhood of twenty-seven thousand.[61] By that time a number of unsavory aspects of the Italians' harsh lives had become well known, principally due to the work of Representative George Scigliano (1874–1906). The first US-born member of his family, Scigliano was raised in the North End and made his life and career there. After winning a number of local political posts, Scigliano was elected to the Massachusetts legislature in 1903, where he took up causes that concerned Italians. They were many: poverty, of course, but also disease—tuberculosis was rampant—and illiteracy. Taken together, there seemed to be little possibility that the dreadful straits of Boston's Italians would improve any time soon.

Perhaps the most direful issue facing the immigrants was crime, and one particularly insidious manifestation was the "padrone system." This scheme, one of forced labor and indentured servitude, was the most prominent topic taken on by Scigliano while he served as a legislator. At its simplest, a padrone, or boss (or, literally, "big daddy") would pay for the passage of an Italian to the United States with the promise that the cost of the passage would be paid off over time with a reasonable fee assessed by the padrone. Once an immigrant was ashore, of course, the terms of the agreement were routinely changed; helpless newcomers had little choice but to follow the padrone's edicts. Those orders, as described by an editor for the *Boston Post*, were often severe: "These men, bound by contract to the *padrone*, must buy the necessaries of life from the contractor's store, live in the miserable shanties which he put up, and often submit to the withholding of the greater part of their pay until the end of the season. When that time comes, the padrone contractor may 'skip' and leave them swindled."[62]

Scigliano had long been familiar with the padroni and their scurrilous actions. In 1904 he legislated against the practice, thus bringing it to the attention of the wider Boston public. Local newspapers reported on padroni abuses regularly, and eventually cases beyond Boston's North End were prosecuted by other states and even the US government, which in 1910 outlawed the padrone system altogether. At Scigliano's June 1906 funeral, attended over several days by more than fifteen hundred Italian mourners, he was heralded not only for his willingness to fight for his disaffected community, but also for his raw courage. Then as now, taking on organized crime was not for the faint-hearted. Scigliano's was the largest funeral procession in the history of the North End, and its long, winding route through Boston's damp streets garnered the attention of most of its citizens.[63] Chadwick could not have been at Scigliano's funeral as he was in Europe at the time; but the plight of the Boston Italians could scarcely have escaped his notice.

Chadwick had completed a dramatic scenario for his proposed opera, *The Padrone*, by December 1911. The idea to prepare a libretto himself occurred briefly, but he knew that his skills were limited. He enlisted the help of David K. Stevens, a composer and arranger in his own right. Stevens's best years still lay ahead of him. Although not a total novice, having written scenes here and there for various projects, *The Padrone* was his first crack at an opera.[64] Stevens would later supply the texts for Hadley's cantata *The Golden Prince* (1914), as well as that composer's best-known opera, *Azora* (1917). Working furiously, Stevens delivered the finished libretto of *The Padrone* to Chadwick on February 18, 1912. After reading it Chadwick was delirious with enthusiasm: "So *at last* I have a *real* book for an opera, for here is action, character, scenic interest and rhythmic lines—all I could ask for." However, with uncharacteristic trepidation he added, "And yet now that it is here I feel a strange lack of confidence about tackling it. Is it laziness or?"[65]

Chadwick began to sketch his first musical ideas for *The Padrone* within three days; he completed his initial draft in May. During the intervening months he had attended American writer and novelist William Dean Howells's seventy-fifth birthday at New York City's swanky restaurant Sherry's—a high-society dining venue fully on a par with the Hotel Savoy and the more storied Delmonico's.[66] Chadwick, of course, had known Howells for years through their association in the St. Botolph Club, and was fully aware of his vital role over the past several decades in America's surge to literary realism. It seems unlikely that Howells's birthday celebration could have inspired Chadwick's work in a direction of more intense realism; after all, the libretto had already been crafted, and Chadwick was working feverishly on the score. But the public acknowledgement of Howells may have given Chadwick additional motivation as he forged ahead on his two-act opera, his single nod to realism, or, in Italian, *verismo*. Verismo works tend to depict life among societies humblest, most vulnerable people—the poor and the uneducated—in locales that are often squalid, where residents usually live in an atmosphere of brutality. Opera's earliest and best known examples of verismo include Pietro Mascagni's *Cavalleria rusticana* (1889) and Ruggiero Leoncavallo's *I Pagliacci* (1891).

A number of traits contribute to making *The Padrone* "realistic." Set in the present day, its plot unfolds in a North Boston neighborhood populated with Italian immigrants. This fact alone separates the opera from many early twentieth-century American works that still found their basis in myths, legends, and fairy tales. *The Padrone*, in English, also features smatterings of a vernacular language that was seldom utilized by New England composers of Chadwick's generation, who tended to cling to a rather more sophisticated, somewhat Victorian tone. Also important was Chadwick's careful attention to vocal declamation.[67] Throughout the opera, he took pains to ensure that his setting of American English was to true to contemporary syllabic emphasis. As elementary as that notion seems, a common complaint among audiences and critics of the day was that English was too often set as though it were German or Latin.

Musically, there is much to admire in *The Padrone*. As one would expect of an opera based on Italian subject matter at this time, resemblances to Puccini abound; there are lively orchestrations, feathery textures that remind one of parts of *Sinfonietta*, and of course Chadwick's writing for brass and woodwinds is exceptional, especially in a number of beautiful chordal passages. The vocal creations are also inventive, although *The Padrone* does not contain a surfeit of soaring lyrical passages. One wonders if Chadwick's disdain for the "stars" of the stage, and perhaps an unwillingness to write brilliant arias for them, contributed to his opera's rejection. While there are several striking choral sections, many of them now sound dated. A most effective, even chilling, scene occurs at the end of the opera when the chorus, singing music of a pastoral style, is suddenly confronted with a murder scene.

Chadwick, contented by his progress on the score, arranged to meet with Met conductor Alfred Hertz at Boston's Tavern Club in May 1912 to review *The Padrone*. Hertz entreated Chadwick to write the principal parts in Italian, as he believed that the reception by Met administrators, by which he undoubtedly meant Gatti-Casazza, would be more positive.[68] This Chadwick had originally intended to do, but, besides the fact that his knowledge of the Italian language was elementary—he had picked up a little over the years, but not much—Chadwick concluded that writing *The Padrone* in Italian would be an artistic misstep.

Work on the score continued through the summer at Die Bude. Stevens visited West Chop at least once to inspect Chadwick's musical treatment, and by early autumn the music was far enough along to share with friends and colleagues. He sought Krehbiel's advice on premiering the opera, possibly in New York, and he enlisted Goodrich to play the score for several Boston Opera principals, including the primary music director Arnaldo Conti. The feedback from each of these encounters was positive. An encouraged Chadwick sent a bound piano-vocal version of *The Padrone* to Gatti-Casazza in early December. By month's end he had orchestrated some 150 pages of the score.

If the reception of *The Padrone* from his own circle had been warm, the reaction among the leaders at the Met was tepid. Shortly after Chadwick had sent his music to New York, he visited the city. While there he learned that Gatti-Casazza had sent a letter to his Boston residence that summoned him to a meeting in New York. In an awful twist of fate, Chadwick missed the appointment because he was already in New York at the Academy and Institute of Arts and Sciences annual meeting and did not receive Gatti-Casazza's post. When he learned of the meeting time, Chadwick rushed to see Gatti-Casazza, who had already departed.[69]

Why might Gatti-Casazza have summoned Chadwick? Perhaps he wished to inform Chadwick of his decision not to perform *The Padrone* in person; or perhaps he had changes to suggest before reconsidering it. Unfortunately, we will never be certain. In early January, 1913, Chadwick received a telegram notifying him that *The Padrone* would not be performed at the Met. It was rejected rather curtly and without explanation, but for "conventional editorial phrases."[70] Chadwick was stunned and eventually even angry, but he was undeterred; he continued his work at a brisk pace. *The Padrone* was completed on June 15, 1913 (see table 12.1).

Soon after *The Padrone*'s official rejection, Chadwick received a communication from Krehbiel, who reported that the Met's staff accompanist, Hans Morgenstern, played it through and "reported unfavorably on it." Krehbiel guessed that Gatti-Casazza "disliked the book because it was a drama of life among the humble Italians (and probably too true to life)."[71] Following the Met's summary judgement, one that could only have been a staggering disappointment for him, Chadwick seldom discussed *The Padrone*.

The Met had not shirked its promise to present American opera. Walter Damrosch's *Cyrano de Bergerac*, the libretto for which was written by music critic W. J. Henderson, was performed a month after Chadwick's score was declined. It was the third American opera produced by the Met. By this time Gatti-Casazza had probably already settled on the fourth American opera: Victor Herbert's *Madeleine* would be premiered in January 1914. Chadwick had known that Herbert was peddling this opera to the Met, and after its lukewarm reception he

TABLE 12.1. Chadwick's Works for the Stage

1884	*The Peer and the Pauper* (Comic Operetta)
	Robert Grant; two acts; unpublished
1894	*Tabasco* (Burlesque Opera)
	Robert Ayres Barnet; two acts; 1894 (piano-vocal score)
1892	*A Quiet Lodging* (Operetta)
	Arlo Bates; two acts; unpublished
1900	*Judith* (Lyric Drama)
	William Chauncy Langdon; three acts; 1901 (piano-vocal score)
1903	*Pontius Pilate* (Opera)
	Henry Copley Greene; three acts; incomplete
1910	*Everywoman: Her Pilgrimage in Quest of Love* (Incidental music to the play)
	Walter Browne; five acts; 1911 (piano-vocal score)
1913	*The Padrone* (Opera)
	David Kilburn Stevens; two acts; unpublished
	(piano-vocal score prepared in 1995)
1917	*Love's Sacrifice* (Pastoral Opera)
	David Kilburn Stevens; one act; 1917 (piano-vocal score)

had hard feelings. Herbert's trifling work, Chadwick undoubtedly thought, had taken the spot that might have been filled by *The Padrone*.

The Padrone's story line revolves around Marta and her two daughters, Francesca and Marietta, a family of immigrants from the Italian village of Trapani who are indentured to Catani, the neighborhood padrone. As the first act begins, in Catani's restaurant, where the family works, Marietta and Dino, a customer, are found flirting. Dino is entranced with Marietta and later discusses her with Francesca, who explains to him that Marietta is promised to another, Marco, from their hometown. Marietta has saved money for Marco's passage to America from her meager earnings as a street tambourine player for Catani, who undoubtedly would not have been pleased to learn that she was spending her money on things other than repaying her debt to him. Catani learns of Marietta's engagement only when she is being congratulated by customers of the restaurant. Having planned to pursue Marietta himself, Catani is angry to hear of her plans to wed. When Marietta refuses to be deterred, Catani pledges to make her his own at any cost. Later, when Francesca reveals to Catani that Marco has a criminal record in Italy, Catani makes plans to alert immigration authorities, who will halt Marco's entry into the US.

Act 2 begins on Boston's docks, where Marietta awaits the arrival of her beloved Marco. But at Catani's insistence, Francesca, who once had been Marco's lover and who is increasingly jealous of Marietta and Marco's plans, informs officials of Marco's felonious past. Marco is promptly detained, and, upon learning about his arrest and Catani's dastardly involvement, Marietta flies into a rage. She seizes a knife and plunges it into Catani as a stunned crowd looks on in fearful disbelief.

The Padrone is a shocker not only for its vicious public murder (killing and death, of course, are common fare in later opera), but also for its portrayal of a seamy and largely unnoticed portion of Boston. Like Stephen Crane's important realist novella, *Maggie, a Girl of the Streets* (1892), which languished briefly until it was "discovered" by William Dean Howells, there was no moral to the story of *The Padrone*. There were no admonitions against the impoverished immigrants or uplifting conclusions that could edify an emotionally overwhelmed audience.[72] There was simply servitude. And despair. And death. This represents a huge artistic leap for Chadwick, whose collaboration with Walter Browne on *Everywoman* was a diametric opposite to this project. *Everywoman*, a somewhat preachy Victorian morality play, could still draw an audience ten years into the new century. It does not, however, represent the cusp of a new artistic movement, nor does it carry the aesthetic weight of *The Padrone*. Unfortunately for its composer, there was no operatic Howells, nor a revered leader of an American opera house who, having recognized its relationship to the nation's most current and potent literary style, might advocate for Chadwick's opera.

The Padrone represents several pivotal accomplishments for both Chadwick and for the history of American opera. First, by simply utilizing an Italian scenario and musical style, he managed to link *The Padrone* to a modern strain of Italian opera. Of course, that linkage might have been stronger had Chadwick heeded Hertz's advice to write Italian dialogue. Second, by embracing the Italian, he eschewed the Germanism that was so often encountered not only on the American operatic stage but also in the concert hall. (We should not forget that Chadwick's most famous work during his lifetime was the very German concert overture, *Melpomene*.) In *The Padrone*, Chadwick also rejected any hints of the American nationalism that continued to gain ground among younger American composers; as we have seen, nationalism affected Chadwick only briefly. Finally, Chadwick loaned his voice to the current of realism that was storming the arts in this period, although his participation in the movement—similar to his involvement in nationalism—was short-lived.

Chadwick's interest in realism fell off following *The Padrone*. At least one comment in his writings reveals him to have been, at best, ambivalent about the movement. Just a few months after he had completed his opera, he heard a fine BSO performance of Brahms's *Tragic* Overture. Lauding the high drama in this score, Chadwick observed that "at no point in it does Brahms descend to realism; his art is too great for that."[73]

Chadwick took up *The Padrone* again in 1919 when he began a correspondence with Frederick Stock, who promised to share the libretto with Cleofonte Campanini, the powerful principal conductor and managing director of the Chicago Opera Company. Stock also promised to consult personally with Campanini on *The Padrone*, but it is not possible to know whether he was able to honor his pledge.[74] Campanini was Italian, of course, and if Gatti-Casazza had reservations about presenting his countrymen in an unseemly light, the Chicago opera leader may have felt the same way. In any event, a performance in the Windy City was not forthcoming, and that was the last time that Chadwick mentioned his operatic masterpiece in writing.

The Padrone, finally staged in 1995 at Connecticut's Thomaston Opera House, is far removed from Chadwick's other dramatic works. *Judith*, for all its allure, is stylistically of the nineteenth century, and that is certainly true of the stage works that pre-date *Judith*. *The Padrone* is emphatically modern not so much in its technical apparatus, but in its character. The reserve and dignity that had been central to Chadwick's aesthetic had been, if not smashed, at least jarred. Few who knew Chadwick's musical style up to this point would have recognized his imagination at play, for it marked a distinct departure from the principles that had motivated him his entire life. On the other hand, given that Boston's seams were bursting with immigrants, and crime, poverty, and desperation were noticeably on the rise, *The Padrone* is plainly a product of its tumultuous time. It reflects drastic changes, to both Chadwick's sheltered Back Bay surroundings and in the art of music, that he had experienced firsthand over the past decade.

And Chadwick's future promised even more turbulent change.

"We Live on *Hope*"
Chadwick's Response to the Great War
1914–1919

Musical Supremacy

On June 28, 1914, Archduke Franz Ferdinand, the nephew of Emperor Franz Joseph, leader of the Austro-Hungarian empire, was assassinated in Sarajevo while carrying out duties as the Inspector General of his uncle's army. That event provided a pretext for what turned out to be the start of World War I, also known as The Great War. Franz Ferdinand's murder was but one more episode in a complicated, ongoing European struggle that pitted the militaristic "Central Powers"—Germany and Austria-Hungary—against the "Allies"—Russia, France, and Britain.[1] The intensifying European conflict would change the way the world thought about war. Not only would it introduce hideous new weapons and technologies into battle, including submarines, flamethrowers, chemical weapons, and others, but the brutality, the sheer number of casualties, would be on a scale not seen in modern times.

For a variety of reasons, the United States wanted nothing to do with "Europe's war." Historian Barbara Tuchman reflected that the prevailing American attitude was "one of self-congratulation that it was none of our affair."[2] A muddled, far away matter, most Americans saw no need to involve the nation in it. Up to this time, the US had not asserted itself militarily on the world stage, and by and large the administration of President Woodrow Wilson was, if not completely isolationist, at least strongly against intervention. For the time being, America would remain neutral.

But that did not mean that America was not impacted; in fact, art music in America was greatly affected. The United States had long been fertile ground for European orchestral musicians, virtuosi, and opera singers who were intent not only on performing in America's major cities and oftentimes riding the rails of the nation's many western and southern performing circuits, but also taking advantage of an increasing willingness on the part of Americans to pay for music. Moreover, the outbreak of the Great War brought foreign artists to the United States in droves, and many never returned to their homelands. Among them one may count many famous artists; Fritz Kreisler, who was renowned as a violinist but was also a gifted composer, arrived in 1914, and Ernest Bloch, praised for his compositions on Jewish themes, in 1916. Countless others of more modest celebrity may be listed among their ranks.

As war burgeoned, some Americans saw in it the possibility of a more potent artistic benefit to the United States than the mere influx of foreign musicians. In an early statement of what would become a crescendoing theme, the *New York Times* ran an opinion by William Sloane Coffin, the respected leader of the city's Metropolitan Museum of Art. With regard to the visual arts, Coffin thought that "the Great War in Europe gives New York an opportunity to become the great art center of the world," and that "the setback to art in Europe will serve as an impetus to American artists."[3] The very next day American baritone Oscar Seagle concurred in a *New York Times* letter to the editor that the "musical supremacy" so desired by Americans could now be achieved. According to Seagle, by October—a mere four months into the war—"that thing we call artistic atmosphere is . . . smashed beyond all hope of immediate recovery" in Europe. Although Seagle had just returned to the US from Sussex, England, where he reported the calm was "scarcely marred," he nevertheless thought that "there are many favorable signs, but if we could only do something in this, the year of our greatest opportunity, if we could bring the American mind to understand that now is the time to place our imprint upon art, to make it as much our own as possible."[4]

By 1916, just two years after the comments offered by Coffin and Seagle, critic Frederick H. Martens could confirm that their hopes had come to fruition. "The third year of the European War," he wrote,

> still bears witness to the survival of strenuous musical endeavor in the countries engaged in the contest: concerts are given, operas are produced; trench-operettas and musical *vaudevilles* reflect its persistence on the very scene of the conflict. Yet the conscription of nations *en masse* and the shifting of the European financial and economic balance to this country have not been without effect. The decreased creative energy in music in Europe has stimulated the creative output in America; recitals and concerts have been more frequent, and a general impetus has been given to composition. . . . In an educational sense the war has done much to break traditions of musical dependence on Europe which had been already rudely shaken before it began.[5]

Although they remained officially neutral, Americans for the most part were disgusted by the spectacle of war in Europe and especially by the atrocities committed by the Germans. By August and early September 1914, the Germans had barreled their way through Belgium, killing thousands of Allied soldiers at the battles of the Sambre, Mons, and the Marne; Germany's military sites were aimed squarely at Paris. These barbarous events compelled the learned, prolific, and celebrated professor of dramatic literature at Columbia University, Brander Matthews, to write a letter to the *New York Times* in which he skewered the antagonists. "Nations are never accepted by other nations at their own valuation," Matthews insisted,

> and the Germans need not be surprised that we are astonished to find them asserting their natural self-appreciation, with the apparent expectation that it will pass unchallenged. The world owes a debt to modern Germany beyond all question, but this is far less than the debt owed to England and to France. It would be interesting if some German, speaking with authority, should now be moved to explain to us Americans the reasons which underlie the insistent assertion of the superiority of German civilization. Within the past few weeks, we have been forced to gaze at certain of the less pleasant aspects of the German character; and we have been made to see that the militarism of the Germans is in absolute contradiction to the preaching and to the practice of the great Goethe to whom they proudly point as the ultimate representative of German culture.[6]

Most Americans would have agreed. For his part, Chadwick read the letter and immediately responded to Matthews, who had become a friend and correspondent: "I read your article on Germans in the New York Times with *glee*, and I must tell you that I have never seen a keener arraignment of German character than you have expressed in your article. . . . To my mind your last paragraph sums up the whole matter."[7] (Chadwick admired Matthews. When, one month later, Mathews gave a speech in honor of Henry Higginson, Chadwick concluded that "everything that he says or writes is so convincing that it is not easy to disagree with him with any success."[8])

Chadwick had certainly been among those hoping for America's musical supremacy, but his growing personal animosity toward German aggression could not at first have been easy for him to admit. He harbored an abiding affection—forged during his impressionable youth—for Germany and the German people, especially Jadassohn and the southern Germans. And not only were his teachers German, but his idols and musical models tended to be German, as well. But Chadwick had long been distressed by Germany's expanding militarism, and he was nauseated by its violent behavior. Some thought that the war in Europe would be short-lived, but several months into it the predictions of a brief skirmish were rapidly giving way to the sense that this would be a protracted, onerous conflict.

Despite his love of Germany, as Europe's war plodded on, Chadwick's stance against the Germans was becoming remarkably resolute.

Tam O'Shanter (1915)

Nine days after Matthews's scathing letter had appeared in the *New York Times*, Chadwick began scoring what would be his most extensive and complex, but in many ways also his most accessible, orchestral composition.[9] *Tam O'Shanter* is a "symphonic ballade" based on the famous poem *Alloway Kirk, or Tam O'Shanter: A Tale* (1791) by Scottish poet Robert Burns (1759–1796). Naturally, given the Scottish pedigree of Burns's poem, Chadwick's *Tam* has a similar ethnic flavor. He had worked with British stylizations before, in his Second Symphony and in several lesser-known works, including the "Irish ballad" *Aghadoe*, completed in 1910 at West Chop. Chadwick was delighted with this piece; following its premiere in 1911 with alto Lilla Ormond (who was also the dedicatee) and conductor Max Fiedler leading the Boston Symphony Orchestra, the composer wrote, "After I am dead someone will discover this piece and make a hit with it."[10] Lamentably, this has not yet happened, but it is something to hope for; Chadwick's light orchestrations and characteristic rhythms are here coupled with a genuinely engaging tale that progresses from the pastoral to the treacherous in the village of Aghadoe ("pronounced approximately like the German 'Ach-du,'" according to a note on the published score[11]). Chadwick had also experimented with a number of "Irish ditties," as he called them, that included the strongly Celtic-flavored songs "Larry O'Toole," "The Lady of the Leith," "Nora McNally," and "The Recruit," which were published together in 1910 as *Four Irish Songs*.[12]

Tam O'Shanter is crafted for a large, modern orchestra of three flutes plus piccolo, a pair of oboes, English horn, three clarinets (one in D), a bass clarinet, two bassoons, four horns, three trumpets, three trombones, a tuba, an extensive percussion battery, harp and strings. Chadwick completed its scoring in just under four months on January 23, 1915, an amazingly short span of time. Perhaps as an indication of their shared British heritage, he dedicated this composition to Horatio Parker.

It has been widely thought that *Tam O'Shanter* unfolds in an episodic form. Yellin described it as a series of six programmatic episodes or "tableaux" that reflect scenes in Burns's work: "(1) the storm; (2) Tam O'Shanter in the storm; (3) trotting homeward past Kirk Alloway; (4) Tam's observation of the witches' revels; and (5) the witches' chase. The sixth section is the coda, which is constructed upon different principles."[13] (Yellin's analysis does not indicate by measure numbers where the various episodes begin and end.) Another musicologist,

TABLE 13.1. The Form of *Tam O'Shanter*

	Introduction	Exposition			Development	Recapitulation	Coda
Part:		I			II		
Section:		1	2		3	4	
Theme:	O	P	S	N	"Scottish dances"	P, S, N	K
Key:		C	f-sharp	b-flat	d		G-flat	C
Measure:	1		66	133	161	201	480	538

Hon-Lun Helan Yang, makes the case for seven episodes.[14] Chadwick clearly informs us that he intended to reflect the action of Burns's great poem, and has done so in thrilling fashion. But I believe that in fact Chadwick's creation is not as episodic as is often supposed. *Tam O'Shanter* bears the outlines of a highly developed variety of sonata form and again demonstrates that Chadwick was able to venture into new areas of expression even as he was unable to leave traditional forms very far behind.

In his extensive preface to the score, Chadwick himself outlines the scenes, although nowhere does he state that he is utilizing sonata form as his underlying model (see table 13.1). Following "a short and stormy introduction" (m. 1), Tam's theme—a bouncy, optimistic, even naïve pentatonic melody—is presented in the horns in C major, the principal key, beginning the exposition (P, m. 66). In one of the cleverest strokes in the piece, the composer sets the secondary theme (S, m. 133) not in the expected dominant key, but in the key of F-sharp minor, related to Tam's C-major theme by a tritone. The tritone relationship of an augmented fourth has long been considered harsh, ignoble, and even evil. Perhaps more surprising is the approach to the secondary theme, in which Chadwick brings into play a stark, German augmented-sixth chord (Bb—D—F—G♯; m. 120), just a dozen measures before the new theme is sounded. Might Chadwick's use of this chord—one that he did not utilize often—to introduce the "wicked" secondary theme indicate his animosity toward the Germans? Chadwick then introduces a new theme (N, m. 161) that represents Kirk Alloway (Alloway Church); it is a noble chorale melody based, according to critic Henry Krehbiel, on a Thomas Ravenscroft hymn tune melody called "Martyrs."[15] It is sounded by the trombones, now in the distant key of B-flat minor.

In one of the more captivating development sections in American music literature, Chadwick presents what may be best described as a protracted fantasy, "a series of dances very much in the Scottish style" (m. 201).[16] Here Chadwick forgoes the expected treatment of the conventional development section. Nowhere do we find the typical rhythmic and harmonic manipulation of motives derived from earlier themes, but rather a succession of dances, some of them rather harrowing and all of them strongly seasoned with Gaelic, an "orgy" that depicts witches reveling in the church. This development area comprises five sub-sections, each in minor keys and each featuring different solo instruments or instrumental groups. Beginning with a fiddle tune played by the viola (D minor, m. 211), the music goes on to feature the upper woodwinds and brass playing the Dies irae, a theme associated with death (G minor, m. 265); the violins (C minor, m. 325); the woodwinds and trumpets (C-sharp minor, m. 381); and a final, more transitional portion in A minor, the relative minor to the C major tonic key.

A recapitulation (m. 480), or what Chadwick called "a short interlude of plaintive character," brings back expected hints of Tam's theme, now in G-flat major, an enharmonic relative to the earlier tritone, F-sharp. "But here it no longer depicts the carousals of the drunken Highlanders," the composer related, rather. "it is transformed into a quiet sustained melody with simple harmonizing, purely lyrical in expression" until longer statements of both Tam's theme and the Kirk Alloway theme are heard (mm. 513 and 523, respectively) alongside snippets of the witches' reels in "a rather extended close." The recapitulation marks the first area of major-key tonality encountered since the initial statement of Tam's theme in the exposition.

Chadwick explained that "the piece ends very quietly with a reminiscence of the Tam O'Shanter theme," a coda in C major (m. 538). He neglected to add that the coda is marvelously tinted with several colorful chord choices including E-flat major (m. 551) and a cadential half-diminished seventh chord (m. 558), harmonies that lend an attractive, piquant effect.

Chadwick's application of sonata style in *Tam O'Shanter* presents two issues that have contributed to its misreading as merely an episodic form. First, Chadwick eschewed traditional development of his ideas through the harmonic twists and thematic transformations expected in sonata form—including fugato, which is present in many of his larger orchestral compositions—opting instead for the dance sequence. While the "development" section is stirring in its own right—by virtue of the furious character of the dances and their utterly entrancing Scottishness—it fails to create the tension that is conventionally resolved by the appearance of the recapitulation. That brings up the second concern, namely that the recapitulation is neither clear nor strong in terms of either the return to the tonic key or the return of the principal theme. It is already apparent that *Tam O'Shanter*'s cohesiveness as a sonata form is not attributable to its harmonic unity but to its thematic content. The recapitulation does not give a strong and clear reaffirmation of Tam's theme, and the result is a conclusion that is somewhat less obvious than might have been possible otherwise. And, not unlike *Adonais*, *Tam*'s appeal to conductors has undoubtedly suffered as a result of its reposeful close. But we are left with the masterpiece Chadwick has given us, and he clearly demonstrated in *Tam O'Shanter* that he continued to grow as an artist. While he did not say farewell to sonata form, he proved that it was remarkably pliable and still an eminently suitable vehicle for expression.

The expansion of the boundaries of form serves to make *Tam O'Shanter* a compelling, meaningful, and important work in the American canon. Moreover, Chadwick reinterpreted the tale to create a document of the era; *Tam O'Shanter* may readily be considered a metaphor for war. Burns's poem depicts a young naïf who leaves a warm, comfortable location only to gallop headlong into a storm through a strange, albeit recognizable, world where he encounters a ghoulish and potentially violent horde that chases him to the very brink of his existence. Once a close call is averted, Tam is left to make his way back in relative calm and quiet. This effectively parallels the image of young men leaving the safety of home to trudge off to war where they meet the enemy in battle before returning.

Although the US government was still neutral on the topic of the war, the European conflict was on the minds of Americans from its first shots, as Matthews's essay indicated. Chadwick was deeply affected by the contrast of his own youthful and sometimes even idyllic experiences in Leipzig and Munich and the warmongering that was now perceived as the chief characteristic of German culture in the first quarter of the twentieth century. With *Tam*, Chadwick left far behind his penchant for abstract orchestral music and the dignified Hellenism that had stimulated him just a dozen years earlier. By choosing Burns's poem as his inspiration, he asserted his own British lineage at a time when he and many of his colleagues struggled to redefine the nature of their relationship to Germany.

Tam O'Shanter was premiered on June 3, 1915, at the Norfolk Festival's Music Shed, a place where by now Chadwick felt very much at home. As a tribute to his close relationship with Stoeckel and the festival, Chadwick offered his work free of charge. Before long, *Tam* had been programmed for ten sets of performances around the United States, by the symphony orchestras of Minneapolis, Chicago, Saint Louis, New York, and Boston. The reviews were roundly favorable. While many lauded the composition for its close connection to Burns's poem, others thought its extra-musical references unnecessary. *Chicago Tribune* critic Eric De Lamarter considered it "a sturdy, fascinating creation. It stands on its own as absolute music, as descriptive music, and as a sort of sardonic humor. It is [a] tribute to the mastery of its composer."[17] To Louis C. Elson it was "the most truly picturesque and dramatic [composition] that we can recall in the

American repertoire. . . . *Tam O'Shanter* is undoubtedly one of the very best of American works and can hold its own with the best European symphonic poem."[18] With one exception, critics avoided the notion that *Tam O'Shanter* could somehow represent an artistic response to the war. In what can only be called an oblique hint at the current struggle, the reviewer for the *Minneapolis Tribune* sensed in Chadwick's score "moral contemplations . . . upon the error of human ways and their dire consequences."[19]

But tension among the audience at Norfolk's Music Shed must have been running high. In May, less than one month before *Tam*'s premiere, a German u-20 submarine had launched a torpedo at the Cunard Steamship Company passenger vessel *Lusitania* off the coast of Ireland. Killed were 1,201 innocent travelers, over half of those passengers on board. Among the dead were 128 Americans.[20]

San Francisco's Panama-Pacific International Exposition (1915)

The tragedy of the *Lusitania* could not halt the long-planned and already-begun celebration in San Francisco, the Panama-Pacific International Exposition, which had commenced on February 20 and would continue until December 4. The exposition celebrated the 1914 completion of the Panama Canal; some accounts also linked the event to the four hundredth anniversary of Balboa's discovery of the Pacific Ocean, but that sidelight is difficult to locate in official exposition publications. The canal was the greatest engineering feat of the era and still ranks as a noteworthy achievement of any age. Costing $352 million and well over five thousand lives, it connected east and west, Atlantic and Pacific, and rendered the lengthy and treacherous shipping route around the southern tip of South America unnecessary.[21]

Chadwick set off for California in June, accompanied by Ida May and former NEC composition student Mabel Daniels, in another of his many trips across the United States (see Appendix 3). Daniels, an NEC standout, was currently the head of the music department at Simmons College, and her renown as a composer was steadily on the rise. The trio did not go directly to San Francisco; their first destination was Los Angeles, to participate in the ninth biennial Festival of American Music under the aegis of the National Federation of Music Clubs. The festival featured four concerts on a single day, June 30, starting at 1:00 p.m.; Chadwick conducted his own music, three movements from the *Symphonic Sketches* ("Hobgoblin" was omitted), with the Los Angeles Symphony Orchestra at the 8:00 p.m. performance at Trinity Auditorium.

The festival's hallmark event, however, was the premiere performance of Horatio Parker's new opera, *Fairyland*, which won the ten-thousand-dollar prize offered by the federation. It was Parker's second prize-winning opera, and if Chadwick had been mildly envious of Parker when the latter's *Mona* won the Metropolitan Opera's ten-thousand-dollar prize, now he was positively bursting with jealousy. When Chadwick first learned that *Fairyland* had won the coveted prize, he remarked that, based on rumors he had heard, the work would never see the light of day because the federation lacked both facilities and money.[22] But performed it was; and while *Fairyland* got off to a rocky start at rehearsals, its premiere went remarkably well. The orchestra, soloists, and chorus performed wonderfully under Alfred Hertz's direction, and the packed houses were exceptionally responsive.

Parker's triumph disgusted Chadwick. The judges for the contest—wholly unqualified in Chadwick's opinion—were Munich-trained Adolf Weidig, a composer and administrator at Chicago's American Conservatory of Music, San Francisco organist Wallace Sabine, and Charles Seeger, a Harvard man who was now chairman of the music department at the University of California at Berkeley. They were charged with the evaluation of the fifty-four scores received. Chadwick learned from one of them that Seeger had preemptively and publicly announced the award in Parker's favor without having consulted with his fellow panelists. This left Weidig and Sabine embarrassed and paralyzed, but for some unknown reason they decided against confronting Seeger on the matter. "It seems incredible," Chadwick grumbled, "that the judges should have allowed such a piece of outrageous injustice to be perpetrated."[23] Chadwick despised Seeger's scurrilousness; it mattered little to him that the competition winner was his former pupil, still his closest friend. To make matters worse, Chadwick's informant even claimed that Seeger had not actually reviewed all the submitted scores; having made his choice, he stopped once he had identified Parker's opera.

As for *Fairyland*'s artistic merits, Chadwick considered some lines "poetic enough in an affected highbrow way," but generally the drama's confusing twists and turns made it difficult to follow.[24] Much of the blame he laid on Brian Hooker's inept libretto, but he also thought that Parker's music had again missed the mark, especially in terms of dramatic pacing. While some critics exclaimed that *Fairyland* had ushered in "a new American school," Chadwick found it simply "labored and dull."[25]

With yet another unsavory operatic episode behind him, Chadwick and Ida May departed for a brief visit to San Diego before embarking on their journey north to San Francisco. Excitement was slowly beginning to build, for the musical activities at the Panama-Pacific Exposition promised to be the grandest since the Chicago World's Fair of 1892.

The Panama-Pacific Exposition had been years in the making. Following a long and rancorous competitive bidding process for the right to host the exposition—New Orleans had been the other leading contender—this event was the last of the great World's Fair–style spectacles. Having been granted presenting authority by President William Howard Taft, San Francisco began construction of the fairgrounds in January 1913. The exposition occupied 635 acres along a three-mile stretch of the bay waterfront, which, in some portions, was a half-mile wide. As with other World's Fairs, massive and elaborately adorned buildings were raised. The major sites included the still-standing Palace of Fine Arts, the basilica-like Palace of Horticulture, and the exposition's centerpiece structure, the Tower of Jewels, which hovered 435 feet above the proceedings, scores of thousands of "Novagems," or colored-glass crystals ("jewels"), hanging from virtually every available surface. When the building was illuminated at night it produced a ravishing effect.[26]

Musical events were held at Festival Hall, a squat, French-inspired building that was easily distinguishable from most of the others, among which the Greco-Roman style of architecture predominated. Festival Hall was easy to find; topped with minarets and covered with statuary, it was also flanked by two decorative Italian towers and was fronted by the Court of Flowers, an impressive flora-laden boulevard that led directly to the hall entrance. Besides paying tribute to the completion of the canal, the exposition, like all the World's Fairs before it, sought to exalt and display the achievements of mankind in all endeavors. Spectators could view innovations in electricity and transportation, ethnological exhibits, a huge number of sporting events and, of course, the arts. And there was another purpose behind the exposition. San Francisco's city leaders sought to showcase their city and its remarkable recovery in the aftermath of the devastating and deadly 1906 earthquake. Their efforts can only be judged a success—when all was said and done, the exposition had accommodated eighteen million visitors.

Chadwick traveled to the exhibition to conduct on "American Composers' Day" (August 1, 1915). That day was but one of scores of such special recognition days, which included "Baptist Day" (June 1), "Loganberry Day" (July 29), "Non-Smokers' Protective League of America Day" (July 15), and "National Society of Americans of Royal Descent Day" (July 27). In something of a postsundown oddity, there was even a "March-King Night" (July 23), a celebration of the immeasurable contribution to American music of John Philip Sousa.

Chadwick's longtime acquaintance George W. Stewart had been enlisted as the Exposition Musical Director. In that capacity he did a marvelous job of luring

FIGURE 13.1. Chadwick (*center*) with an unidentified entourage in California, 1915. Courtesy of New England Conservatory, Boston.

talent—local, national, and international—to San Francisco and providing them numerous performance opportunities (see figure 13.1). One writer noted that "a large part of the regular daily program, indeed, is devoted to music, ten or a dozen concerts going on every day."[27] French composer Camille Saint-Saëns, perhaps the biggest celebrity invited to attend, offered his composition *Hail California* to the exposition. Scored for military band, orchestra, and organ, it is a celebratory work that the composer may well have considered a trifle, for he did not even assign to it an opus number. Sousa's band was featured prominently, and his *Panama March* was composed for the event. Muck arrived with his Boston Symphony Orchestra in tow. And Festival Hall also hosted daily organ recitals in the main venue, which seated three thousand people.

American Composers' Day, a tribute to the works and triumphs of native-born composers, was to be one of the major musical events of the exposition. A crowd numbering two thousand—more than Chadwick expected[28]—gathered to hear the music, but the program lineup was disappointing. Works by Parker

FIGURE 13.2.
Chadwick and Henry Hadley at Bohemian Grove in San Francisco, California, 1915. Courtesy of New England Conservatory, Boston.

and Beach were performed, and Chadwick conducted his own *Melpomene* and *Euterpe* overtures. But the remainder of the concert featured music by relative unknowns. Ernest Kroeger's four-movement suite *Lalla Roohk* was on the program, as were Carl Busch's tone poem *Minnehaha's Vision*, Mabel Daniels's *The Desolate City* for baritone and orchestra, and the prelude from W. J. McCoy's opera *Egypt*. "On the whole," Chadwick exhorted, "the concert was not a powerful argument in favor of American composition. It by no means represented the best that has been done, comprising as it did only the composers who happened to be on the ground. Some who are in the ground would have added distinction to it."[29] Among those "in the ground" were Paine, MacDowell, Dudley Buck, Templeton Strong, and other venerable, deceased American composers whom Chadwick admired. It was surely obvious to sophisticated listeners that the most consequential living American composers—Converse, Carpenter, Hadley, Loeffler, and Stock—were missing from an auspicious occasion.

Following the disappointment of the musical fare at the Panama-Pacific Exposition, Chadwick and Ida May traveled to the renowned redwood grove owned by the San Francisco Bohemian Club (see figure 13.2) for al fresco rehearsals and a performance of *Euterpe*, before they commenced the long journey home. They had mapped out a circuitous return route to Boston, one that would take them north through Portland, Oregon, to Seattle and then on to Vancouver.

Along the way, while still in California, the Chadwicks were guests of publishing baron William Randolph Hearst (1863–1951) and his wife, Millicent Veronica Willson, at their Castle Crags home near Mount Shasta. Stewart had introduced the Chadwicks to Mrs. Hearst a month earlier in San Francisco, when they were invited to stay at the couple's famous residence, Hacienda del Pozo de Verona, in Pleasanton. Always affected by landscapes, Chadwick later remembered the many scenes of natural beauty he encountered—Banff, Lake Louise, and other unique locations—in fine detail. Since leaving Boston, he had spent little time thinking about music. The exposition and its associated diversions provided a much needed, if only temporary, distraction from the stress and anxiety that attended Europe's war. They did not, however, inspire him to compose.

"Nothing to Write": Boston and Muck Again

When Chadwick returned to Boston from the west, he found that life was unexpectedly normal. Much to his surprise, the war had not stifled enrollment at NEC. On the contrary, perhaps because music students were not able to travel abroad safely, enrollment for the new academic year was robust. Organ instructor Henry Dunham observed that the corridors of NEC "were nearly as full of young life as ever. I had about as many pupils as usual, only more women."[30] The number of applications from artists who wished to teach at NEC was also high, due to the limited opportunities for European music instructors in Europe. But if activities at NEC were thankfully normal, even routine, Chadwick's lack of compositional inspiration was hugely bothersome to him. As early as 1914, following his participation in a local saengerfest, Chadwick wondered why he so enjoyed singing in a chorus. "It is about all the musical expression of which I seem to be capable in these days."[31] Within two years he lamented that "for the first time since I can remember I find myself with nothing to write," and indeed very little composition was accomplished in 1916.[32] Chadwick had not suffered a slow creative period since he returned from Germany in 1879, and his current inability to summon energy—let alone inspiration—depressed him.

Chadwick kept a close eye on political and military events, and as they unfolded they began to weigh heavily upon him. He possessed an uncanny ability to see where this conflict was headed, and he already predicted a number of consequences; he even suggested that entry into it by the United States was inevitable. Chadwick was not alone, of course; equally reprehensible in the eyes of Americans to the sinking of the *Lusitania* was the incarceration into internment camps of thousands of prisoners following the German invasion of Belgium in 1916.[33] It was an action than met with enormous American protest.

If 1916 was not a year for musical creation, Chadwick managed to remain busy with matters that required less focus than composing. Musical leaders at the Minneapolis Symphony Orchestra invited him to conduct *Tam O'Shanter* at a January concert. A performance in Chicago was also arranged. The trip, an uncomfortable and arduous winter journey, was made more palatable by a visit to Ida May's brother, Clarence Brooks, who resided with his family in Duluth, and whom she had not seen for over three decades.

Another happy diversion was provided by Chadwick's friend and fellow Duveneck Boy, artist Joseph Rodefor DeCamp, who began his famous oil portrait of Chadwick at this time. DeCamp was recognized as the finest portrait artist in the US, and he produced many of them. This project gave the two men, both of whom were affable characters, a chance to relive old times, swap stories, sing, and, less often, discuss current events.[34]

The same year a number of mostly Harvard men, under the leadership of Walter Spaulding, founded a Composers' Club. Meant to provide a forum for composers to gather for a freewheeling discussion of new music, it provided Chadwick with an excellent counterpoint to his involvement with the more staid and far less musical Thursday Evening Club. Chadwick attended several initial organizational meetings and was urged, as was Charles Martin Loeffler, to be the first president. Loeffler flatly said no, and Chadwick refused at first, but eventually relented: "it is a good cause and I shall help it along until I see some good reason for not so doing. I suspect that there are some turbulent elements in the club already."[35] Over several difficult months the club offered Chadwick an opportunity to assess works by the younger generation of composers and to advise them, although by 1917 the club lacked direction and needed to expand "beyond a little group of Harvard men who compose occasionally" if it was going to be a meaningful enterprise. Chadwick probably was not enthusiastic about the fairly strict administration of the club, which included a constitution and by-laws; meetings even needed to have a quorum. About the membership—which included William Clifford Heilman, Edward Burlingame Hill, Chalmers Clifton, Percy Atherton, Fred Converse, and others—Chadwick tartly noted that "the men who write the least do the most talking."[36] While the club offered him a distraction and musical camaraderie at a time when he needed it, Chadwick resigned in 1917, although he continued to attend meetings well into the 1920s.

As the war worsened, Chadwick avoided discussions of current events. The war created difficulties for American composers and musicians, legions of whom had studied in Germany and had passed most of their lives with a deep reverence for German music and culture. Nowhere was this truer than in Boston. However, citizens of the US who were not residents of coastal and seafaring areas were more ambivalent, for the cause of the nation's entry into the war was closely linked to Germany's closure of America-to-Europe shipping lanes. Bostonians, who knew firsthand the natural dangers of crossing the Atlantic, were willing to fight foreign aggressors who sought to make passage even more treacherous. The sinking of the *Lusitania* had provoked national outrage, and, but for the obstinate reticence of President Wilson, American involvement in the war likely would have come shortly after that attack.

But the *Lusitania* was not an American ship; it was British. That fact, a feeble one to many of Wilson's critics, helped the president to dodge the specter of war.[37] To stem the deaths of more Americans, the congress urged Wilson to forbid travel by Americans on British liners, but the president would have none of what clearly amounted to an abridgement of a citizen's right to move about freely. After many more U-boat attacks, Wilson finally caved in to demands that he threaten to break off diplomatic relations with the Germans. As a result, the Germans ceased U-boat operations in the Atlantic in May 1916.

It would not last. The Germans renewed their commitment to submarine warfare in January 1917, and when, a month later, President Wilson learned of it, he refused to believe it. But two mighty dilemmas forced his hand. First, the Zimmermann telegram revealed the plot crafted by the Germans to involve Mexico on their side in the event that America should declare war on Germany. For its aid to the Germans, the Mexican government was promised the return of its formerly held territories, New Mexico, Texas, and Arizona. Second, in March 1917 Wilson got word that three American merchant ships had been torpedoed with disastrous results. He immediately recognized that he could no longer shrink from the prospect of military engagement. On April 6, 1917, President Wilson signed a declaration of war against Germany; in doing so he was now siding with popular sentiment in the US, for the American populace had grown rabidly anti-German. Within one month of Wilson's declaration, Noël Chadwick trekked to Boston's navy yard to enlist for a four-year hitch in the United States Naval Reserve. "How can one think of music," his father asked forlornly, "when the future holds such dreadful possibilities?"[38]

The Chadwicks were already more familiar with the military than they wished. Theodore had enlisted in the First Regimental Field Artillery unit of the National Guard two years earlier, and in the summer of 1916 that duty kept him frequently away from home; in June war with Mexico seemed imminent, and Theodore was shipped off to Texas.[39] Perhaps remembering his father's objection to his own career desires, Chadwick did not discourage Theodore from joining the armed service; in fact he considered the National Guard a good alternative to a branch that might see more combat.[40] In October, his service in the Guard temporarily over, Theodore had begun a new job close to home; it was one that Chadwick thought would suffice "until war begins."[41] By May 1917 Theodore had been commissioned as second lieutenant, but he remained in the National Guard, even as hundreds of other young Boston men were leaving town for basic training in the regular army. Theodore's talents lay in administration, planning, and recruiting. Following a summer promotion, he traveled daily to Lawrence, where, as the Captain of Battery B, he organized the newly established Second Field Artillery regiment.

Noël's academic achievements had never matched Theodore's. His poor marks had been a matter of some consternation to his father for years, and he dropped out of Harvard in 1914.[42] Chadwick recognized Noël's decided preference for outdoor activities and a far greater tolerance for risk than Theodore possessed. Noël began his active service on August 31 following his certification for flying balloons, airplanes, and dirigibles.[43] By October 26, 1917, he was declared fully qualified for aviation duty, and his service in the Naval Reserve was terminated. The following month he was commissioned as an Ensign in the US Naval Reserve Flying Force at the Dirigible School of the Goodyear Tire & Rubber Company at Akron, Ohio, where he had already reported for further training.[44]

As if his sons' military careers were not weighing on him heavily enough, November 1917 would bring more anguish to Chadwick and musical Boston. Anti-Germanism was escalating, and his friend Karl Muck's brilliant American career was swiftly coming to its unforeseen end.

The Muck controversy erupted in Rhode Island as the BSO was undertaking one of its many concert tours in the Northeast. According to contemporary published reports, Charles A. Ellis, the orchestra's business manager, received at least one telegram from the Rhode Island Council of Defense to request that the BSO perform "The Star-Spangled Banner" at an upcoming concert in Providence. For unknown reasons Ellis failed to share the request with Muck, and the anthem was not played. Muck was accused of having a "deliberately insulting attitude" toward the anthem and the nation, when he stated in imperfect English, "Why will people be so silly? Art is a thing by itself and not related to any particular nation or group. It would be a gross mistake, a violation of artistic taste and principles, for such an organization as ours to play patriotic airs."[45]

Although Muck forged meaningful friendships in Boston, he had long felt out of place in America. Chadwick noticed that Muck was depressed about the onset of the war and completely unable to understand America's sympathy with Britain.[46] At first, Muck's stance was overlooked by an adoring public;

Chadwick intimated that BSO audiences were fully aware of Muck's German allegiance. Nevertheless, he received a rousing round of applause as he went to the podium to begin the final concert of the 1915–1916 season, a potent indication of support for him if not his country. "He probably thinks it was hypocrisy," Chadwick surmised about the applause, "but the audience seemed to make him want to feel that they appreciated his faithful and supremely conscientious work with the orchestra as well as his gifts as a scholar and conductor however much they differ with him as to the ethics of modern warfare."[47] After his ill-advised remarks in Providence about "patriotic airs," however, there followed a tumult the likes of which no one might have imagined.

Within days newspaper editorial writers and distinguished contributors were weighing in on the Muck affair. Composer David Stanley Smith utterly rejected Muck's argument that the national air did not belong on an artistic program, concluding that "the national anthem is never presented with more appropriateness than before audiences that have gathered for serious reflection."[48] Following Providence, the orchestra was set to perform in Baltimore. In a positively unseemly episode, former Maryland governor Edwin Warfield threatened physical harm to prevent Muck's appearance. "I told [the Police Board] that mob violence would prevent it, if necessary, and that I would gladly lead the mob to prevent the insult to my country and my flag. I told them that I knew of a thousand others who would gladly aid in leading the throng."[49] Henry Higginson himself could not avoid the fray, which by now had gotten well out of hand. Higginson threatened that if the topic of the BSO and the anthem continued to inspire public ire, "the orchestra would be disbanded and symphony hall sold."[50]

But Warfield had in fact already organized a rally at Baltimore's Lyric Theatre to protest Muck and the BSO. It featured speeches, a local regimental band, and the promised angry mob. "When the resolutions were read declaring that Dr. Muck should not be allowed to lead the orchestra in this city whether he played 'The Star-Spangled Banner' willingly or unwillingly," reported one journalist, "the applause was deafening. When ex-Governor Warfield, in referring to the musician, said 'he should be in an internment camp,' the applause lasted almost a minute. At its end a woman who had been waving the flag from a box near the stage shouted: 'Muck should have been shot when he said that.'"[51]

Even Chadwick suspected that the BSO harbored traitors. He shared his fears in a letter to Frederick Stock, the German-American conductor of the Chicago Orchestra, who had been able to avoid fealty concerns more successfully than Muck. "There are many members of the Boston Symphony," Chadwick wrote, "who are anything but loyal to this Country, although they are legally naturalized citizens, claim its protection and are willing to take advantage of all its privileges. Whether they will be allowed to continue as members of the Orchestra, I do not know, but if they do I am pretty sure that it will result in smaller audiences at the Concerts."[52]

Circumstances improved for Muck in the following months, although, as always, he kept characteristically silent on personal matters, even among his circle of friends. Locals, however, were becoming increasingly suspicious of him. A year before, when Muck had mysteriously taken ill and missed the BSO's performance of Kelley's *New England* symphony, even Chadwick's support had begun to wane. "Many people think that Muck has no interest in American compositions, an idea which I have tried to defend him from," Chadwick wrote, "but this occurrence will not help matters. Besides it *may* be true."[53] Higginson and the BSO administration continued to defend Muck, and armed guards protected him at least once during a concert trip to New York.[54] The efforts proved to be for naught. Muck was to have led the BSO in a Holy Week performance of Bach's *St. Matthew's Passion* on March 25, but he was arrested as an enemy alien earlier that day and sent to the East Cambridge jail. By April, Muck had been transferred to the makeshift internment camp at Fort Oglethorpe, Georgia, one of three military camps established in the US for the incarceration of German prisoners.[55]

Chadwick's claims of "nothing to write" during this period were exaggerated, although there is no question that following *Tam O'Shanter* his pace slowed. He composed his thirty-minute "pastoral opera" *Love's Sacrifice* in 1916–1917. In a letter to Carl Stoeckel he wrote that the opera "is intended for young people and to be performed out of doors" and expressed the hope that it could be premiered at the Norfolk Festival.[56] That did not happen, but on May 4, 1922, Chadwick reported that "after two previous attempts my little 'Love's Sacrifice' was performed in Jordan Hall. . . . The piece is pretty, idyllic, graceful, but it needs a very refined performance to be effective."[57] Chadwick may have been inspired to compose *Love's Sacrifice* by his recent al fresco performance experience among the giant redwood trees at San Francisco's Bohemian Grove concerts.

Between 1915 and 1918 he also completed *Silently Swaying on the Water's Quiet Breast* (ca. 1916) and several patriotic, war-related compositions including *Land of Our Hearts* (1917), *The Fighting Men* (1918), and *These to the Front* (1918). Chadwick called *Land of Our Hearts*, with John Hall Ingham's text, a "patriotic ode." It was dedicated to the Stoeckels and premiered at the 1918 Norfolk Festival. "Mr. Chadwick's 'hymn' sounded neither better nor worse than the 'potboiler' of a practiced composer," wrote H. T. Parker of its December performance in Boston. He considered it "a frank *pièce d'occasion* designed for general usage, with little imagination and no distinction."[58] *The Fighting Men* and *These to the Front* were set to texts by Mark Antony DeWolfe Howe, whose history of the BSO had appeared in 1914.

The armistice that effectively halted the Great War was reached on November 11, 1918, but the Treaty of Versailles, which would end the war officially and conclusively, was still seven and a half months away. The truce did not prevent casualties, of course, and deadly clashes with the enemy continued across the theater of war. Only days after the armistice, Chadwick lamented that "every day comes news of our New England boys, some of them our friends, being killed or wounded. Ma is wonderful and I think I should go to pieces except for her steadfast courage. We live on *hope*."[59]

American casualties would be a dreadful fact until the signing of the Versailles treaty on June 29, 1919. But, as occurred with so many young servicemen, Noël's hitch ended immediately following the armistice. He had been transferred in early December from Montauk, New York, to the naval air station at Camp May, New Jersey. There Noël was to begin his duties as a dirigible pilot, but on Christmas Eve day, he was relieved from active duty, probably much to his surprise. He left Camp May a week later and beat a path directly for home.

Theodore's return was delayed, perhaps as a result of ongoing skirmishes with the enemy; as a member of the Twenty-Sixth Division he was closer to the battle than his younger brother had been. He had even seen trench warfare at the Battle of Verdun.[60] As Chadwick put it, "We knew he was in the thick of it."[61] The relief was palpable when Theodore arrived at Boston's Commonwealth Pier on April 10, 1919.

The Angel of Death (1918)
During the Muck scandal Chadwick occupied himself with the composition of his final large work for orchestra, a symphonic poem titled *The Angel of Death*. On the heels of the premiere of *Tam O'Shanter*, Chadwick vowed not to write program music again. "Not that I may not try to make something with a poetic motive," he wrote, "but of delineative music I feel I have written quite enough."[62] He had given thought to producing a new work as early as 1915, as he returned home from his summer tour to California and the Panama-Pacific Exposition. In August of that year, while in Chicago, he visited the funerary relief *The Angel of Death and the Sculptor* created by his friend, sculptor Daniel Chester French (see figure 13.3).[63] Chadwick admired the work enormously. French had created

FIGURE 13.3. Daniel Chester French's "The Angel of Death and the Sculptor" (1893). This is a bronze funerary relief for the gravesite of artist Martin Milmore, Forest Hills Cemetery, Jamaica Plain, Massachusetts. Photo, ca. 1900. Courtesy of the Library of Congress Prints & Photographs Division, Detroit Publishing Company Photograph Collection, LC-D4-11944.

the bronze relief more than twenty years before, in 1893. It was a commission from the family of the young Irish immigrant and sculptor Martin Milmore, who died at age thirty-nine, and his brother, Joseph. Both are buried at Forest Hills Cemetery in Jamaica Plain near Boston. Chadwick had first seen French's sculpture at Forest Hills in the company of its creator, at which time he suggested that it would make a fine subject for a symphonic poem. French agreed. What had attracted Chadwick and many others was its representation of the Angel of Death not as a figure of doom, as it had been depicted since medieval times, but as a humane and gentle deliverer from the travails of life. In French's masterpiece the artist—perhaps a depiction of Milmore—is shown at work carving a sphinx, the traditional guardian of ancient temples and the mysteries that lie therein. The imagery is powerful; while his hammer is still in mid-stroke, aimed squarely at his chisel, the artist is summoned by the Angel—the artist himself will soon encounter the greatest mystery of all. Naturally, the depiction of death during the very act of artistic creation was a compelling, highly romantic element of

French's piece. This scene also had extraordinary resonance for Chadwick at this time, when the specter of death—for his sons as they served their country or Ida May and himself as their infirmities increased—had entered his own life.

French's Angel of Death, already a beloved sculpture, gained even greater notoriety in 1917, when a marble copy was commissioned by New York City's Metropolitan Museum of Art. Although the marble replica was not completed until 1926—it was interrupted by French's own ambivalence about the project and his creation of the magisterial Lincoln Memorial in Washington, DC—its iconic stature in American sculpture and its extraordinary craftsmanship added considerably to his already brilliant reputation.

Chadwick began his composition in 1917 and completed it on January 3, 1918. He called *The Angel of Death* a symphonic poem, although there is little to distinguish it from a standard concert overture. (Several months before he commenced this new work, he recalled his *Adonais* overture and lamented, "I wish I could make another overture as good as this one."[64]) An essential element in the work is its mood, which the composer conveys skillfully. One hears throughout the influence of Strauss, particularly strains of *Don Juan* and *Ein Heldenleben*, but also gestures borrowed from Chadwick's own Second Symphony, including its broad melodies and clever rhythmic vocabulary. At its beginning, Chadwick's score is melodious and optimistic, as it depicts the sculptor at work and happy in his enterprise. The temper then changes rather quickly; brass chorales appear and lead to a phantasmagorical development section, one which perhaps marks the passage of the sculptor through the stages of death, followed by his entry into the heavenly realm. As a new theme—one that would not sound out of place at the movie theater—rings, one senses that the Angel of Death is not a foreboding figure at all, but a loving apparition. Although *The Angel of Death* is arguably Chadwick's closest foray into the sound world occupied by Strauss, it nevertheless has a spirit, form, and fluency comparable to some of his earlier works, including *Aphrodite*, *Tam O'Shanter*, and even portions of *Symphonic Sketches*.

The Angel of Death had to wait thirteen months following its completion for its premiere by the New York Symphony under Walter Damrosch's baton. The occasion was a Theodore Roosevelt memorial concert held at the city's hallowed Aeolian Hall on February 9, 1919, slightly more than a month after Roosevelt's death. French attended the memorial and wrote to Chadwick on the very same day. He proclaimed the composer's creation "very noble, very beautiful."[65]

Bostonians, however, considered it mildly insulting that *The Angel of Death* was not premiered in Boston. In an unattributed report in the *Boston Evening Transcript*, written just before the composition's premiere, the writer, almost certainly H. T. Parker, asserted that "it was a pity that music written by a Bostonian composer and suggested by a Bostonian monument should seek and receive [its] first performance in New York, and not from the Boston Orchestra."[66] Clearly *The Angel of Death* had piqued local interest. In the same article, Henry Krehbiel's review of the premiere in the *New York Tribune* was quoted at length:

> The artist's hand is stopped in the middle of his work by Death—a theme which is as proper to the musician as to the poet or plastic artist. For poet and composer, indeed, it goes further in full expression than it could for the sculptor. Mr. Chadwick did not see "Finis" written by the arrested chisel; for him there remained apotheosis achieved despite uncompleted work. And so, after the section of the composition in which we are privileged to imagine the creative activity and the soaring ambition of the artist, threatened by ominous warnings of the fatal catastrophe, which is reached at the first climax of the music, we hear a new beginning of a new song which proclaims ultimate triumph.

The *Transcript* article also quoted from W. J. Henderson's review in the *New York Sun*. Henderson was more succinct and less poetic in his estimation of Chadwick and *The Angel of Death*:

> Mr. Chadwick said what he had to say in idioms clear and purposeful. The development of the music showed the sculptor throbbing with enthusiasm and vigor, suddenly confronted with the solemn challenge of the destroyer, but rising into immortality still triumphant. Sonorous, rich and vibrant music it was.

If Krehbiel and Henderson appreciated Chadwick's music as communicative, well-built, and eminently suited to the occasion, others would disagree. H. T. Parker got his own chance to assess Chadwick's new composition when it was featured on a BSO concert. Pierre Monteux conducted it at Harvard's Sanders Theater on a program that also included Bloch's *Two Psalms* (1912–1914) for soprano and orchestra. Parker related *The Angel of Death* to two of Chadwick's earlier works, *Cleopatra* and *Aphrodite*, both of which he counted among the "willed and manufactured music of Mr. Chadwick's later, more sterile years." Parker complained,

> The rays of Mr. Chadwick's study-lamp, not the heat of creative passion within, warm it. Has he, rich in the laurels of his prime, with a voice on occasion more American than that of any other symphonic composer, need to set down so many pages of barren measures that in his sixties he may still "keep on"? . . . The youngsters, in the comments of the lobby, were not kind to

'The Angel of Death.' They used bad words, slangful words. They called the music "old hat"; they styled the sculptor [i.e., Chadwick], after the manner of musical plays, "a fast little worker." It is not pleasant to hear Mr. Chadwick's music so mocked in these, his latter days.[67]

Chadwick was naturally outraged at this impudent diatribe. He had put up with Parker, whom he considered his *bête noire*, and his opinions for far too long. Chadwick's contempt toward Parker was longstanding, but in recent years it had spiked. Several years earlier he met Horatio Parker's family at a gathering in Norfolk, and, much to Chadwick's distress, there was "another Parker from the simian branch of the family present."[68] Later comments would be harsher than merely calling Parker an ape. After Parker's commentary on *The Angel of Death* appeared, Chadwick vented his disgust:

> In this evening's *Transcript* there was a "criticism" — God save the man! So spiteful, so venomous, so ridiculously insolent, and impertinent not only to me but to the whole audience, who had the poor taste to show signs of liking the *Angel of Death*. That many of our friends are indignant about it [*sic*]. I did not read it but Ma did and told me that it pictured me as a played out old hat with nothing left to say and made very odious references to all my past works, especially in comparison to Bloch of whom I am not worthy to buy a shoestring or a pair of suspenders. Why this little insect should hate me so I can't imagine. I never did anything to him, but I may![69]

"Harmless Lunatics": Chadwick and Modernism

If Chadwick hated Parker and momentarily resented Bloch, it was the general topic of "modern music" that had particularly ignited his irritation of late. During the war years there was a clear escalation of Chadwick's interest in — or at least exposure to — modern music, and he began to comment diligently on BSO performances of it. Muck's programming was nothing if not eclectic, and in recent seasons he had introduced an assortment of new works as well as older but still "modernistic" ones that had been neglected by previous conductors. It should be noted that in his writings Chadwick did not consciously craft detailed analytical essays. Rather, his remarks are first impressions — sometimes no more than fleeting observations — that are peppered with conclusions, some of which he would not hesitate to modify on closer acquaintance with a given composition.

Chadwick delighted in French music; his admiration of scores by Franck, D'Indy, Chausson, and Ravel was swelling. Debussy, however, left him generally dissatisfied. Upon hearing *Pelléas et Mélisande* in 1909, Chadwick acerbically commented that its music, "while being suggestive and often beautiful as mere sound, [is] so monotonous, so similar in characterization, so meagre in resource, that leaving its intrinsic general ugliness out of the question, from *its own standpoint* it is distinctly incompetent."[70] Two movements from Debussy's symphonic suite *Printemps* (1912), played by the BSO in 1914, also disappointed: "The second one is pretty trivial—good fancy music for the theatre but not much more."[71] Chabrier was a favorite, although not unreservedly; Chadwick had just heard the overture to his opera *Gwendoline* when he credited its composer with "an abnormally developed *decorative* sense" if little else.[72] But Chabrier's *España*, he enthused following a 1916 BSO performance, "is positively in a class by itself."[73]

Chadwick's colleague Charles Martin Loeffler, an American composer of Alsatian birth, was one of the earliest practitioners in the US of impressionism. His music was beloved by a small coterie of devoted followers. In 1916 Chadwick advised Loeffler on his new *Hora Mystica* (*The Mystic Hour*), a work for male chorus and orchestra. "In casually looking over the score," Chadwick wrote, "it struck me that it was full of quality and style. It is very elaborate but not difficult for the individual instruments." Chadwick had not always given Loeffler's music such high praise, but this work, he thought, "may become historically important."[74]

Chadwick had few opportunities to hear music from the modern Italian school, but he was familiar with Puccini. The emergence of the Boston Opera, and the increase in local appearances by other companies, gave Chadwick a chance to evaluate fully staged performances. He generally admired Puccini's better-known operas, including *Tosca* and *La Bohème*, citing their "individuality of expression" and "portrayal of the dramatic situation," but he was not always appreciative of the Italian composer's tendency to modernism, despite his own use of some of the very same techniques in *The Padrone*.[75] Chadwick attended the premiere of Puccini's *La Fanciulla del West* at New York's Metropolitan Opera House in 1910. "Apparently Puccini does not intend to be left in the background by Strauss or Debussy," Chadwick complained, "either in bravado of harmonies or gorgeousness of tonal paintslinging and the result is a very lurid specimen of advanced European decadent music in which [there] is quite as much Debussy and Strauss as [there] is natural Puccini."[76] Toscanini conducted, and Puccini himself was in attendance.

During Muck's tenure with the BSO, Chadwick often heard the music of the hyper-Romantic, maximalist German and Austrian moderns. He was curiously ambivalent about Mahler. He admired Mahler's Second Symphony, but the Eighth, which he heard in New York, where Stokowski was touring with his

Philadelphia Orchestra, was more difficult for Chadwick to appreciate: "There are many sublime moments, many of great musical beauty, and some of real dramatic power," but other parts were "dull and groping not to say ugly and meagre in harmonic and rhythmic ideas."[77] And in 1914, when the BSO gave its second performance of Mahler's Fifth Symphony—"by request," as was noted prominently in the program book—Chadwick remarked, "I don't know who requested Dr. Muck to repeat the Mahler symphony. Certainly *I* did not."[78]

Chadwick's stance on Strauss—the most infamous modernist composer for most of Chadwick's life—also fluctuated. He considered the early Symphony in F Minor (1884) "an astonishing piece for a young fellow, but without many indications of his future radicalism."[79] And while he considered *Till Eulenspiegel's lustige Streiche* to be Strauss's immortal masterpiece—"Long may his supremacy continue," Chadwick wrote after a 1916 BSO performance[80]—he was equally certain that *Also sprach Zarathustra* would have a short life in the concert hall: "There are many ignoble spots in it and a great deal of *Bluff*. With all Strauss' infernal talent there is a great lack of really convincing ideas which he tries to cover by heaping up *sound*."[81] His thoughts toward Strauss's *Festival Prelude* were not dissimilar; after condemning its "variety of noise," he wrote, "But as an expression of German arrogance it is undoubtedly a success."[82] Chadwick considered *Tod und Verklärung* the most successful of Strauss's program pieces, but, after hearing Muck perform it in 1915, he noted that "it no longer sounds very daring in either construction or orchestration, and there is not much in it that might not have been done by somebody else."[83] He also heard Strauss's comic opera *Der Rosenkavalier* in the company of critic Richard Aldrich; Chadwick found it disappointing and concluded "there is much that is very common even for light opera."[84]

Perhaps because he was himself an organist, Chadwick was attracted to Bruckner's works, which Muck programmed regularly. While he did not care for the Austrian's Ninth Symphony, one senses Chadwick's own compositional imperatives in a penetrating summation penned in the wake of a 1914 performance. Chadwick groaned, "It seems organically rickety and the material has neither the breadth nor interest of his other symphonies. The continual repetition of two measure phrases, the everlasting organ points, the general lack of *juice* in the orchestration and the eternal rambling without logical sequence or climax make it nothing less than a huge bore."[85] On the other hand, Chadwick was awed by the Austrian prodigy Erich Wolfgang Korngold, whose *Sinfonietta* (op. 5) the BSO played in 1915. Korngold was a talented and imaginative composer, whose gifts were considered by many fully on a par with the likes of Mendelssohn and Mozart. Korngold, still a teenager at the outbreak of the Great War, was an amazingly skilled orchestrator, and his polyphony was "often as daring as Reger or Strauss."[86]

The Australian composer Percy Grainger's music was gaining attention. Chadwick heard the BSO perform Grainger's ingenious composition for orchestra and three pianos titled *The Warriors*. He saw in it a pleasing alternative to rampant modernism and remarked that "this music represents an interesting reaction from the modern French and German tendencies." But, he continued, "I doubt if it has sufficient dignity or intrinsic value to influence matters very much."[87] When Chadwick heard it again at Norfolk in 1917, his attitude changed considerably: "the man really has ideas and once in a while they come to the surface in a genuine expressive phrase or passage." He then scolded Grainger for his extravagant harmonic effects: "All the more he should be ashamed to descend to such brutal sensationalism."[88]

Chadwick had a great deal to say about Sibelius. Following the 1913 Boston premiere of his Fourth Symphony, Chadwick exclaimed, "This Sibelius Symphony is bilious all right! The melodies, such as they are, are crabbed until ugly. The harmony [is] brutally and apparently gratuitously discordant, even to actual cacophony at times. In design and development [it is] a string of puzzles to the orderly mind [and] the instrumentation sometimes thinner than the landlady's proverbial soup." But "he has conviction; he creates atmosphere. He knows what he wants and how to get it, and his heart knows no fear." Chadwick concluded, "Love him we may not, but respect him we must."[89] By the time the two met at the 1914 Norfolk Festival, the Finn was indeed beloved by Chadwick, who had studied Sibelius's music in greater detail. The next year Chadwick would admit, following a BSO performance of Sibelius's First Symphony, that "I have heard nothing for a long time which I like as much as this Sibelius symphony." Chadwick fervently believed that it would become popular in the same way that Tchaikovsky's E minor symphony had. "A careful study of the score shows that he is a conscientious and clever workman."[90]

George Enescu's *Rhapsodie Roumaine* (op. 11, no. 1) "is pretty nearly the most reckless piece I ever heard. This cuss has a simply amazing talent."[91] And after hearing the Boston premiere of Enescu's E-flat major Symphony, Chadwick speculated on the Romanian composer's future as a representative of the French school of composition: "I would not wonder if he turned out to be one of the best ones."[92]

Among the younger group of American composers, Chadwick thought most highly of John Alden Carpenter. He had heard several of Carpenter's works, but upon hearing his First Symphony at the Norfolk Festival in 1917, he wrote, "Without doubt he is a really gifted man, probably the most so of any of the

Harvard bunch since Converse's time."[93] Walter Damrosch conducted Carpenter's imaginative *Adventures in a Perambulator* in 1915 in New York; Chadwick heard it there and observed that, although Carpenter tried too hard to put everything he knew into his first large work (not unlike Chadwick's own example in *Rip Van Winkle* Overture), "it is vivid, graphic, effective and sane and logical enough from his own point of view. Besides it is very ingenious rhythmically with not a little skillful thematic development and genuinely poetic moments."[94]

Despite Chadwick's reservations about his sincerity, Muck took a strong interest in the music of American composers. Critic Louis C. Elson observed with delight that Muck had "taken the American muse under his special guardianship."[95] Muck and the BSO took up Carpenter's *Adventures in a Perambulator* a month after the New York performance. Although on second hearing Chadwick was not moved by its programmaticism, which he thought indistinct, he nevertheless considered Carpenter "astonishingly clever."[96]

Other young Americans attracted Chadwick's notice as well. David Stanley Smith (1877–1949), one of Horatio Parker's Yale University students, wrote a string quartet that was "a very singular and ingenious work, very modern, restless, spasmodic and unmelodious. Interesting no doubt, but more as a puzzle and problem than as a concert expression."[97] His own student Henry Hadley, whose cantata *The Golden Prince* Chadwick performed with NEC forces in 1914, was carving an exceptional career, and his friend Frederick Stock (a German-born composer who many thought not American enough to be considered so) produced a First Symphony (op. 18) to which Muck devoted an unheard of eight BSO rehearsals. Stock's symphony was one of the few compositions Chadwick mentioned that he would like to hear again. He found it "a tremendous work in scope and in mastery of orchestral technique," one that reminded him of Strauss, Mahler, Wagner, and occasionally Brahms.[98]

Edgar Stillman Kelley's *Aladdin Suite* garnered Chadwick's respect, even if he did not particularly care for the composer himself. But he was underwhelmed by Kelley's Symphony no. 2 (*New England*), which he heard at the Norfolk Festival in the summer of 1913. "The scherzo is very clever with many pretty birdcage effects," Chadwick concluded, "some of them rather new and ingenious." Overall the composition was "German through and through and pedantic German at that."[99] Chadwick disliked Kelley personally; he was hugely annoyed by a speech Kelley delivered in Chicago in 1913 in which the younger man "regaled the company with the same old professorial sermon, without a ray of humor and everybody was glad when he sat down."[100]

Another young Harvard composer, Phillip Greeley Clapp, who had once studied with B. J. Lang, wrote a Symphony in E minor. It was premiered by the BSO with Clapp himself conducting. Its unnecessarily enormous orchestra, forgettable angular melodies, and dismal orchestration drew a chilly response: "His thematic invention seems to me weak and sterile. The first theme has some character but not enough to impress itself on the mind through all its permutations and combinations." Chadwick appreciated Clapp's melodic gifts, "But I suspect it started from Richard Strauss." As for the Finale, "it pretends to be a development of all the other themes, but all of these are so vague that [the] result is nothing short of irritating." Clapp, Chadwick concluded derisively, was "another composer not afraid of being up to date."[101]

Naturally, it was the "ultra-moderns" whose music most rankled Chadwick. The features of many new works such as those discussed above, even if trite and poorly crafted, were still intelligible to him. But other compositions, especially ones by Igor Stravinsky, Leo Ornstein, and Arnold Schoenberg, had taken artistic avenues that Chadwick found antithetical to beauty, grace, and expression. He strongly disliked much of Stravinsky's music, although he was not entirely put off by the BSO's 1914 performance of *Fireworks*, which "is said not to represent Stravinsky at his latest—that is[,] his worst."[102] He admired portions of *Petrushka*, which he heard in its original balletic form. "It really is quite wonderful how the music follows and describes the emotions of the marionette. It is impossible to consider it apart from the stage. I believe however that Stravinsky can write some good legitimate music if he tries."[103]

For "ultra-modern" music, the leading composers of which were Schoenberg and the iconoclastic Ornstein, Chadwick had little use. He was incredulous at the 1914 Boston premiere of Schoenberg's *Five Pieces for Orchestra*. "The fact is Schoenberg has in these pieces," Chadwick railed,

deliberately and with malice aforethought sought to found his chord combinations on fourths and sevenths as the rest of us do with thirds and fifths, combined with all imaginable forcing of the instruments. Of course this sets all principles of musical sound entirely aside. There is no beginning, no ending, no triads, no cadences, no melodies, no rhythm (except that occasional ugly snatches of various instruments obtrude), and no harmony except as above described. Why the man went to the trouble of reducing this to a measured notation is not comprehensible. When everything is lawless, what is the good of the police! I would be willing to accept this man as a harmless lunatic were it not for the fact that his earlier works show that he *can* write music of beauty and expression and therefore I suspect him of being a deliberate prostitute—or pervert, which is worse. . . . But he is not alone. A whole school of cacophonists has arisen. Stravinsky, Bartók and even the little New

York Hebrew, Ornstein have gone in for this sort of thing and of course have gained a certain following among the feeble minded. . . . Having spent my lifetime in trying to acquire some musical sense I decline to have it outraged. I prefer to be put on the academic shelf and remain behind times.[104]

In Schoenberg's music Chadwick was witnessing the total decay of artistic precepts he had held sacred since his youth. Ultimately, we must believe that, in Chadwick's eyes, the "lunatics" were not so harmless after all.

"Altschüler"
1919–1930

Teutonic tradition has died hard in music in America.
—H. T. Parker, *Eighth Notes*, 1922

American Music Education and Chadwick's Progeny

Chadwick had been a leader in music education almost since his career began, and he found most of his efforts an uphill climb. While huge musical gains had been made in Boston and elsewhere, he nevertheless was troubled by the inability of serious music to reach a wide population outside major cities and towns. Chadwick constantly found himself fighting the same battle he had been waging since he delivered his tirade in the 1870s to "make good music popular." Music education in primary schools was still not widespread, and the ascendance of popular music in the nineteenth century resulted in a corresponding decline in serious amateur music-making. The major choral festivals that flourished in Chadwick's youth and middle age were disappearing; Chadwick himself saw the fall of the Springfield Festival. In his 1919 essay, "A Plea for Choral Singing," Chadwick detailed the importance of music to his own upbringing and sketched the history of music in Boston. Naturally, it was chronicled with pious respect, but he was disappointed that music's advancement in his beloved New England had not diverged from well-worn paths. "And how is it now?" he asked about the current musical situation:

> In the country, beyond the reach of the trolley, a musical desert, a barren waste broken only by the occasional squeak of a wheezy cabinet organ drooling out a ragtime gospel hymn or a vulgar scrap of vaudeville music issuing from the strident horn of a talking machine. The village blacksmith no longer rejoices to hear his daughter's voice singing in the choir. He goes to town and listens to a paid—and usually overpaid—quartet choir simpering and snickering behind their curtain, and perhaps counting up the receipts from the last funeral, where they have quavered through the favorite hymns of the deceased.[1]

Chadwick lamented several of the most important music-related sociological facts of the era. In the wake of musical professionalism, the development of recorded sound, the rise of popular music, and the steady encroachment of modernism and jazz, there was a precipitous decline in music pursued by the masses as a civilizing activity. Active participation was eclipsed by the ascent of an audience class, that is, passive listeners. What formerly occurred in the home and church—around the hearth or the piano or the pulpit—was now accomplished with paid professionals who worked not strictly for love of the art, but for money.

The position of music in education was evolving. As the practice of music moved farther away from the everyday experience of most people, "music appreciation" began to usurp the place once held by the actual practice of music-making. In a view entirely antithetical to Chadwick's hopes for music in America, music appreciation was becoming a rung on the ladder to social respectability. This was laid out in depressing detail in a vision of music education put forth by the National Federation of Music Clubs in 1912; it was published the following year in an issue of Boston's influential *Journal of Education* devoted entirely to "Music—Its Mission and Message":

> All along the line [of education], music plays an important part. It is as important to have music in the school as it is to have clean windows, adequate ventilation, and sanitation. A half-day in school without music is like a face without a smile, or a desert landscape. Music breeds optimism as [its] absence breeds pessimism. Music in school lends zest to intellectual effort. . . . To appreciate music, vocal and instrumental, raises one in the social scale as definitely as does skill in dress or propriety in manners. Not to be intelligently appreciative handicaps one seriously in social life.[2]

Although the musical situation was the result of many changes in American life, Chadwick cannot escape at least a small measure of responsibility. After all, at NEC he helped to create a professional class of musicians, many of whom adhered to conventions of European musical practice and tradition in composition, performance, and pedagogy. An ascendant professional class further distanced the uninitiated from the musical experience and accelerated the rate at which the common music lover felt alienated. If music itself had become too esoteric in America to inspire the continued activity in it, at least the "appreciation" of music could enhance general knowledge and perhaps even social standing.

Chadwick was not concerned about appreciation; he was concerned about achievement. For years he had denounced those who continued the Boston custom of attending BSO concerts without a full comprehension of what was occurring. Chadwick sought from audiences an understanding of beauty, originality, and technique. Allan Lincoln Langley, who attended Chadwick's composition classes in the composer's later years, related the story of the time Chadwick attended a performance of compositions by NEC students, including one by Langley. Chadwick congratulated Langley on his fidelity to form, but encouraged him to "put something a little more original into it next time." Langley was elated; he declared, "Anyone who had mastered form, even slightly, won the respect of Chadwick: he was to the last an Altschüler."[3]

Chadwick's art emanated from a long European tradition of which he was both proud and protective. First and foremost, this tradition was based on a respect for and adherence to formal principles and the mastery of certain technical aspects of composition: harmony, counterpoint, and orchestration. How can an American composer create an expressive work, Chadwick might have asked, if one did not possess the technical apparatus required to create it? It was a problem he saw in the music of a number of younger composers, among them the upstart Americanist Henry Gilbert. Chadwick was woefully aware that the ideal of form, which had informed his musical style since his earliest days, and which had been paramount since before Beethoven's time, was now being obscured, even openly derided. "Musical America is in the grip of Europe," Gilbert wrote in 1918. "Europe dictates to us what music we shall hear, tells us the kind we should prefer, and, worst of all, insists upon dictating to our composers what kind they should write."[4] Gilbert is rather alarmist here and was responding in part to the anti-German climate of the country. For Chadwick, however, there was much more at stake than mere geopolitics. The cultivation of noble musical influences—once championed by J. S. Dwight and now vilified by Gilbert—seemed to be ending.

But it did not quite end. Music history books, by and large, tell the tale of what is new and "progressive," and leave to history's ash can that which is "traditional" or "old fashioned." Chadwick was indeed an "Altschüler," an "old-schooler," but he influenced American music in ways that resonate to this day. Langley once observed that "in spite of Chadwick's presence, the New England Conservatory somehow did not attract composers of any remarkable talent,"[5] and Chadwick never mentioned the establishment of a "school" of composers in his wake. Over the course of fifty years as a teacher at what had become a prestigious American conservatory, however, there was very little chance that one would not develop.

Among his students were several individuals we have already met, including Parker and Foote. Another was Arthur Whiting (1861–1936) who studied privately with Chadwick beginning in 1882 before he moved on to Munich and Rheinberger. Whiting composed chamber works and a well-regarded *Fantasie for Piano and Orchestra* (1897). His seminal contribution may have been as an advocate for early music. In New York, Whiting organized early music performances in which he played the harpsichord.

Sidney Homer (1864–1953) studied with Chadwick and, like his teacher, ventured to Leipzig and then Munich. He married another NEC graduate, the remarkable singer Louise Beatty Homer, and resided in Paris for a number of years. Homer wrote many instrumental chamber works and published over a hundred songs; his renown today stems from his 1939 memoir, *My Wife and I*.

We have discussed Fred Converse (1871–1940) and his importance in American opera as both a composer and as an administrative leader at Boston Opera. But Chadwick had seen in Converse a remarkable talent long before. After studying with Chadwick at NEC, Converse took the familiar route of study in music with Rheinberger. (By now the reader is aware of Rheinberger's large influence on the course of American music. More than any other figure in Europe, Rheinberger helped ambitious young American composers hone their craft. Comparing Rheinberger to the great and now better-known French teacher of American composers in the 1930s and 1940s, Converse biographer Robert Garofalo has reflected that "in some ways, though not all, Rheinberger may be considered the late nineteenth century German equivalent to Nadia Boulanger."[6]) Converse composed in forms similar to those preferred by Chadwick. Besides four operas there are four symphonies (he sketched a fifth), chamber works, cantatas, and orchestral works, including the imaginative *Flivver Ten Million* (1926) and *American Sketches* (1928). Perhaps influenced by Chadwick was Converse's early concert overture, *Euphrosyne* (op. 15), titled for one of the three Greek graces, another of which was Thalia.

Henry Hadley (1871–1937) had an extraordinary career as a conductor and a composer. His father, Samuel Henry Hadley, had been a music instructor in the Somerville, Massachusetts, public schools, and young Henry was a prodigy. He took lessons with Chadwick both privately and at NEC. Hadley then went to Munich, but studied with Ludwig Thuille, who had himself learned from Rheinberger. Hadley established an enviable conducting career. He led the orchestras of Seattle, San Francisco, and Manhattan; he later founded the Berkshire Music Festival; and he was arguably the best American conductor of his time. Hadley is remembered today for five symphonies, each of which bears a descriptive title, but during his own lifetime his numerous other assorted orchestral works, operas — especially *Azora* (1917) — and cantatas were admired. Following a Harvard Musical Association performance of Hadley's quintet in 1915, Chadwick radiated: "It shows his undeniable gifts very plainly."[7] Through the 1920s the relationship between Hadley and his mentor grew closer, and Chadwick took enormous pride in his student's achievements.

Edward Burlingame Hill (1872–1960) studied privately with Chadwick after he completed a degree with Paine at Harvard. Hill bypassed Germany to take up advanced training with Charles Marie Widor in Paris. Although a composer of imagination, he was hugely influential as a professor of music at Harvard University (over which his grandfather had once presided) from 1908 until 1940. In that post he, like Chadwick, influenced legions of musicians. Among Hill's works are four symphonies and other arresting works for orchestra, including his symphonic poem, the Edgar Allen Poe–inspired *The Fall of the House of Usher* (1919). Hill was among the first Americans to write serious chamber works for wind instruments; included in his oeuvre are his Flute Sonata (1925), Clarinet Sonata (1925) and Bassoon Sonata (1946), among others.

Arthur Farwell (1872–1952) was a young composer with "Americanist" inclinations. He graduated from the Massachusetts Institute for Technology with a degree in engineering in 1895 before taking up study with Chadwick. He then labored variously as an editor and as an administrator before founding in 1901 his own Wa-Wan Press, a publishing house that would cement his place in history by bringing out a large amount of music redolent of folk and Indian influences. Wa-Wan Press was sold in 1912, but Farwell continued to teach, compose, and advocate for an American music free from European influences. Although his own compositional potency was minimal, his vision for Wa-Wan Press has had a lasting influence.

Daniel Gregory Mason (1873–1953) had an impressive family lineage in music, one rivaled only by the slightly more famous Damrosch family. A Harvard man, Mason studied first with Paine and then orchestration with Chadwick, although only briefly. Like Hill (another Harvard grad), Mason sought further study in Paris with Vincent D'Indy. His compositions were appreciated in their day, although none have retained a position in the repertoire. Among them are three symphonies (no. 3 is titled *Lincoln*); a *String Quartet on Negro Themes* (1918); *Fanny Blair*, a folk song fantasy for string quartet; and a great deal of chamber music. Mason was a perceptive critic and the author of a huge number of books and articles. He influenced myriad students as professor of music at New York's Columbia University, where he taught from 1905 until 1942.

Before traveling to Munich for study with Thuille, Mabel Daniels (1878–1971) was tutored by Chadwick. A native New Englander, Daniels's father had once been the president of Boston's venerable Handel and Haydn Society. She wrote orchestral and chamber music, but became well known for her songs and choral works, a number of which drew on sacred themes. Daniels was the head of the music department at Boston's Simmons College for five years, 1913–1918.

Arthur Shepherd (1880–1958) studied composition at NEC with Chadwick, who noted Shepherd's "poetic sensibility and a command of modern harmonic resources which is quite remarkable."[8] Shepherd taught at NEC from 1908 until

1920, taking only a short time off to serve as an army bandmaster in 1918. He occasionally led the NEC Orchestra, and, along with Hadley, is one of the most important conductors from the period to emanate from the conservatory. Shepherd left to become assistant conductor of the Cleveland Orchestra, a post he held until 1926. He remained in Cleveland to teach at Western Reserve University until 1950. Shepherd's composition list is modest. Two symphonies and miscellaneous chamber and vocal works were completed after he left Boston.

William Grant Still (1895–1978) was a black composer who famously studied with Chadwick in the 1920s. Still did not seek an NEC degree; he seems only to have sought out Chadwick for a few lessons in orchestration. He was from a musical family, and by the time he arrived in Boston he had already begun a career as a musician. A prolific composer, Still crafted nine operas, several ballets, and a number of works on American themes (*Kaintuck* for piano and orchestra [1935], for example), as well as works on black themes. These include his *Afro-American* Symphony (no. 1, 1930) and his second symphony, *Song of a New Race* (1937).

A school of American composers having Chadwick's indelible imprint did in fact evolve from his studio. Not all the composers listed were equally influenced by him. Some, like Parker and Hadley, owed much of what they knew about the art of composition to him; others, like Mason and Still, simply intended to pick up what they could in a short time—most often in orchestration—from a respected American master. All of his students composed tonal music in familiar genres and forms and sought, like Chadwick, to express the beautiful. One may add to these countless others who, although they did not become acclaimed composers, went on to populate American orchestras, run private studios, and join college and university faculties in an era when, following the lead of Harvard and Yale, institutions of higher learning were increasingly sanctioning music programs.

Assessing the whole of Chadwick's career, Philip Hale was correct when he asserted that "as a teacher he exerted a wider influence and one that will be more enduring" than his work as an organist, conductor, or even a composer.[9]

Chadwick's Health
Chadwick's slowly declining physical health, which had been a source of discomfort and irritation since he reached his fifties, carried into his later years with even more force. Rheumatism became a problem, and, following a particularly distressful period, he reported, "After six days of dosing and dieting I finally had to give up the struggle and go to bed."[10] Chadwick continued to lose teeth, and his eyesight became increasingly poor (Chadwick wore glasses, although it

was only in his later years that he was photographed while wearing them). As the 1920s approached his pain became chronic, and, although he suffered from a number of maladies, gout remained his most potent enemy. He recorded a typically agonizing month-long bout in 1915:

APRIL 24 TO MAY 1

Pain began in left instep & swelling in the heel. Took Atophan three times a day. Went out only in carriage.

MAY 1 TO 8

Increasing pain extending to left knee. Very bad nights and unable to get out of bed. Took asperine sometimes twenty grains per day.

MAY 8 TO 15

Pains and swelling shifted to right knee and extended to left foot.

MAY 15 TO 20

Pain and swelling somewhat diminished. Had massage [May] 17. 18. 19 and got to library in wheelchair. 20th bad again. Pain back in instep where it started.

[MAY] 20 TO 23

Continued massage and [May] 22 got down stairs on crutches.

[MAY] 23

Went out in auto.

[MAY] 24

Stayed downstairs all day and heard exams [at NEC].

[MAY] 25

Crawled over to NEC in carriage to hear rehearsal of *Tam O'Shanter*. Very tired when I came back. A good deal of pain and next day stayed in bed.

[MAY] 25–29

Considerable improvement. Soreness and inflammation still in both feet but much improved. Can walk a little without crutches.[11]

Gout forced Chadwick to remain at home for days or weeks at a time as the disease invaded his toes, fingers, knees, and elbows; strangely, the symptoms appear much more regularly after the passage of prohibition in 1919. The national prohibition on the consumption of alcohol was effected by the ratification of the eighteenth amendment of the Constitution. Alcohol, with the exception of homemade wine produced in small batches, was prohibited as of January 16, 1920. Chadwick lamented prohibition on Thanksgiving Day, 1919, when he wrote that the holiday dinner included wine and cocktails "perhaps for the last time."[12]

Of course, it wasn't to be the last time. Although the eighteenth amendment would not be repealed until 1933, alcohol was available to those who could find it, afford it, and were willing to break the law to acquire it. In Boston, alcohol had long been a feature of many of the clubs, and at the Thursday Evening Club it remained a highlight. On March 18, 1920, Chadwick dryly noted that, at a gathering that included lectures on snakes, fishing in Florida, and the city of Lowell, "There was Scotch." At another meeting, "There was some rye whiskey."[13] Alcohol was enjoyed among friends—Hadley, for example, would routinely bring Chadwick whiskey or wine—but access to alcohol outside Boston was another matter. "The bite of prohibition is pretty keenly felt as soon as one goes away from home," Chadwick wrote following a trip to Worcester to hear *Judith*.[14] As a regular drinker, Chadwick naturally despised prohibition; it was, he determined, nothing more than "fanatical despotism."[15] He was also quick to note its deleterious effect on American society when, ten years before the amendment would be cast aside, he observed that "this idiotic law has developed a defiance of all law."[16]

Chadwick was nearly constantly in pain starting in 1919. One of his worst bouts of gout, which he endured for four weeks, occurred in 1922, and prompted him to take a steady regimen of codeine, aspirin, and colchicum. By 1924 Chadwick was ready to go to some length to reduce his pain, even if it meant experimentation. That year Chadwick rented from New York a "radium emanator" to help "counteract the uric acid," the cause of gout. "The extent of its healing effect," he admitted, "was questionable."[17]

Gout was not Chadwick's only concern, for his heart ailment was becoming an increasingly alarming burden. Not that it was a total surprise, for Chadwick had noticed "palpitation and pressure on the chest" as early as 1913.[18] And in the first weeks of 1914, he was advised by his physician to lose weight because his increasing girth was putting strain on his heart.[19] A decade later his doctor detected "a slight muscular irregularity in my heart action."[20]

We must also briefly consider Chadwick's mental state. Although it is doubtful that he suffered clinical depression, Chadwick certainly experienced his share of melancholy, which had surfaced during his student years in Leipzig, and again when Theodore Thomas died. As the 1920s progressed, he saw a number of his dearest friends pass—Theodore Presser, Wilhelm Gericke, and Carl Stoeckel all died within the space of a week in 1925—and he sensed that his own life was approaching its end. His family history of life expectancy provided no solace: his brother Henry had lived into his seventies, but his father Alonzo died at age sixty-nine. In November 1920 Chadwick turned sixty-six. Birthdays, which had long provided an annual opportunity for anguish, were becoming increasingly stressful. At one point Chadwick was so blue that he considered—as he had before—ceasing to write in his diary. "I do not want it to reflect," he wrote, "my now nearly habitual pessimistic frame of mind."[21]

Anniversary Overture (1922)

The region once known as Illyria occupies the central portion of the Balkan Peninsula that is situated directly across the Adriatic Sea from Italy. Illyrians comprised a confederation of various tribes that were pressed into the service of Augustus in the early years of the Roman Empire. They were widely hailed as excellent warriors. Still smitten with the ancient, *Illyria* also seems to have been the original title of Chadwick's *Anniversary* Overture, although he also flirted with the idea of calling it *Arcadia*.[22] Sketches for the piece were completed in August 1921. Ledbetter has speculated that Chadwick may have composed it as a companion piece to *Ouverture mignon*, which was also initially titled *Arcadia* when it was sketched in summer 1916.[23] He may have simply renamed *Illyria* upon the realization that he needed a composition to celebrate the silver anniversary of his association with NEC.

Chadwick led the Norfolk Festival Orchestra in the premiere of his new *Anniversary* Overture on June 7, 1922. By then he had conducted five premieres of his music at the festival, and audiences were accustomed to him and his music. There he was able to rehearse and work out problems, which was especially important since the overture was already slated for performance four more times in the upcoming season—in Chicago, New York, and twice in Boston, at Symphony Hall and NEC, respectively. Chadwick shared the Norfolk Festival limelight this year with English composer Ralph Vaughn Williams, whose *Pastoral Symphony* was premiered the same evening.

Chadwick scored his overture for pairs of woodwinds with the addition of piccolo, English horn, bass clarinet and contrabassoon; four horns, three trumpets, three trombones, and tuba; timpani, two percussion parts, celesta, two harps, and strings. He provided program notes for its premiere:

> The overture is constructed on three principal themes, of which the most important consists of the five notes represented by the five black keys of the pianoforte.
>
> This theme appears originally as an oboe solo in the short introduction. In the succeeding Allegro molto risoluto it is proclaimed with great emphasis by the trumpets and horns against an agitated background of strings and wind.
>
> There is a long lyrical passage in D-flat and C major, in which the two other themes are carried on side by side.
>
> The "development" section, which is very animated, is largely made up of

canonic imitations of the first subjects. The theme appears in what is called "symmetrical inversion," by augmentation and diminution and in various intervals of the scale. It reaches a climax in an emphatic restatement of the five-note theme in E-flat minor by the full brass choir, the trombones following half a measure after the trumpets.

The lyrical passage is now recapitulated (in F-sharp and F major) with some variation in form and instrumentation. The overture closes with a very animated coda.

The structure of the work is symphonic, but the atmosphere of it is romantic and at times dramatic. There is no program.[24]

For Chadwick, *Anniversary* Overture was an artistic declaration. As he was completing it, he wrote, "I have been living in the past for so long, that I perhaps have lost confidence; but I *would* like to show some of these young fellows that the old dog is not dead yet."[25] In this period of his life Chadwick was looking for acceptance, even validation, from younger artists. Naturally, the crowds in Norfolk gave Chadwick a warm ovation, but in the audience sat a reviewer for *Musical America* who, although appreciative of Chadwick's technical skills, felt the music was bland. "Sincere and scholarly good writing it proved to be," the critic averred, "but not distinguished, individual or homogenous in its material. In matters of development, canonic imitations, the use of contrary motion, variation, augmentation, diminution, and the like, the hand of a very fine craftsman which Mr. Chadwick never fails to be, is evident."[26]

Chadwick was not surprised. A few weeks earlier he had predicted that "on account of its regularity of form and the occasional unity of its material, they will jam me into the 'old hat' box harder than ever."[27] But he was wrong. Pierre Monteux led the Boston premiere of the overture in December 1922, and H. T. Parker's assessment following the performance was surprisingly complimentary. Chadwick "is eager and warm again," he wrote. The orchestra "missed none of Mr. Chadwick's keen-set detail. They also kept his high spirits." In the *Anniversary* Overture, Chadwick was "looking forward with cheerful ardor and back in no unhappy retrospect; which should be the way of Anniversary Overtures."[28] In some quarters at least Chadwick's declaration succeeded.

Whether because of the geniality of the *Anniversary* Overture, or, more likely, due to the respect extended to an elder composer, criticism of Chadwick and his music was softening. Chadwick could only have been stunned by Parker's kindness. As we have seen, his relationship with critics—and particularly Parker—was not always cordial.

"Troublesome Enemies"

The founding of musical institutions and the establishment of an American school of composers throughout the late nineteenth century was accompanied by a corresponding rise in the profession and professionalism of music journalism and criticism. This development did not bypass Chadwick's notice. From the beginning of his career, Chadwick's music had generated rivers of newspaper ink, and early on much of the commentary was positive. Naturally, as his music became less novel, that changed. Chadwick had a strong disdain for many newspaper critics—men he demeaned as "penny-a-liners" because they were paid according to the number of lines per column they filled—although there were a few he admired. Some became acquaintances, but none became friends.

Having suffered attacks from the *Boston Evening Transcript*'s H. T. Parker for a decade and a half, Chadwick's disgust with him had intensified. At a 1919 performance of *The Angel of Death* in Cambridge, Chadwick, seated in the audience, glanced to the side. "Who should be put into the [nearby] pew," he steamed, "but the person, of all human creation, I most despise!"[29] Chadwick reserved for Parker, perhaps the most important critic relative to his career, a special brand of contempt.

A Boston native, Parker succeeded Apthorp at the *Transcript* in 1905. He was not a novice, having been a correspondent with several newspapers, including the *New York Globe*, for a number of years. Parker was musically informed, although he could not read music; he was better known as a drama critic. A bit eccentric and something of a loner, Parker was not to be found among Boston's social set, and as a confirmed bachelor he devoted the majority of his waking moments to his work.[30] Parker typically signed his reviews "H. T. P.," initials which came to be known ominously as "Hard to Please" by those who considered his critical style too harsh; or "Hell to Pay," by those who simply thought his standards unobtainable.[31]

Parker's vitriol had resonated loudly throughout his reviews of Chadwick's music. One commentary was typical. When Chadwick's works were featured at a 1924 all-Chadwick concert given by the People's Symphony Orchestra of Boston, nearly all the works performed were of an older vintage.[32] The recent songs with orchestra—"Voice of Philomel," "The Curfew," and "Drake's Drum"—were heard. But *Euterpe*, *Lochinvar*, three of the *Symphonic Sketches* ("Hobgoblin" was omitted), and three miscellaneous movements (the orchestrated *Andante* from Quartet in D minor, the Scherzo from the Second Symphony, and the "Romance" from *Suite Symphonique*) garnered the most attention. Parker was surprised that Chadwick's recent tone poems were missing from the program.

"That symphonic vessel," he wrote dryly, "has not seemed altogether congenial to him. Filling it, he has not often been his free and fecund self."[33] It was like Parker to slight works that were not even on the program.

When Parker died in 1934, he received encomia from across the arts world. "His passing is an unbearable affliction," lamented none other than Nicolas Slonimsky.[34] Chadwick might have been mystified by that assessment had he lived to read it.

Chadwick was among the last generation of American musicians to know John Sullivan Dwight, who died in 1895, but whose influence had waned long before. He was quick to note the veteran critic's shortfalls. "Dear old Johnny!" Chadwick exclaimed. "He could neither play, sing, conduct or compose, and probably he had rather a *sweet* tooth for music, but at least he had a profound respect for noble and beautiful things and was not so entirely pig headed that he condemned all that he did not understand."[35] Chadwick's music attracted Dwight's attention immediately—it would be hard to overstate the impact Dwight's enthusiasm for *Rip Van Winkle* Overture had on Chadwick's entry into Boston's musical circles—but since his *Journal* ceased publication in 1881, his influence on the later reception history of Chadwick's music was nil.

Parker was not the only critic toward whom Chadwick was contemptuous. Chadwick considered Henry Krehbiel the first among critics by virtue of his position at the center of New York musical life if not by talent. Chadwick grumbled that Krehbiel "has lorded it over our musical opinion for so long" even though the critic "can't come within forty blocks of reading an orchestral score." He thought that it would be rough justice if, in compositions submitted for a contest, Krehbiel "ought to be made to put in all the missing flats and sharps in the horns and clarinets . . . just to teach him humility."[36]

In one of his more vitriolic moments, Chadwick wrote that "musical critics are a bunch of ignorant, flatulent, diarhoeal shite-pokes, who take to scribbling because they can neither sing, play or conduct or compose."[37] He had long derisively called Apthorp "little Billy," although it seems that he eventually became a tolerable acquaintance. Chadwick enjoyed several pleasant encounters with Richard Aldrich, including an evening spent at the critic's home. Philip Hale raised Chadwick's ire at a Tavern Club meeting when he made several disparaging remarks about composers, and when, in 1912, Hale joined the Thursday Evening Club, Chadwick wrote, "Can't say I think he improves it much."[38] Following a dinner party thrown by Paderewski—during which the great pianist was cozying up to Hale—Chadwick warned that Hale "can be a troublesome enemy as I happen to know."[39] And there were many other critics whom he simply thought unqualified. As concerned the reviewer at the *Springfield Republican*, "While he probably would have been too modest to attempt to report a baseball game or a prize fight," Chadwick seethed, the writer "thought himself entirely competent to criticize singers, singing or even musical compositions."[40]

Music book publishing was also on the rise. In 1908 Chadwick wrote that "one of the significant phases of our present musical era—as a matter of works of permanent and lasting musical worth, is the multiplication of books on music by men of little authority, of less talent and of distinctly vicious literary habits."[41] *Harper's Weekly* critic Lawrence Gilman was a vocal advocate of Debussy's music, the author of a biography of Edward MacDowell, and according to Chadwick was "in the front rank of modern sensationalism." Chadwick had several disagreements with Gilman, whom he once called "our adolescent friend."[42] He had a similarly low opinion of Daniel Gregory Mason, a prodigious author who had been his student ("Whom even *I* was unable to teach much of anything about composition," Chadwick sourly remembered[43]). Rupert Hughes, author of *Contemporary American Composers* (1900), "makes a whole book out of the published opinions of other scribes."[44] Chadwick wished not to lump Dr. Louis Adolphe Coerne, author of *The Evolution of the Modern Orchestra* (1908), in with the penny-a-liners. Coerne, a student of both Paine and Rheinberger, merited a bit more respect on account of his earned PhD degree. But Chadwick nevertheless thought Coerne's book "is simply a compilation of the information on that subject to be found in the dictionaries and encyclopedias and as far as one may judge from a hasty perusal, contains no original matter."[45]

The BSO, Koussevitzky, and "A Bad Humor"

"I am beginning to think that I was a D***** fool," Chadwick grumbled in 1926, "to blow $45.00 for these concerts. They always put me in a bad humor."[46] "These concerts," of course, were those of the BSO, for which he had resumed his subscription. But his immediate complaint concerned the concert he had attended that very day. Chadwick was incensed by its inclusion of Prokofiev's Suite from *The Love for Three Oranges* (1919; rev. 1924) and Bartók's *Dance Suite* (1923) for string orchestra. For Chadwick, the BSO had become a tiresome endeavor; when his subscription lapsed in 1916, he decided not to renew. "It has become a species of slavery to give up every Saturday night, rain or shine, to this peculiarly Bostonese function," he complained.[47] Now led by Sergey Koussevitzky, whose reign over the orchestra would easily eclipse his predecessors' in length and significance, the character of the BSO had changed drastically since the halcyon days of Muck. And with it had changed Chadwick's relationship to the institution he had once loved.

Chadwick saw nine conductors come and go at the BSO; taking full advantage of his reputation as Boston's leading composer, he managed to befriend a number of them. More importantly, he acquainted them with his music (see Appendix 4). Most gave Chadwick a place on their programs, but that situation, which had been crucial for him throughout his career, changed dramatically in the wake of the Great War and the Muck scandal. Muck would be the last of the BSO conductors whose musical background and aesthetic closely mirrored Chadwick's own. His situation had worsened tremendously following two key retirements: Higginson's 1918 departure was swiftly followed by the retirement of longtime orchestra business manager Charles A. Ellis. Higginson's lamentable death the next year left Chadwick on the outside looking in insofar as his relationship with BSO leadership was concerned. Given these circumstances—and Chadwick's declining creativity—there seemed little hope for a Chadwick resurgence.

Henri Rabaud, a Frenchman, had taken over the season after Muck's arrest. Rabaud had broad tastes with a decided preference for Beethoven, Rimsky-Korsakov, and Saint-Saëns, but he also led the orchestra in Chadwick's patriotic *Land of Our Hearts* in December 1918 at a pair of concerts advertised as "Celebrating the Close of the Year of Victory." Chadwick got to know him only slightly; Rabaud stayed with the orchestra just one season before Pierre Monteux was hired. Monteux, an affable personality and a conductor of undisputed genius, embraced his role at a pivotal time in the orchestra's history. Here was an institution that had suffered pervasive anti-German sentiment, as well as the loss of its founder, its manager, and its formerly respected, now despised conductor, all within the space of two years. With a modicum of understatement, M. A. DeWolfe Howe remarked that Monteux "made this orchestra the first to reflect the post-war change in creative musical life."[48]

Monteux's musical interests and repertoire were wide ranging. He is best known today for introducing the American concert-going public to compositions by Stravinsky, including his *Petroushka* (1911), Schoenberg's *Verklärte Nacht* (1917), Ravel's *La Valse* (1920), and Scriabin's Symphony no. 3 (*Divine Poem*, 1904). Chadwick heard the last mentioned in February 1924 and remarked that "I went to sleep three times; I could never do that in Stravinsky or Ravel."[49] Not that Chadwick was a fan of Stravinsky. He attended Monteux's BSO premiere of Stravinsky's *The Rite of Spring* in 1919, which he admitted "was a very remarkable stunt" for both the conductor and the musicians. "The audience was plainly 'flabbergasted,'" Chadwick observed: "Some sensitive souls worked themselves into a state of orgasmic excitement, some were merely bored by the endless racket and din and some, not a few either, were honest enough to resent it as an insult to the Art of Music." Chadwick believed that even Stravinsky's admirers could agree that "this stuff"—he refused to call it music—lacks "repose, dignity, elevation, poetic sentiment."[50] Naturally, Monteux also programmed more accessible, although still cosmopolitan, works: Respighi's *The Fountains of Rome* (1916), Sibelius's Symphony no. 5 (1915), and many others.

Monteux's advocacy of music by British and American composers has gone under-appreciated. Monteux introduced Bax's tone poem *The Garden of Fand* (1916), about which Chadwick effused, "I like this man Bax; he has imagination, style of his own and is an expert colorist."[51] He was less certain of his opinion of Vaughn Williams, whose *London* Symphony (no. 2, 1913) was programmed by Monteux in 1922: "There is very little fast tempo in the piece, which rather leaves the impression of meandering, especially in the first part." Chadwick concluded that he enjoyed Vaughn Williams's music, "but I might change my mind on further acquaintance."[52] Monteux led the *Negro Rhapsody* (1912) by Henry Gilbert, whom had never ranked among Chadwick's favorites. "Henry Gilbert's nigger Rhapsody is not very desirable music," Chadwick sneered. "The material is very poor, not very fertile for development or suggestive for harmony. The everlasting repetition of four bar phrases is walking around the block [i.e., pointless]. The scoring is pretty rough and there is too much brass."[53] Chadwick thought Deems Taylor's suite *Through the Looking Glass* "a very effective and interesting piece and made with quite remarkable skill for the orchestra. This is a 'fellar' to be reckoned with, even if he is a critic."[54]

In 1924 Monteux was honored at a dinner hosted by Boston's Composers Club; he had played many works by club members and his service to the cause of American music was widely hailed. Like many of the BSO's conductors, Monteux also proved to be supportive of Chadwick's music during his five seasons with the orchestra. He conducted the Boston premiere of *The Angel of Death* in his first season (November 1919), and he followed with *Melpomene* (April 1921), *Theme, Variations, and Fugue* (December 1921, with organist Albert W. Snow), and *Anniversary* Overture (December 1922). "Monteux is an excellent conductor," Chadwick stated following the performance of the latter overture, "an extremely conscientious and painstaking disciplinarian and a thorough musician but he does occasionally sacrifice clarity to speed." Chadwick then gibed, "Muck could get both!"[55] Nevertheless, given the BSO's impressive record of performances of American music, Chadwick would have been hard pressed to disagree with critic Carl Van Vechten's 1915 assertion that "it can hardly be said that the American composer has been neglected."[56]

Monteux's departure from the orchestra following the 1923–1924 season was bittersweet. Although he had done much stabilize the organization following the departures of Muck and Rabaud, several run-ins with the musicians became public much to his own detriment. To this may be added the orchestra's strengthening ties to organized labor, which caused enormous tension and even estrangement between the conductor and his players.[57] Chadwick recounted one scene following a magnificent performance in which Monteux motioned for the orchestra to stand and share in the ovation. "All stood up except Fradkin, the concertmaster, who remained in his seat. The audience, of course, was offended and the applause turned to hisses."[58]

Rather than tolerate infighting, the orchestra's new management simply allowed Monteux's contract to expire. There was no question that his term there had been musically superlative and that Monteux had effectively given the BSO new life. H. T. Parker noted that the conductor "leaves spacious memories behind him—the saviour of an illustrious orchestra, the renewer of its prestige, the sustainer of its standards."[59] And Howe reminds us that, with five complete seasons under his belt, Monteux's tenure as the eighth conductor of the BSO had been exceeded only by two of his predecessors, Gericke and Muck.[60]

The ninth conductor of the BSO would also leave an imposing legacy in Boston. Koussevitzky, a Russian émigré, had attended the Moscow Philharmonic Music School as a bassist before becoming a member of the Bolshoi Theater Orchestra. As he matured, Koussevitzky demonstrated something of an entrepreneurial spirit—he cultivated a career as a bass soloist and even composed a number of works for the instrument; he became a successful publisher of music; and he founded several of his own orchestras and concert series in Russia and in western Europe, where he lived before removing to the United States. Koussevitzky's musical biases were obvious: he loved the modernism that emanated from his home country and supported its brilliant composers, who included Medtner, Scriabin, and the young Prokofiev, among others. He was excited by the scintillating musical trends of Paris, and, like many young artists who had abandoned Germany following the Great War, Koussevitzky found that in France he could immerse himself in musical tradition while also cultivating a modernist aesthetic.

Koussevitzky was a charismatic personality on and off the podium, one whose passionate love of the art could appeal to those music lovers who could afford to write the donation checks. Chadwick possessed a similar charisma and recognized it immediately in his Russian colleague. He found Koussevitzky a delightful conversationalist, a good conductor, and "I suspect, an adroit flatterer."[61] But if Chadwick admired some facets of Koussevitzky's work, he had little use for his programming. Chadwick's stance toward Stravinsky had not relented over the years. A 1925 BSO performance featured Stravinsky as both conductor and pianist for renderings of his *Petroushka*, the *Firebird* Suite and the Concerto for Piano and Winds. "His piano playing is very ordinary," Chadwick judged, "but it is only fair to say that his Concerto is no test of a pianist's musical qualities. It is dismal and dry . . . mostly a jumble of bad counterpoint exercises." As for the other two, although vibrantly scored, "they are not great as we understood the word. Clever [to] no end but not much more."[62] By the time Koussevitzky programmed Stravinsky's *Le Chant du Rossignol*, Chadwick was certain that its composer was "inspired by the devil himself. It has every suggestion of evil."[63] Chadwick had a similar response to Koussevitzky's performance in 1924 of Honegger's "Mouvement symphonique" *Pacific 321* (1923), which he complained "might be called 'Racket on a Railway' for all the nobility or poetry there is in it."[64]

Koussevitzky also sought to perform music by the younger generation of American modernists, and Aaron Copland was one of his favorites. Chadwick listened with horror to the February 1925 performance of Copland's Symphony for Organ and Orchestra, and he could not pass on the opportunity to slur his younger colleague. "Copland (Caplan) piece," Chadwick seethed, "is the most impudent and indecent specimen of Hebrew godlessness was have yet heard."[65] Later that year he professed that Copland's new *Music for Theatre* was "a disgusting, indecent mess." And as for Copland's Piano Concerto, Chadwick declared it "silly, obscene, babbling, without a trace of musical melody, harmony or color."[66] The blame for these performances, of course, lay squarely on the Russian conductor: "And 'Witsky' commissioned this Jew to make it! Will it never come to an end?"[67]

Near the end of a disappointing 1925 concert season in which Chadwick found almost nothing he could enjoy, he considered—as he had several times before—giving up his tickets. "It is a question whether it is worthwhile to give up a whole afternoon and $60.00 for such a meagre amount of musical satisfaction."[68] Following the final performance of that year he noted that "there was polite applause for 'Witsky' as a farewell but none of it came from the orchestra," which, Chadwick implied, was just as fed up with the conductor's programming as he was. "I will give him just one more year."[69]

And he did. In fact Chadwick renewed his BSO subscription for both the 1925–1926 and 1926–1927 seasons, neither of which fared much better in his estimation. In May 1927 Chadwick again vowed not to renew for the upcoming season, as "there has been so much hideous music this year."[70] This time, after forty-six years of nearly uninterrupted attendance at BSO performances, he would honor his pledge.[71]

Late Works

"In sheer desperation, for lack of something to do," Chadwick opined while on a 1922 visit to Florida, "I tried to write some notes this morning while walking along the shore of the lake; very uphill work however."[72] Now sixty-seven years old, Chadwick was growing tired and fast losing the inspiration to spend much time at his writing desk. Composition was increasingly a struggle, although the habits that had been developed over five decades did not leave him easily, and he still had the urge to compose. Original musical thought, however, had grown depressingly difficult, and Chadwick lacked the physical stamina to take on large symphonic or operatic projects. He turned his attention to composing new occasional works and orchestrating some of his older ones. These smaller projects kept him active in composing for his beloved orchestra, and avoided the heavy toil of original creation. And now, as had always been true for Horatio Parker, Chadwick relied more heavily on texts for inspiration than at any time in his career.

Chadwick had composed *The Voice of Philomel* and *The Curfew* in 1914, and both were published in piano-vocal versions in the same year. He began orchestrating them at West Chop in 1920. Ovid famously told the story of Philomel in his *Metamorphosis*. In it, Philomel, a Greek woman, is raped; when she threatens her tormentor her tongue is cut out. Following other atrocities toward her, the Olympic gods, in their pity, enabled Philomel's freedom by turning her into a bird. Chadwick's infatuation with the ancient Greeks continued long after their potency among other composers had waned. *The Voice of Philomel* utilized a text by David K. Stevens, with whom Chadwick had created *Love's Sacrifice* and *The Padrone*. It is dedicated to Louise Homer.

The Curfew, to words by Henry Wadsworth Longfellow, was dedicated to Marianne Kneisel, the wife of Chadwick's friend and colleague, Franz. Chadwick used only six of Longfellow's eight stanzas, although he repeated the first two at the end of his composition. The poem's imagery, which includes a curfew bell, fire, books, and song, was a rich source for the composer. Marked Lento espressivo, the mood throughout is somber, and Chadwick makes striking use of pedal point, mild chromaticism, and a variety of textures in the piano part.

One of Chadwick's most poignant compositions is the *Elegy* in memory of his best friend of four decades. "Horatio Parker died this morning in his sleep," Chadwick lamented on December 18, 1919. "Poor fellow, he deserved that boon after all his suffering. . . . This is the first break in the 'Big Four.' Thus, one by one are severed the strands that connect us to a happy past. To me, who have watched Parker from the very beginning, it seems like knocking away the foundations of the house."[73] The three-part *Elegy* was written first for organ and then later arranged for orchestra.

Sidney Lanier's two-stanza poem "The Ballad of Trees and the Master" (1880) was orchestrated by Chadwick in 1920. Chadwick first made a song from Lanier's poem in the late 1890s, and it proved to be an audience favorite. Its ABA form begins in E minor and closes in the major, a triumphant gesture given the darkness of the poem. One instructor, Clarence G. Hamilton, used the song as an example in his textbook *Music Appreciation* (1920), where he compared it to Schubert's *Die Erlkönig*: "In both ballads the music is founded upon a persistent rhythmic accent; but in the Erlking the prevailing emotions are excitement and dread, while the *Ballad of Trees* is calm and dignified. . . . Both ballads are pointed examples of the power of music to intensify and illustrate literary ideas."[74]

Chadwick's orchestral movement titled *Arcadia*, composed in 1916, languished in sketch form until he decided to orchestrate it in 1923. Originally intended for use as a curtain raiser for his stage piece *Love's Sacrifice*, he later changed the movement's title to *Ouverture mignon*, and in 1925 he added a second movement, *Canzone vecchia* (in which he used material from his earlier *Serenade for Strings*), and a third, *Fuga giocosa*. The three movements were combined to form the orchestral suite *Tre Pezzi*. This composition was given its first and last performance in 1931, when it was premiered by Goodrich and the NEC orchestra. The reviews were good. One writer appreciated the sophistication of the overture, which occupies forty-three pages of manuscript score. Its character and instrumentation are reminiscent of the first movement of the *Sinfonietta*. The *Canzone* "has the manner of an old folk song," and the *Fuga* contained "frolic fugues," the writer observed, "based on decidedly humorous motives."[75] A splendid orchestral romp, Chadwick had high hopes for *Tre Pezzi*'s artistic and financial success, but it was not published.[76]

James Russell Lowell's "Salute to the Sacred Dead," the eighth verse of his *Ode Recited at the Harvard Commemoration* (1865), inspired Chadwick's own *Commemoration Ode* (1924).[77] Composed in homage to the fallen heroes of the Great War, it was published by Oliver Ditson's firm in 1928. Over the course of its ABA form it travels from a dolorous C minor introduction ("Salute the Sacred Dead, who went and who return not") through violent, raucous passages ("Blow, Trumpets, Blow") to a final, ultimately triumphant area and a radiant C major close ("Beautiful evermore, and with the rays of morn on their shields").

Chadwick scored his "Pirate's Song" in 1925. It is based on a tune sung by characters in Arthur Conan Doyle's three-part short story, "Captain Sharkey," which is a featured tale in his 1900 book, *The Green Flag and Other Short Stories*. Chadwick wrote to Doyle to request permission to use the text. A wily Doyle instructed, "if you make money out of it you send me £10—but not otherwise."[78]

Fathers of the Free was composed in 1927 for New York University's Hall of Fame. Its words, by the university's chancellor, Elmer Ellsworth Brown, were set for chorus and a small orchestra; Gray published it in piano-vocal score the same year. Chadwick's friend and correspondent Robert Underwood Johnson was the director of the Hall of Fame at the time and undoubtedly spearheaded the commission. *Fathers of the Free* was used as the Hall of Fame's processional music annually until 1941.

Chadwick's "American" Imperative and the Revision of *Rip Van Winkle* (1929)

On June 16, 1919, the NEC Pops Orchestra took up Chadwick's *Rip Van Winkle* Overture in celebration of its premiere in Germany forty years—almost to the day, its composer noted—earlier. The much-lauded Leipzig premiere was followed by triumphant performances in Boston in 1879 and 1880, after which the overture received only two more hearings, in 1883 and 1889, respectively.

But *Rip Van Winkle* found a second life in the world of the American band movement. We know it was arranged for John Philip Sousa's band, although the circumstances surrounding the genesis of the transcription, and that of nearly a dozen other Chadwick compositions, are unknown. Because the score of *Rip Van Winkle* was available only in manuscript form Chadwick undoubtedly had some influence over the band arrangement. Chadwick and Sousa had long been friends but the details of their professional relationship are clouded. Sousa's own band had formed in 1892, following his resignation from the US Marine Corps Band, which he had conducted since 1880. Sousa and Chadwick had several opportunities to meet, including at least as early as the World's Columbian Exhibition in Chicago or perhaps during one of Sousa's numerous concert tours throughout the Northeast. Chadwick was not one to shy away from meeting a renowned musician if he had even the slightest opportunity to do so, and he doubtless would have jumped at the chance to introduce himself to "The March King."

Chadwick and Sousa had much in common besides music. Although the circumstances of their childhoods could scarcely have been more different, they were exact contemporaries (Sousa was born precisely one week before Chadwick). Both were excellent musicians possessed not only of immense musical knowledge, but also a wide general knowledge that was mostly self-developed.

Both men enjoyed the sporting life, intelligent and topical conversation, and a good joke sometimes tinted with sarcasm. Chadwick respected Sousa's weighty position in American music and in later years would often begin his correspondence with the tongue-in-cheek salutation, "My dear St. Philip."

Over the years Sousa utilized a number of Chadwick's scores besides *Rip Van Winkle* (see Appendix 5). Movements from the Second Symphony, the *Sinfonietta in D*, and the *Symphonic Sketches*, as well as several arrangements for band with vocal soloists, found their way into Sousa's repertoire. In 1926 Sousa's band arrived in Boston, where they played the bandmaster's own arrangement of Chadwick's *Tam O'Shanter*. In the only record we have of Chadwick hearing a band transcription of one of his orchestral works, he grumbled, "I got little satisfaction out of it. I could not be reconciled to the loss of string tone even though the clarinets and saxophones played all the notes. Played by Sousa's Band, the whole thing is poorly balanced and ineffective in certain parts."[79] The band arrangement of *Rip Van Winkle* Overture follows the orchestral score faithfully although, like *Tam O'Shanter*, the instrumentation was changed drastically to conform to the requirements of a wind band.

Whatever Chadwick's involvement with the band arrangement of *Rip Van Winkle* may have been, the overture's lure for him subsided until 1929, when he took up the orchestral score again. In February of that year he began its revision; the overture was to be "shortened and materially changed," for Chadwick concluded that it was far too long and had a number of serious structural defects. "But why," he asked, "did Reinecke and Jadassohn who watched it grow week by week let these 'little foxes' go by?"[80] Chadwick intended his new version of the overture to demonstrate the compositional techniques that had proven successful for him in the intervening fifty years since it was first heard. An updated version would also help Chadwick to meet modern expectations of what his music was supposed to sound like. Although *Rip* had never been considered a particularly Americanist overture, Chadwick, as the "Dean of American Music" (a mantle he detested), whose fame in large measure rested on vaguely nationalistic compositions like the Second Symphony, the Fourth String Quartet, and *Symphonic Sketches*, was expected by many to forge a distinctly American sound. He took the task of revision seriously, and *Rip Van Winkle* proved nearly an obsession for Chadwick in the first months of 1929; he composed furiously, and at one point even reported spending six hours a day on the score.[81] His "new" overture was completed on April 16, and the parts were ready before mid-May.

The very next month, June 1929, Chadwick conducted his new *Rip Van Winkle* Overture in a performance at NEC, perhaps in preparation for yet another hearing.[82] It had long been Chadwick's custom to iron out problems in his music using the resources of the NEC orchestra, and he would have seized the opportunity to rehearse and perform his refurbished overture at the conservatory. There he would have plenty of time to locate errors and revisit problematic passages before handing it over to the printers or to another conductor, if indeed those were his intentions.

Within a year after Chadwick's NEC performance, the eminent conductor, composer and music educator Howard Hanson featured the overture at his March 1930 "American Composer's Series" concerts. Produced as a tribute to "Dr." Chadwick, the concert included, besides *Rip Van Winkle* Overture, the more recent *Tam O'Shanter* and *The Angel of Death*. Also on the program were a fanfare by Hanson, who wrote it in honor of Chadwick, and an appearance by Rochester's Chadwick Choral Club, which had been founded in 1925.[83]

Like many of Chadwick's orchestral works, *Rip Van Winkle* Overture is programmatic. In the 1870s Chadwick was reluctant to provide any hints about the music's program beyond what would already have been known to the average American reader. As we have found, most of the time Chadwick preferred to let his music speak for itself. But in *Rip Van Winkle*'s case that reluctance had subsided by the 1920s, when he wrote a preface to the overture's revised version emphasizing that "it is in no sense program music, but to those who see pictures when they hear music a few hints may be useful." Chadwick then provided a program that follows Washington Irving's story faithfully:

> The calm, peaceful introduction may be like the pleasant valley where Rip van Winkle lived. The first theme in the fast tempo may suggest the jolly good-for-nothing which Rip really was. But he was fond of his little daughter, and so the second theme is sweeter.
>
> And when he wandered off into the mountains the little old men made him drink and play "Kegel" with them. Perhaps you hear the knocking of the ninepins and the rolling of the distant thunder. Then Rip goes to sleep and does not wake up for twenty years. There is a long pause in the music to indicate the passage of time.
>
> Then Rip wakes up and goes back to his home where he finds everything changed. All the rest of the overture means the general rejoicing at Rip van Winkle's return.[84]

Rip Van Winkle Overture is best known to us today in its revised version, which differs vastly from Chadwick's original version.[85] Three important changes are immediately apparent: first, the melodic material is altered rhythmically; second, instruments are added and crucial changes are made to the orchestrations; and finally, the overture's length is substantially reduced. As concerns the first point, the rhythmic changes are not widespread throughout the piece; in fact, only the principal theme undergoes dramatic transformation. The modifications are distinct, however, and occur as a means to enhance the "American" feel of the piece. Chadwick's new vision of his protagonist not only dispenses with the regular, rather square rhythms of the original, which were perfectly acceptable to a student composer with an 1870s European musical sensibility, but now the composer positively revels in the flourish, syncopation, and sheer bounce of his latter-day Rip. The character is now far more spirited, more ebullient than his previous manifestation, and echoes of his captivating persona are sounded throughout the overture. Another good example of Rip's rhythmic sprightliness is the metamorphosis that occurs in the final bars, where Chadwick has given the trombones a memorable syncopated passage built on the main theme that bears only a slight resemblance to the original.

Chadwick's instrumentation also changed significantly. The revision features the addition of color instruments, including piccolo; a small battery of percussion comprising bass drum, triangle, and one of Chadwick's favorite percussion instruments, the xylophone; and the tuba. The instruments are used in predictable ways much of the time. The piccolo often doubles the flute part, the tuba doubles the bass line, and the percussion instruments lend additional punctuation to climactic moments. But what is most striking about Chadwick's re-orchestration is not the mere addition of forces; rather, here Chadwick has fully reconsidered the sonic effects utilized in the original and has changed instrumental combinations in order to provide a more sparkling, resplendent sound. Several important examples will suffice to make the point: in the initial measures Chadwick enlivened the music by featuring a solo violin prominently where the bassoon was formerly featured. In the same segment, Chadwick replaced the accompanimental bassoon part with the solo cello. Another provocative orchestration change occurs at the beginning of the secondary theme, where the dark and sultry combination of the horn and clarinet in their low registers has been replaced by the slightly more shimmering combination of horn and flute.

Chadwick's formal revisions to the overture are less obvious than the changes already discussed, but they are no less significant. After years of experience and reflection, Chadwick was clearly bothered by the cumbersome length and the unbalanced design of the original version. The revision is seventy-nine measures shorter than the original, although the proportions of the respective sections have drastically changed. The introduction and exposition sections are nearly identical in both versions, while the length of the development in the revised version has been reduced by forty-one measures. The weightiest changes occur in the recapitulation, where Chadwick eliminated eighty-seven measures of material. The revised coda, however, features forty-seven additional measures, which enabled Chadwick once again to dazzle his audiences with a fiery close.

Hanson conducted the revised *Rip Van Winkle* Overture again in May 1931. On hand was Olin Downes, the influential music critic of the *New York Times*, who commented on the overture in terms that had been sounded by Chadwick's Leipzig critics nearly fifty-two years before. "The performance of the overture, certainly one of the best of Chadwick's works," Downes reported effusively, "was more than emphatic of the place that he holds in native musical art. It is first of all full of invention, and distinguished by a remarkable grasp of form. Conventional as it is harmonically, the spontaneity, humor, and poetical nature of certain portions of the overture more than justify the place given to it on this program and the significance attributed to it."[86]

Had he read it, Chadwick would have appreciated Downes's assessment. As we have seen, after the Great War and into the 1920s, Chadwick thought himself irrelevant. He sought to appeal to modern audiences, but he was unable to stray from deeply ingrained aesthetic principles. By revising *Rip Van Winkle* Overture, Chadwick smoothly brought his first major composition into line both with his mature compositional technique and with his later reputation as a composer of characteristically American music.

The revision of *Rip Van Winkle* Overture would be the composer's last major project. With laudatory reviews of a brilliant little overture, Chadwick effectively left the world in the same manner—musically speaking—in which he had entered it.

Chadwick's Death & Legacy

1931

With him a whole epoch in American music culminated.
—Olin Downes, *New York Times* (1931)

His unswerving creed was that of beauty in expression.
—Henry Hadley, *Musical Courier* (1937)

"Weep for Adonis"

Although gout had been a painful nemesis for decades, Chadwick's heart condition was more worrisome. In late 1930 and into the first months of 1931, problems that had been of concern became severe. "Paderewski dinner and concert," he wrote in his diary on December 27, 1930, "Had a heart attack and could not go." January 15, 1931: "Went to BSO rehearsal. Hadley came to lunch. Beastly cold. Very bad for heart." More comments, each made briefly, sometimes clinically, followed: "Heart attack in the night" (March 5, 1931); later that month, "Bad heart in a.m." (March 31, 1931). After months of scares and struggle, Chadwick's heart finally failed him at his home on 360 Marlborough Street on April 4, 1931.[1]

We learn several intimate details about Chadwick's death from Dr. Hamilton C. MacDougall, who penned an affectionate remembrance of him for publication in the organists' periodical *The Diapason*. (MacDougall had studied counterpoint with Chadwick at the turn of the century, but there is no evidence that they remained in close contact.) As they often did, the Chadwicks were entertaining friends at their home on Saturday evening. "About 10 [p.m.] he excused himself to go to bed," MacDougall reported. "Mrs. Chadwick, hearing a noise, went to the room where he had fallen and tried to help him up, but he died in her arms."[2]

His funeral service, swiftly arranged and conducted on April 7, was led by Rev. Arthur Lee Kinsolving and held at Boston's Trinity Church. Chadwick's attendants and pallbearers included old friends and colleagues: Wallace Goodrich, Ralph Flanders, Fred Converse, Henry Hadley, Edward Burlingame Hill, and Charles Martin Loeffler, among others. He was buried at the iconic Mount Auburn Cemetery in Jamaica Plain, just outside of Boston.

Notice of Chadwick's death in the Boston press was surprisingly cursory. A short, unsigned obituary appeared in the *Boston Evening Transcript* on April 6;

a funeral announcement followed the next day. The *Boston Post* ran a brief page-one article; the *Boston Herald* tucked its short post on page eight. The event stimulated disappointingly few memorial performances. Henry Hadley and his Manhattan Symphony honored Chadwick with a performance of Wagner's *Siegfried's Funeral Music*. It was pronounced "deeply moving."[3] Frederick Stock led his Chicago Symphony Orchestra in two performances of *Melpomene*. "This aristocratic, dignified music was reverently presented," wrote one auditor.[4] In a more celebratory vein, the National Orchestral Association under conductor Leon Barzin performed "Jubilee."[5]

Matters were more controversial in New York. In "Mephisto Musings," an editorial column in the popular periodical *Musical America*, the writer expressed surprise that Chadwick's death did not merit "official notice" by the New York Philharmonic. Although Chadwick was a New Englander, he was, the columnist asserted, of more than just regional importance—he was an American treasure. "Toscanini may not have wanted to do this [tribute] without a rehearsal, which I can understand," Mephisto mused, "but could he not have given the baton to [assistant conductor] Hans Lange?"[6]

In Boston, Goodrich led a memorial concert at NEC, portions of which were broadcast on the radio. It featured *Adonais* and *Ecce jam noctis*, along with works by Horatio Parker and others. Jordan Hall, we are told, was crowded.[7] Perhaps emblematic of how far Chadwick's star had fallen at the BSO, the orchestra performed "Noël" in the composer's honor on a Tuesday matinee program on April 21. It was given without fanfare, although a critic on hand thought Koussevitzky and the orchestra played it "very expressively, con amore."[8] Nevertheless, the tribute seemed a rather curt farewell to the towering composer who had dominated music in Boston since the 1880s.

"Mendelssohn Understood the Business":
Chadwick's Aesthetics, Ideals, and Legacy

Chadwick's legend had dissipated enormously by the time he died. He had long been considered "old hat," he thought, and in 1929, following a performance of his Fifth String Quartet by the New York Quartet, he remarked that the 1898 work was "a relic of the Ice Age."[9] In Chadwick's estimation, his music, tuneful and exultant, did not speak to musicians of a younger generation. Moreover, orchestra performances of his works became more infrequent, and his once exalted position at the forefront of American composition was eclipsed by others who produced works that were more accessible to professionals in recital or to amateur musicians at home. One such composer was Edward MacDowell, who had long given Chadwick an inferiority complex. MacDowell's body of piano music secured his place in American music history, as Chadwick understood when, during a visit to Minneapolis, he spoke before the city's Matinee Musicale Club. The emcee "addressed me as Mr. MacDowell," he wrote, "even after I answered her that Mac was dead. She also told me I was the greatest American composer *next to him*."[10] (Chadwick then quipped, "I wonder how Foote and Parker will like that.")

Recognition and appreciation would reappear slowly. Composer Howard Hanson championed Chadwick and other American composers throughout the 1930s and beyond. In 1943, a dozen years after Chadwick's death, Hanson wrote an article titled "Twenty Years' Growth in America," in which he reflected on the evolution of American music since the 1920s. While Hanson identified the founding in 1923 of the League of Composers as a seminal step in the musical development of the nation, he nevertheless respected and admired the older school of New England composers, especially Chadwick. Hanson, writing in the league's quarterly periodical *Modern Music*, acknowledged "the enormous debt which American music owes to Boston and the New England group" and outlined five important changes in music in America in the post–World War I era, a number of which he thought could be directly attributed to the Second New England school of composers.[11] They included: (1) the improved technical competence of composers; (2) the increase in opportunities afforded composers and a realization by the public that such support was their obligation; (3) the increase in the number of places—conservatories, universities, and private music schools—available for composers to learn their craft; (4) an energetic commingling of the "serious" with the "popular"; and (5) "a growing maturity in the attitude of the casual listener of American music." This final point, Hanson judged, "is indicated by the fact that the sophomoric search for the 'American art-form' has given way to the realization of the complexity of the American scene and an understanding that its artistic expression will be as varied in form as are the components of the country from which it springs. With this understanding has come a tolerance which finds both in the works of Chadwick and of [George] Gershwin manifestations of the American mind, and a maturity which does not demand the exclusion of one because it is not like the other."[12]

Hanson's convincing argument, aimed at garnering support for Chadwick and the New England composers, would not be heeded for decades.

As we have seen, Chadwick did not consider himself a nationalist composer. Perhaps his most definitive statement on the subject occurred in a 1915 interview, during which he boldly proclaimed, "Music, in a broad sense is cosmopolitan and universal; more or less nonsense is talked about a national school of music."[13]

Despite his "American" dalliances, and his experimentation with the "decadence" of impressionism, exoticism, and realism, at its most elemental Chadwick simply admired and sought musical beauty, comprehensible forms, and expert craftsmanship. Like John S. Dwight, he disdained that which he considered ugly.

And music in the modern age had gotten ugly. After hearing two psalms by Ernest Bloch, Chadwick complained that the music was "full of the most awful shrieks, grunts, groans, blasts and general row." He admitted that Bloch had decided talent ("the man has all the skill of Strauss or Stravinsky"), but his music "is totally devoid of a sense of Beauty."[14] Others agreed with his general position. "In an epoch of ferment and anxiety, disturbance and readjustment," said Robert Underwood Johnson in a 1926 speech to a crowd of two thousand at the unveiling of busts at New York University's Hall of Fame for Great Americans, and at which Chadwick's *Commemoration Ode* was to be performed, "when everything is being torn up by the roots to see how it is growing, they [i.e., those represented by the busts] call on us to hold fast to the principles and the unselfish purposes which the men and the women whom they portray have so conspicuously illustrated."[15] Over the course of his career, Chadwick had seen music torn up by its roots. Johnson, an officer in the American Academy and Institute of Arts, eloquently reflected a traditional aesthetic, which Chadwick himself felt deeply. Following a 1909 institute meeting, the composer wrote "I went to bed with a sense of gratitude that my lot has been cast among these idealists, these Visionaries, if you like, who worship beauty for its own sake and are never tired of preaching its gospel."[16] Olin Downes astutely observed that "music has an entirely different physiognomy and outlook than it had when [Chadwick] was at the zenith of his powers."[17]

As for matters of form and technique, Chadwick looked to late Beethoven and the masters of early Romanticism. Although it has been remarkably easy for musicologists to derisively accept the decades-old conclusion that the music by composers of this school is "conservative," in fact, it relied on a rich tradition. Chadwick pursued formal clarity over chaos; a "learned" style, which sometimes included counterpoint, and competent orchestration; light textures rather than the heavy, lengthy, and ponderous styles that were in vogue at the turn of the century (on the maximalism of Mahler's Eighth Symphony Chadwick wrote, "But it is not a symphony in the classical sense for it depends on massive choral effects rather than on convincing development for its effects"[18]); and, above all, he sought the more indefinable characteristics of dignity and nobility. To him, the often frenetic styles of modernism and its accompanying pandemonium were not simply inartistic; they were an affront to all he had loved and tried to emulate his entire life. Chadwick endeavored to achieve a characteristic that was once noticed by a perceptive critic as he listened to the composer's Third Symphony: his music, the critic thought, "can be measured by the classical yard-stick, yet it expresses modern thoughts."[19]

We have already discussed many of Chadwick's musical predilections, especially his dislikes in regard to modern music (Chadwick once admitted that he was considered by some as a "tough old cynic, sneering at Debussy and snoring through Richard Strauss"[20]), but he admired many composers, and his assessments of their works offer a chance to further infer his compositional aesthetic. Chadwick appreciated pleasing melody and coherent formal structure first and foremost, and, as we have seen in our examination of his many orchestral works, he adhered closely to traditional principles; likewise, he appreciated those qualities in others. Upon hearing a 1914 performance of MacDowell's *Indian Suite*, Chadwick concluded that for all the composer's "sneers at the sonata form," he had used it effectively.[21] There was no question that, to Chadwick, sonata form still held enormous possibilities for expression.

Music in a traditional vein garnered Chadwick's respect. After a performance of Brahms's First Symphony by Muck and the BSO, Chadwick remarked that it "puts all its successors into the shade. After all dignity and repose *are* necessary qualities and there is no big music without it."[22] A Bax string quartet contained "bully Irish tunes and rhythms but plenty of modern harmony and very striking instrumentation. It was a comfort to hear some new music that does not depend on the poly-tonal fad for its effects and on unresolved dissonances for a raison d'être."[23] Chadwick admired much of Vaughn Williams's music, if the composer himself, whom he had met at the Norfolk Festival, seemed sedate. He regarded the *Variations on a Theme of Thomas Tallis* as "full of delicate tints; very modern in harmony but logical and sane." As if to further validate Vaughn Williams's music, Chadwick noted that "it contains numberless striking examples of such progressions as are found in the appendix to my Harmony book."[24] In 1912, as Chadwick rehearsed the NEC Orchestra for a performance of Beethoven's Sixth Symphony, he wrote, "But what serenity, what repose, what gladsome melody and buoyancy are in this so-called weakest of Beethoven's Symphonies!!"[25] Others, of course, heard the same traits in Chadwick's music. Olin Downes commented on the pervading personality of the Yankee's music: "This spirit was devotional, earnest, high-minded. It embodied high living and thinking, a deep love of music in its simpler and less complex manifestations and a reliance upon it for solace and inspiration."[26]

Chadwick's approach to composition was workmanlike. For him, music was not just a calling, it was a vocation—after all, he had a family to raise, and music, especially teaching and administration, paid the bills. When it came to composing, he was of a similar mind and approached his work with the mindset of a craftsman. MacDougall reiterated this point when he reflected that "in regard to his own compositions he would always say: 'Last year I *made* so-and-so,' rather than *composed* or *wrote*. I remember his saying once, 'Mendelssohn understood the business.'"[27] The business Mendelssohn understood was that music is an art, but it is also a craft and a profession, and a living can be carved from it if one applies oneself. Another indication of his attitude, perhaps one characteristic of his pragmatic Yankee upbringing, was that Chadwick never agonized over his compositions. He worked hard—constantly and quickly—but at no time did artistic creation engender for him even a hint of consternation. If, especially as a teacher or administrator, Chadwick sometimes took on the mantle of a tyrant, he rarely affected genius. MacDougall recalled that "the brief time I had lessons with [Chadwick] showed me what a clear thinker he was, how destitute of all pomposity, bluster and self-conceit."[28] To Chadwick, composing was all in a day's work.

Chadwick's music figured prominently in the resurgence in the 1980s and 1990s of interest in music by nineteenth- and early twentieth-century American composers. Although his orchestral works had been performed sporadically since his death, especially at NEC, his music did not enter into the repertoire of any professional ensemble. *Melpomene* and various movements of the *Symphonic Sketches* sustained Chadwick's small place in the concert hall throughout the mid-twentieth century. Noteworthy performances of the former were Hans Lange's 1940 concert with the Chicago Symphony Orchestra and Leonard Bernstein's New York Philharmonic performance at Carnegie Hall in 1958. As for the latter composition, John Barbirolli conducted "Jubilee" in a 1937 youth concert in New York, and other individual movements from Chadwick's genial suite were heard on and off for decades on programs throughout the country. In what seems almost an aberration, Fritz Reiner conducted all four *Sketches* in Chicago in 1941.

Musicologist Steven Ledbetter conducted a performance of *Judith* at Dartmouth College in 1977, a keystone event in Chadwick performance history, and one that garnered national attention. For the first time in decades, a serious Chadwick composition was listened to seriously. One critic admired the workmanship and detected "traces of Mendelssohn, Puccini, and Saint-Saëns mixed . . . with Eastern evocations, marches (Chadwick's are nearly identical with Sousa's), and anthem-like music."[29]

It was not until Chadwick's music became widely available via sound recording that his renown surged. Although several recordings had appeared throughout the mid-century in a variety of formats—including those by Karl Krueger, who conducted several orchestras for the Society for the Preservation of the American Musical Heritage, and Jorge Mester and the Louisville Orchestra—it was Julius Hegyi's 1986 recording of the Symphony no. 2 and the three-compact-disc set of Chadwick's chamber music played by the Northeastern String Quartet (produced by Ledbetter) in 1988 that set the stage for a wave of excellent recordings.[30]

Conductors Neeme Järvi and Jose Serebrier, of the Detroit Symphony Orchestra and the Czech State Philharmonic, respectively, led the Chadwick renaissance of the 1990s, with stellar recordings of the composer's best-loved music, as well as a number of seldom-heard pieces. Järvi breathed life into Chadwick's Third Symphony, and Serebrier offered up a thrilling, raucous performance of *Tam O'Shanter*; other cuts are equally valuable. Several well-conceived recordings have followed: the Nashville Symphony Orchestra's 2002 disc includes several unpublished works, and Peter Kairoff's 2005 compilation of Chadwick's piano music, titled "American Character," glimpses a seldom-encountered aspect of Chadwick's compositional personality.

Important writings have also appeared, especially Victor Fell Yellin's valuable 1990 life-and-works biography, *Chadwick: Yankee Composer*, as well as several analytical and bibliographical works. Scholarly articles and editions of his music, including two overtures and the string quartets, have also appeared. From today's vantage point it looks as though Chadwick's growing reputation as a music administrator, teacher, and composer of uncommon ability will not only survive but thrive.

Of course, Chadwick knew that his music and career eventually would stoke historical inquiry. Carl Engel's 1924 *Musical Quarterly* article had already offered that promise. Chadwick himself surmised on several occasions that this composition or that would gain in popularity, or at least appreciation, after his death. And the respected historian of Boston's general culture and the BSO, M. A. DeWolfe Howe, even considered writing Chadwick's biography in the 1920s.[31]

Chadwick cautiously guarded his posthumous reputation, however. In 1927, as he was cleaning his office at the end of the NEC school term, he "destroyed all pencil sketches and all sketches of works which have been published. I do not want any 'sweepings' of the studio to rise up and call me 'Damned.'"[32] With many of his compositional sketches gone, he gave his eldest son custody of his personal writings and effects. As intimate family documents, they were jealously defended against possible intrusion by historians. "I have made this somewhat voluminous record of my childhood," Chadwick wrote to his family in 1917, "not because it is of any special interest to any one at present, but because a future generation may get an idea from it of life in a small New England town while it still retained some of the characteristics of real American life."[33] In 1950 Theodore Chadwick, now approaching his sixties, donated a large number of his father's music manuscripts to the Library of Congress. Many others had already found safe haven at NEC. The memoirs and diaries were not so lucky. Upon Theodore's passing, Chadwick's writings burrowed their way into the deep recesses of family storage. Inasmuch as few in the family were musically informed—and Chadwick's fame had long since faded—there was not a keen awareness of the value of those possessions as music-historical artifacts. Which was just as well; Chadwick would not have wanted them made public.

But after a time, portions, and then whole sections, became available. Now— Chadwick's family and heirs having donated their collection to the loving care of NEC—his documents may and must continue to be mined, for they are essential to a complete understanding of his music and musical life in Boston during his age. Although perhaps never so intended, Chadwick's writings, no less so than his music, are an invaluable piece of America's musical record.

Springfield Music Festivals, Selected Repertoire & Guest Artists (1890–1899)

1890

Beethoven	Symphony no. 5
Bruch	*Fair Ellen* (cantata)
Chadwick	"Scherzo" from Symphony no. 2
Chadwick	*Lovely Rosabelle* (ballad for soloists, chorus, and orchestra)
Dvořák	*Slavonic Dances*
Goldmark	*Sakuntala* Overture, op. 13
Gounod	*The Redemption* (oratorio)
J. C. D. Parker	*St. John* (cantata)
Raff	Symphony no. 5
Wagner	Prelude to *Die Meistersinger*

1891

Grieg	*Peer Gynt* Suite
Liszt	*Les préludes*
E. MacDowell	*Ophelia*
Mendelssohn	*St. Paul* (oratorio)
H. W. Parker	*The Kobolds* (cantata)
Rossini	Stabat Mater
Schumann	Symphony no. 1
Tchaikovsky	Piano Concerto, op. 23; Adele Aus der Ohe, piano

1892

Chadwick	*Phoenix expirans* (cantata)
Dvořák	*The Specter's Bride* (cantata)
Haydn	*The Creation* (oratorio)
G. Henschel	*Hamlet* Suite, op. 50
Rubenstein	Piano Concerto in D Minor; Franz Rummel, pianist

1893

Beethoven	Symphony no. 8
Chadwick	*Melpomene*
Mendelssohn	*Elijah* (oratorio)
Saint-Saëns	*Rouet d'Omphale*
Verdi	Requiem
George E. Whiting	*Dream Pictures* (cantata)

1894

Chadwick	*Lovely Rosabelle* (ballad for soloists, chorus, and orchestra)
Chopin	Concerto in F minor; Vladimir de Pachmann, piano
Handel	*The Messiah* (oratorio)
Mendelssohn	Symphony no. 3 (*Scottish*)
H. W. Parker	*Hora Novissima* (cantata)
Weber	Overture to *Euryanthe*

1895

Beethoven	Symphony no. 3 (*Eroica*)
Saint-Saëns	*Samson et Delilah* (grand opera)
Mendelssohn	Violin Concerto; Franz Kneisel, violin
Mendelssohn	Symphony no. 2 (*Hymn of Praise*)
Mozart	Overture to *The Magic Flute*
Wagner	Overture to *The Flying Dutchman*

1896

Beethoven	*Coriolanus* Overture
Bruch	*Arminius* (oratorio)
Chadwick	*Lochinvar*; Max Heinrich, tenor
Chadwick	*The Lily Nymph* (cantata)
Mackenzie	*Brittania* Overture
Massenet	*Eve* (oratorio)
Schubert	Symphony no. 9 (*The Great*)
Wagner	Overture to *Die Meistersinger*
Weber	*Jubel* Overture
A. Whiting	*Fantasie for Piano and Orchestra*; Arthur Whiting, piano

1897

Brahms	Symphony no. 2
Gounod	Suite from *Philémon et Baucis*
Mendelssohn	*Elijah* (oratorio)
Saint-Saëns	*Samson et Delilah* (grand opera)
Schubert	Symphony no. 8 (*Unfinished*)
Schumann	Piano Concerto; Adele Aus der Ohe, piano
Stanford	*Phaudrig Crohoore* (Irish ballad for chorus and orchestra)
Wagner	Overture to *Rienzi*

1898

Beethoven	Symphony no. 9
Bruch	*Fair Ellen* (cantata)
Chadwick	*Symphonic Sketches*
Dvořák	*Scherzo capriccioso*
Goodrich	*Ave Maria*
Lalo	*Rhapsodie*

Massenet	Suite from *Les Erinnyes*
H. W. Parker	*The Legend of St. Christopher* (oratorio)
Schumann	*Genoveva* Overture
Schumann	Symphony no. 4
Wagner	*Siegfried Idyll*

1899

Bach	Suite in D
Beethoven	Symphony no. 4
Bruch	Concerto in G minor; Olive Mead, violin
Chadwick	*Ecce jam noctis* (for male chorus and orchestra)
Goldmark	*Sakuntala* Overture, op. 13
Mendelssohn	*Elijah* (oratorio)
J. K. Paine	Prelude to *Oedipus Rex*
H. W. Parker	*A Northern Ballad*
Tchaikovsky	Concerto in B-flat; Teresa Carreño, piano

Worcester Music Festivals, Selected Repertoire & Guest Artists (1898–1901)

Forty-First Annual Festival (September 26–30, 1898)

Beach	*The Rose of Avontown* (cantata)
Brahms	Symphony no. 2
Chadwick	*The Lily Nymph* (dramatic cantata)
Grieg	*Olaf Tryggvason* (opera)
Lalo	*Concerto Russe for Violin and Orchestra*, op. 29; Ovide Musin, violin
Massenet	Suite from *Les Erinnyes*
Mendelssohn	*Elijah* (oratorio)
Mozart	Overture to *The Magic Flute*
H. W. Parker	*Hora Novissima* (oratorio)
Raff	Symphony no. 3 (*Im Walde*), op. 153
Rheinberger	Concerto for Organ, op. 137; Wallace Goodrich, organ
Schumann	Concerto for Piano and Orchestra, op. 54; Adele aus der Ohe, piano
Tchaikovsky	*Romeo and Juliet* Overture
Wagner	Excerpts from *Tannhäuser*

Forty-Second Annual Festival (September 25–29, 1899)

Berlioz	*Damnation of Faust* (dramatic legend)
Chadwick	*The Lily Nymph* (dramatic cantata)
Chopin	Piano Concerto in F minor, op. 21; Vladimir de Pachman, piano
Converse	Symphony no. 1 (first movement only)
Haydn	*The Creation* (oratorio)
Mackenzie	*Brittania* Overture
Mendelssohn	*Athalie* Overture
H. W. Parker	*King Trojan* (cantata)
Tchaikovsky	Symphony no. 5
Wagner	Excerpts from *Lohengrin*

Forty-Third Annual Festival (September 24–28, 1900)

Beethoven	*Leonore* Overture (no. 2)
Brahms	*A German Requiem*
Franck	*Les béatitudes* (oratorio)
Glazuonoff	Symphony no. 6
E. MacDowell	*Lancelot and Elaine*
Tchaikovsky	Piano Concerto in B-flat minor; Augusta Cottlow, piano
Verdi	Te Deum
Wagner	Selections from *Die Walküre* and *Rienzi*; E. Schumann-Heink, soprano

Forty-Fourth Annual Festival (September 23–27, 1901)

Beethoven	Symphony no. 2
Bizet	Suite from *Jeux d'Enfants*
Brahms	Symphony no. 3
Chadwick	*Judith* (lyric drama)
Franck	*Les béatitudes* (oratorio)
E. Kelly	*Aladdin Suite*
Liszt	*Concerto Pathetique*; Richard Burmeister, piano
Mackenzie	*Coriolanus Suite*
Massenet	*Phèdre* Overture
Nicolai	Overture to *The Merry Wives of Windsor*
Schumann	Overture, Scherzo, and Finale, op. 52
Wagner	Overture to *Die Meistersinger*

APPENDIX 3

Chadwick's Major North American Travels (1892–1927)

Date	Event/Location	Activity
October 1892	World's Columbian Exhibition (Chicago)	Premiere of *Columbian Ode*
January 1896	St. Louis Choral-Symphony Society	Conducts Symphony no. 2
April 1897	Montreal Festival	Conducts *Lily Nymph*
June/July 1898	Omaha International Exposition	Lecture-demonstrations
January 1907	Ottawa, Canada	Music contest judge
December 1908	Washington, DC	MTNA Convention
January 1910	Chicago Symphony Orchestra	Conducts *Symphonic Sketches*
November 1913	Chicago Symphony Orchestra	Conducts *Melpomene*
June 1915	Ninth Biennial Convention of Federation of Music Clubs (Los Angeles)	Conducts *Symphonic Sketches*
August 1915	Panama-Pacific Exposition (San Francisco)	Conducts *Melpomene* and *Euterpe*
January 1916	Minneapolis Symphony Orchestra and Chicago Symphony Orchestra	Conducts *Tam O'Shanter*
January 1919	Chicago Symphony Orchestra T. Thomas Memorial	Conducts Symphony no. 3 Concert
July 1919	Montreal/Tadaussac/Quebec/Albany	Vacation with Theodore (son)
December 1921	Detroit, Michigan	Silver, Burdett meetings
March 1922	Florida	Health retreat
December 1922	Chicago	Family visit
April 1923	Rochester, New York	Eastman School visit
May 1923	Chicago	Family visit
July 1923	San Francisco, California	Invited to conduct *Tam O'Shanter*
February 1925	Rochester, New York	Eastman School visit
August 1927	Tadaussac/Quebec/Blue Hill	Vacation

Boston Symphony Orchestra Performances
of Chadwick's Music through 1931

Year	Composition	Conductor
1883	*Thalia*	G. W. Chadwick
1884	Symphony no. 2 (2nd movement only)	George Henschel
1886	Symphony no. 2	G. W. Chadwick
1887	*Melpomene*	Wilhelm Gericke
1889	*Melpomene* (twice)	Wilhelm Gericke
1891	Symphony no. 2	Arthur Nikisch
1894	Symphony no. 3	G. W. Chadwick
1896	*Melpomene*	Wilhelm Gericke
1898	*Melpomene*	Wilhelm Gericke
1900	*Adonais*	Wilhelm Gericke
1903	*Melpomene* (Jordan Hall inaugural concert)	G. W. Chadwick
1904	*Euterpe*	G. W. Chadwick
1906	*Cleopatra*	Karl Muck
1907	*Cleopatra* (tour selection)	Karl Muck
1908	*Symphonic Sketches*	Karl Muck
1909	*Theme, Variations and Fugue*	Max Fiedler
1910	*Sinfonietta in D*	Max Fiedler
1911	*Suite Symphonique*	G. W. Chadwick
1913	*Aphrodite*	Karl Muck
1914	Symphony no. 3	Karl Muck
1915	*Symphonic Sketches* (on the California tour)	Karl Muck
1916	*Tam O'Shanter*	G. W. Chadwick
1918	*Symphonic Sketches*	Karl Muck
1918	*Land of Our Hearts*	Henri Rabaud
1919	*Angel of Death*	Pierre Monteux
1921	*Melpomene*	Pierre Monteux
1921	*Theme, Variations and Fugue*	Pierre Monteux
1922	*Anniversary* Overture	Pierre Monteux
1930	*Sinfonietta in D*	Sergey Koussevitzky
1931	*Symphonic Sketches* ("Noël" only)	Sergey Koussevitzky

APPENDIX 5

Chadwick's Music Performed by Sousa's Band (1894–1927)

indicates selection performed on tour

1894	Selections from *Tabasco*
1895	Selections from *Tabasco*
1896	"The Danza"
1898	*Rip Van Winkle* Overture*
1902	*Rip Van Winkle* Overture
1904	"Jubilee" from *Symphonic Sketches**
1905	"Jubilee" from *Symphonic Sketches**
1906	"Jubilee" from *Symphonic Sketches*
1908	"Jubilee" from *Symphonic Sketches**
1909	"Jubilee" from *Symphonic Sketches*
1910	"A Vagrom Ballad" from *Symphonic Sketches*
	"Canzonetta" from *Sinfonietta in D*
	"Jubilee" from *Symphonic Sketches*
1911	"Canzonetta" from *Sinfonietta in D**
1914	"The Maiden and the Butterfly"
	"Jubilee" from *Symphonic Sketches*
1915	"Canzonetta" from *Sinfonietta in D**
1916	"Jubilee" from *Symphonic Sketches*
	Selections from *Tabasco*
1918	The Fighting Men (march)
	"Jubilee" from *Symphonic Sketches*
1923	"Jubilee" from *Symphonic Sketches*
1926	*Tam O'Shanter**
	"The Cricket and the Bumblebee"
1927	*Tam O'Shanter*

*Works and repositories frequently cited are identified in the endnotes
by the following abbreviations:*

BET	*Boston Evening Transcript*
CC-NEC	Chadwick Collection, New England Conservatory
CtY-HPP	Yale University, Horatio Parker Papers
DJoM	*Dwight's Journal of Music*
ICN-FGGC	Newberry Library, Chicago, Frederick Grant Gleason Collection
ICN-TTP	Newberry Library, Chicago, Theodore Thomas Papers
MB-Mu	Boston Public Library, Music Department, Allen A. Brown Collection
NYT	*New York Times*
PPi-GHWP	Carnegie Library of Pittsburgh, George H. Wilson Papers

Prologue: A Chadwick Sketch

1. Slonimsky, "Composers of New England," 26.

2. Olin Downes, "George Whitefield Chadwick—Passing of Dean of American Composers Marks End of Epoch in Native Tonal Art," *NYT* (April 12, 1931): IX/7.

3. "Second New England School" was adopted by H. Wiley Hitchcock in a noble attempt to free its members from the shackles of musical conservatism implied by the word "Classicists" and to locate them within a tradition of American music-making. See Hitchcock, *Music in the United States*, 143.

4. Kearns, *Horatio Parker*, 5.

5. Chadwick, Diary, [after March 27], 1910 (CC-NEC).

1. Chadwick's New England Roots

1. See Broyles, "Music of the Highest Class," 41.

2. Crawford, *America's Musical Life*, 26.

3. For excellent summaries of the controversies surrounding Old Way and Regular Singing, see Crawford, *America's Musical Life* (chap. 2 and 3, 15–55) and Broyles, "Music of the Highest Class" (chap. 2, 33–61).

4. Coffin, *History of Boscawen* (1878); Buxton, *History of Boscawen and Webster* (1933); Boscawen Historical Society, *History: Town of Boscawen, 1933–1983* (1983). The last listed is beyond the chronological scope of this volume.

5. Coffin himself was a fascinating figure. As an army correspondent for the *Boston Journal* in the 1860s, he was reportedly the first news man to inform leaders in Washington that the Battle of Gettysburg had been won by Union forces. In his position as a war correspondent, he had unusual access to Abraham Lincoln; he eventually wrote a respected biography of the assassinated president. See Wingate, "Boston Letter," 234; and Coffin, *Abraham Lincoln* (1893).

6. Coffin, *History of Boscawen*, 485.

7. Boscawen Historical Society, *History: Town of Boscawen, 1933–1983*, 392; letter to the author from Virginia Chadwick Colby, October 3, 2000.

8. Letter to the author from Virginia Chadwick Colby, October 3, 2000.

9. Coffin, *History of Boscawen*, 485.

10. Elson, *History of American Music*, 170. Inquiries to the National Archives regarding Edmund's activities have not yielded confirmation of his war participation. According to the Archives, his files cannot be located (letter from National Archives to the author, September 10, 1999).

11. Coffin, *History of Boscawen*, 485.

12. Chadwick, Diary, June 17, 1925 (CC-NEC). Chadwick was registered member no. 13,980 of Sons of the American Revolution.

13. Letter to the author from Dorothy Sanborn, Boscawen Town Clerk, October 16, 1999.

14. Coffin, *History of Boscawen*, 290.

15. Silver and Silver, *From King's Plantation to Home Town Heritage*, 118–19.

16. Engel, "George W. Chadwick," 441.

17. Getchell, *Fitts Families*, 45–6.

18. Ibid., 69–70.

19. Ibid., 112–3.

20. Moore, *History of the Town of Candia*, 267; 285; 251; 284, 290; 272.

21. Alternate spellings of the family name included Fitts, Fitz, and Fittz.

22. Moore, *History of the Town of Candia*, 380.

23. Asa Fitz, *American School Hymn Book*, preface.

24. Getchell, *Fitts Families*, 200.

25. Moore, *History of the Town of Candia*, 374.

26. Ibid., 378.

27. Moore, *History of the Town of Candia*, 316.

28. Ibid., 316–18.

29. Letter to the author from Dorothy Sanborn, Boscawen Town Clerk, July 26, 2000.

30. Engel, "George W. Chadwick," 441.

31. Boscawen, New Hampshire, Town Records, vol. 3: 309. As with Asa, the family name Fitts is sometimes seen as Fitz; since Fitz Henry signed his own name like the latter, its use has been adopted here; throughout his life he was simply called Henry. See Chadwick, Memoirs, 1880–1893 (CC-NEC).

32. Chadwick, Memoirs, 1880–1893 (CC-NEC).

33. Yellin, *Chadwick: Yankee Composer*, 12. According to Chadwick's grandson, Theodore Chadwick Jr., this news came as a shock to George's heirs, who thought Susan Collins was the original family matriarch; author interview with Theodore Chadwick Jr., June 15–20, 1997.

34. Chadwick, Memoirs, 1880–1893 (CC-NEC). Chadwick also dedicated his First Symphony to her.

35. Chadwick, Diary, November 2, 1911 (CC-NEC).

36. Chadwick, "A Plea for Choral Singing," read before the Dedham Historical Society, November 5, 1919; in file no. RG1.2/E/9/8 (CC-NEC). This paper exists in two drafts.

37. Ibid.

38. According to information provided on a printed program for Chadwick's "The Pilgrims" included in Chadwick, Memoirs, [February 19], 1914 (CC-NEC).

39. Some of this information has been gleaned from an untitled, undated typescript; in file no. RG1.2/G/11/10 (CC-NEC).

40. Ibid.

41. Coffin, *History of Boscawen*, 298–99.

42. "Deacon Gould's book" might refer to Nathan Gould's popular *Social Harmony* (Boston: T. Badger, 1823).

43. Yellin, "George Chadwick and Populist Music," 9.

44. Engel, "George W. Chadwick," 441–2.

45. Elson, *History of American Music*, 170.

46. Chadwick, Memoirs, 1895 (CC-NEC).

47. Engel, "George W. Chadwick," 442.

48. Chadwick, Diary, October 1, 1910 (CC-NEC).

49. Elson, *History of American Music*, 170.

2. Early Life in Lowell, Lawrence, Boston & Michigan

1. Josephine L. Baker, "The Lowell Offering," 5 (1845): 97–100; quoted in Eisler, "The Lowell Offering," 82.

2. Eisler, "The Lowell Offering," 18–19.

3. Dickens, *American Notes*, 111.

4. Ibid., 114.

5. Ibid.

6. Mitchell, "Good Citizens," 117.

7. Interview with Theodore Chadwick Jr., June 15–20, 1997.

8. Rybicki, "The Mill Girls of Lowell," 9–10.

9. Ibid., 10.

10. Ibid., 10.

11. Gross, *Industrial Decline*, 66–7.

12. Dickens, *American Notes*, 117.

13. Eisler, "The Lowell Offering," 33.

14. Dickens, *American Notes*, 118.

15. Suggested by Getchell in *Fitts Families*, 140.

16. Interview with Theodore Chadwick Jr., June 15–20, 1997.

17. Chadwick, Certificate of Record of Birth, November 13, 1854, City of Lowell (file no. 1087): 179.

18. Cole, *Immigrant City*, 17; Wadsworth, *History of Lawrence*, 163.

19. Cole, *Immigrant City*, 49.

20. Ibid., 22.

21. Lawrence City Directories; 1859: 65; 1860: 27; 1864: 62; 1866: 41; 1868–69: 44; 1871: 39; 1873: 43 and 308; 1877: 44.

22. Wadsworth, *History of Lawrence*, 124.

23. Upton, "Musical Societies," 69.

24. Wadsworth, *Quarter-Centennial History*, 130.

25. Chadwick, Memoirs, 1869–1876 (CC-NEC).

26. Ibid.

27. Engel, "George W. Chadwick," 442.

28. Yellin, *Chadwick: Yankee Composer*, 17.

29. Chadwick to George H. Wilson, January 8, 1888 (PPi-GHWP).

30. Ibid.

31. Ibid.

32. Ibid.

33. Chadwick, Memoirs, 1869–1876 (CC-NEC).

34. Ibid.

35. *The [Daily] American*, February 11, 1876; in file no. RG.2/F/2 (CC-NEC).

36. Ibid.

37. Chadwick, Diary, March 18, 1908 (CC-NEC).

38. Chadwick, Memoirs, 1877–1880 (CC-NEC).

39. Engel, "George W. Chadwick," 443.

40. Cole, *Immigrant City*, 27.

41. Wadsworth, *Quarter-Centennial History*, 163.

42. Cole, *Immigrant City*, 132.

43. Chadwick, Memoirs, 1869–1876 (CC-NEC).

44. Cole, *Immigrant City*, 45.

45. Ibid.

46. Gilmore, *National Peace Jubilee*, 2.

47. Henry and Alonzo are listed in Gilmore, *National Peace Jubilee*, 686 and 706, respectively.

48. Foote, "A Bostonian Remembers," 38.

49. Fisher, *Music in Old Boston*, 46–7.

50. Howells, *Suburban Sketches*, 199–201.

51. Ibid.

52. Ryan, *Recollections of an Old Musician*, 198–203.

53. Dunham, *Life of a Musician*, 54.

54. "'America Must Utilize Music, Like Germans' Say Sinfonians," clip dated by hand February 28,1918, in Sousa Press Book, box no. 26, US Marine Band Library, Washington, DC.

55. Chadwick, Memoirs, 1869–1876 (CC-NEC).

56. Ibid.

57. Chadwick, "A 'Touch' of Beethoven," *Neume*, 3 (1907): 35–6.

58. McPherson and Klein, *Measure by Measure*, 37.

59. Chadwick, Memoirs, 1869–1876 (CC-NEC).

60. Ibid.

61. Coffin, *Story of the Great Fire*, 10.

62. Ibid.

63. Chadwick, Memoirs, 1869–1876 (CC-NEC).

64. Salter, "Eugene Thayer," 864.

65. Ibid., 864–5.

66. Chadwick, Memoirs, 1869–1876 (CC-NEC).

67. Elson, *History of American Music*, 170–71.

68. Chadwick, Memoirs, 1869–1876 (CC-NEC).

69. Ibid.

70. The performance occurred on June 19, 1874; the BWV numbers are unknown.

71. Programs located in Chadwick, Scrapbooks, 1874–1896 (CC-NEC).

72. Hector Berlioz, *Grande traité d'instrumentation et d'orchestration modernes* (Paris: Schonenberger, 1843); an English translation appeared in 1856.

73. *The New Prodigal* premiered on December 28, 1874; see Chadwick, Memoirs, 1869–1876 (CC-NEC).

74. *Daily American*, November 17, 1875; in file no. RG.2/F/2 (CC-NEC).

75. *Daily American*, October 6, 1875; in file no. RG.2/F/2 (CC-NEC).

76. *Daily American*, November 17, 1875; in file no. RG.2/F/2 (CC-NEC).

77. Ibid.

78. *Daily American*, December 9, 1875; in file no. RG.2/F/2 (CC-NEC).

79. Foote and Raffy, *Arthur Foote*, 22.

80. "From the Preface to the First Edition" in Coon (ed.), *Richter's Manual of Harmony*, iv.

81. Ibid., v.

82. Engel, "George W. Chadwick," 443.

83. Ibid.

84. Chadwick, "Musical Atmosphere," 138–41.

85. Ibid., 138.

86. Memoirs, 1869–1876 (CC-NEC).

87. Ibid.

88. "Italian Opera," *DJoM* 34/19 (December 26, 1874): 358–9.

89. Santayana, "Intellectual Temper of the Age," 11.

90. Chadwick, Memoirs, 1877–1880 (CC-NEC).

91. Chadwick, "Musical Atmosphere," 138.

92. Chadwick, Memoirs, 1877–1880 (CC-NEC).

93. In 1872.

94. Chadwick, Memoirs, 1869–1876 (CC-NEC).

95. Chadwick, "Theodore Presser," *Etude* 44 (January 1926): 10; Olivet College and Conservatory Catalogue, 1876–1877.

96. Chadwick, "Theodore Presser," *Etude* 44 (January 1926): 10.

97. Williams, *History of Olivet College*, 116.

98. Chadwick, "Theodore Presser," *Etude* 44 (January 1926): 10.

99. Chadwick to Charles Saunders, September 17, 1876 (CC-NEC).

100. Williams, *History of Olivet College*, 92.

101. Olivet College and Conservatory Catalogue, 1876–1877, 49–50. Chadwick is referred to as "Professor" in this publication.

102. Ibid., 49.

103. An Olivet College fire destroyed various records, yearbooks, and miscellaneous resources; letter to the author from Julie Walker, Librarian, Olivet College, 1996.

104. Engel, "George W. Chadwick," 443.

105. Program dated October 9, 1876. See Chadwick, Scrapbooks, 1874–1896 (CC-NEC).

106. Programs located in Chadwick, Scrapbooks, 1874–1896 (CC-NEC).

107. Now known as the Music Teachers National Association.

108. Proceedings of the Musical Teachers National Association, 1877 (Delaware, Ohio: Geo. H. Thompson, Job Printer, 1877): 34–9; also quoted in Yellin, "George Chadwick and Populist Music," 13–14.

109. Ibid. George M. Cohan's "Yankee Doodle Dandy" (1904) follows Chadwick's disparaged recipe.

110. Ibid.

111. Ibid. Emphasis mine.

112. "Tributes to [*sic*] Eminent Men and Women to Theodore Presser," *Etude* 44/1 (January 1926): 10.

113. Engel, "George W. Chadwick," 443. The "op. 11" reflects Chadwick's revised numbering system.

114. Chadwick to Charles Saunders, November 19, 1876 (CC-NEC).

115. Chadwick, "Theodore Presser," *Etude* 44 (January 1926): 10.

116. Chadwick to Charles Saunders, May 18, 1877 (CC-NEC).

117. Engel, "George W. Chadwick," 444.

118. Chadwick to Charles Saunders, September 17, 1876 (CC-NEC).

119. Chadwick, Memoirs, 1877–1880 (CC-NEC).

120. Engel, "George W. Chadwick," 444.

121. Chadwick, Diary, August 4, 1922 (CC-NEC).

122. Chadwick to William Orcutt, *Christian Science Monitor* (undated clipping); in file no. RG1.2/6 (CC-NEC); also cited in Bomberger, "German Musical Training," 71.

3. Chadwick's European Education

1. Chadwick, Diary, [after June 12], 1917 (CC-NEC).

2. "The Piano Factory Fire," *NYT* (September 5, 1877): 5.

3. "Eighty Buildings Burned," *NYT* (September 4, 1877): 1.

4. "The Piano Factory Fire," *NYT* (September 5, 1877): 5.

5. See New York Maritime Register (September 26–October 17, 1877). His departure on the sixth is confirmed in "Departures for Europe," *NYT* (September 6, 1877): 8. It lists J. [*sic*] W. Chadwick and companions Herrmann and Heubach.

6. Chadwick, Memoirs, 1877–1880 (CC-NEC).

7. Ibid.

8. August Wilhelm Bach was not related to J. S. Bach.

9. Bomberger, "German Musical Training," 219.

10. Chadwick, Memoirs, 1877–1880 (CC-NEC).

11. Bomberger, "German Musical Training," 72.

12. Chadwick, Memoirs, 1877–1880 (CC-NEC).

13. Ibid.

14. Ibid.

15. Cited in Bomberger, "German Musical Training," 76 (trans. by Bomberger).

16. For his part, Reinecke fondly remembered Chadwick and other American students in reflections titled "My Pupils and Myself," *Etude* 26/1 (January 1908): 7–8.

17. Chadwick, Memoirs, 1877–1880 (CC-NEC).

18. Program inserted into Chadwick, Memoirs, 1877–1880 (CC-NEC).

19. This information is gleaned from an annotation on the exam concert program.

20. "Correspondenzen," *Neue Zeitschrift fur Musik* 74/1 (June 21, 1878): 273.

21. Ledbetter, liner notes, Northeastern Records 236-CD, 1988.

22. Chadwick to Charles Saunders, July 12, 1878 (CC-NEC).

23. Chadwick to Charles Saunders, May 27, 1878 (CC-NEC).

24. Beveridge, "Sophisticated Primitivism," 25.

25. Ledbetter, liner notes, Northeastern Records 236-CD (1988).

26. Ibid.

27. Chadwick, Memoirs, 1877–1880 (CC-NEC).

28. Ibid.

29. Program located in Chadwick, Scrapbooks, 1874–1896 (CC-NEC).

30. Chadwick, Memoirs, 1877-1880 (CC-NEC).

31. Program located in Chadwick, Scrapbooks, 1874–1896 (CC-NEC).

32. Ibid.

33. Ibid.

34. Chadwick, Diary, October 28, 1925 (CC-NEC).

35. Chadwick, Memoirs, 1877–1880 (CC-NEC).

36. Ibid.

37. Steven Ledbetter, liner notes, Northeastern Records 236-CD, 1988.

38. Chadwick to Charles Saunders, May 10, 1879 (CC-NEC).

39. Ibid.

40. *Musikalisches Wochenblatt* 10 (June 6, 1879): 290.

41. B. B., "Correspondenzen," *Neue Zeitschrift für Musik* 75/1 (20 June 1879): 269.

42. G. Bernsdorf, "Hauptprüfungen am Konigl. Conservatorium der Musik zu Leipzig," *Signale für die Musikalische Welt* 37/41 (June 1879): 642-4.

43. "Euterpe," *DJoM* 41/1035 (January 15, 1881): 15.

44. "Some Recent American Music," *BET* (June 24, 1881): 1.

45. Letter to Charles Saunders, December 17, 1878 (CC-NEC).

46. Ibid.

47. Ibid.

48. Chadwick, Memoirs, 1877–1880 (CC-NEC).

49. Ibid.

50. Easter was observed on April 13; see Bomberger, "German Musical Training," 77.

51. Chadwick, Memoirs, 1877–1880 (CC-NEC).

52. Ibid.

53. Chadwick, Diary, October 1907 (CC-NEC).

54. Chadwick, Memoirs, 1877–1880 (CC-NEC).

55. *Musikalisches Wochenblatt* 10 (July 4, 1879): 334 (trans. by Chadwick).

56. G. Bernsdorf, "Hauptprüfungen am Konigl. Conservatorium der Musik zu Leipzig," *Signale für die Musikalische Welt* 37/41 (June 1879): 642-4 (translation by Chadwick).

57. V. B. "Correspondenzen," *Neue Zeitschrift für Musik* 75/2 (July 4, 1879): 288.

58. Homer, *My Wife and I*, 33.

59. Chadwick, Memoirs, 1877–1880 (CC-NEC).

60. Ibid.

61. Ibid.

62. Ibid.

63. Warner, *Saunterings*, 61–2.

64. Ibid., 64.

65. Ibid., 95.

66. Chadwick, Memoirs, 1877–1880 (CC-NEC).

67. Ibid.

68. Hans von Bülow to E. Spitzweg (May 5, 1871); cited in Bomberger, "German Musical Training," 130.

69. *Baker's Biographical Dictionary*, s.v. "Rheinberger, Josef."

70. Hans-Josef Irmen, *Gabriel Josef Rheinberger als Antipode des Caecilianismus* (Regensburg: Bosse, 1970): 56–7; cited in Bomberger, "German Musical Training," 125.

71. Chadwick, Memoirs, 1877–1880 (CC-NEC).

72. Ibid.

73. Ibid.

74. Bomberger, "German Musical Training," 140.

75. Homer, *My Wife and I*, 34; cited in Bomberger, "German Musical Training," 145.

76. Chadwick, Memoirs, 1877–1880 (CC-NEC); Chadwick's emphasis.

77. Ibid.

78. Bomberger, "German Musical Training," 136.

79. Chadwick to Charles Saunders, September 21, 1879 (CC-NEC).

80. See Yellin, *Chadwick: Yankee Composer*, 26; and McPherson and Klein, *Measure by Measure*, 75.

81. Chadwick, Memoirs, 1877–1880 (CC-NEC).

82. Ibid.

83. Louis C. Elson, "George W. Chadwick—An Appreciation," *NEC Magazine-Review* 7/1 (September–October, 1916): 7.

84. Chadwick, Memoirs, 1877–1880 (CC-NEC).

85. Ibid.

86. Ibid.

87. Chadwick to Charles Saunders, [n.d.], (CC-NEC).

4. Getting Started in Boston

1. "Musical Instruction," *DJoM* (January 1, 1881): iii.

2. Lehrerzeugniß, Hochschule für Musik archives, Leipzig; cited in Bomberger, "German Musical Training," 76.

3. Chadwick, Memoirs, 1877–1880 (CC-NEC).

4. "Here and There," *Musical Visitor* 10/8 (May 1881): 218.

5. Chadwick, Memoirs, 1880–1893 (CC-NEC).

6. "Major and Minor," *Musical Record* 191 (May 27, 1882): 575.

7. Reports to the Prudential Committee (1866–1883), Park Street Church, Boston, May 12, 1882.

8. Ibid., May 25, 1883.

9. Chadwick, Memoirs, 1880–1893 (CC-NEC).

10. Reports to the Prudential Committee (1866–1883), Park Street Church, Boston, June 7, 1886.

11. Chadwick started in September 1884.

12. Unitarianism and Congregationalism were very close cousins in this period. See Willard L. Sperry, "The Unitarian, Universalist and Congregational Churches," in *Fifty Years of Boston*, 594–7.

13. Letter to the author from Jessica Steytler, archivist, Congregational Library, Boston, March 14, 2001.

14. Dunham, *Life of a Musician*, 77.

15. Chadwick, Memoirs, 1880–1893 (CC-NEC).

16. Foote and Raffy, *Arthur Foote*, 34–5.

17. A. Z. Conrad, "Congregationalism," in *Fifty Years of Boston*, 592.

18. Chadwick, Memoirs, 1880–1893 (CC-NEC).

19. Ibid.

20. Chadwick, Memoirs, 1898 (CC-NEC).

21. Chadwick, Memoirs, 1894 (CC-NEC).

22. Dickinson, *Music in the History of the Western Church*, 407.

23. "Concerts of the Month," *Musical Herald* 1/6 (June 1880): 139; "Musical—Triennial Festival," *BET* (May 7, 1880): 1.

24. Chadwick, Memoirs, 1880–1893 (CC-NEC).

25. "Theatres and Concerts—Oedipus at the Globe," *BET* (January 24, 1882): 1; "Major and Minor," *Musical Record* 178 (February 25, 1882): 339.

26. Chadwick, "Orchestral Conductors and Conducting," paper read to Thursday Evening Club on January 18, 1912; in file no. RG1.2/E/9/6 (CC-NEC).

27. Ibid.

28. "Musical," *BET* (January 8, 1881): 3.

29. "Recent Concerts—Apollo Club," *DJoM* 41/1045 (May 7, 1881): 76.

30. Ibid. The full title of Bruch's work is *Frithjof: Szenen aus der Frithjof-Sage* (1864).

31. "Our Musical Hopper," *Church's Musical Visitor* 11/12 (September 1882): 328.

32. "Theatres and Concerts—The Apollo Concert," *BET* (February 11, 1886): 1.

33. Chadwick, Memoirs, 1880–1893 (CC-NEC).

34. "Musical Mention," *Musical Herald* 3/11 (November 1882): 301.

35. "Major and Minor," *Musical Record* 243 (May 26, 1883): 64.

36. Chadwick, Memoirs, 1880–1893 (CC-NEC).

37. Whipple, "Musical Societies," 128.

38. Ibid., 129.

39. Ibid., 128–9.

40. Chadwick, Memoirs, 1880–1893 (CC-NEC).

41. Ibid.

42. Ibid.

43. Ibid.

44. Ibid.

45. Homer, *My Wife and I*, 33.

46. Hadley, *Commemorative Tribute*, 100–1.

47. Chadwick, "Et Arcadia Ego," *Boston Herald* (May 29, 1923): 14.

48. Starr, *Bamboula*, 449, 451.

49. Chadwick, untitled essay; in file no. RG1.2/E/9/5 (CC-NEC).

50. Ibid.

51. Chadwick, Diary, January 26, 1876 (CC-NEC).

52. "Mr. J. K. Paine's New Symphony," *DJoM* 40 (March 27, 1880): 53–4.

53. Ibid.

54. For more on Chadwick's relationship with the Duveneck Boys see Yellin, "Chadwick, American Musical Realist," *Musical Quarterly* 61 (1975): 77–97.

55. Chadwick, Memoirs, 1877–1880 (CC-NEC).

56. Ibid.

57. "Musical Matters — Mr. George W. Chadwick's First Symphony," *Boston Sunday Herald* (February 19, 1882): 3.

58. Chadwick to Charles Saunders, October 7, 1879 (CC-NEC).

59. Chadwick, Memoirs, 1877–1880 (CC-NEC).

60. "Musical Matters — Mr. George W. Chadwick's First Symphony," *Boston Sunday Herald* (February 19, 1882): 3.

61. "Music and the Stage," *Boston Daily Evening Traveller* (February 24, 1882): 4.

62. Rosen, *Sonata Forms*, 324.

63. "Theatres and Concerts," *BET* (February 24, 1882): 1.

64. Louis C. Elson [pseud. Proteus], "Music in Boston," *Church's Musical Visitor* (April 1882): 187.

65. Chadwick, Memoirs, 1880–1893 (CC-NEC).

66. Chadwick, Memoirs, 1877–1880 (CC-NEC).

67. Ibid.

68. Ibid.

5. Chadwick's Boston

1. For a good summary of the Society's purpose and goals see Broyles, *Music of the Highest Class*, 144–7.

2. Elson quoted in Broyles, *Music of the Highest Class*, 8.

3. Broyles, *Music of the Highest Class*, 248–50.

4. Apthorp, *By the Way*, 76.

5. Ibid.

6. Chadwick, "Mr. Chadwick on the Symphony Orchestra" (address delivered at the celebration of Major Henry L. Higginson's eightieth birthday, November 18, 1914), 67 (CC-NEC).

7. Apthorp, *By the Way*, 82.

8. Ibid., 76–8.

9. Ibid., 49–51.

10. J. S. Dwight, "Musica Peripatetica," *DJoM* 36/8 (July 22, 1876): 270–1.

11. Louis C. Elson [Proteus, pseud.], "Music in Boston," *Musical Visitor* (November 1, 1883): 293.

12. Louis C. Elson [Proteus, pseud.], "Music in Boston," *Church's Musical Visitor* (October 1882): 355.

13. Ibid.

14. Louis C. Elson [Proteus, pseud.], "Boston," *Musical Visitor* (November 1, 1884): 292.

15. Stephen A. Emery, "Orchestral Playing," *Musical Herald* 1/1 (January 1880): 20.

16. Bates, *The Philistines*, 174.

17. Higginson, "Account of the Boston Symphony Orchestra," 1911; quoted in Howe, *Boston Symphony Orchestra*, 27.

18. Chadwick, Memoirs, 1880–1893 (CC-NEC).

19. Clifford [only name given], "Correspondence — Boston," *Church's Musical Visitor* (December 1881): 75.

20. Ibid.

21. Louis C. Elson [Proteus, pseud.], "Music in Boston," *Church's Musical Visitor* (July 1882): 270–1.

22. Louis C. Elson [Proteus, pseud.], "Music in Boston," *Church's Musical Visitor* (June 1882): 242–3; Louis C. Elson [Proteus, pseud.], "Music in Boston," *Church's Musical Visitor* (February 1, 1883): 41–2.

23. Louis C. Elson [Proteus, pseud.], "Music in Boston," *Musical Visitor* (June 1888): 151.

24. Chadwick, "Artistic Environment"; in file no. RG1.2/E/9/6 (CC-NEC).

25. Foote, "A Bostonian Remembers," *Musical Quarterly* 23 (1937): 41.

26. Bates, *The Philistines*, 125.

27. Louis C. Elson [Proteus, pseud.], "Music in Boston," *Musical Visitor* (December 1890): 318–9.

28. Ibid.

29. Louis C. Elson [Proteus, pseud.], "Music in Boston," *Musical Visitor* (July 1889): 178.

30. Chadwick to Thomas, July 17, 1882 (ICN-TTP).

31. Chadwick, Memoirs, 1880–1893 (CC-NEC).

32. The manuscript score is held at Firestone Music Library, NEC.

33. "Theatres and Concerts," *BET* (January 15, 1883): 1.

34. Yang, "Overtures and Symphonic Poems," 93.

35. Yellin, *Chadwick: Yankee Composer*, 153.

36. Louis C. Elson [Proteus, pseud.], "Music in Boston," *Musical Visitor* (March 1885): 68–9.

37. Chadwick, Memoirs, 1880–1893 (CC-NEC).

38. "Some Boston Concerts," *Musical Record* 313 (February 1888): 6.

39. "Some Boston Concerts," *Musical Record* 315 (April 1888): 6.

40. Chadwick, Memoirs, 1880–1893 (CC-NEC).

41. Chadwick to Horatio Parker, March 9, 1889 (CtY-HPP).

42. Chadwick, Memoirs, 1880–1893 (CC-NEC).

43. Chadwick to Horatio Parker, November 24, ca. 1885 (CtY-HPP).

44. Canfield, *Henry Hadley*, 43.

45. Chadwick remembered that he resigned in 1890, but printed BOC programs document his leadership through the end of the 1891 season. See BOC Scrapbook (MB-Mu).

46. Chadwick, Memoirs, 1880–1893 (CC-NEC).

47. Chadwick, "Music," in Herlihy (ed.), *Memorial History*, 327.

48. Louis C. Elson [Proteus, pseud.], "Music in Boston," *Musical Visitor* (November 1890): 291.

49. Chadwick, Memoirs, 1880–1893 (CC-NEC).

50. Ibid.

51. Yellin, *Chadwick: Yankee Composer*, 48–9.

52. Chadwick, Memoirs, 1899 (CC-NEC).

53. Dunham, *Life of a Musician*, 216.

54. Ibid.

55. Ibid.

56. Ibid.

57. "Musical Matters," *Boston Sunday Herald* (December 12, 1886): 17.

58. Chadwick, Memoirs, 1880–1893 (CC-NEC).

59. "Music and the Drama," *Boston Daily Advertiser* (April 30, 1885): 4.

60. Howard, *Our American Music*, 328–9.

61. "The Eighth Symphony Concert," *Boston Post* (December 13, 1886): 5.

62. [William Foster Apthorp], "Theatres and Concerts," *BET* (March 10, 1884): 1.

63. Ibid.

64. [Apthorp], "Theatres and Concerts," 1.

65. Unidentified newsclipping (MB-Mu).

66. "The Eighth Symphony Concert," *Boston Post* (December 13, 1886): 5.

67. [William Foster Apthorp], "Theatres and Concerts," *BET* (December 13, 1886): 1.

68. Philip Hale, unidentified clipping (MB-Mu).

69. Higginson to Chadwick, May 21, 1888, in Scrapbooks, 1874–1896 (CC-NEC).

70. Chadwick, Memoirs, 1880–1893 (CC-NEC).

71. [William Foster Apthorp], "Theatres and Concerts," *BET* (December 13, 1886): 1.

72. Chadwick, Memoirs, February 7, 1926 (CC-NEC).

73. Ledbetter, liner notes, Northeastern Records NR 235-CD.

74. Chadwick to Horatio Parker, April 8, 1886 (CtY-HPP).

75. Yellin remarked that Krehbiel detected a resemblance in *Chadwick: Yankee Composer*, 102–3; Betz notes Yellin in String Quartets nos. 1–3, xii.

76. "The American Concerts," *NYT* (November 23, 1887): 5.

77. Krehbiel, *Review of the New York Musical Season*, 36.

78. Mathews, *Hundred Years of Music*, 363–4.

79. Apthorp, "John Sullivan Dwight," quoted in Faucett, *Music in America*, 84–6.

80. Stephen A. Emery, "Musical Criticism," *Musical Herald* 1/7 (July 1880): 149.

81. Horowitz, *Classical Music in America*, 24.

82. Apthorp, "John Sullivan Dwight"; reprinted in Faucett, *Music in America*, 84–6.

83. Louis C. Elson, "The Wagner Festival," *Musical Herald* 5/5 (May 1884): 121.

84. Schabas, *Theodore Thomas*, 131–2.

85. "At Home," *Musical Herald* 9/5 (May 1888): 137.

86. Chadwick, Memoirs, 1880–1893 (CC-NEC).

87. Ibid.

88. See Howe, *Boston Symphony Orchestra*, 60–1.

89. Chadwick, Memoirs, 1880–1893 (CC-NEC).

90. William Foster Apthorp, "Theatres and Concerts," *BET* (December 27, 1887).

91. Bomberger, "Chadwick's *Melpomene*," 323.

92. Chadwick, Memoirs, 1880–1893 (CC-NEC).

93. "Theaters and Concerts," *BET* (March 4, 1889): 6.

94. "Amusements," *NYT* (December 11, 1890): 4.

95. "Theatres and Concerts," *BET* (January 14, 1892): 4.

96. Hale, "Music," *Boston Journal* (January 15, 1892): 4.

97. Chadwick, Memoirs, 1889 (CC-NEC).

98. Chadwick to Parker, March 9, 1889 (CtY-HPP).

99. Hadley, "George W. Chadwick," 101.

100. Chadwick, Memoirs, 1880–1893 (CC-NEC).

101. Ibid.

102. Ibid.

103. "Theatres and Concerts," *BET* (February 1, 1892): 5.

6. Chadwick & America's Vocal Traditions

1. Cutler, *The Gay Nineties* (1927); Beer, *The Mauve Decade* (1926); Brand, *The Reckless Decade* (1995); Twain, *The Gilded Age* (1873) and adopted by Cashman, *America in the Gilded Age* (1984); and Brooks, *The Confident Years* (1955).

2. King, *King's Handbook*, 172.

3. Ibid., 170–2.

4. "George W. Chadwick of Boston Chosen," *Springfield Daily Republican* (August 10, 1889): 6.

5. Ibid., 6.

6. "Phoenix Inter Flammas Exspirans" in Richard Chevenix Trench, *Sacred Latin Poetry* (London: John W. Parker, 1849): 232–3.

7. "Chadwick's Phoenix Expirans," *Springfield Daily Republican*, (May 6, 1892): 5.

8. Philip Hale, "At Springfield," *Boston Journal* (May 6, 1892): 5

9. Ibid.

10. Elson, *Modern Music and Musicians*, 90

11. Chadwick, Memoirs, February 9, 1913 (CC-NEC).

12. Bomberger, "Tidal Wave of Encouragement," 94–5.

13. [Higinbotham], *Report of the President*, 11.

14. Ibid., 278.

15. Ibid., 295.

16. Monroe, *Poet's Life*, 116–8.

17. Ibid., 139.

18. Ibid., 126.

19. [Editorial]. *Musical Visitor* (September 1892): 248–9.

20. Chadwick to Thomas, September 4, 1892 (ICN-TTP).

21. "Of Social Interest," *Springfield Graphic* (October 29, 1892): 16.

22. W. S. B. Mathews, "The Case of the American Composer," *Musical Record* (January 1893): 12.

23. Monroe, *Poet's Life*, 129–30.

24. Ibid., 131.

25. See Stephen Williams, *Cases Argued and Decided in the Supreme Court of the United States*, 367–9, for details of Monroe's lawsuit and Press Publishing Company's countersuit.

26. Chadwick, Memoirs, 1880–1893 (CC-NEC).

27. [Higinbotham], *Report of the President*, 251–3.

28. Ibid., 305. This figure is for operations only; it does not include construction expenditures.

29. Barnet, *Extravaganza King*, 2.

30. Although still an impressive building, some of its former dignity has been lost. As of this writing it is an upscale steakhouse.

31. Chadwick, Diary, November 24, 1914 (CC-NEC).

32. Barnet, *Extravaganza King*, 191.

33. Chadwick, Memoirs, 1894 (CC-NEC).

34. Ibid.

35. Ibid.

36. Ibid.

37. "Theatres and Concerts," *BET* (April 10, 1894): 4.

38. "At the Theatres," *Boston Journal* (April 24, 1894): 7.

39. "New Bills at the Theatres," *NYT* (May 15, 1894): 5.

40. Chadwick, Memoirs, 1894 (CC-NEC).

41. Philip Hale, "Music in Boston," *Musical Courier* (February 7, 1894): 18.

42. "Mr. Seabrooke in Harlem," *NYT* (March 5, 1895): 4.

43. Chadwick to Charles Saunders, September 6, 1894 (CC-NEC).

44. Chadwick, Memoirs, 1894 (CC-NEC). Efforts to locate court documents on this matter have not been successful.

45. "Actor Seabrooke's Finances," *NYT* (December 29, 1898): 12.

46. Chadwick, Memoirs, 1894 (CC-NEC).

47. Fawcett to Chadwick, September 25 and October 27 [year unknown]; in Scrapbook, 1874–1896 (CC-NEC).

48. Chadwick, Memoirs, 1880–1893 (CC-NEC).

49. Chadwick's eldest son, Theodore, had been born nearly four years earlier, on January 5, 1891.

50. Chadwick, Memoirs, 1895 (CC-NEC).

51. H. E. Krehbiel, New York Musical Society program book, December 7, 1895, included in Chadwick, Memoirs, 1895 (CC-NEC).

52. "New York Musical Society," *NYT* (December 9, 1895): 4.

53. Chadwick, Memoirs, 1895 (CC-NEC).

54. Ibid.

55. Chadwick, Memoirs, 1896 (CC-NEC).

56. Ibid.

57. Ibid.

58. "Festival Opens Brilliantly," *Springfield Daily Republican* (May 7, 1896).

59. Ibid.

60. Ibid.

61. "Music in America: G. W. Chadwick," *Godey's Magazine* 132/788 (February 1896): 193–8.

62. Hughes attended the New York premiere.

63. "Music in America: G. W. Chadwick," *Godey's Magazine* 132/788 (February 1896): 193.

64. Chadwick, Memoirs, 1898 (CC-NEC).

65. Philip Hale, "Worcester and Boston," *Musical Record* 454 (November 1, 1899): 488–90.

66. Scott, *Marmion*, 258–61.

67. Chadwick, Memoirs, 1896 (CC-NEC).

68. "Mme. Nordica and Max Heinrich," *Springfield Daily Republican* (May 8, 1896): 6.

69. Henry Krehbiel, "Music — A Concert of American Compositions," *New York Tribune* (April 19, 1909): 7.

70. Chadwick, Memoirs, 1896 (CC-NEC).

71. Chadwick, Memoirs, 1898 (CC-NEC).

72. Chadwick, Memoirs, 1880–1893 (CC-NEC).

73. Chadwick, Memoirs, 1898 (CC-NEC).

74. In a letter to Thomas (May 9, 1894), Chadwick mentioned that he will not need many scores or parts this season (ICN-TTP).

75. Chadwick to Thomas, May 11, 1898 (ICN-TTP).

76. Chadwick, Memoirs, 1896 (CC-NEC).

77. Chadwick, Memoirs, 1898 (CC-NEC).

78. Chadwick to Thomas, July 9, 1900 (ICN-TTP).

79. Chadwick to Thomas, August 13, 1898 (ICN-TTP).

80. Ibid.

81. Chadwick, Memoirs, 1898 (CC-NEC).

82. Chadwick to Thomas, August 13, 1898 (ICN-TTP).

83. Chadwick, Memoirs, 1899 (CC-NEC).

84. Chadwick to Gleason, March 27, 1896 (ICN-FGGC).

85. Ibid.

86. "Of Social Interest," *Springfield Graphic* (November 26, 1892): 12.

87. Chadwick, Memoirs, 1899 (CC-NEC).

88. Chadwick, Memoirs, 1880–1893 (CC-NEC).

89. Chadwick, Memoirs, 1899 (CC-NEC).

90. "Chadwick is Chosen," *Worcester Telegram* (December 21, 1897): 1.

91. "Exit Mr. Zerrahn," *Worcester Telegram* [hand dated December 1897], clipping at Worcester Historical Museum.

92. Morin, *Worcester Music Festival*, 75–6.

93. Chadwick, Memoirs, 1898 (CC-NEC).

94. Ibid.

95. Morin, *Worcester Music Festival*, 77.

96. Worcester Music Festival bulletin, July 17, 1899.

97. Chadwick, Memoirs, 1900 (CC-NEC).

98. Worcester Music Festival bulletin, July 17, 1899.

99. Chadwick, Memoirs, 1899 (CC-NEC).

100. Chadwick to Thomas, September 5, 1900 (ICN-TTP).

101. Chadwick to Thomas, September 21, 1900 (ICN-TTP).

102. Chadwick to Thomas, October 5, 1900 (ICN-TTP).

103. Ibid.

104. Chadwick to Thomas, November 7, 1900 (ICN-TTP).

105. "In the Music World," *NYT* (May 11, 1902): 6.

106. Morin, *Worcester Music Festival*, 80–1.

107. Chadwick, Memoirs, 1901 (CC-NEC).

108. Chadwick, Memoirs, 1899 (CC-NEC).

109. Chadwick, Memoirs, 1901 (CC-NEC).

110. Springfield Festival program guide, sixth season (May 2–4, 1894): 50.

7. Taking Charge at New England Conservatory

1. Bicknell, "Eben Jordan," 210.

2. Ibid.

3. Ibid.

4. The old Boston Music Hall stands today as Orpheum Theatre.

5. Dunham, *Life of a Musician*, 123.

6. Mathews, *Hundred Years of Music*, 456.

7. Louis C. Elson [Proteus, pseud.], "Music in Boston," *Musical Visitor* (July 1885): 181.

8. Chadwick, Memoirs, 1896 (CC-NEC).

9. Chadwick mistakenly remembered that Busoni arrived in Boston under the administration of Tourjée, who had already died.

10. Chadwick, Memoirs, 1880–1893 (CC-NEC).

11. Ibid.

12. Dunham, *Life of a Musician*, 155.

13. Chadwick, Memoirs, 1896 (CC-NEC).

14. Ibid.

15. Chadwick, Memoirs, 1903 (CC-NEC).

16. Chadwick, Memoirs, 1880–1893 (CC-NEC).

17. Chadwick, Memoirs, 1897 (CC-NEC).

18. "Faelten is Out," *Boston Morning Journal* (February 18, 1897): 1.

19. Chadwick to Thomas, February 21, 1897 (ICN-TTP).

20. Ibid.

21. Chadwick, Memoirs, 1897 (CC-NEC).

22. Ibid.

23. Ibid.

24. Ibid.

25. The first edition reads, "Published for the New England Conservatory of Music by The B. F. Wood Music Company, Boston."

26. Chadwick, Memoirs, 1897 (CC-NEC).

27. Chadwick, *Harmony* (1897), preface.

28. Morgan (ed.), *Richter's Manual of Harmony*, v–vi.

29. Chadwick, typescript of speech to MTNA (version 2; 1909); in file no. E/9/6/5 (CC-NEC).

30. Ibid.

31. See Yellin, *Chadwick: Yankee Composer*, 81. Yellin erroneously attributes this quote to the first edition (see also p. 228, fn. 123).

32. Chadwick, *Harmony* (1922), 237.

33. Benjamin Cutter, *Exercises in Harmony: Simple and Advanced Supplementary to the Treatise on Harmony by G. W. Chadwick* (Boston: NEC, 1899).

34. Chadwick to Thomas, November 21, 1902 (ICN-TTP).

35. Chadwick, typescript of speech to MTNA (version 2; 1909); in file no. E/9/6/5 (CC-NEC).

36. Chadwick, Memoirs, 1897 (CC-NEC).

37. McPherson and Klein, *Measure by Measure*, 60.

38. Chadwick, Memoirs, 1902 (CC-NEC).

39. "In the Music World," *BET* (March 8, 1902): 8.

40. Chadwick, Memoirs, 1898 (CC-NEC).

41. Chapple, "New England Conservatory," 5.

42. Chadwick, Memoirs, 1902 (CC-NEC).

43. Chadwick, Diary, October 1, 1914 (CC-NEC).

44. On March 9, 1915.

45. Chadwick, Diary, [after March 9], 1915 (CC-NEC).

46. Louis C. Elson, "George W. Chadwick — An Appreciation," *NEC Magazine-Review* 7/1 (September-October 1916): 7.

8. Chadwick's Instrumental Music

1. "Antonin Dvořák," *The Critic* 558 (October 29, 1892): 236.

2. "Music for the Nation," *Washington Post* (April 20, 1890): 10; reprinted in Faucett, *Music in America*, 105–7.

3. Horowitz, "Dvořák and the New World," 93.

4. Rubin, "Dvořák at the National Conservatory," 56–7.

5. [James Creelman], "Real Value of Negro Melodies," *New York Herald* (May 21, 1893): 28.

6. Antonín Dvořák, Letter to the Editor, *New York Herald* (May 28, 1893): 31; reprinted in Faucett, *Music in America*, 124–5.

7. Ibid.

8. William T. Mollenhauer, "A Reply to Dr. Dvořák and His Negro Melodies," *American Art Journal* 61/10 (June 17, 1893): 224; reprinted in Faucett, *Music in America*, 126.

9. "American Music — Dr. Dvořák's Expresses some Radical Opinions," *Boston Sunday Herald* (May 28, 1893): 23; quoted in Block, "Dvořák, Beach and American Music," 257–9.

10. Antonín Dvořák, Letter to the Editor, *New York Herald* (May 28, 1893): 31; reprinted in Faucett, *Music in America*, 124–5.

11. For the full text see Faucett, *Music in America*, 127–34.

12. From Dvořák to Rus, April 14, 1893. In Milan Kuna (editor), *Antonin Dvořák: Correspondence and Documents*, vol. 3, 1880–1895 (Prague: Barenreiter Editio Supraphon Praha): 189. My thanks to David Beveridge for pointing this out and for permission to use his translation.

13. We may be fairly certain that Dvořák was also familiar with the edition of the poem brought out by his friend Josef Sládek in 1870. My thanks to David Beveridge for pointing this out.

14. Krehbiel, quoted in Beckerman, *Dvořák and His World*, 167.

15. Huneker, quoted in Beckerman, *Dvořák and His World*, 160.

16. From Dvořák to Nedbal, [ca. February 1900]. In Milan Kuna (editor), *Antonin Dvořák: Correspondence and Documents*, vol. 4, 1896–1904 (Prague: Barenreiter Editio Supraphon Praha): 185. My thanks to David Beveridge for pointing this out and for permission to use his translation.

17. Chadwick, Memoirs, 1880–1893 (CC-NEC).

18. Chadwick, Sketchbook, November 20, 1894 (CC-NEC).

19. "Amusements," *NYT* (March 31, 1893): 4.

20. Ibid.

21. [James Creelman], "Real Value of Negro Melodies," *New York Herald* (May 21, 1893): 28.

22. The age maximum had to have changed by 1893 for Chadwick to compete, but we only learn of the change for certain later; see "Dr. Dvorak to Return," *NYT* (January 3, 1897): 11.

23. Dvořák to Chadwick, April 12, 1894; reprinted in "Chadwick's Symphony Wins the Prize," *American Art Journal* (April 21, 1894): 25.

24. Chadwick, Memoirs, 1880–1893 (CC-NEC).

25. Chadwick to Thomas, October 2, 1893, and October 9, 1893 (ICN-TTP).

26. Chadwick to Thomas, October 9, 1893 (ICN-TTP).

27. Chadwick to Thomas, May 9, 1894 (ICN-TTP).

28. Ibid.

29. Chadwick to Thomas, December 15, 1894 (ICN-TTP).

30. Chadwick to Thomas, February 21, 1897 (ICN-TTP).

31. Chadwick, Diary, [after March 29, 1914] (CC-NEC).

32. "Music," *Saturday Evening Gazette* (October 20, 1894): 2.

33. Philip Hale, "Music in Boston," *Musical Courier* 29/17 (October 24, 1894): 18

34. Louis C. Elson, "The Symphony," *Boston Daily Advertiser* (October 22, 1894): 4.

35. See Faucett, *Chadwick: His Symphonic Works*, 81–2.

36. Chadwick to Thomas, October 5, 1900 (ICN-TTP).

37. Chadwick, Memoirs, 1895 (CC-NEC).

38. Ibid.

39. Ibid.

40. H. T. Parker, "Music and Drama," *BET* (February 10, 1908): 11.

41. Philip Hale, "Symphony in 18th Concert," *Boston Herald* (March 23, 1918): 16.

42. Chadwick, Memoirs, 1895 (CC-NEC). It is not clear why Chadwick used in his title the archaic "vagrom" instead of "vagrant."

43. Ibid.

44. Chadwick, Memoirs, 1896 (CC-NEC).

45. I have elaborated on this point in *Chadwick: His Symphonic Works*, 87–8.

46. Howells, *Suburban Sketches*, 211.

47. Chadwick, Memoirs, 1896 (CC-NEC).

48. H. T. Parker, "Music and Drama," *BET* (February 10, 1908): 11; reprinted in Faucett, *Music in America*, 152.

49. Chadwick, Memoirs, 1896 (CC-NEC).

50. H. T. Parker, "Music and Drama," *BET* (February 10, 1908): 11; reprinted in Faucett, *Music in America*, 152.

51. Yellin, "Chadwick: American Musical Realist," 89.

52. See Faucett, review of Yellin's *Chadwick: Yankee Composer* in *Notes* 48/2 (December 1991): 493–5.

53. Unidentified news clipping (MB-Mu).

54. Ibid.

55. Philip Hale, "Symphony in 18th Concert," *Boston Herald* (March 23, 1918): 16.

56. Ledbetter, liner notes for Northeastern Records (NR 234-CD).

57. W. F. Apthorp, "Music and Drama," *BET* (December 22, 1896): 7.

58. See Ledbetter, liner notes for Northeastern Records (NR 234-CD) and Yellin, *Chadwick: Yankee Composer*, 106.

59. Ledbetter, liner notes for Northeastern Records (NR 234-CD).

60. Yellin, *Chadwick: Yankee Composer*, 106.

61. W. F. Apthorp, "Music and Drama," *BET* (December 22, 1896): 7.

62. Chadwick, Memoirs, 1898 (CC-NEC); also recounted in Ledbetter, liner notes for Northeastern Records (NR 234-CD).

63. Chadwick, Memoirs, February 12, 1901 (CC-NEC); also in Betz (ed.), *Chadwick: String Quartets* nos. 4–5, viii.

64. Chadwick, Memoirs, June 15, 1903 (CC-NEC).

65. W. F. Apthorp, "Music and Drama," *BET* (February 13, 1901): 7.

66. Chadwick, Diary, November 7, 1911 (CC-NEC).

67. The compositions were Beethoven's F minor quartet, op. 95, and Brahms's B minor quartet, op. 115.

68. Elson, "Kneisel Quartet Concert," *NEC Magazine and Alumni Review* 4/2 (December 1913): 48.

69. Henry F. Gilbert, "Composer Gilbert on American Music," *NYT* (24 March 1918): 4/9.

70. Ibid.

71. Chadwick, Diary, [after April 16], 1911 (CC-NEC).

72. Ibid.

73. The nature of American music changes in this regard as ragtime, jazz, and other popular musics mature.

74. Chadwick, untitled essay read before the Thursday Evening Club, January 19, 1922; in file no. E/9/8 (CC-NEC).

9. Chadwick, Modernism, & the End of an Era

1. W. F. Apthorp, "Music and Drama," *BET* (February 5, 1900): 8.

2. Richard Aldrich, "Antonin Dvorak and His Music," *NYT* (May 8, 1904): III/3; reprinted in Faucett, *Music in America*, 134–5.

3. Chadwick, Memoirs, 1897 (CC-NEC).

4. Rossetti, *Shelley's Adonais*, vii.

5. For a detailed analysis of *Adonais*, see *Chadwick: Two Overtures* (Faucett, ed.).

6. W. F. Apthorp, "Music and Drama," *BET* (February 5, 1900): 8.

7. From *BET* quoted in Howe, *Boston Symphony Orchestra*, 104.

8. Chadwick, Memoirs, February 3, 1900 (CC-NEC).

9. Ibid.

10. Ibid.

11. Ibid.

12. Chadwick to Theodore Thomas, July 9, 1900 (ICN-TTP).

13. Author interview with Neeme Järvi, May 12, 1998, Singer Island, Florida.

14. Chadwick, Memoirs, February 3, 1900 (CC-NEC).

15. Yellin, *Chadwick: Yankee Composer*, 186; and Ledbetter, "Two Seductresses," 281–301.

16. Chadwick, Memoirs, 1890 (CC-NEC); also in Ledbetter, "Two Seductresses," 287.

17. Chadwick, Memoirs, 1899 (CC-NEC); also in Ledbetter, "Two Seductresses," 285.

18. Ledbetter, "Two Seductresses," 300–1, n.6.

19. Chadwick to Thomas, November 7, 1900 (ICN-TTP). Although he reports to Thomas that *Judith* is complete, the end of the score is dated December 12.

20. Chadwick to Thomas, November 17, 1900 (ICN-TTP).

21. Frederick R. Burton, "The New Opera Judith," *NYT* (September 29, 1901): 2 [magazine supplement].

22. R. R. G., "Judith, Lyric Drama," *BET* (October 28, 1901): 11.

23. Chadwick to Thomas, September 21, 1901 (ICN-TTP); also quoted in Ledbetter, "Two Seductresses," 294.

24. Olin Downes, "Festival Audience Greets Chadwick's 'Judith' Eagerly," *Worcester Telegram* (October 9, 1919).

25. Chapple, "New England Conservatory," 7.

26. Chadwick, Memoirs, 1901 (CC-NEC).

27. "No Other Like It," *Boston Daily Globe* (October 21, 1903): 1.

28. Chadwick, Memoirs, 1901 (CC-NEC).

29. Ibid.

30. Chadwick to Thomas, September 20, 1901 (ICN-TTP).

31. Chadwick, Memoirs, 1901 (CC-NEC).

32. Chadwick to Thomas, September 20, 1901 (ICN-TTP).

33. Chadwick, Memoirs, 1901 (CC-NEC).

34. Parker to Ida May Chadwick, December 13, 1901 (CtY-HPP).

35. Parker to Chadwick, April 19, 1902 (CtY-HPP).

36. Parker to Chadwick, June 11, 1901 (CtY-HPP).

37. See Stebbins, *Making of Symphony Hall*, for a thorough account.

38. Waldo, "Acoustics of Jordan Hall," 54.

39. Ibid., 57.

40. Ibid., 54–61.

41. Ibid., 57.

42. Chadwick, Memoirs, 1901 (CC-NEC).

43. Ibid.

44. Chadwick to Parker, May 2, 1902 (CtY-HPP).

45. Ibid.

46. Greene, *Three Plays in Verse*, 3–47.

47. Chadwick, Memoirs, 1907 (CC-NEC).

48. Greene, *Three Plays in Verse*, 46.

49. Chadwick, Memoirs, [after June 18], 1907 (CC-NEC).

50. Chadwick, Memoirs, 1902 (CC-NEC).

51. Chadwick, Memoirs, 1903 (CC-NEC).

52. Ibid.

53. "In New Jordan Hall," *Boston Globe* (June 23, 1903): 8.

54. Chadwick, Memoirs, 1903 (CC-NEC).

55. Ibid.

56. "No Other Like It," *Boston Daily Globe* (October 21, 1903): 1.

57. Ibid.

58. Ibid.

59. Ibid.

60. Yellin, *Chadwick: Yankee Composer*, 157.

61. Chadwick, Memoirs, 1904 (CC-NEC).

62. R.R.G., "Music and Drama," *BET* (April 25, 1904): 9.

63. "New Overture by Chadwick," *Boston Sunday Herald* (April 24, 1904): 16.

64. Mason Redfern, "Composers of America Display Art," *San Francisco Examiner* (August 2, 1915): 6.

65. NEC orchestra program notes (February 24, 1905) state that *Sinfonietta* was composed expressly for that ensemble.

66. H. T. Parker, "Age Honored, Youth Heard, Heights Won," *BET* (April 26, 1930): 14.

67. R.R.G., "Music and Drama," *BET* (November 22, 1904): 15.

68. *New York Sun* review, hand dated 1910 (MB-Mu).

69. From *Musical Courier*; quoted in Kennedy, *Richard Strauss*, 138.

70. From Huneker, *Mezzotints in Modern Music*; reprinted in Faucett, *Music in America*, 182.

71. Ibid.

72. Chadwick, Memoirs, 1904 (CC-NEC).

73. Ibid.

74. Ibid.

75. Ibid.

76. BSO program notes, December 14/15, 1906.

77. Hale's reading is essentially accurate, although he misinterpreted the opening key, which is not F major but D major; the "melancholy phrase for the viola" appears later than he suggests.

78. Chadwick, Memoirs, 1904 (CC-NEC).

79. Chadwick, Memoirs, 1906 (CC-NEC).

80. Ibid.

81. Philip Hale, "Symphony and Mme. Eames' Recital," *Boston Sunday Herald* (December 16, 1906): 7.

82. W. L. Hubbard, "News of the Theatres," *Chicago Tribune* (March 28, 1908): 8.

83. Chadwick, Memoirs, 1905 (CC-NEC).

84. Hale quoted in Schabas, *Theodore Thomas*, 223.

85. Chadwick, Memoirs, 1905 (CC-NEC).

86. Howard, *Our American Music*, 294.

87. In Chadwick's draft of an unidentified paper; in file no. RG1.2/6/9/10 (CC-NEC).

88. Chadwick to Thomas, July 17, 1882 (ICN-TTP).

89. Chadwick to Thomas, June 20, 1898 (ICN-TTP).

90. Rose Fay Thomas, *Memoirs of Theodore Thomas*.

91. Chadwick, Diary, November 21, 1911 (CC-NEC).

92. Ibid.

10. Chadwick's Grand Tour

1. Chadwick, Memoirs, 1904 (CC-NEC).

2. Parker to Chadwick, June 11, 1901 (CtY-HPP).

3. Chadwick, Memoirs, 1896 (CC-NEC).

4. Howard, *Our American Music*, 334–5.

5. Chadwick to Rheinberger, July 6, 1882, in *Rheinberger Briefe*, V, 162–3; cited in Bomberger, "German Musical Training," 134–5.

6. Kearns, *Horatio Parker*, 208.

7. Chadwick to Parker, [ca. July, 1900] (CtY-HPP).

8. Parker to Chadwick, April 19, 1902 (CtY-HPP).

9. Chadwick, Memoirs, 1905 (CC-NEC).

10. Ibid.

11. Chadwick to Wallace Goodrich, October 7, 1905, inserted into Chadwick, Memoirs, 1905 (CC-NEC).

12. Chadwick, Memoirs, 1905 (CC-NEC).

13. For an interesting discussion of this topic see Von Glahn, *Sounds of Place*.

14. Chadwick, Memoirs, 1905 (CC-NEC).

15. Ibid.

16. Chadwick to Charles Saunders, October 16, 1905, inserted into Chadwick, Memoirs, 1905 (CC-NEC).

17. Chadwick, Diary, [after June 12], 1917 (CC-NEC).

18. "Leipsic Discovers a Boston Composer," *Boston Globe* (December 29, 1905).

19. Chadwick, "A Greeting to '06 from Over the Water"; in file no. RG1.2/E/9/3 (CC-NEC).

20. Chadwick, Diary, July 7, 1906 (CC-NEC).

21. Chadwick, Diary, July 26, 1906 (CC-NEC).

22. Chadwick, Diary, February 28, 1909 (CC-NEC). Chadwick's analysis of Elgar's symphony is one of the longest in the whole of his writings.

23. Chadwick, Diary, July 18, 1906 (CC-NEC).

24. Chadwick, Diary, July 29, 1906 (CC-NEC).

25. Chadwick, Diary, August 2, 1906 (CC-NEC).

26. Chadwick, Diary, July 21, 1906 (CC-NEC).

27. Chadwick, Diary, July 8, 1906 (CC-NEC).

28. Chadwick, Diary, July 9, 1906 (CC-NEC).

29. Chadwick, Memoirs, 1906 (CC-NEC).

30. Thomas was five feet, five inches tall; see Schonberg, *Great Conductors*, 196. Chadwick stated that Thomas was "an inch or two shorter" than himself; see Memoirs, 1905 (CC-NEC).

31. Chadwick, Memoirs, 1895 (CC-NEC).

32. Chadwick, Diary, March 8, 1910 (CC-NEC).

33. Chadwick, Memoirs, 1897 (CC-NEC).

34. Chadwick, Diary, January 9, 1908 (CC-NEC).

35. Ibid.

36. Ives, *Memos*, 183.

37. Chadwick, Diary, October 11, 1912 (CC-NEC).

38. Chadwick, Memoirs, 1877–1880 (CC-NEC).

39. Chadwick to Thomas, June 10, 1903 (ICN-TTP).

40. Chadwick, Diary, October 13, 1908 (CC-NEC).

41. Ibid.

11. Thursday Evenings & the Sea

1. Higginson to Chadwick, January 31, 1906 (CC-NEC).

2. Howe, *Boston Symphony*, 119.

3. Chadwick, Memoirs, 1906 (CC-NEC).

4. Ibid.

5. Ibid.

6. Chadwick, Diary, October 12, 1907 (CC-NEC).

7. Chadwick, Memoirs, 1906 (CC-NEC).

8. Ibid.

9. Chadwick, "Music" in Herlihy (ed.), *Fifty Years of Boston*, 324.

10. Chadwick, Diary, January 29, 1908 (CC-NEC).

11. Chadwick, Diary, May 1, 1909 (CC-NEC).

12. Chadwick, Diary, April 7, 1909 (CC-NEC).

13. Chadwick was notified of his election on November 30, 1906; letter inserted into Chadwick, Memoirs, 1906 (CC-NEC).

14. Chadwick, Diary, January 6, 1908 (CC-NEC).

15. Williams, *Greater Boston Clubs*, 11.

16. Chadwick, Memoirs, 1906 (CC-NEC).

17. Chadwick, Memoirs, [before January 19], 1914 (CC-NEC).

18. Chadwick, Diary, February 4, 1909 (CC-NEC).

19. Chadwick, Memoirs, 1906 (CC-NEC).

20. Chadwick, Diary, March 17, 1915 (CC-NEC).

21. Chadwick, Diary, March 7, 1912 (CC-NEC).

22. Dukes County Deeds Book no. 90 (September 14, 1892): 412–4.

23. Dukes County Deeds Book no. 215 (October 25, 1948): 268.

24. Chadwick, Diary, September 12, 1908 (CC-NEC).

25. Author interview with Theodore Chadwick Jr., June 15–20, 1997.

26. "George Whitefield Chadwick: Twenty-Five Years Director," *NEC Bulletin* 4/7 (August 1922): 3.

27. Chadwick, Memoirs, 1896 (CC-NEC). Also recounted in Ledbetter, liner notes, Northeastern Records 234-CD.

28. Chadwick, Diaries, 1908 and 1909 (CC-NEC).

29. Chadwick, Memoirs, March 27, 1907 (CC-NEC).

30. Chadwick, Diary, February 29, 1912 (CC-NEC).

31. "Philadelphia Orchestra," *Philadelphia Evening Bulletin* (March 30, 1911): 4.

32. "Special Concert in Honor of Convention," *Philadelphia Inquirer* (March 30, 1911): 2.

33. H. T. Parker, "The Symphony Concert," *BET* (April 14, 1911): 12.

34. Ibid.

35. Olin Downes, "Two Novelties by Symphony," *Boston Post* (April 14, 1911): 12.

36. "New York Symphony," *NYT* (February 3, 1912): 11.

37. Unidentified news clipping (MB-Mu).

38. Chadwick, Diary, February 3, 1912 (CC-NEC). The seven-hundred-dollar prize approaches twenty thousand in 2010 dollars.

39. "Philadelphia Orchestra," *Philadelphia Evening Bulletin* (March 30, 1911): 4; "Chadwick Suite is Typically American," in *Musical America* 15/14 (February 10, 1912): 21.

40. Doris Evans McGinty, " 'That You Came So Far to See Us': Coleridge-Taylor in America," *Black Music Research Journal* 21/2 (Autumn 2001): 198.

41. Judith Ann Schiff, "Old Yale: The Battell Connection," *Yale Alumni Magazine* (October 2002); accessed August 13, 2010; available at www.yalealumnimagazine.com/issues/02_10/old_yale.html.

42. "A Big Private Auditorium," *NYT* (December 20, 1909): 2.

43. Arthur B. Wilson, "Community Work in Music (part 2)," *Musician* 14/5 (May 1909): 251.

44. Ibid.

45. Fisher, *Music Festivals*, 48.

46. Chadwick, "Notes on the Norfolk Meeting," *NEC Magazine* 4/4 (June 1914): 117–8.

47. Chadwick, Diary, June 9, 1914 (CC-NEC).

48. Chadwick, "Notes on the Norfolk Meeting," *NEC Magazine* 4/4 (June 1914): 117–8.

49. Henry F. Gilbert, "The American Composer," *Musical Quarterly* 1/1 (1915):174.

50. "A Big Private Auditorium," *NYT* (December 20, 1909): 2.

51. Vaill (ed.), "Report of the Music Committee, 1908," 191–3.

52. Ibid.

53. Ibid.; quote also found in Ledbetter, *Sourcebook*, 169.

54. Richmond P. Paine apparently was not related to John Knowles Paine.

55. George W. Judson, "Noel, Under the Direction of Its Composer, Mr. Chadwick, Delighted," *Winsted Evening Citizen* (June 3, 1909): 1.

56. Chadwick, Diary, May 21, 1909 (CC-NEC).

57. Arthur B. Wilson, "Community Work in Music (part 2)," *Musician* 14/5 (May 1909): 251.

58. Ibid.

59. George W. Judson, "Noel, Under the Direction of Its Composer, Mr. Chadwick, Delighted," *Winsted Evening Citizen* (June 3, 1909): 1.

60. Ibid.

61. Chadwick, Diary, December 18, 1913 (CC-NEC).

62. Chadwick, Diary, October 9, 1910 (CC-NEC). The librettist's name is seen in print as "Browne" and "Brown." The former is used here.

63. "Mr. Henry W. Savage," *NYT* (December 29, 1907): SM7.

64. Ibid.

65. "About *Everywoman*," *New York Daily Tribune* (March 5, 1911): V/6.

66. Chadwick, Diary, October 9, 1910 (CC-NEC).

67. Chadwick, Diary, March 30, 1911 (CC-NEC).

68. Browne, *Acting Version of Henry W. Savage's Production* [from the introduction; unpaginated].

69. Chadwick, Diary, February 5, 1911 (CC-NEC).

70. Chadwick, Diary, [after November 26], 1911 (CC-NEC).

71. Chadwick, Diary, February 26, 1911 (CC-NEC).

72. Philip Hale, "*Everywoman* at the Majestic," *Boston Sunday Herald* (November 14, 1911): 10.

73. "Modern Morality at Herald Square," *NYT* (February 28, 1911): 8.

74. Chadwick, Diary, [after February 27], 1911 (CC-NEC).

75. Chadwick, Diary, August 27, 1911 (CC-NEC).

76. Chadwick, Diary, October 29, 1911 (CC-NEC).

77. Louis C. Elson, unlocated review of the printed score; in Chadwick, Diary, [after March 13], 1914 (CC-NEC).

78. Chadwick, Diary, May 5, 1912 (CC-NEC).

79. Chadwick, Diary, August 27, 1911 (CC-NEC).

80. Preface to the printed score, *Aphrodite* (Boston: A. P. Schmidt, 1911).

81. Perry, *Garden of Hellas*, 42–3.

82. Program notes, Norfolk Music Festival, June 4, 1912.

83. Chadwick, Memoirs, 1906 (CC-NEC).

84. Chadwick, Diary, February 4, 1912 (CC-NEC).

85. Richard Aldrich, "Norfolk Festival a Choral Triumph," *NYT* (June 9, 1912): II/10.

86. Louis C. Elson, "Aphrodite a Brilliant Work," *Boston Daily Advertiser* (April 5, 1913): 5.

87. Philip Hale, "New Fantasie at Symphony," *Boston Herald* (April 5, 1913): 8.

88. H. T. Parker, "Mr. Chadwick's New Tone Poem and its Uneven Quality," *BET* (April 5, 1913): III/14.

12. Opera in Boston, the Met, & *The Padrone*

1. Chadwick, Memoirs, [after March 7], 1902 (CC-NEC).

2. Ibid.

3. Ibid.

4. Chadwick, Memoirs, March 3, 1903 (CC-NEC).

5. McPherson and Klein, *Measure by Measure*, 61.

6. "The Colden [*sic*] Cross Sung by Conservatory Pupils," *Boston Herald* (May 19, 1906): 7.

7. "News of the Day," *BET* (May 12, 1908): 12.

8. Chadwick, Diary, May 11, 1908 (CC-NEC).

9. Chadwick, Diary, October 19, 1926 (CC-NEC).

10. Chadwick, Diary, April 6, 1908 (CC-NEC).

11. Chadwick, "Music" in *Fifty Years of Boston*, 328.

12. Ibid.

13. Chadwick, Diary, December 30, 1907 (CC-NEC).

14. Jackson, *Boston Opera House*, [unpaginated].

15. Chapple, "New England Conservatory," 12.

16. Writing in 1930, Chadwick remembered that only forty-six boxes had been sold; see Chadwick, "Music," in *Fifty Years of Boston*, 328.

17. Ibid.

18. Jackson, *Boston Opera House*, [unpaginated].

19. "New Opera House Cornerstone Laid," (unidentified news clipping dated December 1, 1908); in Chadwick, Diary, [after November 28], 1908 (CC-NEC).

20. Chadwick, "Music" in *Fifty Years of Boston*, 328.

21. "New Opera House Cornerstone Laid," (unidentified news clipping dated December 1, 1908); in Chadwick, Diary, [after November 28], 1908 (CC-NEC).

22. Chadwick, Diary, May 11, 1908 (CC-NEC).

23. Chadwick, Diary, April 29, 1909 (CC-NEC).

24. Chadwick, Diary, February 22, 1912 (CC-NEC).

25. H. T. Parker, "Music and Musicians," *BET* (October 27, 1909): 23.

26. Chadwick, Diary, March 27, 1909 (CC-NEC).

27. "Opera Manager Resigns Office," *Boston Herald* (October 27, 1909): 12.

28. "Boston's Opera House is Ready," *Boston Herald* (October 31, 1909): 11.

29. Chadwick, Diary, November 9, 1909 (CC-NEC).

30. Chadwick, Diary, [after April 2], 1912 (CC-NEC).

31. Chadwick, Diary, April 29, 1909 (CC-NEC).

32. Chadwick, Memoirs, October 27, 1909.

33. Chadwick, Diary, January 6, 1911 (CC-NEC).

34. Ibid.

35. "American Opera, 'The Sacrifice,' is Sung," *NYT* (March 4, 1911): 11.

36. Chadwick, Diary, March 3 [incorrectly dated "May 3"], 1911 (CC-NEC).

37. Chadwick, Memoirs, October 4, 1908 (CC-NEC).

38. Krehbiel to Chadwick, April 24, 1911; included in Chadwick, Diary, 1911 (CC-NEC).

39. Ibid. Nevin, the brother of the better known composer Ethelbert Nevin, studied briefly at NEC. In the early part of the new century, Nevin lived in Montana, where he studied the music of the Blackfeet tribe of American Indians.

40. Gatti-Casazza, *Memories of Opera*, 238.

41. Chadwick, Diary, January 2, 1911 and January 18, 1911 (CC-NEC).

42. Chadwick, Diary, March 4, 1911 (CC-NEC); emphasis Chadwick's.

43. Chadwick, Diary, April 23, 1911 (CC-NEC).

44. Chadwick, Diary, April 1911 (CC-NEC).

45. Krehbiel to Chadwick, April 24, 1911, in Diary, 1911 (CC-NEC).

46. Krehbiel to Chadwick, April 29, 1911, in Diary, 1911 (CC-NEC).

47. Parker was pronounced the winner on May 2, 1911.

48. Daniel Gregory Mason, "Recent Musical Happenings in New York: A Review," *Outlook* (April 13, 1912): 806–8.

49. Richard Aldrich, "'Mona,' New American Opera, Warmly Welcomed at the Metropolitan," *NYT* (March 17, 1912); VII/7.

50. "'Mona' Opera Lauded," *NYT* (March 9, 1913): C6.

51. Chadwick, Diary, May 2, 1911 (CC-NEC).

52. Damrosch to Chadwick, April 14, 1911 (CC-NEC).

53. Chadwick, Diary, May 2, 1911 (CC-NEC).

54. Chadwick, Diary, June 6–8, 1916 (CC-NEC).

55. Chadwick, Diary, [before November 24], 1914 (CC-NEC).

56. Gatti-Casazza, *Memories of Opera*, 238.

57. Ibid., 237.

58. Chadwick, Diary, April 26, 1911 (CC-NEC).

59. Ibid.

60. Chadwick, Diary, May 2, 1911 (CC-NEC).

61. Puleo, *Boston Italians*, 9.

62. *Boston Post* editorial; reprinted in Puleo, *Boston Italians*, 22.

63. Puleo, *Boston Italians*, 28–9.

64. Freeman, "American Realism," 7.

65. Chadwick, Diary, February 18, 1912 (CC-NEC).

66. Chadwick, Diary, March 2, 1912 (CC-NEC).

67. Freeman, "American Realism," 10–11, 34–40.

68. Chadwick, Diary, May 5, 1912 (CC-NEC).

69. Chadwick, Diary, [after December 11], 1913 (CC-NEC).

70. Chadwick, Memoirs, 1913 (CC-NEC); quoted in Yellin, *Life and Operatic Works*, 248–9, and Yellin, *Chadwick: Yankee Composer*, 210–11.

71. Chadwick, Diary, [before February 9], 1913 (CC-NEC).

72. For a good analysis of Crane's story see Shi, *Facing Facts*, 223–30.

73. Chadwick, Diary, October 11, 1913 (CC-NEC).

74. Stock to Chadwick, November 16, 1919 (CC-NEC).

13. Chadwick's Response to the Great War

1. Keegan, *First World War*, 52.

2. Tuchman, "How We Entered World War I," 159.

3. "New York as an Art Centre," *NYT* (October 12, 1914): 8; reprinted in Faucett, *Music in America*, 204–5.

4. "America Has Opportunity," *NYT* (October 13, 1914): 11; reprinted in Faucett, *Music in America*, 205.

5. Martens, "Music," 741.

6. "Germans as Exponents of Culture," *NYT* (September 20, 1914): II/14.

7. Chadwick to Brander Matthews, October 12, 1914, Brander Matthews Papers, Rare Book & Manuscript Library, Columbia University, New York City.

8. Chadwick, Diary, November 18, 1914 (CC-NEC).

9. Scoring began on September 29, 1914.

10. Chadwick, Diary, [after November 19], 1911 (CC-NEC).

11. Chadwick, *Aghadoe* (Boston: A. P. Schmidt, 1911).

12. Boston: A. P. Schmidt, 1910.

13. Yellin, *Chadwick: Yankee Composer*, 147.

14. Yang, *Overtures and Symphonic Poems*, 287.

15. Krehbiel's review of the composition's Norfolk performance relied heavily upon information provided by Chadwick. See Chadwick, Diary, [after June 6], 1915 (CC-NEC). I have not located this hymn tune.

16. Chadwick, *Tam O'Shanter* (Boston: Boston Music Company, 1917): preface.

17. Eric De Lamarter, "Chadwick Conducts Chicago Symphony," *Chicago Tribune* (January 22, 1916): 15.

18. Louis C. Elson, "Brilliant New Work by Chadwick," *Boston Daily Advertiser* (April 29, 1916): 3.

19. Unidentified, untitled article in Chadwick, Diary, 1915 (CC-NEC).

20. Sources differ slightly on the number of Americans killed, as well as the total number killed. These figures are from Keegan, *First World War*, 265.

21. Lipsky, *Panama-Pacific International Exposition*, 8.

22. Chadwick, Diary, October 23, 1914 (CC-NEC).

23. Chadwick, Diary, July 1, 1915 (CC-NEC).

24. Ibid.

25. See Kearns, *Horatio Parker*, 164–5; Chadwick, Diary, July 1, 1915 (CC-NEC).

26. See Lipsky, *Panama-Pacific International Exposition*, 54–5.

27. Wheeler, Edward J., editor, "The European War and the Panama-Pacific — A Monumental Contrast," *Current Opinion* 58 (January–June 1915): 318.

28. Chadwick, Diary, August 1, 1915 (CC-NEC).

29. Ibid.

30. Dunham, *Life of a Musician*, 176.

31. Chadwick, Diary, February 11, 1914 (CC-NEC).

32. Chadwick, Diary, January 1, 1916 (CC-NEC).

33. See Tuchman, "How We Entered World War I," 158–72.

34. Chadwick, Diary, February 21, 1916 (CC-NEC).

35. Chadwick, Diary, [after March 7], 1916 (CC-NEC).

36. Chadwick, Diary, [after February 24], 1917 (CC-NEC).

37. For an excellent account of US involvement in the war see Harries, *Last Days of Innocence*, 61–73.

38. Chadwick, Diary, May 13, 1917 (CC-NEC).

39. Theodore enlisted on May 23, 1915. Unlike for Noël, military service records for Theodore are not yet available; information here has been gleaned from the Diaries.

40. Chadwick, Diary, May 23, 1915 (CC-NEC).

41. Chadwick, Diary, October 23, 1916 (CC-NEC).

42. Chadwick, Diary, April 11, 1914 (CC-NEC).

43. Noël was certified on June 11, 1917; see US Naval Reserve Records (enlistment no. 120-99-96).

44. On November 5, 1917.

45. "Threat to Disband Boston Symphony," *NYT* (November 1, 1917): 10.

46. Chadwick, Diary, October 8, 1914 (CC-NEC).

47. Chadwick, Diary, May 5, 1916 (CC-NEC).

48. "National Anthem's Place," *NYT* (November 4, 1917): II/2.

49. "Ex-Governor Warfield Would Mob Muck," *NYT* (November 5, 1917): 13.

50. "Threat to Disband Boston Symphony," *NYT* (November 1, 1917): 10.

51. "Denounce Muck at Rally," *NYT* (November 7, 1917): 11.

52. Chadwick to Stock, May 7, 1918 (CC-NEC).

53. Chadwick, Diary, January 24, 1916 (CC-NEC).

54. "Arrest Karl Muck as an Enemy Alien," *NYT* (March 26, 1918): 3.

55. For a good summary of events surrounding his arrest see "Arrest Karl Muck as an Enemy Alien," *NYT* (March 26, 1918): 3.

56. Chadwick to Stoeckel, May 17, 1917 (CC-NEC).

57. Chadwick, Diary, May 4, 1922 (CC-NEC).

58. H. T. Parker, "Symphony Concert," *BET* (December 31, 1918): II/8.

59. Chadwick, Diary, November 25, 1918 (CC-NEC).

60. Author interview with Theodore Chadwick Jr. (June 15–20, 1997).

61. Chadwick, Diary, November 25, 1918 (CC-NEC).

62. Chadwick, Diary, [after May 14], 1915 (CC-NEC).

63. French's work is also known as *Death Staying the Hand of the Sculptor*. In Chicago Chadwick would have seen the plaster model from which French created the bronze original. That model gained notoriety when it was exhibited at the World's Columbian Exhibition.

64. Chadwick, Diary, November 24, 1916 (CC-NEC).

65. French to Chadwick, February 9, 1919 (CC-NEC).

66. H. T. Parker, "Music and Musicians," *BET* (February 7, 1919): 12.

67. H. T. Parker, "Week-End Concerts," *BET* (November 13, 1919): 13.

68. Insofar as can be determined, the two Parkers were not related.

69. Chadwick, Diary, November 17, 1919 (CC-NEC).

70. Chadwick, Diary, April 7, 1909 (CC-NEC).

71. Chadwick, Diary, January 24, 1914 (CC-NEC).

72. Chadwick, Diary, April 17, 1915 (CC-NEC).

73. Chadwick, Diary, October 18, 1916 (CC-NEC).

74. Chadwick, Diary, March 27, 1916 (CC-NEC).

75. Chadwick, Diary, December 10, 1910 (CC-NEC).

76. Ibid.

77. Chadwick, Diary, April 9, 1916 (CC-NEC).

78. Chadwick, Diary, February, 1914 (CC-NEC).

79. Chadwick, Memoirs, 1894 (CC-NEC).

80. Chadwick, Diary, October 15, 1916 (CC-NEC).

81. Chadwick, Diary, January 24, 1915 (CC-NEC).

82. Chadwick, Diary, December 13, 1913 (CC-NEC).

83. Chadwick, Diary, October 17, 1915 (CC-NEC).

84. Chadwick, Diary, [after November 18], 1914 (CC-NEC).

85. Chadwick, Diary, January 18, 1914 (CC-NEC).

86. Chadwick, Diary, April 11, 1914 (CC-NEC).

87. Chadwick, Diary, after June 6, 7, and 8, 1916 (CC-NEC).

88. Chadwick, Diary, June 6, 1917 (CC-NEC).

89. Chadwick, Diary, October 25, 1913 (CC-NEC).

90. Chadwick, Diary, January 24, 1915 (CC-NEC).

91. Chadwick, Diary, December 11, 1915 (CC-NEC).

92. Chadwick, Diary, October 24, 1915 (CC-NEC).

93. Chadwick, Diary, [after June 10], 1917 (CC-NEC).

94. Chadwick, Diary, [after November 14], 1915 (CC-NEC).

95. Louis C. Elson, "Brilliant New Work by Chadwick," *Boston Daily Advertiser* (April 29, 1916): 3.

96. Chadwick, Diary, December 24, 1915 (CC-NEC).

97. Chadwick, Diary, November 30, 1915 (CC-NEC).

98. Chadwick, Diary, April 1, 1916 (CC-NEC).

99. Chadwick, Diary, June 3, 1913 (CC-NEC).

100. Chadwick, Diary, [after November 12], 1913 (CC-NEC).

101. Chadwick, Diary, April 12, 1914 (CC-NEC).

102. Chadwick, Diary, December 12, 1914 (CC-NEC).

103. Chadwick, Diary, April 8, 1916 (CC-NEC).

104. Chadwick, Diary, [after December 11], 1914 (CC-NEC).

14. "Altschüler"

1. Chadwick, "A Plea for Choral Singing," paper read before the Dedham Historical Society, November 5, 1919 (version 2); file no. RG1.2/E/9/8 (CC-NEC).

2. "The Vision of Public School Music," *Journal of Education* 78/15 (October 23, 1913): 397–9.

3. Langley, "Chadwick and the New England Conservatory of Music," 52.

4. Henry F. Gilbert, "Composer Gilbert on American Music," *NYT* (March 24, 1918): 4/9; reprinted in Faucett, *Music in America*, 21–2.

5. Langley, "Chadwick and the New England Conservatory of Music," 47.

6. Garofalo, *Converse*, 7.

7. Chadwick, Diary, November 25, 1915 (CC-NEC).

8. Chadwick, Diary, May 16, 1909 (CC-NEC).

9. Hale, quoted in "In Memoriam Mr. Chadwick," *NEC Bulletin* 13/4 (May 1931): 1–4.

10. Chadwick, Diary, April 24, 1915 (CC-NEC).

11. Chadwick, Diary, April-May, 1915 (CC-NEC).

12. Chadwick, Diary, November, 1919 (CC-NEC).

13. Chadwick, Diary, December 2, 1920 (CC-NEC).

14. Chadwick, Diary, October 8, 1919 (CC-NEC).

15. Chadwick, Diary, December 31, 1923 (CC-NEC).

16. Ibid.

17. Chadwick, Diary, April 19, 1924 (CC-NEC).

18. Chadwick, Diary, [after June 15], 1913 (CC-NEC).

19. Chadwick, Diary, January 11, 1914 (CC-NEC).

20. Chadwick, Diary, April 10, 1924 (CC-NEC).

21. Chadwick, Diary, June 22, 1910 (CC-NEC).

22. Chadwick, Diary, August 28, 1921 (CC-NEC).

23. Ledbetter, *Sourcebook*, 49.

24. Chadwick, Norfolk Festival program notes (June 7, 1922).

25. Chadwick, Diary, September 10, 1921 (CC-NEC).

26. Oscar Thompson, "American and British Works Given First Performances at Norfolk, Conn.," *Musical America* 36/3 (June 17, 1922): 1, 5–6.

27. Chadwick, Memoirs, June 7, 1922 (CC-NEC).

28. H. T. Parker, "Current-Chronicle," *BET* (December 18, 1922): 7.

29. Chadwick, Memoirs, November 13, 1919 (CC-NEC).

30. Grace May Stutsman, "H. T. Parker, Noted Music Critic of Boston 'Transcript,' is Dead," in *Musical America* 54/7 (April 10, 1934): 57.

31. Nicolas Slonimsky (editor), *Baker's Biographical Dictionary of Composers*, 6th edition (New York: Schirmer, 1978): 1721. s.v. "Parker, Henry Taylor."

32. The concert occurred on February 17, 1924.

33. H. T. Parker, "Weekend Round Over Bostonian Concert Giving," *BET* (February 18, 1924): I/8.

34. "H.T.P. — Ave Atque Vale," *BET* (April 2, 1934): 10.

35. Chadwick, Memoirs, 1880–1893 (CC-NEC).

36. Chadwick, Diary, September 27, 1908 (CC-NEC).

37. Chadwick, Memoirs, March 29, 1927 (CC-NEC).

38. Chadwick, Diary, January 4, 1912 (CC-NEC).

39. Chadwick, Diary, [after December 28], 1913 (CC-NEC).

40. Chadwick, Memoirs, 1880–1893 (CC-NEC).

41. Chadwick, Diary, September 27, 1908 (CC-NEC).

42. Chadwick, Diary, April 23, 1908 (CC-NEC).

43. Chadwick, Diary, September 27, 1908 (CC-NEC).

44. Ibid.

45. Ibid.

46. Chadwick, Diary, November 12, 1926 (CC-NEC).

47. Chadwick, Diary, October 15, 1916 (CC-NEC).

48. Howe, *Boston Symphony Orchestra*, 144.

49. Chadwick, Diary, February 29, 1924 (CC-NEC).

50. Chadwick, Diary, January 25, 1924 (CC-NEC).

51. Chadwick, Diary, April 17, 1925 (CC-NEC).

52. Chadwick, Diary, June 6, 1922 (CC-NEC).

53. Chadwick, Diary, January 11, 1924 (CC-NEC).

54. Chadwick, Diary, February 15, 1924 (CC-NEC).

55. Chadwick, Diary, December 16, 1922 (CC-NEC).

56. Van Vechten, "Music after the Great War"; reprinted in Faucett, *Music in America*, 193-4.

57. Howe, *Boston Symphony Orchestra*, 144-5.

58. Chadwick, Diary, March 5, 1920 (CC-NEC).

59. Parker quoted in Howe, *Boston Symphony Orchestra*, 150-1.

60. Howe, *Boston Symphony Orchestra*, 151.

61. Chadwick, Diary, April 13, 1927 (CC-NEC).

62. Chadwick, Diary, January 23, 1925 (CC-NEC).

63. Chadwick, Diary, October 30, 1925 (CC-NEC).

64. Chadwick, Diary, October 10, 1924 (CC-NEC).

65. Chadwick, Diary, February 20, 1925 (CC-NEC).

66. Chadwick, Diary, November 20, 1925 (CC-NEC).

67. Chadwick, Diary, January 28, 1927 (CC-NEC).

68. Chadwick, Diary, April 30, 1925 (CC-NEC).

69. Chadwick, Diary, [after May], 1925 (CC-NEC).

70. Chadwick, Diary, May 2, 1927 (CC-NEC).

71. Chadwick reported that while he did not subscribe in 1916–1917, he attended many of the performances; see Chadwick, Diary, [after February 24], 1917 (CC-NEC).

72. Chadwick, Diary, March 15, 1922 (CC-NEC).

73. Chadwick, Diary, December 18, 1919 (CC-NEC).

74. Hamilton, *Music Appreciation*, 368.

75. "New Music by Chadwick," *Musical Courier* 102/14 (April 4, 1931): 16.

76. Chadwick, Diary, December 31, 1925 (CC-NEC).

77. Chadwick, Diary, July 10, 1924 (CC-NEC).

78. Doyle to Chadwick, August 26, 1919 (CC-NEC).

79. Chadwick, Diary, September 19, 1926 (CC-NEC).

80. Chadwick, Diary, February 11, 1929 (CC-NEC).

81. Chadwick, Diary, April 13, 1929 (CC-NEC).

82. One writer erroneously stated that *Rip Van Winkle* Overture received its NEC premiere on May 6, 1930; see *NEC Bulletin* 12/4 (May 1930): 3.

83. "Chadwick Feted in Rochester," *Musical America* 50/6 (March 25, 1931): 4.

84. Chadwick, preface to *Rip Van Winkle* Overture.

85. The overture was published by Birchard (under the auspices of the Eastman School) in 1930. Neeme Järvi and the Detroit Symphony Orchestra were the first to record the overture (revised version). See Chandos 9439 (1996).

86. Olin Downes, "Chadwick Work Played at Festival," *NYT* (May 22, 1931): 28.

Epilogue: Chadwick's Death and Legacy

1. Chadwick's death certificate lists the principal causes of death as arteriosclerosis, angina pectoris, and coronary occlusion. Prostate enlargement was noted as a "contributory cause." See Standard Certificate of Death, Boston, Suffolk County, Commonwealth of Massachusetts, registry no. 3324, certificate no. 685951.

2. MacDougall, "George W. Chadwick," 8. MacDougall apparently got his information from inside sources, for none of his reportage is found in the local newspapers.

3. *Musical America* 51/8 (April 25, 1931): 41.

4. "Chicago Symphony Honors George W. Chadwick's Memory," *Musical Courier* 102/16 (April 18, 1931): 32.

5. "New York Concerts and Recitals," *Musical America* 51/9 (May 10, 1931): 27.

6. "Mephisto's Musings," *Musical America* 51/8 (April 25, 1931): 7.

7. "Memorial to Chadwick," *NYT* (May 20, 1931): V/28.

8. A. H. M. of the *BET* quoted in "In Memoriam Mr. Chadwick," *NEC Bulletin* 13/4 (May 1931): 4.

9. "George W. Chadwick Is Feted by 'Bohemians,'" *Musical America* 49/23 (December 10, 1929): 7.

10. Chadwick, Diary, January 17, 1916 (CC-NEC).

11. Howard Hanson, "Twenty Years' Growth in America," *Modern Music* 20 (January/February 1943): 97.

12. Ibid., 95–6.

13. Chadwick, "Impressions of California," *NEC Magazine Review* 6/2 (December–January 1916): 39.

14. Chadwick, Diary, November 14, 1919 (CC-NEC).

15. "Six Busts Unveiled at Hall of Fame," *NYT* (May 6, 1927): 6.

16. Chadwick, Diary, December 13, 1909 (CC-NEC).

17. Olin Downes, "George Whitefield Chadwick," *NYT* (April 12, 1931): IX/7.

18. Chadwick, Diary, April 9, 1916 (CC-NEC).

19. Unidentified article included in Chadwick, Diary, [after March 13], 1914 (CC-NEC).

20. Chadwick, Diary, [after December 13] 1909 (CC-NEC).

21. Chadwick, Diary, April 24, 1914 (CC-NEC).

22. Chadwick, Diary, [probably January 16], 1915 (CC-NEC).

23. Chadwick, Diary, February 14, 1923 (CC-NEC).

24. Chadwick, Diary, November 23, 1923 (CC-NEC).

25. Chadwick, Diary, January 11, 1912 (CC-NEC).

26. Olin Downes, "George Whitefield Chadwick," *NYT* (April 12, 1931): IX/7.

27. MacDougall, "George W. Chadwick," 8.

28. Ibid.

29. M.D.D., "Debuts & Appearances," *High Fidelity and Musical America* 27/5 (May 1977): 20–1.

30. For a comprehensive discography of Chadwick's music to 1998 see Faucett, *Chadwick: A Bio-Bibliography*, 211–9.

31. Author interview with Theodore Chadwick Jr., June 15–20, 1997.

32. Chadwick, Diary, May 30, 1927 (CC-NEC).

33. Chadwick, Memoirs, 1854–1868 (CC-NEC).

SELECT BIBLIOGRAPHY

Archival Resources

American Academy of Arts and Letters Archives. New York.

Amy Cheney Beach Collection. Milne Special Collections and Archives Department, University of New Hampshire Library, Durham, NH.

Boscawen, New Hampshire, Town Records. Volume 3.

Boston Opera House Records, 1908–1958. Archives and Special Collections, Snell Library, Northeastern University, Boston.

Boston Orchestral Club Scrapbook. Allen A. Brown Collection, Boston Public Library.

[Brander Matthews]. Special Manuscript Collections, Columbia University.

George Whitefield Chadwick Collection. New England Conservatory, Boston.

Essex Institute Historical Collection. Essex Institute, Salem, MA.

Gericke, Wilhelm. Papers. Houghton Library, Harvard University.

Gleason, Frederick Grant. Papers. The Newberry Library, Chicago.

Grant, Robert. Papers. Houghton Library, Harvard University.

Arthur Hartman Collection. Sibley Music Library, Eastman School of Music, Rochester, NY.

Harvard Musical Association. Boston.

Manuscripts Collection. University Libraries, University of Iowa, Iowa City.

National Archives. War Records. Washington, DC.

Parker, Horatio. Papers. Yale University, New Haven.

Sousa, John Philip. Scrapbooks. United States Marine Band Library, Washington, DC.

Strawbridge & Clothier Collection. Hagley Museum and Library, Wilmington, DE.

Thomas, Theodore. Papers (box 1, folder 20). The Newberry Library, Chicago.

Thursday Evening Club Records, 1846–1999. Massachusetts Historical Society, Boston.

Taylor, William Ladd. Papers. Owned by Dr. Ferdinand Brigham; microfilmed by the Archives of American Art, Smithsonian Institution, Washington, DC.

Wilson, George. Papers. Carnegie Library of Pittsburgh.

Interviews/Conversations

Theodore Chadwick Jr. June 15–20, 1997. Duxbury, Massachusetts.

Neeme Järvi. May 12, 1998. Singer Island, Florida.

Victor Fell Yellin. November 15–18, 2001. Atlanta, Georgia.

Books, Dissertations, Editions, and Articles

Adams, John R. *Edward Everett Hale*. Boston: Twayne Publishers, 1977.

"Antonin Dvořák." *The Critic* 558 (October 29, 1892): 236.

Apthorp, William Foster. "John Sullivan Dwight." In *Musicians and Music-lovers and Other Essays*. New York: Charles Scribner's Sons, 1894.

———. *By the Way*. Vol. 2. Boston: Copeland and Day, 1898.

Baker's Biographical Dictionary of Music and Musicians. 3rd ed. Revised and enlarged by Alfred Remy. New York: G. Schirmer, 1919.

Barnet, Anne Alison. *Extravaganza King: Robert Barnet and Boston Musical Theater.* Boston: Northeastern University Press, 2004.

Bates, Arlo. *The Philistines.* Boston: Houghton, Mifflin and Company, 1900; reprint, Charleston, South Carolina: BiblioBazaar, 2007.

Beckerman, Michael, ed. *Dvořák and His World.* Princeton, NJ: Princeton University Press, 1993.

Beckerman, Michael. "The Master's Little Joke: Antonín Dvořák and the Mask of a Nation." In *Dvořák and His World,* edited by Michael Beckerman. Princeton, NJ: Princeton University Press, 1993: 134–54.

Beer, Thomas. *The Mauve Decade.* New York: Alfred A. Knopf, 1926.

Bergen, Peter. *Old Boston in Early Photographs, 1850–1918.* New York: Dover, 1990.

Betz, Marianne. "Sinfonie und Orgel." *Musik und Kirche* (January/February 2005): 28–33.

Beveridge, David. "Sophisticated Primitivism: The Significance of Primitivism in Dvořák's American Quartet." *Current Musicology* 24 (1977): 25–36.

———. "Non-traditional Functions of the Development Section in Sonata Forms by Brahms." *The Music Review* (February 1990): 25–35.

———. "Dvořák and Brahms: a Chronicle, an Interpretation." In *Dvořák and His World,* edited by Michael Beckerman. Princeton, NJ: Princeton University Press, 1993.

Bicknell, Thomas. "Eben Jordan, Mus. Dr." *Education: An International Magazine,* 3 (September 1882–July 1883): 208–11.

Bierley, Paul Edmond. *The Incredible Band of John Philip Sousa.* Urbana: University of Illinois Press, 2006.

Block, Adrienne Fried. "Dvořák, Beach and American Music." In *A Celebration of American Music: Words and Music in Honor of H. Wiley Hitchcock,* edited by R. Crawford, R. Allen Lott, and Carol Oja. Ann Arbor: University of Michigan Press, 1990.

———. *Amy Beach: Passionate Victorian.* New York: Oxford University Press, 1998.

Bomberger, E. Douglas. "The German Musical Training of American Students, 1850–1900." PhD diss., University of Maryland, 1991.

———. *"A Tidal Wave of Encouragement": American Composers' Concerts in the Gilded Age.* Westport, CT: Praeger, 2002.

———. "Chadwick's *Melpomene* and the Anxiety of Influence." *American Music* (Fall 2003): 319–48.

Boscawen Historical Society, Inc. *History: Town of Boscawen, 1933–1983.* Boscawen, NH: Compiled and published by the society, 1983.

Bowles, Edmund A. "Karl Muck and his Compatriots: German Conductors in America during World War I (and How They Coped)." *American Music* 25/4 (Winter 2007): 405–40.

Brand, H. W. *The Reckless Decade.* Chicago: University of Chicago Press, 1995.

Brooks, Van Wyck. *The Confident Years.* New York: Dutton, 1955.

Browne, Walter. *Acting Version of Henry W. Savage's Production of Everywoman: Her Pilgrimage in Quest of Love.* New York: H.K. Fly Company, 1908.

Broyles, Michael. *"Music of the Highest Class": Elitism and Populism in Antebellum Boston.* New Haven: Yale University Press, 1992.

Buxton, Willis G., compiler. *The History of Boscawen and Webster from 1883–1933.* NH: Printed by W. B. Ranney Co., 1933.

Canfield, John C. "Henry Hadley: His Life and Works." Ed. D. diss., The Florida State University, 1960.

Cashman, Sean Dennis. *America in the Gilded Age.* 3rd ed. New York: New York University Press, 1993.

Chadwick, George Whitefield. *Harmony: A Course of Study.* 1st ed. Boston: B.F. Wood, 1897.

——. "Musical Atmosphere and Student Life." *New England Conservatory Magazine* 9/4 (May 1903): 138–41.

——. *Harmony: A Course of Study.* 55th ed. Boston: B.F. Wood, 1922.

——. *Memoirs, Diaries and Scrapbooks.* Boston: New England Conservatory (CC-NEC). This collection comprises mostly unpaginated and undated manuscript materials.

——. Two Overtures: *Rip Van Winkle* and *Adonais*, edited by Bill F. Faucett. Middleton, WI: A-R Editions, 2005.

——. String Quartets, nos. 1–3, edited by Marianne Betz. Middleton, WI: A-R Editions, 2006.

——. String Quartets, nos. 4–5, edited by Marianne Betz. Middleton, WI: A-R Editions, 2007.

Chapple, Joe Mitchell. "The New England Conservatory." *National Magazine* (July 1908): 5–12.

Clapham, John. *Dvořák.* New York: W. W. Norton, 1979.

Coerne, Louis Adolphe. *The Evolution of Modern Orchestration.* New York: Macmillan Company, 1908.

Coffin, Charles Carleton. *The Story of the Great Fire, Boston, November 9–10, 1872.* Boston: Shepard and Gill, 1872.

——, compiler. *The History of Boscawen and Webster from 1733 to 1878.* Concord, NH: Printed by the Republican Press Association, 1878.

——. *Abraham Lincoln.* New York: Harper & Brothers, 1893.

Cole, Donald B. *Immigrant City: Lawrence, Massachusetts, 1845–1921.* Chapel Hill: University of North Carolina Press, 1963.

The Columbian Gallery: A Portfolio of Photographs from the World's Fair. Chicago: Werner Company, 1894.

Conwell, Russell H. *History of the Great Fire in Boston, November 9 and 10, 1872.* Boston: B. B. Russell, 1873.

Coon, Oscar, ed. *Richter's Manual of Harmony.* New York: Carl Fischer, 1912.

Cowley, Robert, ed. *The Great War: Perspectives on the First World War.* New York: Random House, 2003.

Crawford, Richard. *America's Musical Life: A History.* New York: W. W. Norton, 2001.

Cutler, R. V. *The Gay Nineties: A Book of Drawings.* Garden City, NY: Doubleday, Page & Co., 1927.

Cutter, Benjamin. *Exercises in Harmony: Simple and Advanced Supplementary to the Treatise on Harmony by G. W. Chadwick.* Boston: New England Conservatory, 1899.

De Koven, Reginald. "The Modern Revolt in Music." *North American Review* 186/624 (November 1907): 360–69.

Dickens, Charles. *American Notes for General Circulation*. London, 1842; reprint, London: Penguin Classics, 1985.

Dickinson, Edward. *Music in the History of the Western Church*. New York: Charles Scribner's Sons, 1902.

Doyle, Arthur Conan. *The Green Flag and Other Stories*. New York: P. F. Collier and Son, 1900.

Dunham, Henry M. *The Life of a Musician Woven into a Strand of History of the New England Conservatory*. New York: Richmond Publishing and Printing Company, 1931.

Duveneck, Josephine. *Frank Duveneck: Painter-Teacher*. San Francisco: John Howell, 1970.

Dykstra, Andrea. "George Whitefield Chadwick and the Shaping of American Orchestral Music: A Study of Performance and Composition in the Late Nineteenth and Early Twentieth Century." PhD diss., Michigan State University, 2004.

Eisler, Benita. "The Lowell Offering": *Writings by New England Mill Women (1840–1845)*. Philadelphia: Lippincott, 1977.

Elson, Louis C. "George W. Chadwick—An Appreciation." *NEC Magazine-Review* 7/1 (September–October 1924): 7.

———. *The History of American Music*. New York: Franklin, 1925.

———, ed. *Modern Music and Musicians*. Vol. 2, *Encyclopedia*. New York: University Society, 1912.

Engel, Carl. "George W. Chadwick." *Musical Quarterly* 10 (1924): 438–57.

Faucett, Bill F. *George Whitefield Chadwick: His Symphonic Works*. Lanham, MD: Scarecrow Press, 1996.

———. *George Whitefield Chadwick: A Bio-Bibliography*. Westport, CT: Greenwood Press, 1998.

———. *Music in America, 1860–1918: Essays, Reviews and Remarks on Critical Issues*. Hillsdale, NY: Pendragon Press, 2008.

Fisher, William Arms. *Notes on Music in Old Boston*. Boston: Oliver Ditson, 1918.

———. *Music Festivals in the United States: An Historical Sketch*. Boston: American Choral and Festival Alliance, 1934.

Fitz, Asa. *The Primary School Song Book*. Boston: Phillips & Sampson, ca. 1843.

———. *The Congregational Singing Book*. Boston: Phillips & Sampson, ca. 1848.

———. *School Songs for the Million*. Boston: Fitz, Hobbs & Company, ca. 1850.

———. *The American School Hymn Book*. Boston: Crosby, Nichols & Company, 1855.

———. *The Sacred Minstrel*. Boston: Hickling, Swan and Brown, ca. 1856.

———. *The Harmoniad and Sacred Melodist*. Boston: Bela Marsh, ca. 1857.

———. *The National School Songster*. Boston: D. C. Colesworthy, ca. 1870.

Foote, Arthur, and Walter Spalding. *Modern Harmony: Its Theory and Practice*. Boston: Arthur P. Schmidt, 1905.

Foote, Arthur. "A Bostonian Remembers." *Musical Quarterly* 23 (1937): 37–44.

Foote, Arthur, and Katherine Foote Raffy. *Arthur Foote, 1853–1937: An Autobiography*. Norwood, MA: Plimpton Press, 1946.

Freeman, Charles Spence. "American Realism and Progressivism in Chadwick's *The Padrone* and Converse's *The Immigrants*." PhD diss., The Florida State University, 1999.

Gänzl, Kurt. *The Encyclopedia of the Musical Theater.* 2nd ed. New York: Schirmer, 2001.

Garraty, John A., and Peter Gay. *The Columbia History of the World.* New York: Harper & Row, 1988.

Gatti-Casazza, Giulio. *Memories of Opera.* New York: Charles Scribner's Sons, 1941.

Getchell, Sylvia Fitts. *Fitts Families: A Genealogy.* Concord, NH; Concord Offset Company, 1989.

Gilmore, Patrick S. *History of the National Peace Jubilee.* Boston: Lee & Shepard, 1871.

Gould, Nathaniel D. *The Sabbath School Harmony.* Boston: Gould, Kendall and Lincoln, 1841.

———. *Church Music in America.* Boston: A. N. Johnson, 1853.

Greene, Henry Copley. *Three Plays in Verse: Pontius Pilate, Saint Ronan of Brittany, Théophile.* New York: Scott-Thaw, 1902.

Gross, Laurence F. *The Course of Industrial Decline: The Boott Cotton Mills of Lowell, Massachusetts, 1835–1955.* Baltimore: Johns Hopkins University Press, 1993.

Hadley, Henry. *A Commemorative Tribute to Chadwick.* Publication no. 77. New York: American Academy of Arts and Letters, 1932.

Hale, Edward Everett. *A New England Boyhood.* New York: Cassell Publishing Company, 1893; reprint, Upper Saddle River, NJ: Literature House, 1970.

Hale, Edward Everett Jr. *The Life and Letters of Edward Everett Hale.* Boston: Little, Brown, and Company, 1917.

Hamilton, Clarence G. *Music Appreciation.* Boston: Oliver Ditson Company, 1920.

Harries, Meirion and Susie. *The Last Days of Innocence: America at War, 1917–1918.* New York: Random House, 1997.

Heerman, Norbert. *Frank Duveneck.* Boston: Houghton Mifflin, 1918.

Herlihy, Elisabeth, ed. *Fifty Years of Boston: A Memorial Volume Issued in Commemoration of the Tercentenary of 1930.* Boston: Subcommittee on Memorial History of the Boston Tercentenary Committee, 1932.

[Higinbotham, H. N.] *Report of the President to the Board of Directors of the World's Columbian Exhibition.* Chicago: Rand, McNally & Company, 1898.

Hitchcock, H. Wiley. *Music in the United States: A Historical Introduction.* 3rd ed. Englewood Cliffs, NJ: Prentice Hall, 1988.

Holloway, Jean. *Edward Everett Hale: A Biography.* Austin, TX: University of Texas Press, 1956.

Homer, Sidney. *My Wife and I.* New York: Macmillan, 1939.

Horowitz, Joseph. "Dvořák and the New World: A Concentrated Moment." In *Dvořák and His World*, edited by Michael Beckerman. Princeton, NJ: Princeton University Press, 1993.

———. *Classical Music in America.* New York: W. W. Norton, 2005.

Howard, John Tasker. *Our American Music.* New York: Thomas Y. Crowell, 1930.

Howe, M. A. DeWolfe. *The Boston Symphony Orchestra, 1881–1931.* Boston: Houghton Mifflin, 1931.

———. "John Knowles Paine." *Musical Quarterly* 25/3 (July 1939): 256–67.

Howells, William Dean. *Suburban Sketches.* New York: Hurd and Houghton, 1871.

———. *Letters of an Altrurian Traveller.* Gainesville, Florida: Scholars' Facsimiles and Reprints, 1961.

Huneker, James. *Mezzotints in Modern Music*. New York: Charles Scribner's Sons, 1899.

Ives, Charles. *Memos*, edited by John Kirkpatrick. New York: Norton, 1972.

Jackson, Frank H. *Monograph of the Boston Opera House*. Boston: W. A. Butterfield, 1909.

Johnson, Robert Underwood. *Poems of War and Peace*. Enlarged from the First Edition. New York: Published by the Author, 1917.

Kearns, William K. *Horatio Parker, 1863–1919: His Life, Music, and Ideas*. Metuchen, NJ: Scarecrow Press, 1990.

Keegan, John. *The First World War*. New York: Knopf, 1999.

Kennedy, Michael. *Richard Strauss: Man, Musician, Enigma*. Cambridge: Cambridge University Press, 1999.

King, Moses, ed. *King's Handbook of Springfield, Massachusetts*. Springfield, MA: James D. Gill, 1884.

Krehbiel, Henry E. *Review of the New York Musical Season, 1887–1888*. New York: Novello, Ewer & Company, 1888.

Langley, Allan Lincoln. "Chadwick and the New England Conservatory of Music." *Musical Quarterly* 21 (1935): 39–52.

LaRue, Jan. *Guidelines for Style Analysis*. 2nd ed. Warren, MI: Harmonie Park Press, 1995.

Ledbetter, Steven. "Chadwickiana at the New England Conservatory." Paper presented at the annual mid-winter meeting of the Music Library Association, Cambridge, Massachusetts, 2 March 1978.

———. *George W. Chadwick: A Sourcebook*. Revised preliminary version. (Unpublished, 1983.)

———. Liner notes to George W. Chadwick's String Quartet nos. 4 and 5. Portland String Quartet. Northeastern Records NR 234-CD (1988).

———. Liner notes to George W. Chadwick's String Quartet no. 3 and Quintet for Piano and Strings. Portland String Quartet. Northeastern Records NR 235-CD (1988).

———. Liner notes to George W. Chadwick's String Quartet nos. 1 and 2. Portland String Quartet. Northeastern Records NR 236-CD (1988).

———. "Two Seductresses: Saint-Saëns' Delilah and Chadwick's Judith." In *A Celebration of American Music*, edited by Richard Crawford, et al. Ann Arbor: University of Michigan Press, 1990.

Lipsky, William. *San Francisco's Panama-Pacific International Exposition*. San Francisco: Arcadia Publishing, 2005.

Longfellow, Henry Wadsworth. *The Song of Hiawatha*. (With illustrations by Frederic Remington, Maxfield Parrish, and N. C. Wyeth.) Boston: Houghton, Mifflin & Company, 1890.

MacDougall, Dr. Hamilton C. "George W. Chadwick: An Appreciation of a Distinguished Life." *The Diapason* (May 1, 1931): 8.

Macy, Arthur. *Poems*. Introduction by William Alfred Hovey. Boston: W. B. Clarke Company, 1905.

Martens, Frederick H. "Music." In *The American Year Book: A Record of Events and Progress, 1916*, edited by Francis G. Wickware. New York: D. Appleton and Co., 1917.

Mathews, W. S. B. *A Hundred Years of Music in America*. Philadelphia: Theodore Presser, 1900.

Mazzola, Sandy R. "Bands and Orchestras at the World's Columbian Exposition." *American Music* 4/4 (Winter 1986): 407–24.

McPherson, Bruce, and James Klein. *Measure by Measure: A History of New England Conservatory from 1867*. Boston: The Trustees of New England Conservatory of Music, 1995.

Miller, Eleanor L. "The History and Development of the New England Conservatory of Music." B. M. thesis, New England Conservatory, 1933.

Mitchell, Brian C. "Good Citizens at the Least Cost per Pound: The History of the Development of Public Education in Antebellum Lowell, 1825–1855." In *The Continuing Revolution: A History of Lowell, Massachusetts*, edited by Robert Weible. Lowell: Lowell Historical Society, 1991.

Monroe, Harriet. *A Poet's Life*. New York: Macmillan, 1938.

Morgan, John P., trans. *Richter's Manual of Harmony*. New York: G. Schirmer, 1867.

Morin, Raymond. *The Worcester Music Festival: Its Background and History, 1858–1946*. Worcester, MA: Worcester County Musical Association, 1946.

Moore, J. Bailey. *History of the Town of Candia*. Manchester, NH: George W. Brown, 1893.

"Noel Chadwick Returns to Naval Aviation Career in St. Louis Executive Post." *News Times* (St. Louis, MO) March 26, 1942.

Oates, Stephen B., ed. *Biography as High Adventure*. Amherst, MA: University of Massachusetts Press, 1986.

O Broin, Leon. *Fenian Fever: An Anglo-American Dilemma*. New York: New York University Press, 1971.

One Hundred and Fiftieth Anniversary of the Settlement of Boscawen and Webster, August 16, 1883. Concord, NH: Republican Press Association, 1884.

Orcutt, William Dana. *Celebrities Off Parade*. Chicago: Willett, Clark & Company, 1935.

Paine, John Knowles. "The New German School of Music." *North American Review* 116/239 (April 1873): 217–45.

———. *The History of Music to the Death of Schubert*. Boston: Ginn and Company, 1907.

Parker, H. T. *Eighth Notes*. 1922; reprint, Freeport, NY: Books for Libraries Press, 1968.

Perry, Lilla Cabot. *From the Garden of Hellas: Translations into Verse from the Greek Anthology*. New York: United States Book Company, 1891.

Pollack, Howard. *Harvard Composers: Walter Piston and His Students from Elliott Carter to Frederick Rzewski*. Lanham, MD: Scarecrow Press, 1992.

———. *Aaron Copland: The Life and Work of an Uncommon Man*. New York: Henry Holt and Company, 1999.

———. *John Alden Carpenter: Chicago Composer*. Urbana: University of Illinois Press, 2001.

Puleo, Stephen. *The Boston Italians*. Boston: Beacon Press, 2007.

Rafferty, Oliver P. *The Church, the State, and the Fenian Threat, 1861–75*. New York: St. Martin's Press, 1999.

Railey, Julia Houston. *Mater Musica*. Boston: New England Conservatory, 1929.

Rheinberger, Josef. *Briefe und Dokumente seines Lebens*, edited by Harald Wanger and Hans-Josef Irmen. Vaduz: Prisca, 1982-7.

Rosen, Charles. *Sonata Forms*. Revised edition. New York: W. W. Norton, 1988.

Rossetti, W. M., and A. O. Prickard, eds. *Shelley's Adonais*. 2nd ed. Oxford: Clarendon Press, 1903.

Rubin, Emanuel. "Dvořák at the National Conservatory." In *Dvořák in America, 1892–1895*, edited by John C. Tibbets. Portland: Amadeus Press, 1993: 53–81.

Ryan, Thomas. *Recollections of an Old Musician*. New York: E. P. Dutton, 1899.

Rybicki, Verena. "The Mill Girls of Lowell." In *The Lowell Mill Girls: Life in the Factory*, edited by JoAnne B. Weisman. Lowell, Massachusetts: Discovery Enterprises, 1991.

Rydell, Robert W. *All the World's a Fair*. Chicago: University of Chicago Press, 1984.

Salter, Sumner. "Eugene Thayer." *The Musician* 17/12 (December 1912): 864–65.

Santayana, George. "Intellectual Temper of the Age." In *Winds of Doctrine and Platonism and the Spiritual Life*; reprint, Gloucester, MA: Peter Smith, 1971.

Schabas, Ezra. *Theodore Thomas: America's Conductor and Builder of Orchestras, 1835–1905*. Urbana and Chicago, Illinois: University of Illinois Press, 1989.

Schlereth, Thomas J. *Victorian America: Transformations in Everyday Life*. New York: HarperPerennial, 1992.

Schonberg, Harold C. *The Great Conductors*. New York: Simon and Schuster, 1967.

Scott, Walter. *Marmion: A Tale of Flodden Field*. 3rd ed. Edinburgh: Constable and Company, 1808.

Shi, David. *Facing Facts: Realism in American Thought and Culture, 1850–1920*. New York: Oxford University Press, 1995.

Silver, Walter Theo, and Linnea Stadig Silver. *From King's Plantation to Home Town Heritage: Boscawen and Webster, New Hampshire*. Portsmouth, NH: Peter E. Randall, 1977.

Slonimsky, Nicolas. "Composers of New England." *Modern Music* 6 (February–March 1930): 24–27.

Starr, S. Frederick. *Bamboula: The Life and Times of Louis Moreau Gottschalk*. New York: Oxford University Press, 1995.

Stearns, Harold E., ed. *Civilization in the United States: An Inquiry by Thirty Americans*. New York: Harcourt, Brace and Company, 1922

Stebbins, Richard Poate. *The Making of Symphony Hall, Boston*. Boston: Boston Symphony Orchestra, 2000.

Strang, Lewis C. *Famous Stars of Light Opera*. Boston: L. C. Page & Company, 1900.

———. *Celebrated Comedians of Light Opera and Musical Comedy in America*. Boston: L. C. Page & Company, 1901.

Taruskin, Richard. *Music in the Early Twentieth Century*. Oxford and New York: Oxford University Press, 2010.

Thomas, Evan. *The War Lovers*. New York: Little, Brown and Company, 2010.

Thomas, Rose Fay. *Memoirs of Theodore Thomas*. New York: Moffat, Yard and Company, 1911.

Thomas, Theodore. *A Musical Autobiography*. 2 vols. Edited by George P. Upton. Chicago: McClurg, 1905.

Tibbetts, John C., ed. *Dvořák in America, 1892–1895*. Portland, Oregon: Amadeus Press, 1993.

Tourjée, Eben. *The Chorus Choir*. Boston: Oliver Ditson, 1875.

———. *Ye Centennial: A Quire Book for Folke Old and Younge*. Boston: Oliver Ditson, ca. 1875.

———. *Select Anthems for Choirs, Choral Societies and Conventions*. Boston: Musical Herald Company, 1884.

———. *The New England Conservatory Method for the Piano-Forte*. Boston: Oliver Ditson, 1898.

Tourjée, Leo Eben. *For God and Music: The Life Story of Eben Tourjée, Father of the American Conservatory*. Los Angeles: Leo Eben Tourjée, 1965.

Tower, James E., ed. *Springfield Present and Prospective: The Sources of its Charm, Its Advantages, Achievements and Possibilities, Portrayed in Word and Picture*. Springfield, MA: Pond and Campbell, 1905.

Trench, Richard Chevenix. *Sacred Latin Poetry*. London: John W. Parker, 1849.

Tuchman, Barbara W. "How We Entered World War I." In *Practicing History*. New York: Ballantine Books, 1981.

Twain, Mark, and Charles Dudley Warner. *The Gilded Age*. Hartford: American Publishing Co., 1873.

Upton, George P. "Musical Societies of the United States and their Representation at the World's Fair." *Scribner's Magazine* 14/6 (July–December 1893): 68–83.

Vaill, J.H., ed. "Report of the Music Committee, 1908." In *Litchfield County Choral Union* (Vol. 1). Norfolk, CT: 1912.

Von Glahn, Denise. *The Sounds of Place: Music and the American Cultural Landscape*. Boston: Northeastern University Press, 2003.

Wadsworth, Horace Andrew. *History of Lawrence, Massachusetts*. Lawrence: Hammon Read, 1880.

Waldo, Frank. "The Acoustics of Jordan Hall of the New England Conservatory." *New England Conservatory Magazine* 10/2 (January 1904): 54–61.

Warner, Charles Dudley. *Saunterings*. Boston: J.R. Osgood & Co., 1872; reprint, HardPress.net: n.d.

Weible, Robert, ed. *The Continuing Revolution: A History of Lowell, Massachusetts*. Lowell, Massachusetts: Lowell Historical Society, 1991.

Weisman, JoAnne B., ed. *The Lowell Mill Girls: Life in the Factory*. Lowell, MA: Discovery Enterprises, 1991.

Wheeler, Edward J., ed. "The European War and the Panama-Pacific — A Monumental Contrast." *Current Opinion* 58 (January–June 1915), 315–20.

Whipple, George M. "Sketch of the Musical Societies of Salem." In *Essex Institute Historical Collections* (vol. 23): 72–80, 113–33. Salem, MA: Salem Press, 1886.

Whitehill, Walter Muir. *Boston: A Topographical History*. 2nd ed. Cambridge, MA: Belknap Press of Harvard University, 1968.

Williams, Alexander W. *A Social History of the Greater Boston Clubs*. Barre, MA: Barre Publishers, 1970.

Williams, Stephen K. *Cases Argued and Decided in the Supreme Court of the United States* (Book 41). Rochester, NY: Lawyers Co-Operative Publishing Company, 1901.

Williams, Rev. Wolcott B. *A History of Olivet College, 1844–1900*. Olivet, MI: n.p., 1901.

Wingate, Charles E. L. "Boston Letter." *The Critic* 558 (October 29, 1892): 234.

The World's Fair: Being a Pictorial History of the Columbian Exposition. Mansfield, OH: Estill & Company, 1893.

Yang, Hon-Lun Helan. "A Study of the Overtures and Symphonic Poems by American Composers of the Second New England School." PhD diss., Washington University (St. Louis), 1998.

Yellin, Victor Fell. "The Life and Operatic Works of George Whitefield Chadwick." PhD diss., Harvard University, 1957.

———. "Chadwick: American Musical Realist." *Musical Quarterly* 61 (January 1975), 77–97.

———. "George Chadwick and Populist Music." Paper delivered as part of the "Musicology Lecture Series," SUNY-Buffalo, April 11, 1983.

———. *Chadwick: Yankee Composer*. Washington, DC: Smithsonian Institution Press, 1990.

Zuck, Barbara A. *A History of Musical Americanism*. Ann Arbor: UMI Research Press, 1980.

Journals and Newspapers

American Art Journal
Boston Daily Advertiser
Boston Daily Traveller
Boston Daily Evening Traveller
Boston Evening Transcript
Boston Globe
Boston Herald
Boston Journal
Boston Morning Journal
Boston Post
Boston Sunday Herald
Chicago Tribune
Christian Science Monitor
Church's Musical Visitor
The Critic
Current Opinion
The Daily American (Lawrence, Massachusetts)
Dwight's Journal of Music
The Etude
Godey's Magazine
The Musical Herald
The Musical Record
The Musical Visitor
The Musician
Musikalisches Wochenblatt
Neue Zeitschrift für Musik
The Neume
New England Conservatory Magazine
News Times (St. Louis)
New York Post
New York Sun
New York Times
New York Tribune
North American Review
The Outlook
Philadelphia Evening Bulletin
Philadelphia Inquirer

San Francisco Examiner
Saturday Evening Gazette
Signale für die Musikalische Welt
Springfield Daily Republican
Springfield Graphic
Winsted (Connecticut) Evening Citizen
Worcester Telegram
Yale Alumni Magazine

Recordings

Chadwick, George Whitefield. *Five Pieces* (1905); *Three Waltzes* (1890); *Six Characteristic Pieces*, op. 7; *Two Caprices* (1888); *Three Pieces for Children* (1928); *Chanson Orientale* (1895); *Nocturne in D-flat* (1895); *The Aspen* (1925). *American Character: Piano Music of George Whitefield Chadwick*. Peter Kairoff, piano. Albany Troy 745 (2005).

———. *Tam O'Shanter*; *Melpomene*; *Symphonic Sketches*. Czech State Philharmonic. Jose Serebrier. Reference Recordings RR-64-CD (1995).

———. *Aphrodite*; *Suite Symphonique*; *Elegy*. Czech State Philharmonic. Jose Serebrier. Reference Recordings RR-74-CD (1996).

———. Symphony nos. 2 and 3. Detroit Symphony Orchestra. Neeme Järvi. Chandos 9685 (1998).

———. Symphony no. 2; *Symphonic Sketches*. Detroit Symphony Orchestra. Neeme Järvi. Chandos 9334 (1995).

———. *Rip Van Winkle* Overture; *Tam O'Shanter*; *Melpomene*. Detroit Symphony Orchestra. Neeme Järvi. Chandos 9439 (1996).

———. String Quartet nos. 1 and 2. Portland String Quartet. Northeastern Records. NR 236-CD (1988).

———. String Quartet no. 3; Quintet for Piano and Strings. Portland String Quartet. Northeastern Records. NR 235-CD (1988).

———. String Quartet nos. 4 and 5. Portland String Quartet. Northeastern Records. NR 234-CD (1988).

———. *Tabasco March*. *The Golden Age of the American March*. The Goldman Band. Richard Franko Goldman. New World Records 80266-2 (1976).

———. *Thalia*; *Melpomene*; *Euterpe*. Nashville Symphony Orchestra. Kenneth Schermerhorn. Naxos 8.559117 (2002).

———. *Sinfonietta in D Major*; Symphony no. 3. *Our Musical Past* (vol. 6). Royal Philharmonic Orchestra. Karl Krueger. Library of Congress OMP-107 (1968).

Web Resources

"Trans Mississippi & International Exposition." Website of the Omaha Public Library. www.omahapubliclibrary.org/transmiss/about/about.html. Accessed August 19, 2009.

INDEX